1922 portrait of Ernest Hemingway by Henry Strater (courtesy of Museum of Art of Ogunquit Permanent Collection)

READING HEMINGWAY
The Facts in the Fictions

by
MIRIAM B. MANDEL

The Scarecrow Press, Inc.
Metuchen, N.J., & London
1995

British Library Cataloguing-in-Publication data available

Library of Congress Cataloging-in-Publication Data

Mandel, Miriam, B.
 Reading Hemingway : the facts in the fictions / by Miriam B. Mandel. — 1st ed.
  p.   cm.
 Includes bibliographical references and index.
 ISBN 0-8108-2870-7 (alk. paper)
 1. Hemingway, Ernest, 1899–1961—Knowledge and learn-ing—Dictionaries. I. Title.
PS3515.E37Z459   1995
813'.52—dc20   94-14481

This book is for Jerry

CONTENTS

LIST OF ILLUSTRATIONS

ACKNOWLEDGMENTS

A reference work is of necessity a joint project. Annotating Hemingway's nouns and names has been an international endeavor, and I am glad to acknowledge the help offered by informed minds in England, France, Israel, Italy, Puerto Rico, Spain, Switzerland and the United States. Of the many people I consulted, not a few did considerable research on my behalf. Without their help even this incomplete step towards a full annotation of Hemingway's work would not have been possible. Whatever infelicities, omissions and errors mar this book are fully my responsibility. I hope that users of this book will respond to its shortcomings by completing the task here begun.

In preparing the various entries I have relied on the holdings of the library of the University of Barcelona, the National Library of Cataluña, the Biblioteca Nacional in Madrid, the library of the Museo del Ejército in Madrid, and the public and university libraries in Pamplona, Navarre, Spain. The work could not have been completed without the resources of the Hemingway Collection at the J.F. Kennedy Library, the Widener Library of Harvard University, and the Elias P. Sourasky Library of Tel Aviv University. My particular thanks to Kevin Donnelly at the Reference Desk of the Reading Room at the Widener; to Geula Wolffson of the Inter-Library Loan Department at Sourasky Library; and to the archivists and curators of the Hemingway Collection, who were unfailingly friendly and helpful: Megan Floyd Desnoyers, Lisa Middents, and Stephen Plotkin.

Librarians and curators at many other institutions wrote long, informative and friendly letters in answer to my queries. My special thanks to D. J. Penn, Keeper of the Department of Exhibits and Firearms, Imperial War Museum, London; and to Emily Clark, Assistant Librarian, Chicago Historical Society, Chicago, IL. Thanks also to Candace Eaton and Zelda Gilman, of the Little Traverse Historical Society, Petoskey, MI; Barbara Kotzin, Cheltenham Township Historical Commission, Cheltenham, PA; Lisa Schwarzenholz, Archivist, Wyandotte County Historical Society and Museum, Bonner Springs, KA; Thomas P. Wollenzien, President, Sheridan County Historical Society, Sheridan, WY; Paul Fees, Senior Curator, Buffalo Bill Historical Center, Cody, WY; Benedict K. Zobrist, Director, Harry S. Truman Library, Independence, MO;

Karl Crosby, Serial Reference Specialist, the Library of Congress, Washington, DC; Virginia S. Wood, Reference Librarian in the General Reading Rooms Division, the Library of Congress, Washington, DC; Michael Grace, S.J., University Archivist, Loyola University, Chicago, IL; Nicholas Varga, College Archivist, Loyola College, Baltimore, MD; Tom Hambright, Local and State History Department, Monroe County May Hill Russell Library, Key West, FL; Chris Renz, Research Correspondence, National Geographic Society, Washington, DC; Bryan Kennedy, Researcher, Smithsonian Books, Washington, DC; Robert Gottlieb, *The New Yorker* magazine, New York, NY; Michael Culver, Curator, Museum of Art of Ogunquit, Ogunquit, ME; David F. Setford, Senior Curator, Norton Gallery & School of Art, West Palm Beach, FL; Morris Buske, Historian, the Ernest Hemingway Foundation, Oak Park, IL; Joyce Ann Tracy, Curator of Newspapers and Periodicals, the American Antiquarian Society, Worcester, MA; News International Newspapers Ltd., 1 Virginia St. London; D. Fullin, Centro Documentazione, *Corriere della Sera,* Milan; and Pierluigi Tagliaferro, Vicedirettore, *Il Gazzettino,* Venice.

For information on alumni, special collections, and other matters relating to their universities and schools, my thanks to Rebecca J. Bates, Curatorial Assistant, Harvard University Archives; Rick Ryan, Biographical Section, Office of Alumni Records, Princeton University; Eustace D. Theodore, Executive Director, Association of Yale Alumni, Yale University; Gould P. Colman, University Archivist, Cornell University; Adele A. Lerner, Archivist, the New York Hospital-Cornell Medical Center, New York, NY; Mary E. Foy, Assistant Dean/Registrar, Johns Hopkins University School of Medicine; Carley R. Robison, Curator of Manuscripts and Archives, Knox College, Galesburg, IL; and Patrick M. Finn, Director of Admissions, Canterbury School, New Milford, CT.

For information on military and diplomatic personalities, my thanks to Floriane Truninger, Research Officer, Principles, Law and Relations with the Movement, International Red Cross, Geneva; Jerry Knoll, Public Inquiry Center, National Headquarters of the American Red Cross, Washington, DC; Suzanne Christoff, Assistant Archivist, U.S. Military Academy at West Point, NY; Perry D. Jamieson, Historical Services Division, Office of the Air Force Historian, Bolling Air Force Base, Washington, DC; Tab Lewis and Joseph Dane Hartgrove, both of the Civil Reference Branch, National Archives, Washington, DC; Karl E. Cocke and William J. Webb, Staff Support Branch, Center of Military History, Department of the Army, Washington, DC; Frederic Pasquier, Etat Major de la Marine, Paris; the staff at the Cultural Center of the Italian Embassy, Tel Aviv; and Denise Pessah, British Council, Tel Aviv.

For information about various sports, sports figures and sports equipment, my thanks to Robert Lorenz, Consultant to the Museum of Montreux; M. Guenot, Registre du Commerce, Vevey; R. Stadler, Staatsarchiv des Kantons Zurich; Francois Och, Chairman and Managing Director, Och Sport, Zurich; Robert Buscaglia, Office de l'état civil, Geneva; Jean-Etienne Genequand, Archives d'Etat, Geneva; M. Jekiel, Union Cycliste Internationale, Geneva; and to Bengt-Erik Bengtsson, International Ski Federation, Oberhofen, all of whom wrote me from Switzerland. In the United States, my thanks to Doris Jean Waren, Librarian, Keeneland Association, Inc., Lexington, KY; Kathryn Schrade, Registrar, National Museum of Racing and Hall of Fame, Saratoga Springs, NY; Howard Bass, Thoroughbred Racing Communications, Inc., New York, NY; Theresa C. Fitzgerald, Librarian, The Blood-Horse, Lexington, KY; Ross A. Phelps, Taurine Bibliophiles of America, La Crescent, MN; Alanna Fisher, Curator, The American Museum of Fly Fishing, Manchester, VT; Robert W. Brown, President, The American League of Professional Baseball Clubs, New York, NY; Jeff Elijah, Director of Publications, International Baseball Association, Indianapolis, IN; Gary Van Allen, Research Associate, National Baseball Hall of Fame and Museum, Inc., Cooperstown, NY; Ray Leverton, Curator-Manager, U.S. National Ski Hall of Fame, Ishpeming, MI; Scoop Gallello, President, International Veteran Boxers Association, New Rochelle, NY; and Ben Primer, University Archivist, Seeley G. Mudd Manuscript Library, Princeton University Archives, Princeton, NJ.

For information on boats, ships, marine exploration and marine life, my thanks to R. M. Browning, Jr., Historian, U.S. Coast Guard, Washington, DC; A. J. Booth, USN, Deputy Director of Naval History, Office of the Chief of Naval Operations, Washington, DC; C. F. Wise, USN, Deputy Director of Naval History, Naval Historical Center, Washington, DC; Lysle B. Gray, Executive Director, American Boat and Yacht Council, Inc., Millersville, MD; R. P. Dinsmore, Woods Hole Oceanographic Institution, Woods Hole, MA; José I. Castro, U. S. Department of Commerce, National Oceanic and Atmospheric Administration, Miami, FL; Paul J. O'Pecko, Reference Librarian, Mystic Seaport Museum, Mystic, CT; Richard Hart, Reference Librarian, Greenwich Library, Greenwich, CT; and Dot Wensink, Researcher, New England Aquarium Library, Boston, MA.

For information on medicine, medical literature, and pharmacology, my thanks to Rita Mtz. Buxó, Librarian, Real Academia de Medicina de Barcelona; Marguerite Fallucco, Archives, American Medical Association, Chicago, IL; Carolyn A. Hough, The Science Bookshelf, Ann Arbor, MI; and Jennifer Bell and Cliff Neuman, both of Tel Aviv.

For details relevant to music and composers, I am indebted to Jean

Rainwater, Librarian, and Rosemary Cullen, Curator, both at the Harris
Collection, John Jay Library, Brown University; Wayne D. Shirley,
Music Specialist, Music Division, Library of Congress, Washington,
DC; and my daughter Naomi Mandel, possessor of much arcane musical
knowledge and a fine researcher.

For information about the histories and products of their companies
and businesses, I am grateful to many people in England: D. Preston,
Public Relations Officer, Rolls-Royce Motor Cars, Crewe, Cheshire;
Peter Baines, Chief Executive, Rolls-Royce Enthusiasts Club, The Hunt
House, Paulerspury, Towcester, Northants; A. W. Bailey, Factory
Manager, Rowntree Sun-Pat, Cheshire; A. J. W. Lokatis, Director, Boss
& Co., Ltd., London; Suzanne Quail, Administrator, Pantry Buying
Office, Harrods, Knightsbridge, London; G. V. Hamilton, Managing
Director, Fortnum & Mason, Plc., London; and John Hunt, Publicity
Manager, Rolex, London. In the United States, my thanks to Lisa C.
Schlegel, Public Relations Representative, Hershey Foods, PA; Gabor
M. Korody, founder of Korody-Colyer Corp., CA; Dan L. Fapp, Jr.,
Public Affairs, Sears Company, Sears Tower, Chicago, IL; Mary Louise
Brown, Curator of Collections/ Assistant Archivist, Anheuser Busch
Companies, St. Louis, MO; Marc A. Shafir, Public Relations, and Diana
Harkin, Advertising, Rolex, New York, NY; Patricia Champier, Man-
ager, Louis Vuitton, Copley Place, Boston, MA; Carol Smith, Aber-
crombie & Fitch, Columbus, OH; and David Hull, Manager of Store
Operations, Burberrys, New York, NY. Thanks also to Veronique
Brown-Claudot, Public Relations Officer, Hotel de Crillon, Paris;
Vicenzo Finizzola, Manager, Hotel Gritti Palace, Venice, Italy; Mariani
G. Luigi, Manager, Grand Hotel des Iles Borromees, Stresa; the
Manager of the Hotel Cavour, Milan; and Arrigo Cipriani srl., Harry's
Bar, Venice.

To friends and colleagues at home and abroad, whose various areas of
expertise helped me to understand how much Hemingway knew about
so many different things, I owe a particular debt. My thanks to
Gianfranca Balestra, Barry Barancik, Gabriel Beiner, Gavriel Ben-
Ephraim, Brian Bell, Giovanni Cecchin, Barnaby Conrad, Hjalmar Flax,
Noam Flinker, Moshe Frankel, James L. Gamble, Jr., Julian Goldberg,
Mavis Goldberg, Robert Griffin, Barry Gross, Judy Hen, Joseph J.
Feeney, S.J., the late Daniel A. Fineman, Murray Grant, Barry Gross,
Barbara Hochman, Jonathan Kandell, Bernice Kert, Alan Marbe, Gene
D. Phillips, S.J., Robert Rockaway, Robert Roripaugh, Bruce Rosen-
berg, Ernest Schwiebert, Aharon Shai, Paul Beekman Taylor, Marvin
Turk, Laura Watson, and Rizik Zuabi.

Although the details of Hemingway's life were not my primary focus,
they are highly relevant to the study of his art. All Hemingway scholars
are indebted to the magnificent contributions made by Carlos Baker,

Jeffrey Meyers, Michael Reynolds, and other biographers and biographical critics. I have found the community of Hemingway scholars to be unusually generous and supportive, and none more so than my old friend Peter L. Hays, of the University of California at Davis, who read an early draft and saved me from more mistakes than I care to remember. I am heavily in his debt. I also want to thank two new friends: Paul Smith, of Trinity College, who read the entire final draft, and Susan F. Beegel, editor of *The Hemingway Review,* who gave fine scholarly and practical advice—getting to know them has been one of the pleasures of making this book. At home, my colleagues Hana Wirth-Nesher and Zephyra Porat read sections of the manuscript and supported my efforts in every way possible.

For technical assistance and support I am grateful to Ronnie Abraham, Joe Alpher, Idalia Ortiz Gabriel, Evelyne Goldblatt, Kay Skeist, Roy Horowitz, and particularly to John Strommer, who supplied hardware and software and converted me from one system to another. A special thanks to my daughter Jessica Mandel, whose technological expertise enabled me to survive a variety of computer crises. My thanks also to Deborah Guth-Cohen and to Monique and Isadore Jutrin, who helped me with translations from the French. The translations from German, Italian and Spanish are my own.

During the writing of this book I was the recipient of much generous and stimulating hospitality. I want particularly to thank my dear relatives Mirek and Tinka Kerner, Marianne and Luis S. Axtmayer, Marilyn and Harry Cagin, and Shirley and Iván Rodríguez and their children. Old friends, who are, after all, the best, offered meals, beds, and refuge. I am grateful to Alma and Dan Rolfs, Diane and John Strommer, and especially to Andrea and Roy Horowitz, who eased my passage into and out of the United States as I traveled to libraries and conferences. They helped me survive months of research necessarily spent away from home.

I am grateful to the United States-Israel Education Foundation and to the John F. Kennedy Library Foundation for grants awarded in 1990 and 1992, and to the Cohen-Porter Fund of the English Department at Tel Aviv University, for additional support. Tel Aviv University generously provided the free time I needed to finish this project. My family and friends must be commended for having survived years of Hemingway crises, Hemingway jokes, Hemingway readings, Hemingway ups and Hemingway downs. But largest of all is the debt I owe my husband, without whose well-equipped mind and steady heart I could not have sojourned so happily in this good country.

January 1994
Tel Aviv University

USER'S GUIDE

This reference guide is intended for readers of Hemingway and is therefore closely keyed to Hemingway's novels. Its nine chapters correspond to Hemingway's nine novels, and in each chapter entries are arranged alphabetically to provide easy access. Readers who require information about a person, animal or cultural artifact mentioned by any one of Hemingway's narrators or characters will find it quickly by turning to the chapter which is devoted to that particular novel. For readers who recall a name but not the novel in which the name appears, the Index at the end of this volume collects all names into a single alphabetized list. Alphabetization is according to the English alphabet, the Spanish letters *ch, ll, ñ,* and *rr* being treated as *c, l, n,* and *r.*

The beginning of each chapter supplies the date of the first American edition of the novel and a short paragraph identifying the time and place of the action. The first endnote to each chapter briefly identifies the historical and literary prototypes for the fictional characters, as these have been established by Hemingway and his family, friends, biographers, and critics. The entries themselves form the major portion of each chapter.

TYPES OF ENTRIES

The entries fall into three broad categories: People / Characters, Animals, and Cultural Constructs.

1) *People / Characters.* In most chapters, the largest number of entries refers to the real people and the fictional characters who appear or are mentioned in that Hemingway novel. Full cross-references enable the reader to access these figures through their nicknames, pen names, noms de guerre, and other pseudonyms. Places and objects which are named after people (the Hotel Cavour in Milan, the Père Lachaise Cemetery in Paris, the Stokes mortar) are listed under Cavour, Lachaise, Stokes.

In addition to proper names, the reader will find entries for generic nouns, as the population of each novel dictates. Nameless characters, identified only by their professions, are grouped under headings such as bartenders, doctors, drivers, flower-sellers, porters, waiters, and the like. Readers interested in Hemingway's use of nameless, undefined background figures are directed to entries such as background characters, crowds, customers, men and boys, women and girls.

2) *Animals.* Fictional and historical animals are listed only when they are mentioned by their own names (the mare Lysette, the cat Boise, the dog Kibo), not when they appear as part of the landscape (hungry dog crossing the street) or in the imagery ("You have the pleasant air of a dog in heat"). An exception is the chapter on *The Old Man and the Sea,* which includes the unnamed animals (the galano shark, the Mako shark, the warbler) which come to the notice of the main character.

3) *Cultural Constructs.* Specific cultural constructs identified by name or nickname in the text (e.g., the Madrid newspaper *ABC,* the novel *Mr. Britling Sees It Through,* the poem "Thanatopsis," the movie *Birth of a Nation, Newsweek* magazine, the Free Masons, the Salvation Army, the Order of Merit) are also included and annotated.

TEXT OF THE ENTRIES

The entries may be composed of as few as two or as many as six of the following elements:

1) *Asterisk.* An asterisk * preceding the entry heading indicates that the item is discussed, mentioned, or recalled, but does not appear as part of the present action of the novel. In *The Sun Also Rises,* for example, Jake Barnes speaks about Brett Ashley's husband and Bill Gorton mentions the boxer Tiger Flowers. The entires for these absent characters begin with an asterisk: *Ashley and *Flowers, Tiger.

2) *Entry Heading.* All items are listed as they appear in the Hemingway text, even if the text presents the name in an incomplete or misspelled form. Thus, the American baseball player Frank Frisch is listed under *Fritsch, which is how the name is misspelled in *The Sun Also Rises,* and the French writer Henri Monfreid is listed under *Montfried, the doubly misspelled version of his name which appears in *Islands in the Stream.* For Spanish names and nouns, however, I have silently added accents and amended *n* to *ñ.* These marks, which the Hemingway texts usually omit, do not affect the alphabetical order of the entries, and they may help readers with pronunciation.

Because nicknames feature prominently in Hemingway's work, each proper name is followed by nicknames, pet names, and diminutives by which the character is known. Nicknames which are presented in the Hemingway text (Daughter, Devil, Rabbit) are enclosed in parentheses to distinguish them from given names. Names and nicknames of historical characters which are not presented in the Hemingway text are offered to the reader as part of the annotation, i.e., the text in square brackets.

3) *Text in Square Brackets.* If the item is historical (the prohibitionist Wayne B. Wheeler, the horse Traveller, the movie *Birth of a Nation*), not fictional, the entry supplies information culled from sources outside the novel. This "external" or extra-textual material is enclosed in square brackets [ ] to distinguish it from material provided by the Hemingway text itself. Within the square brackets, I supply as much material as I think could be useful, such as full first and family names; nicknames and pseudonyms; nationality, profession, and birth- and death-dates; and a biographical sketch, including titles of paintings, compositions, books, and other outstanding achievements, with pertinent dates. The less familiar the historical figure, the more information I thought it proper to offer. Thus the entries for *Crittenden and *Och are longer than the entries for *Hitler and *Shakespeare. For historical animals I trace the etymology or significance of the name (if any) and/or the events, occasions, and people which made the animal well-known. For cultural artifacts like books, newspapers, movies, songs, and organizations, I offer dates of composition, first performance or publication, summary of contents, historical overview, and other relevant information. Entries for purely fictional people, animals, or artifacts do not require bracketed material, although occasionally a fictional character has a historical name (Harry Morgan, Thomas Hudson) which requires annotation.

4) *Sources and Documentation.* To make the entries as easy to read as possible, most of the documentation has been relegated to the endnotes at the end of the book. Information which is generally available in dictionaries like Webster's, in the *Encyclopaedia Britannica,* or in the *Encyclopedia Americana* (e.g., birth and death dates of André Gide or J. S. Bach, or the titles of their works), is assumed to be common knowledge not requiring documentation beyond a listing of such basic reference books in the list of Works Consulted. The endnotes document information obtained from more specialized sources such as legal and medical dictionaries, sports and music encyclopedias, daily newspapers, annual volumes updating encyclopedias, including the *Britannica* and *Americana,* and reference works written in languages other than English. When the entry is controversial, the endnote may also offer a summary of scholarly debate. Full bibliographical details are provided in the list of Works Consulted.

All direct quotations, even if they are from easily available sources like the *Encyclopaedia Britannica,* are documented parenthetically immediately following the quoted material.

5) *Hemingway's Use of the Item.* Each entry contains a short paragraph which identifies the occasion and context in which the item occurs in the Hemingway text, with page references to the widely-available Scribner editions, as listed at the end of this User's Guide.

6) *Page Numbers Indicating Quoted Speech.* Page numbers presented separately at the end of the entry indicate direct speech as it occurs in monologue, dialogue or general conversation. Free indirect speech, interior monologue, or dialogue presented without quotation marks is generally not included.

ORGANIZATION OF THE MATERIAL

Alphabetical Order. Within each chapter, the entries appear in alphabetical order. Fictional and historical characters are listed by their surnames. If the Hemingway text does not provide the surname (Joan of Arc, el Greco, a character known simply as Guy or Eddy), the character is listed according to the first or given name. Occasionally a missing surname can be supplied from outside sources; in such cases, the reader is directed by a cross-reference to the main entry under the surname.

Names beginning with Mc or Mac are alphabetized according to the spelling offered by the Hemingway text. Saints are alphabetized according to their names, not under San, St. or Saint. Names which include el, de, van, von and the like are generally listed according to the substantive and not to the preposition or article preceding it: thus, de la Rosa is listed under R for Rosa, el Greco under G for Greco, and Otto von Bismarck under B for Bismarck. When the more commonly accepted form of the name includes the preposition or article, however, the name is listed accordingly; thus, Vincent Van Gogh is listed under V for Van Gogh. Personalities best known by their professional names (Michael Arlen, Greta Garbo, Jean Harlow) are listed under those names, their real names being supplied within square brackets as part of the entry.

Cross-references. A generous sprinkling of cross-references is provided to guide the reader through the maze of nicknames and professional names to the full entry for each character. In addition, cross-references lead the reader (1) to other, relevant materials in the same chapter, or (2) to the same item in another chapter, or (3) to another item in another chapter. For example:

(1) The entry on Stonewall Jackson in *Across the River and Into the Trees* (*ARIT*) refers the reader to another entry in the same chapter by indicating (see also Hill). If A. P. Hill had been mentioned by name in the Jackson entry, the insertion of (q.v.) after his name would also inform the reader that an entry exists for Hill in that same (*ARIT*) chapter.

(2) The reader may be referred to the same item in another chapter: in the *ARIT* entry for Jackson the parenthetical pointer (See also *FWBT*) directs the reader to an entry for Jackson in the chapter on *For Whom the Bell Tolls*.

(3) The cross-reference might be to another item in another chapter (See also Hill in *FWBT*).

I have used the following editions and the abbreviations, which are recommended by the Hemingway Society:

ARIT	*Across the River and Into the Trees.* 1950. New York: Scribner's, 1978.
DIA	*Death in the Afternoon.* 1932. New York: Scribner's, 1960.
DS	*The Dangerous Summer.* 1960. New York: Scribner's, 1985.
FTA	*A Farewell to Arms.* 1929. New York: Scribner's, 1957.
FWBT	*For Whom the Bell Tolls.* 1940. New York: Scribner's, 1968
GE	*The Garden of Eden.* New York: Scribner's, 1986.
GHA	*Green Hills of Africa.* 1935. New York: Scribner's, 1963, 1987.
Islands	*Islands in the Stream.* New York: Scribner's, 1970.
MF	*A Moveable Feast.* New York: Scribner's, 1964.
OMS	*The Old Man and the Sea.* New York: Scribner's, 1952.
SAR	*The Sun Also Rises.* 1926. New York: Scribner's, 1954.
THHN	*To Have and Have Not.* 1937. New York: Scribner's, 1965.
TS	*The Torrents of Spring.* 1926. New York: Scribner's, 1954, 1972.

INTRODUCTION

Literary and critical revolutions happen more or less quietly. One of the noisier of such revolutions occurred in Paris in the early 1920s, when poetry and prose, painting and music burst old boundaries and exploded into new forms. Most visible among the revolutionaries was brash, young, handsome Ernest Hemingway: the tallest, most muscular and, perhaps, the fastest and noisiest of the lot. He was "the lad" who "whittled a style for his time," so forceful that it earned him the Nobel Prize "for the influence he has exerted on contemporary style."[1] He changed the shape of the sentence and taught us a new way to read. And all this happened so quickly that long before he died, he was firmly entrenched in the canon. The revolutionary had become the establishment.

One of the things Hemingway taught his readers was the technique which Susan Beegel has called "the craft of omission."[2] As early as 1932, Hemingway informed us that his texts were more complicated than they seemed:

> If a writer of prose knows enough about what he is writing about he may omit things that he knows and the reader, if the writer is writing truly enough, will have a feeling of those things as strongly as though the writer had stated them. The dignity of movement of an ice-berg is due to only one-eighth of it being above water. A writer who omits things because he does not know them only makes hollow places in his writing.[3]

Interviewed by George Plimpton in 1958, Hemingway elaborated:

> I always try to write on the principle of the iceberg. There is seven-eighths of it underwater for every part that shows. Anything you know you can eliminate and it only strengthens your iceberg. It is the part that doesn't show. If a writer omits something because he does not know it then there is a hole in the story. . . . I have tried to eliminate everything unnecessary to conveying experience to the reader so that after he or she has read something it will become a part of his or her experience and seem actually to have happened. This is very hard to do and I've worked at it very hard.[4]

For some time now, readers have accepted that a great deal of material underlies the deceptively accessible surface of Hemingway's prose, and that this submerged material is essential to our understanding of the texts. Biography and psychology became the first focus for Carlos Baker, Philip Young, and other scholars attempting to uncover this alarmingly large mass of absent materials. Such a focus, natural and endemic to the study of all great artists, was particularly attractive to students of Hemingway, a man famed for his exploits as well as for his work, a writer who constantly referred to recognizable contemporary characters and events. No surprise, then, that this approach has yielded an extraordinarily rich harvest of books.[5]

The critical shift from biography to intellectual and cultural backgrounds was ushered in by two important events in the early 1980s: the opening of the Hemingway papers at the John F. Kennedy Library and the publication of two fine books: James D. Brasch and Joseph Sigman's *Hemingway's Library: A Composite Record* (1981) and Michael S. Reynolds' *Hemingway's Reading, 1910–1940: An Inventory* (1981). The Hemingway Collection allows us to examine how the art was made; the records of Hemingway's reading reveal how the mind that made that art was furnished. The variety, depth and range of those intellectual furnishings shocked many readers and destabilized the critical clichés about the simplicity of Hemingway's art. His prose is certainly elegant and beautiful, but it is far from simple: it is constructed out of a complicated mass of knowledge which we have barely begun to examine.

By drawing our attention to what Hemingway read and studied, Reynolds, Brasch and Sigman performed an invaluable if as yet under-valued service. Their work was so thorough that one critic could write, with great assurance, of the "well documented" fact "That Hemingway was a voracious reader and that his reading helped to shape his fiction."[6] But we are so unused to looking for the intellectual furniture in this particular artist's mind that even when we stumble across it, we miss it. Thus, another critic complains that, while it is clear that the author can think, "his fiction contains none of that conspicuous intellectual paraphernalia," none of "that give and take of cultural allusion which so often does more than anything else to place a writer as an intellectual."[7] The revolution which is taking place in Hemingway studies has begun to shift our attention away from the man, from his passion for blood sports and his troubles with his father, mother, wives, and sons, in order to focus on the relationship between the work of art and the cultural trappings which support it. Much of this submerged material has to do with what Hemingway read and knew—an impressive mass of material which I hope this book will begin to define.

Hemingway did not always approve of contemporary readings of his work. Not only did he decry the critics' penchant for biographical and

Freudian readings, but he was mightily miffed that they refused to see the intellectual dimensions of his work. Even today, Wyndham Lewis' "dumb ox" image is more readily remembered than Hemingway's own insistence that "A good writer should know as near everything as possible." "Ideally," Hemingway wrote to Malcolm Cowley, "a man should know everything." To Bernard Berenson he remarked that "A writer should know too much." From the beginning to the end of his life, Hemingway insisted on education. Although he went to war instead of to university, the tens of thousands of books in his various libraries clearly indicate that the action-hungry, hard-drinking, jet-setting cult hero was, above all, a learned man. His scholarship was multi-lingual and cross-cultural and, as often happens with auto-didacts, idiosyncratic: he read about Renaissance painting, classical architecture and American history and literature. He studied the art and folklore of the Spanish bullfight and the African hunt, the history and design of English and American weaponry, the writings of ancient and modern military strategists and theorists, the biology and habits of the animals he admired. A man who helped shape his time, he was also immersed in the facts, rumors, and scandals of his various environments. To his almost compulsive reading he brought an analytical mind and an impressively retentive memory.

Inevitably, the extensive knowledge he acquired underlies the fiction. But, in accordance with his "iceberg" theory, Hemingway does not tell us the "everything" which we now know he knew. He argued that if "everything" is included in the art, the results can be disastrous: "You know Ezra [Pound] can't leave any erudition true or false out of a poem and what the results are sometimes. . . . Erudition shouldn't show."[8] The withholding of information is a deliberate esthetic decision of an artist who insisted that his work be read carefully, by informed readers. To such an audience, the deeply embedded material remains available. Hemingway's contemporaries, for example, could often supply the withheld information suggested by the many people, artifacts, and even animals that appear or are mentioned in the novels, and were able to apply that knowledge to the text. The passage of time, however, has distanced us from that material.

Similarly, readers who share all of Hemingway's many interests—history, boxing, skiing, hunting, fishing, travel, language, literature, painting, war, and the Catholic church, to name just a few—will recognize not just the names he mentions, but the connotations evoked by references to people or events connected with these topics. Few of us can claim to know all these contexts, just as few of us are familiar with the governments, languages, literatures, and sports of the various countries Hemingway visited, studied, or lived in. Lacking the contexts, we may easily misread or under-read his work.

Introduction

While working on this book, I have been surprised at how much material the details of the novels have enabled me to uncover. Most of the proper names in the novels are historical, referring to people, events, animals, books, songs, and organizations which we have forgotten or, perhaps, never knew. Working with the assumption that every detail in Hemingway's work is potentially significant, I have attempted to annotate, but not to interpret, Hemingway's novels. I began by aiming for comprehensiveness and objectivity, but realized soon enough that the first was probably unattainable and the second a chimera: selection and organization are themselves interpretive acts. Even so, my aim has been to provide material for interpretation, to identify and flesh out detail, to recover embedded materials and forgotten contexts which readers might find suggestive or useful for interpretation. In the process I have, of course, formed opinions, but these are a by-product and not the moving force for the making of this book.

Because Hemingway's prose is multi-layered, he appeals to a variety of readers. Hence his continuing appeal to popular as well as academic audiences. He can be read by any reader who brings intelligence to the task: he is not impenetrable. But like every great artist, he rewards those whose reading is informed and whose scrutiny is thoughtful. To all such readers, who stumble on a detail and want the embedded facts that underlie the fiction, I offer this book.

THE TORRENTS OF SPRING

A ROMANTIC NOVEL
IN HONOR OF THE PASSING
OF A GREAT RACE

———

ERNEST HEMINGWAY
AUTHOR OF "IN OUR TIME"

Scribner dust jacket for the first edition of *The Torrents of Spring* (courtesy Charles Scribner's Sons, an imprint of the Macmillan Publishing Company; and by permission of the Houghton Library, Harvard University)

CHAPTER I

THE TORRENTS OF SPRING
A ROMANTIC NOVEL IN HONOR
OF THE PASSING OF A GREAT RACE

(1926)

A parody of Sherwood Anderson's *Dark Laughter* and, less directly, of his *Many Marriages, The Torrents of Spring* relates the adventures of two heroes: the war veteran Yogi Johnson, who fears he has lost his interest in women, and the would-be musician and writer Scripps O'Neil, who marries one woman after another. The action takes place in late winter and early spring, in Mancelona and in Petoskey, Michigan.[1] The book is composed of four sections, each introduced by a quote from Henry Fielding (q.v.); four Author's Notes to the Reader; and two Post Scripts.

American Mercury. See *Mercury.*

*the anarchists. Scripps' father used to take him to see the monument erected in memory of the Chicago anarchists; the boy would have preferred to visit the amusement park near-by (9; see Chicago anarchists).

*Anderson, [Sherwood. American novelist and short story writer, 1876–1941. Anderson's novels include *Windy McPherson's Son* (1916), *Marching Men* (1917, about coal miners, not about soldiers), *Poor White* (1920), *Many Marriages* (1923), *Dark Laughter* (1925, his only best-seller), *Beyond Desire* (1932), and *Kit Brandon* (1936). He was a master of the short story: "I Want to Know Why," "Death in the Woods," and "I'm a Fool" are among his best. Anderson is remembered for his collection *Winesburg, Ohio* (1919).]
    The Torrents of Spring is a deliberate parody of the subject matter and style of *Dark Laughter* by "that fellow Anderson" (53; see also Fred).

*Ariel. [An airy spirit, servant to Prospero in Shakespeare's *The Tempest*.]
Mandy suggests this name for Scripps' bird (39).

*Austin, Mary [Hunter. American novelist and playwright, 1868–1934. Austin lived many years in the American southwest where she observed and studied the desert and the American Indian. Several of her books deal with Indians and their environment: *The Land of Little Rain* (1903, a sympathetic description of desert life), *The Basket Woman* (1904, a collection of short stories), *The Arrow Maker* (1911, a play), and *The American Rhythm* (1923, includes studies of American Indian songs). Other books, like *Isidro* (1905), deal with the freedom of the individual spirit.]
A picture of this contemporary author adorns the committee room of the sophisticated town Indians' club (65).

the bartender. See Bruce.

*The Beggar's Opera. [A play with songs or "airs," by John Gay, English poet and playwright, 1685–1732. *The Beggar's Opera* mocked Italian opera, much in vogue among fashionable audiences of the day, and served as an "exposure of the corrupt political methods of Sir Robert Walpole" (Cecil A. Moore, "Introduction," *Twelve Famous Plays of the Restoration and Eighteenth Century* [New York: Modern Library, 1933], xx). First performed in 1728, it was enormously successful. Gay wrote a sequel, *Polly* (or *Polly Peachum*), in 1729, which Walpole angrily banned from the stage. Only a few years before the writing of *TS*, *The Beggar's Opera* enjoyed a successful revival at the Lyric Theatre, Hammersmith, London, running for more than three years, from 5 June 1920 to 17 December 1923.[2] In 1928 the composer Kurt Weill (1900–1950) and the playwright Bertold Brecht (1898–1956) produced *The Threepenny Opera,* a modern rendition of Gay's work.]
When the drummer suggests that if Scripps' bird is a parrot it could be named Polly, a common name for such birds, Mandy, always anxious to show off her erudition, correctly but irrelevantly adds that *The Beggar's Opera* has a character named Polly (40).

*Bender, [Charles Albert] (Chief Bender). [American baseball player, 1883–1954. Between 1903 and 1914 Chief Bender, a Chippewa Indian, won 193 regular season games and six World Series games for his team, the Philadelphia Athletics. In 1915 he played for Baltimore (Federal League) and in 1916 and 1917 for Philadelphia (National League); all told he scored 212 major league victories and had 128 losses. After retiring from professional baseball, Chief Bender coached at the United

States Naval Academy, 1924–1928. He was elected to the Baseball Hall of Fame in 1953.]

A picture of this famous Indian baseball player adorns the committee room of the pseudo-British club of the sophisticated town Indians (65).

the bird. The bird accompanies Scripps on his adventures, traveling inside his shirt from Mancelona to Petoskey. Its identity and sex are never firmly established: it may be a hawk, a falcon, a robin, a parrot (40); it reminds Diana of an osprey (19, 84); it could be either male or female (40). The names Ariel, Puck, and Polly (qq.v.) are suggested for it, but none is adopted. Although originally dead (8), the bird is able to peck at Scripps, eat ketchup and beans at Brown's Beanery, and sleep. It is the only thing that Diana salvages from her marriage to Scripps (84).

The Birth of a Nation. [D. W. Griffith's epic movie about the American Civil War and its aftermath was first released in 1915. The movie, written by Griffith and Frank Woods, is based on Thomas Dixon's novel *The Clansman* and reflects the novel's anti-black bias. It presents exciting battle scenes and a dramatic "rescue" by the Ku Klux Klan. D. W. Griffith (1875–1948) used the innovative film techniques he had developed, such as cross-cutting, flashback, fade-in, and fade-out. Other important films by Griffith were *Intolerance* (1915), *Broken Blossoms* (1919) and *Orphans of the Storm* (1921).]

Yogi complains that "the last part" of Willa Cather's popular war novel was based on the movie *Birth of a Nation* (57) and not on first-hand experience (see Cather).

*Blackstone. See Hartman.

Bookman. [A monthly literary magazine, published from 1895 to 1933, the *Bookman* was modeled on the English magazine of the same name. It was a conservative magazine, devoted to literature and criticism. Although it published English and American authors, it favored and encouraged Americans. See also Farrar, who edited the magazine from 1921–1927.][3]

Diana and Scripps subscribe to the *Bookman*. In her competition with Mandy over the affections of Scripps, Diana arms herself with literary anecdotes from this magazine (43).

Borrow, Mr. One of the two very old men (the other is Mr. Shaw, q.v.) who "make all the pumps" which compete in "the big international pump races" (30). He hand-crafted the Peerless Pounder (q.v.).

Speaks: 30–31.

*Brickley, [Charles Edward (Charlie,] Charley). [American football player, stock broker, and advertising salesman, 1891–1949. Often called football's greatest field-goal kicker, he kicked thirty-four goals in three seasons, was twice named to Walter Camp's All-American team, and was the captain of the Harvard team. He made football history in 1913, when he kicked five field goals in one game and thus brought Harvard to a 15–5 victory over Yale. He is reputed to have kicked field goals even when his eyes were injured and he couldn't see the goal posts. He and Eddie Mahan (q.v.) made Harvard University an almost unbeatable football team in 1911–1915; their coach was Percy Haughton. After graduation Brickley became head coach at Boston College and in 1920, after his military service, he opened his own brokerage business, Charles E. Brickley & Co. Between 1920 and 1927, he was charged with larceny three times, acquitted twice, convicted the third time, and sentenced to twelve months in jail. In later years he ran a health club in the Hotel Roosevelt in New York and worked as an advertising salesman.][4]

Thoughts of Harvard University bring Charley Brickley and Eddie Mahan to Scripps' mind (38).

*Brodie, [Stephen] (Steve). [American saloon keeper, actor, and publicity seeker, 1858–1901. A strong swimmer, Brodie achieved a modest reputation as a life-saver in New York. In July 1886, he jumped off the Brooklyn Bridge into the East River (a distance of about 175 feet) on a bet. This spectacular feat brought him notoriety and wealth: Brodie became a professional bridge-jumper, touring the country and appearing as a well-paid circus stuntman. When he opened his saloon on the Bowery, he continued to appear in the news: he was arrested for abducting his future wife, was stabbed once, handed out umbrellas to surprised passers-by on rainy days, and gave free meals and free funerals to the poor people in his neighborhood. In 1894 he began his theatrical career, as subject and star of a sketch entitled "One Night in Brodie's Barroom." The *New York Times* reported his death on 1 April, 1898; the next day a headline proclaimed "Steve Brodie Very Much Alive" (*New York Times*, 2 April, 1898, 14:2). Although at least one person was killed attempting to repeat Brodie's feat, enthusiasm for bridge-jumping survived even Brodie's death. Hemingway might have read about swimmer Daniel Carone's 1921 leap, performed in front of movie cameras and reported on the front page of the *New York Times* (11 April, 1921). Two months after *The Torrents of Spring* was published, Peter McGovern also jumped, driven by a sudden "desire to try the stunt that made 'Steve' Brodie famous" (*New York Times*, 13 July, 1926, 10:3); he suffered only a few bruises.]

In one of his nonsensical, mock-Andersonian lists, Yogi mentions Steve Brodie, defining him as someone who had "taken a chance" (75).

Brown, Brown's Beanery. [*Polk's Petoskey City and Emmet County*

Directory for the year 1903 lists Dr. George C. Braun as the owner of the New Braun Hotel and Restaurant, located at 210-212 Howard Street, Petoskey, Michigan. The establishment boasted a Lunch Counter and Dining Room specializing in chicken and fish. Until the late 1930s, Braun's was owned by John George Braun.][5]
Brown's Beanery is the setting for much of the action: Scripps and his bird meet both Diana and Mandy while eating beans, and all the main characters gather here in the last section of the novel. The owner, though not identified as Mr. Brown, appears briefly (78).

*Browne [General Sir Samuel J.] (Sam). [English soldier, 1834–1901. Browne captured the strategically important fort of Ali Masjid in the Khyber Pass at the outbreak of the second Afghan War in 1878, at the close of which the British were in control both of the Khyber Pass and the Khyber tribes. The Sam Browne belt, named after this officer, is a leather belt which has a shoulder strap attached to it.]
When Johnson finally tracks down the beautiful woman who had seduced him in Paris, he sees that she is a prostitute. Preparing for dalliance, her client divests himself of his Sam Browne belt (80; see also the officer).

Bruce. The black bartender at the town Indians' club, he is "an eccentric . . . and a good-hearted chap" (64). He speaks in a thick dialect and laughs the "high-pitched, uncontrollable . . . dark laughter of the Negro" (64), a direct reference to Anderson's novel *Dark Laughter* which Hemingway is parodying.
Speaks: 64, 66, 67.

*Buque, Marquis of. [Probably Ninian Edward Crichton-Stuart (1883–1915, killed in action), second son of the 3rd Marquess of Bute. Ninian was MP for Cardiff (1910–1915); he was Lt.-Col., 6th Battalion, Welch Regiment. As 2nd Lieut., 3rd Battalion of this same Regiment, Ford was stationed at Cardiff Castle.]
Mandy reports that he was extremely wealthy and served in Ford Madox Ford's regiment (85–86; see also Gosse).

*Carlisle Indian School. [At the end of the 19th century, the American government stopped distributing funds for sectarian education and instead established a federally-operated system of schools. For the Indian population, boarding schools were set up where young Indians, living apart from their families and tribes, could be educated as "Americans." Many army forts were converted into such schools, among them the one in Carlisle, Pennsylvania. The Carlisle Indian School, founded by General Richard Henry Pratt in 1879, established the system of "outing," placing its students in the homes of white families where they could learn "the

American way of life.'' The school achieved national prominence through its extraordinary athletes; it was closed in 1918.]⁶

Several of the people whose portraits hang in the Indians' club house had been associated with the Carlisle Indian School (see Thorpe, Warner). The two woods Indians whom Yogi befriends ''had been to Carlisle'' (55).

*Carpentier, Georges. [French boxer, 1894–1975; light-heavyweight champion of the world, 1920–1921, and European champion in four different weight classes. He fought and lost to Jack Dempsey in 1921 and to Gene Tunney in 1924. He retired in 1927 (after the publication of *TS*) and was elected to the Boxing Hall of Fame in 1964. After his retirement he ran a restaurant in Paris.]

Diana includes Georges Carpentier in her list of people whom she considers strange (41).

*Caslon, [William. English engraver and typefounder, 1692–1766. Caslon's clear and legible type, which secured him the patronage of English and European printers, modernized book-production, making books look as we know them today, rather than printed imitations of hand-produced manuscripts. The typeface he designed between 1720–1726, known as Caslon, is particularly legible; hence the printer's maxim, ''When in doubt, use Caslon.'' Caslon's son carried on the business after his father's death.]

In an Author's Note to the Reader, Hemingway dismisses the printer and then lists several printer-related items, including the print-type ''twelve-point open-face Caslon'' (46).

*Cather, Willa [Silbert. American novelist, 1873–1947. Cather was born in Virginia but grew up in Nebraska; many of her novels explore the clash between materialistic and spiritual values as these relate to the American frontier she knew. She also drew on her past for the many immigrants who appear in the novels. Cather is best known for *My Antonia* (1918) and *Death Comes for the Archbishop* (1927). *One of Ours* (1922), which is seldom read today, was a best-seller in its day and brought Cather the 1923 Pulitzer Prize. It presents the career of Claude Wheeler from his childhood on an American farm to his death on a European battlefield during World War I.]

Yogi Johnson, himself a war veteran like Hemingway, objects to the production of war stories by non-combatants, although the example he mentions, Cather's war novel, was very popular among ex-servicemen (57). The narrative insists that ignorant civilians should not write about such serious issues as war because ''Literature has too strong an effect on people's minds'' (57).

*Caxton, [William. English printer, c.1422–1491. Caxton was the first English printer. He learned printing in Cologne (1470–1472), set up a press in Bruges (1474) at great personal expense and there printed his own translation of Raoul Le Fevre's *Recueil des Histoires de Troye,* the first book printed in English. In 1476 Caxton translated and published another book, *The Game and Playe of the Chesse,* which treats chess as an allegory of life. That same year he returned to England and set up a press at Westminster which produced about 100 items, including Chaucer, Malory, Gower, Lydgate and many devotional works.]

In an Author's Note to the Reader, Hemingway mentions Caxton, Gutenberg and Caslon (qq.v.), three important printers (46).

Century Magazine. [*Scribner's Monthly, an Illustrated Magazine for the People* (1870–1881) was bought by the Century Company in 1881 and became *The Century Illustrated Monthly Magazine* (1881–1929). Hemingway's reference is to this magazine which, under the editorship of Glenn Frank (1921–1925), focused on public affairs and short stories and carried fewer illustrations than previously: "it had a distinctly literary tone" (Mott, *A History of American Magazines* III, 479). Hewitt H. Howland, who followed Frank as editor (1925–1930), deemphasized fiction. In 1930 *Century Magazine* was bought by *Forum* (q.v.); the resulting *Forum and Century* continued publication until 1940. In the mid-1920s, when Hemingway was writing *The Torrents of Spring, Century, Harper's,* and *Scribner's* were important, well-established literary magazines. See also Frank, *Scribner's,* Van Doren.]

In her pitiful attempt to compete with the buxom Mandy and her literary anecdotes, Diana reads the leading literary publications, including *Century* (44).

*Cézanne, [Paul. French painter, 1839–1906. Cézanne, one of the greatest of the post-impressionists, influenced many 20th-century artists and artistic movements; he is considered a forerunner of Cubism. Cézanne insisted on personal expression and on the integrity and independence of the painting itself. He is best known for his landscapes. Cézanne was born into a well-to-do family; while he was still a young man, his father settled an allowance on him that freed him from money worries. Cézanne never had to earn his living.]

When he decides to take the job at the pump factory, Scripps comforts himself that other artists, including Cézanne, had also done menial labor (23).

*Chicago anarchists. [An active society of anarchists rose up in Chicago in 1884; they opposed big business as well as governmental institutions, and encouraged strikes and other forms of labor unrest. In May 1886, a strike against the McCormick works resulted in a riot, during which several strikers were killed by police. The Chicago anarchists met at Haymarket Square the next day to protest the incident and propound their revolutionary views; the police interfered, a bomb was thrown, seven policemen were killed and many others injured. Although the bomb-thrower could not be identified, the courts condemned seven anarchists to death and one to 15 years' imprisonment, on the grounds that they were morally conspirators and accomplices in the killing, having advocated violence in the pursuit of their political goals. Of the seven condemned to death, two had their sentences commuted to life imprisonment, one committed suicide and four were hanged in November, 1887: Albert Parsons, Adolf Fischer, George Engle, and August Spies. In 1893 the surviving three anarchists were pardoned by Governor J. P. Altgeld, who felt that insufficient evidence had been presented and that both the jury and the judge had been prejudiced against the defendants. The case, known as the Haymarket Affair, roused great passion. A massive monument was erected in the anarchists' memory in Waldheim Cemetery, Chicago. It shows the figure of a woman (Justice) looking ahead into the future; partially obscured by her draperies is a fallen worker, on whose head she is placing a laurel wreath. The inscription at the base reads: "The day will come when our silence will be more powerful than the voices you are throttling today."][7]

Seeing the engineer (q.v.) on the train with "his hand on the throttle," Scripps is reminded of the inscription on the Anarchist Memorial Monument, which he recalls only imperfectly. Scripps, who was a small boy when he last saw the monument, misremembers the impressive central figure as "a black angel" (9).

*Clemenceau, [Georges Benjamin Eugene. French physician, editor, writer, translator, and statesman, 1841–1929; premier of France, 1906–1909, 1917–1920. Clemenceau, an ardent republican, was jailed for a short period for his opposition to Napoleon III (1808–1873; emperor of the French, 1852–1870). His four years in the United States in the late 1860s strengthened his commitment to the principle of separation of church and state. When he returned to France in 1870, he began his political career, serving as mayor of Montmartre and as a member and later president of the Paris Municipal Council and entering national politics with his election to the Chamber of Deputies of the Third Republic in 1876, where he served for nine years. In the 1880s he was a powerful member of the opposition; in 1893 he was accused of dishonesty and involvement in the Panama Canal scandals and, losing the next election, was out of politics until 1902. In those nine years he turned his energies to writing and journalism: he wrote a play set in China, the novel *The Strongest*, the philosophical treatise *Great Pan*, and a considerable amount of criticism. In 1897 he founded the daily *L'Aurore,* which published *J'Accuse* (1898), Emile Zola's famous attack on the establishment which had framed Alfred Dreyfus. Clemenceau's own writings on behalf of Dreyfus filled seven volumes (1899–1903). In 1902 he was reelected to the Senate and in 1906, at age 65, he became Minister of the Interior and, a few months later, Prime Minister. When his government fell in 1909 he returned to journalism, founding the daily *L'Homme Libre* in which he urged France to prepare for war against the Germans. He was recalled to politics in 1917, when at age 76, he served both as War Minister and Prime Minister. He is credited with leading France from defeat to victory, and was appointed chairman of the Paris Peace Conference, in which he argued that severe conditions be imposed on Germany, conditions which his Allies rejected. In the years of his retirement Clemenceau wrote *Au soir de la pensée* (1927), a book on the painter Claude Monet in 1928, and *Grandeurs et misères d'une victoire,* published posthumously in 1930.]

Diana includes Joan of Arc and Clemenceau in a list of "strange" French people (41).

*CMR [Cape Mounted Rifles. Other initials: DSO (Companion of the Distinguished Service Order), GR & I (Grand Rapids & Indiana Railroad), MC (Military Cross), VC (Victoria Cross), qq.v. Also see Order of Merit.]

The taller of the Indians, a veteran of World War I, identifies his unit, the Cape Mounted Rifles, and various military decorations by their initials (58).

*the coiffeur in Paris. The first and only anecdote which Diana tells Scripps is about her first visit to Paris, for the Exposition [there was one in 1889 and another in 1900]. When they first arrived, Diana recalls, she and her mother visited a hairdresser (20). When Diana's mother mysteriously disappears and is replaced by an elderly general, the coiffeur testifies that he saw Diana with the general, not with her mother (21). In his Final Note to the Reader, the author explains that the police had forced the coiffeur to lie (90; see also *concierge,* doctor, driver, police). Hairdressers appear in several other novels: see the hairdresser in *FTA,* *the hairdresser in *THHN,* Jean in *GE.*

*the *concierge*. [The *concierge* is the resident caretaker, doorkeeper, and janitor; in short, the person in charge of a hotel or other tenanted building. See also *SAR* and *MF.*]

When Diana's mother disappears from the hotel in Paris, the *concierge* insists that Diana had arrived with a French general, and shows her the (altered) register to support his claim that her mother had not stayed at the hotel (21; see also the coiffeur, doctor, driver, police).

the cook at Brown's Beanery. He is a black man and, like Bruce, is good at his work, talks in dialect, and laughs "a high-pitched, haunting laugh" (41) reminiscent of the "dark laughter" of Sherwood Anderson's black characters. He throws the naked Indian woman out of Brown's Beanery (78; see also 17, 20, 23, 34).

*Coolidge, Dr. [John Calvin (Silent Cal). American lawyer and politician, 1872–1933. Coolidge became 30th President of the United States when his predecessor, Warren G. Harding, died in 1923; he was elected President in 1924 but refused his party's nomination in 1928. The Republican Coolidge was President of the United States at the time of the events of the novel; he is also mentioned in *SAR* and *GE*.]
    Scripps, "talking wildly," speaks out against Coolidge (18).

*Coxey, [Jacob Sechler. American businessman and politician, 1854–1951. Coxey was a social reformer, interested in solving financial problems in general and unemployment in particular. After the Panic of 1893, Coxey led groups of unemployed, known as Coxey's Army, to Washington, D.C. to demand federally funded employment in public works. He reached Washington with only 500 people; the leaders of the march were arrested for walking on the Capitol lawn.]
    Yogi Johnson, walking aimlessly with the two woods Indians through the cold streets of Petoskey, compares the three veterans to the unsuccessful marchers of Coxey's Army (73). Yogi and his friends eventually head for Brown's Beanery.

*Cree. [A tribe of North American Indians of Algonquin stock, like the Fox (q.v.), who live mostly in the Canadian provinces of Manitoba and Saskatchewan. Both the Plains Cree and the Woodland Cree were expert game hunters. The Woodland Cree language and culture resemble that of the Ojibwa, who are also of Algonquin stock.]
    When he offers to propose Yogi for membership to the Indians' club, Red Dog asks Yogi which tribe he belongs to: "Sac and Fox? Jibway? Cree, I imagine" (65). When he discovers that Yogi is not an Indian at all, he angrily kicks him out of the club.

the crowd. Several groups, all masculine, congregate in different places: in the barber shop (14–15; see also 27), the pump factory (28–29), and the town Indians' club (61, 64; see also men and boys).

*the crowd. Yogi recalls other crowds, also predominantly masculine: the voyeurs at the Paris night-club (80), the combatants at a football game or on the battle field (55–57; see also Coxey, *men).

*Crowninshield, [Francis Welsh] (Frank). Crowninshield was also known by the pseudonym Arthur Loring Bruce. American editor, critic and humorist, 1872–1947. He published two magazines, *Bookman* (1895–1900) and *Metropolitan Magazine* (1900–1902), and was the art editor of *Century Magazine* (1910–1913) as well as the long-time editor of *Vanity Fair* (1914–1935). He also wrote *Manners for the Metropolis* (1908) and *The Bridge Fiend* (1909).]

   Although Diana is desperately trying to keep up with the literary scene in order to hold on to Scripps, she paradoxically finds that she doesn't have time to think about a number of important contemporary literary figures, such as Marianne Moore, e.e. cummings, and Frank Crowninshield (41).

*cummings, e[dward] e[stlin]. [American poet, novelist, painter, 1894–1962. Cummings' first novel, *The Enormous Room* (1922), was based on his experiences as an inmate in a French prison during World War I; he had been charged with treasonable correspondence but was later exonerated. In his poetry cummings experimented with format, rhythm, spelling, punctuation, and language. He achieved fame for his collections of poetry such as *Tulips and Chimneys* (1923), *Vi Va* (1931), *No Thanks* (1935), *1 X 1* (1944) and *95 Poems* (1958). One of his books, published in 1930, has no title. He spelled his name in lower-case letters.]

   Diana reflects that now that she is married she has little time to worry about French cabinet crises or other matters such as e.e. cummings and his novel (41).

*Custer, General [George Armstrong. American soldier, 1836–1876. Custer earned steady promotions during the American Civil War, achieving the rank of major general. After the Civil War Custer was appointed to the Seventh U.S. Cavalry, winning a major victory against the Cheyenne in 1868 and engaging the Sioux in battle several times over a period of years. In 1876 he and his companies, totalling less than 700 men, faced about 4000 Sioux under the leadership of Chief Sitting Bull. Custer and more than 200 of his men were killed at Little Big Horn; this famous battle was depicted in a widely-distributed advertisement for Anheuser-Busch beer. The ad is mentioned in *FWBT* and *THHN*, s.v. Custer; Anheuser-Busch is mentioned in *Islands*, and Custer and his wife in *ARIT*.]

   A picture of General Custer adorns the committee room of the pseudo-British club of the sophisticated town Indians (65).

*Dawson, Franky. Yogi mentions that "Dawson was killed" at the pump races in Italy (30).

Detroit News. [Daily newspaper established in 1905 and published continuously since then. In 1960 it merged with the *Detroit Times* to form the *Detroit News and Times.*]

The drummer (q.v.) reads this newspaper throughout the novel (36, 82) and takes it with him when he exits (82).

*the *Dial,* the *Dial* prize. [*Dial* magazine was published from 1880 until 1929. Established in Chicago, it was a staid monthly journal of criticism. But under the editorship and co-ownership of Scofield Thayer (1919–1926), who moved it to New York, it became one of the leading "small" literary magazines which published modern art, innovative fiction and poetry, and encouraged young talent.[8] Hemingway recalls that the *Dial* award was $1,000 (*MF* 123); literary historians put it at $2,000. The first such prize went to Sherwood Anderson in 1921; subsequent awards went to T. S. Eliot (1922), Marianne Moore (1924), and e.e. cummings (1925), among others. The *Dial* (q.v. in *MF*) rejected Hemingway's work.]

Scripps has published two stories in the *Dial* (33). Diana Scripps mentions the magazine and its prestigious prize (41; see Moore, Seldes, and Thayer).

Diana. See Scripps, Diana.

*Diana's parents. Diana claims that her father and Gladstone (q.v.) were schoolfellows (34) in England, and that her mother, also named Diana (42), disappeared mysteriously in Paris (21–22, 90; see also coiffeur, *concierge,* doctor, driver, police).

*the doctor. A doctor was called in when Diana's mother suddenly took sick in the hotel in Paris. Diagnosing bubonic plague, he "warned the authorities," who promptly caused Diana's mother to disappear (90; see also police).

*Dodge, Mabel. [Full name: Mabel Ganson Evans Dodge Sterne Luhan. American writer and patroness of the arts, 1879–1962. She wrote *Lorenzo in Taos* (1932, about D. H. Lawrence's years in Taos, New Mexico), *Taos and Its Artists* (1947), and an autobiographical series, *Intimate Memories* (1933–1947). Her fourth husband, Antonio Luhan, was a Pueblo Indian, and in her later years she preferred Indian civilization to the Italian and New York high society she had known earlier.][9]

A signed picture of this writer adorns the town Indians' club (65).

*Dos Passos, John [Roderigo. American novelist, 1896–1970. His controversial first novel, *Three Soldiers* (1921), derived from his service in the French Ambulance Service, the Red Cross, and the U. S. Medical

Corps during World War I. *Manhattan Transfer* (1925) paints a picture of New York City, and the trilogy entitled *U.S.A.* (1930–1936) discusses the American experience in the first three decades of the 20th century. Hemingway and Dos Passos were good friends in the 1920s but the friendship soured in the late 1930s. See also *GHA*.]

In an authorial note, Hemingway praises Dos Passos' work and personality and reports that Dos Passos admires Hemingway's work in progress (i.e., *The Torrents of Spring,* 68); later we hear that Dos Passos has left Paris and gone to England (77).

*the driver. He had driven Diana and her mother from the train station to the hotel in Paris from which Diana's mother mysteriously disappeared. Called in the next day by the police who are investigating the disappearance, he denies seeing Diana's mother (22). The mystery is cleared up in the last few paragraphs of the book (90).

the drummer. [A commercial traveler or traveling salesman who drums up business for his company.]

The drummer is a habitué of Brown's Beanery, admired by Scripps for his "sound ideas," like determining the sex of the bird before giving it a name (40). Although he is married (36), this salesman seems to have all his meals at Brown's Beanery, where he eats steak and potatoes and reads the *Detroit News,* q.v. He is eventually considered "an old friend" of Scripps, Diana, and Mandy (82). He wants to tell O'Neil "about a pretty beautiful thing that happened to me" (i.e., a sexual adventure or "travelling salesman" story) but refrains because Mandy and Diana are listening (41).

Speaks: 36, 40, 78, 79, 82.

*DSO. [The Distinguished Service Order (DSO) was founded on 6 September 1886 by Queen Victoria. To be eligible, one must be an officer and have been mentioned "in despatches for meritorious or distinguished service in the field, or before the enemy." It is often but not necessarily awarded for gallantry under fire ("Knighthood" and "Medals," *Encyclopaedia Britannica,* 11th ed., XV: 861 and XVIII: 17). James Ellis notes that in World War I slang, the initials DSO "stood for 'dick shot off'."]

The taller of the two Indians, who attained the rank of major in World War I, was awarded two British decorations, the DSO and the MC (q.v.) (58).

*Emerson, [Ralph Waldo. American essayist, philosopher, and poet, 1803–1882. Emerson helped define the great American transcendentalist movement. He is best known for essays such as "Self-Reliance," "Compensation," and "The American Scholar." Emerson worked his way through Harvard as a messenger and waiter.][10]

When he decides to take the job at the pump factory, Scripps comforts himself that Emerson had also done menial labor (23).

the engineer. Scripps sees an engineer and a fireman on a passing train; Catherine Bourne sees a similar engineer and fireman on a moving train (*GE* 78). The vision of the working man reminds him of the Chicago anarchists (q.v.). The connection is presented through the word ''throttle'' (9).

The Enormous Room. Novel by e.e. cummings (q.v.).

*Enright, Ethel. [An Enright family lived in Oak Park, Illinois, Hemingway's home town. Elizabeth Enright (Mrs. Robert Gillham, 1909–1968) was the author of about fifty short stories, many of them for children. Among her best known books are *Thimble Summer,* for which she was awarded the 1938 Newbery Medal, and the *Gone-Away Lake* series (1955–1957).][11]
    The telegrapher at the train station in Petoskey mentions that he knew a girl named Ethel Enright in Mancelona (13).

*Eton. [A prestigious English school which prepares boys for university and has a particularly close relationship with King's College, Cambridge. Both Eton and King's College were founded by King Henry VI in 1440. See also *GE*.]
    Diana claims that her father and Gladstone were together at Eton (34).

*Farrar, John [Chipman. American editor and poet, 1896–1974. As a very young man, Farrar become editor of *Bookman,* 1921–1927, giving it ''a somewhat more personal and attractive air'' and making it ''a kind of working guide to the current literary movements'' (Mott, IV, 458). From 1921–1924 the magazine had a department, ''The Literary Spotlight,'' which presented ''short, sometimes caustic sketches of contemporary writers'' (Mott, IV, 439). After editing the *Bookman,* Farrar was editor, vice president and finally chairman of the board of the publishing house Farrar & Rinehart (1929–1944) and chairman of the board of Farrar, Straus & Giroux (1946–1974).]
    Diana memorizes Farrar's editorials in the vain hope of keeping her husband (43).

*Fielding, Henry. [English lawyer and novelist, 1707–1754. Fielding studied law and was called to the bar in 1740. His great works—*Joseph Andrews* (1742), *Tom Jones* (1749) and *Amelia* (1751)—helped establish and define the English novel. In *The Torrents of Spring* Hemingway quotes from Fielding's ''Author's Preface'' to *Joseph Andrews* (full title: *The History of the Adventures of Joseph Andrews, and of His Friend Mr. Abraham Adams. Written in Imitation of the Manner of Cervantes, Author of Don Quixote).* When Hemingway wrote *The Torrents of Spring, Joseph Andrews* was seen as a take-off on Samuel Richardson's popular novel *Pamela.* It presented similar situations and characters: the title character Joseph Andrews, for example, is introduced as the brother of Richardson's servant-heroine Pamela Andrews (he turns out to be the son of an important family), and his virtue, like Pamela's, is under attack. But Fielding's real parody of *Pamela* was *Shamela* (not definitively recognized as Fielding's work until twenty years after the publication of *The Torrents of Spring*).[12] Today *Joseph Andrews* is read not just as parody but also as social satire and, more importantly, as a forerunner of the great *Tom Jones.* Similarly, *The Torrents of Spring* might be reconsidered in the context of Hemingway's other work, and not dismissed simply as a parody of *Dark Laughter,* though it certainly is that. See also *MF.*]

Hemingway takes the epigraphs which introduce each of the four parts of *The Torrents of Spring* from Fielding (unnumbered pp. 1, 25, 49, 71).

the fireman. O'Neil sees a fireman on a passing train (9; see also the engineer).

*Fitzgerald, F. Scott. [American writer, 1896–1940. Fitzgerald's early work—*This Side of Paradise* (1920) and two collections of stories, *Flappers and Philosophers* (1920) and *Tales of the Jazz Age* (1922)— were popular successes. His best novel is the beautiful *The Great Gatsby* (1925); it was followed by *Tender Is the Night* (1934) and the unfinished *The Last Tycoon.* Edmund Wilson collected some of Fitzgerald's essays, stories, letters, and autobiographical pieces in *The Crack-Up,* published posthumously in 1945. Fitzgerald and Hemingway had a complicated relationship. See *MF.*]

In an Author's Note to Reader, Hemingway pokes fun at his often intoxicated friend, who overstays his welcome and then sits down in the fireplace (76).

*Foch, [Marshal Ferdinand. French military leader, 1851–1929. Foch had argued for a single, unified allied command but his recommendations had been rejected, and France's forces, led by General Joffre, remained independent of their British allies for much of World War I. When Foch was given control of allied forces late in World War I (May 1918), Haig and Pétain, the commanders of the British and French armies respectively, both came under his orders; they were soon joined by American forces, led by General Pershing. By July, the Allied forces had turned almost-certain defeat into victory, largely due to the military genius of Foch. Foch was elevated to the rank of Marshal of France. He is the author of *Des princips de la guerre* (1903) and *De la conduite de la guerre* (1904).]

Scripps wishes he had served in World War I, like Foch (37) and Joffre (q.v.).

*Ford, Ford Madox [Hueffer. English novelist, critic, and historian, 1873–1939. Ford published his short but sophisticated novel, *The Good Soldier,* in 1915; the enormous *Parade's End* appeared between 1924 and 1928. He was founder and editor of *The English Review* (1908– 1911) and editor of the *Transatlantic Review* (1924–1925). Although Ford published early Hemingway stories in the *Transatlantic Review* and invited Hemingway to serve on its editorial board (in Ford's absence, Hemingway edited the August 1924 issue, of which Ford did not approve), Hemingway did not like him (see *MF*). Ford collected his anecdotes and literary memories of the Paris years in *It Was the Nightingale* (1933).]

The narrator confides to the reader that he gets his boring literary anecdotes from Ford (47); Mandy's pointless anecdotes also derive from Ford, whom she considers a good friend (85; see also *MF*).

the foreman at the pump factory in Petoskey. He is a short man (5) who hires Scripps, affects Australian slang and claims to be an Australian (28–29). When the chinook threatens, he gives the men a day off (51); when the chinook doesn't materialize, Johnson thinks that the foreman will ''catch hell'' or perhaps be fired (60; see also *manufacturers).

Speaks: 5, 28.

Forum. [This magazine, published from 1886 to 1950, began as a staff-written quarterly. In 1909 it became a monthly and developed a strong emphasis on literature and art, earning ''a reputation for excellence'' under the editorship of Henry Goddard Leach (1923–1940). In 1930 *Forum* absorbed *Century,* becoming *Forum and Century* (Mott, IV, 518).]

Diana subscribes to many literary magazines, including *Forum,* in the hopes that its literary anecdotes will help her hold on to Scripps (43).

*Fox. [An Algonquin tribe, like the Cree (q.v.), whose former range was central Wisconsin. In order to strengthen themselves for their wars with the Ojibways (q.v.) and the French, the Fox allied themselves with the Sac (Sauk) tribe in about 1780.]

In order to propose Yogi for membership to the Indians' club, Red Dog needs to know his lineage and mentions several tribes, including the Fox and the Sac (65).

*Frank, Glenn. [American editor and educator, 1887–1940. Frank edited the *Century Magazine,* 1919–1925, and was president of the University of Wisconsin, 1925–1937. He wrote a daily column syndicated in American newspapers and several books: *The Politics of Industry* (1919), *An American Looks at His World* (1923), *Thunder and Dawn: Studies in the Outlook for Western Civilization* (1932), and *America's Hour of Decision* (1934).]

The narrative indicates that *Century Magazine* (q.v.) had a new editor to replace Glenn Frank, who "had gone to head some great university somewhere" (44).

*the Fratellinis. [An Italian family of clowns. The father, Gustavo Fratellini (1842–1905) was an acrobat, clown, and horse-back performer. Of his many sons, three took up the profession: after ten years touring Russia and Europe with the Salamonsky Circus, they joined the Medrano Circus of Paris during World War I. They were the most famous clowns in the period between the world wars: Pablo (1877–1940) played the placid, self-satisfied bourgeois; Francisco (1879–1951), the chubby dreamer, stuffed into a sparkling sequined and spangled outfit; and Alberto (c. 1886–1961), the hirsute buffoon whose make-up (heavy eyebrows, big red nose and mouth) is now standard for clowns. See also *DIA*.]

Now that she is married, Diana no longer has time to read the [*Manchester*] *Guardian* [*Weekly*] and keep herself informed about English and French affairs. She has lost track of a number of "strange people," including the Fratellinis (41; see Seldes).

*Fred Something. [Fred Grey, World War I veteran and wealthy manufacturer of automobile wheels, is the husband of Aline, with whom Bruce Dudley elopes in Sherwood Anderson's novel *Dark Laughter* (1925). On the night he meets Aline, Fred, who has been upset at a party, recalls the war: "Thoughts dancing in the brain—horror. One night, in the time of the fighting, he went out on patrol in No Man's Land and saw another man stumbling along in darkness and shot him. The man pitched forward dead. It had been the only time Fred consciously killed a man. You don't kill men in war much. They just die. The act was rather hysterical on his part. He and the men with him might have made the fellow surrender. They had all got the jimjams. After it happened, they all ran away together. . . . Hang on! Grip it with your fingers, your soul! Sweetness and truth! It's got to be sweet and true. Fields—cities—streets—houses—trees—women" (Anderson 198–99). Hemingway's character Yogi Johnson quotes sections of this passage. Throughout *The Torrents of Spring* Hemingway ridicules Anderson's style, particularly his penchant for rhetorical questions, fragmented sentences, and lists of phrases and words, like the list just quoted.]

Yogi Johnson has read an unnamed but easily identifiable book by "that fellow Anderson" in which the character named "Fred Something . . . killed a man" in wartime and has since been haunted by his action. Yogi, also a veteran, feels no such remorse for killing committed during wartime. He argues that Anderson misrepresents war and soldiers (53; see also Cather).

Gallienne. See *Le Gallienne, Eva.

*Gardner, Oscar. A co-worker at the pump factory about whom we know only that "a strange and beautiful thing had happened" to him (52–53). The sexual adventures of the drummer, the foreman, O'Neil and Diana, and Yogi Johnson and the prostitute are represented by this and other euphemisms (e.g., "a wonderful thing"; 5, 35, 41, 80).

*Gladstone, [William Ewart. British orator and politician, 1809–1898. He served Queen Victoria as prime minister four times: 1868–1874, 1880–1885, 1886, 1892–1894. As a boy, Gladstone studied at Eton (q.v.)]
Diana claims that her father and Gladstone were schoolfellows at Eton (34).

*Gosse, Professor (Sir Edmund) [William. English poet, playwright and critic, 1849–1928. Gosse was a prominent figure in the literary life of London and a friend of Henry James. In addition to his poetry and plays he published critical studies of Thomas Gray (1882), Jeremy Taylor (1903), Sir Thomas Browne (1905), and Algernon Charles Swinburne (1917). Gosse is credited with introducing Scandinavian literature to the English-speaking world with his influential *Studies in the Literature of Northern Europe* and his translations and biography of Ibsen. A professor of English literature at Cambridge University, he was knighted in 1925. His autobiographical *Father and Son* (1907) describes his relationship with his father, Philip Henry Gosse (1810–1888), a very religious man and a famous scientist.]
Mandy mentions Professor Gosse in her literary anecdotes about Henry James (38) and the Marquis of Buque (85–86).

*GR & I. [Grand Rapids & Indiana Railroad; see CMR.]
Scripps walks along the tracks of the GR & I railroad (8) and watches the train go by (9–10; see also 3, 87).

*Grock. [Swiss clown, 1880–1959. Charles Adrien Wettach changed his name to Grock in 1903. He was famous for both his musical and acrobatic skills. Much of his humor came from his mistake-filled performances on the twenty musical instruments he played. His autobiography, *Die Memoiren des Königs der Clowns,* was published in 1956; the English translation, *Grock, King of Clowns,* appeared the next year.] Mrs. Scripps mentions all the "strange . . . French" people she no longer has time to worry about. Her list veers off to include the Swiss clown Grock, the Italian clowns known as the Fratellinis, and several expatriate American writers (41; see Seldes).

the *Guardian* see *Manchester Guardian Weekly*

*the guide. Johnson recalls the Paris guide whom he hired to show him Parisian night-life. The guide finally took him to a house where Johnson saw the woman he had been searching for; she was having intercourse with a soldier while an audience peered at the show through slits in the wall (80).

*Guitry, [Alexandre-Georges] (Sacha). [French actor, dramatist, movie director, 1885–1957. Son of the actor Lucien Guitry, Sacha Guitry achieved success with his first play, *Nono,* at age 21. The prolific Guitry wrote over 130 plays, producing and acting in most of them. He also wrote, directed, and produced movies. He married five times; his most famous wife was the actress and singer Yvonne Printemps (q.v.), whom he married in 1917 and divorced in 1934 and for whom he wrote many plays. Guitry was awarded France's highest honor (the Legion of Honor, 1936) and was elected to the Académie Goncourt in 1939. His autobiography, *If I Remember Right,* was published in 1935.]
He is one of the many French people Mrs. Scripps no longer has time to worry about (41; see Seldes).

*Gutenberg, [Johann, né Johannes Gensfleisch. German printer, c.1398–1468. The Gutenberg (Mazarin) Bible is generally considered the first book printed from movable type.]
In an authorial note to the reader, Hemingway dismisses printers with a rhetorical question which he answers by mentioning several early printers (46; see also Caslon, Caxton).

*Hamsun, Knut. [Pseudonym of Knut Pedersen. Norwegian author, 1859–1952. Knut Hamsun made two visits to the United States (1882–1884 and 1886–1888) during which, according to various reports, he worked as a farmer, grade-school teacher, shoe maker, dock worker, sheriff's assistant, coal trimmer and, as Mandy says, street-car conductor in Chicago. A leader of the neo-Romantic movement, he opposed technology and urbanization and advocated a return to nature. In his later works he presented aggressively individualistic and independent characters, realistically portrayed. Hamsun's best-known books were *Hunger*

(1890), which became a best seller, and *The Growth of the Soil* (English translation, 1920), awarded the 1920 Nobel Prize for Literature. Other titles: *Pan* (1920), *Segelfoss Town* (1925), *Mysteries* (1927), *The Women at the Pump* (1928), *Vagabonds* (1930), *August* (1931), *The Road Leads On* (1934), *The Ring Is Closed* (1937), *Look Back on Happiness* (1940). Hamsun favored the Germans during both World Wars. He was tried and convicted of collaborating with the Nazis, fined $85,000, committed to a psychiatric hospital in Oslo and then, because of his reputation and age, released in 1950.]

The last of Mandy's literary anecdotes is about Knut Hamsun (86).

Harper's Magazine. [The four Harper brothers were the founders of the publishing house Harper and Brothers and of several magazines. *Harper's New Monthly Magazine* was founded by James Harper in 1850. The management of the magazine was taken over by his brother Fletcher Harper, who later established *Harper's Weekly* (1857) and *Harper's Bazar* (1867). Under the editorship of Henry J. Raymond (1850–1856), *Harper's New Monthly Magazine* published mostly British authors, including Dickens, Thackeray, Trollope, and Hardy. When Henry M. Alden became editor (1869–1919), the focus turned to American fiction and a separate English edition was published abroad. In 1925 the name of the magazine was shortened to *Harper's Magazine* and it was commonly called just *Harper's*.][13]

Hoping to keep Scripps, Diana subscribes to *Harper's Magazine* which, as the narrative accurately reports, is "in a new format . . . completely changed and revised" (43).

*Hartman. [The 1923 Chicago city directory listed the main retail store of the Hartman Furniture and Carpet Company at 228–234 S. Wabash Street; the Blackstone Hotel was and is at 636 S. Michigan Street, one block east and four blocks south of the store, in Chicago's prestigious Loop area.][14]

As a boy, Scripps loved to watch the large, garish flashing electric sign of Hartman's furniture store as his mother slept on the ground at the site of "what is now probably the Blackstone Hotel" (10–11).

*Harvard, John. [English clergyman, 1607–1638. Harvard, a graduate of Emmanuel College, Cambridge, and a recent immigrant to the Massachusetts colony, willed his library and half his estate to the proposed school, which opened as Harvard College in 1640. On the statue of John Harvard which stands in front of University Hall, "his shoes feature large buckles which may be presumed to have been silver or silver plated."][15]

Mandy's mention of Henry James takes Scripps' mind to Boston, the home of the James family and of Harvard University; he recalls that John Harvard's shoes sported "silver buckles" (38).

*Hemingway, [Ernest Miller. American writer, 1899–1961. Author of the current narrative.]
In numerous humorous authorial asides to the reader, Hemingway advertises himself, his friends, and his novel.

*Hutchinson, [Arthur Stuart-Menteth. India-born British journalist and writer, 1879–1971. The son of a British general who wrote several military textbooks, Hutchinson studied medicine before turning to journalism. He rose to the editorship of the *Daily Graphic*. In World War I he served with the Royal Engineers and after the war wrote a popular novel, *If Winter Comes* (1920), and his autobiography, *A Year that the Locust. . .* (1935). His books are romantic and sentimental.]
Yogi attributes the famous last line of Shelley's "Ode to the West Wind" to Hutchinson, who quoted part of it in the title of his novel (3).

*Huysmans, [Joris Karl. French novelist of Dutch descent, 1848–1907. His first novel, *Marthe* (1876), depicts the life of a courtesan; the next few novels present everyday life in realistic detail: *Les Soeurs Vatard* (1879), *En Ménage* (1881), *A vau-l'eau* (1882), and others. In *A Rebours* (1884) he parodied current innovations in literature and art; the novel was a literary sensation. His later novels deal with mysticism and religion: *La Cathédrale* (1898) celebrates Catholic ritual and the cathedral at Chartres. Other novels of this later period feature the hero Duval who appears in several novels and is attached to a Benedictine monastery in *L'Oblat* (1903). Huysmans was nominated by Edmond de Goncourt as a member of the Académie des Goncourt.]
Yogi recalls a street in Paris named after the writer Huysmans (74).

the Indian squaw. The wife of the shorter Indian, she shows up naked at Brown's Beanery and is immediately and forcibly removed. She carries a papoose on her back and inspires lust in Yogi, who feared he had lost all desire for women, and in Scripps, who thinks about her even as he proposes to Mandy (86–87). Yogi follows her joyfully into the frozen night, shedding his clothes as he goes (87; see also 79 and Salvation Army).

Indians. Some of Hemingway's sharpest parodies involve stereotypes about Indians, "the simple aborigines, the only real Americans" (57). Two Indians walk past O'Neil (14); they may be the same two who pick him up later, play pool with him and take him to the Indians' club (see the woods Indians). Most of the workers at the pump factory are Indians; they wear breech-clouts and hum as they work (29). Indians also frequent the sophisticated Indians' club, where they read magazines, play pool, and dress in evening clothes (61, 64; see the town Indians). Also see Cree, Fox, Ojibway, Sac; see Indians in *FWBT*.

*the inspectors. They check the workers at the end of the day to make sure that they don't steal anything from the pump factory (30).

*James, Henry. [American novelist and essayist, 1843–1916. James's sophisticated stories and novels explore human behavior and motivation. Many deal with the experience of the naive, well-meaning American among sophisticated Europeans: "Daisy Miller," *Portrait of a Lady* (1881), *The Ambassadors* (1903), *The Golden Bowl* (1904). For the New York edition of his work James prepared prefaces for the various volumes, in which he explains the development of his art and his experiments with narrative techniques such as point of view. James became a British subject in 1915 and was awarded the Order of Merit (q.v.) in 1916. See also *MF*.]

The narrative correctly identifies James as an American living in England. Mandy's first literary anecdote is about James receiving the British Order of Merit on his deathbed (38–39).

*James, William. [American psychologist, philosopher, and educator, 1842–1910. A graduate of Harvard University, William James taught there from 1872 until his death. He was one of the founders of pragmatism.]

When Mandy speaks about Henry James, Scripps correctly associates him with his brother William and with Harvard University (38).

*James's nurse. See the nurse.

*Jibway. See Ojibway.

*Joan of Arc. [French heroine and saint, 1412–1431. Dressed as a man, she routed the English and enabled Charles the Dauphin to be crowned Charles VII at Rheims in 1429. Betrayed to the English, she was burned at the stake for heresy and sorcery in 1431. She was canonized in 1920.]

Diana includes Joan of Arc in a list of French people whom she considers to be "strange" (41).

*Joffre, General [Joseph Jacques Césaire. French soldier, 1852–1931. Joffre was the commander in chief of the French armies before and during much of World War I. Outnumbered and overpowered by the German forces at the outset of the war, Joffre retreated until, at the Marne, he turned to fight the Germans and achieved an impressive victory. His conduct of the war after this event led to heavy losses and much dissatisfaction. In December 1916 Joffre was replaced by General Nivelle. In 1917 and 1918, Joffre, by then elevated to the rank of Marshal of France, played a largely ceremonial role. See also Foch.]

Scripps suggests that Joffre might be the general who was awarded Diana's mother's room when she disappeared mysteriously in Paris (21). In his Author's Final Note to the Reader, Hemingway explains that the general was given Diana's mother's hotel room when she died suddenly of bubonic plague (90; see also 37).

Johnson, Yogi (White Chief). One of the workers in the pump factory in Petoskey, the main character of Parts III and IV of *The Torrents of Spring*. A World War I veteran, Johnson is "a chunky, well-built fellow . . . [who] looked as though he had been through things" (28). His eagerness to go to war (29), the centrality of the war experience in his life (29), his war wound (59), his sexual inadequacy as a result of war-time experience, the effect of war on his literary opinions (57) are all familiar motifs to Hemingway's readers. Although a figure of fun, he is treated more straightforwardly than any other character in the novel because, as Hemingway explains, "We want the reader to like Yogi Johnson" (46; see also women and girls).
Speaks: 29–31, 54–55, 57–67, 73–76, 79–81 (also much indirect speech and interior monologue)

*the *Katzenjammers*. [*The Katzenjammer Kids* was a comic strip developed by Rudolph Dirks in 1897. Based on the work of German caricaturist Wilhelm Busch (1832–1908), whose *Max und Moritz* quickly became a best-seller, the *Katzenjammers* comic strip details the misadventures of two boys. It was syndicated in the Hearst newspapers and enjoyed a long run, outliving its creator. In 1952 Joe Musial (American cartoonist, 1905–1977) became the ghost artist, drawing the Katzenjammer Kids and several other popular comic strips for many years.[16] The German word *katzenjammer* means a hangover, the dumps, the blues.]
While "talking wildly," Scripps peppers his remarks with German, claiming that the "*polizei* . . . give me the *Katzenjammers*" (18).

*the king. [George V (1865–1936); king of Great Britain, 1910–1936. Early in 1916, King George and his government awarded the Order of Merit to Henry James.]
Mandy repeats her oft-told anecdote about Henry James receiving the prestigious Order of Merit (38–39).

*Lauder, Harry. [Professional name of Sir Hugh MacLennan. Scottish music-hall comedian, singer, and songwriter, 1870–1950. Lauder first played an Irish comic but became famous for his Scottish acts, appearing in kilt and glengarry in his many tours of England, the United States (22 tours, 1909–1932), South Africa, and Australia. An extremely popular entertainer, he organized the first entertainments for soldiers at the front

during World War I, and was knighted in 1919, the first music-hall star
to be so honored.][17]
    Scripps' fascination with things English, which attracted him to
Diana, extends to Scotland and to Harry Lauder (37).

*Lawrence, D[avid] H[erbert. English essayist, poet, and novelist,
1885–1930. The earlier novels, *The White Peacock* (1911) and *Sons and
Lovers* (1913), are autobiographical. In later novels like *The Rainbow*
(1915), *Women in Love* (1920), *Aaron's Rod* (1922) and *Lady Chatterley's Lover* (1928), Lawrence argued for the natural, physical life as a
source of strength and spirituality. In search of this ideal, Lawrence
traveled to Italy, Australia, Mexico, and New Mexico. His interest in the
Aztec and Pueblo Indians resulted in *The Plumed Serpent* (1926), which
glorifies the Aztec religion and the god Quetzalcoatl, and *Mornings in
Mexico* (1927), which presents the Indian as an eternal presence,
connected to nature. See also *MF*.]
    A picture of D. H. Lawrence hangs in the pseudo-British club of the
sophisticated town Indians (65).

*Le Gallienne, Eva. [London-born American actress, producer, and
director, 1899–1991. A successful Broadway actress, Le Gallienne
founded and directed the Civic Repertory Theatre in New York in 1926,
in order to present important foreign plays at low prices; the Company
collapsed in 1935. In 1946 Le Gallienne helped found the American
Repertory Theater. She was also connected to the National Repertory
Theatre, directing and acting in many productions of classics. She
translated and starred in many Ibsen plays, translated Hans Christian
Andersen, and appeared in Barrie's *Peter Pan*. She wrote a study of the
actress Eleanora Duse, *The Mystic in the Theatre* (1973), and two
volumes of memoirs: *At 33* (1934) and *With a Quiet Heart* (1953).][18]
    Diana lists her among "the French . . . a strange people" (41).

*Lewis, [Harry] Sinclair. [American novelist, 1885–1951. Lewis was a
severe critic of his contemporary American society. He wrote social
satires such as *Main Street* (1920), *Babbitt* (1922), and *Elmer Gantry*
(1927). He rejected the Pulitzer Prize (for *Arrowsmith*, 1926) and was
the first American to receive the Nobel Prize for Literature (1930).
Hemingway knew and disliked Lewis, whom he satirized as the ugly,
nameless American writer in *ARIT*.]
    In an authorial note, Hemingway invites his readers to bring him their
own writing "for criticism or advice" to the Café du Dome in Paris,
where Hemingway spends most of his afternoons discussing literature
with Sinclair Lewis and Harold Stearns (47).

*the librarian. She gives Johnson a book by Anderson (q.v.). Worried by his lack of interest in women, Johnson thinks about why he hadn't found the librarian attractive (53).

*Literary Digest. [Founded in 1890, the Literary Digest was published continuously under that name until it merged with Time in 1938. Its most important features were its reviews and condensations of articles recently published in other periodicals. The Literary Digest covered six areas: politics, sociology, education (including literature and art), science and philosophy, religion, and miscellaneous. In the 1920s the magazine enjoyed a huge circulation of over one million readers.][19]
   In order to compete with Mandy's fund of literary anecdotes, Diana consults the Literary Digest Book Review (43).

London Mercury. See Mercury.

*Longfellow, Henry Wadsworth. [American poet, translator, and educator, 1807–1882. Longfellow knew many languages and was professor of modern languages at Harvard, 1835–1854. His poetry was sentimental and immediately popular. Among his prodigious output are Ballads and Other Poems (1842), Evangeline (1847), The Courtship of Miles Standish (1858) and Tales of a Wayside Inn (1863). Perhaps his most famous poem is The Song of Hiawatha (1855), a long narrative poem glorifying the statesman and "civilizer" Hiawatha and describing his adventures, his rule, and his prophecy: the white people will come and offer a new religion, which Hiawatha advises his people to accept. Although Hiawatha was most probably a Mohawk and consequently part of the Iroquois nation, Longfellow associates him with the Ojibway, who are part of the Algonquin nation. See Manitou.]
   The town Indians have hung two portraits of this romanticizer of the Indians in their club's committee room (61, 65).

*Lorimer, George Horace. [American editor and publisher, 1868–1937. Lorimer edited the Saturday Evening Post from 1899 to 1936, during which time its circulation rose from less than two thousand to over three million. He paid well for fiction which would have a wide appeal. See also MF.]
   As editor of Saturday Evening Post (q.v.), Lorimer bought one of Scripps' stories for $450 (14, 18).

*Lousy. See O'Neil, Lucy (Lousy).

*Lowell, James Russell. [American poet, critic, editor, diplomat and teacher, 1819–1891. Lowell published two influential collections of poems early in his career (1844, 1848). He was the first editor of *The Atlantic Monthly* (1857–1861) and also edited *The North American Review* (1864–1872). He served as minister to Spain (1877) and to England (1880–1885). An influential critic and professor of modern languages at Harvard University (1855–1876), he encouraged the development of an authentic American literature at home and fostered respect for it abroad.]

When he decides to take the job at the pump factory, Scripps comforts himself that other artists, like Lowell, had also done manual labor (23).

*Lucy. See O'Neil, Lucy.

*Mahan, [Edward W.] (Eddie). [American football player, coach, and investment banker, 1892–1975. As a Harvard undergraduate, Mahan was elected all-American in 1913, 1914 and 1915. He is considered the greatest half-back in Harvard's history. He was also a fine baseball player, leading Harvard to victory against the Boston Red Sox, then world champions, in a 1916 exhibition game. In World War I Mahan served in the Marine Corps; after the war he coached many years for Harvard and other schools. He eventually became an investment banker.[20] See also Brickley.]

Thoughts of Harvard University lead Scripps to think of Eddie Mahan and Charley Brickley, both spectacular football players during their undergraduate years at Harvard (38).

Manchester Guardian Weekly (the *Guardian*). [Founded as a weekly in 1821, it became a daily, known as the *Manchester Guardian*, in 1855. In August 1959 it became *The Guardian*, under which name it is still issued in England today as a daily. In 1919 the newspaper launched *The Manchester Guardian Weekly*, an overseas weekly edition which offered a selection of items from the daily *Manchester Guardian*. The newspaper "has always maintained an independent liberal stance and was once called 'Britain's non-conformist conscience' " (*Britannica*, 1990 ed.). It offers news and features on art and literature.]

Diana reads the overseas *Manchester Guardian Weekly*, which Scripps also likes. After she is married, Diana no longer has time to read the *Guardian* (33–34, 41).

Mandy. The buxom young waitress at Brown's Beanery loves to tell pointless literary anecdotes, mostly derived from her friend Ford Madox Ford (q.v.), which fascinate Scripps (38–39). Although Diana spends most of her short married life scouring book reviews for anecdotes with which to charm her husband, Scripps inevitably succumbs to Mandy's physical and intellectual attractions. As the novel ends, the fickle

Scripps' attention turns to the naked Indian squaw while Mandy is "talking on. Telling literary reminiscences. Authentic incidents" (87). Speaks: 35–40, 84–86.

*Manitou. [Translation: mystery or supernatural. In Algonquin philosophy, Manito or Manitou is the pervading spirit or god who rules over the forces of nature. Longfellow's poem *The Song of Hiawatha* mentions "Gitche Manito, the mighty/ He the Master of Life" who gathered all the Indian nations and spoke to them of peace. The "Notes to the Poem" define "Gitche Manito" as "the Great Spirit, the Master of Life."][21]
     When Yogi is about to speak to the two woods Indians about war, one of them refers to "gitchy Manitou the Mighty" (54).

*the manufacturers. The absentee owners of the pump factory. Johnson thinks that they are cold, manipulative, and interested only in profits (51, 60; see also the inspectors).

*MC. [The Military Cross (MC) is a British award, instituted in 1914, for which only officers (i.e., captains, junior officers, warrant officers, and all higher ranks) are eligible. If the medal is awarded repeatedly, a bar listing the various battles or occasions which merited the award is added to the medal ("Numismatics," *Encyclopaedia Britannica,* 1954 ed., XVI: 638–39).]
     The taller of the two Indian war veterans, a major, was awarded the Military Cross, with bar (58), as well as the DSO (q.v.); both are British awards.

*McCarthy's barber shop. A thriving barber shop in Petoskey. Although it looks very inviting, Scripps twice walks past it without entering, once because he is looking for food (14–15) and once because he is looking for a job (27; see also men and boys).

men and boys. The narrative shows us several unnamed men having their hair cut, getting a shave, waiting their turns, and lounging in a barber shop (14–15; see also 27). Many men and boys work in the pump factory (28; see also Indians). A pedestrian stares at O'Neil (5).

*men and boys. As he thinks about war, Johnson conjures up soldiers and discusses their behavior (54–57); developing his analogy between war and football, Johnson mentions the man who plays center (55). An unseen, unidentified man brings the ribbon and decoration of the Order of Merit to Henry James as he lies on his deathbed (38). O'Neil wonders about the unseen passengers on a train (10).

*Mencken, Henry L[ouis. American writer, journalist, editor and critic, 1880–1956. H. L. Mencken was a controversial and influential critic of American democracy who nonetheless insisted on the independence of the American literary scene, rejecting the idea that "culture" can exist only according to British and European patterns. He became literary editor of *The Smart Set* in 1908 and then co-editor, with George Jean Nathan, from 1914 to 1923. He and Nathan founded and edited *The American Mercury* (q.v.). Mencken wrote *The American Credo* (1920), *The American Language* (1919, revised 1921, 1923, 1936), and many other books. His six collections of critical essays, *Prejudices* (1919–1927), were very influential, but in the 1930s Mencken's popularity and influence declined.]

At first Scripps purports to admire Mencken: when he leaves Mancelona, he heads for Chicago because Mencken had defined that city as "the Literary Capital of America" (10). He drops that plan—Chicago is too far away—and begins to worry about Mencken's interest in him (19). By the end of the novel he doesn't "give a damn about Mencken any more" (83). [Scripps' rejection of Mencken may be due to Mencken's negative review of Hemingway's *In Our Time* (Meyers, 168) and to his rejection of Hemingway's submissions to *American Mercury* (Reynolds, *The Paris Years*, 236). See also Mencken in *SAR*.]

*Menken, S[olomon] Stanwood. [American lawyer and publicist, 1870–1954. Hemingway, who volunteered for service in World War I and was wounded in Italy, would certainly not have admired Menken, who opposed American intervention in World War I. In 1914, Menken was active in the American Relief Committee, which evacuated Americans from Europe. He also helped organize the National Security League, an isolationist, militaristic organization that urged America to prepare herself for war but to fight only at home, in case of invasion. A letter he wrote in support of William Randolph Hearst's newspapers, which also argued for strengthening the national defense and staying out of international conflicts, tainted him with that newspaper chain's reputation for being pro-German.[22] As a result of the ensuing scandal, Menken resigned the presidency of the National Security League. However, he was re-elected to that position twice again and served as chairman of the board from 1925 until 1933. The ironical dedication of *The Torrents of Spring* is part of the satirical plan of the novel; it was dropped from most later editions, although it was retained in several printings of the English edition (published by Cape; see Scribner's Sons), which misspelled Menken as Mencken.][23]

Hemingway dedicated *The Torrents of Spring* to Mencken (q.v.) and to Menken, "In Admiration."

*Mentor. [An unusual magazine which devoted each issue "to a single topic" in order "to give readers authoritative information from specialists'' in a variety of fields. The magazine was published under this policy from the time of its founding (before World War I) until 1929, when new editors sought to increase its circulation by diversifying its contents. In 1930 the magazine was sold to World Traveler Magazine Corporation.][24]

Mentor is one of the many magazines the elderly Diana reads in order to accumulate anecdotes with which to charm her straying husband (43).

Mercury, American Mercury, London Mercury. [Literary magazines. The English magazine, *London Mercury,* ran from 1919 to 1939; in its last few years it merged with another English magazine, the *Bookman,* being known from 1936–1938 as the *London Mercury and Bookman.* In 1939 it was absorbed by another magazine, *Life and Letters.* The *American Mercury* was, as its title indicated, the American counterpart of the *London Mercury.* Founded in 1924 by George Jean Nathan and H.L. Mencken (q.v.), who had co-edited *The Smart Set* for several years, the *American Mercury*'s goal was to present ''the whole gaudy, gorgeous American scene.'' As part of the argument that Americans should develop their own style and not depend on English literary fashions, *American Mercury* encouraged young authors to submit essays, poetry and fiction that had been rejected in other, more conservative journals; they published innovative young American writers like Sherwood Anderson, Eugene O'Neill and Carl Sandburg, but rejected everything Hemingway submitted. Under Mencken's editorship (1924–1933) the magazine had a strong literary section. Under the editorship of Lawrence E. Spivack (1944–1950) the magazine became politically conservative, a trend which intensified ''until in later years the content had become an unalloyed rabid anti-Communism with overtly anti-Semitic overtones.'' During Spivack's editorship the masthead prominently displayed H. L. Mencken's name (but not Nathan's) and inaccurately boasted of ''51 years of continuous publication.][25]

In her attempts to hold on to her husband, Diana constantly reads literary magazines. Although she is English, she abandons the *London Mercury* for the *American Mercury,* ''just to please Scripps.'' But when he fails to respond to ''a wonderful editorial . . . about chiropractors,'' Diana knows that ''She had lost him'' and walks out of the novel ''clutching . . . the copy of *The Mercury* to her breast'' (83–84; see also 78).

*Meyers, [John Tortes] (Chief). [American baseball player, 1882–1971. Chief Meyers, a Cahuilla Indian, played catcher for New York, Brooklyn, and Boston, from 1909–1917. He played for the New York Giants in the World Series of 1911, 1912 and 1913, setting a record in the 1911 World Series by throwing out twelve runners. In 1917 he led all the major league catchers in batting, with an eight-year average of .297

and a lifetime average of .291. After retiring from professional baseball, Meyers worked for the Bureau of Indian Affairs.][26]

A picture of this famous Indian athlete adorns the committee room of the pseudo-British club of the sophisticated town Indians (65).

*Moore, Marianne [Craig. American poet, 1887–1972. Moore's poetry is experimental, with a complex rhyme pattern and a rich variety of images, drawn from scholarly sources as well as from contemporary culture. Her poetry often mentioned animals, plants, baseball, subways, and tricorn hats. Among her collections of poems are *Poems* (1921), *Observations* (1924, awarded the *Dial* Prize, q.v.), *Selected Poems* (1935), *What Are Years?* (1941), *Collected Poems* (1951; Pulitzer Prize, 1952), *Like a Bulwark* (1956), and *O To Be a Dragon* (1959). She was awarded the National Book Award for Poetry and the National Medal for Literature. Chosen by Scofield Thayer to succeed him as editor of the *Dial,* Moore served in that capacity from 1926 until the journal folded in 1929.]

Diana feels that now that she is married she no longer has time to worry about Marianne Moore, the *Dial* and the *Dial* prize (41), although these literary matters, when discussed by the buxom Mandy, are irresistible to Scripps.

New York Times. [Morning daily paper, founded in 1851. In 1896 the paper was bought by Adolf Ochs, under whose ownership it achieved its international reputation for excellent reporting of national and international affairs. Ochs removed fiction from the main sections of the paper; he established the *New York Times Index* in 1913 and added the Sunday magazine and the Literary Section, which reviews recently published books.]

Diana subscribes to the Literary Section of this newspaper in order to arm herself with the literary anecdotes she hopes will keep Scripps' attention focused on her and not on the comely Mandy (43).

*the nurse. Henry James's nurse is a character in the first literary anecdote Mandy relates to Scripps. Henry James's last words were addressed to his nurse (38–39).

the officer. As he observes a British officer preparing to make love to the beautiful woman who had previously seduced him, Johnson realizes that his own love-making had also been observed. The knowledge makes him lose all interest in sex (80–81).

*Ojibway [or Ojibwa. A large Indian tribe first reported living in Michigan's Upper Peninsula, now also residing in northern Minnesota and along Lake Superior and Lake Winnipeg. The Canadian group (the Saulteurs) number about 20,000; the U.S. group about 30,000, most of them of mixed blood. They are associated with the Algonquin nation and speak an Algonquin language.]

In order to propose Yogi for membership to the Town Indians' club, Red Dog needs to know his tribal affiliation and so asks if he is a "Jibway" (65; see Cree).

O'Neil, Diana. Scripps' second wife; see Scripps, Diana.

*O'Neil, General. Scripps' father was a composer in Chicago (9), a Confederate army general (15) or both.

*O'Neil, Lucy. Scripps' first wife, with whom he lived in Mancelona. Like Anderson's Sponge Martin and his wife (in *Dark Laughter*), Scripps and his first wife enjoyed getting drunk together (4). When he misplaces her after four days of drinking (4), he leaves Mancelona.
Speaks: 6.

*O'Neil, Lucy (Lousy). Scripps' daughter by his first wife. Lousy recalls Sponge Martin's daughter, Bugs, who couldn't stay away from the boys, in Anderson's *Dark Laughter*.]

With other girls and boys, Lousy spends long hours at the Mancelona High School, learning about sex (6).

*O'Neil, Mrs. Scripps' mother, an Italian, hopes that her son will be a composer like his father (9–11). Scripps recalls that as a boy he and his mother, reduced to beggary, slept in the streets of Chicago (10–11). She had objected when General Sherman burned her house (15–16).
Speaks; 11, 15–16.

O'Neil, Scripps. The main character of the first two sections of *The Torrents of Spring,* a bigamist. When he misplaces his first wife, Lucy (q.v.), he sets off for Chicago in search of a new life, but ends up in Petoskey instead. He is a "tall, lean man with a tall, lean face" (3), literary ambitions (he has sold a few stories and is a sucker for literary anecdotes), and a short attention span where women are concerned: he marries the elderly Diana almost immediately after meeting her; is attracted to Mandy a short while after he has married Diana; and is lusting after the naked Indian squaw even as he claims Mandy as his woman (86–87). He works at the pump factory in Petoskey.
Speaks: 7–9, 11–14, 17–23, 27–31, 33–34, 36–40, 45, 78–79, 83–86.

Order of Merit. [Founded by Edward VII on the occasion of his coronation in 1901, this honor is awarded to individuals who have distinguished themselves in the British military or naval services or in

science, art, and literature. The order does not convey a title and has no
classes. Membership is restricted to 24 British, and may be awarded to
foreigners at the discretion of the Sovereign. Early in 1916 it was
awarded to Henry James (q.v.), who had become a British subject in
1915. James died in February, one month after receiving the honor.]
   Mandy's first anecdote correctly reports that James was awarded the
Order of Merit on his deathbed (38).

the owner. See Brown, the owner of Brown's Beanery; see also the
manufacturers.

the papoose. The baby travels on the back of its mother, who refuses to
let Yogi Johnson carry it for her (87; see also the Indian squaw).

*Parker, Harry. A friend of Scripps O'Neil, Parker met a "poet chap"
whose lines he quoted often. Although now he can barely remember the
lines Parker quoted to him, Scripps claims he once set them to music.
The lines seem to be the lyrics of "Home, Sweet Home" (6).[27]

*Parkman, Francis. [American historian and horticulturist, 1823–1893.
As a boy, Parkman became interested in Indians and dedicated himself
to fishing, trapping, woodcraft, and Indian lore, in preparation for his trip
West. His journal of that experience, including his life with the Sioux
Indians, was first published as *The Oregon Trail* in the *Knickerbocker
Magazine* (1847) and then as *The California and Oregon Trail* (1849).
It contains "a remarkable ethnological study of the Indians . . . Parkman
charged Fenimore Cooper with lack of realism in his portrayals of Indian
characters" (*Reader's Encyclopedia,* 836). Later books include *Conspiracy of Pontiac* (1851) and *Discovery of the Great West* (1869), the
latter being part of his history of the French and Indian wars, which he
expanded to include the whole of Anglo-French relations in North
America. Encouraged to take up gardening for his health, Parkman
became an expert horticulturist, writing *The Book of Roses* (1866). He is
best remembered for the autobiographical, adventure-filled *The California and Oregon Trail* ("Parkman," *Oxford Companion to American
Literature*).]
   A photograph of this famous chronicler of Indian life hangs in the
town Indians' club (65).

*the Peerless Pounder. The absurdly handcarved steel pump "that won
the pump race in Italy" (30; see Borrow).

*Phelps, William Lyon. [American educator and literary critic, 1865–
1943. Phelps was a professor of literature at Yale University (1892–

1933) and author of *The Advance of English Poetry* (1918) and *The Twentieth Century Theatre* (1918), as well as several collections of essays (on Russian novelists, 1911; on modern dramatists, 1921; on American authors, 1924). From 1922 until his death he wrote the column "As I Like It" for *Scribner's Magazine* (q.v.), as well as a widely syndicated newspaper column, by means of which he popularized the study of the humanities.][28]
Diana reads Phelps' column in *Scribner's* (43).

*Picasso, [Pablo Ruíz. Spanish painter, sculptor, and ceramicist, 1881–1973. Picasso was one of the founding forces of cubism and surrealism. His many famous works include *Les Demoiselles d'Avignon* (1907) and *Guérnica* (1937).]
When he decides to take the job at the pump factory, Scripps comforts himself that other artists had also done menial labor: he claims that [like Carmen in Bizet's opera], Picasso began his working life in a cigarette-factory (23).

Poisoned Buffalo, Mr. One of the sophisticated town Indians Johnson meets at their club (62).

*the police, policeman. The French police, informed that Diana's mother had died of bubonic plague, "hushed the whole matter up" in order to prevent wholesale panic among Parisians and among the many tourists who had come to the city for the great exposition [probably the international exhibition of 1889]. They efficiently altered the evidence and arranged for the witnesses to present false testimony (21, 90; see also coiffeur, *concierge*, doctor, driver). An American policeman orders young Scripps O'Neil and his mother "to move along" (11).

*Polly. Common name for parrots. When the drummer suggests this name for Scripps' bird, Mandy adds that Polly [Peachum] is a character in [John Gay's] *The Beggar's Opera* (q.v., 40).

*Printemps, Yvonne [Wigniolle. French operetta singer, actress, comedienne, and movie star, 1894–1977. She made her stage debut in 1907 at the age of 13 and joined the Folies Bergère at age 15. She and her husband Sacha Guitry (q.v.) came to New York in 1926 amid much fanfare to present his *Mozart*, which was a success. She starred in many musical comedies and operettas and in several films, including *La Dame aux camélias* (1934), *Trois Valses* (1934), *Le Duel* (1940), and *Le Valse de Paris* (1940). In 1934 she divorced Guitry and married the actor Pierre Fresnay, who often played opposite her on stage and in the movies.[29] See Seldes.]
Yvonne Printemps is included in the long list of "strange people" Mrs. Scripps no longer has time to worry about as she scurries about

acquiring literary anecdotes with which she hopes to entice her husband away from the competition (41).

*Puck. [A mischievous goblin in Shakespeare's *A Midsummer Night's Dream*.]

When Mandy suggests the Shakespearean name Ariel as a name for Scripps' bird, Diana competitively suggests "Puck" (39).

*Pullman, [George Mortimer. American industrialist, 1831–1897. Pullman was a cabinetmaker who worked on railroad coaches to make them more comfortable for travelers. He built the first modern sleeping car, which proved very popular and profitable. In 1867 he was able to establish the Pullman Palace Car Company, and in 1880 he built the town of Pullman, Illinois to house the company and its workers. Like the communities established by Hershey (q.v. in *Islands*), Pullman was controlled by the man who built it, its schools, medical facilities, and social benefits determined by the company, which rejected interference by the American Railway Union. In May, 1894, the workers went on strike to protest a wage cut. The strike eventually stopped all train traffic in and out of Chicago. President Cleveland sent in federal troops, who were violently resisted by the strikers. After many injuries and the loss of several lives, the strike collapsed.]

Scripps watches a train with Pullman cars (9–10).

*the reader. A construct whom the author confides in, teases, cajoles, and flatters. Hemingway explains the novel to the reader and invites the reader to make changes in it and to recommend it to friends (46–47, 67–69, 76–77, 89–90).

Red Dog. The Indian at the club who acts as host to Yogi Johnson, whom he has mistaken for a fellow Indian. When he discovers that Yogi is a "Swede," he threatens him with a gun (66). Red Dog works at the pump factory in Petoskey.

Speaks: 61–66.

*Renoir, [Pierre Auguste. French impressionist painter, 1841–1919. Renoir broke with the impressionist movement in the 1880s; his later work is associated with the post-impressionists. He is especially famous for his studies of nudes and his pictures of women and children, including such masterpieces as *Madame Charpentier and her Children* (1878), *Bathers* (1884, 1887), and *After the Bath* (1895).]

When he decides to take the job at the pump factory, Scripps comforts himself that other artists had also done menial labor: Renoir had been a carpenter (23). [Not likely: his father, recognizing his son's talent, apprenticed Renoir as a decorator of porcelain in a Paris factory at age 13.]

*Rodin, [René François Auguste. French sculptor, 1840–1917. Rodin was considered the foremost sculptor of his time and perhaps the greatest portraitist in the history of sculpture. Among his best known pieces are *The Thinker, Adam and Eve, Balzac,* and *The Kiss.*]
When he decides to take the job at the pump factory, Scripps comforts himself that other artists, including Rodin, had also done menial labor (23). [True only insofar as sculpture is done with the hands. Rodin was apprenticed to an ornament maker at age 14 and later worked for architectural sculptors, doing decorative stonework.]

*Rumsey, Dr. [The 1903 edition of *Polk's Petoskey City and Emmet County Directory* lists the address of Dr. James E. Rumsey as 633 Pleasant Street. Mr. Brad Leech, City Planner of Petoskey and an expert on Hemingway landmarks, believes that the house Yogi passed belonged to a Dr. Ramsdell.][30]
As they walk into Petoskey, Yogi and the two Indians pass the house of Dr. Rumsey (59).

Running Skunk-Backwards (Chief). One of the urbane Indians whom Johnson meets at their club. He is descended from the legendary native reputed to have sold Manhattan "for a few strings of wampum," some of which he gives to Johnson (63–64).
Speaks: 63.

*Sac. [Sometimes spelled Sauk. A North American tribe of Indians whose territory included the Fox River valley and Green Bay area in Wisconsin. The Sauk allied themselves with the Fox Indians (q.v.) about 1780.]
In order to propose Yogi for membership to the Indians' club, Red Dog needs to know Yogi's tribal affiliation. He asks him if he is a Sac Indian (65).

*Saintsbury, [George Edward Bateman] (Professor Whatsisname). [English educator, prolific critic and literary historian, 1845–1933. Educated at Oxford University (B.A., 1868), Saintsbury worked as a journalist and literary critic in London from 1875 to 1895, when he became professor of rhetoric and English literature at Edinburgh University. In addition to publishing many articles and books on English and French literature, literary history, and literary criticism, Saintsbury was also a connoisseur of wines, whose popular *Notes on a Cellarbook* (1920) led to the founding of the Saintsbury Club. His anecdotes about literary personalities he had known during his London years appeared in

A Last Scrap Book (1924; see "Saintsbury," *Oxford Companion to English Literature,* 5th ed.]

Together with Professor Gosse (q.v.), Professor Saintsbury appears in the first and the last of the literary anecdotes with which Mandy captures Scripps' heart (38–39, 85–86).

*Salvation Army. [An international Christian organization dedicated to preaching the gospel and offering charity to the needy. It was established in London in 1865 by William Booth, a Methodist minister, and now operates in over eighty countries. As its name indicates, the Salvation Army follows a military model: members are organized into corps and divisions, and the commanders (ministers) wear uniforms. The Salvation Army runs soup kitchens and shelters for the poor. It also collects used and discarded clothes, furniture, and other household goods which are cleaned and repaired and then sold or given away at their various stores. Their religious services are informal and joyous, often accompanied by instrumental music.]

The two destitute Indian war veterans (the woods Indians, q.v.) intend to join the Salvation Army (58, 67; see also 88).

Saturday Evening Post, the *Post.* [Published 1821–1969 as a weekly. Originally a newsweekly which offered both news and fiction, the *Post* slowly increased its emphasis on fiction (but not its circulation or reputation) as it went through various owners and editors. Under the ownership of Cyrus H. K. Curtis and the editorship of George Horace Lorimer (1899–1936) it became very popular (circulation of three million) and carried a lot of advertising, which enabled it to pay well for stories which its editors felt would please its large readership (no experimental fiction). It published F. Scott Fitzgerald but rejected all the short stories the young Hemingway submitted.[31] See also *MF*.]

Scripps has published one story in the *Post* and two in the more experimental *Dial.* Although grateful for the $450 he got from the *Post* (18), Scripps approves of Brown's Beanery because it does not advertise in this slick weekly (16–17; see also Lorimer).

Saturday Review of Literature. [Founded in 1924, it appeared until 1982. Under its first editor, Henry Seidel Canby (1924–1936), it presented book and drama reviews and fairly conventional literary commentary, generally maintaining this format for many years. In 1952 it shortened its name to *Saturday Review* and expanded its coverage to include film, music, travel, etc.][32]

In her pitiful attempts to keep Scripps' attention from wandering to the young and buxom Mandy and her literary anecdotes, Diana stands "in the snow" waiting for the arrival of this weekly journal (43).

*Scribner's. [Scribner's Magazine (1887–1939). A few years after Scribner's Monthly was sold to the Century Company and became the Century Illustrated Monthly Magazine, Scribner's publishing house launched Scribner's Magazine, a journal devoted to criticism, contemporary fiction (including Hemingway's) and art. Scribner's soon joined the Century and Harper's (qq.v.) as one of the country's leading literary magazines. Its editors were Edward L. Burlingame (1887–1914), Robert Bridges (1914–1930), Alfred Dashiell (1930–1936), and Harlan de Baun Logan (1936–1939).][33]
Hoping to hold on to Scripps by quoting literary anecdotes to him, Diana reads William Lyon Phelps (q.v.) in this literary magazine (43).

Scribner's Sons. [American publishing family. Charles Scribner (1821–1871) founded the publishing house which bore his name. His son, also named Charles (1854–1930), became head of the firm in 1879 and founded Scribner's Magazine (q.v.) in 1887. The founder's grandson, the third to be named Charles Scribner (1890–1952), was Hemingway's publisher. They had a very friendly relationship over the many years of their association; see Scribner in OMS. In the English editions of The Torrents of Spring, the reader is advised to communicate with Jonathan Cape (English publisher, 1879–1960); in 1921 Cape and George Wren Howard founded the publishing firm of Jonathan Cape, Ltd., which published both English and American authors, including Sinclair Lewis, Eugene O'Neill, Robert Frost and Ernest Hemingway.]
Addressing the reader directly, Hemingway advises us to report complaints to his publisher, [Charles] Scribner's Sons, who will revise the novel accordingly (77).

Scripps. See O'Neil, Scripps.

Scripps, Diana. An elderly English woman who worked as a waitress at Brown's Beanery until she married Scripps O'Neil, whereupon she became Diana Scripps (not O'Neil). She attracts Scripps with her British accent, her connection to Wordsworth (19, 37), and her anecdote about losing her mother in Paris (20–22); they marry the day after their first meeting. For most of her short married life, Diana tries to hold on to her husband. To compete with the many attractions of the younger, well-endowed Mandy (q.v.), Diana feverishly reads literary reviews and magazines and even memorizes editorials (43), but to no avail. She eventually accepts the loss of Scripps, who gives her the bird as she leaves (84).
Speaks: 17–23, 33–36, 38–39, 45, 83–84.

*Seldes, Gilbert [Vivian. American journalist, critic and editor, 1893–1970. In several books—The Seven Lively Arts (1924), The Movies and *the Talkies* (1929), and *The Great Audience* (1950)—Seldes examined contemporary culture. Under the pseudonym Foster Johns, he wrote a novel, *The Wings of the Eagle* (1929), and several detective stories. He published in the *Dial* (q.v.) and was an associate editor for that important literary magazine from 1920 to 1925. Joost explains the logic of Diana's list: it lists people whom Hemingway disliked because of their association with the *Dial*, and it displays an internal logic as well: "Some of the French names—Carpentier the boxer, followed by Sacha Guitry and Yvonne Printemps (Parisian actors, then man and wife), and the circus clowns and acrobats (Grock and Les Fratellinis)—bring to mind Gilbert Seldes . . . his name by a process of association followed upon those of Grock and Les Fratellinis because in his book *The Seven Lively Arts*, Seldes had tried to bring together the fine arts and the popular arts of the music hall, the circus, and the comic strip" (153).]

Seldes is one of the many people, French and otherwise, whom Diana no longer has time to think about (41).

*Shakespeare, [William. English poet and dramatist, 1564–1616.]

Scripps describes him as "that old writing fellow" and attributes to him Plato's remark that "Might makes right" (9; see also Ariel, Puck).

Shaw, Mr. Henry. A very old man who works at the pump factory in Petoskey, he is "probably the greatest living pump-maker." He correctly predicts that Scripps "won't have no difficulty" finding a wife (30; see Borrow).

Speaks: 30–31.

*Sherman, General [William Tecumseh. American soldier, 1820–1891. During the Civil War, this Union general led the campaign against Atlanta, Georgia, burning most of the city after it fell. During his "march to the sea" through Georgia in 1864, he encouraged his troops to loot and burn. His philosophy was that the enemy must be broken completely if victory is to be achieved.]

Scripps' mother recalls that the General personally supervised the burning of her house (15–16).

Speaks: 15–16.

*Sidney, Sir Philip. [English poet, soldier and statesman, 1554–1586; author of *Astrophel and Stella*. When fatally wounded, Sidney "passed a cup of water to another wounded man, saying, 'Thy necessity is greater than mine' " ("Sidney," *Oxford Companion to English Literature*, 3rd ed.).]

Yogi alludes to Sidney's selflessness when he describes the various stages in the development of good soldiers (57).

*Simmons, Walt. [A family named Simmons lived next door to the Hemingways on Kenilworth Avenue, Oak Park, Illinois. Hemingway was friendly with Isabelle Simmons (1901–1964) and mentioned her brother Charlie in "Soldier's Home" (see *Simmons in *In Our Time*).]
Walt Simmons was Scripps' friend. He had "heard" the cry of "dumb terror" emitted by a horse who had been hit by a bus (7).

*Sitting Bull. [Chief of the Sioux nation, c.1831–1890. Sitting Bull resisted the encroachments of the American settlers, most notably at the battle of Little Big Horn (1876) in which General Custer and over 200 of his men were killed. Chief Sitting Bull was killed at the battle at Wounded Knee Creek, 29 December 1890; see *Custer and *Sioux in *FWBT*.]
The Indian whom Yogi meets at the club says he is not related to the famous Sioux chief of the same name who fought against Custer (q.v.).
Speaks: 63.

*Spalding, Albert. [American violinist and composer, 1888–1953. Spalding studied in Italy and made his concert debut in Paris in 1905. After a European tour he returned to the United States and appeared to great acclaim in Carnegie Hall, New York City, in 1908. He served as liaison officer in the Aviation Corps Signal Services in World War I. He returned to the concert stage in 1919 and continued his successful career as soloist until his retirement in 1950. Spalding composed several pieces for violin, including two violin concerti and a sonata for violin and piano. He wrote his autobiography, *Rise to Follow* (1943), and a novel, *A Fiddle, a Sword, and a Lady* (1953).]
Scripps thinks briefly of going to Paris, as Spalding did (7).

*Stearns, Harold [Edmund, American journalist and social critic, 1891–1943. Stearns' first book, *Liberalism in America: Its Origin, Its Temporary Collapse, Its Future* (1919), indicated his discontent with American society. In his second book, *America and the Young Intellectual* (1921), Stearns accused American society of stifling the development of the individual. The following year he edited a symposium, *Civilization in the United States: An Inquiry by Thirty Americans* (1922), which sharply criticized American leaders for fostering provincialism, materialism, and conformism. Stearns' subsequent expatriation was understood as a political statement. Dubbed as "America's foremost expatriate," he worked in Paris as a journalist for much of the 1920s, during which time he wrote the Peter Pickem racing column for the Paris *Tribune* and for the London *Daily Mail* and was foreign talent scout for the publishing house of Boni & Liveright, who had published Hemingway's *In Our Time* and whose rejection of *The Torrents of Spring* freed Hemingway to associate himself with Scribner's. After his return to the United States in 1929, Stearns wrote *The Street I Know* (1935) and *America, a Re-Appraisal* (1937).]

In an Author's Note, Hemingway reports that he often discusses literature with Stearns (47; see Lewis).

*Stein, Gertrude. [American writer, 1874–1946. Stein wrote *Three Lives* (1909), *The Making of Americans* (1925), and *The Autobiography of Alice B. Toklas* (1933). In several volumes she tried to explain her innovative style and grammar, which emphasized verbs and relied on automatic writing: *Composition and Explanation* (1926), *How to Write* (1931), *Narration* (1935), and *Lectures in America* (1935). As a young writer in Paris, Hemingway showed her his stories and received advice and criticism from her. Stein is mocked in *FWBT* and *MF*.]

Although he admires her, Yogi wonders what will come of "her experiments in words" (74–75).

*Stravinsky, [Igor Feodorovich. Russian composer, conductor, and pianist, 1882–1971. Stravinsky became a French citizen in 1934 and an American in 1945. An innovative composer, he achieved notoriety with his early pieces, the groundbreaking ballets *The Fire Bird* (1910) and *Petrouchka* (1911; title role danced by the great Vaslav Nijinsky); both of these were choreographed by Sergei Diaghilev and performed in Paris by his company, the *Ballets Russes*. Stravinsky wrote several other ballets, many based on Russian motifs, for this great choreographer and, later, for George Balanchine. He also wrote ballets, operas, an opera-oratorio (*Oedipus Rex*, 1927), a violin concerto (1931), and several songs and symphonies. The disturbing metrical shifts, unconventional orchestration, and powerful dissonance of *The Rite of Spring* caused a riot at its first performance (Paris, May 1913) and marked, according to many critics, the birth of modern music. In reaction to romanticism, Stravinsky incorporated classical idioms, subjects, and forms (like the oratorio and the sonata-form), into his decidedly modern music. In the 1950s and 1960s he became interested in serialism, an application of Schoenberg's twelve-note scale. Stravinsky is undoubtedly one of the foremost composers of the 20th century.]

Scripps, the son of a composer and himself a would-be composer (he wrongly claims credit for writing the music for "Home Sweet Home," q.v.) mourns that alcohol has affected his hearing so that now train whistles sound "more lovely" to him than Stravinsky's music (7).

*Stuart, Gilbert [Charles. American portrait painter, 1755–1828. After four years as a student of Benjamin West, in London, Stuart set up his own studio, becoming an extremely successful portraitist: he painted George III and the future George IV. In Paris Stuart painted Louis XVI. Although he was successful in London, Stuart lived beyond his means and had to work his way back home from Scotland in 1773 or 1774 on a collier ship; there is no indication that he worked as a blacksmith.[34] Back in the United States he painted several presidents, governors, generals, and other leading figures. His painting of George Washington became the authoritative likeness.]

When he decides to take the job at the pump factory, Scripps comforts himself that other artists had also done manual labor. Gilbert Stuart, he claims, had worked as a blacksmith (23).

*Suckow, Ruth. [American novelist and short-story writer, 1892–1960. Suckow's stories appeared in the magazine *The Smart Set* and its successor, *American Mercury,* in *Scribner's Magazine* and in *Harper's* (qq.v.). Her early work includes *Country People* (1924), *The Odyssey of a Nice Girl* (1925), *Iowa Interiors* (1926), and *The Bonney Family* (1928). Most of her fiction is based on the Iowa of her youth.]

Diana reads a story by this popular contemporary author in *Century Magazine* (45).

*Tarkington, [Newton] Booth. [American novelist and dramatist, 1869–1946. His best known works, *Penrod* (1914) and *Seventeen* (1917), present a comic-romantic view of a boy's coming to manhood. Tarkington won two Pulitzer Prizes, for *The Magnificent Ambersons* (1918) and for *Alice Adams* (1921).]

Just as he rejects Sherwood Anderson's fiction as not true to life, Yogi disparages Tarkington's novels (53).

the telegrapher. He works at the train station in Petoskey and is the first person Scripps meets there.
Speaks: 12–13.

"Thanatopsis," "To a Water Fowl." [Poems by William Cullen Bryant (American lawyer, poet, and editor, 1794–1878), written when the poet was seventeen years old. Bryant gave up the practice of law in favor of editorial work, editing the New York *Evening Post* from 1829 until his death. His major collection, *Poems,* appeared in 1832.]

To console himself for having to work in the pump factory, Scripps argues, with erratic accuracy, that many great artists engaged in menial work. Even the young telegraph boy, he thinks, may be writing poems like "Thanatopsis" and "To a Water Fowl," poems that will make him famous (23).

*Thayer, Scofield. [American editor and critic, 1889–1982. Thayer was a staff member and contributor to the *Dial* in 1918. At the end of 1919, Thayer and J. S. Watson, Jr. bought the controlling interest in the *Dial* and moved it from Chicago to New York. Thayer edited the journal from

December 1919 to 1925; although he had resigned as editor-in-chief in 1925, he continued as consultant to the magazine and vice president of the Dial Press and the Dial Publishing Company until 1929. In the early 1930s Thayer was a patient of Sigmund Freud; for the last forty years of his life he lived as a recluse in New York City. He left an important art collection valued at over $10 million to the Metropolitan Museum of Art.][35]

When Scripps is "talking wildly," he claims that "Scofield Thayer was my best man" (18).

*Thorpe, [James Francis] (Jim). [American athlete, 1888–1953. Thorpe, who was part Algonquin Indian and part Irish, was an outstanding and versatile athlete. He played football, lacrosse and baseball at the Carlisle (Pennsylvania) Indian School, being named All-American halfback in 1911–1912 and winning both the decathlon and pentathlon in the 1912 Olympics (Stockholm). From 1913 to 1920 he played professional baseball for the New York Giants, and from 1921 to 1925 he was a professional football player for various teams. In 1950 he was voted "the greatest football player and male athlete of the first half of the 20th century" ("Thorpe," *Oxford Companion to Sports and Games*).]

A picture of this great Indian athlete hangs in the committee room of the town Indians' elegant club (65).

"To a Waterfowl." See "Thanatopsis."

Torrents of Spring. [Short novel by Ivan Sergeyevich Turgenev (Russian playwright and novelist, 1818–1883), published in 1872. Hemingway claimed to have read all of Turgenev (*MF* 133); he borrowed *The Torrents of Spring* twice from Sylvia Beach's famous lending library, in 1925 and in 1928, and bought his own copy in 1929 (Reynolds, *Hemingway's Reading*, 194; Jake Barnes reads this author in *SAR*, where the name is spelled Turgenieff). Turgenev took his title from an old song, which he quotes at the beginning of his novel:

> The laughter-filled years,
> The happiest days—
> Like the torrents of spring
> They've all rushed away!]

Hemingway took his title from Turgenev.

the town Indians. Employed by the pump factory, they are a mix of clichés: they run a speakeasy which looks like a Hollywood version of a British club (it has a brass-decorated bar, a committee room, a locker room and a swimming pool) and speak like British officers until they discover that

Yogi, whom they had taken for "one of us," is a "Swede," at which point they suddenly start to behave like gangsters, threatening Yogi with a gun and beating up the two woods Indians. See also Red Dog, Sitting Bull, Poisoned Buffalo, and Running-Skunk Backwards.
Speak: 61–66.

*Ulric, Lenore. [Alternate spelling: Ulrich. American stage and screen actress, c.1894–1970. Ulric often played the role of *femme fatale*. Her many stage and screen credits include *Kilmeny* (1915), *The Better Woman* (1915), *Intrigue* (1916), *The Heart of Paula* (1916), *The Son-Daughter* (1919), *Tiger Rose* (1923), *Peter Pan* (1924), *Capital Punishment* (1925), *Camilla* (1936), *The Fifth Column* (she played Anita; the play opened on March 6, 1940, at the Alvin Theater, New York, and ran for 87 performances), and *Antony and Cleopatra* (1947). For her performance in *The Harem* (1924), she wore veils as part of her costume. When she played in *Peter Pan* (she did not have the title role), Ulric was 30 or 32 years old.][36]
Scripps finds that Diana resembles the aging actress Lenore Ulric, who had played in *Peter Pan* and who "always went about veiled" (20).

*the Van Dorens. [The two Van Doren brothers, Carl Clinton (1885–1950) and Mark Albert (1894–1972) were prominent literary figures. Both were professors of English at Columbia University for many years, both authored many books, and both won Pulitzer Prizes: Carl for his *Benjamin Franklin* (1938) and Mark for *Collected Poems* (1939). The Van Doren family was heavily involved with the weekly journal *The Nation*: Carl was literary editor from 1919 to 1922 and his wife Irita from 1923 to 1924; she also served on the editorial staff (1919–1922) and was the magazine's advertising manager (1922–1923). Mark was literary editor from 1925 to 1928, and his wife, Dorothy Graffe Van Doren, was on the staff of the *Nation* from 1919 to 1936, serving as associate editor for the last ten of those years. Carl continued his association with *Nation* for several years, regularly contributing essays and the feature "The Roving Critic" (1925–1926). In addition, Carl became the literary editor of *Century* (1922–1925) when Glenn Frank was editor-in-chief.[37] See also *Century* and Frank.]
Diana, who reads *Century Magazine,* notices that the work of this gifted family appears more frequently now that the magazine is run by "a new editor" (44).

*Vanity Fair. [New York weekly, established in 1868 and bought by Condé Nast in 1913. *Vanity Fair* was a sophisticated review of current economic, political, and literary events until it was bought by and incorporated into *Vogue* (1936).][38]

Diana includes *Vanity Fair* in the long list of things she no longer has time to worry about (41).

*VC. [Victoria Cross, Britain's most prestigious decoration, instituted by royal warrant, 29 January 1856 and supplemented by subsequent royal warrants. It is inscribed "For Valour" and is awarded in recognition of "some signal act of valour or devotion" performed "in the presence of the enemy" ("Medals," *Encyclopaedia Britannica,* 11th ed., XVIII: 16). Cantwell has also been awarded this honor (*ARIT* 18).]
The smaller of the two Indians, who lost both arms and both legs at Ypres, was awarded the Victoria Cross (58).

*waitress. Johnson worries because the waitress who served him does not arouse him sexually (51–52; see also librarian, women and girls).

*Warner, Glenn [S. (Scobey, Pop). American lawyer and football coach, 1871–1954. Although he graduated law school and was admitted to the New York Bar, Warner made football coaching his career. From 1898 to 1939 he coached for several colleges and universities, developing the double wing-back formation and several new offensive maneuvers, such as the mousetrap, the screen pass, the reverse play and the unbalanced line. He coached the Carlisle Indian School's football team for many years (1898–1914); the combination of his coaching and the outstanding performance of athlete Jim Thorpe (q.v.) brought the Indian team national fame.]
A picture of this legendary coach adorns the committee room of the town Indians' club (65).

*Wells, H[erbert] G[eorge. English educator, novelist, and historian, 1866–1946. H. G. Wells' major works include *The Time Machine* (1895), *The War of the Worlds* (1898) and *The Outline of History* (1920). See also *Mr. Britling Sees It Through* in *FTA*.]
In an authorial intrusion, Hemingway reports that H.G. Wells had worried that the reader might consider "this story" to be autobiographical (68–69).

White Chief. The woods Indians' nickname for Yogi Johnson (54, 57–60, 73–75, 79, 81, 88).

*White, Stewart Edward. [American lawyer and writer, 1873–1946. White wrote more than fifty books, many of them based on his own adventures in the American West, where he went camping, hunting, and prospecting for gold, and on his two trips to Africa. The American West is the setting for *The Claim Jumpers* (1901), *The Blazed Trial* (1902), *Arizona Nights* (1904), *The Forty-Niners* (1918), the trilogy *The Story of*

California (1927) and *Wild Geese Calling* (1940). In later years White was interested in spiritualism and claimed that his last few books had been dictated to him by his late wife.]

A picture of this author hangs in the committee room of the town Indians' club (65).

women and girls. Yogi Johnson worries that he has lost his desire for women: he sees but does not desire a librarian, a waitress, and "a group of girls" (52). The sight of the naked Indian restores desire and memory: Johnson remembers that while he was on leave in Paris an unnamed "beautiful woman" picked him up, seduced him, disappeared, and was later revealed to be a performer, having intercourse with a soldier for an audience who looked through slits in the walls. Realizing he had been observed in this way, Johnson was rendered incapable of sexual feeling (79–81).

the woods Indians. Two grotesquely caricatured Indians on their way to join the Salvation Army (q.v.) become Yogi's companions. One is tall and the other short; both speak in grunts and Hollywood clichés (54). They listen respectfully to Yogi's war stories although both are heavily decorated World War I veterans themselves (58), and the smaller of the two "got both arms and both legs shot off at Ypres" (59). Even with four artificial limbs, he is a successful pool shark (59–60, 64–65). He loses one of his artificial limbs when they are thrown out of the town Indians' club (67); later he loses his wife to Yogi (87; see Indian squaw).

Speak: 54, 57–60, 67, 73–76, 79, 81, 88–89.

*****Wordsworth, [William. English Romantic poet, 1770–1850; poet laureate of England, 1843–1850. Wordsworth's famous poems include "Lines Composed a Few Miles above Tintern Abbey" (published in *Lyrical Ballads*, 1798), "Ode: Intimations of Immortality" (1807), "Ode to Duty" (1807), and many longer works, like *The Excursion* (1814) and the posthumously published *The Prelude* (1850). Wordsworth is closely associated with the Lake District in northwestern England.]

Scripps is first attracted to his second wife, Diana, because she comes from the Lake District: "Wordsworth's country, you know" (19). He thinks of details from several of Wordsworth's poems: "A field of golden daffodils" is a reference to or a misquoting of "a crowd, / A host, of golden daffodils" in the poem "I Wandered Lonely as a Cloud" (37).

Yogi. See Johnson, Yogi.

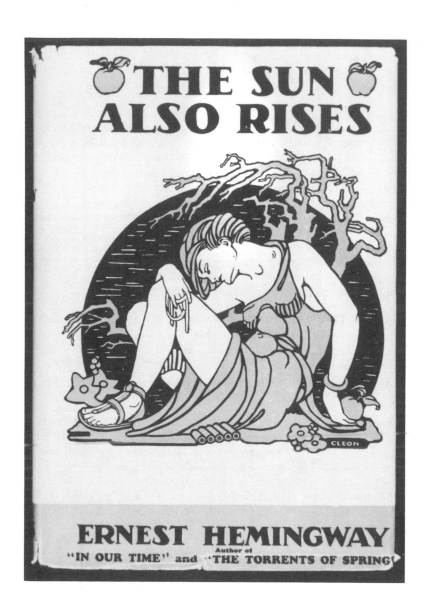

Scribner dust jacket for the first edition of *The Sun Also Rises* (courtesy Charles Scribner's Sons, an imprint of the Macmillan Publishing Company; and of the Hemingway Collection, J.F. Kennedy Library)

CHAPTER II

THE SUN ALSO RISES

(1926)

The action of the novel takes place in the mid-1920s, in France and Spain.[1]

absinthe. [A green, anise-flavored alcoholic drink whose main ingredient used to be wormwood, a substance so toxic that absinthe has been banned in Switzerland and France; its importation into the U.S. has been illegal since 1912. At the time of the novel absinthe was controversial but not illegal in Spain, where it is drunk in the late 1920s by Catherine and David Bourne (*GE* 38–39) and in the late 1930s by Robert Jordan (*FWBT* 50–51, 56–57; see entry for absinthe in *FWBT*), as well as by several characters in Hemingway's short stories. Absinthe has the reputation of being an aphrodisiac and of being addictive; excessive use is said to result in disorientation, insomnia, and even insanity. For a thorough discussion of this drink, see Doris Lanier, "The Bittersweet Taste of Absinthe." David Bourne describes the special equipment required for the proper preparation of absinthe drinks (see *GE* 38–39; see also *Guardia Nacional and Pernod in *GE*).]

After the first bullfight, Bill Gorton and Jake Barnes order absinthe (164). Brett joins them, drinking it from special "absinthe glasses" (166–67). Hobin, who is often defined as Ashley's double, drinks "imitation absinthe" (14–15). After the last bullfight, Gorton and Barnes again drink absinthe; Jake has four of them and is "very drunk" (221–23). See Pernod. The characters also drink goodly amounts of beer, brandy (Fundador is a favorite), rum punch, whiskey, and wine, as well as mixed drinks like Jack Roses and martinis (41, 73, 244–45) and exotic but unpalatable liqueurs like Izzarra (233).

*the Alexander Hamilton Institute. [Founded in 1914, this organization published books on investments, business and management.[2] It was named for Alexander Hamilton (American statesman, 1757–1804, killed in a duel by Aaron Burr) who supported the movement for American independence and fought in the American Revolution. He argued for a strong central government, established the Bank of the United States, and insisted on tight connections between federal government and financial institutions. Hemingway probably ran across the Alexander Hamilton Institute when he was writing copy for *The Cooperative Commonwealth* (subtitled "The Weekly Magazine of Mutual Help"), a publication of the Cooperative Society of America, for which Hemingway worked a few months, 1920–1921. The Cooperative Society of America, based in Chicago, "perpetrated an enormous fraud," its managers and owner embezzling $15 million in the two and a half years of its existence. The venture collapsed in 1921 (Meyers, *Hemingway,* 57). The Alexander Hamilton Institute, on the other hand, has been productive for over seventy years. Among its publications are titles like *Investments* (1917, part of a series of texts for a business course), *Women in Industry* (1918, about women's work during World War I), and a series called *Modern Business Lectures* (1917–1919). Jake remarks that the Alexander Hamilton Institute "was a good thing" (43), implying that it was already defunct, but the Institute was active as late as 1979, when it published James H. Taylor's *Strategic Planning for the Successful Business: How to Profitably Guide your Business into the Future.*]

Harvey Stone scorns Mencken, saying that he attracts only the sort of people who read the business treatises published by the Alexander Hamilton Institute (43).

*Algabeño. [Professional name of José García Rodríguez, Spanish matador, 1875–1947. Algabeño was a popular and successful matador who suffered many gorings, often in the hands. Hard-working, honest, and especially skillful with the muleta, he was able to maintain top ranking until his retirement in 1912. His son, José García Carranza (Pepe Algabeño, Algabeño II, Algabeño) is a more direct prototype for the Algabeño of this novel. He was born in 1902 and killed in the Spanish Civil War, in 1936. This matador had great power and strength but lacked the stamina, determination, and style which had made his father famous. He was a great womanizer. In 1923 the younger Algabeño fought in Pamplona on 12 and 13 July, delivering brilliant performances on both days. In 1924 he also appeared twice in Pamplona, on 11 and 13 July, with equal success. In 1925, he was scheduled to appear at the *gran corrida extraordinaria* of 11 July, with Belmonte and Lalanda, but on the preceding day he was injured in Madrid, at a special *corrida* in benefit of the Red Cross: he was hurt in the hip and arm and had to cancel his Pamplona engagement. Cayetano Ordóñez (Niño de la Palma, on whom Hemingway's Pedro Romero is based) took his place.[3] See also García Rodríguez and García Carranza in *DIA*. By giving the fictional Algabeño a hand injury and a weak character, Hemingway conflated the historical father and son.]

Jake and Montoya speak of Algabeño as a young matador corrupted by foreigners. Romero tells Jake that Algabeño was wounded in the hand "today in Madrid" (172, 185).

*Alger, [Horatio, Jr. American novelist, 1832 or 1834–1899. Alger wrote about 125 popular books for children, all based on the premise that a boy who works hard and eschews temptation will rise to power. Ragged Dick was his most famous hero, although Tattered Tom also starred in a long series of books. An ordained Unitarian minister, Alger was associated with the New York Newsboys' Lodging House, whose "homeless waifs" became his heroes. Alger's titles reveal his major motifs: e.g., *Bound to Rise: The Story of a Country Boy* and *Mark Mason's Victory or the Trials and Triumphs of a Telegraph Boy.* Alger also wrote several biographies of self-made statesmen.]

Jake thinks that W. H. Hudson's books are about as realistic as Horatio Alger's, and scorns Cohn for taking Hudson literally (9).

Ambassador. The unnamed American ambassador and his wife,[4] who are in Pamplona for the fiesta, invite Pedro Romero and Marcial Lalanda for coffee, an invitation Montoya and Jake decide not to deliver to Romero (171–72). The ambassador sees Romero perform (215).

Americans. Barnes, Cohn, and Gorton are Americans. A few other Americans, including the American ambassador to Spain (q.v.), show up for the fiesta in Pamplona (179). Several Americans have come from Biarritz to the fiesta in Pamplona (179; see the English; see *women and girls).

the archivist. Jake arranged for the archivist in Pamplona to buy him bullfight tickets every year and sent him money from Paris. Jake visits him in his office in the Ayuntamiento (City Hall, 96).

*Ashley. Brett's second husband, whom she intends to divorce. Lord Ashley is the ninth in his family to hold the hereditary title of baronet. Traumatized by his Navy service, he always slept with a loaded revolver. Eventually he threatened to shoot Brett (203). Barnes explains to Cohn that Brett did not love Ashley when she married him (39). He reports to Gorton that Ashley is a bona-fide aristocrat, "In the stud-book and everything" (76).[5]

Ashley, Brett (Lady Ashley). One of the expatriate crowd in Paris, she is a beautiful, charming, "modern" woman, with a large capacity for drink

(59). She fell in love with Jake when he came for treatment to the hospital where she served as a V.A.D. (Voluntary Aid Detachment, like Barkley in *FTA*) during World War I. Now thirty-four years old (38), she is divorcing her second husband in order to marry Mike Campbell. Her brief affair with Robert Cohn doesn't engage her emotions; she falls in love with the young bullfighter Pedro Romero but sends him away because she knows she would be "bad for him" and she does not want to be "one of these bitches that ruins children" (243). See end-note 1.

Speaks: 22–29, 32–34, 53–65, 74–75, 79–84, 134–44, 157–59, 162, 165–69, 175, 177–87, 206–9, 211–13, 217, 241–47.

*Ashley, Brett's family. Jake tells Cohn that after Brett's lover died of dysentery, she married two other men, neither of whom she loved, and is now engaged to Campbell (38–39; see 76). Brett mentions "Mummy" (58; see parents).

bargemen. Jake sees bargemen on the River Seine; he considers it a pleasant sight (41).

barman, bartender. Several bartenders serve drinks in the novel (182). The barman in Burguete refused payment (129); the one at the Palace Hotel in Madrid makes good drinks and is polite and discreet (244–45; see also George, waiters). The bartender in Biarritz gets handsome tips from the spendthrift Mike Campbell (229). When he leaves Cohn and Clyne at the Café Select, Jake speaks to the barman but does not order a drink (51).

Speaks: 244–45.

Barnes, Jacob (Jake). The first-person narrator. An American (from Kansas City, 21, 86, 107) news correspondent stationed in Paris, he loves Brett Ashley but has been rendered impotent by a war wound which deprived him of his penis but not of sexual desire. Although he tries not to think about this trauma, he still suffers occasional "bad times," mostly at night. Jake works hard, then takes off for a few days of fishing with Bill Gorton in Burguete, a week of fiesta in Pamplona with Brett, Robert Cohn and Michael Campbell, and then a few days of rest by himself. When Brett ends her affair with Pedro Romero, he goes to Madrid to rescue and comfort her.

Speaks: 6–7, 9–17, 21–29, 32–34, 37–40, 42–48, 51–65, 70–78, 80, 82–89, 95–96, 98–102, 104, 107–10, 113–18, 120–25, 127–31, 133–34, 137, 139–41, 143–45, 153, 156–58, 160–69, 171–72, 174–78, 181–85, 187, 189–95, 197–204, 206–10, 213, 217–18, 222–24, 227, 230–32, 239–47.

the Basques. [The Basque provinces are in the north of Spain. The main occupations are farming, fishing and sheepherding; the religion is Roman Catholicism. Most Basques speak Spanish, although there is a separate, non-Indo-European Basque language called Esquara or Euskara. The Basques consider themselves an independent nation, part of which lies in Spain and part in France. The Basques defeated Charlemagne at Roncesvalles in 778 CE.]

Many Basques travel on the bus from Bayonne to Burguete. They share their wine and wine-drinking expertise with Jake and Bill, make jokes and strike Bill as being "swell people" (104). One of them impresses his fellows with his command of English (103–108; see also 91).

Speak: 104–7.

Belfort. See Denfert-Rochereau.

"The Bells Are Ringing for Me and My Gal." [Correct title: "For Me and My Gal." Popular song, copyright 1917. Music by George W. Meyer, lyrics by Edgar Leslie and E. Ray Goetz. Publisher: Waterson, Berlin & Snyder, N.Y. The song, which rejoices in a forthcoming small-town wedding, extols old-fashioned values:

> The bells are ringing for me and my gal.
> The folks are singing for me and my gal.
> Everybody's been knowing to a wedding they're going
> And for weeks they've been sewing, every Susie and Sal!
> They're congregating for me and my gal.
> The parson's waiting for me and my gal.
> And some day there's gonna be a little home for two or three or four
>   or more
> In Loveland, for me and my gal!

This hit song was still popular in 1932, when it was featured in the movie *For Me and My Gal,* starring Judy Garland, George Murphy and Gene Kelly.]

Bill Gorton sings about "Irony and Pity"[6] to the tune of "For Me and My Gal" (113–14).

Belmonte [García, Juan (Terremoto, Juan Terremoto). Spanish matador, 1892–1962, by his own hand. Belmonte's career began inauspiciously: he had only four years of formal schooling, his family was poor, and he did not manage to attract an influential patron who could smooth his way. His first successes, in 1912, were due to his individual, even idiosyncratic style: a reckless, aggressive performer, he took unbelievable risks and was injured, although lightly, in almost every fight. His unconventional style was controversial from the beginning, the purists decrying his lack of elegance and grace, his apologists lauding his strong personality and courage. Crowds rushed to see this daredevil. In 1914 he and Joselito met for the first time in the ring, the first of many such joint performances in which each learned from the other and the nature of bullfighting was changed. As he achieved polish and control, Belmonte suffered fewer gorings, while maintaining his revolutionary closeness to the bull. The season of 1917, in which Belmonte appeared in 97 *corridas,* is thought by many to be his most triumphant, although in 1919 he fought 109 times, killing 234 bulls and suffering very few accidents. Belmonte's newly acquired sophistication and control alienated the public that had formerly rushed to see him risk his neck: people now accused him of coldness, self-interest and, most damningly, of lack of *afición* (passion for the art of bullfighting). Early in 1923 Belmonte announced his retirement. But the enormous fees he could command and his love of the art, which had grown as his understanding of its subtlety developed, lured him back to the ring: his performances, though few, were increasingly masterful. In 1925 he fought in one festival and 19 *corridas,* among them the *gran corrida extraordinaria* in Pamplona (11 July 1925), heading a bill which also included Marcial Lalanda and Cayetano Ordóñez; the bulls were from the Gamero Cívico ranch (see Miura). Belmonte stayed at the Hotel Quintana (q.v. in *DS*), where he was serenaded by crowds of admirers; he received a standing ovation when he entered the bullring. His performance with his first bull was not distinguished, but he was politely applauded. During his second performance that day, Belmonte was smacked by the bull, which knocked the sword out of his hand. Belmonte killed the bull only after several tries. The audience responded with a mixture of applause and derisory whistles. One reviewer wrote that although Belmonte showed himself to be a skillful artist, a master of the cape and the muleta, he certainly could have fought more closely to the bull. He also indicated that "one can see in Belmonte's face that the matador is in poor health." Belmonte fought the full season in 1926, showing himself a fully mature master of all aspects of the fight, including the final act, the killing itself, in which area he had previously drawn much adverse criticism. In 1927 he consistently drew high praise from critics and fellow matadors, although the public continued to accuse him of coldness. Belmonte retired at the end of the 1927 season, after a severe goring; when he emerged from retirement again in 1934, at age 42, he was unable to achieve his former greatness. He was still fighting, albeit in Portugal, as late as 1937. During his long, spectacular, and controversial career, Belmonte changed the nature of the sport by fighting closer to the bull than was previously thought possible.[7] See also *DIA,* in which Belmonte is treated more generously than he is in *SAR.*]

Jake reports that Belmonte is past his greatness. In his youth, Belmonte always worked close to the bull and consequently drew great crowds. Now Belmonte can only provide a pale copy of the bullfighting style he had established and is, therefore, scorned by the public. The description of Belmonte's face, while accurate [photographs show a dominant lower jaw], emphasizes the contrast he offers to the handsome Romero; Belmonte has a "long wolf jaw," a "wolf smile," a "wolf-jawed smile" (212–15, 221). Both Belmonte and Romero stay at the Hotel Montoya.

bicyclists. A group of Frenchmen and Belgians engaged in a long-distance race; they are accompanied by their trainers and managers. The cyclist who holds the lead suffers from boils. They spend the night in San Sebastián, where their manager talks to Jake (235; see also Bottechia).
Speaks: 236.

*Blackman, Charley. [The Blackman family of St. Louis were close friends of the Richardsons, whose daughter Hadley became the first Mrs. Hemingway: "Hadley's best friend throughout her girlhood was Elsa Blackman," whose home she found "lively and inviting" (Diliberto, 17–18). The name Blackman also appears in the 1916 Directory of the First Congregational Church of Oak Park, Illinois: Mr. and Mrs. Lewis R. Blackman, of 143 N. Harvey Ave., Oak Park, were, like the Hemingways, members of the church (Hemingway Collection: Other Materials, Church Papers). Charley Blackman seems unrelated to either of these two families, but his last name may derive from them.]
Blackman is a Chicagoan who seems to have lent Campbell some money which he failed to repay. Blackman is among those who attack Campbell at the Bar Milano in Pamplona (189; see also creditors).

Bocanegra. The bull that killed Vicente Girones during the running of the bulls in Pamplona (but see endnote 1). He was killed by Pedro Romero in the bullfight later that same day, and his ear was awarded to the bullfighter, who gave it to Brett (196–199, 219–221).

the bootblacks (*limpiabotas*). Mike and Bill think it a good joke to have the bootblacks polish Mike's boots over and over again (172–73; see also *DIA*). Bootblacks are also seen in San Sebastián (237).
Speaks: 173.

Botín's. [The restaurant, named "Antigua casa sobrino de Botín" (Ancient House [of the] Nephew of Botín), occupies the site of an ancient inn at 17, Calle de los Cuchilleros, off the Plaza Mayor of Madrid. In 1725 the large, handsomely tiled oven was added, presumably by the Botín family, and over the years the guest rooms were converted into small, comfortable dining rooms. Today's menu still emphasizes roast suckling pig.[8] For other bars and restaurants, see cafés.]

Jake and Brett have lunch at Botín's (245–46).

*Bottechia, [Ottavio. Italian bicyclist, 1894–1927. The son of a poor family, Bottechia fought in World War I and was taken prisoner in Caporetto. After the war he became a professional cyclist, first for the Bianchi and then for the Ganna companies, placing second in the Tour de France in 1923. During 1924 and 1925, his most successful years, he raced mostly in France, winning the Tour de France in both those years. In 1926 he suffered from unspecified health problems. On 3 June 1927 he suffered an accident and died two weeks later.][9]

The team manager tells Jake that the bicycle race has been uninteresting after Bottechia dropped out (236).

boxer. Robert Cohn was taught boxing (3) and knocks out Jake (191, 199, 200–01), Mike (201) and Pedro Romero (201–02), whom he "hurt . . . most badly" (206, 213, 219; see also Kelly).

*boxers. Bill Gorton saw a boxing match in Vienna in which a black boxer knocked out the "local white boy" and ended up in jail. According to the promoter, the black boxer had agreed to throw the match; he told Gorton that he was unable to do so because the white fighter was so inept that even with the aid of his opponent he couldn't win (71–72). Bill and Jake see another boxing match in Paris (81; see also Ledoux and Francis).

Speaks: 71.

*the boxer's family. Gorton reports that the black boxer he saw in Vienna has a wife and family in Cologne (72).

the boy. See men and boys.

Braddocks, Henry. A writer, one of the expatriate crowd in Paris. Jake describes him as one of Cohn's two friends, Jake being the other one (5). Braddocks and his crowd run into Jake and Georgette at a restaurant; they all go to a dancing-club (17–19). When Braddocks meets Jake again later that evening, he tells him about the "corking row" Georgette made at the bal musette (28; see also endnote 1).

Speaks: 17–19, 28.

Braddocks, Mrs. Henry's wife, a Canadian. She accepts at face value
Jake's jokes about Georgette. See Jo.
   Speaks: 17–18, 21, 28–29.

Brett, Lady Ashley. Jake explains that she is Lady Ashley, not Lady
Brett; Brett is her first name (38). See Ashley, Brett.

*Bryan, [William Jennings. American orator and politician, 1860–1925.
Bryan graduated from Illinois College in 1881 and read law at the Union
College of Law in Chicago for the next two years. Over the years he
supported a series of unpopular causes, all of which were defeated: he
favored the silver standard, was a pacifist who opposed American
participation in World War I, supported prohibition, and argued for a
fundamentalist reading of the Bible (he was a Presbyterian). He ran for
President of the United States on the Democratic ticket and was defeated
all three times (1896, 1900, 1908). He edited and wrote the leading
articles of the *Commoner,* a weekly newspaper (later a monthly) which
he established in 1901 in order to advance his campaigns in favor of the
common man and against the wealthy and influential businessmen of the
East, whom he accused of controlling the country. Bryan helped draft the
legislation which outlawed the teaching of evolution in the public
schools in Tennessee. He served as prosecutor in the famous Scopes or
Monkey trial, July 1925, in which John T. Scopes was tried for teaching
Darwin's theory of evolution. He died 26 July 1925, a few days after the
conclusion of the Scopes trial. Gorton mocks the pompous,
fundamentalist Bryan, whose old-fashioned values and style are unacceptable to the next generation. The same generational conflict governs
the jokes about Manning (who was anti-divorce), Mencken (who
rejected Hemingway's fiction), and Wheeler (who was anti-drink; see
also *Mr. Britling Sees It Through* in *FTA:* the young Frederic rejects the
middle-aged Britling's post-war affirmation of religion and patriotism).
The insistence on Catholic universities (Loyola, Notre Dame, Fordham,
Holy Cross) may reflect the anti-Catholic prejudice current in the United
States in the 1920s. See also Roman Catholics and priests.]
   Bill Gorton mocks Bryan's rhetorical style and alludes to the Scopes
trial with a reference to "simian fingers" [identified by Hinkle as a
quote from H. L. Mencken ("Re Query," 4)]. Bill falsely proclaims his
affection for Bryan. Jake informs Bill that Bryan has died (121–22).[10]

*bull-breeder. The narrator reports that Belmonte goes to his friend's
ranch to pick safe bulls for his fights (215).

bullfighters. [The term (*torero* in Spanish) applies to all who fight the
bull, including the picadors, banderilleros and other members of the

matador's crew. Also necessary are the sword-handlers, dressers, and the various bullring servants who handle the equipment (211–13). The highest ranking bullfighter is the graduated *matador de toros,* like Belmonte, Lalanda, Romero and Villalta (qq.v.).]

The two matadors who perform with Romero on the first and second days of the fiesta are far inferior to him (164, 167). On the last day Romero performs with Lalanda and Belmonte (qq.v.). Each of these matadors has his own *cuadrilla* (crew). We see picadors (212, 216, 219), banderilleros and swordhandlers (211, 213; see also Romero's *cuadrilla*).

*bullfighters. Jake prays for "all the bull-fighters" (97). Montoya has photographs of bullfighters in his room and likes to talk about bullfighters (131–32).

bus drivers, cab drivers. See drivers.

cafés. The characters visit or stroll past a number of bars, cafés and restaurants in Paris, among them the Nègre Joyeux (77), the Napolitain (13–14, 22), the Café de Versailles (6), the Café Aux Amateurs (77), the Dingo (36, 81), the Café de la Paix (40), the Dôme (29, 42, 46), the Rotonde (29, 42, 78), and the Closérie des Lilas (29, 45, 74–75, 78). The last four of these still flourish under their original names. A copy of Mike Strater's portrait of Hemingway hangs in the Closérie des Lilas, and a small brass plaque with his name is set into its bar (a similar plaque marks the spot at the Floridita Bar, q.v. in *Islands*). The Café aux (or des) Amateurs, on the Place de la Contrescarpe, is now called La Chope, and the Dingo ("The Crazy Man") at 10, rue Delambre, became the Auberge du Centre. For descriptions and more addresses, see Leland's *A Guide to Hemingway's Paris* or Fitch's *Walks in Hemingway's Paris;* for handsome photographs of these cafés and of other Parisian landmarks mentioned in Hemingway's fiction, see Gajdusek's *Hemingway's Paris.* I have provided separate entries for Damoy's, Foyot's, the Select, Wetzel's, and Zelli's, which were named after their founders; also see Lecomte. The Chope de Nègre [et Taverne des Sports], 13, rue du Faubourg, now defunct, is mentioned but not visited (237). The Café aux Amateurs and the Closérie des Lilas are described in some detail in *A Moveable Feast.* The Closérie des Lilas is also remembered by Thomas Hudson (*Islands* 58). In Pamplona, Spain, the characters often sit at the Café Iruña (today a pilgrimage stop for Hemingway fans) and get into fights at the Bar Milano (188) and the Café Suizo (189–92). Jake and Brett eat and drink at Montoya's Hotel and at Botín's (qq.v.).

Campbell, Michael (Mike). Brett Ashley's fiancé. The scion of a rich family, he is careless about money and is now an "undischarged bankrupt'' (79) who "can't write checks" (229). He overspends his allowance and sticks other people with his bills: Brett pays for the hotel (229–30) and Jake for the rented car (230–31); Mike even borrows money from Montoya (192). Although he claims not to mind Brett's lovers, he objects to Robert Cohn's hanging around her in San Sebastián and Pamplona and, when Brett goes off with Pedro Romero, stays almost continuously drunk, getting into fights and making vulgar and derogatory remarks about Jews, bullfighters, and English people. See creditors.

Speaks: 78–83, 134–37, 141–44, 157–59, 162, 165–69, 173, 175–80, 188–92, 199–204, 206–7, 210, 223–24, 228–31.

*Campbell's family. They are rich (38, 63) and provide him with an allowance (229). Before he came to Paris, Campbell was visiting his mother in Scotland (38, 78). See *parents.

carabineers. See guards.

Catholics. See Roman Catholics.

chambermaid. See maids.

chauffeur. See drivers.

children. The children and nannies Jake sees in Bayonne (232) and San Sebastián (237) suggest an ordered life which contrasts sharply with the disorder and violence of Pamplona. Older children play soccer (91) and hang around, looking at Jake's rented car (94) and wandering up to the bus (130). See Girones' family, men and boys, parents.

*children. Cohn and Krum's children are mentioned but not seen in the narrative (4, 36, 47). Clyne expected to have children some day (47).

*Circe. [In Greek legend, a dangerous enchantress who turns men into swine. In Homer's *Odyssey,* Circe changes Odysseus' companions into swine, but he forces her to break the spell. Milton Cohen finds that the Circe myth is relevant to our understanding of Brett Ashley and of the sexual politics at work in the novel.]
  Mike admires Cohn's comparing Brett to Circe (144). See Bacchus in *FTA* and *FWBT.*

*Cliquot, Veuve Cliquot. ["Veuve" is the French word for widow. The widow Cliquot was the daughter-in-law of Philippe Cliquot (or Clicquot), banker and wool merchant who founded the famous champagne-producing firm in 1772. Her brother Ponsardin joined the firm, which since mid-19th century has been known as Veuve Cliquot-Ponsardin (Rheims).]

When Count Mippipopolous announces he knows a "fellow" who owns large vineyards, Brett asks if his name is Veuve Cliquot (57).[11]

Closérie des Lilas. See cafés.

Clyne, Frances. A "forceful," opportunistic (according to Barnes), European-educated, unpublished American writer (5, 47) who lived with Cohn in the States and in Europe and now wants to marry him. When their three-year-old affair collapses, she attacks him bitterly. She eventually goes to England (45–51; see also 6, 22, 69, 222). See endnote 1.
    Speaks: 17–19, 46–51.

*Clyne's family. Clyne mentions her mother and the husband she divorced as quickly as possible (no alimony) when she took up with Cohn (46, 47, 49). See *parents.

Cohn, Robert. A 34-year-old American writer now living in Paris, he wrote a fairly successful first novel but is now having difficulties writing the second one; he used to support and edit a literary magazine (5). Divorced from his first wife, he is living with Clyne and has enjoyed the attentions of "several women" (8) when he meets and falls in love with Brett. After their brief affair, he hangs around her even though she, Mike Campbell, and Bill Gorton insult him publicly. When he hears that Brett has gone off with Pedro Romero, he is very upset, picking fights and crying. After beating up the bullfighter, Robert Cohn leaves Pamplona. Jake, who used to think that Robert is "frank and simple" and that he reads "too much" (3, 4), develops an angry, negative attitude that colors the retrospective narrative and intensifies the anti-Semitic tone provided most explicitly by Campbell and Gorton; see Jews. See also boxer.
    Speaks: 6–7, 9–13, 21–22, 37–40, 43–46, 48, 89, 95–96, 98–101, 134–35, 138, 140–42, 153–54, 159–62, 165–66, 177–78, 180–81, 190, 193–95.

*Cohn's family. Robert's late father left him more than $50,000, most of which Robert has "lost" (4). His mother comes from a prominent New York family.[12] She gives her son a monthly allowance of $300 (5). Cohn has an ex-wife and three children (4, 47; see *painters).

*the colonel. An Italian colonel visited Jake when he was hospitalized for his war wound (31).
    Speaks: 31.

*"The Colonel's Lady and Judy O'Grady." [The speaker in Rudyard Kipling's popular poem "The Ladies" reports that he "learned about women" from four women of various colors, ages, nationalities, temperaments and social standing. He enjoins the reader to "be warned by my lot (which I know you will not) / An' learn about women from me!" and follows this with the last stanza:

> What did the Colonel's Lady think?
>   Nobody never knew.
> Somebody asked the Sergeant's wife,
>   An' she told 'em true!
> When you get to a man in the case,
>   They're like as a row of pins—
> For the Colonel's Lady an' Judy O'Grady
>   Are sisters under their skins! (Kipling, II: 265–67).]

Afraid he has upset Jake by his reference to Henry James' accident and its suggestion of castration, Bill assures Jake that he's "a hell of a good guy" and tries to return the conversation to its former humorous plane through sexual jokes, including his reworking of Kipling's last line (116).

the *concierge*. The *concierge* at Jake's hotel in San Sebastián brings him police forms, telegraph blanks (234) and two telegrams from Brett (238–39). The *concierge* or manager at the Hotel Montana in Madrid is unattractive, formal and honest (240–41, 243; see also Duzinell and manager; see also *concierge* in *MF*).
  Speaks: 238–39, 240.

the conductor. On the train to Bayonne, he accepts bribes but does not deliver favors (84–85).
  Speaks: 85.

*the cook. One of Frances Clyne's many complaints about Robert Cohn is that he neglected to inform the cook that he wasn't coming home for lunch (46; see also the secretary).

*Coolidge, [John Calvin (Silent Cal). American lawyer and politician, 1872–1933. Coolidge became 30th President of the United States when his predecessor, Warren G. Harding, died in 1923. Coolidge was elected President in 1924 but refused his party's nomination in 1928. The Republican Coolidge was President of the United States at the time of the events of the novel. As his nickname indicates, he was known for his pragmatic, laconic New England style.]

When Jake says that he didn't dream during his nap, Gorton puns on the word "dream" and ironically mentions President Coolidge as an example of a visionary businessman (124).

cop. See *policeman.

correspondents. Jake is a newspaperman, as are Krum and Woolsey (qq.v.). They attend a briefing with several other correspondents (36).

*counsel. Mike Campbell recalls that during the legal bankruptcy proceedings both he and his lawyer were drunk (136–37).

*creditors. Mike Campbell had to declare bankruptcy. He reports offhandedly that he "Probably had more creditors than anybody in England" (136). He borrows money from most of the other characters (192; see also 189) and mentions his creditors often (200; see also Blackman, the English, partner, tailor).

*Crillon, [Louis des Balbes de Berton de. French soldier, c.1541–1615. Crillon was a distinguished soldier who fought for Kings Henry III and Henry IV. He was admired and befriended by Henry IV, who called him "the bravest of the brave," a phrase later quoted by Napoleon (in reference to Marshal Ney, q.v. in *ARIT*). In 1788 his descendant, François-Félix-Dorothée Berton des Balbes, Count of Crillon, acquired a mansion facing on the Place de la Concorde "and bestowed upon it his name." The Crillon family sold the property to the Société des Grandes Magasins et des Hotels du Louvre in 1907. The remodeled mansion opened as the elegant Hotel Crillon in 1909. The famous façade of the hotel matches that of the Department of the Navy, from which it is separated by the Rue Royale. The two façades were commissioned by King Louis XV, designed by the noted architect Jacques-Ange Gabriel, and built in the mid-18th century. The famous and luxurious Hotel Crillon, located at 10 Place de la Concorde, has hosted royalty, heads of state, and famous artists and performers.[13] See George.]
Brett arranges to meet Jake at the Crillon but doesn't keep her appointment (29, 41). Gorton stopped at the Crillon for a few drinks; he saw Harvey Stone there (73).

the critic. See Hernández Ramírez, Rafael.

the crowd. Cohn and Barnes have a drink "and watch the evening crowd" in Paris; later Barnes watches the crowd alone (13–14); he also watches a crowded daytime scene by himself (35). People crowd into a dancing club (see proprietor) in Paris. In Pamplona, peasants arrive to shop (150), but the real crowds show up for the San Fermín fiesta early in July. The fact that the church is crowded (208) and that many people watch the religious procession (155) reminds us that the fiesta is in honor of St. Fermín (q.v.) and is attended by the town's "dignitaries, civil and religious" as well as "a guard of soldiers" (155). The revelers frequent the wine shops (155–59) and restaurants (160–61, 191, 205, 211) and fill the streets and squares of Pamplona (152–53, 157, 159, 164, 178–79, 195, 205, 207, 222, 224). A crowd goes to inspect the bulls (137, 138, 140), runs before the bulls (160, 196, 200; see 150), buys tickets for the fights (190, 195) and drifts towards the bullring, which soon fills up (170, 197, 211–12). During the fight the crowd expresses its disapproval of Belmonte, hurling insults, "cushions and pieces of bread and vegetables" at him (214). Pleased by Romero, they clap and shout (217, 219), wave their handkerchiefs (220) and carry him triumphantly out of the bullring on their shoulders (221; see also dancers). Buses and trains transport crowds of people (98, 103–6). See dancers, the English, men and boys, women and girls.

Speak: 157–59, 213.

*the crowd. Bill reports that the crowd at the boxing match in Vienna got rowdy when the "local white boy" was defeated (71). We hear the roar of the crowd at the bullring (160).

customs officers. See guards.

*Damoy's. [One of the more than 2,000 branches of Julien Damoy's chain of epiceries, located at 113–17, Boulevard du Montparnasse (Leland 21).]
     Barnes and Gorton walk past Damoy's (78).

dancers. Groups of people in various stages of intoxication dance, often around or near Brett, both in Paris (19–20, 62) and in Pamplona (153–56, 157, 159, 164–65, 170–71, 220, 222; see 161). In Pamplona, dancing is a mostly male activity, the men and boys being accompanied by bands, drums, and fifes. As Bill notices, "They dance differently to all the different tunes" (165). Boys dance around the dead bull Romero has just killed (220). The members of various local dancing and drinking societies accompany the body of Girones home for burial (198).

*Davidson, Jo. [American sculptor, 1883–1952. Davidson studied in New York and then in Paris, where he lived from 1907 until the outbreak of World War II. He became famous for his busts of famous contemporaries, including Presidents Woodrow Wilson and Franklin D. Roosevelt, American General Pershing, French Marshal Joffre, Hollywood magnate Adolf

¡VIVAN LOS FORASTEROS Y TODOS LOS PAMPLONICOS! (Hurray for the foreigners and all the Pamplonese!) *Zig Zag,* 19 July 1923 (courtesy of the Hemingway Collection, J. F. Kennedy Library)

"Hurray for Wine! Hurray for the Foreigners!" was painted on the banner.

"Where are the foreigners?" Robert Cohn asked.

"We're the foreigners," Bill said.

From *The Sun Also Rises,* p. 154.

Zukor, millionaires John D. Rockefeller and Andrew Mellon, and several writers: Anatole France, Sinclair Lewis, James Joyce, G. B. Shaw, Gertrude Stein and H. G. Wells. He did more busts of famous men and women than any other sculptor of his time. He charged hefty fees. Davidson wrote *Between Sittings: An Informal Autobiography* (New York: Dial Press, 1951). Hemingway provided texts for Davidson's *Spanish Portraits* (New York: The Georgian Press, 1938).]

Gorton figures that Davidson is not an artist, but one of "our biggest business men" (124).

*Davis, Jefferson. [American statesman, 1808–1889. He was elected senator from Mississippi in 1847 and 1858 and argued for secession when Lincoln was elected President in 1860. The Southern Congress chose him as provisional President of the Confederacy in February 1861; he was elected to the office in 1862 and held it until 1865. In May 1865 the victorious North charged him with two counts of treason, and he was held in jail without trial or bail for two years. In 1867 he was released on bail; he was never tried but benefited from the general amnesty of 1868. He wrote *The Rise and Fall of the Confederate Government* (1881).]

For the post-war generation, old heroes are irrelevant and the new sexual freedom is sometimes problematic. After he expresses his fondness for Jake, Bill, embarrassed by his emotional outburst, makes jokes about "faggots," claiming that "That was what the Civil War was about": both Abraham Lincoln and Jefferson Davis had been in love with General Grant (116).

*Delambre, [Jean-Baptiste Joseph. French astronomer, 1749–1822. Delambre studied latitudes and longitudes as well as astronomical measurements. He wrote several books on measurements and a multi-volume history of astronomy.]

Brett and Jake walk along the Rue Delambre (83).

*Dempsey, [William Harrison (Jack). American prize fighter, 1895–1983; world heavyweight champion, 1919–1926. Dempsey became heavyweight champion by defeating Jess Willard in 1919; in 1921 he defended the championship against Georges Carpentier, whom he knocked out. He toured Europe in 1922, defeated the challenger Luis Firpo in 1923 and lost the championship to Gene Tunney on 23 September, 1926; he retired after losing a second Tunney fight in 1927. Dempsey came out of retirement for a year, 1931–1932 (to fight 56 exhibition bouts), and again in 1940. He was the first boxer to draw a million-dollar gate. His autobiography is entitled *Massacre in the Sun* (1960).[14] At the time of the action of the novel, he was the reigning champion. See also *GHA* and *Islands*.]

The post-war generation is looking for new champions: Bill Gorton tells Jake that he had seen "a whole crop of great young light heavyweights" in New York, any one of whom "was a good prospect to grow up, put on weight and trim Dempsey" (70).

*Denfert-Rochereau, [Pierre Marie Philippe Aristide. French engineer and military man, 1823–1878. Denfert-Rochereau fought in the Crimea and Algeria, but his fame rests mainly on his defense of the town of Belfort, in eastern France, during the Franco-German War of 1870–1871. The German troops had cut Belfort off from the interior of France and had laid siege to the town. Colonel Denfert-Rochereau, who commanded the fortress which dominates the town, organized a formidable opposition to the besiegers. Belfort, the town's castle and several nearby towns fought back during the winter of 1870–1871, but were ordered to surrender in the general armistice agreement of February 1871. In Paris, the Place Denfert-Rochereau displays "a small bronze version of Bartholdi's *Lion* in commemoration of Colonel Denfert-Rochereau's successful defense of Belfort in 1870–71" (*Michelin Paris, 1990*). The Parisian street named after this colonel runs into Boulevard St. Michel at Place Louis Marin, where there was a monument in honor of Joseph Bienaimé Caventou (1795–1877) and Pierre-Joseph Pelletier (1788–1842), professors at the School of Pharmacy credited with isolating many medically important substances, including strychnine in 1817, brucine in 1819, and quinine in 1820. Pelletier also discovered narceine, an alkaloid of opium, in 1832, and toluene, also known as methylbenzene, in 1838. Leland points out that during World War II the Germans "filched the metal" of which the statues were made "and now a half-nude stone woman—La Guerison—reclines there" (Leland 56), her right hand held to her forehead in an attitude of pain. The inscription identifies the two chemists as discoverers of quinine and benefactors of humanity. Each man is honored by a large medallion which shows him in profile and by a tablet which lists his name, academic title, and dates. Under each tablet are a carved caduceus, a water spigot and a trough. The two memorials are on opposite sides of the base which supports the statue of the woman.]
Where the Boulevard St. Michel meets the Rue Denfert-Rochereau, Jake and Bill see the statues of the inventors of quinine (72).

dignitaries. See crowds.

Dingo. See cafés.

diplomat. See *Nouvelle Revue Française*.

Dôme. See cafés.

drivers. The bus driver who takes Jake, Bill and a crowd of Basques from
Bayonne to Burguete drives fast (104), climbs "steadily" (108) and
stops three times (105, 106, 109). Bill and Jake take another bus from
Burguete to Pamplona (130). Jake often rides cabs, both taxis and
horse-drawn cabs (15–16, 24–28, 36–37, 41–42, 51, 74, 75, 89, 137,
140, 240, 243, 247). Bill, Mike and Jake also hire a car and a chauffeur
for the journey from Bayonne to Pamplona (91–94) and again for the
journey back: they travel together from Pamplona to Hendaye, where
Mike gets dropped off, after which Bill and Jake continue to Bayonne,
where Bill takes the train; the chauffeur drives Jake on to his hotel and
is paid by Jake (228–32; see also Henry).
    Speaks: 231–32.

the drummer. A black musician who works at Zelli's; his accent
indicates he's American (62).
    Speaks: 62, 64.

*Dun, R[obert] G[raham. American economist and businessman, 1826–
1900. R. G. Dun rose from clerk to partner (1854) to sole owner (1859)
of the Mercantile Agency, an organization founded in 1841 in response
to the growing size and complexity of the American financial community. This agency, the first to supply businesses and investors with
information about the strength and solvency of firms throughout the
United States, became R. G. Dun & Co. in 1859. In 1933 it merged with
the Bradstreet Co. to become Dun & Bradstreet, Inc.]
    Jake remarks that Cohn takes romantic travelogues as literally as one
reads R. G. Dun reports (9).

Duzinell, Madame. The *concierge* in Jake's building, she gives him his
mail (30) and vets his visitors, forbidding entry to those she considers
unworthy (32, 53). She disapproves of Brett, who comes to see Jake at
4:30 AM after a night of drinking and partying, but after receiving 200
francs (54), Mme. Duzinell suddenly recognizes that Brett is wellborn
and well-bred (52; see also 30, 34, and *concierge*).
    Speaks: 32, 52–53.

dwarfs. [Five larger-than-life heads worn by costumed actors form part
of the frequent processions during the week of the San Fermín fiesta.
They represent a stylized Grandmother, a Japanese man and woman, a
Councilman and a Mayor. As part of the giants' retinue, they walk about
seriously, shaking hands with the adults and giving candy to the
children. They look small in comparison to the giants (q.v.), and their

large heads (90 cm. tall and 70 cm. wide) dwarf the wearers' bodies, hence the names *cabezudos* (large-heads) or *enanos* (dwarfs). Some can move their eyes. The people who wear them look out from openings in the chins or, in the case of the Mayor, through the mouth. They were made in 1875. More recent are the six "kilikis," smaller than the dwarfs but much uglier, as their names indicate: Caravinagre (vinegar-face), Verrugón (warty), Barbas (bearded), Patata (potato), Coleta (pigtail), and Napoleon. These carry "weapons" with which to "protect" the giants and frighten the children. Another six figures, the *zaldikos,* represent horses; they hang from the shoulders of men whose red-garbed torsos emerge from the center, making them look as if they were riding the horses. They are nameless and, like the "kilikis," equipped with "weapons."][15]

Dancing giants and dwarfs with "whacking bladders" form part of the spectacle during the fiesta of San Fermín (155, 222).

the editor and publisher. [Robert Fleming convincingly argues that Robert Cohn is reading the trade journal *Editor & Publisher,* "published since 1884 for an audience of newspaper editors, publishers, and reporters," and that Jake is working by himself ("Re Sources," 3). Hinkle argues that the editor, publisher and Jake are all the same person, a variant of the "me, myself, and I" formula, and that Jake is working by himself: "When Jake finished working, he locked the office. Evidently no one else was there" (Hinkle, "Some Unexpected Sources," 33).]

As punctuated, the narrative suggests that three people—Jake, his editor and publisher—work hard at the newspaper office (12).

Edna. A pretty girl Bill Gorton knew in Biarritz. They meet again in Pamplona and Mike flirts with her (180). Edna goes with Mike and Bill to the Bar Milano, where the two men get into several fights and are expelled by the police. She tells Jake that she has "kept them out of four fights" (188). See also 195, 200, 222. See endnote 1.

Speaks: 188–89, 191–92.

*Edna's friend. She did not accompany Edna, going to bed with "a headache" (180).

the English. A group of English and American tourists vacationing at the fashionable sea resort of Biarritz in south-west France have come to Pamplona (179). Mike probably owes money to some of them. He and Bill get into several fights with the "Damned English swine" and display great drunken solidarity in the face of these "stupid" English "bastards" who have insulted Mike (188, 189; see also 205). Although

moved by Romero's performance (215), the "Biarritz crowd" are
generally ignorant about bullfighting (217) and keep aloof from the
festivities, the women observing the celebrants through their lorgnons
(180). Later Jake, Mike and Bill have some drinks at Biarritz (229–30).
See Edna.
  Speak: 218.

fathers. See parents.

*Fermín, San. [Spanish prelate, c. 2nd century CE. Since the 17th
century, Sts. Fermín and Francisco Javier have been joint patron saints
of the province of Navarre; the patron saint of the city of Pamplona is St.
Saturnino. St. Fermín was the son of Firmo, President of the Senate of
the then-Roman city of Pamplona and an early convert to Christianity.
Firmo, baptized by St. Saturnino, brought up his son in the faith and
Fermín became a great evangelizer and the first bishop of Pamplona. He
was martyred by being beheaded (hence the red neckerchiefs worn
during the fiesta, 154) for his faith in Amiens, after baptizing more than
three thousand converts. In 1591 Pamplona, where St. Fermín had a
great following, asked that his feast day be changed from the fall, the
time of his martyrdom, to July 7, to coincide with the important
mid-summer fair and market. A reliquary in the shape of the saint resides
in the large chapel of San Fermín in the church of San Lorenzo in
Pamplona; the chapel was completed in the early 18th century, although
Fermín has been worshipped in that church since the 14th century. Place
of honor in the chapel is held by a silver statue of the saint, which
displays fragments of his bones. This reliquary is taken in procession
from the Church of San Lorenzo, through the city, and back to the
Church.][16]
  The narrative reports that the statue of the saint was carried ceremonially through the streets at the beginning of the fiesta (152–53, 155). His
name is spelled out in fireworks (179), and people come to pray in his
chapel (153, 155, 198, 208).

fireworks. See Orquito.

*Flowers, Tiger [(The Georgia Deacon). American boxer, 1895–1927.
Tiger Flowers boxed from 1918 to 1927, fighting in 149 professional
bouts. He was 5'10" and weighed 160 lbs. On 10 November, 1924
Flowers fought two bouts in Philadelphia, winning both fights by
knock-outs in the second round. He became world middleweight
champion on 28 February, 1926, when he defeated Harry Greb in a
fifteen-round fight. He lost the crown to Mickey Walker (USA) in
December of the same year. In 1927, Flowers lost only one of the

eighteen bouts he fought before dying in November "from the effects of an operation" (Fleischer 145). Like the boxer Gorton saw in Paris, Tiger Flowers was black.][17]

The black boxer Bill Gorton saw in Paris resembled Tiger Flowers, "only four times as big" (71).

flower-women. Jake sees them on his way to work (35).

*Ford. [American family of automotive industrialists, millionaires and philanthropists. The founder of the company was Henry Ford, inventor and automobile manufacturer, 1863–1947. Ford supported the publication and distribution of the anti-Semitic book, *The Protocols of the Elders of Zion.* He also owned two anti-Semitic newspapers: the *Dearborn Independent* appeared from 1920 to 1927, when it was forced by court order to stop publication; the *International Jew* continued to appear for several decades. Ford dealers were required to stock and promote the sale of these anti-Semitic tracts. Part of Ford's dream for improving American life was to rid the society of Jews (q.v.).]

When Jake says that he didn't dream during his nap, Gorton puns on "dream," mentioning Ford as an example of a visionary businessman (124).

*Foyot's. [The Hotel Foyot, which closed in 1938, was situated at 33 Rue de Tournon, with a south entrance at 22-bis Vaugirard. "The rooms at the Foyot were not too expensive, but the hotel's restaurant was fairly dear. The cuisine, however, drew raves from virtually everyone" (Hansen 98). This restaurant, open from 1848 until 1932, was rated "the best restaurant in the Latin Quarter" by Baedeker (Leland 31). See *FWBT.*]

When Georgette Hobin turns up her nose at Lavigne's restaurant, Jake suggests she go by herself and pay for her own meal at the expensive Foyot's (16).

*France, Anatole. [Nom de plume of Jacques Anatole François Thibault. French novelist and literary critic, 1844–1924. Anatole France was awarded the Nobel Prize in 1921. His most important titles include *Thaïs* (1890), *The Red Lily* (1894), *The Garden of Epicurus* (1894), *Contemporary History* (a collection of four novels, 1897–1901), *Joan of Arc* (1908), *The Path of Glory* (1915), *Literary Life* (1884–1894), and *The Procurator of Judea* (1922). Anatole France was a famous, influential man of letters. His death in 1924 would have recalled him and his achievements to the characters' attention. Clyne probably doesn't know that Anatole France was 35 years old when his first volume of stories, *Jocaste et le chat maigre* (1879), was published, and 37 when his first novel appeared (*The Crimes of Sylvester Bonnard,* 1881). Cohn, who is 34 years old, has already published his first novel and is working on a second.]

In her angry attack on Cohn, Frances Clyne compares him to Anatole France, recently dead at the age of 80, in order to emphasize the thirty-four-year-old Cohn's lack of achievement (50–51).

*Francis, Kid. [Real name: Francisco Buonaugrio. Born in Marseille, France, 7 October, 1907. He was 5'4" and weighed 118 lbs. His boxing career extended from 1923 to 1935. On 9 June, 1924, the teen-aged Kid Francis beat the ex-champion Ledoux (q.v.) in a twelve-round fight (Fleischer, 148) which Hemingway saw (Reynolds, *The Paris Years,* 297). Kid Francis was defeated three times (13 September, 1928; 10 July, 1932; 16 April, 1934) by Panama Al Brown, who held the bantam-weight crown from 1929 to 1935. See endnote 17.]

The narrative mentions Kid Francis as the boxer who fought Ledoux, dates the fight June 20, and describes it as "a good fight" (81).

*the Fratellini. [An Italian family of clowns. The father, Gustavo Fratellini (1842–1905), was an acrobat, clown, and horse-back performer. Of his many sons, three took up the profession: after ten years touring Russia and Europe with the Salamonsky Circus, they joined the Medrano Circus of Paris during World War I. They were the most famous clowns in the period between the world wars: Paul or Pablo (1877–1940) played the placid, self-satisfied bourgeois; Francisco (1879–1951), the chubby dreamer, stuffed into a sparkling sequined and spangled outfit; and Alberto (c.1886–1961), the hirsute buffoon whose make up (heavy eyebrows, big red nose and mouth) is now standard for clowns. Max, Louis, and Nino were the next generation of Fratellini clowns. See also *TS* and *DIA*.]

Bill informs Jake, who has been living in Paris, that the phrase "Irony and Pity" is currently popular in New York, "just like the Fratellinis used to be"[18] (114; see also "The Bells Are Ringing for Me and My Gal").

*Fritsch, [Frank Francis] (Frankie, [the Fordham Flash). Correct spelling: Frisch. American baseball player and manager, 1898–1973. Frisch played baseball at Fordham University, where he was also captain of the baseball, football, and basketball teams. In 1919 he signed on with the New York Giants, with whom he played all infield positions except first base. In 1927 he joined the St. Louis Cardinals, playing second and third base until 1937. He batted .316 over 19 years. Retired as a player, he became team manager for the Cardinals (1933–1938), the Pittsburgh Pirates (1940–1946), and the Chicago Cubs (1949–1951). He was

elected to baseball's Hall of Fame in 1947. At the time of his death Frisch still held the National League record for playing in the most world series games (50) and for hitting the longest home run ever.][19]
After their first bottle of wine, Jake and Bill Gorton tipsily argue about which Catholic university, Holy Cross or Fordham, was Frisch's alma mater (122; for the emphasis on Catholic universities, see Bryan and students).

*Gallo. Professional name of a great family of bullfighters. See Gómez Ortega, Rafael and José.

*Gayarre [Garjón, Sebastián Julián. Spanish operatic tenor, c.1843–1890. Born to a poor Navarrese family, Gayarre had the good luck to be discovered by the singing teacher Eslava, who not only taught him but also underwrote his voice studies with famous teachers in Madrid and Milan. Gayarre rapidly became an international star, reputed to have a repertory of more than fifty operas. He collapsed dramatically in the middle of a performance and died a few days later. Ornate statuary decorates his tomb in his home town of Roncal.[20] In the 1920s Pamplona had two major theatres, the Olympia and the Gayarre. In 1932, Hemingway noted that "They tore down the old Gayarre" (*DIA* 273), but today's city still has a theatre by that name.]
The narrative mentions the Theatre Gayarre, in Pamplona (153).

*George. The barman at the Hotel Crillon, Paris. Jake has a drink with him (a Jack Rose, q.v.) while waiting for Brett, who doesn't appear (41). George prepares the same drink for Gorton, who admires the barman because he's "never been daunted" (73; Gorton may also have been drinking Pernod, q.v.; see also barman).

Georgette. See Hobin, Georgette; and Leblanc, Georgette.

the German. See the maître d'hôtel.

giants. [The Pamplonese giants are a group of eight hollow, elegantly attired papier-maché figures which represent the rulers, a King and a Queen, from four continents: Europe, Asia, Africa and America. Each statue is supported by a four-legged wooden framework which is hidden by the long skirts of the costume. They are about 3.9 meters tall (4.2 m. when carried) and range in weight from 59 kg. (the European Queen, 130 lbs.) to 66.5 kg. (the African King, 146 lbs.). They are made to march and dance by a person who stands inside the framework; this requires no little strength and skill. Pamplona's giants appear in daily processions during the fiesta of San Fermín. The current figures were made in 1860 by Tadeo Amorena, but giants were used in Navarre for religious and royal festivities since the sixteenth century; fictional references trace them back to the thirteenth century. Tafalla, Tudela, Estella and several other Navarrese towns also possess giants, which are occasionally brought together for day-long marches and displays: in 1986, 49 giants marched together in Tudela, and similar large displays have taken place in Pamplona. See endnote 15.]

The giants and dwarfs (q.v.) are seen during the fiesta in Pamplona (155, 222).

girls. See women and girls.

Girones, Vincente. A 28-year-old farmer who has come to Pamplona for the fiesta. Gored early in the morning, during the running of the bulls, he dies a few hours later of his wounds (196–98; see also 204, Bocanegra, and endnote 1).

Girones' family. Vicente Girones' widow and two young children come to Pamplona to take his body back to their home near Tafalla (198; see dancers).

*[Gómez Ortega, José] (Joselito). [Spanish matador, 1895–1920. Descended from bullfighters on both his mother's and father's side of the family, Joselito showed great talent as a boy and had a great following even before his investiture as *matador*. His performances in the bullring were almost consistently magnificent; he mastered all aspects of bullfighting and fought with grace, gallantry, bravery and great art. Joselito's early death caused a great national outpouring of grief.[21] See also *DIA* and *FWBT*.]

Jake explains that Joselito was a great bullfighter who fought smoothly and dangerously close to the bull, as Romero does. Lesser bullfighters, however, fool the public with the "appearance of danger . . . while the bull-fighter was really safe" (168).

*[Gómez Ortega, Rafael] (el Gallo). [Spanish matador, 1882–1960; older brother of the great Joselito. A temperamental bullfighter, haunted by fears and fantasies, el Gallo was unpredictable in the bullring. He was a picturesque improviser, capable of great artistry, widely acknowledged as one of the outstanding bullfighters of all time. His best years were 1910–1914. Possibly under pressure from his brother, he retired in 1918 but came out of retirement the next year, spent the next several seasons in Latin America, and was still fighting in 1935. He is remembered for his extraordinary personality, enormous talent, inimitable style, and erratic and inconsistent behavior, both in and out of the ring.[22] See also *DIA* and *FWBT*.]

Discussing why women are drawn only to young bullfighters, Jake says that "The old ones get fat" and Montoya adds that some, like Gallo, go "crazy" (172).

Gorton, Bill (Old Bill). A successful American writer who comes to Europe for a holiday. After spending a few days in Paris with his good friend Jake, he goes to Vienna, where he rescues a black boxer (71–72; also 81), and to Budapest. After a few more days back in Paris, he and Jake enjoy a quiet fishing interlude in Burguete. He likes Mike and Brett, drinks with them in Pamplona, defends Mike in the brawl at the Bar Milano, and joins their attacks on Cohn. He returns to the States after the fiesta. See endnote 1.
   Speaks: 70–80, 85–89, 95–96, 98–99, 101–2, 104, 108–10, 113–18, 120–25, 127–30, 133–34, 136, 141–42, 145, 154, 156, 158–59, 161–66, 173, 175, 179–80, 188–89, 193, 199–202, 204, 206, 210–11, 213, 219, 221–24, 227–31.

*Grant, [Ulysses Simpson. American military and political leader, 1822–1885. Grant was Commander-in-Chief of the Union forces during the American Civil War and was made a full general in 1866, the first man after Washington to be raised to that rank. He was the 18th President of the United States, 1869–1877. His *Personal Memoirs* (1885–1886) deal with his military career.]
   After he verbalizes his liking for Jake, Bill, embarrassed by his emotional outburst, makes jokes about "faggots" and about heroes, claiming that both Abraham Lincoln and Jefferson Davis had been in love with General Grant (116).

guards. The military and civil guards are visible but not obnoxious. French and Spanish border guards (carabineers) check documents and are not too concerned about the occasional breach of the border (92–93, 109). A customs officer checks luggage (130, 233). See policemen, soldiers.
   Speak: 92–93, 109.

*gypsies. Before the fiesta starts, they set up a camp nearby (150); Brett has her fortune told (151; see also *FWBT*).

*Hadley. See Hemingway, Hadley Richardson.

*Hamilton. See Alexander Hamilton Institute.

*Hardy, [Thomas. English architect, novelist and poet, 1840–1928. Hardy published his first novel, *Desperate Remedies,* in 1871, when he was 31; the next year saw *Under the Greenwood Tree,* and in 1873 he published *A Pair of Blue Eyes.* His major novels are *Far From the Madding Crowd* (1874), *Return of the Native* (1878), *The Mayor of Casterbridge* (1886), *Tess of the D'Urbervilles* (1891), *Jude the Obscure* (1896), and the trilogy *The Dynasts* (1903–1908). He was granted many honors and awards, including the Order of Merit in 1910. At the time of the action and writing of *SAR,* Hardy was the undisputed sovereign of English letters.]

Frances Clyne tells Robert Cohn, who is 34, that he can be considered a young writer only in comparison with Anatole France (q.v.), who had died recently at age 80, or Thomas Hardy, who was then in his mid-80s (50).

Harris. A "very pleasant" Englishman (125) who plays bridge and goes fishing with Jake Barnes and Bill Gorton in Burguete. They invite him to Pamplona, but he prefers to spend the few remaining days of his holiday fishing for trout. He gives Jake and Bill a dozen hand-tied flies (130). Jake notices that, like Brett, he "talked with inflected phrases" (149); he speaks Spanish "quite well" (129).
    Speaks: 126–130.

Harvey. See Stone, Harvey.

*[Hemingway,] Hadley [Richardson. 1891–1979; married to Ernest Hemingway, 1921–1927. Hadley married Paul Scott Mowrer in 1933. See also *MF.*]
    Hemingway dedicated *The Sun Also Rises* to his first wife, whom he was divorcing, and to his son.

*[Hemingway,] John Hadley Nicanor. [Son of Ernest and Hadley Hemingway; born 1923. See also Villalta.]
    Hemingway dedicated this novel to his wife and young son.

Henry. Count Mippipopolous' chauffeur brings in wine (56–57, 64–65).
    Speaks: 57, 65.

*Henry's bicycle. See James, Henry.

Herald. See the *New York Herald.*

[Hernández Ramírez,] Rafael. [Spanish bullfight critic, known by his nom de plume, Rafael. He was the bullfight critic of the Madrid publication *Informaciones.* His major work, *Historia de la plaza de toros de Madrid,* was published in 1955.][23]

The Madrid bullfight critic Rafael has come to see Romero perform. He is very circumspect (173–74).
Speaks: 174–76.

Hobin, Georgette. A prostitute Jake picks up. They have dinner and go to a club where Jake jokingly introduces her to the Braddockses as his fiancée, Georgette Leblanc (q.v.). After Jake and Brett leave the club together, Georgette gets into a fight; Braddocks reports that she called the daughter of the club's owner a prostitute and delivered herself of other offensive phrases (28). Georgette has bad teeth. Frances mentions Hobin and Brett in the same sentence (46); Jake confuses Brett and Georgette (32); the two women are often linked.[24]
Speaks: 14–20.

*Hoffenheimer.[25] Harvey Stone tells Jake that Mencken described Hoffenheimer as "a garter snapper" (43).

homosexuals. Brett arrives at a dancing club with several homosexuals, who dance with Georgette Hobin (20–21; see Lett and Prentiss).

Hubert. A young boy, the son of an American couple from Montana whom Jake and Bill Gorton meet on the train from Paris to Bayonne. Hubert likes to go swimming (87).
Speaks: 87–88.

Hubert's parents. A comfortable, middle-aged couple on their first trip to Europe. They speak in clichés: "See America first!"[26] "That's the way men are" and "You know how the ladies are" (85–86). They voted against Prohibition, although the wife disapproves of strong drink. They are going to Biarritz.
Speak: 85–88.

*Hudson, W[illiam] H[enry]. English naturalist and writer, 1841–1922, born in Argentina. Hemingway read many of his books: *The Purple Land that England Lost* (1885), *The Naturalist in La Plata* (1892), *Hampshire Days* (1903), *Green Mansions* (1905), *Nature in Downland* (1906), *The Land's End: A Naturalist's Impression in West Cornwall* (1908), *Afoot in England* (1909), *South American Sketches* (1909), *Adventures Among Birds* (1913), *The Book of a Naturalist* (1919), *Birds in Town and Village* (1920), *A Hind in Richmond Park* (1922). After reading Hudson's *Far Away and Long Ago,* Hemingway noted that "Hudson writes the best of anyone" (qtd. in Reynolds, *Hemingway's Reading,* 139.]
Cohn identifies with the hero of *The Purple Land* and wants Jake to

go with him to South America to repeat his romantic and improbable adventures. Jake, who has also read *The Purple Land,* considers it "a very sinister book if read too late in life" (9).

Jack Rose. [The Jack Rose cocktail is made of one ounce applejack, 1/2-ounce grenadine, and the juice of one lime, shaken with cracked ice and strained into a chilled cocktail glass.]
   Jake and Bill Gorton drink this American cocktail at the Crillon (41, 73; see George).

*[James,] Henry. [American short-story writer, novelist and essayist, 1843–1916; best known stories include "Daisy Miller" (1879), "The Turn of the Screw" (1898) and "The Beast in the Jungle"; major novels include *Portrait of a Lady* (1881), *The Wings of the Dove* (1902), *The Ambassadors* (1903) and *The Golden Bowl* (1904).]
   Bill and Jake joke about a bicycling accident which reportedly made Henry James impotent (115–16). They seem to think that "he's a good writer" (116).

Jews. Robert Cohn is Jewish (4; see endnote 1), and Frances Clyne probably is too. The other characters are anti-Semitic in a way fashionable when Hemingway was writing. Anti-Semitic remarks are made by Bill Gorton (96, 101, 162, 164), Brett Ashley (184), and Mike Campbell (177, 203, 206, 210, 230). The question of Jews and of anti-Semitism in the novel has occupied several critics, including Josephine Knoff and Barry Gross. Gross rejects the frequently provided excuse that the characters' anti-Semitism was "regrettably commonplace" and suggests that anti-Semitism may be the central moral issue in this novel, "the litmus test for immoral behavior" ("Dealing with Robert Cohn," 124, 129). See also Ford and Moses.

Jo. [The common noun "jo" (variant spelling, joe; plural, joes) is a Scottish term of endearment. The word is also an obsolete form of the modern "joy."]
   Jo is one of the women at the dancing club to which Jake brings Georgette. Brett jokes that Jake's bringing a prostitute to a place frequented by Brett, Frances Clyne, Mrs. Braddocks and other expatriates is "wrong" and "an insult to all of us" because "It's in restraint of trade" (22). Jo may be Mrs. Braddocks' first name or nickname.

*John Hadley Nicanor. See Hemingway, John Hadley Nicanor.

*Joselito. See Gómez Ortega, José.

*Katherine. See Kirby, Mr. and Mrs. Aloysius.

*the keeper. Mike says he will ask the gamekeeper at his family's estate to forward two fishing rods, one for himself and one for Bill Gorton (82, 90). Neither Mike nor the fishing rods arrive at Burguete.

*Kelly, [John H.] (Spider Kelly). [American boxer and trainer, d. 1937; champion of the Paperweight class (less than 100 lbs); Flyweight and Bantamweight champion. Kelly turned professional in 1887 and was unbeaten for the next 13 years. From 1903 until his death in 1937 he was boxing coach at Princeton University (except for the war years, during which he appeared in exhibition fights to raise funds for the war effort). He was nicknamed "The Spider" because, in his black tights, he "resembled a nervous insect . . . as he bounced around the ring."][27]
    The narrative reports that Spider Kelly was boxing coach at Princeton when Cohn was a student there (3). Kelly's training seems to have stayed with Cohn, who at age 34 beat up the 19-year-old Pedro Romero (see boxers).

kids. See children.

*the King [George V, 1865–1936; king of Great Britain, 1910–1936.]
    Mike Campbell tells Jake, Bill, and Robert about having been invited to "this wopping big dinner" at which the King and the Prince of Wales (q.v.) were expected (135; see also Wilson, Henry).

*Kirby, Mr. and Mrs. Aloysius. They send Jake an announcement of their daughter Katherine's wedding. Jake doesn't recognize the name (30).

*Klan. [In 1865 the Ku Klux Klan was founded in Tennessee to protest the victory of the anti-slavery Union forces and to maintain "white supremacy." Klansmen dressed in white robes and killed blacks and radical Reconstructionists. In 1915 a broader-based organization was formed, dedicated to terrorizing and killing Catholics and Jews as well as blacks and those who promote the well-being of these minorities. An illegal, secret society for much of its history, it was very active in the 1920s.]
    Bill's remark about the Klan to the priest is very offensive (88).

Krum. An American news correspondent living in Paris. He claims to envy Jake for leading what seems to him a carefree life (36–37).
    Speaks: 36–37.

*Krum's family. Krum takes for granted the family Jake can never have. They keep him from visiting the "in" cafés (q.v.) frequented by Jake (36).

Lalanda [del Pino], Marcial. [Spanish matador, 1903–1990. Like many great matadors before him, Lalanda was a child prodigy, developing a great reputation and an enthusiastic following even before his elevation to *matador.* Lalanda went from success to success in 1922, fighting in 79 *corridas* and increasing his already large following. Minor accidents reduced the number of his appearances to 50 (still an impressive number) in 1923; a serious wound in 1924 kept him out of the ring for a month. Whenever he performed, however, his success was astounding. In 1925 he fought 75 engagements, more than any other bullfighter that year. Among them were three *corridas* in the San Fermín fiesta.

On Thursday, 9 July, 1925, Lalanda appeared in Pamplona in a special *corrida de prueba:* four matadors fought, each one killing one bull, unlike the usual *corrida,* during which three matadors fight six bulls. Lalanda, who fought the second bull, shared the bill with Antonio Márquez, Martín Agüero and Cayetano Ordóñez. Lalanda's passes were warmly applauded but he had to try several times before he managed to kill the bull. During one of these attempts, his sword bounced off the bull and into the *barrera,* fortunately without injuring anyone. The taurine critic thought Lalanda's performance disappointing and described the afternoon as "boring." On Saturday, 11 July, 1925, Lalanda performed in Pamplona again, this time with Juan Belmonte and Cayetano Ordóñez (qq.v.), in the *gran corrida extraordinaria.* The six bulls were provided by the Gamero Cívico ranch (see Miura). Lalanda fought the second and fifth bulls of the afternoon, being hurt by the second when it lifted its head while Lalanda was attempting a *descabello* (death blow, coup de grâce). The matador fell unconscious at the same moment that the bull died. Lalanda was awarded the ear. In spite of his injury, Lalanda performed a masterful *faena* (work with the red cape which precedes the kill) with the fifth bull (his second one), was carried around the ring in triumph, and was awarded both ears and the tail. Lalanda clearly outperformed both Belmonte and Ordóñez on this afternoon.

The last fight of the 1925 fiesta took place on Sunday, 12 July. The Pablo Romero bulls were fought by Márquez, Lalanda (his head bandaged due to the preceding day's injury), and Ordóñez, in that order. Lalanda's first bull of the day was a brave, handsome animal, but Lalanda seemed unable to kill him, the job being finished by his *puntillero;* the audience whistled its disgust at Lalanda. With his second bull Lalanda performed very creditably, killing the bull elegantly on the second try. Although the audience clapped loudly and long, Lalanda refused to be carried triumphantly around the ring; one reviewer suggests that the refusal might have been due to pain and exhaustion, or perhaps to his having been offended by the derogatory whistles that had followed his first performance of that afternoon.

In 1926, in spite of a long illness which reduced his appearances to 54, his skillful mastery of all aspects of the fight attracted international admiration. Two serious gorings in 1927 seemed only to increase his courage, and the next few years established him as one of the all-time masters of the art. Lalanda, who maintained his standing at the top of his profession until his retirement in 1942, was known for his control, discipline, courage, and great knowledge of the bull, which he could dominate even when fighting *de rodillas* (on his knees). A paso doble written in his honor was entitled, "Marcial, eres el más grande" ("Marcial, you are the greatest").[28] See also *FWBT* and *DIA*.]

Jake prefers Romero to the slightly older Lalanda, claiming that the latter performs in the post-Belmonte, "decadent" style of bullfighting which gives the impression of danger without really endangering the bullfighter. Jake argues that since Lalanda is already corrupted [presumably by women and foreigners] the American ambassador's flattery poses no danger (171; see endnote 4). Lalanda performs on the last day of the fiesta with Belmonte and Romero (212, 215); he "had a big day" (219), but his performance is not described.

L'Auto. [Probably a reference to the French journal *L'Auto-carrosserie,* subtitled "Revue pratique des industries de la voiture" (a practical journal of the automobile industries). It was published from 1911 to 1914 and from 1919 to the end of 1938 (*Catalogue Collectif des Périodiques,* I: 515).]

Jake reads back issues of this magazine, left behind by the bicyclists (238).

Lavigne and Madame Lavigne. [The owners and managers of the Nègre de Toulouse, an inexpensive restaurant located at 157-59 Boulevard de Montparnasse, where the Hemingways often had dinner with Harold Loeb, Kitty Canell, Ford Madox Ford, and others. The restaurant, which "offered exotic, inexpensive meals" (Hansen, 144), no longer exists.[29] See also *MF*.]

Lavigne serves the liqueurs at the restaurant where Jake and Georgette Hobin have dinner (19). His wife also works in the restaurant (16). Later that night, Jake passes the closed restaurant on his way home (29).

*Leblanc, Georgette. [Famous French actress and singer, c.1867–1941. Leblanc acted the feminine lead in many plays by Maurice Maeterlinck, who both wrote and translated plays for her. She and Maeterlinck were associates for twenty years; their famous salon was the meeting place for the artists and intellectuals of the period. Their separation was accompanied by scandal and followed by Maeterlinck's marriage to a younger woman. In addition to starring in Maeterlinck's plays, Leblanc was also a fine interpreter of Ibsen. She is the author of *Souvenirs: My Life with Maeterlinck* (1932).][30]

Jake jokingly introduces Georgette Hobin, a prostitute, as Georgette Leblanc (18).

Lecomte, Madame. [Owner and manager of Rendezvous des Mariniers, a small hotel and inexpensive restaurant at 33 Quai d' Anjou on the Ile St. Louis. It was "a handy meeting place for American editors, writers, and critics," many of whom had offices nearby (Hansen, 35–36), and popular with local boatmen (Leland, 64). The restaurant no longer exists.]

Madame Lecomte remembers Bill Gorton, who had been there in 1918, and "made a great fuss over seeing him." Even so, Bill and Jake have to wait 45 minutes for a table because the restaurant, reputed to be "quaint," has become popular with American tourists (76).

Speaks: 76–77.

*Ledoux, [Charles (Kid Ledoux). French boxer, born 1892. Ledoux was 5'1/2" tall and weighed 116 lbs. He began to box professionally in 1909, interrupted his career to enlist in 1914, resumed professional boxing after World War I, and retired in 1924. He was the European featherweight champion from 1920 to 1924, when he forfeited the title. In February 1924, he won the French featherweight title from Edouard Mascart in a fight that lasted twenty rounds (Fleischer, 231–32). On 9 June, 1924, Ledoux fought and lost to Kid Francis (q.v.), his junior by fifteen years, who was just beginning his career. See endnote 17.]

Mike praises Ledoux (79) but he doesn't go to the fight. Jake and Bill do go: "It was a good fight" (81).

*Lemoine, Cardinal [Jean. French prelate, c. 1250–1313. Cardinal Lemoine was the representative of Pope Boniface VIII (pope from 1294 to 1303) in France. Soon after the Pope's accession, relations between King Philip IV (the Fair) and the Pope became strained over Boniface's attempt to exempt papal officials from French taxes. In 1302 Boniface issued *Unam sanctam,* "one of the strongest official statements of the papal prerogative ever made," and the conflict between Church and monarchy reached a crisis. The imperious Pope was arrested as he was about to excommunicate the King. He was freed after a few days and returned to Rome. Although he was the Pope's representative in France, Cardinal Lemoine had sided with the King in this conflict. The college he founded in 1303, at Rue Saint-Victor, Paris, was in operation until

1793. When they first came to Paris, Ernest and Hadley Hemingway lived at 74, Rue du Cardinal Lemoine.][31]

After dinner, Jake Barnes and Bill Gorton walk along the Rue du Cardinal Lemoine to the Place de la Contrescarpe (77).

*Lenglen, [Suzanne. French lawn-tennis player, 1899–1938. In 1914, when she was 15 years old, Lenglen won the world championship in women's tennis, singles and doubles. She was the French women's singles champion in 1920–1923, and in 1925 and 1926 won both the French singles and doubles crowns. She was the Wimbledon singles champion in 1919–1923 and won both the singles and doubles championship (with Elizabeth Ryan) in 1925. In 1926, after a quarrel with a Wimbledon referee, Lenglen turned pro, but her career as a professional was short. Lenglen's graceful moves earned her the nickname, "the Pavlova of tennis." Her "high emotion and fierce desire for victory" made her performances exciting and dramatic. She wrote *Lawn Tennis* (1925), *Lawn Tennis for Girls* (1930), and *Tennis by Simple Exercises* (1937).][32]

Jake thinks that Cohn is as competitive as Lenglen, although his temper is milder (45).

Lett. Lett is a tall, dark homosexual. He and his crowd come with Brett to the club where she meets up with Jake and the Braddocks. He dances with the prostitute Georgette Hobin (20–22).[33]

Speaks: 20.

*Lincoln, Abraham. [American statesman and folk hero, 1809–1865; 16th president of the United States (during the Civil War), 1861–1865. His most famous pronouncements include the Emancipation Proclamation (January 1863), the Gettysburg Address (November 1863), and the Second Inaugural Address (January 1865). He was assassinated by actor John Wilkes Booth at Ford's Theater in Washington, D.C., a few months after the beginning of his second term as President. See also *Fifth Column.*]

After he expresses his fondness for Jake, Bill, embarrassed by his emotional outburst, makes jokes about "faggots." He jokes that the leaders of both the Union and Confederate forces were really fighting for the sexual favors of General Grant (116).

Lion de Belfort. See Denfert-Rochereau.

Lourdes. See Roman Catholics.

maids, chambermaids. A chambermaid brings beer (201) and is ordered to bring drinks (204). Because Jake has exposed Romero to Brett, Montoya refuses to talk to him and instead sends a maid with the bill

(228). An unfriendly maid opens the door for Jake at the hotel in Madrid (240–41; see also *concierge,* manager, and women and girls).
Speaks: 204.

maître d'hôtel. A German with a "dirty little pink-and-white smile" at the restaurant near Montoya's hotel. Bill and Jake think he is "damned snotty" and eat elsewhere (209–10).
Speaks: 209.

the manager. The manager of the bicyclists talks to Jake (236–37; see also the bicyclists). The manager of the Hotel Montana in Madrid is honest (243; see *concierge*).

*Manning, Bishop [William Thomas. English-born American Protestant Episcopal bishop, 1866–1949. Ordained in 1892, Manning served as rector of Trinity Church in New York from 1908 until 1921, when he was consecrated as Bishop of New York, thus becoming the head of the wealthiest Protestant Episcopal diocese in the United States, a position he held until his retirement in 1946. During much of his career Manning was associated with the funding and building of the huge Cathedral of St. John the Divine, said to be the largest church in the United States. Manning's conservative and often controversial positions made him a newsworthy figure. A militantly conservative high churchman, he opposed the marriage of divorced persons and campaigned vigorously against companionate marriage and the easy dissolution of such marriages by mutual consent. About to separate from his first wife, Hemingway would have disagreed with Bishop Manning's strict views of marriage and divorce. The joke lies in the incompatibility between the reality and what Jake and Bill claim: being a generation younger than Bishop Manning, they could not possibly have gone to any university with him. And Bishop Manning, being Episcopalian, had no connection with Loyola University, a Catholic institution.[34] See also Bryan.]
    As they start drinking their second bottle of wine, both Jake and Bill tipsily insist that each studied at Loyola University with Bishop Manning (122).

Marcial. See Lalanda, Marcial.

*[Marlowe, Christopher. English dramatist and poet, 1564–1593. Among his best-known plays are *Tamburlaine the Great* (1590), *Edward II* (1594), *The Tragicall History of Doctor Faustus* (1604), and *The [Rich] Jew of Malta* (1633). He was admired by Shakespeare, who quoted and apostrophized him in *As You Like It.* Gorton alludes to the famous passage in Marlowe's *The Jew of Malta*:

Father Barnardine: Thou has committed—
Barabas: Fornication—but that was in another country;
and besides, the wench is dead (IV, i, 40–43).]

In their jokes about the taxidermist, Gorton substitutes "animals" for
Marlowe's "wench" (75).

*Márquez [Serrano, Antonio. Spanish matador, 1898–1988. A matador
of the first rank, Márquez maintained a great following and full
schedules from 1923 until 1928, when health problems forced him to
accept fewer engagements. He lost six weeks of the 1929 season because
of a serious goring. Worried about his health, his family and friends
convinced him to retire at the end of the 1931 season. Retirement did not
suit him: he made a few appearances in 1933, always with great success,
and prepared to return to a full schedule in 1936, but the outbreak of the
Spanish Civil War disrupted his plans. He was an artistic, knowledgeable matador, with a polished style and unerring sense of timing, but
some critics argue that he lacked commitment and spirit (*afición*).
Márquez fought twice in Pamplona in 1923: with Luis Freg and Nicanor
Villalta (qq.v. in *DIA*) on 6 July, and with Villalta and Joselito Martín on
8 July. In 1925 he fought in Pamplona on 7, 9, and 12 July, sharing the
last two bills with Marcial Lalanda and Cayetano Ordóñez (qq.v. in
DIA). On 7 July Márquez was masterful with both his bulls, being
accorded a triumphant march around the ring for his first bull (*vuelta al
ruedo*) as well as the ear of his second bull. The 9th of July was a *corrida
de prueba* (four matadors fighting one bull each): parts of Márquez's
performance were applauded but on the whole he disappointed the
audience, who applauded the dead bull as it was being dragged out (the
arrastre) and whistled at the bullfighter to indicate their disapproval. On
the 12th he began well but killed the bull so badly that the audience
applauded the dead bull during its *arrastre*. His second performance that
day was a mirror image of the first: mostly undistinguished at the
beginning but ending with a good *faena* and an impressive sword thrust
which killed the bull quickly.[35] See also *DIA*. The American ambassador
was living in San Sebastián during the fiesta; he and his party drove in
to Pamplona for the festivities of 9 and 11 July, returning to San
Sebastián in the evening; see endnote 4.]
   Márquez and Lalanda drove to San Sebastián, where Montoya
expected them to spend the night (171–72).

*Mason, A[lfred] E[dward] W[oodley]. British author, 1865–1948. A
failed actor and minor playwright, Mason was a popular and prolific
author of spy, adventure, detective, and historical fiction. He was a
member of Parliament, 1906–1910, and did "notable secret service

work,'' 1914–1918. Among his early works are *A Romance of Wastdale*
(1895), *Miranda of the Balcony* (1899), which first brought him fame,
and *The Four Feathers* (1902, film version 1939). Later works include
They Wouldn't Be Chessmen (1935), *Musk and Amber* (1942), and the
Inspector Hanaud series which began with *At the Villa Rose* (1910). Jake
reads Mason's story ''The Crystal Trench,'' which forms part of a
collection entitled *The Four Corners of the World* (New York: Scribner's, 1917), pp. 177–201. Jake's report of the story is quite accurate:
after the foolhardy young husband Mark was killed in a climbing
accident, the nineteen-year-old widow, Stella Frobisher, consults an
expert who predicts the precise day when her husband's body would
emerge from the crevasse into which it had fallen. The wife waits the
prescribed twenty-four years, as does Dennis Challoner, the young
lawyer who has fallen in love with her. Mark Frobisher's body,
preserved in ice, emerges on schedule, but when it is exposed to the
elements it disintegrates into dust. A gold locket Mark was wearing
reveals the picture of a ''pretty and quite vulgar'' girl, clearly not Stella.
Challoner attempts to protect Stella from the truth, telling her that the
locket contains a portrait of her, but she knows that ''He had no locket
with a portrait of me,'' whereupon ''the sun leapt into the sky and
flooded the world with gold'' (Mason, 200–1), apparently to celebrate
Dennis and Stella's release from the unsavory Mark.]

Waiting to have lunch with Bill after his first morning of fishing in
Burguete, Jake reads most of this ''wonderful story'' by Mason,
summarizing the plot accurately. Fortunately, Bill's arrival interrupts his
reading (120) before the story deteriorates too far into romantic implau-
sibility.

matadors. In addition to Belmonte, Lalanda, and Romero (qq.v.),
unnamed matadors perform at the Pamplona bullring (164, 167, 169).

*McGinty. [The name of this fly seems to derive from the ''unusual
naive and pugnacious Irish song'' called ''Down Went McGinty to the
Bottom of the Sea,'' written by Joseph Flynn and first performed at the
Hyde and Behman theater in Brooklyn about 1889. The McGinty fly,
popular before World War I and familiar to the trout fishermen of
Hemingway's generation, is a wet fly; it looks like a bee.][36]
Bill fishes for trout with a McGinty fly (118).

men and boys. In addition to the nameless men who are identified by their
professions (bartenders, bicyclists, bootblacks, bullfighters, drivers, porters, waiters, etc.), several unnamed, undefined men appear in the novel.
Such unobtrusive background characters give a feeling of activity and
enlarge the scope of the novel.

Jake sends for a boy to take his dispatches to the train station (12). Unnamed men sprinkle the streets to settle the dust (90, 150). In Paris a man prints an ad on the sidewalk; nearby, others display their wares to tourists and passers-by (35). Some men work on the roads in the middle of the night (25). A boy in Paris sells Jake a newspaper (46), and a man in Bayonne sells fishing equipment to Jake and Bill (90; see keeper). An old man without a passport is stopped at the border (92). In Pamplona, several workmen get the town ready for the fiesta (149–50) and the hawkers and gypsies (q.v.) set up their booths and tents (150). Boys watch while the men release the bulls from their cages (138–39) and while the fireworks are prepared (221); two men take the tickets of the people who are entering the bullring (137) and a man incites a bull (139). Later, a man shows Jake where to buy a leather wine bottle, the salesman displays his wares, and a worker in the shop informs him the price is right (156); an old man talks with Cohn and Gorton in a bar, another man advises Brett how to handle Romero's cape (213). In the street, an ugly reed-pipe player attracts the children to him like the pied piper of Hamelin (154). A happy boy and girl swim and sun themselves in San Sebastián (235); another pair of lovers crosses a bridge (77). See also Basques, crowds, dancers).
    Speak: 139, 156, 213.

*men and boys. Several nameless men are mentioned but not seen. Bill reports that he saw two boxers, a promoter and a music student in Vienna (71–72; see also boxers and students). He "recognizes" the men depicted in a monument (72, see Denfert-Rochereau). Cohn reports that he met a bilingual old man (100). Mike tells a story about giving away medals, mentioning the owner of the medals and the man who was sent to fetch the medals (136; see tailor). Men often come to Montoya's hotel to discuss bulls and bullfighting; Jake meets and is accepted by some of them as a true aficionado (132). Mike mentions friends of his in San Sebastián who would not invite Cohn (142), some of whom are probably men. Similarly, Jake mentions friends of his in Paris (69), and Clyne sarcastically mentions Cohn's French-speaking friends (51) and her own "friends," whom she is going to visit in England (49). Brett mentions that she knows and is known by "too many people" (33).
    Speak: 49, 132.

*Mencken, [Henry Louis. American writer, journalist, editor and critic, 1880–1956. H. L. Mencken was a controversial and influential critic of American democracy who nonetheless insisted on the independence of the American literary scene, rejecting the idea that "culture" can exist only according to British and European patterns. With George Jean Nathan, he founded and edited *The American Mercury* (1924–1933), the

American version of the influential English journal, *Mercury*. He wrote
The American Credo (1920), *The American Language* (1919, revised
1921, 1923, 1936), and many other books. His six collections of critical
essays, *Prejudices* (1919–1927) were very influential. Mencken started
working as a reporter for the Baltimore *Morning Herald* in 1899, when
he was only 19. He had attended the Baltimore Polytechnic Institute
(*National Cyclopaedia of American Biography*) but did not go to Holy
Cross or any other Catholic university. See endnote 34; see also *TS*. For
an explication of Bill's remark, "Don't eat that, Lady—that's
Mencken," see Hinkle, who argues that through free association Bill
transforms the chicken leg Jake is holding into "cock of Mencken . . .
Menckensprick. . . . That Jake follows Bill's train of thought seems clear
from Jake's comment: 'You're cock-eyed' " ("Re Query," 4).]
      Tracing Cohn's dislike of Paris to Mencken, Jake complains that "So
many young men get their likes and dislikes from Mencken" (42).
Harvey Stone claims to know Mencken personally, reports some of his
witty remarks and then disparages him (43). Jake and Bill joke about
Mencken during lunch, Bill claiming that he went to Holy Cross with
Mencken and Bryan (q.v.) (122; see also Manning).

*the miniature-painter. See painters.

*Mippipopolous, Count. A rich, fat man who claims to have been in
seven wars and four revolutions and displays his arrow wounds to Jake
and Brett (60). He owns candy stores in the U.S. (32) and likes expensive
cigars, wines, and restaurants; he declares that he knows "the values"
and that he is "always in love" (60, 61). He offers Brett $10,000 to go
to Biarritz with him. Brett identifies him as "quite one of us" (32; see
97). He calls Jake "sir" and "Mr. Barnes" and addresses Brett as "my
dear." See Henry and Zizi; see endnote 39.
      Speaks: 28–29, 56–64

*Mippipopolous' father. Because he was friends with Zizi's father,
Mippipopolous feels obliged to support Zizi (63).

*Miura. [A breed of bull, famous for its deadliness. The strain was first
registered in Madrid in 1849, by don Juan Miura, who established the
family's first ranch in Seville. The breed remained in the family and was
registered by several generations of heirs (see *DIA*). The bulls were so
fierce that in 1908 many bullfighters demanded higher wages for
fighting Miuras, sparking off a great controversy in Madrid. Miuras were
fought in Pamplona on 8 July, 1925; the local taurine reviewer described
them as big but not particularly brave. As a result, the *corrida* was
disappointing. They may be famous and expensive, the reviewer wrote,

but let Miura keep them. The Miura and Gamero Cívico bulls were unloaded in Pamplona on 4 July 1925.][37]
Miura bulls were fought in the Pamplona bullring (169; see 131, 145).

Montoya, Juan (Juanito). Owner and manager of the Hotel Montoya in Pamplona. He caters to aficionados of the bullfight (131–32). Because Jake has *afición,* Montoya saves good rooms for him (94, 131; also see 84) and consults him about the American ambassador's potentially dangerous interest in Pedro Romero (171–72). But after Jake exposes Pedro to Brett and the rest of their crowd, Montoya ignores him, refusing to nod (177), smile (209) or "come near us" (228) for the rest of the fiesta. See endnote 1; also see Quintana in *DS.*
    Speaks: 99, 130–31, 144–45, 162–64, 171–72.

*Montoya's sister. Many bullfighters have given Montoya autographed portraits of themselves, dedicated to him and to his sister (131–32).

*[Moses. Biblical hero who led the Jewish people out of Egypt and across the desert to the Promised Land (Canaan). He received the Torah (Pentateuch, Five Books of Moses) but smashed the tablets in anger when he saw the people worshipping the golden calf. He smote a rock with his brother Aaron's rod, instead of speaking to it as God had commanded him to. Because of his public disobedience to God, Moses was not permitted to enter the Promised Land.]
    The narrator reports that when Robert Cohn looks at Brett Ashley, "He looked a great deal as his compatriot must have looked when he saw the promised land" (22).

*Mumms, Baron. [Correct name: Mumm. The Mumm family, German Protestants who never became French citizens, founded the champagne-producing firm in 1827. In World War I the French government declared that the firm was owned by enemy aliens and confiscated it. In 1920 the firm was put up for auction; its new owners retained the Mumm name and slogan: "Mumm's the word for champagne."]
    Count Mippipopolous claims to know the Baron Mumms (*sic,* 56–57). He drinks this champagne at all hours of the night and day (32, 56) and has a "Dozen bottles" packed in a hamper for a picnic breakfast (33; see also Cliquot).

Nacional. [Professional name of the four Anlló brothers, who made their careers as bullfighters in the 1920s. Ricardo (Nacional, Nacional I) and Juan (Nacional II) were matadors, Eduardo (Nacional III) was a skillful *banderillero,* and Ramiro (Nacional IV) a *matador de novillos* (killer of young bulls, usually three-year-olds). Ricardo (1891–1977) was a brave, serious, and knowledgeable matador with a respectable but not great following. Gored seriously in 1920 and again in 1921, he recovered his powers fully each time, without losing his nerve. Although his 1922 season was very successful, he never captured the public's affection. He had very few engagements in 1923, fought only ten times in 1924, less in 1925, and retired in 1927. Juan (1897–1925) was brave and iron-willed and had three successful seasons before he died. But he was not an artistic performer; his reputation and popularity were due more to his forceful personality than to his skill. Nacional and Nacional II performed in the 1924 Pamplona bullfights, each one fighting in three *corridas*; on 10 July they appeared together, sharing the bill with Chicuelo (q.v. in *DIA*). They did not perform during the 1925 fiesta of San Fermín.[38] See also Anlló in *DIA*.]

Pedro Romero mocks Nacional as a conventional, uninspiring bull-fighter. He mimics the expression on Nacional's face to show Brett the popular conception of "what bullfighters are like" (186).

Napolitain. See cafés.

Nègre Joyeux. See cafés.

The New York Herald, the *Herald.* [In 1924 the daily *New York Herald* (founded in 1887) merged with the *Tribune* to become the *New York Herald Tribune* and as such launched a European edition (1924–1966) which eventually merged with the *New York Times International* to form the *International Herald Tribune* (1967–present).]

Jake and Georgette Hobin pass the Paris bureau of this newspaper on their way to dinner (15). Jake buys a copy of the New York *Herald* in Bayonne (232).

*Ney, Marshal [Michel. French military hero, 1769–1815; one of the original 16 marshals of France. First a Republican, Ney became a Bonapartist, later a royalist and finally, sent out by Louis XVIII to stop Napoleon, he joined Napoleon once again. After the French defeat at Waterloo (1815), Ney was convicted of treason and shot. He was a great military hero and a politically controversial figure. See also *ARIT* and *MF*.]

Jake passes a statue of Marshal Ney as he walks home (29).

Nouvelle Revue Française. [Important French journal of literature and literary criticism. Founded in 1909, the monthly stopped publication between September 1914 and May 1919 but has been published continuously since then. In 1925, when Paulhan became editor, the journal became interested in foreign literature and expanded its scope to include large questions of thought, art, psychology, and philosophy. Over the years the journal has become more conservative. See also *GE*.] At a news briefing, Jake listens for half an hour to "a young Nouvelle Revue Française diplomat" who has nothing important to communicate (36).

nurses. See children.

*O'Grady, Judy. See *"The Colonel's Lady and Judy O'Grady."

Old Bill. Barnes' affectionate rendering of Bill Gorton's name, spoken once (116).

Orquito, don Manuel. [Correct spelling: Oroquieta. The local newspaper, *El pensamiento Navarro,* reports that the elaborate fireworks display which marked the beginning of the 1923 fiesta was the work of "the well-known and accredited pyrotechnists, Mr. Oroquieta and his son" (7 July, 1923, 1:3, my translation). The Oroquietas prepared most of the displays presented at the three fiestas (1923, 1924, 1925) that Hemingway attended before writing this novel. Fireworks were and still are an integral part of the celebrations, and are announced in the published schedule of events, which also lists the *encierro,* the appearances of the giants and dwarfs, concerts, bullfights, and other *espectáculos* and performances. On the 9th and 10th of July, 1925 the weather was rainy, windy and cold; spectacular fireworks were presented nonetheless. The text mentions various types of fireworks, including the rocket or *chupinazo* which marks the beginning and end of the daily 6:00 AM *encierro* (153, 154, 159, 160, 180, 196, 197, 221–22). Nowadays the *encierro* begins at 8:00 AM, to accommodate television crews and hung-over tourists. Pilar recalls the long string of firecrackers, the *traca,* which she saw in Valencia (*FWBT* 85).]
    Orquito and his son have trouble setting off the fireworks at the fiesta of San Fermín in Pamplona (178–79; see 221–22).

*painters. A miniature-painter ran off with Mrs. Robert Cohn (4). Jake's *concierge* refuses admittance to a skinny painter who obviously hasn't tipped her (53; cf. the *concierge*'s treatment of Evan Shipman, *MF* 136).

parents. Parents are sometimes seen with their children (see Girones' family, Hubert's parents, Orquito, proprietor; also see children).

*parents. Absent, unseen mothers are mostly ineffective and often mocked. Michael Campbell, Brett Ashley and Bill Gorton refer ironically to mothers and old-fashioned values (63, 58, 78, 102; see also

Kirby, Mr. and Mrs. Aloysius). Mike jokes that bullfighters are drunkards who beat their mothers (168). Frances Clyne's mother is unable to provide financial support (49). Robert Cohn's mother fares better than most: she is able and willing to supply money on a regular basis (5, 47) and is not vilified by her son. Dead fathers, on the other hand, provide financial and social protection for their sons (see Cohn's family, Mippipopolous' father, Zizi's father).

Paris Times. Newspaper which Jake buys (46).

*partner. Mike seems to blame his former partner for his financial problems, but accepts a drink from him (79, 137; see also creditors).

*Paula. Frances Clyne's friend, who fails to show up for her luncheon date with Frances (46).

Pernod, [Henry-Louis. "In 1797 . . . Henry-Louis Pernod in France first produced the drink called absinthe, using the recipe originated by [Dr.] Ordinaire" (Lanier, 282). Absinthe is based on wormwood, which is so toxic that, at the time of the action of the novel, it was banned in the U.S., France, and several other European countries; it was still legal in Spain, where it is drunk by characters in this novel (see absinthe), by Robert Jordan (*FWBT* 50–51, 56–57), and by the Bournes (*GE* 38–39, 62–66, 69; also see Pernod in *GE*).]
   In Paris, Hobin and Barnes drink Pernod; Gorton also seems to be drinking it (73). The narrator describes this drink and its effects (14–15; 73).

pharmacy. See Denfert-Rochereau.

pilgrims. [In 1858, the fourteen-year-old Marie Bernadette Soubirous (1844–1879) claimed that the Virgin Mary had appeared to her at Lourdes. A church was built and consecrated on the site, and many sick people claimed to have been healed of their ills there. In June 1925, the peasant girl was elevated to sainthood (St. Bernadette), and more people than usual made pilgrimage to Lourdes.]
   Seven carloads of American Roman Catholics are mixing pleasure with pilgrimage to holy sites, traveling to Rome, Biarritz, and Lourdes (86). They fill up the dining-car and delay Jake and Bill's lunch until 4:15 PM (85–88; see also priests, Roman Catholics).

*P.L.M. [Paris-Lyon-Marseille train line. In Hemingway's fine story "A Canary for One," from the collection *Men Without Women,* the characters travel the Marseille-Paris route by train. The approach to Paris allows the narrator of that story to see abandoned train cars and "fortifications [which] were levelled" but over which, in 1926 (the date of composition of the story), "grass had not grown." Reminders of war are connected to the break-up of the characters' marriage, and the loss of a happy, pre-war, pre-divorce time is connected to that particular part of the journey, which seems to be the same terrain Jake remarks upon.]

Jake feels that a very short section of the P.L.M. line, just a few miles southeast of Paris, makes the traveler feel "dead and dull" (41; cf. Raspail).

*policeman. Cohn complains that the only adventure that ever befell him in the Quarter is that he was stopped by "a bicycle cop" (12; see Edna).

policemen. One policeman smiles at Jake as the homosexuals pass him to enter the club in Paris (20; see 19); another raises his baton to stop Brett and Jake's progress down the Gran Via in Madrid (247). In Pamplona, police try to keep drunks out of the path of the running bulls (196, 200).

porters. The porter at the City Hall in Pamplona brushes dust off Jake's coat (96). Another porter carries Bill's bags onto the train in Bayonne (231). When Jake takes the train the next morning he is also helped by a porter, whom he does not overtip (233).
Speaks: 96.

postman. He brings a telegram from Brett, summoning Jake to Madrid (238). Telegrams are also delivered by Montoya (99) and a girl (127).

poules. See prostitutes.

Prentiss, Robert. A "rising new novelist" from New York, probably a homosexual. Jake walks away from him (21).[39]
Speaks: 21.

the President. [A high-ranking representative of the civil authority always presides over the legal and ceremonial aspects of the bullfight. He receives the salutes of the bullfighters, gives the signal that the fight can begin, decides if a bull is unworthy and needs to be replaced, determines whether any of the laws governing the fight have been breached, settles disputes and determines which and how many trophies (one ear, two ears, tail, hoof) are to be awarded. He represents the state at the bullfight.]

At the bullfight, the President performs his ceremonial duties: he makes a grand entrance (212), receives the bullfighter's salute (214, 219), rules that the bull is fit (217) and awards an ear to Romero (220).

priests. Several priests accompany the American Roman Catholics on the train; Bill, who is hungry and "difficult," offends one of the priests (86–88; see also Klan, pilgrims). Hubert's father refers to Catholics as "snappers" (87; i.e., mackerel snappers, because Catholics ate fish on Fridays, formerly a meatless day).
  Speaks: 88.

*Primo de Rivera, [General Miguel. Marquis of Estella. Spanish lawyer, soldier and politician, 1870–1930. Primo de Rivera's early military service was in the Spanish provinces of Cuba, the Philippines and Spanish Morocco (see Riff). He seized control of the Spanish government in 1923 and was dictator until 1930, when the Republic was established and he went into exile in France, dying in Paris a few months later. The Spain of *The Sun Also Rises* is under his tyrannical rule.]
  Bill dares Jake to "Make some crack" about the dictator to the Spanish girl who waits on them at the inn in Burguete (114).

*Prince of Wales [1894–1972; ruled Great Britain as Edward VIII for ten months in 1936. After he abdicated in order to marry the twice-divorced American Wallis Simpson, he was known as the Duke of Windsor.]
  Mike Campbell says he had been invited to a banquet at which the King and the Prince of Wales were expected (135; see also Wilson, Henry).

*promoter. See *boxers.

proprietor, proprietor's family. The proprietor of a dancing club in Paris plays the accordion (19); he is joined by a banjo-player (23). The proprietor's wife and daughter serve the customers (19; see 28). Their place is crowded.
  Speaks: 23.

prostitutes (*poules* in French). In Paris, Jake watches the prostitutes and then picks one up (14; see Hobin, Georgette).

the publisher. See the editor and publisher.

*publishers. Cohn's first book was praised and published by "a fairly good" publishing house (8–9).

Rafael. See Hernández Ramírez, Rafael.

*Raspail, [François Vincent. French scientist, journalist, and politician, 1794–1878. In 1830 the Republicans, led by Lafayette, opposed the monarchists, or Orleanists, who supported a modified form of monarchy with Louis Philippe as king. Louis Philippe was elected king in July, but the Republicans, and in particular the socialists among them, were dissatisfied with this government (called the "July monarchy" or "the bourgeois monarchy") which lasted from 1830 to 1848. Raspail founded several dissident organizations and established two opposition journals, *Le Reformateur* in 1834 and *L'Ami du peuple* in 1848. Louis Phillippe was forced to abdicate by the February Revolution of 1848, and the provisional government which replaced the monarchy immediately established national workshops to ease the plight of the unemployed. But the workshops were a disappointment, the government dissolved them, and the workers, who had been instrumental in bringing about the February Revolution, found that their desperate conditions had not improved under the government they had helped install. In May and June 1848, Raspail was among those who led civilian uprisings against the provisional government. The government called out the Army and the National Guard and ruthlessly put down the June rebellion: "The battle, the sorry battle, was fierce and lasted for four days. . . . In all there were several thousand dead. . . . Thousands of the insurgents were deported, in mass and without trial, the socialist party was broken, and its papers were suppressed" (Malraux, 410). Raspail was deported; he lived in Brussels for eleven years before being allowed back to France by the general amnesty of 1859. In later years he was elected to public office. He was a noted botanist and chemist, author of *Nouveau système de chimie organique* (1833) and *Nouvelles études scientifiques* (1864). It is probably a vague memory of having read about the massacres of the June rebellion of 1848 that makes Jake dislike the Boulevard Raspail; cf. P.L.M.]

Jake rides a taxi along the Boulevard Raspail with Brett (27) and twice by himself, once after Brett fails to keep their appointment (41–42), and again after he witnesses Clyne's attack on Cohn (51). Riding on that street is unpleasant for him (41–42).

riau-riau. [A loud shout which marked the beginning and end of the verses of the popular waltz, *La alegría de San Fermín* ("The Joy of San Fermín," music by Miguel Astráin, lyrics by María Luisa Ugalde). The waltz was formally incorporated into the fiesta's program in 1909, as a musical accompaniment to the procession in which the city officials, accompanied by the giants, dwarfs (qq.v.) and the crowds, march to the Church of San Lorenzo to hear Vespers. The term "¡Riau! ¡Riau!" has come to denote the whole procession, from the City Hall to the Church. In 1915 crowds of young people considerably delayed the progress of the civil authorities towards the Church of San Lorenzo; this disrespectful behavior was repeated in subsequent years, until the singing of the waltz was banned, as were rude gestures and odd dress. Not surprisingly, the ban merely ensconced the custom (of opposing and delaying the authorities) more firmly among the celebrants, the "¡Riau! ¡Riau!" becoming a cry of defiance. Topical verses are added each year, criticizing the councilmen and their policies, and in recent years radical and separatist groups have used it to express political opposition. In the 1920s the "¡Riau! ¡Riau!" usually lasted about an hour; in 1980 it lasted five and a half hours, the waltz being played 170 times. In some years the "¡Riau! ¡Riau!" has completely prevented the city's councillors from reaching the church.][40]

The singing and shouting of the riau-riau are part of the San Fermín fiesta (153, 155).

*Riff. [Sometimes spelled Rif. The hilly region along the Mediterranean coast of Morocco, contested territory until Morocco became an independent country in 1956. Both Spain and France colonized this area; local resistance led to heavy fighting. See Abd el Krim in *FWBT* and *ARIT*.]

When he is served jam, Jake is tempted to ask the Spanish waitress "what kind of a jam . . . they've gotten into in the Riff," but Bill dissuades him from making this "Very poor" joke (114; see endnote 6).

*Rockefeller, [John Davidson, 1839–1937; both he and his son (1874–1960) were successful American industrialists and philanthropists. Rockefeller Sr. expanded Standard Oil Co. until it dominated the U.S. oil-refining industry. The company later broke up into different branches: Esso, Hess Oil, Standard Oil of Ohio, etc. He founded the University of Chicago (1892), the Rockefeller Institute for Medical Research (1901), and the Rockefeller Foundation (1913).]

Jake's remark that he didn't dream during his nap inspires Gorton to list a variety of "dreamers," including Rockefeller (124).

rockets. See Orquito.

Roman Catholics. Roman Catholicism is the overwhelmingly predominant religion of both France and Spain, which means that most of the background characters (crowds, dancers, maids, waiters, etc.) are Catholics. The fiesta in Pamplona honors the province's patron saint, St. Fermín (q.v.); the fiesta begins with "the big religious procession" (155). Bullfighters, who face death whenever they enter the bullring, are usually devout Catholics; prayer is a standard part of the pre-bullfight ritual and many bullfighters travel with a portable chapel. In honor of St. Bernadette, recently elevated to sainthood, many Catholics are visiting shrines in Rome and Lourdes (86; see 51). Jake Barnes himself is Catholic, but the religion cannot ease his pain (87, 124). The Roman Catholic religion is an important issue in this novel: it is one of the old institutions which no longer work in the post-war world. Other institutions, like education, marriage, and patriotism, are also shown to be largely irrelevant to this generation. See also Klan, parents, pilgrims, priests, and students.

Romero, Pedro. [Famous Spanish matador, 1754–1839, native of Ronda. Trained by his father, Juan Romero, himself an outstanding practitioner of the art, Pedro Romero attracted royal attention as a young man and appeared for many years before the court, giving consistently magnificent performances. His career was long and impressive: he never suffered a wound and he killed, it is claimed, all his bulls on the first try. In 1830 he was appointed to the faculty of the newly formed bullfighting school in Seville; when a student found himself in difficulties the 76-year-old Romero attracted the bull away from the student and toward himself, standing still when the bull charged and dispatching him on the first try. He is considered one of the masters of all time, legendary for the length and excellence of his career.[41] See also Romero in *DIA*. Hemingway exalts his fictional bullfighter by naming him Pedro Romero and giving him the same birthplace (173). The fictional Romero is modeled on the young Cayetano Ordóñez (1904–1974), also a native of Ronda. Ordóñez performed in Pamplona on 7, 9, 11 (when he replaced Algabeño, q.v.) and 12 July, giving his best performance on the last day, when he was awarded an ear for his first bull, which he killed elegantly on the first try.[42] See Ordóñez in *DIA* and *DS*.]

Romero is a 19-year-old matador (163, 167, 174, 244), about 15 years younger than the other main characters. Jake recognizes the beauty and honesty of Romero's style (168). In addition to his skill, Romero possesses the virtue of modesty: he is pleased when his work is praised but discusses it in a professional, impersonal way (174). Like the paragon after whom he is named, Romero is as honest and honorable in his personal dealings as he is in his art. Unlike Mike, who lets Brett pay the hotel bill at Pamplona, and like Jake, who always pays his own bills and often those of his companions, Romero pays the hotel bill in Madrid. Although badly bruised by Robert Cohn (201–2, 219), Romero fought so brilliantly that he was awarded Bocanegra's ear; he gave it to Brett.

Speaks: 163, 173–76, 185–86, 219, 221.

Romero's *cuadrilla* (crew). Romero's older brother serves as his *banderillero* (174); he cuts the ear which Romero gives to Brett (220). We also see his sword-handler and three hangers-on (163). The "hard-eyed people at the bullfighter table" disapprove of Jake and Brett's intervention in the life of Romero (187; see Americans). Brett reports that Romero's "people" are "very angry" about her (207). See bullfighters.

Speak: 163, 219.

Pedro Romero, *Anales del Toreo* (1873)—courtesy of the Hemingway Collection, J. F. Kennedy Library

*Romero's women. Romero told Brett that he had been involved with only two women before he slept with her (245).

Rotonde. See cafés.

runners. In Bayonne several hotels send hotel buses and "hotel runners" to meet the incoming trains (89).

*Sanchez Taberno. [Correct spelling: Sánchez Tabernero. Family name of the owners of a large and well-known bull-breeding ranch whose bulls, under this family's name and emblem, were first presented to the public in Madrid in 1882. Esteban Domeño, on whom Girones is based, was gored by a Santa Coloma bull during the *encierro* of 13 July, 1924 (see endnote 1), and not by one from the Sánchez Tabernero ranch. The bulls for the 1925 *corridas* came from the Villar, Miura, Cándido Díaz, Gamero Cívico, and Pablo Romero ranches. Bocanegra is a fictional construct.]

Bocanegra, the bull which killed Vicente Girones (q.v.), came from the ranch and stock of Sanchez Taberno (*sic,* 199).

*Sarasate [Navascués, Martín Melitón. Known as Pablo Sarasate. Spanish violinist and composer, 1844–1908. Sarasate's father, himself a musician, recognized his son's talent and arranged for the boy to study with a series of teachers. Sarasate began his perfoming career in 1861, in Paris, and soon achieved international fame. His compositions include *Jota de San Fermín* (opus 36). Born in Pamplona, he returned regularly to the city, which established a museum in his name and named its Conservatory for him. In 1903 the handsome Paseo de Valencia was renamed Paseo de Sarasate.][43]

Well-dressed people stroll along the Paseo de Sarasate (207).

*Scott, Dred. [American slave, c.1795–1858. In a famous case, 1856–1857, the U.S. Supreme Court judged that Dred Scott, a black person descended of slaves, had no civil rights or standing in court even though he had lived for years in free territory. Although the judgment went against him, Scott was declared a free man in 1857.]

After he verbalizes his affection for Jake, Bill attempts to defuse the atmosphere with a string of jokes, including one about Dred Scott (116).

*the secretary. During her tirade, Clyne scathingly mentions a secretary whom she caused Cohn to fire at the beginning of their relationship (49–50). Cohn has also enjoyed the attentions of a few other women (8). Jake has a secretary (69).

the Select. [This café, named after its owners, opened in 1925 at 99 Boulevard du Montparnasse. Madame Select "was an imposing figure, with sternly arched eyebrows, high color, and heavy bosom." Her husband did the cooking (Hansen, 121–22). The characters visit other cafés and restaurants (see café).]

The Select is "this new dive" (36) often frequented by the main characters. Barnes goes there by himself (41, 81) and with others (27, 42, 48–51, 75, 78).

soldiers. Soldiers accompany the dignitaries at the religious ceremonies in Pamplona (155). Officers stroll about the town in the evening. In San Sebastián, Jake sees a soldier who is missing an arm (237); the postman "looked very military" (238). See crowds, guards, Primo de Rivera.

the *sommelier* [wine steward]. Count Mippipopolous orders a bottle of old brandy from the wine steward at the restaurant to which he invited Jake and Brett for dinner (61–62; see 33).

Speaks: 62.

A Sportsman's Sketches. [Ivan Turgenieff's great collection of portraits and stories (1847–1851), in which he realistically and sympathetically describes the miserable conditions of Russian peasants. The collection was widely read in Russia and may have contributed to the movement for the emancipation of the serfs.]

In Pamplona, Jake Barnes rereads *A Sportsman's Sketches* (147–49; see also Turgenieff).

*Stein, Gertrude. [American writer, 1874–1946. Stein was an important experimental writer and art collector. In 1903, she moved to Paris with her brother. Her salon at 27, rue de Fleurus, attracted such important writers as Anderson, Fitzgerald, Ford, Pound and Hemingway. She collected the innovative art of the young painters of the period and was herself the subject of a portrait by Picasso. She experimented with automatic writing, colloquial dialogue, repetition, and various aspects of grammar to produce a new, unadorned style. She wrote stories (*Three Lives,* 1909), poems (*Tender Buttons,* 1914), opera (*Four Saints in Three Acts,* with music by Virgil Thomson, 1934), thinly veiled autobiography (*The Autobiography of Alice B. Toklas,* 1933, and *The Making of Americans,* published 1925), and theoretical and critical essays (*Composition and Explanation,* 1926; *How to Write,* 1931; and *Narration,* 1935). In *MF* Hemingway explains that Stein's famous "lost generation" remark, to which he takes strong exception, originated not with her but with the owner of the garage that serviced her car (*MF* 29). Thinking it over, Hemingway concludes that "all generations were lost by something and always had been and always would be," although he resents "her lost-generation talk and all the dirty, easy labels" (*MF* 30–31). Stein is mentioned in *TS*, parodied in *FWBT*, and figures prominently in *MF*.]

The first of the two epigraphs in *The Sun Also Rises* is credited to Gertrude Stein; the second is from *Ecclesiastes*.

Stone, Harvey. An American living in Paris. He drinks heavily and hasn't eaten anything for five days because his money hasn't arrived. Jake, who recently lost 200 francs to Harvey, lends him another 100 (42–43) and goes to see him (51). Harvey's scorn for Mencken (43) and Cohn (44) is shared by Jake and Bill Gorton. Gorton, who sees Harvey a couple of weeks later, reports that he "Doesn't eat any more" (73) and that he likes to be alone "like a cat" (43, 73).[44] Jake likes Harvey Stone (see endnote 1; see also Stearns in *MF*).
Speaks: 42–44.

students. Jake sees students walking towards their universities (35). Cohn is a graduate of Princeton (3, 4), and Gorton met a music student in Vienna, jokingly connected to Harvard (71). Bill and Jake joke about various universities they have not attended, all of them Catholic schools with powerful sports teams which kept them in the news: College of the Holy Cross, Worcester, Mass; Fordham University, Bronx, New York; University of Notre Dame, Notre Dame, Indiana; and Loyola University in Chicago (122–23).

*tailor. Mike's tailor lends him military medals which belonged to another customer; Mike gives them away to various girls (135–36; see also creditors).
Speaks: 135.

*taxidermist. Jake and Bill joke about taxidermists and stuffed animals (72–76).

*Tiger Flowers. See Flowers, Tiger.

Le Toril. [Subtitle: *Revue Tauromachique Indépendante Illustrée.* French bullfighting newspaper, established March 1922, in Toulouse. It was a four-page weekly during the long bullfighting season (spring through fall) and a monthly during the winter. The articles cover Spanish, French, Portuguese, and Central and South American taurine events; most are signed by taurine critics with Spanish pen names like Aguilita, Amarguras, and don Cándido. A large drawing of a bull adorns the title of the newspaper; smaller illustrations accompany the headings of some of the articles. Among the regular columns is one entitled

"Torigrammes," usually presented on p. 2. It consists of a variety of short news items: coming events, announcements of gorings, changes in schedules, retirements, marriages, arrivals and departures of important bullfighting personalities, and so on. Jake misremembers its title as "Cornigrams." "Petite Correspondance" is a very occasional column, appearing on the last page. The Hemingway Collection has several issues of *Le Toril,* 1926–1928; Jake would have been reading an earlier issue. The other paper Jake reads is probably *Le Torero,* subtitled *Revue Taurine Française,* established 1891, and also published weekly during the season and monthly in the winter. After more than 60 years both papers look yellow (Other Materials: Bullfight Materials).]
    Jake reads *Le Toril* from beginning to end (30).

the trainers. See the bicyclists.

*Turgenieff, [Ivan Sergeyevich. Alternate spelling: Turgenev. Russian novelist and short-story writer, 1818–1883. Author of *A Sportsman's Sketches* (1847–1851), *A Month in the Country* (play, 1850), *A Nest of Gentlefolk* (1859), *Fathers and Sons* (1862), *Smoke* (1867), *The Torrents of Spring* (1872) and *Virgin Soil* (1876). Hemingway admired Turgenieff's detailed and vivid presentation of physical, social, and psychological detail. See also Turgenev (*sic*) in *TS* and *MF.*]
    In Pamplona, Jake rereads *A Sportsman's Sketches* (q.v.) (147–49).

*Veuve Cliquot. See Cliquot.

*Villalta [Serris, Nicanor. Spanish matador, 1897–1980. After a long but inauspicious apprenticeship, Villalta had an outstanding afternoon in Madrid in 1922, which launched his career. Throughout the 1920s he triumphed often in the bullring and developed a great following. Villalta performed often, was seldom hurt, and was often awarded the bull's ears. At the time of the novel he would have been a famous man at the height of his powers. The early 1930s saw a decline in his performance; he retired in 1935. He returned to the ring after the Civil War, when he was in his 40s, and enjoyed fine seasons in 1940, 1941, and 1942, finally ending his long career in 1943. A matador of the first rank, he was a serious, even solemn artist.[45] Hemingway admired this extremely tall, accomplished bullfighter and named his first-born, John Hadley Nicanor, after him. See also *DIA.*]
    Romero insists that Bill Gorton looks like Villalta (176).

*Villar. [The ranch of don Francisco Villar de Zamora provided the bulls for the first *corrida* of the 1925 fiesta of San Fermín. They were fought by Antonio Márquez, Martín Agüero, and Cayetano Ordóñez on the afternoon of 7 July.][46]

Montoya announces the arrival of the Villar bulls (131); he does not think much of them (144–45; see Miura).

waiters. Waiters, bartenders, hotelkeepers and restaurant owners are important characters in Hemingway. They are usually presented sympathetically.
Several waiters serve drinks to the characters (14, 153, 166, 206). One waiter sells Jake's unused ticket for the bullfights (161); another "saved chairs for the others" (164). A waiter in Bayonne offers advice about restaurants and liquors and gets a good tip (232–33); two waiters wait for the Count, Jake and Brett to leave so they can go home (61). The only waiters we see serving food are the overworked men on the crowded train from Paris to Bayonne (87, 88). We occasionally see a waiter get paid (137). Waiters move bystanders away from the injured Jake (191). At the beginning and end of the novel, waiters hail cabs for Jake and Brett (24, 247). Waiters in Pamplona perform several important thematic functions: their preparations foreshadow the destructiveness of the fiesta and indicate the return of normality afterwards (153, 227). After Jake has compromised himself and endangered Pedro Romero, a waiter silently cleans up (187). A waiter denounces the violence that accompanies the fiesta (197). And finally a waiter sits alone "with his head in his hands" (192), an image of exhaustion, sorrow and desolation.
Speak: 87, 195, 197–98, 232.

*waiters. In Hemingway's economical prose, waiters do not have to appear in order to perform their duties; see 18, 19, 146, 150, 157, 159, 172, 180, 222–23 *et passim.*

waitresses. Three waitresses return happily from the bullring (199). See women and girls.

watchman. By the end of the fiesta, everyone is tired, including the night watchman (199).

Wetzel's. [Also spelled Vetzel's. A "hangout for newsmen" at 1, Place de L'Opéra and Rue Auber, Vetzel's was a brasserie (Leland, 80).]
Jake and Cohn have beer and snacks at Wetzel's (37).

*Wheeler, Wayne B[idwell. American lawyer and prohibitionist, 1869–1927. Wheeler was a fervent champion of legislation to enforce prohibition. He organized support for "dry" political candidates, helped formulate state and national prohibition legislation, "prosecuted over 2,000 saloon cases . . . and defended the constitutionality of prohibition laws before state and federal courts and the Supreme Court of the United States." During World War I Wheeler worked successfully for legislation to prohibit all alcoholic beverages in the U.S. Navy, including all its vessels, training stations, and land installations. Wheeler's B.A., earned in 1894, was from Oberlin College, Ohio, which was then closely associated with the Women's Christian Temperance Union (WCTU).[47] Jake and Bill could not possibly have gone to college with this famous prohibitionist, who is about thirty years older than they are. See also Bryan and Manning.]

During their tipsy lunch on the banks of the Irati River, Jake and Bill Gorton both claim to have gone to college with Wayne B. Wheeler, Bill insisting that they were together at Austin Business College, where Wheeler was class president, and Jake claiming that he and Wheeler were together at Notre Dame (123).

Wilson-Harris. See Harris.

*Wilson, [Sir] Henry [Hughes. British military man and politician, 1864–1922. Wilson distinguished himself during World War I. He was field commander of the British Army's IV Corps, 1915–1916; assumed the Eastern Command in 1917; became chief of the British general staff and principal military advisor to Prime Minister David Lloyd George in 1918; and was promoted to Field Marshal and created Baronet in 1919. After the war, the Irish-born Wilson disagreed with England's Irish policy; he was refused reappointment as chief of staff, resigned from the Army, and was elected to the House of Commons (Ulster). An ardent supporter of Anglo-Irish unionism, he was shot and killed on his doorstep in London by two revolutionaries from the Irish Republican Army, 22 June, 1922.]

Mike recalls going to an elegant dinner-party at which the Prince of Wales and the King were expected. Because of the murder of Wilson, the royal personages did not come "and no one wore any medals" as a sign of mourning (135).

women and girls. Several unnamed women, most of them Spanish, appear in the novel. Hemingway uses the word "girl" more often than "woman," thus suggesting youth and inferior social position. The following listing is probably not complete.

Several women travel on the bus to Burguete (103). Two women serve drinks at a roadside stop (106). A fat woman and girl run the inn where Jake and Bill stay (109–11, 113–14) in Burguete; a girl brings Jake a telegram from Robert Cohn (127). The girls of Pamplona promenade in the square (150); one girl fills Jake's wine skins (157). A woman and three girls stare at Brett as she walks by (137); a girl takes lunch on a tray to Brett and Romero (210). Old women sweep out the boxes in the bullring (150). In San Sebastián, where Brett and Robert had "lived together" (194), Jake sees a happy young couple: the girl "was browning her back" (235). Jake also noticed another happy young

couple in Paris (77). Three girls sit at Count Mippipopolous' table (64; see Zelli's); two chic girls sit with the bicyclists (236). We also see a few other French girls: one fries potato chips and serves stew (77), another displays and sells marionettes (35; see also Edna, maids, prostitutes).
Speak: 109–10, 127

*women and girls. Several women are mentioned but do not appear in the narrative. When he suggests to Robert and Frances that they go to Strasbourg, Jake adds that he knows a girl there whom they could contact (6). In New York, "several women were nice" to Cohn (8). Mike once gave away medals (which were not his; see tailor) to a few girls in a nightclub (136). When he tries to help an old lady with her bags, they fall on him (78; he was probably drunk). Jake reports of an American woman currently in Pamplona that she "collects bull-fighters" (172; see endnote 4). See Romero's women.

Woolsey. American news service correspondent working in Paris. Jake shares a taxi with him and Krum after a news briefing (36–37).
Speaks: 36.

Zelli's. [Joe Zelli, an American, made a fortune by supplying overpriced drinks, loud music, and a friendly welcome at his nightclub located at 16 bis Rue Fontaine, Pigalle, in Montmartre. Zelli's featured the leading musicians, singers, dancers, comedians, and burlesque artists of the day. Its owner and manager "made a particular point of remembering names and developed this talent to so remarkable a degree that he could greet Americans by name from the second visit on" (Al Laney, qtd. in Gajdusek, 130). The window of Zelli's was full of "photographs of his entertainers and bar girls (topless)" who were available for the customers (Hansen, 268). Leland describes it as a tourist trap, no longer in business (81–82).]
    Count Mippipopolous patronizes Zelli's, where he is soon surrounded by three of Zelli's girls (64). He orders a champagne picnic from the club's kitchen (33). Zelli's is "crowded, smoky, and noisy" (62).

Zizi. [French slang for penis (Leland, 82).]
    Zizi is the (nick)name of a "little Greek portrait-painter, who called himself a duke." He is supported by his patron, Count Mippipopolous, who doesn't like him, the implication being that Zizi is a homosexual (63; see endnote 39). Brett dismisses Zizi as a "Rotten painter" (33). Zizi introduces Brett and Mippipopolous (28).
    Speaks: 28.

*Zizi's father. He and Count Mippipopolous's father were friends (63), which seems to support Zizi's claim to an aristocratic title.

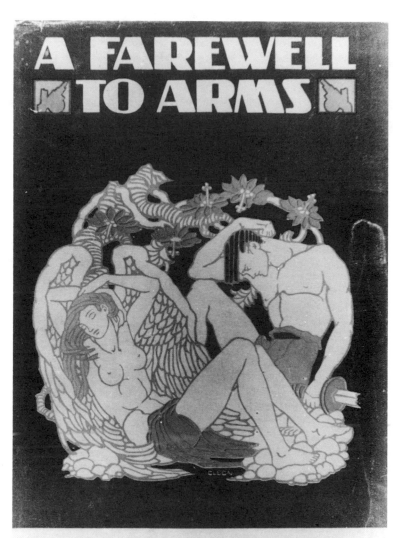

Scribner dust jacket for the first edition of *A Farewell to Arms* (courtesy Charles Scribner's Sons, an imprint of the Macmillan Publishing Company; and of the Special Collections and Archives, Knox College Library, Galesburg, Illinois)

CHAPTER III

A FAREWELL TO ARMS

(1929)

The action takes place in Italy and Switzerland during World War I.[1]

the adjutant (sergeant-adjutant). Even as Henry is being treated for his wounds, the adjutant prepares his report, writing down the doctor's testimony that Henry was wounded by enemy action, in order to protect Henry from the possibility of court-martial for "self-inflicted" wounds" (59). He represents the bureaucracy of the Italian Army and suggests the disaffection rampant among its troops. See also *alpini,* battle police, Emilio, Italians, mechanics.

Speaks: 59–60.

"Africana." [*L'Africaine* (The African Woman) is an opera by Giacomo Meyerbeer (real name: Jakob Liebmann Beer, German composer, 1791–1864), who began it in 1838 and did not complete it until 1863; the libretto was by the popular and prolific librettist Augustin Eugène Scribe (1791–1861). The long, five-act opera was in rehearsal when its composer died. It premiered in Paris, 28 April, 1865. Meyerbeer's operas were exciting theatrical spectacles, very popular in the 19th century but seldom performed in the 20th. According to the Press Office of the Scala Opera House, *L'Africaine* "was not performed in Milan" during World War I.[2] The opera boasts exotic settings (Lisbon and Africa) and crowd scenes populated by scores of soldiers, sailors, bishops, Brahmin priests, and Indians. Among the leading male characters are the Grand Inquisitor, the Grand Brahmin, an admiral named don Diego, and the King of Portugal, named don Pedro. The two main parts for tenors are the characters of the explorer Vasco de Gama and don Alvar, the former having a long, passionate aria, "O paradis sorti de l'onde," early in Act IV, in which he praises the island of Madagascar, comparing it to the Garden of Eden and claiming it triumphantly as a possession of Portugal.]

The tenor Simmons bursts into an aria from ''Africana,'' singing very loudly (242).

Aldo. See Bonello, Aldo.

*alpini. [The Italian Alpine troops are recruited from and trained to fight in mountainous terrain. Two decrees established these troops and organized them into 15 companies, grouped into four regiments. They were enlarged to six regiments in 1882, at which time artillery brigades were added. At the beginning of World War I the *truppe alpini* numbered 179 companies (52 battalions); they had expanded to 274 companies (88 battalions) by 1918. Like Italy, other countries also created special alpine forces, among them France (*Chasseurs des Alpes),* Germany *(Alpenkorps),* Austria *(Kaiserjager),* Switzerland, Spain, Poland, Chile and Argentina.]³

According to the mechanics, Italian troops are uncommitted to the war effort, their only motivation to fight being their desire to protect their families from the stiff reprisals meted out to the relatives of defectors. Among the few who are willing soldiers are the *alpini* (49; see also 276, *bersaglieri, carabinieri, granatieri).*

the American Garibaldi. See Garibaldi.

the Americans. [Frederic Henry is the only American to appear in Books I, III, IV and V. The Americans we see in Book II are few, far from the front, and not particularly impressive: the vice-consul McAdams, Mr. and Mrs. Meyers, Crowell Rodgers and two other unnamed patients at the American Hospital, and the singers Edgar Saunders and Ralph Simmons, both of whom have taken Italian names to further their careers. The Cunningham family and most of the staff at the American Hospital are probably Americans; Moretti's family in San Francisco may have become naturalized citizens. Henry is called ''the American Garibaldi'' (76). See also the aviators, the soldier with the hernia, and the British.]

The narrative reports that ''many'' Americans have volunteered for service in the Red Cross; eventually we hear that the United States has joined the Allied war effort (75).⁴ Henry attempts to cheer the major with exaggerated reports of how many American troops are being trained (165).

*Anthony, Saint. [Egyptian hermit and ascetic monk, c.251–c.350. As a young man, Anthony gave away his large inheritance and became a hermit. The devil offered a variety of temptations, all of which Anthony resisted. He attracted a following, men who prayed and ate together but otherwise lived in solitude. St. Anthony is considered the father of monasticism. His feast day is January 17. Stoneback writes that "Saint Anthony is chiefly invoked for the return of lost property, secondarily invoked for the protection of the pregnant, thirdly for the protection of travellers" ("Lovers' Sonnets," 50).]

When Henry bids farewell to Catherine, she gives him the medal of Saint Anthony which she has been wearing. Henry thinks the medal was stolen from him when he was wounded (43–44; see *FWBT*).

*Aosta, Duke of [Emanuele Filiberto Vittorio Eugenio Genova Guiseppe Maria. Italian aristocrat and soldier, 1869–1931. Emanuele Filiberto was the second Duke of Aosta and Commander of the Third Army during World War I. He was appointed General in 1920 and Marshal of Italy in 1926. He was a first cousin of King Vittorio Emanuele III. His father, Amadeo Ferdinando (1845–1890), was the first Duke of Aosta; this Amadeo was the younger brother of King Umberto I (1844–1900) and thus the uncle of Umberto's son, King Victor Emanuele III, who ascended the throne in 1900. The second Duke of Aosta, son of Amadeo the first Duke, was therefore the King's cousin.][5]

The narrative incorrectly identifies the current Duke of Aosta as the King's uncle; he is the King's cousin, born the same year as the King (their fathers were brothers). The narrative correctly asserts that the Duke of Aosta stood at the head of the Italian Third Army (36–37).

Astra. [Weapons marked "Astra" are the product of the Spanish weapons manufacturer Esperanza y Unceta (later known as Unceta y Compañía), originally of Eibar and later of Güérnica. In 1911 they produced their first automatic pistol, the 6.35 caliber "Modelo Victoria," which was later produced in larger calibers (Hernández Menéndez, 188–92; he does not, however, specify larger-caliber variants of the 1911 Victoria). In 1916 Unceta produced a modified version of the 9mm Campo Giro Model 1913, calling it the Astra Model 1913–16. In 1921 they launched Models 300, 400, and 600, the first of which is a 7.65 caliber pistol, but it was produced after World War I and therefore could not have been issued to Henry. Perhaps he had an Astra 9mm Campo Giro, which "is basically a blowback operated pistol with a very heavy recoil spring wrapped around the barrel" (Ezell 442).][6]

Henry is dissatisfied with the Astra 7.65 caliber that he is required to carry at all times (29).

*the Austrians. [Although the Austrians are the enemy, Henry seems to bear them no ill will. He speaks of their army contemptuously (36), but even more contemptuously of the Italians (q.v.) under whom he serves.

The Italians advanced upon the Austrian lines in 1916 and 1917 (Book I) but in late October 1917, the Austrians and Germans inflicted a terrible defeat on the Italians; the resulting retreat from Caporetto dominates the beginning of Book III. See also Franz Joseph. Henry describes the ''Austrian sniper's rifle,''which he has hung over his and Rinaldi's beds, in sensuous detail (11).]

In the course of the long war, rumor, speculation and wishful thinking are rife: ''Maybe the Austrians would crack'' (37; see also Americans, British, French, Germans, Italians).

the aviators. An unseen American serving in the French air force writes to Henry about his adventures (136). Henry sees a few aviators at the Cova café in Milan (119) and others on the train from Milan to Stresa (243). Aviators, who are always seen in groups, emphasize Henry's isolation and seem to make him uncomfortable with his non-combatant status, both before and after his defection.

Aymo, Bartolomeo (Barto). A kind, conscientious Italian driver, under Frederic Henry's command in the Ambulance Corps. He works hard during the retreat from Gorizia to Pordenone, evacuating the wounded. While the other drivers sleep before evacuating the hospital equipment, Aymo cooks spaghetti for them. During the retreat, he gives a ride to two frightened young girls (see virgins). Eventually Henry, Aymo, and the other two drivers have to abandon their ambulances and continue the retreat on foot. Suddenly, Aymo is shot in the back of the neck; he dies within minutes (189–214).[7]

Speaks: 190–193, 195–196, 199–200, 204–5, 207–12.

*Aymo's family. Henry, who had become fond of Aymo, intends to write a condolence letter to Aymo's family (214).

*Babe Ruth. See Ruth, George Herman.

Baby, Old Baby. Rinaldi's favorite nicknames for Frederic Henry (32, 40–41, 63, 66, 67, 167, 186).

the baby. See Young Catherine.

*Bacchus. [In Roman mythology, the god of wine and fertility. Ceremonies to worship Bacchus were often drunken and orgiastic. Legends associated with the Greek god Dionysus were also applied to the cult of Bacchus.]

During a tipsy postprandial discussion about drinking, the major and Henry mention Bacchus repeatedly (39–40; see *FWBT*).

the barber. A middle-aged Italian who shaves the convalescing Henry in the American hospital in Milan but refuses to talk to him or to receive payment because he thought that Henry was an Austrian (although the porter had said "American") officer (90–91; see barbers in *FWBT).*
Speaks: 90–91

*barber. Henry goes to a barber in Milan for a shave (134).

*Barbusse, [Henri. French poet, novelist and journalist, 1873–1935. Barbusse was deeply affected by his military service during World War I. Wounded twice, he was discharged in 1917 because of his wounds and cited for gallantry. Barbusse became a pacifist, a critic of his society and eventually a communist. *Le Feu,* an anti-war novel which won the prestigious Prix Goncourt in 1916, details the terrible life of the French soldier on active duty. It was translated into English as *Under Fire: The Story of a Squad* (1917). In his "Introduction" to *Men at War: The Best War Stories of All Time,* Hemingway praised Barbusse's *Under Fire* as "The only good war book to come out during the last war. . . . His whole book was a protest and an attitude. The attitude was that he hated it. . . . Its greatest quality was his courage in writing it when he did." Hemingway adds that "the writers who came after [Barbusse] wrote better and truer than he did" (xv).]
Count Greffi recommends Barbusse's novel *Le Feu* to Frederic Henry (261).

Barkley, Catherine (Cat, Madame, Madame Henry). A beautiful blonde British woman who has been working with the Voluntary Aid Detachment (V.A.D.) since late 1915 (Brett Ashley, q.v. in *SAR,* was also a V.A.D.). When we meet her she is a veteran of almost two years of army service and still "nearly crazy" (30) over the loss of her fiancé (q.v.). Her experiences have made her an uncompromising realist (20) who rejects conventions like marriage (but not militantly; see entries for husband and wife) and patriotism and takes full responsibility for herself (246). She first meets Frederic Henry in the spring of 1917; their love consumes her. Although she is a conscientious nurse and fond of her colleagues, she unhesitatingly abandons job and friends to be with Frederic Henry. She tries to erase the past (both his and hers), shuns other people, and wants to bury her own identity in that of Frederic Henry (115). When Henry is sent for treatment to the American Hospital in Milan, she manages to get herself transferred there. By the time he is returned to the front, she is pregnant. She escapes with him to Switzerland, where they spend an idyllic winter in the mountains. After more than twelve hours of hard labor and a Caesarean delivery, Catherine is exhausted, gray, and weak. She begins to hemorrhage and dies in the night. For an excellent reading of this controversial character, see Sandra Whipple Spanier's "Hemingway's Unknown Soldier."

Speaks: 18–20, 22–27, 29–32, 42–43, 91–93, 102–6, 112–16, 124–26, 129–32, 136–41, 147–57, 246–52, 257–58, 266–69, 272–85, 293–310, 312–19, 322–26, 330–31.

*Barkley's family. Only Catherine's father is mentioned: he has gout (154; see children and the fiancé).

the barmaid at a little inn in Switzerland. She serves drinks and sells chocolate (296–97).
Speaks: 296–97.

the barman at the Grand Hotel. See Emilio.

Barto. See Aymo, Bartolomeo.

Bassi, Fillipo Vicenza. An Italian officer in Frederic Henry's outfit at Gorizia. He and Henry engage in a drinking contest which Henry abandons in order to visit Catherine (40). When Henry returns in the fall, Bassi is no longer there and no one mentions him; the implication is that he was killed during the heavy fighting that summer.
Speaks: 40.

battle police, military police. In a futile attempt to control the retreating troops and to find a scapegoat for the defeat at Caporetto, the officers of the Italian military police call aside Italian officers who for whatever reason look suspicious to them. These hapless men, accused of being deserters or German infiltrators (221–25), are questioned briefly, sentenced to death, and handed over to the *carabinieri* (q.v.; see also floorwalkers, games) for execution. The battle police stop and question Henry and precipitate his defection (222–25), after which he must avoid the military police (239). As Emilio points out, after the defeat, the battle police arrest people indiscriminately (264, 265; see 250–52).
Speak: 222–25.

beards. Although they usually indicate virility, beards in this novel seem to signify an ineffective, spectatorial or non-combatant position. Soldiers on active duty do not grow beards, because they do not fit into gas masks; beards are grown only by nurses (76–77) and Swiss woodcutters (i.e., strong men, but civilians, 302–3). One of the ineffective doctors in Milan sports a beard (95), and after his defection Henry himself grows a beard. Catherine approves of it (304), but Henry recognizes that it is ill-suited to aggressive pursuits like boxing (311). In his white hospital gown, Henry feels he looks "like a fake doctor with a beard" (319).[8]

bersaglieri. [Light infantry group, established 18 June, 1836, whose specialty is rapid deployment and rapid firing. The original single company was expanded to seven (two battalions) during the national uprisings in 1848 and their number continued to grow. They played an important part in the Crimean War, the Italian *Risorgimento* and the reunification of Italy (see Cavour), the Italo-Turkish war of 1911–1912, and World War I. In 1899 the first company of bicycle-mounted *bersaglieri* was established; in 1904 a *bersaglieri* museum opened in Rome. After World War II they were fully integrated into the Italian army, ceasing to exist as separate units. They have entered the Italian language in the adjectival phrase *alla bersagliera,* denoting an intrepid, independent, and aggressive manner. The *bersaglieri* uniform is dark green, and they wear picturesque hats with large cock-feather plumes.][9]

Moving towards Plava on the Isonzo River (May 1917), Henry's men discuss the *bersaglieri,* who are supposed to play a major role in the coming battle. The mechanics describe them as wide-chested, healthy men (a description repeated by Aymo, 199) but deride them as "fools" for being so militaristic. They remark that even among these aggressive troops there have been defectors (48–49). Men walking towards the battle ground "wearing red fezzes" are identified as *bersaglieri* (44).

Biffi's. [An elegant café at the Galleria Vittorio Emanuele, near the cathedral in Milan.]

Henry and his drunken visitors mention all the places Henry will visit during his convalescence, Biffi's among them (76). Later, Frederic Henry and Catherine Barkley do enjoy a dinner at Biffi's (112; see also *MF*).

Black Pig.

The lieutenant (Rinaldi) claims that *Black Pig* destroyed his faith; he recommends it to Henry (7–8). The priest denounces the book as "filthy and vile" (7).

Bonello, Aldo. A driver in the ambulance Corps. He is under Henry's command during the retreat in October 1917, evacuating first the wounded and then the hospital equipment. He claims to be a socialist and is not committed to the war effort: he says he likes a retreat better than an advance because the drink is better, but when the retreat turns out to be unpredictably dangerous, he deserts, believing that an enemy prison is safer than the countryside (217; see also endnote 7). He gives a lift to two sullen sergeants (qq.v.) from the Engineering Corps. When

Henry shoots and wounds one of them, Bonello obtains his permission
to "finish him" (207). Bonello doesn't know how to fire a gun (204).
  Speaks: 34–35, 188–93, 195, 199–202, 204–12, 214–15.

*Bonello's family. Because Bonello's desertion endangers his family,
Piani asks Henry to report that Bonello was taken prisoner (219; see also
grenatiere's family).

*[Borromeo, Vitaliano. Italian aristocrat, d. 1690. The Borromean Islands,
a group of four islands in Lake Maggiore, near Stresa, take their name from
the Borromeo family. Count Vitalio Borromeo is responsible for the
chateau and terraced gardens for which Isola Bella is famous. The other
three islands are Isola dei Pescatori, which, as its name indicates, contains
a fishing village; Isola Madre, the largest of the four; and Isola San
Giovanni, off Pollanza. In spite of its name, the Grand Hotel des Iles
Borromees, in Stresa, has no connection to the Borromeo family. It was
established by the Omarini brothers soon after the unification of Italy in
1861, and was so successful that in 1868 a new wing was added. The
opening of the Sempione Tunnel in 1906 made Stresa more accessible, and
the number of tourists increased. Hemingway visited Stresa in September
1918 (Baker, *Life,* 51); when he returned in October 1948 he signed the
hotel's celebrities book and added "an old client" after his name.][10]
  Henry and Catherine stay at the elegant Grand Hôtel & des Isles
Borromées (*sic,* 244). Emilio and Henry row out past Isola Bella and
have a drink at the Fisherman's Island (255).

the boy. See men and boys.

*the British. [The British are consistently presented in a favorable light.
Henry approves of the British gunners and ambulance drivers (37,
57–61, 163); Gino also admires the British (181). As the fighting
intensifies, the British appear at the front in increasing numbers (10);
they are also seen in Milan, where the British major shows himself to be
well-informed (119, 133).[11] Catherine Barkley exemplifies all the
British virtues: courage, intelligence, humor and witty understatement.
See also drivers, the English driver, the English Major, and the fiancé.]
  Henry's several meetings with the British increase his appreciation for
them: "I wish that I was with the British" (37).

Britling. See *Mr. Britling Sees It Through.*

Brundi. An Italian officer in Henry's outfit in Gorizia. When Henry
returns in the fall, Brundi is gone, probably a victim of the heavy
fighting that summer (173; see also Bassi).

*Cadorna, [Luigi. Italian general, 1850–1928. Cadorna was in charge of preparing Italy's armed forces for World War I and served as Chief-of-Staff during the first thirty months of the conflict. His campaigns in the Tentino, Gorizia (August 1916) and Bainsizza (1917) were successful though overshadowed by the major defeat of the Italian army at Caporetto (October 1917), which led to his being removed from his position as Chief-of-Staff.][12]

The narrative identifies Cadorna as the Italian General of the Second Army. Just as the mechanics scorn the Italian soldiers, Frederic Henry finds their leadership inadequate. He wishes they were commanded by Napoleon (q.v.) instead of by the "fat and prosperous" Cadorna (36).

the Captain. One of the officers in Henry's outfit in Gorizia, the Captain loves jokes. He translates his own vulgar jokes into "pidgin English" so Henry will understand (although Henry's Italian is excellent), and constantly teases the priest (7–9). When Henry returns in the fall, after the Italian army has fought hard and suffered many losses over the summer, the Captain is not there. The implication is that he, like Bassi and Bundi, has been killed. Most of the army doctors in the novel have the rank of medical captain (see doctors and soldiers; see also endnote 31).

Speaks: 7–9.

carabinieri. [(V. E. soldiers, airplanes). Troops armed with carbines, established on 13 July, 1814 by royal decree of Vittorio Emanuele I and closely connected to the royal house of Savoy and the head of state, for whom horse-mounted squadrons of *carabinieri* serve as personal guard. They are empowered to keep civil and military order; in the novel they carry out the orders of the battle police (q.v.). After World War I the *carabinieri* enjoyed special favor during Mussolini's fascistic regime. Their wide hats earned them the appellation "airplanes" (224).][13]

Two *carabinieri* stop Henry (24), two others are seen in Milan (157–58). The mechanics despise these troops, who they claim shot fellow Italian soldiers (49). We see *carabinieri* behaving in just this fashion during the retreat: acting upon orders of the battle police (q.v.), they pluck officers out of the retreating masses, stand guard over them before and during their questioning by the battle police, and then shoot them (221–25; see also 232 and headgear).

*Caruso, [Enrico. Italian tenor, 1873–1921. Caruso appeared over 600 times at the New York Metropolitan Opera and was one of the first singers to make records. He was internationally famous not only for his magnificent voice and his dramatic performances at opera houses in North and South America and in Europe, but also for molesting women in Italy, England, and the United States. The most famous of these cases began on 17 November, 1906, when the front page of the *New York Times* reported that Caruso had been arrested for accosting a woman in front of the Monkey House at the Central Park Zoo. The case was front page news almost every day for the rest of that month. Between 1909 and 1912 Caruso was sued repeatedly by the soprano A. Giachetti, who claimed he had fathered her child. In 1912 Caruso was sued by another Italian woman, E. Ganelli, for breach of promise; a Milan court found him guilty. In 1913 he was "rebuked" by the English courts for annoying a woman in a London hotel. In 1914 he was again sued for breach of promise, convicted, and required to pay a "substantial sum" to settle the case (*New York Times,* 1906–1918). See also "Fathers and Sons" in *Winner Take Nothing.*]

When Henry goes away on leave (winter 1916–1917) his fellow officers ask him to buy a record player and records of Caruso (9). Almost a year later, in response to Rinaldi's letter (135–36), Henry brings him some records (167).

Cat. Henry's nickname for Catherine Barkley (e.g., 156–57, 266, 284, 285, 298, 310, 312, 320, 330, 331).

Catherine. See Barkley, Catherine; and Young Catherine. In *GE,* the young wife is named Catherine Bourne; she also calls her husband by her first name.

Cavalcanti. One of the Italian officers who enlivened the mess in Gorizia. When Henry returns from Milan in the fall of 1917, he finds only the priest, Rinaldi, and the major. Rinaldi misses Brundi, Cavalcanti, and Cesare (173).

*Cavour, [Count Camillo Benso. Italian aristocrat, patriot and politician, 1810–1861; leading figure of the *Risorgimento,* prime minister, 1852–1859. In 1847 Cavour founded the newspaper *Il Risorgimento,* which rapidly became a powerful voice calling for Italian independence and unification. Cavour advocated constitutional monarchy, as opposed to republican democracy or church-affiliated government. In achieving his goal he had to contend with local princes, internal factionalism, Austrian domination, and European and Church politics. During the *Risorgimento,* the period of Italy's emergence as a national entity (1815–1870), Cavour's party, which advocated unification under the royal family of Savoy, emerged as the most powerful. In February 1848, King Charles Albert was induced to grant a charter of liberties and thus connected himself to the *Risorgimento;* he abdicated in favor of his son Vittorio Emmanuele II in 1849, who also supported Cavour's efforts. Cavour, who rose to high position in the government, convinced France (through territorial concessions) to join the Italian forces against the Austrians, who ruled most of Italy. After several setbacks and complications, much of the north and center of Italy was united. Cavour joined forces with Garibaldi (q.v.), who had gained control of the southern provinces, to complete a large part of the unification of Italy. The negotiations with Garibaldi were difficult, and soon after the exhausted Cavour took ill and died. He lived long enough to see Vittorio Emanuele II proclaimed king of a united Italy in 1861. Cavour, a great patriot, fought the same enemy facing Frederic Henry: the Austrians. The original Hotel Cavour was damaged during World War II; the present Hotel Cavour, built in 1959, is part of a block of buildings that includes a bank, a cinema, a library, and shops. It is located on the Piazza Cavour, Fatebene Fratelli 21, Milan.][14]

When he first thinks of taking Catherine to a hotel, Henry envisions a visit to the Hotel Cavour in Milan (37–38). Eventually, they do go to a hotel in Milan, but it isn't the Cavour (153–54).

*censorship. Wartime censorship is strict in Italy. Letters are read (25, 155) and official postcards with printed messages are issued. Henry crosses out all the messages except the one reporting that "I am well" (36). Newspapers are also censored (292).[15]

Cesare. One of the "good old priest-baiters" who enlivened the mess at Gorizia in the spring of 1917. Like Brundi, Cavalcanti, Rocca, the Captain, and many others, he is no longer there when Henry, who had spent the summer convalescing in Milan, returns to Gorizia in the fall (173).

*the chamois hunter. See the woodcutters.

*Chicago White Sox. See White Sox.

children. Children peek in through the windows of the train at wounded soldiers (77). Children hold menial jobs and run errands (see men and boys).

*children. Catherine and Henry speculate about the children they will have (103; see Young Catherine and the nurse). Catherine falsely claims that they already have four children (293) and that they have been married four years (294).

civilians. In this war novel, most of the background characters are soldiers. Some scenes, however, do present civilians, albeit briefly: in

Milan, Henry gazes at "people going by" (147) and sees "streetcars
. . . full of people going home" (150). Civilians and some convalescing
and off-duty soldiers crowd the San Siro race track (128). While war
rages on in Italy, the Swiss enjoy the pleasures of civilian life. In the
evenings, Swiss villagers often come to the Guttingens' inn for a drink
(291). Shopkeepers in Montreux welcome Henry and Catherine's patronage (292). In addition to drinking, Henry enjoys walking through
Montreux, sitting in cafés, watching passers-by (311), and boxing (see
the professor). While Barkley is dying, the café near the hospital is
crowded with civilian customers (328–29). See barmaid, conductor,
crowds, hairdresser, men and boys, women and girls, and woodcutters.

*civilians. Henry and Barkley are told that the people of Montreux are
"extremely courteous and friendly" (283).

*Cleopatra. [Queen of Egypt, 69–30 BCE. The daughter of Ptolemy XI.
According to custom, Cleopatra married her brother Ptolemy XII and,
after his death, her brother Ptolemy XIII. She had a son, Caesarion (later
Ptolemy XIV) with Julius Caesar and, after Caesar's death, was romantically involved with Marc Antony. She committed suicide by having an
asp bite her. Cleopatra is supposed to have been enchantingly beautiful.]
   The jovial doctor who X-rayed Henry's legs insists that Miss Gage is
more beautiful than Cleopatra (95).

the *concierge*. We see the *concierge* at the hotel in Stresa (244) and in
Lausanne (308; see the manager and porters; see also *SAR*).

*the *concierge*. See *the porter or *men and boys.

the conductor. The Swiss motorman and conductor drive the electric
train up the mountain (295).

Corriere Della Sera [*(Evening Courier)*. Founded in Milan in 1876 as an
evening paper, the newspaper retained its name when it became a morning
daily. In 1885 the paper was bought by the wealthy Crespi family, textile
manufacturers who gave it complete editorial independence. It is a highly
respected paper, noted for its political independence, its reliable reporting
of both national and international affairs, and its literary style.]
   Henry reads this Italian newspaper (135, 292; see also censorship,
newspapers).

*cowards. [When his wife asks him to stay home, Caesar replies,
"Cowards die many times before their deaths;/ The valiant never taste of
death but once" (Shakespeare's *Julius Caesar,* II.ii, 32–33).]

When Henry says that "Nothing ever happens to the brave," Catherine rejects the platitude, reminding him that "They die of course." Catherine also rejects Shakespeare's distinction between cowards and brave men, arguing that "The brave dies perhaps two thousand deaths if he's intelligent" (139–40).

Croats, Croatians. [From 1091 until 1918, Croatia was united to Hungary, except for the periods of Turkish occupation (1526–1699), French occupation (1809–1813), and Austrian annexation (1849–1868). By its connection to Hungary, Croatia was part of the Austro-Hungarian empire, which was dissolved in 1918, at which time it joined in uneasy confederation with five other republics to form Yugoslavia.] Croatians are seen at the front lines, on the Austrian side (182, 186). See crowds.

crowds. Most of the crowd scenes involve Italian soldiers: the train at the Milan station is full of soldiers, and more get on as the train approaches the eastern front (158–59). Italian and Austrian soldiers are massed at the Bainsizza, including Croats and Magyars (qq.v., 182, 186). During the retreat we see crowds of Italian soldiers and officers, a German battalion, and many civilians, who join the retreating army, bringing their possessions with them (198). The crowd is so massive that it seems "The whole country was moving" (218). A more cheerful crowd of soldiers gathers at San Siro (128). See also battle police, civilians, soldiers, the wounded.

*crowds. Crowds protest the war, which has taken almost 200,000 lives (133).

Cunningham, Mr. [John L. Cunningham, born 1858, was a banker in Palo Pinto, Texas. Cunninghams of that same generation were bankers in Bisbee, Arizona, a small but booming copper-mining town. The Texas Cunninghams had one daughter; the Bisbee Cunninghams had three daughters and three sons. I have not been able to discover if any of these Cunninghams were in Italy during World War I.] Mr. Cunningham is the banker who cashes Frederic Henry's sight drafts (76, 131). He is one of the "people we knew" at the race track (128).

Cunningham's family. Henry and Catherine meet the banker, his wife and daughters at the horse races in San Siro, near Milan (131; see 128).

customers. See civilians and crowds.

DelCredo, Enrico [Henry of the Creed]. Stage name of Ralph Simmons (120).

*doctor. We hear that Catherine's doctor in Montreux has advised her not to go skiing and to drink beer to keep the baby small because her hips are "rather narrow" (294; see 293).

doctors. As an ambulance driver, Henry knows many of the doctors (46). Before the offensive in the spring and again before the retreat in the fall, Henry goes into the medical tent and speaks with the medical officers from whom he takes his orders. The orders are telephoned to the medical tent and are usually changed at the last minute (51–52, 187). During the battle, several blood-stained Italian doctors are seen at the dressing station (57–58). When he is wounded, Henry is first tended by a medical sergeant (57) and then by a captain who works quickly, makes jokes, gives him a drink, and has one himself (59–60). The doctors at the field hospital were also "very nice and . . . very capable" (74–75; see 62). Most of the doctors have the rank of medical captain; the highest-ranking doctors are majors (52–53, 98; see Valentini and endnote 31). See also nurses, Rinaldi, and stretcher-bearers.
   Speak: 52–53, 59–60, 187.
   In contrast to the pressured, hard-working front-line doctors, the nameless house doctor at the American Hospital in Milan is incapable of making medical decisions and calls in a pair of equally incompetent doctors (Vanella and Varino, qq.v.) for consultation. The house doctor is quiet, small (94), and repeatedly described as "delicate" (95, 97, 98). He is more concerned about his private clinic in Lake Como (84, 86–87, 93) than with the war wounded. Both his medical incompetence and personal manner repel Henry. Needless to say, this house doctor, like the unpleasant Miss Van Campen and Ettore Moretti, doesn't drink (98); it is he who diagnoses Henry's jaundice (142). Also in Milan, Henry is X-rayed by an "excitable, efficient and cheerful" doctor (94–95) and operated on by Valentini (q.v.).
   Speak: 95–99.
   The Swiss doctors are all civilians. The doctor in Lausanne advises Catherine to go to the hospital (312). The first doctor who attends Catherine in the Lausanne hospital soon turns over his duties to Henry, while he eats, rests, and smokes. Several doctors operate on Catherine and tend to the baby. All are incompetent and misleading, first announcing that her labor is proceeding "very well" (316), that a Caesarean is safe (321), that the baby is "magnificent" (325), and that Catherine is "all right" after the operation (325). The last of these doctors attempts to offer condolences, to discuss the operation, and to drive Henry to his hotel; Henry rejects all his offers (331–32; see also the nurses).
   Speak: 312, 316–21, 325, 330–32.

drivers. As their officer, Henry is often in the company of ambulance drivers, among whom there were many casualties. During the Italian offensive of May 1917, Passini is killed, Gordini and Henry are badly wounded, and the remaining two drivers, Gavuzzi and Manera, are also hurt. During the retreat in October of that year, Aymo is killed, Bonello deserts, and Piani is last seen when the battle police grab Henry. Several nameless military drivers appear in the novel (42–45, 163); sometimes Henry also drives (33; see also Gino, Peduzzi). The British ambulance drivers also suffered heavy losses (37). Like the Italians, they perform well during the May offensive (57–61), and Henry entrusts his equipment to them (58; see the English driver).

Civilian drivers provide transportation in Italy (128, 150–51, 157–58, 239, 240, 244; see also 242) and Switzerland (281, 284–85, 311, 313).

Emilio. Barman at the Grand Hôtel & des Isles Borromées in Stresa. Although he is now too old to be drafted, Emilio says that if the Italian Army were to conscript him he would leave the country rather than serve (255). He tells Henry where Catherine is staying, warns him that there are plans to arrest him, and helps them escape to Switzerland, giving them his boat against payment sometime in the future, and providing them with directions, sandwiches, wine, and good brandy. See endnote 10.
Speaks: 244–45, 253–56, 264–66, 268–69.

the engineer. When he defects, Henry sees but is not seen by the engineer of the train on which he hitches a ride to Milan (229; see soldiers). See the sergeants from the Engineering Corps.

the English driver. The ambulance driver to whom Henry entrusts two of his ambulances when Passini is killed and he and Gordini are too badly wounded to drive is English. In order to get immediate medical attention for Henry at the field dressing station, this English driver announces that Henry is the son of the American President Wilson (58) and of the American ambassador to Italy (59). After Henry's wounds are bandaged, the English driver takes Henry from the dressing station to the field hospital. Like Henry, he speaks Italian fluently. See also the British and drivers.
Speaks: 57–59, 61.

the English Major. Henry meets him at the club in Milan in September, before he returns to active duty in Gorizia. The Major tells Henry that the war is going very badly for the Italians and predicts that the Allies will lose the war. Henry notes the "great contrast between his world pessimism and personal cheeriness" (134; see also the British).
Speaks: 134.

Enrico. The Italian major's nickname for Frederic Henry (172, 175).

Enry. Italian mispronunciation of Henry.

Federico. Italian for Frederic.

Ferguson, Helen (Fergy). A Scottish nurse serving in Italy. She is very attached to Catherine, transferring with her from the British hospital in Gorizia to the American Hospital in Milan (where Henry is convalescing) and later going with her to Stresa, where she cries in anger and frustration when Henry shows up and takes Catherine away (246–48). Throughout she attempts to protect Catherine and keep her from Henry: she warns him not to get Catherine pregnant and objects to Catherine's frequent night duty, insisting to Henry that Catherine must rest (108–9). Ferguson rejects the notion of marriage between Henry and Catherine (108). Henry likes her but doesn't understand the nature of her attachment to Catherine or the sexual jealousy that makes Ferguson hate him: he "never learned anything about her except that . . . she was very good to Catherine Barkley" (108) and thinks that she would not like "what we have" (i.e., a passionate, illicit heterosexual relationship).[16] Catherine, who is more perceptive about the nature of Ferguson's attachment to her, tells him he doesn't "know much" (257). Ferguson naturally rejects all of Henry's offers of friendship (109, 247; see also Gage).
    Speaks: 20–21, 41, 108–9, 130, 246–48.

*Ferguson's family. We hear only about her brothers (108).

Fergy. Catherine and Frederic's nickname for Helen Ferguson (108, 109, 247–48).

*Le Feu. Anti-war novel by Henri Barbusse (q.v.).

*the fiancé. Catherine's fiancé was killed in France, at the battle of the Somme. They had known each other since childhood and had been engaged eight years, during which time they did not sleep together. The war and his death have taught Catherine that the conventions which governed her and her fiancé as they were growing up no longer apply (18–19). In her relationship with Frederic she discards convention and makes her own rules.

*the fiancé's mother. After her son was killed, she sent Catherine his swagger stick (18–19).

fishermen, the fishermen's island. The fishermen at Isola dei Pescatore [a small island in Lake Maggiore, near Isola Bella] are seen mending their nets (255). See Borromeo.

fish-face. Piani's nickname for the major (190).

*the floorwalkers. [Store managers, whose task is to direct the movement of customers and keep track of sales and salespeople.]
   Frederic justifies his desertion with an image from the business world. He figures that, having lost his equipment and his personnel "as a floorwalker loses the stock of his department in a fire" (in Frederic's case, gunfire) and having almost been shot by the army in which he served (ostensibly because of his accent, see battle police), he now "had no more obligation" than the floorwalkers would if they had been shot for having "an accent they had always had" (232).[17]

France. See the French.

*Franz Joseph. [Hapsburg ruler, 1830–1916; Emperor of Austria, 1848-1916; King of Hungary, 1867–1916. During his reign, Austria subdued Hungary and Sardinia in 1849 but lost Lombardy in 1859 and Venice in 1866. In 1867 his empire became the Dual Monarchy of Austria-Hungary. The assassination of his grand-nephew Franz Ferdinand touched off World War I.]
   To bait the priest, the Major claims that the Church supports the enemy, and that the head of the Church "loves" the head of the Austro-Hungarian empire (7; see the Pope).

Fred. Ettore Moretti's nickname of Frederic Henry (123).

Frederic. See Henry, Frederic.

Fredi. Another of Rinaldi's nicknames for Henry (175).

*Free Masons. [The "Free and Associated Masons" is an ancient secret fraternal organization committed to charitable works. Established in the Middle Ages in England as a guild for the stone masons engaged in building cathedrals and other large monuments, it adopted symbols from the mason's trade, from architecture, geometry, and Egyptian mythology. The society developed strongly ethical and philanthropic positions. By the early eighteenth century the society, no longer merely a craftsman's guild, was open to all men, regardless of creed; members not engaged in the trade of masonry, including the many aristocrats who joined, were designated as "associated" Masons, and a well-defined hierarchy was established. Although one of the basic tenets of the organization is belief in the "Great Architect of the Universe," several European lodges dropped this statute, thus enabling atheists to join the organization and, of course, incurring the hostility of the Roman Catholic Church, which, even before this anti-religious tendency emerged, viewed the large and influential membership of the many lodges as a threat to its own position. The Church first persecuted and then excommunicated Free Masons.]

The atheistic major rejects even the Free Masons [with its historical belief in a Supreme Being]. Rinaldi describes it as "a noble organization" (8).

*the French. [In World War I, some of the heaviest fighting in the west took place in France. The British lost enormous numbers of men in the three bloody battles in and around Ypres (a Belgian town on the French border, 1914, 1915, 1917) and the French also suffered heavy casualties in the valley of the Somme River. Dispirited French troops mutinied in May 1917. The French continued to suffer terrible losses until May 1918, when Marshal Ferdinand Foch was put in control of Allied forces in France. By July Foch had turned almost certain defeat into victory. Military historians are largely agreed that he achieved the Allied victory. See Foch in *ARIT*.]

Barkley, who has been in service since late 1915, is well-aware of the horrors of war. She was witness to events in France, and predicts that the Allies will "crack" first in that country (20; see the fiancé). By spring 1917, the general feeling is that "the French were through"; Rinaldi reports that French soldiers mutinied and were shot (37; Hemingway discusses this mutiny in "Old Newsman Writes," rpt. White, 196–97). The British major summarizes the general attitude about the progress of the war: "We were all cooked" (133–34).

Gage, Miss. A nurse at the American hospital in Milan to which Henry has been transferred. She washes him, drinks with him, and hides his empty bottles from Miss Van Campen. Henry keeps asking her if Miss Barkley has arrived, and Miss Gage lets him know when she finally comes. Henry likes Miss Gage and calls her "a fine girl" (89). Miss Gage also likes him; it is not surprising that she does not like Catherine. Gage is a contrast to Ferguson, whom Henry also calls "a fine girl" (109), but whose fondness is all for Catherine.

Speaks: 84–90, 93, 107, 109–11, 144–45.

games and play-acting. The important motif of games is introduced early in the novel, with the captain's finger-shadow game (8–9). Important issues are consistently linked to games. Henry compares his pursuit of Catherine to "a chess game" (26) and "a [card] game, like bridge" (30); card games reappear during the happy interlude in Montreux (see *Hoyle) and the tragic denouement in Lausanne (318, 329). Henry and Count Greffi discuss war and religion while playing billiards (260), and when he discusses bravery and self-knowledge with Catherine, Henry makes a reference to baseball (140). Later, war seems as irrelevant to him as college football (291). There are also word games, puns, and jokes (38, 39, 91, 245, 261).

Costumes and false or mistaken identities abound. German infiltrators are said to wear Italian uniforms (216), Henry removes his insignia in order to seem an enlisted man (227–28) and later borrows Simmons' clothes to seem a civilian (242); the borrowed outfit makes him feel like "a masquerader" (243). Wearing a white coat, Henry looks "like a fake doctor" (319; see also beards). Many other examples of false or assumed identity can be cited: Simmons and Saunders assume Italian names and pretend to have successful careers. Henry is said to be the son of the American President and of the American ambassador (see the English driver). He is also mistaken for a Frenchman (60), just as the Italian soldier with the hernia is mistaken for an American (35), and the British driver flatters himself that his accent is so good that he is mistaken for an Italian (58). The ambulance drivers are given "a false feeling of soldiering" (17). Mrs. Meyers assumes a motherly role towards the soldiers (119). Catherine pretends Henry is her fiancé; Henry speaks the lines she dictates to him and pretends to be in love with her. Later they pretend to be married (see *children); they also pretend to be cousins, tourists and students (280); the Swiss guards pretend to believe these stories (281). As Henry says, "It's like a comic opera to-day" (285). Catherine's fiancé's swagger stick is "like a toy riding-crop" (31), and even the horse Japalac is disguised.[18] The battle is called a "show" (43 ff), the regulation steel helmets are "theatrical" (28; see headgear), and even the road is disguised and looks "like the entrance at a circus" (46). The pervasive play-acting makes real people seem false. The Italian leaders are described in visual and spatial terms (36–37) so that they seem to be the subjects of a painting, not real people. And "a legitimate hero" wearing medals he has really earned is discredited and dismissed as a boor (124).

*Garibaldi, [Guiseppe. Italian patriot and soldier, 1807–1882. Garibaldi fought in civil wars abroad (Brazil and Uruguay); in Italy he fought against Austrian and French intervention in Italian affairs (1848–1849). With his volunteer militia, the Red Shirts, he wrested Sicily and Naples from the Bourbon king Francis II, thus liberating southern Italy from foreign rule. He attempted unsuccessfully to conquer the Papal States in

1862 and 1867. With Guiseppe Mazzini (a republican, 1805–1872) and Cavour (q.v.), the charismatic Garibaldi was a leader of the Italian *Risorgimento* (1815–1870), the movement to expel foreign powers from Italy and to unify the various states into one nation.]

When Henry drunkenly describes himself as a patriot sacrificing himself for Italy, Rinaldi calls him "the American Garibaldi" (76).

Gavuzzi. An ambulance driver under Henry's command. Like the other drivers (Manera, Passini, and Gordini), he was a mechanic in civilian life and he hates the war. He and Manera carry the wounded Henry to the dressing station, dropping him twice when shells fall near them (56). Although slightly wounded himself, Gavuzzi continues to drive soldiers from the dressing station to the field hospital.

Speaks: 48, 51, 53–54.

George. The headwaiter at the Gran Italia, Henry and Catherine's favorite restaurant in Milan,[19] is "a fine waiter" (112), saving tables for the two lovers, ordering their meals, recommending good wines, and lending Henry money (76, 113; see waiters).

Speaks: 113.

Georgetti. He is a young man traveling on the train when Henry is transferred from the Italian field hospital in Gorizia to the American Hospital in Milan. Henry recalls the painful trip with long delays; he and Georgetti got drunk and were sick on the floor of the train. Georgetti seems to have a shoulder wound (77–78; see children).

*the German. A wealthy German had owned and furnished the villa now housing the British hospital near Gorizia. The many marble busts with which he decorated it strike Henry as expensive, depressing and undistinguished (28).[20]

the Germans. The Germans inspire more fear than the Austrians (87). In contrast to the exhausted Italians, Germans "were ruddy and healthy-looking" (211). They are described in terms of their equipment: they have steel helmets, carbines, and stick bombs; they ride in a staff car or on bicycles (210–11). A German battalion passes the retreating Italians who are relieved not to be seen by the enemy (218).

*the Giants. [The New York Giants are a professional American baseball team, members of the National League since the 1880s. Managed by John J. McGraw from 1902 to 1932, the Giants won ten National League championships. They lost the 1917 World Series to the White Sox (q.v.). See games; see also McGraw in *OMS*.]

In late September (after the league season is over and just before the World Series), Henry reads about the New York Giants (136).

gifts. Henry is the object of much generosity. He receives a St. Anthony's medal from Catherine (43), money from his grandfather (76, 135), a bottle of cognac from Rinaldi (69), a silhouette-portrait from an unnamed man (135), clothes from Simmons (242), the get-away boat from Emilio (268; we never hear that Henry sent the 500 francs he promised), and vermouth, newspapers and mosquito netting from the priest (69). Catherine is given her fiancé's stick by his mother (18–19), and Henry gives Rinaldi records of Caruso (167). Remarkably few gifts are given in other novels: Diana is given a bird in *TS*; Harris gives hand-tied flies to Jake and Bill in *SAR*, Romero gives Brett the bull's ear, Mike Campbell gives away medals that aren't his, and the Count is generous with champagne; in *THHN* Morgan buys trinkets for his daughters; in *FWBT* Santiago gives Jordan a bottle of whiskey and the bullfighter Rafael gives his manager a tiepin; food is given to Santiago in *OMS*. But see gifts in *ARIT*.

Gino. The Italian officer in charge of the ambulances while Henry is recuperating (164–65). When Henry returns to Gorizia in the fall of 1917, he hears about the terrible summer. Gino confirms that "it really had been hell" (182) and adds that the shelling continues, the soldiers are tired, and food is scarce. Like Henry, Gino is interested in and knowledgeable about military tactics, history, and theory, but his interest is more than academic: unlike the priest and the drivers, Gino is "a patriot" (185) and committed to the war. He is popular with his fellows: "a nice boy" (182; see also 181).
    Speaks: 182–84.

Giovanni, Edouardo. Stage name of Edgar Saunders (120).

girls. See women and girls.

Gordini, Franco. He is the quietest of the four ambulance drivers under Henry's command at Gorizia and, like the others, a professional mechanic and an unwilling soldier. While he and Henry are in the medical tent looking for food, the attack begins. Henry and Gordini run out to bring the macaroni and cheese to the others. Shells fall as they eat: Gordini is wounded but even so he manages to help Henry (57–58). Later he ascribes heroic acts to Henry so that he will be awarded a silver medal (63).
    Speaks: 51, 58.

granatiere's family. Passini reports how the family of one of the cowardly grenadiers suffered for his dereliction of duty: not only was their son shot, but the family was placed under house arrest, denied voting rights and treated as outcasts (48–49; see also Bonello's family).

granatieri. [Originally, soldiers who, in addition to their regular equipment and weapons, carried and hurled grenades; hence their name. Infantry soldiers who possessed the requisite height and strength were chosen and trained to be grenadiers. In the late seventeenth century, *granatieri* were detached from their companies and organized into separate units. In 1796 various companies were organized into full battalions of grenadiers, and in the 1850s and 1860s, as the various provinces rejected Austrian rule, they formèd their own regional battalions of grenadiers. Italian *granatieri* are required to be at least 1.75 meters tall (5'10''), and the noun, both in the masculine and feminine, denotes a tall, strong person.][21]

Manera describes the *granatieri* as tall, which "was a joke" at which "They all laughed" (48). [The joke probably refers to excesses or deficiencies in other parts of their anatomies.] Recalling a battle in which the *granatieri* refused orders to attack, the mechanics mock them, not for their refusal to fight (an attitude which the mechanics share) but for the cowardice of these tall, elite troops (49). Many of those frightened grenadiers were shot by the *carabinieri* (see also battle police). The mechanics remark that, as their commanding officer, Henry should forbid such disloyal remarks, but Henry is already disassociated from the war.

Greffi, Count. A retired diplomat said to have served the governments of both Austria and Italy, he knows Henry from previous visits to the Grand Hotel in Stresa. He invites Henry to play billiards and, as usual, Henry loses. They drink champagne and talk about books and growing old. The Count is 94 and intends to live to 100 (254). He tells Henry that he detects signs of aging in himself: he finds it easier now, for example, to speak Italian. His expectation that he would "become devout" as he got older has not been fulfilled (263). See also Metternich and endnote 1.
    Speaks: 259–263.

*Greffi's family. The Count reports that they all "died very devout" (263). His niece, who has come with him to Stresa, reminds Henry of his own grandmother (254, 258).

grooms. Grooms lead the horses around before the race at San Siro (128).

guards. See soldiers.

gunners. See the British.

Guttingen, Mr. and Mrs. They own the chalet in Switzerland where Catherine and Henry spend a happy winter. Mrs. Guttingen had been a maid in a hotel and her husband had been a headwaiter; they saved for years to buy their chalet. Catherine and Henry seem to be their only guests, but in the evenings people stop by to drink wine and beer. Their son is in Zurich studying to be a headwaiter (289–91, 297; see also 307–8 and endnote 1). See Gangeswisch in *MF* and the Aurol family in *GE*.

Speak: 307.

the hairdresser. A "very cheerful" woman, "the only person we knew in Montreux" (292). Catherine lies to her, telling her that she and Henry already have four children (293).

Speaks: 293.

headgear. Caps, helmets, and even gas masks appear often in the novel. The Italian military cap is treated as legitimate headgear: it makes Henry look "less beautiful" but "more military" (135). It reflects its wearer's condition or situation: when the officers disport themselves at the whore house, the prostitutes play with their caps (30), and the stretcher-bearers who are waiting for a tip hold their caps in their hands (83). When Aymo is killed, Piani carefully retrieves his cap and covers his face with it (214). Henry loses his cap in the river when he deserts (227). In contrast to the cap, the Italian steel helmet is rejected by all right-thinking soldiers: it is ill-fitting (33), "uncomfortable and too bloody theatrical" (28); Henry's helmet hangs unused in his room in Gorizia (11), and "most" soldiers simply "slung [their helmets] from their packs" (33; but see the man with the hernia, 36). The Italian officers, however, are equipped with "better fitting helmets" (33) which they do wear. The despised *carabinieri* (q.v.) wore either steel helmets or "the wide hat" which earned them the nickname "airplanes" (157, 224, see also 222). The despicable Italian battle police wear their steel helmets, but of their victims, "Only two of us had steel helmets" (224), which they probably were not wearing. In contrast, the disciplined, well-equipped Germans "all wore . . . helmets" and in that army the helmet, not the cap, represents the soldier: "we could see the German helmets moving" (210–11). The distinction between cap and helmet extends to the British and the Swiss. The British ambulance driver who is clearly "one of us" wears a cap (163), but the Swiss soldier who makes Henry and Catherine nervous as they row to freedom "wore . . . a helmet like the Germans" and, like them, "had a healthy-looking face" (277). The importance of headgear extends to civilian life: although Henry takes the shirts and pants Simmons offers him, he "would not wear Sim's hat" and bought a new one instead (243; see also beards).

the Head Nurse. Catherine's superior at the British Hospital in Gorizia. She likes Italian but not Italians (22–23).

Helen. See Ferguson, Helen.

Henry, Catherine. Catherine Barkley identifies herself as Catherine Henry (313) and is called Mrs. Henry and Madame Henry (see wife).

Henry, Frederic (the American Garibaldi, Baby, old Baby, Enry, Enrico, Federico, Fred, Fredi, Henry, Mr. Henry, Signor Tenente, Tenente).[22] A young American volunteer serving in the Ambulance Corps of the second Italian army during World War I; he holds the rank of lieutenant (Italian, *tenente*). Henry supervises the drivers and vehicles used in transporting the wounded from the battle-field dressing stations to clearing stations and hospitals (16). Like Barkley, he joined the war effort in 1915, and by the time he meets Catherine in the spring of 1917 he is already disenchanted with the Italian army (see the Italians), from which he defects in late 1917. His first person narrative about love and war is retrospective.[23]

Speaks: 8–9, 11–13, 15–23, 25–27, 29–32, 34–36, 40–44, 47–61, 63–73, 81–93, 95–99, 102–110, 113–16, 119–26, 129–32, 135–41, 143–45, 147–59, 164–80, 183–84, 187–93, 195–215, 217–23, 237–42, 244–48, 250–69, 271–85, 293–301, 303–10, 312–19, 321–32.

*Henry's family. Henry is not overly fond of his family (304). He relies on his grandfather for money (76, 135; see 304) and mentions his grandmother (258), his step-father (154), and his "relatives" (244).[24]

House doctor. See doctors.

*Hoyle, [Edmond. English systematizer of the laws of backgammon and several card games, c.1672–1769. His books *A Short Treatise on Whist* (1742, followed by many editions) and *Laws* (1760) codified the rules of whist and were authoritative for over a century, when clubs dedicated to the game gradually began adopting new rules. His codification of the rules of backgammon (1743) is still considered authoritative. His name often appears in the titles of books describing all sorts of card games. The phrase "according to Hoyle" means "according to the rules of authority; correctly" (*The Random House Dictionary of the English Language,* College edition, 1968; the phrase appears in several other dictionaries as well and was current in the 1920s).]

Catherine and Henry acquire a copy of a book by Hoyle and amuse themselves with card games (290; see also games and play-acting).

*Hugo. [The publishing house of McKay produced a series of books for Hugo's Institute for Teaching Foreign Languages, with titles like *Hugo's English Self-taught for the Spanish, Hugo's English Self-taught for the French* and *How to Avoid Incorrect English.*]
   Rinaldi studies "Hugo's English grammar" in order to improve his English (17) and impress Miss Barkley.

*the hunter. See the woodcutters.

husband. Henry is identified as Barkley's husband (317, 319, and by implication). See wife.

Ireland, [John. Irish-born American Catholic churchman, 1838–1918. Ireland was appointed the first Archbishop of St. Paul, Minnesota, in 1888. A controversial public figure, he advocated state support and inspection of Catholic schools and opposed foreign-language church schools in the United States. These policies were attacked by both Catholics and non-Catholics.]
   Henry has never heard of this Archbishop, but when the priest speaks seriously about him Henry politely pretends to be knowledgeable about "the injustices [the Archbishop] had received" (38).

the Italians. We see large numbers of Italians going from place to place. The trains are crowded with Italian troops (158–59) and during the retreat the roads are choked with soldiers and civilians (qq.v.; also see crowds and wounded). Italian soldiers are compared unfavorably to the British (q.v.). Catherine makes several unkind remarks about Italians: she explains to Henry that he hasn't really defected, because "It's only the Italian army" (251; also see 149 and the head nurse), and she finds that Moretti (q.v.), the Italian war hero, is "conceited" and "dreadful," inferior to the more modest British heroes (124). Italians are exaggeratedly polite (130), which makes them, in Catherine's eyes, "awful" (131). Foreign nurses have skills the Italians lack, and they don't think much of the Italians' ideas of propriety (see nurses). Henry does not hold the Italian army in great esteem, having joined it merely because "I was in Italy . . . and I spoke Italian. . . . I was a fool" (22, 256). The Italian army seems "funny" and unreal to him (26). He even despises the Italian pistol and helmet he has been issued (29; see headgear)[25] and is embarrassed by the Italian army's salute (23). Altogether, the Italian military system gives him only "a false feeling of soldiering" (17). The Italians are presented as unprepared for the Austrian attack (182–83), and Henry is angry at the disorganization which allows the Germans to advance so easily (211).

*the Italians. In September 1917, even before the defeat at Caporetto, war-weary Italians have marched in protest "against the war" (133), as the French (q.v.) did in May 1917.

Japalac. [If Crowell Rodgers' assumption that this black horse "was dyed that color" is correct, then Japalac is probably a fake name, to go with the fake color. Valuable French race horses were sent away (mostly to the south of France but sometimes to other countries) for safety during World War I; such a horse might have been registered to run (illegally) under a different name in Italy. As an unknown, it would have attracted few bettors and paid handsome returns when it won.[26] In any case, I have not been able to find a horse by that name in the official stud books. See also jockeys.]

Even before the race, the racehorse Japalac stands out among the inferior Italian horses (127); he wins the race by fifteen lengths (129). Henry, Catherine, Ferguson and Rodgers bet on this suspect black gelding at the horse races in San Siro, near Milan.[27] The odds on him were 35 to one, but due to crooked last-minute betting he paid less than even money (128–30).

*the Japanese. During the drunken farewell party that precedes Henry's transferral to the hospital in Milan, Rinaldi and the Major discuss various countries. Henry describes the Japanese as "a wonderful little people fond of dancing and light wines" (76; see 75).

jockeys. Jockeys are seen astride horses before, during, and after the races (128–29, 131). In the fixed race, Japalac's jockey tries unsuccessfully to hold him back (129).

*Kempton and the boys. Crooked gamblers who place last minute bets at the rigged horse races in San Siro (129–31), so that the winning horses don't pay well. Meyers knows they have doctored the betting on Japalac but is "angry" when he discovers that the next race is similarly rigged (129, 131).

*the King. See Vittorio Emanuele.

*The Lancet. [Prestigious English medical journal, established in 1823 and published continuously to today. The Lancet frequently announces important medical advances.]

Rinaldi brags that he will write up his medical exploits for publication in The Lancet (64).

the lieutenant. See Rinaldi.

*Light For Me. [A horse by this name ran in Auteuil in November, 1925.]
Henry and Catherine bet on Light For Me at the San Siro races near Milan (131; also see Japalac).

Mac. See McAdams.

the machine-gunner. The machine-gunner, who is on leave and working as a tailor in Milan (146), saves a seat on the train for Henry, but when Henry comes to claim it other soldiers protest (158). Henry gives up the seat to the Italian officers who claim it, but tips the machine-gunner and the porter anyway. Although the porter, a civilian, comfortingly suggests that some soldiers will detrain, making Henry's trip more comfortable, the machine-gunner correctly predicts that additional troops will board the train as it moves towards the front (159).
Speaks: 159.

Madame, Madame Henry. See wife.

*Magyars. [Hungarians and therefore closely associated with the Austrians. The Austro-Hungarian empire was dissolved in 1918. See Franz Joseph.]
Gino reports that Magyars have joined the Austrian lines (182). See also crowds.

the Major (Maggiore, Signor Maggiore, the old man, fish-face). The commanding officer of Frederic Henry's outfit in Gorizia is a physician (58; see endnote 31) and an atheist (8; see also Free Masons). He drinks and jokes at the officers' mess (39) and when he visits Henry at the field hospital (75). He is friendly but somber at the dressing station before and during the shelling in which Henry is wounded (47–48, 52–53). When Henry returns to Gorizia in September, the Major looks worn and shrunken and his mustache has turned gray (164, 172; see 47). He no longer jokes; the terrible fighting over the summer has convinced him that "It's all over" (165). Foreshadowing and justifying Henry's desertion, he says, "If I was away I do not believe I would come back" (165). He has arranged for Henry to be decorated (164; see also Gordini). A major is head of a ward at the field hospital (74). For a discussion of the rank of major or medical major, see doctors.
Speaks: 7–9, 14, 52–53, 58, 75–77, 164–66, 172–76.

the manager. The manager of the hotel in Milan rents Henry and Catherine a room, rides the elevator with them, shows them to their

room, and stations the waiter outside their room to make sure they pay before leaving (151–52, 156; see *men and boys and waiters).
  Speaks: 151–52.

Manera. One of the ambulance drivers under Henry's command. Like the others (Gavuzzi, Passini, and Gordini), he was a mechanic in civilian life and he hates the war. He and Gavuzzi carry the wounded Henry to the dressing station, dropping him twice when shells fall near them. Manera fetches a medical sergeant to bandage Henry's legs (57). Although slightly wounded himself, Manera continues to drive soldiers from the dressing station to the field hospital.
  Speaks: 47–51, 53, 56–57.

*Mantegna, [Andrea. Italian painter and engraver, 1431–1506. His art is characterized by skillful foreshortening, solidly modeled figures, and correct anatomical details. Important works include the *Triumph of Caesar, Martyrdom of St. Christopher, Madonna della Vittoria.* The famous *Dead Christ with Two Angels* is part of the collection of the Brera Palace in Milan, where Henry probably saw it. H. R. Stoneback writes that "Mantegna, like Hemingway, is one of the great students and teachers of perspective and exactitude, of a sharp precision that compels the observer to relive the austere glory of his vision" ("Lovers' Sonnets," 51–52). Both Barbara Greenclose and Kenneth Johnston identify *The Dead Christ* as the "bitter" Mantegna painting.]
  Frederic Henry and Catherine agree that Mantegna is "very bitter. . . . Lots of nail holes" (280). Henry recalls the motif of the crucified Christ when he shows Catherine his injured hands and jokingly remarks, "There's no hole in my side" (284).

*Manzoni, [Alessandro Francesco Tommaso Antonio. Italian poet and novelist, 1785–1873. Manzoni's major works are *Il Clinque Maggio* (1821, inspired by the death of Napoleon) and *I Promessi Sposi* (1822, revised and republished by the author over the next few years), both of which won him great fame. *I Promessi Sposi* is considered by many the greatest Italian prose work of the 19th century. Manzoni's writing had wide appeal and influenced the formation of modern Italian, the standardization of the language reflecting the national *Risorgimento* (the political movement that achieved the independence and unification of Italy, see Cavour). Manzoni also wrote a treatise on the Italian language. The author's last years were saddened by many losses, including those of his wife and seven of his nine children. His own death was considered a national loss, and Verdi's famous *Requiem,* premiered at the first anniversary of Manzoni's death, is dedicated to his memory. Manzoni is buried in Milan.]

When he daydreams about taking Catherine to a hotel in Milan, Henry thinks of walking along the Via Manzoni (37). Several details of the daydream, including the clicking elevator, become fact on their last afternoon together before Henry returns to the front (151–52; see 118).

*Marvell, [Andrew. English politician and poet, 1621–1678. Marvell was tutor to the daughter of Lord Fairfax and later to Cromwell's ward. In 1657 he was appointed secretary to John Milton and in 1659 he was elected to Parliament. Most of his poems were published posthumously, including the famous "To His Coy Mistress" (q.v.).]
Henry quotes two lines from the poem; Catherine correctly attributes them to Marvell (154; see also 311).

McAdams (Mac). The American vice-consul in Milan. Henry runs into him in Milan (119) and again at the horse races in San Siro (130). He is a quiet fellow.[28]
Speaks: 121–23.

the mechanics. Gavuzzi, Gordini, Manera and Passini (qq.v.), all of whom had been mechanics in civilian life, serve as ambulance drivers in the Italian Army. Even before the Italian offensive [May 1917] in which Henry is wounded, they display a marked distaste for war. See also drivers.

medical captains, medical majors. See doctors.

men and boys. One unnamed old man earns his living by cutting out silhouettes, first for two girls and then for Henry. He refuses payment and tells Henry to give the finished profile to his girl, but we never hear what Henry did with the likeness (134–35; speaks: 135).[29] At the entry gate at San Siro, men refuse payment from soldiers in uniform (128). A boy buys wine for the wounded Henry (77); a boy carries Catherine's package from the lobby to the bedroom in the hotel in Milan (151–52); another boy comes to take Catherine's order for a drink at San Siro (132); a man in Stresa gives Henry information (244); a boy carries Henry and Catherine's luggage into the Hotel Metropole in Montreux (285); and a boy works in the café near the hospital in Lausanne (318). Also see soldiers, waiters, and women and girls.

*men and boys. When Henry daydreams about taking Catherine to a hotel in Milan, a *concierge,* a porter, an elevator boy and a boy delivering wine are part of the imagined scene (37–38). When Henry telephones for a cab, an unseen man promises to send one immediately (313).

*Metternich[-Winneburg, Clemens Wenzel Lothar. Austrian diplomat, 1773–1859. Metternich was an important figure during and after the Napoleonic era. He was Austria's ambassador to France (1806–1809) and Minister of Foreign Affairs (1809–1848), during which time he negotiated the marriage between Napoleon and Marie Louise (1810) and the Austrian alliance with France (1812). Then, to restrain Napoleon's expansionism, he helped form the Quadruple Alliance of 1814 (England, Austria, Russia, and Prussia) against Napoleon. At the Congress of Vienna he sought to restrict Russian expansionism to the west and negotiated an important position for Austria within the German confederation. He was a leading figure in the Holy Alliance of 1815 (Russia, Austria and Prussia), which sought to preserve the political status quo in Europe. He argued that the balance of power existing in Europe was, like the Hapsburg monarchy, divinely ordained. He insisted that only large blocks of power could maintain stability. His repressive Karlsbad Decrees (1819) were an attempt to suppress liberalism in Germany. The rise of nationalism, expressed in the revolutions of 1848, marked the end of his influence. The era between 1815 (the end of the Congress of Vienna) and the revolutions of 1848 has been called the Age of Metternich. Count Greffi, himself an Austrian diplomat, had been 35 years old when Metternich died in 1859 at the age of 86. By connecting Greffi to Metternich, the narrative makes the old Count the representative of almost 150 years of European history.]

The narrative accurately presents Count Greffi as being old enough to have known Metternich (254).

Meyers, Mr. A short, elderly American now living in Milan with his wife. Henry tells Catherine that Meyers is a convicted criminal (125) who has inside information on the horses. Although not generous with tips, Meyers does give advice to Crowell Rodgers, towards whom he feels kindly because he, like Crowell, has problems with his eyes. Henry runs into him in Milan and again at the San Siro racing track. Mr. Meyers never drinks.
Speaks: 119, 129–31.

Meyers, Mrs. A large, loud, well-meaning American woman now living in Milan with her husband. She visits the American Hospital often, bringing wine and cakes for the soldiers, whom she calls "my boys" and "my dear boys." Her husband refuses to advise her about the horses and so she always loses money at the races at San Siro.
Speaks: 119, 129.

M.O.B., the Montreux Oberland Bernois railway. [The Bernoise Alps and the high Oberland Valley, to the east of Montreux, offer beautiful scenery and sport.]

The M.O.B. is recommended to and used by Barkley and Henry (282, 295–96). The Swiss officials' description of this area (283) recalls the priest's description of the Italian mountainous area, the Abruzzi (9; see also 13).

Moretti, Ettore. An Italian lieutenant, 23 years old. He had been living and studying in San Francisco and was in Turin visiting his parents when war was declared, whereupon he joined the Italian army. Although "a legitimate hero" (124), his patriotism seems to be only skin-deep: he says he would like to be in the American army, because the pay is so good. McAdams accurately describes him as "a militarist" (123). Moretti is universally disliked because he is a braggart (124). He returns to the front while Henry is still recuperating in Milan (133).
Speaks: 120–24.

*Moretti's family. Moretti's parents live in Turin and an uncle is in San Francisco. His sister who, like Ettore, had been living with the uncle, is about to graduate from normal school (teacher training college, 124).

the motorman. See the conductor.

[*Mr. Britling Sees It Through.* Novel by H. G. Wells (English writer, 1866–1946), published in 1916. Mr. Britling, as his name indicates, represents a large segment of the British population. Wells presents him as an intelligent, bumbling, kindly, somewhat eccentric English writer. He has a teen-aged son by his late first wife, whom he loved passionately, and younger children by his second wife, to whom he is unfaithful. The novel records his responses to the war: surprise and shock when it broke out; then a surge of patriotic confidence that victory would come inevitably and rapidly; then dismay mixed with pride when his son and namesake, Hugh, lies about his age and enlisted; disgust at the British War Office's mishandling of material and of people; intense worry for his beloved son; and finally, after the son is killed, the conviction that "Religion is the first thing and the last thing, and until a man has found God and been found by God, he . . . works to no end. . . . Our [dead] sons [both British and German] have shown us God" (442). The novel ends with a glowing pastoral view of England. Both Catherine and Henry reject the old-fashioned values—religion and patriotism—affirmed by Britling: they have "seen through" those platitudes. Greffi seems to indicate that the book accurately reflects the British response to the war; he probably does not endorse that response. The novel was a best-seller in its day (i.e., at the time of the action of *A Farewell to Arms*). For a discussion of the French translation as a source for Greffi's error, see Hinkle, "Seeing Through." Hinkle does not indicate whether the translation was available at the time of Greffi's and Henry's conversation.]

Count Greffi misremembers H. G. Wells' title, calling the book *Mr. Britling Sees Through It.* Frederic Henry, who has read the book and catches the mistake, explains to Greffi that the main character "doesn't see through it" and that the book is not "any good." Greffi recommends the book as a "a very good study of the English middle-class soul" (261).

*Napoleon [Bonaparte. Corsican-born French general, master tactician, politician, economist, and opportunist, 1769–1821. Napoleon I was a military genius who came to dominate much of Europe. In Italy he defeated the Austrians in 1796, conquering much of the north of Italy and establishing the Cisalpine Republic in Lombardy. In the treaty of Campo Formio (October 1797) the French kept the Cisalpine Republic but ceded Venetia to the Austrians. After defeating Austrians and Russians at Austerlitz (December 1805), Napoleon annexed the Venetia to his growing Kingdom of Italy. Napoleon was undefeated until he was outmaneuvered by the Russians in 1812: by retreating into Moscow, the Russians drew Napoleon deeply into Russia where, far from its supply lines, his army starved and froze when winter came. The retreat from Moscow decimated the Napoleonic Continental army. Napoleon was defeated again in Leipzig (1813) and suffered a final defeat at the hands of his old enemies, the British (Waterloo, 1815). The Congress of Vienna (1814–1815) stripped France of most of its empire, returning Lombardy and Venetia to Austria. In 1859, almost fifty years later, Napoleon's nephew, Napoleon III, joined with the Italians to expel the Austrians from Italy in return for territorial concessions (Savoy and Nice). In 1859 the Italian and French armies defeated the Austrians at the battles of Magenta and Solferino, their advance across northern Italy halted not by Austrian military might, but by Napoleon III's making a separate peace with the Austrians at Villafranca di Verona, July 1859, a move which greatly angered the Italians. The famous quadrilateral to which Henry refers is formed of Verona, Peschiera, Mantua and Legnago. The Austrians reinforced this area when it was in their possession, but lost it to the French, both under Napoleon I (1796) and Napoleon III (1859). See Cavour; see also Napoleon in *FWBT.*]

Frederic Henry believes that, unlike the present Italian leadership, Napoleon would have waged war on the plains, where he could defeat the Austrians (118). He repeats this opinion just before the Italian defeat (182–84). Henry generalizes that "any Napoleon" could defeat the Austrians and would prefer to have "a Napoleon" as commander instead of General Cadorna (36). He also quotes the lesson Napoleon learned in Russia: "An army marches on its stomach" (201).

*the New York Giants. See *the Giants.

The News of the World. [Sunday newspaper, founded in London in 1843 and still published today. In 1712, a tax of a halfpenny per sheet was levied on British newspapers, causing the demise of most cheap newspapers. During the next century, the tax was slowly increased, reaching a maximum of fourpence in 1815. When the heavy tax was reduced, cheap newspapers began to appear again, among them *The News of the World* (1843), which offered a successful combination of sex, scandal, sport and conservative politics. After several reductions, the tax was completely repealed in 1855, at which point many more cheap weeklies sprang up; most of them did not last long. The well-established, lurid crime sheet, *The News of the World,* not only outlived most of its competition but steadily increased its circulation. In 1943 it was reputed to be the Sunday paper with the largest circulation in the world. It was the first British paper to be bought by Rupert Murdoch (1969).]

The priest "makes big preparations" before visiting Henry (65), assembling appropriate presents: mosquito netting, a bottle of vermouth and several English newspapers, not locally available, which he had sent away for. One of the newspapers that the priest thinks Henry would enjoy is the scandalous *The News of the World* (69).

newspapers. When he is not at the front, Henry reads Italian, English and American newspapers avidly. Hospitalized in Milan, he has the porter bring him newspapers (87, 95; also see 117, 135, 141) as well as magazines (117; see also 290). He even reads outdated papers (136). After the retreat and his defection from the army, Henry pointedly avoids the papers (243, 250), but he soon resumes reading them (253, 291, 292, 308, 310, 320, 329). It is interesting that only two other characters are seen reading papers. Although his eyes were injured, Crowell Rodgers "read the racing papers" (127), and an old man at the café near the hospital reads a paper and objects to Henry's reading it from across the table they share (328–29). See also *Corriere della Sera, The News of the World,* and censorship.

the night-watchman. At the hotel in Lausanne, the night-watchman opens the door for Henry and Catherine when they wait for the taxi which will take them to the hospital (313).

*the nurse. Looking forward to a happy future, Guttingen invites Henry and Barkley to return to the mountains with the baby and "the nurse" who will tend it (307).

nurses. Male nurses tend the wounded soldiers (74, 76–77) at the Italian field hospital; a medical sergeant (male nurse or paramedic, not a doctor) bandages Henry's wounds (57). Female British nurses are kept at some distance from the fighting. At the American Hospital in Milan, there are four female nurses—Ferguson, Gage, Walker, and Barkley, the latter called a nurse although she is only a V.A.D. (Voluntary Aid Detachment and therefore lacking formal nursing training)—too many for four patients (103). These foreign nurses submit to the Italians' code of behavior in order to be allowed to work in Italy (25, 117–18), but none of them thinks of reporting or upbraiding Catherine when she does precisely what the rules were designed to prevent. Unlike their Italian counterparts, the nurses at the American Hospital are able to make a bed while the patient is in it, "an admirable proceeding" (85, 62). In Lausanne, several unnamed female nurses take care of Catherine; student nurses hurry in to observe the Caesarean operation (324). Nurses give Henry the bad news that the baby is dead and that Catherine is dying; two nurses absorb Henry's anger after Catherine dies (331–32). See doctors.

    Speak: 314–16, 322, 324–32.

*Ochs Brothers. [Correct spelling: Och. A family-owned Swiss sporting-goods store, founded in 1837. By 1905 the business was listed under the names of the brothers Jules-Albert Och (1867–1951) and Ami-Auguste Maurice Och (1879–1955). The successful business expanded, the 1920 catalogue listing ten shops and outlets throughout Switzerland, with the main store located at 2 and 4, rue de la Marche, Geneva. The Montreux branch, located at 12, Avenue du Kursaal, Montreux-Chatelard, opened in 1905; it was sold to H. Bornand, a resident of Montreux, in 1923. The catalogues for the years 1906–1920 indicate that the Och shops offered a wide range of well-made sports clothes and equipment, including toboggans, which were available in four models ranging in price from 22 to 35 Swiss Francs. These toboggans were narrow (43 cm.) and long (either 120 or 150 cm.), made of wood which curves up and back at the front end. The illustration and description indicate that the Canadian toboggan does not have runners; the wooden board itself slides down the snowy surface. The rider or riders who, according to the brochure, can lie, sit or stand, guide it by lifting the left or right-hand corners of the front end. The catalogue also lists Canadian sleds (called "luge" in French, "schlitten" in German) with runners and brakes, but the toboggans are sold under that name: "toboggans du Canada" in French, "Canadische toboggans" in German. The Montreux store that is recommended to Henry was called Och Frères. Like most of the Och outlets, it had to be closed during the financially troubled 1930s. The Zurich branch, established in 1911, is "the only point of sales existing under the name of Och" today. It is located at Bahnhofstrasse 56/58, Zurich.][30]

Henry is advised that Ochs Brothers *(sic)* of Montreux sell excellent toboggans imported from Canada (283).

orderlies. Orderlies perform a variety of duties. One sits behind the desk at the British Hospital (29), others announce meals (172), bring food (52, 172, 175) and candles (175), usher people in and out (42, 68, 73), make beds (177), and take care of the wounded: Henry's orderly at the field station pours water on his wounds, opens wine bottles, brushes off flies, and so on (62–64, 69).
Speak: 64, 172.

*Othello. [The title character in Shakespeare's play is a black general who is tormented by the suspicion that his young wife is unfaithful; he finally strangles her. Othello cries out, "Farewell the tranquil mind! farewell content!/Farewell the plumed troops and the big wars . . . Farewell! Othello's occupation's gone!" (III.ii, 348–57). Like Othello, Frederic bids farewell to the arms of war and of his beloved.]
When Frederic remarks that he had always had "something to do" in the army, Catherine teases him by referring to him as "Othello with his occupation gone." Frederic recognizes the allusion and crudely rejects the comparison, referring to Othello's black skin and his jealousy (257; see also endnote 16. The same racism accompanies Cantwell's remarks about Othello in *ARIT*).

Passini. An ambulance driver under Henry's command at Gorizia. He is rather talkative, defeatist and dispirited, explaining to Henry and the other three drivers (Manera, Gordini and Gavuzzi) that war is horrible and interminable (50). Horribly wounded in the legs at the time that Henry is, he screams and bites himself in pain and soon dies of his injuries (55; also see Gino and Randolfo in *ARIT*).
Speaks: 47–51, 54–55.

patients at the American Hospital. In addition to Crowell Rodgers and Frederic Henry (qq.v.), the hospital holds two more American patients, both hospitalized for illness rather than wounds (107–8). See endnote 1.

*Paul, Saint. [Paul of Tarsus, originally named Saul. Paul's missionary travels and his letters and epistles did much to define, strengthen and spread Christianity. He exhorted men and women to "Flee fornication" (I Corinthians 6: 18), advising that it is "better to marry than to burn" (I Corinthians 7: 9). He also advised Timothy to "Drink no longer water, but use a little wine for thy stomach's sake and thine often infirmities" (I Timothy 5: 23). The feast day of Sts. Peter and Paul is June 29.]

Rinaldi is familiar with St. Paul's remarks about wine (171, 173) but objects to his ban on sensuality (173).

*the peasants. The priest tells Henry about the generous, humble peasants of the Abruzzi (73).

Peduzzi. A driver in the Italian ambulance service. In October 1917, when Henry returns to Gorizia, Peduzzi drives him to the front-line post at Bainsizza, where Henry relieves Gino. Peduzzi then drives Gino back to Gorizia (175, 185).

*Pfeiffer, G[ustavus] A[dolphus (Gus). Gus was Pauline Pfeiffer Hemingway's uncle. His great wealth came from Sloan's Liniment, the Richard Hudnut line of perfumes, and William Warner Pharmaceuticals. Gus Pfeiffer was extremely generous to his niece and her husband, financing most of their Key West house as well as their safari to Africa (1933–1934). See also endnote 5 in *THHN*.]
Hemingway dedicated *A Farewell to Arms* to G. A. Pfeiffer.

Piani, Luigi. One of the three ambulance drivers under Henry's command during the retreat from Bainsizza to Pordenone, he is a big, rough-spoken man (218). Piani, whom Henry describes as an anarchist (191), is really a socialist (208) who scorns war (217). He does not condemn Bonello for deserting. After losing their equipment, witnessing the death of Aymo and the desertion of Bonello, Piani and Henry are left alone together. They come close to the Germans but "nothing happened" as they walk alone through the night and eventually rejoin the main body of the retreat (218). Henry discovers that when separated from his army comrades Piani "was much gentler" (220). See also Aymo, Bonello, Bonello's family.
Speaks: 189–90, 192–93, 198, 201, 204, 206–11, 213–15, 217–21.

*Piani's family. Piani has a wife (220).

play-acting. See games and play-acting.

police. See battle police.

*police. Simmons wonders if Henry is "fleeing the police" and correctly informs him that in Switzerland he will "just have to report" to them (241). In Switzerland, Henry and Catherine are told "to report to the police" of whatever city they go to (282), although this is just a formality (283).

*the Pope [Benedict XV. Secular name: Giacomo della Chiesa, 1854–1922; Pope from 1914 to 1922. Benedict XV strove to maintain a neutral stance during World War I, refusing to condemn either side but tacitly condoning German and Austrian infractions of international law. Benedict's attempt at neutrality, in itself repugnant to both sides, was seen by the Allies and in particular by the Italians, as support for the Austrians. In addition, most Cardinals of the Church were pro-Austrian, increasing the Allies' antipathy for the Church's position. During Benedict's reign the prestige of the Papacy declined, and he was excluded from the peace negotiations.]

To aggravate the Italian priest, the Major voices the generally held opinion that the Church supports the enemy (7; see Franz Joseph).

porta feriti. See stretcher-bearers.

*the porter. Henry imagines taking Catherine to a hotel in Milan. The imagined scene is full of details, including a subservient porter and a *concierge* (37; see *men and boys).

the porter's wife. She is a matronly woman (146) who did Henry's mending when he was in the American Hospital. Like her husband, she claims to be fond of Henry, cries when he leaves for the front, and embraces him happily when he returns to Milan after the retreat and his defection (240).
    Speaks: 146, 240.

porters. Like orderlies and *concierges* (qq.v.), porters do a number of odd jobs. A porter at the American Hospital in Milan sends Henry and the stretcher-bearers up in the elevator, meets them upstairs, and receives a tip; he "was very kind" (83). He buys wine and newspapers for Henry (87, 95), gets rid of the empty bottles (143), finds him a barber (90), and holds a seat on the train for him (146, 158; see the machine-gunner, who also accepts a tip from Henry). The porter is happy when Henry returns to Milan, tells him where Catherine is, promises not to tell anyone he has seen Henry, and refuses a tip (239–40). When the lovers abandon Stresa, the "second porter" at the Grand Hotel supplies an umbrella and innocently entreats them not to "stay out in the storm" (267); another porter offers assistance at the train station in Milan, where it is also raining (157; see the night-watchman).
    Speak: 82–83, 91, 159, 239–40, 267.

*the priest. A French priest, jailed for embezzling, is the subject of an "informative" anecdote told by Rocca (39). When Barkley is dying, Henry offers to call a priest (330).

priests. In the field hospital, a priest is called in to give last rites to a dying solder (74). Henry is friendly with the unnamed young priest who serves in his outfit in Gorizia; he calls him "father" (68–70), although only out of "politeness" (72). This priest defines his love of God in terms of service and self-sacrifice (72), and predicts that Henry will come to love like that. He good-naturedly tolerates the officers' crude jokes, brings the wounded Henry several thoughtfully chosen presents (see *The News of the World*), and writes him "a dull letter" when Henry is recuperating in Milan (135). He differentiates between officers and patriots ("people who would make war") and others, like the drivers and himself, "who would not make war" (71; see the mechanics). After the difficult summer, the priest seems older and more confident (177–78). His traditional wisdom is contrasted both with Rinaldi's secular pessimism and with Count Greffi's philosophical acceptance of life. One of the most clearly retrospective passages in the novel involves Henry's recognition that he eventually managed to learn, and to forget, what the priest "had always known" (14; also see endnote 23). The priest is associated with the pure, cold mountains.

Speaks: 7–9, 13–14, 38–39, 68–73, 173–80.

*the priest's family. His father, "a famous hunter" (9; see also 73) is still alive; his mother seems to have died long ago (72). The priest assures Henry that his family would be happy to have him as their guest in the beautiful mountain region of Abruzzi; Henry does not accept the invitation (13). The mountains of Switzerland where he and Catherine love each other and are happy recall the idyllic Abruzzi family life offered by the priest. See also *the peasants.

the professor. An ineffective boxing teacher. Henry amuses himself by "occasionally scaring the professor" during the boxing lessons he takes from him in Lausanne (311).

the proprietor of the wine shop in Milan. A sharp fellow, he realizes that Henry is a deserter and offers to sell him false papers (237–39).

Speaks: 237–39.

*prostitutes. See *women and girls.

Rinaldi (Rinaldo, Rinaldo Purissimo, Rinaldo Sporchissimo, Rinin). A handsome young Italian surgeon in Henry's outfit at Gorizia; he holds the rank of lieutenant (11).[31] He is Henry's roommate and friend; they drink and joke easily together. Rinaldi has a lively mind: we see him reading and studying (17, 27; also see *Black Pig*). Henry acknowledges that Rinaldi, like the priest, is wiser than he is (170), but whereas the

priest's wisdom is generous and optimistic (72). Rinaldi insists that progress is impossible, that people cannot become wiser (171). Rinaldi jokes that of the three things he likes (liquor, sex, and his work), the first is harmful and the second short-lived (170); only the work gives real satisfaction (170). He defines himself as "All fire and smoke and nothing inside" (66). Although he claims to have no principles, he risks arrest by refusing to carry a gun (29) and not only renounces Catherine Barkley (with whom he claims to be in love) when she and Henry become interested in each other, but even helps Henry court her, sobering him up before he goes to visit her (40). But because Rinaldi is given to levity, it is difficult to define his feelings or convictions. Rinaldi visits Henry twice in the field hospital (63, 75) and writes him in Milan (136). When Henry returns to Gorizia in the fall of 1917 Rinaldi looked "a little thinner" (166); he is "very tired and over-worked" and suffering from syphilis (175). After he deserts, Henry thinks of Rinaldi rather often (233, 298, 327). See also Caruso, *The Lancet,* and salvarsan.
    Speaks: 7–9, 11–13, 17, 20–21, 27, 32, 37, 39–41, 63–67, 75–77, 166–75.

Rinaldo, Rinin. The priest's nicknames for Rinaldi (173–75). Henry also calls him Rinin (169) and Rinaldo Sporchissimo (the dirtiest; 171). Rinaldi calls himself Rinaldo Purissimo (the purest).

Rocca. An Italian officer in Frederic Henry's outfit at Gorizia. He tells one of the several anti-clerical jokes which enliven the officers' mess (39). When Henry returns in the fall, no one mentions him or the others who were killed during the heavy fighting of the summer of 1917.
    Speaks: 39.

Rodgers, Crowell. A young American who, like Henry, is a patient at the American Hospital in Milan (108; also see patients). Rodgers makes friends with Henry and Catherine and, knowing they are lovers, tries not to disturb them at night (108). He goes with them and Ferguson to the horse races at San Siro (127–30). In September he is shipped back to the United States (133).
    Speaks: 130.

*Romulus. [In Roman legend, the founder of Rome. Romulus and his twin brother Remus were the children of Rhea Silvia and the god Mars. Cast adrift in a basket on the Tiber River, they came safely to land, were suckled by a she-wolf, and raised by a farmer. They decided to found a city on the place where they emerged from the Tiber River. Eventually Romulus killed Remus, founded Rome by himself c.750 BCE., enjoyed a long reign, and was worshipped as the god Quirinus after his death.]

After too much wine, someone (probably Henry) discourses on Rome and talks about "Romulus suckling the Tiber" (76).

*Rubens, [Peter Paul. Flemish painter, 1577–1640. Rubens is considered by many as the foremost painter of the Flemish school. He was successful and popular in his own time, established a large studio and with the help of his apprentices produced over 2,000 works, including many large altar pieces. He painted many portraits for the Spanish, French, and English courts. His figures are realistic, sensuous, often heroic, painted in glowing colors.]

Catherine mentions Rubens as she and Henry prepare to back up their story that Catherine is in Switzerland as an art student. Henry characterizes Rubens' figures as "large and fat" (280).

*Ruth, [George Herman] (Babe). [Popular American baseball player, 1895–1948. Babe Ruth pitched for the Boston Red Sox (1914–1919), for whom he won 87 and lost 44 games. He joined the New York Yankees in 1920 as an outfielder; he set many records, including the longstanding ones for most home runs in one season (60 in 1927) and for most home runs in major-league play (714). He is author of *Babe Ruth's Own Book of Baseball* (New York, 1928).]

Henry reads in old American newspapers that Babe Ruth was "then" [i.e., as opposed to now, the time of writing the narrative] pitching for Boston (136; also see endnote 23).

*salvarsan. [Scientific name: arsphenamine. An arsenic-based drug, salvarsan was the first successful treatment of syphilis. It was developed in 1909 by the German bacteriologist Paul Ehrlich and was the standard treatment for syphilis until the discovery of penicillin by Sir Alexander Fleming in 1941. It contains bismuth but not mercury. Mood swings and erratic behavior, such as Rinaldi exhibits in Book III, can be caused by mercury or by the later stages of syphilis. Rinaldi errs by treating himself with mercury. The drug is also mentioned in *FWBT*.]

Rinaldi, who is treating himself for syphilis with mercury, incorrectly defines salvarsan as a "mercurial product" (175; see endnote 31).

Saunders, Edgar. (Professional name: Edouardo Giovanni) [A singer named Edoardo de Giovanni sang at the Scala Opera House on 9 January, 1914 *(Parsifal)* and on 5 February, 1915 *(Loreley)*.][32]

The tenor Saunders is studying singing in Milan. Henry has a drink with him, Simmons, Moretti, and the American vice-consul. Saunders has very little to say; the conversation is dominated by Moretti (120–23).

Speaks: 120–21, 123.

the sergeant-adjutant. See adjutant.

Sergeants from the Engineering Corps. Two sullen Italians who claim that during the retreat they were separated from their unit; Bonello gives them a ride in his ambulance. They are unsavory characters, looting the countryside (Henry makes them return a stolen clock), disobeying orders, and refusing to help their comrades. Henry, who has never killed anyone (94), shoots and wounds one of them. Bonello (q.v.) obtains Henry's permission to kill the wounded sergeant (204; see also 199, 202, 205–6). The other sergeant gets away.
    Speak: 195, 200, 201, 203–4.

Sim. Nickname for Ralph Simmons (123, 241–42).

Simmons, Ralph (Sim. Professional name: Enrico DelCredo). Like Saunders, a tenor studying singing in Milan. He is first presented as an unattractive braggart (120), but when Henry turns to him for help, Simmons speaks honestly (241) and acts generously, giving Henry his own clothes. In this second scene Simmons sounds British; he speaks of "the bloody front," says that Henry is "awfully polite" and calls him "my dear fellow." See Africana and Tosca.
    Speaks: 120–23, 240–42.

sisters. See the virgins.

*Skoda, [Emil von. Czech engineer and industrialist, 1839–1900. Skoda began his career as an engineer in a small machine shop in Pilsen, Czechoslovakia, which he soon acquired. Skoda also bought and built other machine shops and forges, which eventually produced locomotives, turbines, business machines, and heavy armaments such as tanks and guns. The Skoda Works, later called the Tenin Works, became one of the largest steel and armament producers in Europe. The Skoda howitzer is a very short large-caliber howitzer, used, as a mortar is, for firing at troops behind cover.]
    Just before they are wounded, Henry and the mechanics remark that the Austrians "have big Skoda guns" (54).

soldier with the hernia. An unsuccessful Italian deserter. He discarded his truss in order to enlarge the rupture and thus get himself exempted from further military service. Because he has no medical papers Henry cannot pick him up and take him to a hospital, away from the fighting. Henry advises him to "fall down . . . and get a bump on your head" (35), which the soldier does.[33] But by the time Henry comes to pick him up, his own regiment has come back for him. He has been to Pittsburgh

[Pennsylvania], speaks English, and is mistaken for an American by the driver.
　　Speaks: 34–36.

soldiers. In addition to the many soldiers who have names, the novel is crowded with unnamed soldiers and officers (see the English driver, the English major, the British, the Austrians, the Germans, the Italians, Croats, Magyars). Italian soldiers march to the May 1917 attack (45–46), after which many lie wounded or dead at the dressing station (56–57). Outside the field hospital, a soldier prepares crosses to place on graves (75); at the railroad yards outside Verona a soldier gives Henry water and an orange and refuses the penny Henry offers (78). In Milan, the soldiers in the building next to the hospital are so near that Henry can smell their morning coffee and overhear them talking (101–2). Two drunk soldiers sit at the wine bar in Milan (237), and a soldier embraces his girl "tight up against the stone" of the cathedral in Milan (147; see women and girls). The train Henry takes from Milan to the front is crowded with soldiers; Henry argues with a captain who, like himself, is returning to the front after recuperating from a wound (158–59; see also porters and the machine-gunner). A captain receives confusing orders about when the retreat from Caporetto is to begin (187); during the retreat itself, huge masses of Italian soldiers, officers, equipment and civilians are seen (194–199, 218; see also crowds). After he deserts, Henry evades the several Italian soldiers who guard the trains that carry armaments (228–29) as well as the Italian customs guards *(guardia di finanza,* see *alpini)* patrolling Lake Maggiore in a motorboat (276; see also the Swiss navy). A Swiss soldier returns Catherine's wave (277), another carries their bags and waits for a tip (281, 284), and Swiss soldiers arrest Henry and Catherine after breakfast (279; speak: 279–81). See also battle police, crowds, doctors, stretcher-bearers, Swiss lieutenant, Swiss officials, and the wounded.

*soldiers. A few unnamed soldiers are discussed but not seen: Moretti claims that he shot the soldier whose hand-grenade injured him (122). During the trip from Stresa to Switzerland, Henry is afraid to be seen by "a sentry" or by the guards on patrol, but fortunately no such soldiers materialize (276–77).

stretcher-bearers *(porta feriti* in Italian). They carry the wounded men to the medical tent and put them into ambulances to be taken to hospitals (52–53, 55–60, 81–83). There are not enough stretchers for the many wounded (56–57). In Milan, the stretcher-bearers carry Henry into the

hospital; he tips them (81–83). See also doctors and wounded; see also stretcher-bearers in "Under the Ridge" in *Fifth Column.*
   Speak: 81–82.

Swiss civilians. See civilians.

Swiss lieutenant. A lieutenant at the Swiss customs house questions Henry and Catherine, who tell him they are cousins, that they were in Italy as students, and that they have come to Switzerland as tourists, When he sees they are well supplied with money, the lieutenant "became less haughty" (281). He confiscates their boat and sends them to the Swiss officials (q.v.) at Locarno.
   Speaks: 279–81.

*Swiss lieutenant's father. He owns a hotel which his son recommends to Henry and Catherine (281).

*Swiss navy and Swiss troops. Henry remarks that he and Catherine are lucky to have evaded the Swiss navy who patrol Lake Maggiore (276; see soldiers).

Swiss officials. They issue provisional visas to Henry and Catherine (281). Like the Swiss lieutenant, they respect money and each tries to attract Henry and Catherine's trade for his favorite town. As Catherine notices, Switzerland is "so practical" (281). See also soldiers.
   Speak: 282–83.

*Titian. [Tiziano Vecelio. Venetian artist, 1477–1576. This long-lived master painted grand subjects in the grand manner of the High Renaissance. His masterpieces include portraits of high-ranking individuals as well as paintings dealing with pagan and religious subjects, like the *Rape of Europa* and the *Pieta*. He found patrons both in the Church and the royal courts of Europe and was the favorite painter of Holy Roman Emperor Charles V. He is known for his sumptuous coloring, particularly his reds.]
   As she and Henry prepare to back up their story that Catherine is visiting Switzerland in order to study art, Catherine indicates that she has heard of Titian. Henry contributes the adjective "Titian-haired" (280).

"To His Coy Mistress." [Andrew Marvell's witty poem (published posthumously in 1681) is in the form of a logical argument. In the first section the speaker explains that ladylike coyness "were no crime" if the young man had unlimited time for wooing her. The second section, which Henry quotes, is about the quick passage of time: if the lady continues to be coy, happiness will elude them, and then only the "worms shall try / That long-preserved virginity." In the final section the would-be lover urges, therefore, that the lovers should "sport us while we may." Henry appropriately and correctly quotes from the middle section of the poem:

> But at my back I always hear
> Time's winged chariot hurrying near.

The next few lines of the poem (unquoted) anticipate the death of the loved woman and the young man's final action (in Henry's case, the writing of the novel/song:

> And yonder all before us lie
> Deserts of vast eternity.
> Thy beauty shall no more be found,
> Nor, in thy marble vault, shall sound
> My echoing song.]

Henry's quote is precipitated by a honking car (154), the modern equivalent of "Time's winged chariot hurrying near." Marvell's lines are echoed at the end of the idyllic mountain interlude: the lovers feel "as though something were hurrying us" (311).

*Tosca. [The female lead in Giacomo Puccini's popular opera of the same name. The opera was first performed in Rome and London, 1900, and in New York in 1901. Like most of Puccini's operas, it was highly acclaimed from the beginning. The beautiful Floria Tosca is the central figure. The villain of the piece, the policeman Scarpia, lusts after her and plots to kill her lover, Cavaradossi. News of Napoleon's victory over the Austrians at the Battle of Marengo (June 1800) heartens Cavaradossi in Act II. The opera offers two roles for tenors: Cavaradossi and Cavaradossi's friend Angelotti. *Tosca* was performed at the Scala Opera House on 2 February, 1917 and for seven subsequent performances, with Amedeo Bassi as Cavaradossi and Dentale as Angelotti.][34]
    Simmons brags about his performance in *Tosca* and claims that he is scheduled to appear in that opera in Milan, at the Scala Opera House (120). Later he recants the first claim and modifies the second (241).

Valentini, Dr. The surgeon who operates on Henry's knee at the American Hospital in Milan. He holds the rank of major. When the "delicate" house doctor and his two consultants (Varino and Vanella) decide that Henry has to wait six months for an operation, Henry insists on another opinion. The house doctor provides Dr. Valentini, who is cheerful and breezy, flirts with Catherine, drinks with Henry, and offers to operate the next morning. The operation lasts more than two hours and is successful (99–100; see 231; also see doctors).

Speaks: 99–100.

Van Campen. The rather starchy superintendent of the American Hospital in Milan is a snob (86). Because she thinks that Catherine "came from very good people," she accepts the obvious fabrication that Catherine and Henry "were great friends" (118). She does not allow non-prescription alcoholic beverages (86); when she finds empty bottles in Henry's armoire, she accuses him of "producing jaundice with alcoholism" (144) in order to avoid returning to the front, and sees to it that he loses his leave. Not surprisingly, she and Henry dislike each other.

Speaks: 86–87, 143–44.

Vanella, Dr. The more talkative of the two doctors whom the house doctor of the American Hospital consults about Henry's knee. He has a beard, holds the rank of first captain, and is extremely cautious; he wants to wait six months before operating on Henry's knee (96). Henry rejects this doctor and demands another opinion (98).

Speaks: 95–97.

Varino, Dr. One of the two doctors with whom the house doctor of the American Hospital in Milan consults in order to determine treatment for Henry's knee. He carries the X-rays but does not contribute an opinion during the consultation (96–98). He holds the rank of captain (see endnote 31).

Speaks: 96.

vice. [Catherine's progress from feeling "like a whore" in the gaudy Milan hotel room to feeling at home in it and describing it as "fine" and "lovely" (152–53) recalls Alexander Pope's remarks:

> Vice is monster of so frightful mien,
> As, to be hated, needs but to be seen;
> Yet seen too oft, familiar with her face,
> We first endure, then pity, then embrace.

(*Essay on Man,* II.217–220); see also Pope in "The Sea Change," *Winner Take Nothing.)*]

Catherine reports that "Vice is a wonderful thing" (153).

the virgins. During the retreat Aymo offers a ride to two frightened teen-age sisters; they nod when asked if they are virgins. They speak "a dialect" but understand "the vulgar word" Aymo uses; it reduces them to tears (195, 196). When he can no longer help them, Henry gives them money and sends them off (199, 200, 202, 205–6; see also the sergeants from the engineering corps.).

*V.E. soldiers. [The initials refer to King Vittorio Emanuele I, who established the *carabinieri* (q.v.)]
   Discussing the disaffection evinced by the majority of Italian troops, the mechanics mention the few militaristic units, among them the *alpini* and "These V.E. soldiers" (49).

*Vittorio Emanuele [III, 1869–1947; king of Italy, 1900–1946. A member of the royal house of Savoy, rulers of Sardinia under whom Italy achieved unification (see Cavour). Vittorio Emanuele III ascended to the throne when his father, Umberto I, was assassinated at Monza on 29 July, 1900. He was King of Italy during both World Wars. During World War I he spent much of his time near the front. When the Austrians broke through at Caporetto, the King urged that the Italian army retreat no further than the Piave River. Some military historians argue that his refusal to retreat any further was instrumental in convincing England and France to transfer support troops from the western front to the Italian lines.
   Vittorio Emanuele III was unable to check Mussolini's rise to power, and although he arrested Mussolini in 1943 and named his son Umberto lieutenant governor in 1944, he could not preserve the monarchy, which was defeated in a plebiscite in 1946, at which point both Vittorio Emanuele and his son went into exile.[35] See also Aosta.]
   In contrast with the large Germans and their imposing equipment, the King of Italy is consistently described as a small, unimpressive man (36; see also 4, 6) who rides by quickly in unimpressive cars (4).[36] Henry considers him to be an ineffectual leader. Bonello jokes that he will "sleep in the king's bed" and "with the queen" (192).

waiters. An unnamed and sometimes unseen waiter brings two bottles of wine and a good meal to Henry and Barkley's room in the hotel in Milan; the good food makes them feel "fine" and the wine soon makes the vulgar room "fine . . . lovely . . . nice . . . splendid" (153; see vice). He calls for a carriage, holds an umbrella over them when they enter it, and accepts a tip (156–57; see manager). A waiter at the hotel in Stresa brings drinks and meals (308–9) during their three-week stay there. At the hotel in Lausanne a waiter brings drinks and dinner (309–310). At the café near the hospital in Lausanne, an old man behind the bar serves

Henry an early breakfast (315; see also 318) and a middle-aged waiter with "a kind face" serves him a late lunch and dinner (318, 328–29). See also Emilio.

Speak: 157, 310, 315, 318, 328–29.

waitress. A "splendid clean-looking woman" serves Henry and Catherine their first meal in Switzerland (278–79).

Speaks: 278.

Walker, Mrs. The elderly nurse at the American Hospital in Milan is defined in negatives: she is unprepared and unwilling to receive Henry, who is the first patient to arrive at the hospital. She can't read his papers because she doesn't know Italian, she can't make up a bed for him because she doesn't have the keys to the supply rooms, and she can't offer him treatment because the doctor isn't there. Eventually Henry takes command of the situation; in her frustration and helplessness, Mrs. Walker cries. Later that day she helps Miss Van Campen make the bed (85).

Speaks: 82–83.

watchman. See the night-watchman.

*weapons. Sabers and swords, employed in one-to-one combat, are associated with romance and the picturesque (20, 149), attitudes made obsolete by World War I.[37] The cruel present is dominated by more impersonal weapons like pistols (149, 204), rifles (219), and anti-aircraft guns (101–2). See also Skoda.

["Western Wind." Anonymous medieval lyric: "Westron wind, when will thou blow?/ The small rain down can rain./ Christ, that my love were in my arms,/ And I in my bed again." Frederic Henry's line, "Blow her again to me" (197), may derive from Tennyson's long poem "The Princess, A Medley" (1847), which contains the line "Blow him again to me." Charles R. Anderson also finds traces from the prayer, "Now I lay me down to sleep" ("Hemingway's Other Style," in Baker, *Critiques;* see also Benson, 109–10). Another possible source is Walt Whitman's poem, "Out of the Cradle Endlessly Rocking," written in 1859 and included in a section entitled *Sea-Drift* in the 1881 edition of *Leaves of Grass*. In the poem, the speaker cries: "Blow! blow! blow! / Blow up sea-winds along Paumanok's shore; / I wait and I wait till you blow my mate to me" (ll. 52–54). Thomas Hudson quotes from "Western Wind" *(Islands,* 413–14).]

Frederic Henry quotes parts of "Western Wind" (or some other poem) to himself when he longs for Catherine (197).

162 Reading Hemingway

*the White Sox. [The Chicago White Sox, a professional American baseball team, have been associated with the American League since it was recognized in 1901, in which year they won the first League championship. They won the World Series in 1906 and 1917. See *the White Sox in *OMS,* the action of which occurs after the great White Sox scandal of 1919. Lewis points out "that at the time of Frederic's retrospectively writing his story, the 1917 White Sox had become the Black Sox of 1919" *(The War of the Words,* 120–21.]

In late September, 1917, Henry reads in the old American newspapers at the hospital that this team was winning its league's pennant (136; see also *the Giants).

wife. Although they are not married, Henry calls Barkley his wife (245 *et passim,* see 294, 315; see also 221, 232) and she considers herself married (e.g., 154, 315). Catherine encourages the doctor, the hairdresser, and the Guttingens to think she and Henry are married (294, 293, 307); she calls herself Catherine Henry when she checks herself into the hospital (313), where she is called Mrs. Henry (321, 330, 331), Madame Henry (316, 326), and Madame (314, 327; see also 307). The narrative contains several married women, among them Mrs. Cunningham, Mrs. Guttingen, Mrs. Meyers, the porter's wife, and the absent Mrs. Piani (see *Piani's family). The text does not indicate whether Mrs. Walker is married or a widow; the Mrs. may be honorary. See also husband.

*Wilson, [Thomas Woodrow. American professor and politician, 1856–1924; 28th President of the United States, 1913–1921. Wilson was awarded the Nobel Peace Prize (1919) for advocating the establishment of a League of Nations.]

The English driver tells the Italians that Henry is Wilson's son in order to get preferential treatment for him when he is wounded (58).

women and girls. The novel presents only a few unnamed women. In Milan, a woman runs the armorer's shop where Henry buys a gun (148–49). Catherine and Henry see a soldier and his girl embracing (147) and later assume the same position (150), wrapped in his cape as they stand against a wall. A girl sweeps in the early morning (81), another girl waits at table in Stresa (249). Two giggling girls have their silhouettes cut out; Henry follows their example (135, see men and boys). In Lausanne, a woman admits Catherine to the hospital (313–14), and another woman works in the café near the hospital (318). See wife and the virgins.

Speak: 148–49, 313–14.

*women and girls. Prostitutes are talked about but not seen. In addition to the prostitutes in Milan and other large cities, there are two bordellos (one for officers, one for enlisted men) at Gorizia. The officers talk of prostitutes and sexual adventures (5–6, 8–9, 11–13, 64–65). The prostitutes are evacuated during the retreat from Caporetto (188–89). At the garish hotel in Milan, Catherine feels briefly "like a whore" (152, 294). She asks Henry about the women he slept with before he met her (105, 115, 299) and recognizes realistically that he will have "another girl" after she has died (331).[38]

woodcutters. During their long wintry walks, Henry and the pregnant Catherine stop to rest and drink hot wine at an inn which is favored by the local woodcutters and by a chamois hunter who sports gold earrings (302–3; also see beards).

*Woolworth, [Frank Winfield. American merchant, 1852–1919. Woolworth founded the successful national chain of five-and-ten-cent stores that bears his name. The Woolworth building, designed by Cass Gilbert and completed in 1913, is sixty stories high (779 feet). It is located at Broadway and Park Place, New York City, and was, at the time of the action, the tallest office building in the world, a distinction which passed to the Chrysler Building (77 stories, 1,046 feet tall) when it was finished in 1929.]
  Catherine, who would like to visit the United States and see Niagara Falls and the Golden Gate Bridge, is not interested in the Woolworth Building or the Chicago stockyards (295).

*World Almanac [and Book of Facts. Annual guide which began publication in 1868 and is still a popular reference work today.]
  Catherine consults the World Almanac to find out about her and the child's status under American law: the Almanac tells her that when she and Henry marry, she will become an American citizen and the child will be legitimate (294).

the wounded. Many wounded and dying soldiers appear in the narrative (60, 61, 74–75, 77, 186; see 187). See also stretcher-bearers.

Young Catherine. Catherine and Henry variously refer to their unborn child as a boy who may grow up to be a general (141) or a jockey (293), and as a girl named Young Catherine (157, 293, 304, 306, 307). In his dream, Henry refers to the baby as "he" (197). The baby, a boy, is stillborn (324–27). See children and the nurse.

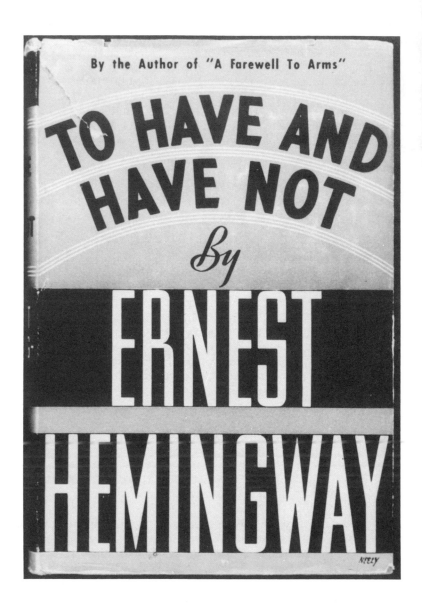

Scribner dust jacket for the first edition of *To Have and Have Not* (courtesy Charles Scribner's Sons, an imprint of the Macmillan Publishing Company; and of the Hemingway Collection, J. F. Kennedy Library)

CHAPTER IV

TO HAVE AND HAVE NOT

(1937)

The action takes place in Havana, Cuba, and Key West in 1933–1934 (see *Machado and *Roosevelt). Although it is often defined as a (failed) novel of social protest, *To Have and Have Not* contains remarkably few references to contemporary historical figures or to current events.[1]

Adams, Captain Willie. A nice old man who earns his living as Morgan used to: by taking amateur fishermen out on his boat, the *South Florida*. A local man (i.e., a Conch), Willie protects Morgan, who has turned to rum-running, from the Washington politicians (Harrison and his secretary, Willis, qq.v.) he has on board. Morgan describes him as "a good skate" (77, 86). In spite of Adams' help, Morgan's boat is impounded.
Speaks: 77–79, 82–84.

Al. Morgan's nickname for Tracy (144).

Albert. See Tracy, Albert.

*Allen, Gracie. [Full name: Grace Ethel Cecile Rosalie Allen. American comedienne, c. 1895–1964. Gracie Allen started her career as part of an Irish sisters act. With straight-man George Burns, who became her partner in 1923 and her husband in 1926, she played "Dumb Dora" and "Lamb Chops" in a fast, funny, popular cross-talk act. Burns and Allen performed in theatres (1926–1932), had their own long-lived radio show, "Burns and Allen" (1932–1949), and made several movies, including *Big Broadcast* (1932), *College Swing* (1938), *Honolulu* (1939), and *Two Girls and a Sailor* (1944). They were successful on television as well, with a long-running show on CBS. Gracie Allen retired in 1958.[2] See also Burns, George in "My Old Man," *In Our Time*.]

Relaxing at home after his first illegal adventure, during which he killed one Chinaman and cheated twelve others, Morgan listens to Gracie Allen on the radio (64).

Alzira III. Yacht owned by the rich, virtuous, and happy family gently satirized at the end of the novel (239–40).

*Bach, [Johann Sebastian. German organist and composer, 1685–1750. See *ARIT.* A sarabande is a dance or dance tune.]
Wallace Johnston has his steward play a recording of a Bach "Sarabande" (228, 230–31).

*Baldwin, Stanley. [British politician, 1867–1947. From 1881 to 1885 Baldwin was at Harrow (established 1571), one of England's great public (i.e., private) schools. He then went to Trinity College, Cambridge, earning his B.A. in 1888. Exclusive schools like Harrow and Cambridge provide valuable connections and easy access to power; their alumni tend to keep in touch with each other and with their *alma mater.* After graduation, Baldwin managed his family's companies for twenty years, not entering the House of Commons until 1908. He was the leader of the Conservative party from 1923 to 1937, serving as Prime Minister three times during that period, which includes the time of the action of the novel. He was created first Earl of Bewdley in 1937.]
The users of the tonic manufactured by the father (q.v.) are as grateful and "as loyal to it as . . . Stanley Baldwin is to Harrow" (240; see also Tompkins).

bartenders. The novel presents three nameless bartenders, one at Freddy's (202–3, 209) and two at the Lilac Time (194). The narrative identifies Freddy's bartender as "nigger" (202) and "Negro" (203, 209); Joey calls him "that big boogie" (209). Freddy Wallace and the proprietor of the Lilac Time (qq.v.) also tend bar.
Speaks: 209.

*Bates. The maid of Dorothy Hollis (242).

Bee-lips. See Simmons, Robert.

Big Boy, Big Shot. Simmons' mocking epithets for Morgan (130, 132).

Big Lucie's daughter. She comes into Freddy's bar with another girl; they may be prostitutes (93; see women and girls).

Big Rodger. See Rodger.

blacks ("niggers"). [The widespread prejudice against blacks, Chinese, Jews, and other minorities results in the characters' and narrator's unselfconscious use of offensive epithets like "nigger," "chink" and "mick" (186). The word "nigger" is particularly prominent, appearing on almost every page of chapter 1 (narrated by Morgan) and chapters 6 and 8 (third person narration); an interesting variant is "niggery looking" (249). Occasionally the word "Negro" is used: see bartenders and fisherman. Also see Chinese and Jews.]

Wesley (q.v.) is identified as "the nigger" (67 ff), as are the man whom Morgan hires to help with the bait (10 ff), the man who shoots Pancho and his two companions (6–8), the bartender at Freddy's (202) and most of the black characters in the novel (see men and boys, *men and boys).

the bouncer. See Wallace.

Bradley, Helene. A rich, lustful, aging beauty with a penchant for writers (150; see also 139). She slaps Richard Gordon when he cannot continue making love to her in the presence of her husband (188–90).
   Speaks: 189–90.

Bradley, Tommy. Helene's rich, fat husband likes to give parties in their "big winter home" in Key West. He condones and even observes his wife's infidelities (189; see also 229).

the broker. Unaware that Morgan is planning to transport Chinamen illegally, the broker arranges clearance for Harry's boat (28, 36, 39). Although Morgan told him that he intends to make the crossing to the United States alone, the broker later adds Eddy Marshall's name to the crew list, thus unwittingly saving Eddy's life (61–62; see 40).

Cap. Eddy Marshall's nickname for Harry Morgan (24, 25); also Adams' title for Harrison, who has rented his boat and his services for the day (78).

Cappie, Cappy. Roberto's nickname for Morgan (152, 155–57, 159–60).

Captain. Johnson calls Morgan "Captain" but treats him as a servant (22). Sing also calls Morgan "Captain" (34; see also Coast Guard officers).

Carpenter, Henry. Johnston's "temperamental" (231) and occasionally compliant homosexual companion. He lives off his diminishing trust fund and his charm. He eventually commits suicide (227–33).
   Speaks: 228–31.

*Carpenter, Mrs. She established a trust fund for her son Henry which the bank has mismanaged (232).

the chauffeur. See the driver.

*Chicha, Chicha's. She runs an establishment [probably a house of prostitution] in the poor section of Key West (193).

Chief. Marshall's nickname for Harry Morgan (52).

the Chinese ("Chinks"). [During much of its colonial history, Cuba imported Chinese as well as black African slaves to work the sugar and tobacco plantations. Importation of slaves from China had ceased by 1871, and slavery was outlawed in 1886. Because illegal Chinese immigrants provide cheap labor on the mainland, the smuggling of Chinese has become profitable and the lives of the Chinese have become cheap. Morgan usually refers to the people and their language as "chink" (chapter 4 *et passim*) and believes they have a peculiar smell (58, 61); he objects to Eddy Marshall's calling them "yellow rat-eating aliens" (57). See blacks and *women and girls; also see Chinese in *Islands*.]

In his first excursion into illegal activity, Morgan makes a deal with the crooked Mr. Sing (q.v.), who hires him to transport twelve Chinese men from Cuba to Tortugas, where Sing had falsely told them they would be picked up by a schooner, presumably for transport to the United States. The men have been charged a hefty fee by Sing, who has no intention of providing the transportation he has promised them. Morgan's role in the scam is to take the Chinese out in his boat and then get rid of them. Morgan takes his cut from Sing ($100 a head), loads the unfortunate men into his boat, kills Sing and returns the twelve Chinese to Cuba. He keeps their money (51–58).

Speaks: 57–58.

Coast Guard officers and men (Captain and mate). [On the southwestern corner of Key West is a U.S. Coast Guard Base, Fort Zachary Taylor (built 1844–1846, named after the U.S. President). A U.S. Naval Station was established at Key West in 1823; see watchman.]

The waters around Key West are patrolled by a Coast Guard boat and airplane (156–58, 162). Towards the end of the novel, the Coast Guard finds and tows in Freddy Wallace's boat, the *Queen Conch,* with its cargo of four dead Cubans, their guns, and bags of stolen money; they transfer Morgan to their own boat. Concerned with the legal aspects of the events, the Captain and his mate reassure the sheriff that except for shifting two of the bodies (248), they have not tampered with the

contents of the boat.[3] They are unable to understand Morgan's last words (224–25) and incorrectly assume that the Cubans shot each other over "how to split the money" (250). Two Coast Guardsmen jump into the water to rescue Mrs. Tracy (252). The dead bodies are "covered with Coast Guard blankets" (253).
    Speak: 223–26, 247–50, 253.

*Colt, [Samuel. American firearms manufacturer and inventor, 1814–1862. Colt patented a breech-loading pistol in Europe (1835) and in America (1836). In 1848 he opened his noted arms factory in Hartford, Connecticut. Colt revolvers were widely used in opening the American West.]
    During the Depression, many failed businessmen shot themselves with this gun (238; see Smith and Wesson).

Conch, Conchs. [A conch is "The spiral, one-piece shell of certain sea mollusks," most of which are edible. In colloquial usage, the word refers to "an inhabitant of the Bahamas and other neighboring islands" (*Webster's New Twentieth Century Dictionary, Unabridged,* 2nd ed., 1956). According to McLendon, the inhabitants of Key West are called Conchs because "their forefathers had in essence said that they could survive on conch meat for the sake of their beliefs"; McLendon does not define these beliefs. Less flatteringly, he also defines "Conchs" as "end-of-the-liners who wanted to be left alone" (*Papa,* 157, 73). In *THHN* the word seems to refer to the year-round inhabitants of Key West, most of them poor, as opposed to "the winter people" (262) like the Bradleys and Laughtons.]
    The native population of Key West, hit hard by the Depression, is denigrated by others and by themselves (27, 96, 98, 156, 193 *et passim*). In the context of their poverty, honesty is a luxury although, as Morgan recognizes, some "Conchs" refuse to steal (148). Morgan enjoys the solidarity and protection offered by fellow Key Westers, who stand with him against threatening outsiders like the customs men (118; see 43) and the big shots from Washington (82–83; see Adams).

the consul. [An American official in Cuba, he obtains permission for American boats to work in Cuban waters.]
    Morgan paid the consul for processing and clearing his boat so he could take his customer, Mr. Johnson, out fishing (9; see also delegate).

the cooler. One of the veterans (q.v.). He "cools" or calms his violent fellows by knocking them out (204–5; see also Slappy and Wallace).

crowds. The bars at Key West are usually crowded at night (194, 200). The bar-restaurant in Havana (the Pearl of San Francisco Café) attracts

customers who eat, drink, and play dominoes (30). Crowds are often associated with violence: one crowd is drawn to the Pearl (Perla) Café, scene of the shoot-out at the beginning of the book (8); the crowd at Freddy's bar drinks and fights (200–19; also see the veterans); and many people gather to see the bullet-riddled bodies of Morgan and the Cubans brought ashore (227–28, 242, 250–54; see *Isleño;* see also crowds in *SAR, FWBT* and *GE.*).
   Speaks: 251–52.

Cubans. [The military dictatorship of Fulgencio Batista (q.v. in *Islands*) has engendered much illegal activity among the Cubans, and Morgan, who is generally unsympathetic to Cubans and their revolution (164, 168) is slowly drawn into it. Both he and Marie blame Cubans for his bad luck (86, 148, 258, 260). Because they speak Spanish, Cubans are sometimes identified as Spanish (39) or *gallegos* (from the Spanish province of Galicia, 30, 49).]
   Three Cubans who are in political trouble try to hire Morgan to transport them out of Cuba; they are killed in a shoot-out (3–8; also see Pancho). A young Cuban sculls for Mr. Sing (50–53, 63). Four Cuban revolutionaries rob a bank at Key West and hire Morgan to transport them to Cuba: they are Roberto, Emilio (qq.v.), and two nameless men who speak only Spanish and are seasick on the boat. Morgan shoots all four; one of them manages to wound Morgan fatally. Most of the crowd (q.v.) waiting at the pier are Cubans. See also men and boys.
   Speak: 3–5, 100–3, 152, 155–58, 162–69.

*Cubans. Emilio mentions the Cuban peasants, who suffer under the present political regime, and the Cuban army, whose members "suck the blood from the nation" (166–67).

*Custer, [George Armstrong. American army officer, 1836–1876. Custer was killed fighting the Sioux Indians in the battle at Little Big Horn. This battle was the subject of a famous lithograph distributed by Anheuser-Busch to taverns and beer-sellers throughout the country, to advertise the company's major product, Budweiser beer. The lithograph, prepared by F. Otto Becker (1854–1945), was based on Cassilly Adams' large (16'5" by 9'6") canvas entitled "Custer's Last Fight." Becker, who relied more heavily on Adams' working sketches than on the finished painting, "produced a much smaller painting . . . and one considerably different in detail from Adams'."[4] See also "Custer" and "Anheuser-Busch" in *FWBT.*]
   A picture of Custer's Last Stand against the Indians adorns Freddy's bar at Key West (123).

the Customs House Officers. [During Prohibition (1920–1933) the production, transportation and sale of liquor were illegal. At the time of the action of the novel, Prohibition had been repealed and liquor was legal, but imported spirits had to go through U.S. customs. Harry attempts to take liquor from Cuba to the United States without going through customs and paying import duties.]

After Morgan's failed attempt to smuggle rum from Cuba to Key West, Customs impounds his boat. In order to transport the four Cuban bank robbers and their stolen money from Key West to Cuba, Morgan steals back his own boat; the next morning, two Customs men question him about it (118–19). Although Morgan denies all knowledge of the boat's present whereabouts, it is quickly found and impounded again (120).

Speak: 118–19.

the delegate. A government official in Cuba who takes bribes and does not notice the illegal transfer of the Chinese, which takes place quite near his house (49–50).

*dentists. They have their offices in Key West (194).

the deputy (the sheriff's deputy). See Johnson, Roger.

the dockmaster. At the sheriff's request, he arranges to light up the Coast Guard pier when the wounded Morgan is brought ashore (248).

Speaks: 248.

doctor. He waits at the Coast Guard pier for the wounded to be brought in (247) and later informs Marie that Morgan has died (254, 256; see also 260). Although not a physician, Harrison (q.v.) is also a doctor (79); because of his many degrees he is referred to as "this big alphabet man" (83).

Speaks: 247, 254, 256.

*the doctor. When they are wounded, Wesley and Morgan wish for a doctor (72, 85, 86); later, Morgan mentions the doctor who amputated his arm (92). The grain broker (q.v.) disregards his doctor's advice that he abstain from liquor for three months (233, 238).

Donovan, Donovan's. [Fuentes describes this as well as other Cuban locales visited by Morgan. He reports that Donovan's was a disreputable Cuban bar and that "The building where Donovan's was housed has long since been demolished" (*Hemingway in Cuba*, 95–96).]

Waiting in Havana for Johnson to pay him for three weeks' charter of his boat, Morgan has a drink at Donovan's and talks "with the old man" (presumably Donovan himself) who tells him that Eddy Marshall and Johnson had been drinking there together the previous evening (26; see Hatuey).

driver. One of the men who shoots the three young Cubans at the beginning of the novel wears "a chauffeur's white duster"; he is shot by Pancho (6–7). The taxi driver who takes the armed Cubans from the bank they have just robbed to Morgan's boat is not killed by the gunmen; instead, they cut his belt and pants and leave him on the dock in his underwear (152–53; see 133–34). Another taxi driver picks up MacWalsey and the beat-up Gordon in front of Freddy's bar and convinces MacWalsey that Gordon can find his own way home (219–22; see also Jesús).
    Speaks: 219–21.

Eddie. One of the satirized idle rich on board the yachts at the pier to which the unconscious Morgan and the dead Cubans are towed. He is big, handsome, married to a rich woman, and too drunk to satisfy his lover, Dorothy Hollis (241).

*Eddie's wife and in-laws. They are wealthy (241; see also *the grain broker's family).

Eddy. See Marshall, Eddy (Eddie).

Emilio. One of the four Cuban revolutionaries who rob a bank in Key West to finance their movement (see *Machado). Emilio is sober (169), soft-spoken, young (100), and confusedly idealistic, claiming to "hate terrorism" while engaging in armed robbery and murder (167). His earnest attempts to justify the revolution do not convince Morgan (168). The fact that Roberto allows Emilio, who is ignorant about sailing (159), to steer the boat indicates to Morgan that the Cubans are off guard and not, as he had feared, plotting to take over the boat. Emilio is the first to be killed by Morgan.
    Speaks: 100, 102–3, 155–58, 163–69.

*the Esthonians (Intrepid Voyagers). [Estonia was conquered by Russia early in the 18th century, proclaimed its independence in 1918 and signed a peace treaty with Russia in 1920. In 1934 President Konstantin Pats canceled the small country's democratic institutions and assumed dictatorial powers. In 1939 the country's military bases were taken over by the USSR, and Estonia became one of the Soviet republics in 1940. In 1934 the population was 1.1 million.]

The narrative mentions but does not show two of the 324 sailor-journalists who travel and send home reports on the state of the world. They are sun-burned, happy, well-paid, and indifferent to the poverty and violence around them. Their columns are popular back home (240–41).

the father. The "generous, sympathetic, understanding" paterfamilias of the rich, "pleasant, dull and upright" (238) storybook-happy family who are mocked by Hemingway. His wealth comes from an over-priced but effective tonic (240).[5] In contrast to the crafty, worried grain broker (q.v.), this honest, exceedingly virtuous manufacturer sleeps soundly at night (239). He is oblivious to the misery and poverty around him (see also Frances, the mother, and Tompkins).

*F.E.R.A. man. [Man working for the Federal Emergency Relief Administration; see *Roosevelt.]
Mrs. Laughton (q.v.) is so unattractive that only "a writer or a F.E.R.A. man [would] have a wife look like that" (137).[6]

fisherman. A black fisherman is headed for the fish market with his unprofitable catch of grunt (143).

*fishermen. As he explains fishing techniques to Johnson, Morgan cites the professional "market fishermen" (18).

Frances. The "lovely" daughter of the exaggeratedly virtuous, rich, and dull family, she innocently dreams of her fiancé, unaware of the dead and dying have-nots who are being towed to the pier nearby (239; see also the father, the mother, and Tompkins).

Frankie. An old friend of Morgan's, he hangs around the docks in Havana, unemployed and usually drunk (28; see also 26). When Morgan's customer, Johnson, leaves Cuba without paying him, the desperate Morgan asks Frankie (who, although deaf, seems to hear Morgan perfectly well) for help. Delighted to be asked, Frankie immediately arranges Morgan's deal with Mr. Sing and thus facilitates Morgan's descent into illegal activity.
Speaks: 27–30, 35–36, 39–40.

Freddy, Freddy's. See Wallace, Freddy.

*Friedrichs, Herman. He tells Bee-lips that Customs officials have found and seized Morgan's boat (120).

gallegos. [People from the province of Galicia in north-west Spain, facing the Atlantic Ocean. Galicia is divided into four districts: La Coruña, Lugo, Orense, and Pontevedra. Because the mountainous area offers little arable land, Galicians have migrated to the New World in such large numbers that in Latin America people of Spanish descent are sometimes called *gallegos* even if they or their ancestors came from a different section of Spain. For their language, see *gallegos* in *FWBT*.]

The narrative refers to *gallegos* twice (30, 49).

*Garrison, Garrison Bight. [A "bight" is "a bend or small bay between two points of land . . . a curve in a river, coast line, etc." (*Webster's New Twentieth Century Dictionary, Unabridged,* 2nd ed., 1956). The bight on the northern shore of Key West received its name not from a person but from its connection to the Army post that "was established in 1831 and was the only thing on that part of the island . . . the army barracks site is now known as Peary Court."[7] McLendon mentions the "Garrison Bight charterboat anchorage" where, in Hemingway's time, the fishermen on "charterboats . . . daily brought their prizes in to hang on racks" (*Papa,* 130, 26; also see 53). The Garrison Bight still docks charter boats.]

When he is injured, Morgan takes his boat to the Garrison Bight (85, 86). Later, with the Cubans aboard, he recalls a speedboat currently at the Garrison Bight (155; see *Ray).

Genghis Khan. [Mongol conqueror of central Asia, 1167–1227.]

The lascivious Mrs. Laughton comments that Morgan resembles Genghis Khan (136). Marie Morgan also admires her husband's "broad mongol cheek bones" (128).

girls. See women and girls.

*G men. [Government men, FBI agents; see Hoover.]

The deferential Willis flatters his boss by telling him that he can capture criminals single-handedly, without the help of federal agents (82).

Gordon, Helen (Sweetheart). Introduced halfway through the novel, she is part of a secondary plot which does not involve Morgan. A Catholic, she married Gordon against her family's wishes, and apparently not in the Church; at his insistence she has disobeyed the Church's ban on contraception and abortion (186; see endnote 1). She insults him angrily and announces that she is leaving him to marry MacWalsey. She is beautiful (138; see endnote 6).

Speaks: 138–41, 176, 182–88, 190–92.

*Gordon, Helen's parents. They were poor, Irish and Catholic, and objected to Gordon, a non-believer who refused to be married in the Church. Her father, a boiler-maker, drank, got into fights, and was unfaithful to his wife, but even so, Helen considers him a better man than her husband Richard (185, 187).

Gordon, Richard (Dick). One of the more successfully presented characters in the novel, Helen's husband is a tanned, handsome second-rate novelist. He is writing his fourth book, about "a strike in a textile plant" (196, 209; see endnote 1). Three characters in *THHN* comment on Gordon's books: Nelson Jacks, the intellectual Communist, describes them as "shit" (210); Joey, who hasn't read them, opines that they are "fine" (210); and Herbert Spellman, who is deranged, "liked them all" (195). Gordon uses his profession as an excuse for self-indulgence, claiming that his long hours in the bars of Key West and his affair with Helene Bradley supply material he needs for his writing (140). But the novel shows that he misreads Marie Morgan (176–77) and has failed his wife. Richard Gordon is attacked physically as well as verbally; he is slapped twice by Helene (189–90) and beaten up by Wallace (218–19). At the end of the novel, he stumbles away, his face bloody; to Marie he looks pitiful (255; see also the Jewess).
Speaks: 138–41, 176, 182–92, 194–207, 209–14, 216–18, 220–21.

the grain broker. One of the rich yacht-owners sketched at the end of the novel as contrast to Albert Tracy, Harry Morgan, and the other "have nots" (in the financial, not spiritual sense). He is a shrewd, ruthless, hard-drinking sixty-year-old businessman, for whom clever deals and large profits have been more important than human relationships or moral issues. While the reader waits to learn whether Morgan is alive or dead, the grain broker worries because the Internal Revenue Bureau, which he outsmarted five years ago, is now investigating him. Alone and forbidden the comfort of liquor, the rich grain broker cannot sleep (233–38).

*the grain broker's family. His wife's money had served the grain broker as the "original capital" on which he built his fortune. The unsatisfactory marriage lasted twenty years; they have been divorced for ten years. The grain broker dismisses his two sons as "fools" (235).

*the hairdresser. He lightened Marie's hair when she was 26 years old; she has been a bleached blonde ever since (258–59; see also Jean in *GE*).

the happy family. See the father, the mother, Frances.

*Hardy, [William and John James (J.J.). English manufacturers of fishing tackle and "famous fly dressers and tournament casters, as well as widely experienced fishermen." J.J. Hardy won more casting championships than any other tournament caster in British history, becoming world salmon- and trout-fly casting champion at the Crystal Palace Exposition, taking the Franco-British tournament held at London in 1908, and remaining the British casting champion until at least the 1930s. In 1872 William and J.J. founded the Hardy Brothers company in Alnwick, Northumberland, with an office in London. A third brother, Lawrence, managed the company, which supplied well-made rods and other fishing equipment. The Hardy family has developed a number of different types of fishing rods and holds several patents for various devices and improvements they have designed. Hemingway owned two Hardy reels and two Hardy fishing rods, one of which (the five-ounce, eight-and-a-half-foot-long Hardy Fairy) is now displayed in the American Museum of Fly Fishing. Hardy tackle has long been prized by fishermen.[9] In August 1934 Hemingway estimated the cost of reels for fishing for marlin at "two hundred and fifty dollars apiece" ("Out in the Stream: A Cuban Letter," rpt. White, 191).]

Morgan's fishing rod is equipped with a Hardy reel. When his customer Johnson (q.v.) disregards Morgan's instructions and therefore loses both the huge fish he hooked and the expensive rod and reel, Morgan informs him that the reel originally cost $250.00, but that the price has since gone up (21; see also 24, 27).

Harrison, Dr. Frederick (Cap). [Perhaps a reference to Francis Burton Harrison, American politician, 1873–1957. Harrison earned a B.A. in 1895 and an LL.B. in 1897, and was Democratic member of Congress from New York, 1903–1905 and 1907–1915. In 1914 he and H. T. Rainey co-authored the Harrison Narcotic Act "which established strict federal control over traffic in narcotic drugs in the United States and its possessions." His major work was done in the Philippines (ceded to the United States after the Spanish-American War, 1898). Harrison was appointed governor-general of the islands in 1913, a position he resigned in 1921 with the recommendation that a Filipino be appointed to that post. In 1935 the Philippines were granted the interim status of Commonwealth, and in 1936 Harrison became the first American to be appointed an honorary citizen of the Philippines, and was invited to serve as advisor to the three Philippine presidents who led the island to full independence in 1946. The *National Cyclopaedia of American Biography* also reports that Harrison "enjoyed hunting and fishing" (XLVI 24) but I can find no evidence that he fished in Key West.]

Harrison is a self-important, self-righteous politician who has chartered Willie Adams' boat for a day of fishing. Noticing that Morgan is wounded, he correctly concludes that Morgan was smuggling liquor and determines to take him into custody (81), an attempt foiled by Adams. Harrison later reports his suspicions as fact, filing an affidavit "that he saw the boat unloading liquor" and thus causing Morgan's boat to be impounded (97, 118; also see doctor). In reference to Harrison's many degrees, Adams describes him as a "big alphabet man" (83). His secretary blurts out that Harrison has been appointed "governor-general of—" (80).

Speaks: 78–84.

*Harrow. See Baldwin; see also Eton in *TS* and *GE*.

Hatuey, Hatuey Beer. [Hatuey was an Indian *cacique* (chief) of the Arawak tribe, who migrated to Cuba from his native Hispaniola (Haiti), after his own people had been exterminated by the Spanish conquistadors. In Cuba he incited the native islanders to rise up against the Spanish, as a result of which the Spanish burned him to death. Hatuey beer is made by the Bacardí Company, famous for its rum. See Hatuey in *OMS*.]

A bottle of Hatuey beer costs Morgan ten cents, five cents less than his meal (30). Morgan also drinks beer at Donovan's (q.v.), in other bars, and on board his own boat (26). Eddy and Johnson also drink beer on the boat (19, 22); that beer is named Tropical (27).

Hayzooz. Mispronunciation of Jesús (q.v.).

Hollis, Dorothy. An "extraordinarily pretty" (243) nymphomaniac, one of the several rich people sketched at the end of the novel. She is vain, unfaithful to her dying husband, and frustrated by her lover (see Eddie). Unable to sleep, she worries about her desirability to men, takes a luminol and then masturbates in order to fall asleep (241–46).

*Hollis, John. The husband of Dorothy Hollis, he is a "highly paid Hollywood director" dying of liver disease (241).

Honey. Marie Morgan's affectionate nickname for her husband Harry (114, 126–27) and for one of her daughters (255).

*Hoover, J[ohn] Edgar. [American lawyer and criminologist, 1895–1972. He was the director of the Federal Bureau of Investigation (FBI) for almost half a century, from 1924 to 1972. Hoover strengthened the Bureau by establishing the FBI Laboratories in 1932 and the National Crime Information Center in 1967. Aggressively anti-Communist, he saw himself as the guardian of democracy at home and abroad, and was accused of excessive zeal in his pursuit of suspected subversives. His agents and investigators were known as G men.]

As he sets out to "capture" the law-breaker Morgan, Frederick Harrison describes himself as being as aggressive as Hoover, but more modest (82). Nelson Jacks, a war veteran and now a Communist supporter, claims that the United States government, including Hoover and Roosevelt (q.v.), want "to get rid of us" (206).

Irydia IV. A yacht moored in Key West on whose deck stands Dorothy Hollis (q.v.). As the Coast Guard boat comes in to the pier to unload the four dead Cubans and the unconscious Harry Morgan (qq.v.), its lights illuminate the *Irydia IV* (241–42).

"Isle of Capri." [Popular song, copyright 1934. Music by Will Grosz, lyrics by Jimmy Kennedy. Publisher: Peter Maurice Music Co., Ltd. The song tells of a man who lost his heart to a beautiful but unavailable (because she is married) woman on the romantic Italian island of Capri:

> 'Twas on the Isle of Capri that I found her
> Beneath the shade of an old walnut tree
> Oh, I can still see the flow'rs blooming 'round her
> Where we met on the Isle of Capri.
>
> She was as sweet as a rose of the dawning,
> But somehow fate hadn't meant her for me.
> And tho' I sailed with the tide in the morning
> Still my heart's on the Isle of Capri.
>
> Summer time was nearly over
> Blue Italian sky above
> I said, "Lady, I'm a rover,
> Can you spare a sweet word of love?"
>
> She whispered softly, "It's best not to linger,"
> And then as I kissed her hand I could see
> She wore a plain golden ring on her finger;
> 'Twas good-bye on the Isle of Capri.]

At Freddy's place, the veterans, who are all far from their wives and sweethearts, play this song on the juke-box (200).

Isleño (the islander). The narrator comments that the crowd at the dock enjoyed seeing the bodies of the four dead Cubans as much as, many years ago, they had enjoyed seeing the body of the lynched *Isleño* (253; see also *the Negro in *FWBT*).

Jacks, Nelson. A tall, educated, liberal veteran with a distinctive scar (203) who comments sardonically on himself and the other veterans: they are all, he says, "desperate . . . completely brutalized" both by the war and by the present government's ill-treatment of them (206). He proudly identifies himself as a communist (204, 206). He has read Gordon's books and thinks they are "shit" (210). His remark about "pleasure" (203) suggests he has read Alexander Pope as well (see vice in *FTA* and Pope in "Sea Change," *Winner Take Nothing*). See Spartacus and Wellington; also see endnote 18.
  Speaks: 203–7, 209–10.

*Jacobson, Jon. The well-paid captain of the happy family's yacht, the *Alzira III*. Unaware of the violence and misery around him, he sleeps peacefully while the dead and dying are towed in (240).

Jesús (Hayzooz). A recently married young Cuban taxi-driver who has brought a customer in to buy rum at Freddy's, he is teased by Rodger about the paternity of his new baby.
  Speaks: 119–20.

*Jews. The narrator seems to share the characters' prejudices. Listing various landmarks, the narrative mentions "five Jew stores" (193; see also blacks and the Jewess; see Jews in *SAR*).

*the Jewess. A character in the book Gordon is writing. Spellman's silly suggestion that Richard include a stereotypical "beautiful Jewish agitator" (197) unwittingly underlines the triteness of Gordon's conception—he has been working on just such a figure (177).

Joey (Red, Slappy). One of the dazed, brawling war veterans at Freddy's bar. A retired boxer (215), he is addicted to violence. He likes to watch it (207–9), inflict it, and endure it (201–3). He and Poochy fight frequently and regularly (214). After so much violence and, perhaps, an attack of syphilis (see Sampson), Joey's memory is vague. He and Poochy are comic characters.
  Speaks: 201–3, 208–14.

*Joey's wife. Joey insists he has "the finest little wife in the world" but cannot remember where she is and whether or not she is Ginger Rogers (q.v.). His side-kick supports Joey in all his assertions about this ideal, misplaced wife (211–12; also see Poochy).

*John Thomas. [In D. H. Lawrence's *Lady Chatterley's Lover*, "John Thomas" is Mellors' and Constance Chatterley's pet name for his penis.]

When Richard Gordon hears that John escorted his wife home, he sarcastically asks, "And what's his last name? Thomas?" (184).

Johnson. An ill-mannered tourist who has chartered Morgan's boat for a week of deep-sea fishing. Because he consistently disregards Morgan's instructions, he loses a beautiful big black marlin and Morgan's expensive tackle (see Hardy) and is pulled overboard as well. He leaves Cuba without paying Morgan the $825 he owes him. Flat broke and unable to replace his tackle, Morgan turns to criminal activity (see Frankie).
　　Speaks: 8–11, 13–19, 21–25.

Johnson, Roger (Sheriff). The thin, friendly sheriff of Key West (199) does his job well. He skillfully separates two brawling veterans at Freddy's bar, supervises the unloading of bodies and money at the Coast Guard Pier, correctly identifies one of the dead Cubans as the murderer of Simmons (q.v., 250), recognizes that the body of Albert Tracy is missing, and tends to his widow (252–53). He and his deputy cover the Cubans' bodies with blankets (253). He is friendly with Gordon. See endnote 18.
　　Speaks: 199–201, 247–53.

Johnston, Wallace (Wally). A rich, well-educated composer, 38 years old, the owner of the yacht *New Exuma II* is oblivious to the dramatic events that have drawn a crowd to the Coast Guard pier. He is said to have "rather special pleasures," which involve "bus boys and sailors, and one thing and another" (232, 229–30). He is petty and unpleasant: he pointlessly curses his steward (229), bullies a watchman (q.v.), sneers at the Bradleys (to whose party he has just been), and alternately insults and wheedles his guest and lover, Henry Carpenter (q.v.). See endnote 18.
　　Speaks: 227–31.

Juan. See Rodríguez, Juan.

*Kermath. [The Kermath Manufacturing Co. was established in Detroit, Michigan, about 1910. Unlike most of the machine shops and engine manufacturers that catered to the rapidly growing automotive industry, Kermath specialized in marine work. Under the presidency of John B. Farr, the company expanded rapidly, dominating the market with its "12-horsepower four-cylinder, four-cycle marine engine with a 3-1/2-inch bore and 4-inch stroke," which it produced in large quantities and sold at a low price. In response to market demand, the Kermath Manufacturing Co. decided to expand its repertoire, designing and producing a variety of engines, a policy which weakened the company financially. Farr eventually decided to concentrate production on the "two cylinder four cycle 4-8-horsepower" and the lighter "one cylinder, four cycle 3-horsepower" models. In the 1920s, as boat-owners began to demand faster engines, the company added other models: the 35-horsepower model was soon replaced by the "70-horsepower four cylinder high speed engine . . . and the culmination in progress thus far [early 1920s] . . . has resulted in the six-cylinder 100-horsepower marine engine for fast runabout work, giving speeds up to 34 miles per hour." By 1925, the company was considered "among the largest and most note-worthy manufacturers of marine engines in the world" (*Power Boating* 27.12 [Dec. 1925]: 56). In the 1920s and 1930s Kermath produced only gasoline marine engines.][10]

Morgan's boat has a "Hundred horse Kermath" [gasoline] engine (31) and a second engine, added later (85).

the kid who sculls for Mr. Sing. See Cubans.

*Larson, Captain Nils. He commands a crew of twelve on Wallace Johnston's yacht, the *New Exuma II* (231).

Laughton, James (Papa). An unproductive writer, he wears glasses, a mustache and shorts (129). Like the Gordons and the Bradleys, he is wintering at Key West; he and his wife come often to Freddy's bar. See endnote 18.
Speaks: 130, 134–36, 139–40.

Laughton, Mrs. An unattractive, vulgar, muscular blonde, she is a tourist in Key West. She finds Morgan attractive and makes lewd remarks to him. Her husband tries ineffectually to protect her from Morgan's insults.
Speaks: 129–30, 132, 135–41, 149–50.

*Lindbergh, [Charles Augustus (Slim). American aviation pioneer, 1902–1974. The first person to fly solo nonstop from New York to Paris (in May 1927), Lindbergh attracted a great deal of admiration and became an international celebrity. Morgan would have seen pictures of his monoplane, "The Spirit of St. Louis," on the front pages of the newspapers. His two-year-old son was kidnapped and killed in 1932; Bruno Richard Hauptmann, although claiming innocence, was convicted of this crime (1935). The notorious case resulted in the "Lindbergh Laws," which prescribe the death penalty for the kidnapper if harm comes to a kidnapped child. Subsequent "Little Lindbergh Laws" imposed stringent penalties for the kidnapping of children. During

World War II Lindbergh expressed pro-German sentiments but he modified this position late in the war and flew fifty missions against the Japanese (as a civilian, not in any military capacity). In the 1960s he became a conservationist, devoting considerable effort to save the humpback and blue whales as well as other endangered species. He wrote *We* (1927), *Of Flight and Life* (1948), the Pulitzer prize-winning *The Spirit of St. Louis* (1953), and *The Wartime Journals of Charles A. Lindbergh* (1970).][11]

The flying fish remind Morgan of "the picture of Lindbergh crossing the Atlantic" (12).

*Luger, [George. Austrian firearms developer, 1849–1923. In 1898, Luger invented a semiautomatic hand weapon which had a toggle-joint breech mechanism; on recoil after firing, this mechanism would open to receive a new cartridge from the magazine in its grip. The pistol was known as the Parabellum 1900 in Europe and as the Luger in the United States.]

During the shoot-out in Cuba, Pancho shoots the chauffeur with his big Luger (7–8).

*Machado [y Morales, Gerardo. Cuban businessman and politician, 1871–1939; dictatorial president of Cuba, 1925–1933. After his election to the Presidency in 1925, Machado reneged on his campaign promises to fight corruption, becoming a practitioner of the art himself. Through a constitutional amendment, he extended the presidential term from four to six years and secured his re-election through various non-democratic means. His authoritarianism and corruption, coupled with the financial pressures of the Depression, led to the revolution which made the equally repressive Fulgencio Batista (q.v., in *Islands*) the most powerful politician in Cuba from 1933 until the advent of Fidel Castro in 1959. Machado lived in Miami from the time of his deposition, August 1933, until his death a few years later. Machado was in power during "Part One" of *THHN;* Parts II and III take place after he fell from power (see p. 95).]

To finance their revolution [against the recently-installed government backed by Batista] four Cubans rob a bank and hire Morgan to transport them and their stolen money to Cuba. One of the Cubans explains to Morgan that the current military-backed regime is better-armed than its predecessor and just as corrupt: it has absorbed "every kind of crook, bully and informer of the old days of Machado" (167; see 158).

MacWalsey, John. [Jack Hemingway includes a Dr. McWalsey in a phrase that means "liquor": "we'd all had more than a few nips of the stuff that killed Dr. McWalsey" (*Misadventures* 313 *et passim*).]

MacWalsey is an unattractive (129), blue-eyed (212) professor visiting Key West. His field is said to be economics (139), but he is interested in etymology (129–30, 216) and place names (135). His heavy drinking is excused as a response to the death of his wife (q.v.). He disapproves of himself for getting involved with Helen Gordon (222) and is kind to her husband (219–21). See endnote 1.

Speaks: 129–30, 135–36, 216–22.

*MacWalsey's wife. She died seventeen years ago "during the influenza epidemic in 1918" [which killed over 20 million people] (217, 222).

Marshall, Eddie or Eddy. Morgan's sometime assistant, he had been "a good man on a boat once, before he got to be a rummy" (18). Eddy arranged for Johnson to charter Morgan's boat, in return for which Morgan hired him on for $4.00 a day. When Johnson leaves Key West without paying Morgan, Morgan blames Eddy, whom he considers to be unreliable and unlucky. Not wanting any witnesses, Morgan refuses to take Eddy when he engages to transport the Chinamen (37–38), but Eddy puts himself on the crew list (62–63), stows away, and witnesses Morgan's murder of Mr. Sing. Morgan doesn't worry about this because even if Eddy talks, "who believes a rummy?" (63).

Speaks: 9, 11, 13, 14, 19, 21–22, 24–25, 37–39, 42–59, 62–63.

the mate. See Coast Guard officers.

men and boys. The novel has a considerable population of poverty-stricken men and boys. In addition to the poor men who have names (Frankie, Marshall, Morgan, Tracy, Wesley) or can be defined by their jobs (driver, sailor, waiter), we see several unnamed, undefined, and mostly unemployed men and boys, black and white, Cubans and Americans, who populate the docks, bars and streets of Havana and Key West. A beggar drinks from a fountain; several "bums" sleep in the streets of Havana (3). A black boy works for Morgan on the boat, putting bait on the fishing hooks for a dollar a day (10–11). A consumptive boy "that works around the docks" was paid a dollar to deliver a grisly photograph to Frankie, instructing him to give it to Morgan (39–40). A few men lounge at the bar at Freddy's place at mid-morning (118). An "old man . . . who sells the rubber goods specialties" comes to Freddy's for liquor (91). Some of these background characters (e.g., Marshall and the unnamed man he picks up) are "rummies" (64). All these people suggest the many "have nots" of the Depression-stricken 1930s. The "winter people," who do not share the troubles of the impoverished permanent residents, are seen "laughing" at the end of the novel (262; see also the blacks, Chinese, Conchs, Cubans, crowds, and veterans).

*men and boys. Several unnamed men and boys are mentioned but do
not act or appear in the narrative. Marie Morgan, for example, recalls a
black man who "said something to me and Harry smacked him" (258).
A black man is murdered offstage and his picture sent to Morgan as a
warning (39). It is said that degraded old men in New York let "you
. . . piss in their beards for a dollar" (207) and that various men are
employed by Johnston to satisfy his sexual needs (229). Unseen,
unnamed rich men have been reduced to poverty and suicide by the
unscrupulous grain broker (237; see also *Cubans).

*Mongol. [In the 13th century the Mongolian Empire included parts of
Europe and most of Asia and the Pacific. See Genghis Khan, Tamerlane
and Tartar.]
    Both Mrs. Laughton and Marie Morgan (qq.v) remark on Morgan's
high cheekbones, associated with the Mongol people (128).

Morgan, Harry (Big Boy, Big Shot, Cap, Cappie, Captain, Captain
Harry, Cappy, Chief, Daddy, Hon, Honey). [Hemingway's main character is named after the Welsh-born pirate Sir Henry Morgan (c.1635–
1688). Legend has it that Morgan was kidnapped as a child, sold as a
slave, and transported to the British colony of Jamaica, where he began
his career as a pirate. In the contested waters of the Caribbean, Morgan
attacked Spanish ships and colonies, participating in a number of raids
against Spanish-owned Cuba. Morgan was so effective on the seas that
he was named commander-in-chief of all Jamaican war-ships, "to levy
war on the Spaniards and destroy their ships and stores, the booty gained
in the expedition being the only pay" ("Morgan, Sir Henry" *Encyclopaedia Britannica,* 11th ed., XVIII: 833). In addition to the activities
commissioned by the governor of Jamaica, Morgan undertook several
raids on his own behalf. Infamous for his cruelty and debauchery, he
amassed a great personal fortune through threats, ransom money, and
looting. When England and Spain made peace, Morgan was arrested and
summoned to England. He managed to ingratiate himself with the King,
who pardoned him, knighted him, and appointed him lieutenant-
governor of Jamaica, to which he returned in 1674. His political career
there was as rowdy as his buccaneering had been. The story of his life
is readily available in a number of sources, among them *Howard Pyle's
Book of Pirates* (New York and London: Harper & Brothers, 1921),
a collection of articles written by Pyle and published in *Harper's
Magazine* over a period of forty years. The first chapter of this book,
"Buccaneers and Marooners of the Spanish Main" contains the
Morgan material (pp. 14–21; the article was first published in August
and September, 1887). Hemingway acquired this illustrated book in
1932 (Reynold's *Hemingway's Reading,* 171), and the father in the short

story "A Day's Wait" (*Winner Take Nothing*) reads from it to his sick son.]

The central character of the novel, Morgan is 43 years old (115), handsome, well-built, and graceful; he loves his wife but not his daughters. Morgan, who used to be a policeman in Miami, goes from taking tourists deep-sea fishing off Key West to transporting illegal immigrants, to murder, rum-running, and finally taking four Cuban outlaws from Key West to Cuba. He kills all four but is fatally injured and dies.

Speaks: 3–5, 8–19, 21–25, 27–40, 42–59, 61–64, 67–77, 83, 85–87, 91–104, 108–28, 130–35, 144–45, 148–69, 171, 173, 224–25; several short and two longer interior monologues, 105–7 (chapter 10), 174–75. Morgan narrates Part I (chapters 1–5).

Morgan, Marie. Harry's 45-year-old wife (115), formerly a prostitute (175), is presented sympathetically. Although she is "big now and ugly and old" (260) and her daughters object to her coarse bleached hair, her husband loves her and she is still passionately responsive to him (112–15).[12] She embodies a number of Hemingway's concerns: the role of hair in sexual attraction (258–60), the problem of how to endure sleepless nights and of how to survive when "everything inside of you is gone" (261, 260). Although devastated by Morgan's death, she has the strength to pull herself together and go on.

Speaks: 64, 112–17, 125–28, 251–56; long interior monologue, 257–61.

Morgan's daughters. Three undifferentiated, nameless girls. Morgan and Marie wonder why they never had sons (126, 127); they don't particularly like their daughters (126, 127, 257) although they provide well for them (26, 64, 147, 257). The girls, who seem very nice, cry and pray for their father (254–55; also see 113–14, 116, and Honey).

Speak: 125, 254–55.

the mother. One of the rich yachts-people, she is a "handsome, wholesome, well-kept woman," an avid gardener and generally well-liked. Because of her and her family's great virtue, she enjoys the luxury of sleeping well (239; see also the father, Frances, and Tompkins).

*mothers. Joey swears by his mother (207); Poochy's mother is dead (212; see also Rodríguez).

Navy, Navy Yard. See Coast Guard and watchman.

New Exuma II. [Exuma is the name of an island group in the Bahamas, including the Exuma Cays and Great Exuma, the largest island. They are separated from Cat Island by Exuma Sound.]

Wallace Johnston's elegant yacht carries a crew of twelve. She is moored at Key West, near the Coast Guard pier to which the dying Harry Morgan is brought (228). The other expensive boats are also numbered, in the order of presentation: see *Alzira III* and *Irydia IV*.

"niggers." See blacks.

*Palmer, [Frank Thomas. American manufacturer, 1857–1944. In 1888 Frank T. Palmer established the Mianus Electric Co., which manufactured telephone and electrical supplies. In 1894 this successful company moved to Cos Cob, Connecticut, and was expanded to include marine motor engines and, eventually, launches. The company was known as Palmer Brothers (for Frank T. and his brother Ralph Louis, born 1860), as the Palmer Engine Works, and the Palmer Engine Company. Their gasoline marine engines incorporated the innovations which, as electricians, they devised for their product. Most notable of these was the jump spark system (*Motorboat* 21.7 [10 April, 1924]: 59). The Palmer Brothers' 1907 catalogue boasts that "The Palmer Motor is in use in every civilized country in the world and gives absolute satisfaction." The Heritage Engine Collection, which reprinted the 1907 Palmer catalogue in April 1985 (Vol. 2, No. 4), writes that "Palmer prices were generally higher than the competition yet their products sold well because they were of high quality and very reliable." In 1907 Palmer Brothers advertised a two-cycle self-lubricating motor, which generated from 1-1/2 to 11 horse-power, and a four-cycle motor, which generated from two to thirty horse-power. In the 1930s they built heavy-duty commercial, hand-started gasoline engines which were very popular. The cylinder head was called an "octopus" because it was so big. The company, a leader in the field, also made diesel engines in the 1940s. They went out of business in 1972.][13]
Willie Adams' boat had a "two-cylinder Palmer" engine (79).

Pancho. One of the three young, well-dressed Cubans who offer Morgan $1,000 apiece to take them to the States on his boat (3–5); they are in some sort of political trouble. His offer is refused by Morgan, who is trying to make his living without breaking any laws. Pancho is killed in the gun battle immediately after his conversation with Morgan (8).

Papa. [Hemingway was often called Papa by relatives and friends.]
Mrs. Laughton addresses her husband as Papa (130).

*peasants. See *Cubans.

Poochy ("the other Vet," Joey's sidekick). One of the World War I veterans in Freddy's bar, he and his demented room-mate Joey (q.v.) fight every night (214–15). Poochy's mind has been affected by "the rale" so that now "he don't know where he is" (216).[14]
 Speaks: 202–3, 209–14.

*Porter, [William R. American businessman, 1871–1953. The son of Florida's first health officer, Porter was the owner of the Porter-Allen Insurance Company and president of the First National Bank. He also owned Porter Dock, at the end of Duval Street, Key West, Florida, where the Ocean Key House Resort stands today (see endnote 7).]
 The Cuban bank-robbers want Morgan to pick them up at the Porter Dock (110), but he insists on a safer spot (132).

the proprietor of the Lilac Time (a Key West bar). A Cuban who tries to cheer up Richard Gordon by making him special drinks. He explains Herbert Spellman's problems to Richard.
 Speaks: 194–95, 198–99.

the quartermaster. He steers the Coast Guard boat which brings the dying Morgan back to Key West (223; see also Coast Guard officers).

Queen Conch.[15] Freddy Wallace's boat, a 34'-long white and green craft valued at $1,200. Because his own boat has been impounded, Morgan leases the *Queen Conch* from Freddy in order to run the four Cubans back to Cuba (131). With all her passengers dead or dying, the *Queen Conch* is towed back to Key West by the Coast Guard. The boat was damaged in the shoot-out between Morgan and the Cubans (178; see also Robby).

*Ray. Owner of the fast speedboat which carries mail between Cuba and Key West. Worried that a fast boat might catch up with him and the criminals he is transporting to Cuba, Morgan reviews the present locations of the four speedboats he knows about in Key West: Ray's speedboat is out on a mail run (154), Walton's boat is at Taylor's ways, a third boat is "up along the keys" and the fourth is "laid up in the Garrison Bight" (155).

*Richard, Richard's. [Probably a misspelling for Richards.]
 The owner/manager of the bar located outside the city of Key West, at which Simmons introduced Morgan to the four Cubans (99–103) and at which he drinks most of the evening (108). His wife is Freda Richards (q.v.).

Richards, Miss Freda. Formerly a prostitute, she is now married to Richard (q.v.) (99). She speaks pleasantly to Morgan and Tracy.
   Speaks: 99, 103.

Red. Several people address the red-headed Joey as Red (203, 213, 215). Jacks is identified as "a red" (i.e., a Communist; 204).

*Robby. Good boatbuilder who built the *Queen Conch* (223; see endnote 15).

Roberto. One of the four Cubans (q.v.) whom Morgan has undertaken to run back to Cuba. He has a big, deep voice, speaks English, and is spokesman for his partners. He kills Simmons during the robbery and Tracy soon after boarding the *Queen Conch* (153); he drunkenly threatens to kill Morgan. Emilio (q.v.) judges him to be "a good revolutionary but a bad man" (158).
   Speaks: 99–103, 152–63, 169.

Rodger, Big Rodger. One of the patrons at Freddy's bar, he teases Jesús about the paternity of his new baby.
   Speaks: 119–20.

*Rodríguez, Juan. One of the local ne'er-do-wells who, according to Tracy, "would steal from his own mother" (102). His lawyer is Simmons, who allegedly reports him to the authorities so that he will be "indicted again so he [Simmons] can defend him" again (102, 91).

*Rogers, Ginger. [Stage name of Virginia Katherine McMath. American film actress and dancer, 1911—. Ginger Rogers and Fred Astaire (q.v. in *GHA*) were a famous dancing team whose musical comedies include *Flying Down to Rio* (1933) and *Top Hat* (1935). She starred in several non-musical movies, like *Bachelor Mother* (1939) and *Kitty Foyle* (1940), for which she won an Academy Award. She continued making films through the 1940s and 1950s.]
   The deranged veteran Joey claims to have a wife who he thinks may be Ginger Rogers (212; see Joey's wife).

*Roosevelt, [Franklin Delano. American politician, 1882–1945; 32nd President of the United States, 1933–1945. In 1933, Roosevelt launched the New Deal and other plans for economic recovery, including the Social Security Act, the Federal Emergency Relief Administration (FERA), and the Works Progress Administration (WPA, 1935), which attempted to create jobs for the unemployed. The veterans in *THHN* come to Key West from the Civilian Conservation Corps (CCC).

According to Carlos Baker, Hemingway "believed . . . the persistent rumour that these men were an embarrassment to Roosevelt's New Deal" and had been "shipped . . . to Florida to get them out of sight" (*Life* 270). When a hurricane killed almost a thousand CCC workers in 1935, Hemingway was angry that the men, mostly war veterans, had not been evacuated and blamed Roosevelt for their deaths. The action of the novel occurs during the Roosevelt administration, but before the devastating hurricane of September 1935.]

Tracy describes his work in a federal program, for which he earns $7.50 a week (94–96); Adams reports that the government pays $6.50 a week (81).[16] Nelson Jacks' criticism of the American government's treatment of World War I veterans (206) echoes Hemingway's.

sailors. A sailor on a British freighter looks at Morgan as he sets out to pick up the Chinese whom he intends to defraud (41). Another sailor sits in the street of the "jungle town" of Key West (194; see *men and boys).

*sailors. The crew of the *New Exuma II* is mentioned but not seen (231).

*Sampson, Benny. A boxer said to have infected Joey with "the rale" (i.e., syphilis) by rubbing the open sores on his shoulders "under Red's nose or across his puss" (215; also see Suds and endnote 14).

Sheriff. See Johnson, Roger.

*Sidney, Sylvia. [Stage name of Sophie Kosow. American film star, 1910—. One of Paramount Studio's biggest stars in the 1930s, Sidney lived modestly and specialized in unglamorous roles, often playing poor or criminal female characters. Short, slim, and large-eyed, she presented an image of vulnerability and helplessness which won her large audiences in the Depression of the 1930s. Among her movies of that period are *City Streets* (1931), *Street Scene* (1931), and *You Only Live Once* (1937). She made a few unremarkable movies in the 1940s and 1950s and appeared often on TV.][17]

Herbert Spellman, who insists he is in love with Sylvia Sidney, wants Gordon to write her into his book (197).

Simmons, Robert (Bee-Lips). A notoriously crooked Key West lawyer (91). His current clients are four Cubans (q.v) who intend to rob the local bank and, with Morgan's assistance, decamp to Cuba. Simmons acts as intermediary between Morgan and the Cubans. He also helps Morgan steal his impounded boat out of the Customs dock and then, when the Customs officials retrieve it, helps Morgan convince Freddy Wallace to lease him his boat for the dangerous operation. Simmons even encourages Freddy to deposit his security money in the bank, although both he and Morgan know that the bank will be robbed that afternoon. The Cubans kill Simmons during the course of the robbery (165, 250). See endnotes 1 and 18.

> Speaks: 91–93, 101, 103, 108–11, 120–22, 130–34.

Sing, Mr. (the Chink). A "smooth-looking," smooth-talking Chinese crook who promises transportation to illegal Chinese immigrants, collects high fares from them, and sends them to their deaths. He engages Morgan to transport twelve such Chinamen, suggesting that Morgan "land them wherever your best judgment dictated" (32). Morgan loads the Chinese, collects the $1,200 from Mr. Sing, and then kills him (53).

> Speaks: 30–35, 52.

*Skull and Bones. [In the nineteenth century private undergraduate societies devoted to a particular interest (like journalism, sport, drama, or music) and, more importantly, senior societies (membership restricted to seniors) evolved at Yale University; they were important indicators of student success. The three leading secret senior societies were and are Wolf's Head, Scroll and Key, and Skull and Bones, the latter (founded in the early 1830s) being the oldest and most prestigious. The societies provided their members with valuable connections in the academic, professional, and business worlds. Though somewhat more open today, the societies still operate on exclusionary principles. In 1991, when Yale seniors invited six women into Skull and Bones, irate "alumni . . . sneaked into the sepulchral clubhouse . . . and changed the locks" (*Newsweek,* April 29, 1991, p. 38).]

Harold Tompkins (q.v.), who was popular among his classmates, was a member of Skull and Bones. The narrative suggests that he is loyal to his society and, by extension, to other "Bones" men and to Yale University (239–40; also see Baldwin).

Slappy. Nickname for Joey (q.v.). One of the veterans, who has taken upon himself the task of "cooling" (i.e., knocking out) his more belligerent fellows, advises Joey to "Shut up, slappy" (205).

*Smith, [Horace. American inventor and gun manufacturer, 1808–1893. In 1853 Smith became partners with Daniel Baird Wesson (1825–1906); they patented a new repeating action which they incorporated into a pistol. The Smith & Wesson Company (1855) continues to be one of the foremost weapons manufacturers.]

Morgan has a Smith & Wesson from his days as a policeman in Miami (44) which he takes but doesn't use during his dealings with Mr. Sing and the Chinese.

*soldiers. See *Cubans.

South Florida. A white charter boat captained by Willie Adams (78; see Palmer).

*Spartacus. [Thracian slave who led a revolt against Rome, known as the Slave or Gladiatorial War (73–71 BCE); died 71 BCE. Spartacus served in the Roman Army, defected, was captured, enslaved, and designated a gladiator. He and several other captives escaped, their band growing rapidly to a force large enough to win a series of battles and gain control over much of southern Italy. Their revolt was put down by Crassus and Pompey. The German Spartacus party or Spartacists was founded in 1916 and became the German Communist Party in 1918.]
   Nelson Jacks (q.v.) would like to organize his fellow veterans to protest the government's mistreatment of them, as Spartacus organized his fellow slaves to protest against Rome (206).

Spellman, Herbert (Harold). The scion of a wealthy family, he is mentally unstable. His family have installed him and a companion-nurse in Key West, where he is well known to the proprietor of the Lilac Time, a local bar. He thinks of himself as an animal (a stork, a winged horse, etc.) and insists that being crazy is the only way to be happy (197). He claims to have read and liked all of Gordon's books (195–98). See endnote 18.

*Stalin, [Joseph. Russian politician, 1879–1953; Premier of the Soviet Union, 1941–1953. Real name: Josif Dzhugashvili. Stalin exterminated political opposition by means of purges in the 1930s. In 1939 he formed a non-aggression pact with Nazi Germany and assumed the Premiership when Germany invaded.]
   Emilio attempts to justify the criminal behavior of the Cuban revolutionaries by comparing them to Stalin (166).

the steward. The polite, white-jacketed steward of Wallace Johnston's yacht, the *New Exuma II,* brings drinks and puts records on the record player (228). On another boat, the steward brings the grain broker a drink (238).

suckers. See endnote 8.

*Suds. A World War I veteran reputed to have gotten syphilis "off a girl in Brest" (215).

Sweetheart. Richard Gordon addresses his wife as "sweetheart" only once (138).

*Sweetwater. A colorful Cuban, he is a "character" in the local community (120).

*Tamerlane. [Timur i leng (Timurleng, Timurlane, the lame Timur). Mongol conqueror, c.1333–1405. Tamerlane tried to reunite the empire of Genghis Khan (c.1167–1227), whom he claimed as an ancestor. He assumed control of the Tartars (1392) and defeated the Turks (1402), building a huge empire and gaining a reputation for cruelty. He died during an invasion of China.]

When Mrs. Laughton lasciviously admires Morgan, her husband taunts her that maybe the next person to enter Freddy's bar will be Tamerlane (136; see Tartar).

*Tartar [or Tatar. The Tatars are a Turkic-speaking people, originally nomadic but later settling in Siberia (also known as Tartary) and in the Crimea (Little Tartary). Their name comes from Tata or Dada, a Mongolian tribe under whose leadership these nomadic tribes conquered parts of Asia and Europe in the thirteenth century. The Tatar Invasion of 1241 (led by Batu Khan, a grandson of the Mongol conqueror Jenghiz or Genghis Khan) reached into Hungary and Germany. See Genghis Khan, Tamerlane; see Tartar in *FWBT*.]

Mrs. Laughton thinks Morgan looks "like a Tartar or something" (136).

the taxi driver. See driver.

*Taylor, Ed. Walton's speedboat is presently moored at Taylor's ways (155; see *Ray).

*Thomas. See John Thomas.

*Thompson, [John Taliaferro. American soldier and inventor, 1860–1940. Thompson held many patents for improvements and innovations in automatic small arms. In 1920 he patented the Thompson submachine gun (Tommy gun), the weapon of choice for the gangsters who flourished during Prohibition (1920–1933). Accurate, fast, and reliable, the Thompson submachine gun weighs just under ten pounds.]

The black man who drives up and kills three Cubans in Havana is armed with a Thompson (6–7; also see Luger and Pancho). Roberto uses a Thompson gun during and after the bank robbery (151–52); he kills Simmons and Tracy with it (151, 153, 158, 165, 250). Morgan kicks it overboard (160–61) and soon after kills Roberto, Emilio and the two other Cuban revolutionaries with his own Thompson (170–72), obtained in Cuba where such guns cost only $45 (147, 162). Before picking up the Cubans, Morgan had loaded and carefully hidden his Thompson on Wallace's boat (127–28, 142–43, 163). When the *Queen Conch* is towed back to Key West, Morgan's Thompson gun is found (249; also see 173). Morgan had also armed himself carefully before going to pick up the Chinese (see Winchester).

*Tompkins, Harold. Fiancé of Frances (q.v.). Among the satirical sketches of the rich tourists at the end of the novel, Hemingway includes this successful, unassuming, and widely admired Yale graduate (239), who fits in perfectly with Frances' "pleasant, dull and upright family" (238). The narrative adds that such fine fellows are usually failures in bed (239; see also Skull and Bones).

Tracy, Albert (Al). An unemployed fisherman, he is a parallel character to Morgan, whom he has known since childhood (98). Both he and Morgan are married with three children, both have been hit hard by the Depression and are unable to find work in their professions. But where Morgan has turned to illegal activities, Tracy has remained honest, working on government-sponsored programs for $7.50 a week (94; see *Roosevelt). Morgan thinks Tracy is "dumb" but he respects his abilities and character (105). Tracy is tempted when he hears that Morgan is going to earn quick money for transporting "somebody" to Cuba, accepts (or perhaps really believes) Morgan's white-wash of the situation, and joins him. The Cubans kill him as soon as they board the boat (153). Tracy narrates Chapter 9.
Speaks: 93–100, 104, 122, 137, 144–45, 151–53.

Tracy, Mrs. Albert. Like Marie Morgan, she is an unattractive and realistically-presented middle-aged woman who loves her husband. Financial difficulties have strained the marriage (104, 144). She becomes hysterical at the pier while waiting for the arrival of Wallace's boat, on which Tracy had sailed with Morgan. In a grotesque scene, she falls into the water, loses her dentures, and is unable to enunciate properly (252). Realizing he is not on board, she screams to express a "grief . . . greater than she could bear" (253).
Speaks: 251–53.

*Tracy's family. Like the Morgans, the Tracys have three children (95, 104).

*Trumbo, [Howard. American engineer, c.1875–1931. Hambright writes that "Trumbo was a dredging engineer hired by the Florida East Coast Railroad to fill the 148 acre site for the railroad yard. Trumbo Point [at the entrance to the Garrison Bight, on the north-central coast of Key West] was the railroad yard until the 1935 hurricane put the Key West extension out of business. After finishing the dredging project in 1912 Trumbo moved to Cuba. . . . The area is now known as the Trumbo Point Annex of the U.S. Naval Air Station, Key West" (see endnote 7). McLendon describes Hemingway's arrival at Key West in 1928: "the steamship . . . crawled east to west around the belly of the island . . . on the western side of the island, the three massive piers of the Trumbo docks presented themselves" (*Papa,* 20–21; McLendon mentions the Trumbo pier again on p. 23 and the Trumbo Club on p. 147).]
    As he approaches Garrison Bight, the injured Morgan sees the Trumbo Dock (86).

*Van Brunt, Margaret. Hostess of a party at which Herbert Spellman claims he met Richard Gordon (196).

the veterans. They work on nearby islands and come to Key West on pay day for an evening of drinking and fighting at Freddy's bar (201–16). One of them, suspected of cadging drinks, has his jaw broken by another (205; see also the cooler, crowds, Jacks, Joey, *mothers, Poochy, and *Roosevelt).
    Speak: 201–16,

the waiter. He serves Morgan a substantial, inexpensive meal (30).

Wallace. The burly bouncer at Freddy's bar, he removes brawling customers from the premises (208, 214). When Richard Gordon hits MacWalsey, Wallace knocks him out (218–20).[18]
    Speaks: 208, 214–15, 218–19.

Wallace, Freddy. Owner and bartender of Freddy's (spelled Freddie's, 91), a successful bar in Key West which is the setting for several scenes in the novel. Morgan describes him as "the only son-of-a-bitch in this town I *would* trust" (133). Nevertheless, he double-crosses him, leasing Freddy's boat, the *Queen Conch* (q.v.), under false pretences (147). See endnotes 1 and 18.
    Speaks: 93, 108, 118–19, 123–24, 130–32, 134, 136–38, 148–49, 207–8.

*Walton. Owner of a speedboat which Morgan thinks he or Simmons might hire to transport the Cubans from the dock near the bank out to where his own boat is hidden (106, 155). Morgan abandons this plan when his boat is re-confiscated by the Customs agents and he uses Freddy Wallace's boat instead. See *Ray and *Taylor; see endnote 7.

*War Aces. [This monthly appeared from April 1930 until July 1932. The veteran who enjoys reading it seems unaware that in 1933, the time of the action of the novel, it is no longer published. The Library of Congress, which holds a complete run, has classified it as "pulp fiction." The veteran's admiration for War Aces indicates the quality of his literary judgment. The magazine is also mentioned in "Night Before Battle," The Fifth Column and Four Stories of the Spanish Civil War.]
Hearing that Gordon is a writer, one of the veterans at Freddy's Bar asks him if has published in Western Stories or in War Aces (210).

the watchman. Morgan steals his impounded boat, which is kept by Customs, without being seen by the night watchman, who does hourly rounds but spends most of his watch at the gate (110). Later, another watchman, a short Cuban with a long mustache, has orders not to let anyone enter the yacht basin, to which the Queen Conch is being towed by the Coast Guard, but two yachtsmen (Carpenter and Johnston, qq.v.) arrogantly push past him and, unaware of the drama going on nearby, enter the dock and go to their boat (227). The yacht basin where these two easily-foiled watchmen work used to be a U.S. Navy installation (see 95, 110, 199, 227) and is now (i.e., at the time of the action of the novel) also used by the Coast Guard (q.v.) as well as by yachts-people.
Speaks: 227.

*Wellington, [Arthur Wellesley, first Duke of Wellington. British soldier and statesman, 1769–1852. Wellington served in India from 1796 to 1805. From 1809 to 1813 he was Commander in the Peninsular War, during which Britain helped Spain repulse the French. Wellington defeated Napoleon at Waterloo, Belgium, in 1815. From 1828 to 1830 he served as Prime Minister of England.]
Jacks, the bitter Communist, sarcastically compares his fellow veter-ans to Wellington's soldiers (205–6).

Wesley ("the nigger"). Morgan's companion in the ill-fated rum-running expedition in which both men are wounded by the police. Wesley complains of great pain from his leg wound; Morgan eventually loses his arm. See blacks.
Speaks: 67–74, 76–77, 85–86.

Western Stories. [Probably *Street & Smith's Western Story Magazine,* known popularly as *Western Story.* A weekly for most of its history, it began publication in 1912 and appeared throughout the 1920s and 1930s.][19]

Upon hearing that Gordon is a writer, one of the veterans asks him if he writes for *Western Stories* (210; see *War Aces*).

Willie. See Adams, Captain Willie.

Willis. Sycophantic secretary to Frederick Harrison (q.v.), with whom he has gone fishing on Adams' boat.
Speaks: 79–82.

*Winchell, [Walter. American journalist, 1897–1972. After military service during World War I, Winchell worked as a vaudeville performer. He joined the staff of the sensationalist New York *Evening Graphic* in 1924 as a gossip columnist, moving to the *Daily Graphic* in 1929. Although his reporting was often inaccurate, Winchell became an influential reporter of the private lives of the rich and famous. With his syndicated columns and weekly radio show, he had an audience of over 25 million. His trademarks were "his rapid speech and the clicking of a telegraph key."][20]

Dorothy Hollis worries that she won't know if and when she has turned into "a bitch" because Winchell doesn't relay that sort of information (244).

*Winchester, [Oliver Fisher. American industrialist, 1810–1880. Winchester, who had worked as a carpenter's apprentice, a clerk, a construction worker, and a successful shirt manufacturer, bought into a weapons company in 1857, reorganized it, and renamed it the Winchester Repeating Arms Company.]

In addition to his Thompson gun and his Smith and Wesson .38 police special (qq.v), Morgan has a pump-gun and a Winchester 30–30 which he normally hangs "right over the wheel" of his boat, "where I could reach them" easily should the need arise (44). He makes a similar arrangement on Freddy Wallace's boat, hanging his Thompson within easy reach but where it won't be visible to his passengers (142–44). When he goes to pick up the Chinese, Morgan arms himself with the police special (44) and makes sure that Eddy knows how to use the pump-gun and the Winchester (48).

women and girls. Two unnamed women support and restrain Mrs. Tracy (251, 252). Prostitutes wait for customers in the "jungle town" of Key

West (194; also see Chicha, Chinese and crowds), but prostitution and gambling seem to be outlawed (93; see Big Lucie's daughter).

*women and girls. The grain broker has slept with a number of unseen, unnamed women (234); he has reduced other women and girls to poverty by his financial speculations and miscalculations, forcing them to take in boarders or to work as dentists' assistants (237–38). A girl is accused of having given syphilis to Suds (215). Three Chinese women are said to service the many Chinese illegally employed in Cuba; Frankie explains that the "Government no let" more Chinese women in (36).

WPA. Works Progress Administration (120; see *Roosevelt).

FOR WHOM THE BELL TOLLS

TOLLS

Ernest Hemingway

Scribner dust jacket for the first edition of *For Whom the Bell Tolls* (courtesy Charles Scribner's Sons, an imprint of the Macmillan Publishing Company; and of the Hemingway Collection, J.F. Kennedy Library)

CHAPTER V

FOR WHOM THE BELL TOLLS

(1940)

The action takes place in the mountains northwest of Madrid, Spain, late in May 1937 (see *FWBT* 153, 165, 194).[1]

ABC. [Madrid's oldest daily newspaper was founded in 1903 as a weekly and became a daily in 1905. Its founder and owner, Torcuato Luca de Tena y Alvarez-Ossorio, maintained control of the paper until his death, after which the ownership and editorship passed to his son, Juan Ignacio Luca de Tena, who in 1928 added a separate Andalusian edition, published in Seville. *ABC* consistently supported the monarchy and the Church. During the Civil War, when most monarchist and nationalist papers were suppressed in Republican-held areas, the Madrid *ABC* was allowed to appear, albeit under Republican censorship. Even so, it was among the most informative and reliable papers of the period. The Seville *ABC* was one of the few nationalist papers allowed to continue publication without any Republican interference. When Madrid fell to the Nationalists, *ABC* was returned to its owners and resumed its former political stance.[2] Because so many different factions among the Republicans and the Nationalists published their own papers, buying and reading a particular newspaper was tantamount to proclaiming one's political affiliation. See journalists.]

Rogelio Gómez angrily accuses Pepe, a Republican officer, of reading *ABC*, thus impugning his loyalty to the cause. When Pepe mildly criticizes *El Mundo Obero,* the paper he is actually reading, Andrés escalates his accusation, from *ABC* to *El Debate* (398). Pepe has aroused Gómez's ire by refusing him access to Lieutenant-Colonel Miranda and thus preventing the transmission of Jordan's important message to General Golz.

*Abd el Krim, [Mohammed ben. Moroccan nationalist leader, c.1882–1963. The son of a Berber chieftain who was killed fighting the Spanish, Abd el-Krim organized fierce resistance against European colonialism in northern Morocco. In 1921 he gathered an army of tribesmen who were victorious against a Spanish force of more than 20,000. He wrested much of Morocco from Spain and France, but was eventually forced to surrender to French and Spanish forces in 1926. In 1927, while being transported to France, he jumped ship and ended up in Cairo, Egypt, from where he continued to energize the militant Riffian nationalists. After much upheaval, Morocco became independent in 1956. Abd el Krim's adventurous life inspired the operetta *The Desert Song* and the novel and film *Beau Geste*. See Berbers. Both Jake Barnes and Colonel Cantwell refer to the Moroccan conflict (*SAR* 114, *ARIT* 230).]

The narrative describes Valentín González (el Campesino) as "an ex-sergeant in the Spanish Foreign Legion who had deserted and fought with Abd el Krim" (229).

absinthe. [A green, anise-flavored alcoholic drink made with worm-wood, a toxic substance, and flavored with anise. See absinthe and Pernod in *SAR*.]

Jordan drinks absinthe (50–51, 56–57), which he carries in a pocket flask (48). He likes it (204, 228), and it seems not to affect him adversely (see Pernod and *Guardia Nacional in *GE*). He also drinks wine and whiskey. See drunkards.

the adjutant. See Gómez's staff.

*Agincourt. [A village in northern France near which the small army of Henry V of England defeated the larger army of the French in October 1415. The English had the advantage of a new weapon, the longbow, and the French were weighed down by their heavy armor, which immobilized them in the rain and mud. The small English army lost 13 men-at-arms and about 100 foot soldiers; the French lost over 5,000 men. Because they did not have enough men to guard their many prisoners as well as continue the battle against the considerable number of remaining Frenchmen, the English killed most of the French who had surrendered.]

Well-versed in the history of warfare "from Agincourt down," Jordan believes he can learn from the mistakes of earlier commanders and plan his own battles successfully (200).

Agustín. One of the guerrilla fighters of Pablo's band, he is a good judge of people and a kind-hearted friend. He recognizes that Pablo is clever (94) but untrustworthy: early on he places his trust in Jordan and warns him to guard his materials (46). He insults and even slaps Pablo to precipitate a showdown between Jordan and the gang's leader; after the bridge has been destroyed he quickly realizes that Pablo has cold-bloodedly killed the five men he had recruited. His feelings are strong but not out of control: although he hates Pablo (e.g. 384), he argues against the "filthiness" of selling him to the Fascists. His desire to kill fascists is as strong as sexual passion (286), but he can control it when necessary (280–82). Similarly, although he loves María (290–91), he does not force his attentions on her or allow his emotions to interfere with his commitment to Jordan. At the end, he helps carry the injured Jordan, cries when he realizes how serious the wound is, and promises him to look after María. He is also a good friend to Santiago, wanting to rush to his aid when the distant sound of shooting indicates that el Sordo's men are fighting (294). His language is unrelentingly foul. See 280–81, 381, 403, 406, 461.

Speaks: 44–46, 92–95, 207, 209–11, 213–16, 218, 221–24, 227, 271–72, 277–78, 282–86, 288–95, 383–85, 388, 402, 406–9, 435, 450–51, 453–57, 465.

*Alejandro. He and Elías (q.v.) are the leaders of a guerrilla group. Pablo recruits some of their men and horses to help out in the bridge-blowing (389–92), and kills them after the action is completed so that there will be enough horses for his own people's get-away (450–57; see 403–4). See also Elicio and Pepe.

*Americans. [Americans who joined the International Brigades were grouped into the Washington and Lincoln Battalions (q.v. in *Fifth Column*), but Jordan seems to have no particular friends among these. The Americans he recalls are mostly military figures (see Custer, Grant, Jackson, Kilpatrick, McClellan, Mosby, Quantrill, Sheridan, Sherman, and Stuart), firearms manufacturers (Lewis and Smith), artists (Garbo, Gilbert, Harlow, the Marx brothers, Stein, Strater) and his family and friends (Hickok, Strater, Thompson, and Weaver). He also mentions President Coolidge and the Sioux.]

Jordan recalls visiting the Headquarters of the International Brigades in Madrid (234–35). See the various members of the Jordan family; see also *women and girls.

anarchists. See FAI.

Andrés. See López, Andrés.

*Anheuser-Busch lithograph. [In 1888, Adolphus Busch acquired the large (16′5″ by 9′6″) canvas entitled "Custer's Last Fight," painted by the American painter Cassilly Adams in 1884. Busch (1839–1928) wanted to use the painting, with its popular and controversial subject matter, to promote his company's product, Budweiser beer. Accordingly, he commissioned F. Otto Becker (1854–1945) to make a lithographic print;

Custer's Last Fight (courtesy of the Anheuser-Busch Companies, St. Louis, Missouri).

Becker, who used Adams' working sketches, "produced a much smaller painting . . . and one considerably different in detail from Adams'." Becker's color lithograph was distributed to taverns and beer-sellers throughout the country. It carries the legend "Custer's Last Fight," under which appear a few lines of small print, followed by "The Seventh Regiment of U. S. Cavalry" in italics, and "Anheuser-Busch Brewing Association" in large clear capital letters. Custer is shown lying on the ground, in a little clearing in the center of the picture, firing his gun, which emits a puff of smoke, at the encroaching Indians; his hat covers his hair.[3] It is probably this nationally distributed lithograph which hangs in the town Indians' club in Michigan (*TS* 65), in Freddy's bar in Key West, Florida (*THHN* 123), and in "the poolroom" at Red Lodge, a town in Carbon county, southern Montana (*FWBT* 339; Red Lodge is also mentioned on p. 337 of this novel). For Custer, see *ARIT* and *Islands*.]

Jordan recalls "the old Anheuser-Busch lithograph" which shows a blond Custer, armed but helpless "as the Sioux closed in around him" (339).

Anselmo (*viejo*, old man). Aged 68, Anselmo is the oldest and most philosophical member of Pablo's band. He is a committed Republican, a reliable soldier (although he worries he might run away from battle), and a knowledgeable guide. Although a good shot and an avid hunter, he kills the enemy very reluctantly. In obedience to revolutionary principles, he has given up prayer and the Church, but he still worries about sin and feels that the killing will have to be atoned for: "I think there must be some form of civic penance organized that all may be cleansed from the killing or else we will never have a true and human basis for living" (196). When he realizes that Berrendo has cut off the heads of Santiago (el Sordo) and his men, he breaks into prayer (327). He is killed by a "piece of steel" when the bridge is blown up (446). Both his reliability and his moral sensibilities make him a strong contrast to Pablo. He is mentioned often (161, 178, 180, 181, 190, 204, 225, 259, 266, 271, 280, 292, 381, 385, 400, 402, 406, 437–38, 446, 455).

Speaks: 1–3, 9–16, 19–20, 22, 24–30, 34, 36–44, 46–47, 52, 54, 77–78, 83, 198–200, 205, 209, 254, 278, 283–86, 295, 327–32, 360, 384, 388, 407–10, 435–37, 439–40, 444; several short interior monologues, 191–94, 196–98, 327, 442–43.

*Anselmo's wife. Anselmo is "glad she died before the movement" because she "would not have understood" (197) all that it demands: the painful estrangements caused by political differences, the rejection of the church, the killing (cf. Santiago's wife in *OMS*, who was also religious).

*Anthony, Saint. [Egyptian hermit and ascetic monk, c.251–c.350. As a young man, Anthony gave away his large inheritance and became a hermit. He withstood a variety of temptations and gathered a following of men who, like him, lived in solitude. He is considered the father of monasticism. His feast day is January 17. In an earlier novel, the main character was given a Saint Anthony medal (see *FTA* 43–44).]

In her letter to her brother, who was killed by Jordan, Concha had written that she was praying to Saint Anthony and to other saints and Virgins "to protect him" (303).

*Asensio [Torrado, José. Spanish soldier, 1892–1961. A professional military officer, Asensio joined the Republican cause, rising to the rank of general. He established military training schools for the Republicans and was appointed subsecretary to the Minister of War in Largo Caballero's government. The Republican defeats in Toledo, Talavera de la Reina, Illescas, and Málaga (February 1937) made him unpopular, especially among the communists, who mounted a smear attack. Asensio was arrested in September 1937 on the charge of treason but charges were dropped and he was released in 1938. After the war he lived in New York, where he died in 1961.][4]

In his anger at Pablo's treachery, Jordan generalizes that all Spanish leaders ("Largo, Prieto, Asensio, Miaja, Rojo, all of them" [369]) betray their people.

*Bacchus. [In Roman mythology, the god of wine and fertility. Ceremonies to worship Bacchus were often drunken and orgiastic. Legends associated with the Greek god Dionysus were also applied to the cult of Bacchus.]
    Instead of the customary blessing, "Vaya con Dios" (Go with God, God be with you), Jordan says "Go with Bacchus" to Pablo (204; see *FTA*; see also Circe in *SAR*).

*Bach, [Johann Sebastian. German organist and composer, 1685–1750. His preludes, fugues, inventions, sonatas, concerti and church compositions are masterpieces of the Baroque period. Titles familiar to every generation of music lovers include Books I and II of *The Well-Tempered Clavier,* the Brandenburg Concertos, the Goldberg Variations, the *Magnificat,* and the *Mass in B Minor.*]
    Jordan compares his feelings about being a member of the International Brigades to what he feels in the presence of great art: "embarrassing to speak about . . . and yet it was authentic as the feeling you had when you heard Bach" (235).

barber. [In late 1936 and early 1937, the anarchists' revolutionary activity in Barcelona aroused the opposition of the Russian and communist elements within the Republicans and particularly in the International Brigades, who were more interested in fighting the enemy without (the Nationalists) than in effecting social revolution within. They felt that the energy expended on social concerns was detracting from the war effort (see CNT and POUM). In Barcelona, social revolution was the central concern, and the working people, most of them anarchists (see FAI) had the upper hand early in 1937. At that time, Orwell wrote, "there was a belief in the revolution and the future. . . . In the barbers' shops were Anarchist notices (the barbers were mostly Anarchists) solemnly explaining that barbers were no longer slaves" (*Homage to Catalonia,* 4). The anarchist uprising was put down in June 1937. *FWBT* consistently presents the anarchists as undisciplined and unreliable Republicans— Pilar calls them "crazies" and Andrés' meeting with them is tension-packed and funny. The presentation of barbers as prone to political excess is not new in Hemingway: see the barber in *FTA*.]
    Pepe mocks Rogelio Gómez (q.v.), who had been a barber in civilian life, for his emotionalism: "thy emotion bores me. It was for that reason that I always shaved myself" (397–98).

*barber. The barber in María's home-town was shot by the fascists. His body lies in the doorway of the barbershop where María and other girls are shaved and humiliated before they are raped (352–53).

*Belgian boy. Of the six boys from his small town who volunteered for the International Brigades, he is the only one still alive. Devastated by his experiences, he cries constantly (136). See Belgians in *ARIT*.

*Berbers. [An ancient Caucasoid people, inhabitants of north Africa, forming most of the population of modern Libya, Algeria and Morocco. The origin of the Berbers is unknown; they have been linked variously to the ancient Phoenicians, the Caucasians, the Basques and the Celts. Conquered by the Arabs in the seventh century, a majority of the Berbers became Moslems and joined with the Arabs in conquering Spain. When Spain and France colonized north Africa, the Berbers who had lived in these countries for hundreds of years resisted them fiercely. See also Abd el Krim, Moors, and Iberians.]
  Thinking about Spain's violent history, Jordan cautions himself not to mythologize "the Berbers and the old Iberians" (286–87).

*Berlitz, [Maximilian Delphinus. German philologist, 1852–1921. Berlitz came to the United States in 1869 and founded the Berlitz School of Languages in 1878. He devised the system of total immersion: classes are conducted entirely in the language to be learned, the student gaining a speaking knowledge of the language by means of question-answer sessions. The formal study of grammar is delayed until the student is fluent in the new language. The system was successful and the Berlitz School of Languages now operates in many countries. Berlitz's grandson Charles, b. 1913, inherited the Berlitz empire; he speaks about 30 languages.]
  Many of the Spanish Republican military leaders are Russian-trained and therefore speak Russian. As Jordan remarks, Modesto "never learned his Russian in Puerto de Santa María [his home town] although he might have if they had a Berlitz School there" (230).

Berrendo, Lieutenant Paco (the second officer). One of the Carlist cavalry who attack Santiago and his men. He correctly interprets el Sordo's shots and the band's subsequent silence as a trick designed to convince them that all the guerrillas are dead; he therefore refuses to go up the hill with Captain Mora. Berrendo survives the hilltop battle, and shoots the fatally wounded Joaquín "quickly and . . . gently," makes the sign of the cross over him, says a prayer for his own dead men, deplores war as "a bad thing," and then orders his men to cut off the heads of Santiago's men, pack them up in a poncho, and take them back to camp

(322, 325). He himself admits that "taking the heads is barbarous" although necessary for "proof and identification" (326). At the end of the novel, he comes within shooting range of Robert Jordan (471; see also Carlists, cavalry and Mora).

Speaks: 314–15, 317–18, 322, 326.

*Bess. [At Nordquist's L-Bar-T Ranch in Wyoming, which Hemingway visited several times in the 1930s and 1940s, he rode "a horse that he loved, a black mare named Old Bess with a white streak on her face" (Baker, *Life,* 214). Hemingway calls her "Bess," capitalizing the adjective "old" only when it occurs at the beginning of a sentence ("A Paris Letter, February 1934"; rpt. White, 169–70).]

Jordan recalls the mare "old Bess" (337).

bicyclists. See cyclists.

*Blanquet. [Professional name of Enrique Belenguer Soler. Spanish bullfighter, 1881–1926. An excellent, left-handed banderillero, Blanquet worked with the outstanding matadors of his time. In spite of his intelligence and skill, he was unable to rescue the great matadors José Gómez Ortega (Joselito), Manuel Granero, or Miguel Baez (Litri), all of whom were killed in fights at which Blanquet was serving as banderillero. Blanquet was the subject of a short novel by Agustín de Foxá (q.v. in *DS.*)][5]

Pilar correctly says that this *peón de brega* (bullfighter who works in the *cuadrilla* or crew of a matador) worked for Joselito and Granero. She claims that although he was not a gypsy, Blanquet had the gypsies' ability to smell death on a person about to die (252–53).

Speaks: 251.

Bob. The brakeman's nickname for Robert Jordan (406).

*Borrow, [George Henry. British amateur lawyer, editor, philologist, translator, and author, 1803–1881. As an agent for the British and Foreign Bible Society, Borrow traveled widely in Russia and Spain (1835–1840) and wrote several autobiographical travelogues: *The Zincali, or The Gypsies in Spain* (1841) and *The Bible in Spain,* which offers a vivid picture of Spain and which is generally considered his best book (1843; the full title of the 1896 edition was *The Bible in Spain: or, the journeys, adventures, and imprisonments of an Englishman in an attempt to circulate the Scriptures in the peninsula*). Other books include *Romano lavo-lil, Word-Book of the Romany, or, English Gypsy Language; Lavengro: The Scholar, the Gypsy, the Priest* (1851) and its sequel, *The Romany Rye* (1857).]

Jordan admires Borrow's and Ford's books about Spain (248).

*brakeman on the train. When Jordan left home to go away to school, the brakeman on the train commented that "Dad seemed to take your going sort of hard, Bob" (406; see the conductor).
Speaks: 406.

*Brueghel. [Also spelled Bruegel or Breughel. Family of great Flemish painters, which included Pieter the Elder (c.1525–1569), his sons Pieter the Younger (1564–1638) and Jan (1568–1625) and his grandson Jan the Younger (1601–1678). Their workshops were major centers of Flemish art for over a century. Pieter the Elder is best known for his vibrant, detailed landscapes and his witty presentations of peasant life. The Prado Museum in Madrid has a large collection of Brueghels, including Pieter the Elder's famous "The Triumph of Death" (1562) which shows Death triumphing over all worldly things. See *Islands.*]
Jordan compares his feelings about being a member of the International Brigades to his feelings when he saw "Mantegna and Greco and Brueghel in the Prado . . . an absolute brotherhood with the others who were engaged in it" (235).

*bullfighters. [Bullfighting was practically suspended during the Spanish Civil War (1936–1939), although occasional fights were celebrated under the auspices of the Nationalists, mostly to raise funds (see Lalanda). The bullfight, an integral part of Spanish culture, enters the narrative largely through Pilar's reminiscences; Andrés López also recalls the *capeas* (amateur bullfights) in his town (364–66).]
As a younger woman, Pilar had lived with three matadors and had known many of the bullfighting personalities of the day (see Blanquet, Chicuelo, Gómez Ortega, Granero, Lalanda, and Rosa). She had often visited the Madrid bullring, where she witnessed the fatal goring of the matador Manuel Granero (see also *crowds, Finito, Finito's assistants, and horse contractor).

*Burns, Emil. [Economist, 1889–?. Burns compiled *A Handbook of Marxism* (New York, 1935; republished in 2 vols, New York, 1970) which contains passages from Marx, Engels and others, as well as a bibiliography, index and glossaries. Burns' other publications of the 1930s include *Russia's Productive System* (New York, 1930), *The Only Way Out* (New York, 1932), *The Roosevelt Illusion* (London, 1934), and *Money* (1937).][6]
Karkov approves of Burns' *Handbook of Marxism*, which Jordan has read (244).

*Calvo Sotelo, [José. Spanish lawyer, economist and politician, 1893–1936. A brilliant young man, Calvo Sotelo was elected governor of

Valencia at age 28; two years later, when Primo de Rivera (q.v. in *SAR*) seized power, he was invited to join the national government. From 1925 to 1930 he served as Finance Minister; his major concerns were the stabilization of the currency and the nationalization of the petroleum industry, the latter being a contributing factor in the defeat of Primo de Rivera in the 1930 election. The day after the election Calvo Sotelo fled Spain, living first in Lisbon and then in Paris. He returned to turbulent Spain in 1934. An eloquent orator and writer, he was instrumental in forming the National Block, a loose confederation pledged to strong central government, the monarchy, and the church. His attacks on the Republic were as passionate as his propaganda for the National Block. In July 1936 he was taken from his home and murdered. His funeral was heavily attended. He wrote often on financial, legal and parliamentary issues, including *Estudio económico de la hacienda española* and *El capitalismo contemporáneo y su evolución*. During his years of exile he wrote *En defensa propia, Mis servicios al estado, La voz de un perseguido* (2 vols.) and *Un proceso histórico*.][7]

The narrative describes Calvo Sotelo as "a true Spanish fascist," and correctly reports that he was assassinated before the action of the novel. Karkov, who wants to write a book "which will explain many things which it is necessary to know," is studying "all of Sotelo's writings and speeches. He was very intelligent and it was very intelligent that he was killed" (244).

Camarada. See Comrade.

*el Campesino (the Peasant). See González, Valentín.

Carlists. [Carlism is a militant Spanish political movement born in the early 1830s when King Ferdinand VII abdicated and named his daughter Isabella as his successor. Carlists claimed that under Salic Law, which recognizes only male succession, Carlos (Ferdinand's brother) and not Isabella (Ferdinand's daughter) was the true heir to the throne. Carlists enjoyed the strong support of the Roman Catholic Church and were particularly strong in the northern provinces. During the Spanish Civil War they joined forces with Franco. Their militia was known as the *requetés*. See also Nationalists.]

The cavalryman whom Jordan shoots early in the morning after the snowstorm (265–66) was a Carlist, recognizable from his insignia (265, 269). More Carlists are seen later on (280–82, 325–27, 471; see soldiers). See *Concha.

*Carmen. A friend of Karkov's mistress (357).

*Castro, don José (don Pepe). A horse dealer, one of the fascists being held in City Hall on the day when the Republicans, led by Pablo, took over the town. He, the town's other fascists, and the priest were all hacked to death when Pablo allowed the mob to enter the building (123–25; see horse contractor).

cavalry. Mounted, well-equipped Nationalist soldiers appear in large numbers: Jordan and his men see one contingent (280–82), looking for their fellow, whom Jordan has killed (see Carlists). With Berrendo (q.v.), they show up again at the end of the novel (471). They are the same men who fought Santiago (el Sordo) and his band on the hilltop (chapter 27) and whom Primitivo, Jordan and Anselmo see after the battle (325–27, 330; see Mora and the sniper). See soldiers.

*Charles. See Thompson, Charles.

chauffeur. See driver.

*Chicuelo. [Professional name of Manuel Jiménez Moreno. Spanish matador, 1902–1967. In spite of his great reputation and popularity, Chicuelo did not perform as often as he could have. The 1920s was his triumphant decade, even though in 1922 and 1927 he turned down many contracts, as he did throughout the 1930s, mostly due to illness. Since his appearances were generally praised, he was able to maintain his following in spite of the reduced number of fights. During and after the Spanish Civil War (1936–1939) he continued to perform, though infrequently; he retired in 1951. Chicuelo was a skillful, talented performer, well-educated in the art of bullfighting. The son and nephew of bullfighters, he also had the benefit of being well-connected in the bullfight world. He excelled in all aspects of the fight and in spite of frequent illness and a seeming lack of ambition, he enjoyed a long career in the ring.][8]
Pilar explains that only a few people, like herself and Blanquet, have the ability to smell death on a doomed person. Chicuelo, she explains, could not smell death on the bullfighter Manuel Granero (q.v.), even as he stood next to him on the day Granero was fatally gored (251–52).

*Chub. See Weaver, Leland Stanford.

Club Finito. A fan club for the bullfighter Finito (q.v.).

CNT. [Confederación Nacional del Trabajo (National Confederation of Labor), a national umbrella organization, founded in 1910 by several local anarcho-syndicalist organizations, some of which later split off to join the Communist Party of Spain. During the Spanish Civil War, the CNT remained a small but identifiable left-wing group within the Republican forces. See FAI, POUM, UHP. The Communist Party rejected the leftist position that social revolution could be pursued at the same time as the fight against the Nationalists, hence the narrative's description of the CNT and FAI supporters as "crazies." The egalitarian, revolutionary left opposed the hierarchical communist discipline which Jordan accepts as necessary.]

The Republican sentries who challenge Andrés are emotional, violent "crazies" who shout, "Viva la F.A.I. Viva la C.N.T. . . . Viva el anarco-sindicalismo and liberty" (374).

Speak: 372–75.

the company commander. In a humorous scene depicting the confusion rampant in the Republican Army, the Republican company commander and his fellows threaten, question, and delay Andrés as he tries to transmit Jordan's important message to General Golz. Eventually the company commander conducts Andrés to Captain Rogelio Gómez, the battalion commander and his superior officer (396). Andrés figures these emotional, violence-prone characters are anarchists (374; see FAI).

Speak: 372–77.

Comrade (Camarada). Communist-inspired egalitarian title with which Republicans replace honorifics which indicate class relationships. Karkov, for example, calls Jordan "Comrade" and "Comrade Jordan" (241, 243; see also Comrade in *Fifth Column*). Agustín complains that the Republican government "moves further to the right each day," the change being indicated by the fact that "they no longer say Comrade but Señor and Señora" (285). Jordan takes forms of address seriously (65–66; see don Roberto), as does Joaquín (132).

Comrade Dynamiter. Joaquín's nickname for Jordan (132, 134).

Comrade General. See Golz.

*Concha, Concha's family. Sister of the Carlist cavalryman Jordan kills early in the morning after the snowfall. Jordan reads the letter she had written her brother, reporting that their parents were in their usual state of health and that many boys from their town had been killed (302–3). The cavalryman's fiancée had also written him (303). See Carlists.

the *concierge*. The *concierge* at the Hotel Gaylord in Madrid collects the weapons of all the people who enter the building where Karkov lives. A policeman sits at the *concierge*'s desk (356).

*the conductor on the train. He witnesses a farewell scene between Jordan and his father, a scene which Jordan recalls when he bids farewell to María (405; see the brakeman).

contractor. See horse contractor.

control patrol. See soldiers.

*Coolidge, [John Calvin (Silent Cal). American politician, 1872–1933. He became the 30th President of the United States when his predecessor, Warren G. Harding, died in office in 1923. The Republican Coolidge was elected President in 1924 but refused his party's nomination in 1928. He was known for his straightforward, laconic New England style.]

Jordan compares the taciturn, unimaginative Fernando to Coolidge (201).

*Copic, [Vladimir. Croatian politician, 1891–1938. Copic represented the Yugoslav Communist Party in Moscow. A veteran of the Austro-Hungarian Army, he followed Gall as commander of the XV International Brigade. Copic was the XV International Brigade's leader "throughout its four major campaigns, and one year of almost continuous front-line service. To his uninterrupted command is due, to a great extent, the welding of the various Brigade units into a capable fighting force which has won for itself a foremost reputation in the Spanish Republican Army" (The Book of the XV Brigade, 23). When Gall commanded the XV Brigade, most notably in the Battle of Jarama (Republican defense of Madrid, February 1937), Copic served as the Brigade's political commissar. His iron discipline won him many enemies, particularly among the Americans, who sustained terrible losses when Copic and Gall disregarded Robert Merriman's report on field conditions and insisted on a doomed attack on the heavily fortified hills nearer the Jarama River on February 27, 1937; Copic later attempted to court-martial members of the Lincoln Brigade, including Merriman, for insubordination.][9]

The narrative identifies Copic as a self-seeking member of the International Brigade who endorses the generally unwise decisions of the commander André Marty in order to advance his own career (421–22).

*the coroner. After Jordan's father shot himself, the coroner who conducted the inquest returned the suicide weapon to Jordan, who dropped it into a lake (337).

Speaks: 337.

*Cortez [or Cortés, Hernando. Spanish explorer, 1485–1547. During the course of several journeys to the Spanish colonies in the New World,

Cortez amassed great personal wealth and influence. Commissioned to explore and conquer Mexico, he at various times disregarded the orders of the Spanish king as well as those of the colonial rulers, in order to further his own interests. When Cortez first met the Aztec ruler Montezuma, he was ceremoniously received as an embodiment of the god Quetzalcoatl. Cortez responded by taking Montezuma hostage, appropriating Aztec treasure and destroying much of their architecture. He was finally mistrusted by both the Spanish and the Aztecs.]

In his anger at Pablo's theft of his equipment, Jordan curses all Spanish leaders, including the *conquistadores* "Cortez, Pizarro, and Menéndez de Avila all down through Enrique Líster to Pablo" as betrayers of their own people (354; see 370).

crowds. On their way to deliver Jordan's message to Golz, Andrés and Gómez pass crowds of tanks and Republican personnel massing for the offensive (412 ff; see soldiers).

*crowds. Although the action involves only the members of Pablo's and Santiago's gangs, several crowd scenes are embedded in the narrative. Pilar paints a verbal picture of public aspects of the bullfighter's life: the crowds at the Valencia feria (84), at the inauguration of Club Finito (186–88), and at the Madrid bullring on the day Granero was fatally gored (251–52). To these major bullfighting scenes Andrés adds the picture of a small-town *capea* (amateur bullfighting, 364–66). Jordan also describes a fair, complete with merry-go-round, wheel of fortune, and the smell of fried fish (225).

The cruelty of crowds is represented from various angles. Pilar's vivid description of how Pablo organized the Republican takeover of his home town (100–27) includes a dissertation on drunkenness and mob psychology (104–5, 111–26; see particularly 116–17). Her report is balanced by María's memories of the fascist takeover of her home town, during which many people, including her parents, were killed and she herself was raped (350–53); her story is echoed in Joaquín's brief report of what the fascists did to his family (138–39). To these Jordan adds his childhood memories of an American mob, a Ku Klux Klan lynching in Ohio (117; see *the Negro; see also crowds in *THHN*).

Members of the crowd (drunks, fools, peasants, a man, someone, etc.) speak: 102, 105–15, 117–22, 124–26.

Other off-stage crowd scenes include the party at Karkov's apartment in the Hotel Gaylord, which presents several political and military leaders of the International Brigades in Madrid (356–59), and the crowd of La Granja, suggested by the laconic Fernando (81).

*Cruz. See Juan de la Cruz, San.

*Cuatro Dedos [Four Fingers]. A cobbler in Pablo's home town, Cuatro Dedos supported Pablo when the Republicans took the town and killed the fascists. In the City Hall, Cuatro Dedos and Pablo stood guard over the town's fascists, prodding them out into the plaza, one by one, to be killed by the townspeople (110; see also 120–21, 124).

the cup. [When he is in Gethsemane, Christ prays, "O my father, if this cup may not pass away from me, except I drink it, thy will be done." The fullest account of this event is provided in the Gospel according to St. Matthew, which reports that Christ spoke about the cup three times, "saying the same words" the second and third times (Matthew 26:39, 42, 44; see also Mark 14:36 and Luke 22:42). Although Jordan cannot remember the quotation precisely, Hemingway has him follow the same rhetorical pattern.]

Trying to remember the relevant quotation, Jordan mentions "that cup" three times, using the same words for the last two of these references (181).

*Custer, George [Armstrong. American soldier, 1839–1876. A West Point graduate, Custer served in the Union forces under McClellan (1862) and Sheridan (1864) and was frequently promoted during the American Civil War, achieving the rank of major general. After the Civil War Custer was appointed to the Seventh U.S. Cavalry, winning a major victory against the Cheyenne in 1868 and engaging the Sioux in battle several times over a period of years. In 1876 he and his companies, totaling fewer than 700 men, faced about 4000 Sioux under the leadership of Chief Sitting Bull. Custer and over 200 of his men were killed in this famous battle at Little Big Horn; the Montana site is now a national monument. Many military historians have argued that Custer bears much of the blame for the disaster at Little Big Horn: he attacked from a position of weakness and he discarded the original timetable for the battle. Custer's apologists contend that the size of the opposing force was not known and that he was forced to attack when the Sioux became aware of his presence and the plan for a surprise attack became irrelevant. Custer wrote *My Life on the Plains* (1874); his wife, Elizabeth Bacon Custer (q.v. in *ARIT*), who accompanied him on many of his frontier expeditions, wrote several books about their experiences.]

Jordan, who admires Custer, "felt resentment" when his grandfather spoke about him disparagingly (339; see 337–38; see also McClellan, Sheridan, Sioux, and Anheuser-Busch lithograph).

*cyclists. To involve all his fellow villagers equally in killing the fascists of his town, Pablo arranged them in two facing rows, between which the doomed fascists had to pass, to be beaten and killed and then thrown off the cliff. Pilar, a gifted storyteller, uses images from sports and religion to make the picture vivid to her audience: the men of the town stood ''as they stand in a city to watch the ending of a bicycle road race with just room for the cyclists to pass between, or as men stood to allow the passage of a holy image in a procession'' (104).

*de la Rosa, Juan Luis. See Rosa de la Garquén, Juan Luis de la.

*de Palencia, Finito. See Finito.

el Debate. [Madrid newspaper, established 1908 or 1910 by Angel Herrera Oria. It espoused liberal Catholic democratic views and became a mouthpiece for the Confederación Española de Derechas Autónomas (CEDA). During the Spanish Civil War it managed to offend both sides of the conflict. The Republicans suspended its publication several times because the Church supported the Nationalists. The Nationalists also suppressed it in Nationalist-held territories because the paper, although Catholic in orientation, presented moderate views. After the Civil War, *El Debate*'s positions were too left-wing for Franco's government, which soon forced the paper to cease publication.][10]
   This newspaper was read by the Catholic fascists in Pablo's home town (116). An angry Gómez maligns a fellow Republican by remarking that ''*El Debate* . . . is your paper'' (398).

*dentists. The Falangists who cut off María's hair seemed like mad, nightmarish dentists to her (351).

*Dolores. See Ibárruri Gómez, Dolores.

don. See don Roberto.

*Donne, John. [English metaphysical poet and churchman, c.1572–1631. Donne was Dean of St. Paul's Cathedral, London, 1621–1631. Among his best-known poems are ''Death Be Not Proud,'' ''Go and Catch a Falling Star,'' ''The Flea,'' ''Batter My Heart, Three Person'd God'' and ''A Valediction: Forbidding Mourning.'']
   Hemingway took the epigraph and title of this novel from Donne's *Devotions Upon Emergent Occasions*, Meditation 17.

don Roberto. [The honorific don is an acronym for the phrase *de origen noble* and is therefore not used by Republicans, who insist on equality and call each other comrade. Like religion, the class system is difficult to erase from the Spanish mind; María, Joaquín and Anselmo, all good Republicans, resort to prayer, and the words don, doña, señor, señora, and señorita surface occasionally. See Comrade, slogans.]

Jordan objects when Pilar jokingly calls him don Roberto (65–66) because "the form of address . . . is like a flag" (66; see 112). Pablo and Jordan insultingly call each other don (212–13; see 204). The conservative Fernando cannot rid himself of the word and repeatedly calls Jordan don Roberto (209, 210, 257, 259, 260, 407, etc.).

drivers. We see several drivers. Following Jordan's instructions (77), Anselmo observes the traffic moving on the road, noting "the chauffeur, red-faced and steel-helmeted" (191) who drives officers of the Nationalists' General Staff. When Jordan blows the bridge, a truck stops and its Nationalist "driver and the two men who had been with him" (446) run for cover. We also see Republican drivers. As Gómez and Andrés ride on their motorcycle through the Republican forces, they are stopped by a road accident which has snarled up traffic; the driver of a smashed truck is told to get his vehicle off the road so the Republican convoy can continue on its way (413), but he (like the armored car driver, see *drivers below) seems paralyzed by the set-back.

Speaks: 413–14.

Andrés passes many vehicles and their drivers (414–15, 427). The Republican Marty has a driver (417; see Marty's staff). See Vicente.

*drivers. Two *guardias civiles* detained a cart driver (14). A frightened armored car driver (a Republican) refuses to dislodge the body of his dead gunner from under the steering wheel and drive his vehicle through the embattled Madrid streets to the bullring, where it is needed for the Republican defense of the city. Jordan rectifies the situation and thus enables the successful Republican action (240–41). See Montero; cf. Russians, three wounded.

Speaks: 240–41.

drunkards. Pablo drinks heavily and prompts Pilar's remark that drunks are worse than thieves, blackmailers and murderers (208; see 116–17, Bacchus and Shakespeare).

*drunkards. Santiago (el Sordo) remarks that Englishmen drink heavily (142). Pilar speaks of the drunkenness that accompanied the murder of the fascists in Pablo's town (115–16 *et passim*); she connects drunkenness with anarchists and other "useless characters" (104–5, 117–18, 121–23, 126; see *crowds, Martín, the Negro, and Rivas).

*Durán [Martínez, Gustavo. Spanish pianist, composer and artist, 1906–1969. When the Civil War broke out, Durán joined the Communist Party and the 5th Regiment of the Republican Army, in which he achieved rapid promotion. He was commander of the XI International Brigade and, when the brigades were reorganized into two divisions, commander of the 69th Division and finally of the XX Army Corps. He was in charge of SIM (Military Investigation Service) in Madrid, but Minister of Defense Indalecio Prieto relieved him of this position, charging that Durán had made some appointments without obtaining proper authorization. After the Civil War Durán lived in exile in Britain, Cuba and the United States. Hemingway knew and admired him, but turned against him in the 1940s. In the early 1950s, Durán was investigated by Senator McCarthy's powerful anti-Communist committee, after which he left the United States. Associated with various departments of the United Nations, Durán worked in Chile, the Congo, and Greece, where he is buried.[11] See also *Fifth Column*.]

Known as "a composer and lad about town" before the Spanish Civil War, Durán received military training from the Russians and quickly became "a damned good general commanding a brigade" (335). With the other Russian-trained Spanish leaders, he is often at the Hotel Gaylord in Madrid. Karkov praises him (246; see 340).

*Durruti [Domínguez, Buenaventura. Spanish mechanic, anarchist, and revolutionary, 1896–1936. Durruti organized strikes, robbed a bank, deserted from the Spanish Army in 1917, escaped to France and from there organized an attempt on the life of King Alfonso XIII which failed. Returning to Spain he participated in the murder of Juan Soldevilla Romero, Archbishop of Zaragoza (in 1923), after which he fled Spain again to foment revolution in South America. He was often jailed, in Spain and elsewhere. During the Civil War he commanded a group of about 2,500 anarchists and attempted to impose communism, some say on pain of death, in the areas he occupied. He led a column of about 2,000 troops (Cortada reports the number as 5,000) in the defense of Madrid. He died in confusing circumstances: he may have been killed by Nationalist agents, or by disaffected or rival factions among his own (Republican) troops. His death was a blow to the Republicans and a huge crowd attended the funeral. His two brothers, both falangists (fascists), were also killed during the Civil War: one, suspected of disloyalty, was killed by his own men; one was killed by the Republicans.][12]

The narrative identifies Durruti as a Spanish leader shot by his own troops (370). [Jordan may be referring to the falangist brother or to the various rumors about how Durruti was killed.]

*Dutch boy. [A little boy who, according to legend, stuck his finger in a hole in the dike and thus saved his country from flooding.]

Jordan thinks that he would rather live a long life with María than risk his life to save a nation or cause, as was done by the Dutch boy at the dyke, Horatius at the bridge, and the Greeks at Thermopylae (164).

Duval. A Frenchman and Golz's chief of staff. He receives Jordan's dispatch and understands its significance, but by the time he finally manages to reach Golz on the phone, the attack has already started and cannot be stopped (421, 427–28, 430). See endnote 1.

Eladio. See López, Eladio.

*Elías. With Alejandro, the leader of a band of guerrillas that operates in the same neighborhood as those of Pablo and Santiago. Santiago doesn't trust Elías' men for the job of blowing up the bridge (146), but Pablo recruits some of them on the night before the attack (145, 389; see Alejandro).

Elicio. One of the five men recruited by Pablo to help in the attack on the bridge. After the attack Pablo kills all five and uses their horses for the get-away. See Alejandro.
  Speaks: 395.

*Estremadura. [The western section of Spain, which contains the provinces of Cáceres and Badajoz. The impoverished agricultural workers of the region, mostly anarchists, fought against the Nationalists who, by 1937, had gained control of Cáceres province as well as much of Badajoz. In that year, "Major fighting took place in Estremadura," but the Republicans steadily lost ground and the entire region came under the control of the Nationalists (Cortada 189–90).]
  Jordan has blown up several enemy trains in Estremadura, which he mentions several times (24, 148, 162, 233, 287; see 210; see also *Gómez).

FAI. [Federación Anarquista Independentista or Federación Anarquista Ibérica (Federation of Independent or Iberian Anarchists), one of the many factions loosely connected to the Republican cause and identified by their red-and-black neckerchiefs. They advocated complete equality, collective ownership of land and industry by the workers, and government by workers' groups. One of the largest leftist groups, they were particularly strong in Barcelona and the Basque provinces. For the conflict between anarchists and communists, see POUM.]
  Pilar is contemptuous of the anarchists, whom she represents as drunkards (q.v.) in her narrative about the Republican takeover of Pablo's hometown (120–26). Karkov has a similarly low opinion of the anarchists (247). Andrés concurs, defining them as "the crazies; the ones with the black-and-red scarves" (374). Jordan and Agustín also disparage the anarchists (236, 285, 305). See CNT and *crowds.
  Speak: 120, 372–75.

*Falangists. [The Spanish Falange, a fascist party founded in 1933 by José Antonio Primo de Rivera (1903–1936, son of the dictator Miguel Primo de Rivera, q.v. in *SAR*). The Falangists emphasized the Catholic and monarchic traditions of Spain. In 1937 the Falange merged with the Carlists (q.v.), the resulting Falange Española Tradicionalista becoming Franco's official party after the fall of the Republic. Franco overpowered the party, the rest of its leadership holding very little power after the 1940s. See Franco and Nationalists.]

The attack on María's town was carried out by the Falangists and the *guardia civil* (q.v., 351).

Speak: 351–53.

*fascists. Pilar recalls the day in which "more than twenty" (103 ff.) fascists in Pablo's town were killed, including Castro, García, González, Martín, Montalvo, Rivas, and Rivero (qq.v.). The fascists are wrongly reported to be "fighting among themselves" (357). The word "fascist" indicates the enemy generally, although Anselmo distinguishes between fascists, who are despicable, and simple, probably unwilling soldiers, who are to be pitied even if they are the enemy (192–93).

Fernandito. Both María and Pilar address Fernando by this diminutive (84, 254).

Fernando (Fernandito). One of Pablo's band. He is 35 years old, has a cast in one eye, does surveillance at La Granja, and brings back reliable reports (80). Fernando is basically against change: he likes Pilar's cooking, for example, because it's always the same, and he disliked Valencia when he visited it because it was different from what he was used to. He thinks that Robert Jordan, an American, should teach English, and not Spanish; Spanish should be taught by Spaniards. He is consistently reliable, precise, literal and occasionally bombastic and bureaucratic. Pilar says of him, "this one doesn't joke," and yet Fernando provides much of the humor of the novel. He dies in great pain but bravely (442, 455; see also 186, 198, 268, 292–93, 385).

Speaks: 80–86, 92, 190, 199–201, 209–10, 217–19. 223–24, 250, 252, 254, 257, 259–60, 327–28, 383, 388, 390, 407, 440–42.

Fiat planes. [The Italian Fiat company (Fabbrica Italiana Automobili Torino) was founded in 1899 by Giovanni Agnelli and incorporated in 1906. Since 1910 Fiat has been the largest firm in Italy, specializing in cars, trucks and other vehicles, but producing aviation engines and components as well. The small, fast tank coming up the road towards the bridge is a Fiat (453, 455, 458). The Fiat planes Jordan sees are probably the CR-32 biplane fighters. The Italians (who sent 75,000 men to fight for Franco) were anxious to test their equipment under battle conditions. The Fiat CR-32, which carried two Breda-Safat machine guns and could achieve a speed of 355 kilometers per hour, was flown by Italian and Spanish pilots as early as 1936. Since the Nationalists obtained 380 such planes, mass fighter formations such as the ones Jordan sees were not unusual. The Fiat G-50, which was faster than the CR-32, and the Fiat BR-20, which was better armed, also formed part of the Nationalist Air Force but in much smaller numbers.[13] The observation planes (278–79, 299–300, 302, 306) may also be Fiats. María and Jordan recognize the beauty of the planes (161, 467). See also Fiat planes in "Night Before Battle" in *The Fifth Column*.]

Jordan counts 27 Fiats flying in formation towards La Granja (74, 76, 132), the first indication that the Nationalists are massing for a counter-offensive. See also Heinkel and Junker.

*Finito de Palencia. [Bullfighters are often known by their place of origin, like Finito de Valladolid (q.v. in *DIA*); Palencia is both a province and its capital city. Pilar's Finito seems to be a fictional character.]

The bullfighter Finito was Pilar's lover for five years. Pablo recalls him as a good bullfighter but "handicapped by his short stature" (184; see 182). Pilar admired his professionalism and courage: he was always fearless and skillful in the ring, performing well for his fans in spite of his tuberculosis, his wounds, his pain, and his fear of bulls. She recalls their trips to Valencia (84–86) and Madrid (252). After his greatest triumph, in Valladolid [just south of Palencia], a fan club named itself Club Finito and gave a banquet in his honor. Unable to eat and coughing blood, Finito drank heavily that evening; he died soon after (182–90). See la Niña de los Peines, el Niño Ricardo, Pablo Romero, Pastora, Retana, Ricardo, and President.

Speaks: 86, 183, 186, 188–89; see 55.

*flyer. See Russians, three wounded.

*Ford, [Richard. English lawyer and writer, 1796–1858. Ford is best remembered for *Handbook for Travellers in Spain* (1845) and *Gatherings from Spain* (1846), which was part of Hemingway's Key West library. See also *DIA*.]

Like the narrator of *Death in the Afternoon,* Jordan admires Ford's books on Spain (248; see Borrow).

*Foyot's. [The Hotel Foyot, which closed in 1938, was situated at 33 Rue de Tournon, with a south entrance at 22-bis Vaugirard, the Latin Quarter of Paris. "The rooms at the Foyot were not too expensive, but the hotel's restaurant was fairly dear" (Hansen, 98). Hemingway stayed

at the hotel on 7–9 May, 1927; he married Pauline on 10 May, 1927; at that time the hotel was owned by Lavernoile (Hemingway Collection: Other Materials, Hotel Receipts). The hotel is also mentioned in *SAR*.]
    Jordan recalls "Foyot's old hotel" (51; for Jordan's background, see Jordan, Robert).

*Franco [Bahamonde], Francisco (Generalissimo). [Spanish soldier, 1892–1975; dictator from 1939 until his death. During his early army service in Morocco, Franco was often cited for bravery. At the military uprising which signaled the beginning of the Spanish Civil War, Franco took control of Spanish Morocco in July 1936. In September 1936 the Nationalist forces named him head of state and Commander of Southern Forces. In March 1939 Franco emerged as dictator, consolidating the Nationalists, Carlists and Falangists (qq.v.) and establishing a repressive government which tolerated no opposition or criticism. Franco was born in El Ferrol, in the province of La Coruña in northwest Spain (the area known as Galicia), as was Pablo Iglesias (q.v.).]
    Anselmo mentions that Líster and Franco are both *gallegos* (q.v.) and therefore "either very intelligent or very dumb and brutal" (193, see 230; also see *gallegos* in *THHN*).

*Fuente Ovejuna. [Or *Fuenteovejuna*. Historical comedy by Lope de Vega (q.v.), based on the town's uprising against their abusive and tyrannical governor in 1476. The play is named after the town where the events took place (north-west of the city of Córdoba, close to the border between the provinces of Córdoba and Badajoz). The play, first published in 1619 but written sometime between 1611 and 1618, is one of Lope de Vega's masterpieces. In an impressive scene dominated by the head of the slain tyrant and the royal arms of Ferdinand and Isabella, the citizens proclaim loyalty to the King and Queen and rehearse the answers they will give when interrogated about the murder. Both during this rehearsal scene (III, xiv) and during the judicial inquiry itself (III, xix), each citizen gives the same response: "*Fuenteovejuna lo hizo*" (Fuenteovejuna did it). Asked who Fuenteovejuna is, each one answers that every one of its inhabitants represents the whole town. Reporting back to the King, the Judge explains that in spite of his having tortured three hundred citizens, including ten-year-old children, he was unable to uncover the murderers and that the King must either pardon the village or kill all its inhabitants. The King and Queen of course issue a general pardon, the village always having been loyal to them. The ideology of the play clearly appeals to the Communist Karkov, but the American Jordan is basically committed to individual rather than collective responsibility (see slogans). In addition, as a professor of literature he has more stringent standards than Karkov does.]

Kashkin had told Jordan that Karkov thought *Fuenteovejuna* was "the greatest play ever written." Jordan does not hold the play in the same high esteem (231).

*Galdós. [Full name: Benito Pérez Galdós. Spanish novelist and playwright, 1845–1920. He is admired for his profound observations and vigorous style. Among his best known titles are *Doña Perfecta* (1876), *Gloria* (1877) and *Marianela* (1878).]

American undergraduates like to discuss literature with their instructors, but Jordan thinks that, even if he survives the war and returns to teaching, he and María will not host such discussion groups about "admirable dead" writers like Galdós, Lope de Vega, and Quevedo (164–65).

*Gal, Gall, General Gall. [*Nom de guerre* of Janos Galicz. Hungarian communist; adopted Soviet citizenship, 1919. An inept, unpopular commander in the International Brigades, General Gall led the XI and XV International Brigades (established in December 1936) during the battle of the Jarama, February 1937. He suffered heavy casualties, including more than 300 from the Lincoln Battalion alone. He led the battle of Brunete, July 1937, more successfully. When the five International Brigades were reorganized into two International Divisions, Gall was appointed commander of the 35th Division, composed of the XI, XIII and XV Brigades. The appointment probably reflected his political connections rather than his military abilities. "Virtually all sources except official Communist ones agree that Gall was a vain, egotistical, brutal man and the worst of the International Brigade generals" (Richardson, 72). He was executed by Stalin, probably 1938.[14] See Copic.]

The narrative identifies Gall as a Hungarian, an unpopular leader of the International Brigades (233). Marty mentions that Golz hated Gall (421), and Gall himself knows that "They don't like me down there" (359).

Speaks: 358–59.

gallegos. [People from Galicia, in north-west Spain, an area comprised of four provinces. Galicians were and are known for their independent spirit. The feudal lords of Galicia resisted the Spanish crown throughout the Middle Ages. In the 19th century, this area offered tough opposition to Napoleon. In the 20th century the Galician Francisco Franco (q.v.) was one of the leaders of the Army's rebellion against the Republic. Galicia was once part of Portugal; the distinctive Galician dialect resembles Portuguese. See *gallegos* in *THHN*.]

Anselmo can tell "from hearing them talk" that the sentries (q.v.) at the bridge are *gallegos* (193), as are Franco and Líster (qq.v.) (230).

*el Gallo. See *Gómez Ortega, Rafael.

*Garbo, [Greta. Stage name of Greta Gustaffson. Swedish-born American actress, 1905–1989. Greta Garbo came to the United States in 1925 and made her first film, *The Torrent,* in 1926. In the 1930s the beautiful actress starred in many films: *Anna Christie* (1930), *Mata Hari* (1931), *Grand Hotel* (1932), *As You Desire Me* (1932), *Queen Christina* (1933), *Camille* (1937), and *Ninotchka* (1939). She also appeared in two film versions of Tolstoy's *Anna Karenina:* the silent film with John Gilbert (1927) and the talking remake with Fredric March (1935). Her last movie was *Two Faced Woman* (1941); after her retirement she lived in seclusion in New York. Extraordinarily beautiful and talented, she was not limited to the traditional roles of ingénue and femme fatale.]

Jordan cannot believe his good fortune in having found someone like María and thinks that perhaps she is a vividly-remembered dream, like his dreams about sleeping with Garbo and Harlow (q.v.) (137).[15] María also remembers seeing a Garbo film (346; see also *Gilbert and *Harlow).

*García, don Benito. The mayor of Pablo's town and therefore the first person forced to cross the square between the two rows of waiting townsmen and farmers on the day the Republicans captured the town. Pilar, an eyewitness to the terrible events of that day, tells the story in vivid detail: as García passed the first few men, nothing happened. Then a tenant farmer, who felt that the mayor had dealt unjustly with him, struck García, after which he was beaten until he fell. With the help of some of the others, the farmer who had struck the first blow dragged don Benito to the end of the two rows of men and threw him off the cliff (108–9; see 116).

*Gaylord, Gaylord's, Hotel Gaylord. [The 1940 *Guía-Directorio de Madrid y su provincia* (Bailly-Baillière-Riera, 85, 319, 448) locates "Gaylord's Apartments, hotel y restaurante" at number 3, Alfonso XI street (a handsome street near the Parque del Retiro). In that directory there is no listing for Velázquez 63, the numbers on that street jumping from 61 to 65 (*Guía Directorio,* 670).]

Karkov lives at the Hotel Gaylord, which seems to be the headquarters of the powerful, Russian-supplied faction of the International Brigades. Jordan recalls several meetings at Gaylord's, where good food and drink are available (228 ff.), in contrast with the more ascetic atmosphere at the headquarters of the International Brigades, located at Velázquez 63, Madrid (234–35). For the friction between the communist and other factions in the Republican Army, see barber, Lerroux, and POUM. Jordan has adopted the Russian focus.

*Gellhorn, Martha. [American journalist, war correspondent, and novelist, 1908—; third wife of Ernest Hemingway, 1940–1945. Gellhorn had

published her first novel, *What Mad Pursuit* (1934), and had completed a collection of short stories, *The Trouble I've Seen* (1937), when she met Hemingway in Key West, Florida, in December of 1936. Their romance flourished in Spain during the Spanish Civil War. She is author of *A Stricken Field* (1940), *The Heart of Another* (1941), *Liana* (1944), *The Wine of Astonishment* (1948), *The Honeyed Peace* (1953), *Two by Two* (1958), and *Travels with Myself and Another* (1978).]
Hemingway dedicated *For Whom the Bell Tolls* to Martha Gellhorn.

*Gilbert, Jack. [Stage name of Jack Pringle, American film actor, 1897–1936. Gilbert played several minor parts before achieving stardom. He was acclaimed as "the perfect lover" and played the romantic lead in many films in the 1920s, such as *He Who Gets Slapped* (1925), *The Merry Widow* (1925), *The Big Parade* (1925), *Flesh and the Devil* (1927), and *The Cossacks* (1927). He starred with Greta Garbo in *Love* (1927), based on Tolstoy's novel *Anna Karenina*. Because his voice was weak he was unable to make the transition from silent film to sound.]
In Jordan's erotic dream Garbo was as beautiful and sexy as she was when she played opposite Jack Gilbert (137).

gloria (mystical ecstasy). To express her feelings during orgasm, María uses the phrase *la gloria* (379; see 380, 386). See el Greco, Juan de la Cruz, and *saetas*.

Golz (Comrade General). [Karl Swierczewsky (General Walter) is thought to be the model for General Golz. The Polish Swierczewsky (1896–1947) was a professional soldier. When the Spanish Civil War erupted he recruited volunteers in Paris to accompany him to Spain to fight for the Republican cause. He commanded the XIV International Brigade and then the 35th, taking part in most of the important actions of the Republican army. He is considered one of the best officers of the International Brigades. When Hemingway's Polish translator asked Hemingway why he had not presented Swierczewsky under his real name or under his *nom de guerre* (General Walter), Hemingway replied: "He was such a spendid man and splendid soldier that I wouldn't dare to present him in fictitious situations, and put in his mouth fictitious words" (Meyers, *Hemingway*, 605, n. 16).]
The narrative presents Golz as a Soviet-trained general who commands the 35th Division of the Spanish Republican Army. Jordan admires him (233; see 162). Although he is in charge of the attack on the bridge and the advance on to the town of La Granja, he worries from the beginning that interference or the incompetence of his superiors will undermine the operation. The operation does go as planned, but the fact that the enemy had knowledge of it and had prepared a counteroffensive

renders it pointless. Internal suspicion prevents Jordan's important information about the counteroffensive from reaching Golz in time for him to act on it: the attack has already started and cannot be stopped. The more Jordan thinks about all that Golz has told him, the more he admires him (168–69; see 17, 167, 226, 228, 232, 339–40; also see Walter). Golz is mentioned in conversation at Karkov's party (359) and by Gómez and other Republicans (375, 385, 397, 399, 400, 412, 416, 417, 421, 469).
Speaks: 4–8, 428–30; see 423.

Golz's staff. A Polish- or Russian-speaking member of Golz's staff "growled" at Golz not to make anti-Soviet or anti-communist jokes (8). Golz's Chief of Staff is Duval (q.v.).

*****Gómez.** ["General Gómez" was the *nom de guerre* of Wilhelm Zaisser, German schoolmaster and communist (1893–1958) who supported the Republic, rising to commander of the XIII International Brigade.][16]
Jordan, who believes in discipline, clearly disapproves of "That swine Gómez in Estremadura" who lacks the courage to obey orders (162).

Gómez, Capt. Rogelio. A barber in civilian life (396, 417), he is a dedicated and aggressive Loyalist, Commander of the First Battalion of the 65th Brigade. He does his best to help Andrés deliver Jordan's dispatch: gives him a drink, drives the motorcycle himself, threatens a minor official who refuses them access to Lieutenant-Colonel Miranda, and finally, when Marty refuses to forward the dispatch, argues vehemently with him and curses him (396 ff.). Marty arrests Gómez and Andrés; they are released by Karkov, who enables them finally to deliver the dispatch to Duval, Golz's Chief of Staff. Duval phones the message to Golz, but by this time the attack is underway (chapters 40 and 42). See company commander.
Speaks: 397–98, 414–22, 427.

Gómez's staff. The narrative mentions Gómez's orderly, motorcyclist, and adjutant. Gómez sends his orderly to wake up his motorcycle driver. When he decides to drive the motorcycle himself, Gómez puts his adjutant in charge of the battalion (396).

*****[Gómez Ortega], José (Joselito).** [Spanish matador, 1895–1920. Joselito is considered by most taurine critics to be the best matador of the 20th century. He showed great talent as a boy and had a large following years before his promotion to full matador. By 1912, when he was 17, he reigned supreme among matadors. His performances in the bullring were almost consistently magnificent; he mastered all aspects of bullfighting and fought with grace, gallantry, bravery and great art, becoming a legend in his own time. Until his death, Joselito and Juan Belmonte (q.v. in *SAR*) dominated

the bullring, defining the 1910s as a golden age of bullfighting. His death at the horns of the bull Bailaor in Talavera de la Reina, on 16 May, 1920, shocked the public. Joselito was widely mourned.][17]
The narrative correctly identifies José as a matador killed in the ring at Talavera (251–53). Blanquet claims that he could smell death on José, as he did later on Manuel Granero (q.v.).

*[Gómez Ortega], Rafael (Gallo). [Spanish matador, 1882–1960; older brother of José (q.v. above). At the peak of his career, 1910–1914, he was a picturesque improviser, capable of great artistry and widely acknowledged as an outstanding bullfighter. He retired in 1918, possibly under pressure from his brother, but came out of retirement the next year. He spent the next several seasons in Latin America and was still fighting occasionally in 1935. He is remembered for his extraordinary personality, enormous talent, inimitable style, and erratic and inconsistent behavior, both in and out of the ring.][18]
Pilar's narrative illustrates this bullfighter's unconventional behavior: one day, his manager recalls, Rafael suddenly kissed and flattered him and gave him an expensive diamond stick pin. The manager, familiar with Rafael's devious ways, claims that he immediately and correctly interpreted Rafael's extravagant professions of loyalty and affection to mean that the bullfighter intended to sign on with another manager (187).
Speaks: 187.

*González, don Federico. The owner of the mill and feed store in Pablo's town was, according to Pilar, a committed fascist. He was the second man (after the Mayor, don Benito García, q.v.) to be beaten to death when Pablo and his men took the town. Pilar describes the event: Pablo brought González, at gunpoint, to the beginning of the double line of armed Loyalists; there don Federico stood, paralyzed by fear, until one of the men walked over to him and clubbed him. Galvanized by this first blow, don Federico ran quickly and silently as the two rows of men beat him with flails. At the end of the line he fell, was picked up and thrown over the cliff into the river (109–10).

*González, Felipe. According to Pilar, he (like Pilar herself and like Blanquet, q.v.) had the gypsy's ability to smell death. The smell was so pungent on the bullfighter Sánchez Mejías (q.v.) that Felipe would leave the saloon Villa Rosa whenever that bullfighter walked in (254).

*González, Valentín (el Campesino). [Militant communist, 1909–1985. A colorful, controversial and famous Republican leader, el Campesino presented an image of tough, untutored individualism. He rejected the authority of others but insisted on his own power and demanded immediate obedience from his inferiors. Trained in Russia, he glorified communism and guerrilla warfare, earning great popularity for his daring exploits and his successful leadership of Republican troops in the early battles of the Civil War; he rose to the rank of lieutenant colonel. Later in the war, however, his reputation declined: he seems to have lost interest in his men and in the conflict, and some say he became a coward, hiding from battle. After the war he went to Russia, was interned in a camp (because he opposed Stalin), escaped, went to Iran, was returned to Russia, interned, escaped again, and finally landed in Paris from where he denounced communism. Author of *Vida y muerte en la URSS, Comunista en España y antiestalinista en la URSS,* and *Yo escogí la esclavitud.* González had been a works contractor before committing himself to political activity.][19]

In the narrative, Valentín González appears as a Russian-trained brigade commander of the Republican forces. Because the Republic needed leaders who appeal to the large agrarian population, he was nicknamed ''el Campesino'' (the Peasant); he is not really a peasant but a trained soldier and guerrilla (229; see Abd el Krim). Brave and sometimes indiscreet, González is one of the Russian-speaking clique who frequent the Hotel Gaylord in Madrid (229–30). Jordan admires and trusts him (246; see 234), even though he thinks him indiscreet (230).

*Gracía, Concepción. [Gracía is an unusual family name, and may be a typographical error for the more common García. The name Gracia, without the accent (Grace), might well be Concepción's middle name. As several critics, Spanish and American, have pointed out, the Spanish in Hemingway's work is full of mistakes (see Barea, ''Not Spain But Hemingway,'' and Josephs, ''Hemingway's Poor Spanish'').]

María's best friend was taken prisoner by the Falangists (q.v.) at the same time as María and probably suffered the same treatment. María tells Robert that as she was being dragged out of the barber shop, beaten, gagged, and with her head shaved, Concepción was being dragged in. When Concepción finally recognized María, she began screaming and didn't stop (353).

*Granero [Valls, Manuel] (Manolo). [Spanish bullfighter, 1902–1922. Investiture as matador, 1920; confirmed in Madrid 1921. A talented and accomplished violinist, the adolescent Granero made equally rapid progress when he suddenly turned his attention to bullfighting, acquiring a large following even as a novice. He was graduated as a full-fledged matador in Sevilla on 28 September, 1920, under the auspices of Rafael Gómez Ortega (q.v.), this *alternativa* being confirmed, as tradition requires, in Madrid, on 22 April, 1921, by Manuel Jiménez Moreno (see Chicuelo). In 1921, his first full season as matador, he was lightly gored four times; even so, he managed almost a hundred appearances that season, being hailed as a fine, elegant fighter, a fit successor to José Gómez Ortega (q.v.). He shared bills with other great matadors like Juan Belmonte and Ignacio Sánchez Mejías (q.v.; see Belmonte in *SAR* and *DIA*). His 1922 season began triumphantly but ended after only thirteen *corridas*, Granero being fatally gored by Pocapena (q.v.), the second bull he faced on 7 May, 1922. When Granero stood, sword in hand, ready to kill Pocapena, the bull charged suddenly, veered to the right, gored him in the right thigh, flung him to the ground, pushed him up against the *barrera,* and crushed his head against the wood. Granero died minutes after reaching the plaza's infirmary. On the same bill that day were Juan Luis de la Rosa and Marcial Lalanda (qq.v.), the latter confirming his *alternativa.*][20]

Pilar claims she was at the Plaza de Toros in Madrid on the day Granero was killed: "The horn entirely destroyed the cranium" (252; see 251, 253; also see *Blanquet).

*Grant, [Ulysses S(impson). American military leader, 1822–1885; 18th President of the United States, 1869–1877. After several successful military campaigns, Grant was appointed Commander-in-Chief of the Union forces in the American Civil War; he accepted Lee's surrender at Appomattox Courthouse in 1865 and was made a full general in 1866. His *Personal Memoirs,* 2 vols., is a highly respected military narrative. Grant drank heavily and smoked cigars.]

Jordan admires good military leadership, regardless of ideology. He recognizes the genius both of Union leaders like Grant and Sherman and of Confederate leaders like Stonewall Jackson and Jeb Stuart; he regrets the lack of such leadership "on either side" of the Spanish Civil War (233; see also 227).

*el Greco ["the Greek," pseudonym of Kyriakos Theotokopoulos, painter and sculptor, c.1541–c.1614. He was born in Crete but was active in Italy, where he was known simply as "the Greek." He came to Spain in 1576 or 1577 and, unable to get a court appointment, settled in Toledo. His highly individual style is noted for its emphasis on vertical lines, particularly in the elongated human figures, and, in the religious pictures, the almost mystical religious fervor. The Prado Museum, which Jordan visited, has many of el Greco's portraits and religious paintings, including the famous "Crucifixion," "The Adoration of the Shepherds" and "The Pentecost."]

Thinking of María's phrase *la gloria* and of the mystical state it represents, Jordan is reminded of el Greco (380; see also 235).

guapa (handsome, brave). Robert, Pilar and Santiago (el Sordo) address María as *guapa.*

Guardia Civil (civiles). [A national body, the *guardia civil* replaced various separate provincial law-enforcement agencies. It was established by three royal decrees (28 March, 12 April, and 13 May, 1844). Its members receive military training; the supreme commander carries the rank of field marshal. They wear distinctive black patent-leather hats, are well-armed and -mounted (see Mauser and Velázquez) and are organized into *tercios,* one *tercio* (q.v.) representing a military district or division.[21] Their training and organization predisposed them to support the insurgent Army during the Spanish Civil War: "42,000 chose to support the Nationalists, while the remaining 27,000 remained loyal to the Republic" (Cortada, 131).]

Pablo began the takeover of his town by dynamiting the barracks of the Civil Guards: two men were killed in the explosion, several others died in the ensuing shoot-out, and the last four, who surrendered, were shot by Pablo in the back of the head (99–102, see 115). According to Pablo, one of the officers killed himself (100). Pilar is rebuked for wearing one of their hats (107–8; see also *Paco). Pablo has killed at least two more *guardias* (14) and blinded another (219). Falangists (q.v.) and *guardias civiles* carry out the attack on María's town (351).

Speak: 100–2.

guards. See *Guardia Civil,* sentries and soldiers.

*Guy. See *Hickok, Guy.

gypsies. [Over the centuries gypsies have exerted a strong influence on the spirit, language, dress and folklore of Spain, their contribution being most easily recognized in flamenco music and dance. Their grace and daring are particularly valued in the bullring. Even so, they remain foreign to mainstream Spanish society.]

Pilar, who has gypsy blood, can smell death (252–56), read palms (33–34; see 27, 252, 387, 467) and feel the earth move (174–75); she tolerantly allows that not all gypsies have these abilities and that some non-gypsies are also capable of these things (see Blanquet). On a darker note, she says that "The mind of the gypsy is corrupt" (68).[22] Anselmo claims that because the war has lifted so many social constraints, gypsies have reverted to "bad" tribal behavior (40). He explains that gypsies enjoy drinking, dancing, stealing, and killing; he sees gypsies as living according to their own code, rejecting universalist moral imperatives like "Thou shalt not kill" (40). Jordan finds them irresponsible and untrustworthy, as "worthless" in wartime as "the physically and mentally unfit" (276), but does not express these feelings when he speaks to Rafael (19). Pilar recalls other gypsies, among them bullfighters, singers, and musicians (185, 187, 253–55; see Gómez Ortega,

Rafael; la Niña de los Peines; el Niño Ricardo; see also 467; see Indians).

the Gypsy. See Rafael.

*Hans. See Kahle, Hans.

*Harlow, [Jean. Stage name of Harlean Carpenter. American actress, 1911–1937, died of uremic poisoning. In her short career, Harlow starred in several movies, including *Hell's Angels* (1930), *Public Enemy* (1931), *Beast of the City* (1932), *Dinner at Eight* (1933), *Hold Your Man* (1933), *Bombshell* (1933); *Saratoga* was released posthumously. She married three times: Charles Fremont McGrew in 1927, Paul Bern in 1932, and Harold Rosson in 1933. Harlow created the fad for the platinum blonde.][23]
Jordan has often dreamt that Harlow came to his bed (137; see also Garbo).

*Heinkel, [Ernst Heinrich. German aircraft designer, 1888–1958. The son of a well-established family of artisans, Heinkel abandoned his studies and turned to the manufacture of aircraft in 1909, after visiting the International Exposition of Aviation. He joined the Hansa Company, which produced aircraft used by the German armies in World War I. In 1922 he established his own factory, the Ernst Heinkel Flugzeugwerke, which developed into the Heinkel Gruppe. Several of his craft won prizes in various national and international races; in 1938 the German General Ernst Udet (q.v. in *ARIT*) set the world speed record of 634.37 kilometers per hour in a Heinkel 112. Heinkel ultimately held 22 international flight records. The Heinkel 111, one of his most famous designs, could carry two tons of cargo at a speed of 375 km/hr (about 235 mph).][24]
Jordan, Pablo and Rafael are dismayed to see many enemy planes flying overhead. Jordan estimates pretty accurately that the Heinkel 111s are flying at a speed of 250 miles per hour (76; see 75, 86–87, 132). They are preceded and followed by Fiat pursuit planes and indicate that the Nationalists have learned of the planned Republican attack and are massing for a counter-offensive. Nationalist bombers attack Santiago's hilltop (320–21; see 312, 323; see also Fiat and Junker).

*[Hickok,] Guy. [American journalist, 1888–1951. Hickok met Hemingway in 1922, traveled with him to Italy in 1927 and to Spain in 1929. He was chief of the Paris office of the *Brooklyn Daily Eagle* until 1933, after which he returned to the United States (Meyers, *Hemingway,* 83–84; Baker, *Life,* 629).]
Guy is a friend of Jordan's in the United States (381).

*Horatius [Cocles, Publius. A legendary hero of ancient Rome. In the sixth century BCE, he and two companions heroically defended the first entrance of the Sublican bridge (i.e., the one on the far bank of the River Tiber) from the attacking Etrurians (Etruscans or Tuscans), keeping the enemy at bay while the Romans demolished the bridge in order to prevent invasion. After the bridge fell and Rome was secure, Horatius jumped into the Tiber and swam across the river to Rome. The Roman historian Livy presented an account of Horatius' actions in *The History of Rome, Book II;* Hemingway included the passage in the anthology he edited, *Men at War: The Best War Stories of All Time* (1942; New York: Bramhall House, 1979), 221–22. According to Livy, Horatius accused the Etrurians of being "slaves of haughty tyrants who . . . came to oppress the liberty of others" (222). The parallels between democratic Rome and Loyalist Spain, and the emphasis, in both instances, on the destruction of a bridge, connect Jordan to Horatius, Jordan's denial inviting rather than rejecting the comparison. Unlike Jordan, however, the Roman hero survived, "swam across safe to his party," and was given many public honors and "as much land . . . as he could plow in one day" (*Men at War,* 222).]

Jordan would like to avoid heroics and early death in order to live a long life with María (164; see Dutch boy).

Hordan, Hordown. [Whore-down or whore-done; Spanish pronunciation of Jordan's name.]

Golz jokes that Jordan has "a funny name in Spanish" (7). See Hotze.

*horse contractor. [In *Death in the Afternoon,* the horse contractor is presented as a greedy, despicable character who, rather than provide new horses to replace those which have been gored, stuffs his wounded horses with sawdust, sews them up, and returns them to the ring. Such weak, frightened horses endanger the lives of the picadors who ride them. The narrator says scornfully that "you may have all the horse contractors I have ever met" (*DIA* 187).]

Before becoming a revolutionary, Pablo worked for a horse contractor. Before that, he worked with pack horses for many years (182, 190). Don José Castro (q.v.) was also a horse contractor (123).

Hotze. [The Spanish rendering of Golz's name sounds either, like a sneeze or like "hots" or "hots-eh."]

Golz jokes that if he had known more about Spanish pronunciation he would have chosen a different *nom de guerre* (7).

Hungarian general, Hungarian divisional commander. Two Hungarian commanders with the rank of General were Gal and Lucasz (qq.v.). Lucasz was 41 when he was killed at Huesca, and the Hungarian at the

Hotel Gaylord is seven or eight years older (358). His age, as well as his admission of his unpopularity with Golz and other Republican figures (233, 359), suggests that this Hungarian is Gal (q.v.).[25]

husband. After Jordan pledges himself to María and promises her a more formal ceremony, they call each other husband and wife (354). See wife.

*[Ibárruri Gómez], Dolores (la Pasionaria). [Spanish politician and patriot, 1895–1989. The uneducated daughter of a miner, she rose rapidly in the ranks of the Spanish Communist Party, becoming a member of the Central Committee. She was elected member (from Asturias) of the Republic's Parliament. Her fiery oratory energized the Republican cause. She coined the Republican motto, "¡No pasarán!" ("They shall not pass!" in a speech of 19 July, 1936); she spoke a passionate farewell to the International Brigades when they were repatriated (November 1938). After the Civil War she lived in the USSR and continued her political activity in exile; she was Secretary-General of the Spanish Communist Party. After the death of Franco, she returned to Spain. She wrote two autobiographical volumes, *El único camino* and *Me faltaba España*; her collected speeches and articles were published in 1938.[26] Hemingway attacks her by presenting her slogans as empty, appealing only to the young or to those who, like the pompous *Izvestia* correspondent, accept propaganda as fact. See also Pasionaria in *ARIT*.]

La Pasionaria has reported that the fascists were quarreling among themselves in Segovia. The emotional *Izvestia* correspondent represents the many Republicans who were heartened by this news, by her rhetoric in general, and by "that great voice where pity, compassion and truth are blended" (357; see 358). On the hilltop battle, Joaquín quotes her slogans (308–9; see *Izvestia* and slogans).

*Ibárruri's family. [In 1916 the young Dolores Ibárruri married Julián Ruiz Gavina, a miner five years older than she, by whom she had six children. Four children died in infancy: Ester (1916–1919); Amagoya and Azucena, two of the triplets born in 1923; and Eva (born and died in 1928). The remaining triplet, Amaya, and the only son, Rubén (b. 1920 or 1921, d. 1942) survived childhood; Amaya was the only one to outlive her mother. By 1934, having been jailed several times for her political activities and increasingly called away to speak and attend meetings, Ibárruri decided to send Amaya and Rubén to school in Russia. At the time of the action of the novel, Rubén was 16 or 17 years old and still studying in a Russian military academy, a fact which aroused much criticism of la Pasionaria. Even according to his mother, who was eager to defend her son from the charge of malingering, Rubén did not come to Spain to fight until July 1938 (the Battle of the Ebro), when he served under Modesto (q.v.); thus the report that he was safely sitting out the war in Moscow reflects the truth of the situation in May 1937, when one of Santiago's band makes this accusation. When the Republic fell, Rubén was briefly interned in a concentration camp in France, after which, like his mother and many other Republicans, he lived in the USSR. Rubén served in the Soviet Army during World War II and was killed in the defense of Leningrad, September 1942. Amaya grew up and married in Russia, becoming the mother of la Pasionaria's only grandchildren: Fyodor, Dolores and Rubén.][27]

One of Santiago's men mocks Joaquín's admiration for la Pasionaria, claiming that she has sent her son to Russia, where he can safely sit out the war (309, 311).

*Iberians. [Ancient inhabitants of Spain, believed to have migrated from Africa to the Iberian Peninsula (i.e., Spain and Portugal) in prehistoric times.]

Jordan theorizes that pre-Christian, murderous impulses still survive among the Spaniards, giving them an almost spiritual passion for killing. But then he cautions himself not to romanticize the ancient peoples of the Iberian peninsula (287).

*Iglesias, Pablo. [Spanish union leader and a socialist politician, 1850–1925. Iglesias was instrumental in establishing the Spanish Socialist Party, which he eventually headed. He was president of the Unión General de Trabajadores (UGT) and edited the newspaper El Socialista, the official organ of the Spanish labor movement. Brought up in an orphanage, he was sympathetic to the plight of the working class. His unremitting efforts to obtain better conditions for the workers led to his being imprisoned eight times.][28]

In his anger and depression at Pablo's theft of his equipment, Jordan curses all Spaniards and their leaders, excepting only Pablo Iglesias. But even Iglesias, Jordan thinks, might not have been able to live through the Spanish Civil War without compromising his principles (370).

Ignacio. One of the members of Santiago's guerrilla band. He holds the tripod of the automatic rifle as Santiago (el Sordo) fires it at the oncoming planes. Ignacio is killed by one of the bombs; his dead body covers that of the wounded Joaquín (320–22; see Santiago).

Speaks: 321.

*Indians. Jordan's grandfather was involved not only in the Civil War but also in American campaigns against the Indians (338). Jordan's own memories of Indians are peaceful and often involve the sense of smell (260); Pilar's bed seems to him to smell like that of an Indian (360). Pilar combines "gypsy blood" (28) and "high Indian cheekbones" (298). Both groups feel kinship with animals: like gypsies, Indians "believe the bear to be a brother of man" (40).[29] But Jordan recognizes that both gypsies and Indians can be cruel to their enemies (40, 336). Santiago looks like an Indian (141).

el Inglés (the Englishman). Because he speaks English, Jordan is called an Englishman by most of the characters (e.g., 290–91). He tells María, "I'm not an *Inglés*" (159); he is an American. Mora (q.v.) looks like an *Inglés* (316, 319).

*Italians. [Italy was a major supplier of both troops and materiel to the Nationalists during the Spanish Civil War; see Fiat.]
    Jordan enjoyed hearing how the XII International Brigade defeated an Italian contingent (233; see Kahle, Hans). He worries that enough Italian troops have joined the Nationalists to enable them to be deployed on two fronts (334).

Izvestia [(News or Announcements). Daily newspaper published in Moscow; founded in 1917 in Petrograd as an organ of the Bolsheviks; it moved to Moscow in 1918. From the beginning the paper functioned as "the organ of the Central Executive Committee of the USSR and the All-Russian Central Executive Committee. It deals with the life of the Union and autonomous republics . . . as well as the development of the economy and culture of the peoples of the USSR." In the 1930s, the paper supported the five-year plans for economic advance and "extensively reflected the heroic labor and creative initiative of the masses and the leading and directing role of the Communist Party in the building of socialism." The paper not only informed its readers of governmental policy but also interpreted international events in the light of these policies. Even after World War II, the paper was concerned with "the ideological education of the Soviet people" (*Great Soviet Encyclopedia*, X: 521). By 1932 it had a circulation of 1.5 million.]
    One of *Izvestia's* correspondents in Spain tells Karkov that he has heard from la Pasionaria the heartening news that the fascists are fighting among themselves. He waxes lyrical about la Pasionaria and then goes off to write his report about her, which will be inaccurate (357–58), since the battle referred to is probably the one between Santiago and the Nationalists. See Ibárruri and journalists.

*Jackson, [Thomas Jonathan] (Stonewall). [American soldier, 1824–1863. A graduate of the American Military Academy at West Point, Jackson fought in Mexico. Finding military service in peacetime irksome, Jackson resigned his commission and taught military science and

strategy at Virginia Military Institute from 1851 to 1861, during which
time he lost his first wife, remarried, traveled in Europe, and became
intensely religious. When the Civil War broke out, Jackson became
Colonel of Volunteers for the Confederate Army, rapidly gaining fame
and promotion. He acquired his nickname by standing against the Union
forces "like a stone wall." Military historians rank Stonewall Jackson
among the most effective of the Confederacy's generals, second only to
Robert E. Lee. He was strict, fervently committed to the cause, and an
outstanding tactician. He is remembered for his great victories in the
Shenandoah Valley, the second battle of Bull Run, and the battle at
Fredericksburg, all in 1862. He was killed accidentally, probably shot by
his own troops who mistook him and his men for Union cavalry.
Cantwell quotes Jackson's famous last words (*ARIT* 307).]
    Jordan admires effective military leadership like that of Stonewall
Jackson (233; see also Grant).

*Joaquín. A peasant from Pablo and Pilar's home town who is nervous
about participating in the flailing of the fascists, which Pablo organized
when he captured the town. Pilar reports that he asked whether women
would be included and was relieved when she assured him that no
women would be killed. He is sweating heavily and crying because he
has never killed anyone (105–6).
    Speaks: 105–6.

Joaquín. An 18-year-old member of Santiago's guerrilla band. His
pigtail (the traditional *coleta* worn by bullfighters) indicates that his
ambition is to become a bullfighter. Joaquín participates in the blowing
up of the train and helps carry María, who had been on that train, to the
safety of Pablo's camp (132–33). He is proud of his souvenir from that
operation, a steel helmet which he wears during the band's last battle
(308). He rejects complexity and relies on charms and formulas: he likes
"military terms because it makes orders clearer and for better discipline" (132), rejects all criticism of la Pasionaria, recites her slogans to
keep up his nerve when the hilltop position is under siege (308–9), and,
when the enemy planes attack, abandons his Republican training in
mid-sentence and reverts to the formulas of Catholic prayer (321). The
only member of Santiago's band to survive the air bombing, he is shot
by Lieutenant Paco Berrendo (320–22; see slogans and Santiago).
    Speaks: 131–34, 138–41, 308–9, 311, 321.

*Joaquín's family. Santiago's young associate, Joaquín, reveals that the
fascists killed his father, mother, sister and brother-in-law. They hold
another sister in prison and his other brother-in-law is hiding in the hills;
Joaquín does not expect him to survive the war (138–39).

*Jockey Club. [Located at 127, Boulevard du Montparnasse, the Jockey Club was one of the "in" night clubs of Paris in the 1920s, where pleasure-seekers and society figures would gather. "Decorated by Hilaire Hiler, painted by Utrillo, the Jockey drew the likes of [the model] Kiki . . . and [the sensational black dancer] Josephine Baker," beautiful women who appeared in the nude. Leland reports its current address, 146, Boulevard du Montparnasse (*Hemingway's Paris*, 43).]

Remarking that the acquisition of horses has undermined Pablo's commitment to a political cause and turned him into a grasping capitalist, Jordan thinks that the next step for him will be the snobbish desire to see and be seen at places like the Jockey Club (16).

Jordan, Robert (Bob, Roberto, don Roberto, Hordan, Hordown, husband, *el Inglés*, Comrade Dynamiter, don Juan Tenorio). Jordan is an American college instructor at the University of Montana at Missoula [founded 1893], where he teaches Spanish language and literature (163–65, 209–210, 335). Drawn to the Spanish Civil War by professional, political, and personal interest, he takes a leave of absence and arrives in Spain in the summer of 1936 (165; the Civil War broke out in July 1936). A demolitions expert, he has blown trains in Estremadura (q.v.). He also fought at Carabanchel and Usera during the Republican defense of Madrid (237, 304) and now, in late May 1937, he has been commissioned to destroy a bridge in the Sierra de Guadarrama northwest of Madrid, in order to prevent reinforcements from reaching the fascist positions which Golz will attack. When he realizes that the fascists are massing forces for a counter-offensive, Jordan suggests that the attack be cancelled or postponed, but by the time his message reaches Golz, the Republican aerial attack has already begun. Cued by the sound of the planes, Jordan successfully carries out his assignment, although he correctly suspects that the entire operation is doomed and that his own action and the several deaths it entails, including his own, will serve no purpose. Jordan's background is varied: he witnessed a lynching in Ohio (116–17), played football, probably in college (438), has worked on a variety of engineering and demolition projects (165), has visited Spain frequently over a ten-year period (4, 248), has been to Paris (16, 51), sailed to Cuba (260), and is familiar with the sharks of the Gulf Stream (87). He has written a book about Spain and hopes to write another (248; see 87, 134, 163, 165). During the last few days of his life, Jordan has come to know the members of Pablo's gang, prepared his attack on the bridge, conducted an intense love affair, revealed some of his history and philosophy, and learned to value the present. See Kashkin; also see endnote 1. For Jordan's political development, see Golz, Karkov, Largo Caballero, and *Russians, three wounded.

Speaks: 1–15, 18–34, 37–47, 49–53, 56–58, 60–62, 65–73, 75–84,

87–92, 96–100, 103–4, 116–17, 128–29, 131–32, 134, 138–53, 155–61, 170–82, 190, 198, 202–13, 217, 220–22, 226–27, 232, 238, 240–57, 259–64, 266–72, 274–80, 282–301, 303, 323–25, 329–33, 341–50, 352–55, 360–62, 370–71, 378–81, 384–85, 387–90, 392, 394, 402–10, 435–40, 445–48, 450–51, 453–65, 468; several long and short interior monologues.

*Jordan's family. Jordan admires and identifies with his paternal grandfather, who led "irregular" troops in the American Civil War (339, 233), much as Jordan is doing in the Spanish Civil War, and was knowledgeable about military history. Jordan often thinks of his grandfather (66–67, 335–40, 369, 386, 467, 469; see also Custer, Kilpatrick, Mosby, Quantrill, Sheridan, Republican). See endnote 1.
    Grandfather speaks: 336–37, 339.
    Jordan is an only child (381). His father was a doctor whose emotionalism embarrasses his son (405–6, 410). His suicide is a troubling issue for Jordan, although at the end of the novel he is ready to kill himself (66–67, 337–40, 386, 405–6, 469). Jordan thinks of his mother seldom and without affection, calling her "that woman" and blaming his father for letting her "bully him" (339).
    Father speaks: 405.

*Jordan's women. See wife and *women and girls.

*José. See Gómez Ortega, José.

journalists. The newspapers published by the various factions on both sides of the conflict indicate both the importance of the press and its lack of objectivity (see, for example, 249). A person's political affiliation could be deduced from the newspaper he read, hence the various taunts about who is reading what (see *el Debate*). In addition, newspapers (which can be read by the enemy) pose a threat to security. According to the military, journalists, who disseminate information as well as disinformation and propaganda, "should be shot" (358; see 228). Jordan suspects that even Karkov, whom he admires, subordinates journalism to politics: Karkov uses the power of the press, as well as of his political connections, to intimidate Marty (424–25) and to aggrandize Miaja (237; see *Izvestia* and *Pravda*). The "puffy-eyed" journalist at Karkov's apartment is mocked for being so gullible as to believe Ibárruri (357–58). Russian journalists live in luxury, with "electric stoves in their rooms" (347; Philip Rawlings and Dorothy Bridges are similarly well-equipped in *Fifth Column*).
    Speaks: 357–58.

*Juan de la Cruz, San. [(St. John of the Cross). Spanish priest, poet and theologian, 1542–1591. His secular name was Juan de Yepez y Alvarez; in religion his name was Juan de San Matías. After meeting St. Theresa of Avila and undertaking, with her, to reform the Carmelite Order, he took the name Juan de la Cruz. He founded several monasteries of the Discalced (Barefoot) Carmelites, a much stricter order than the unreformed Carmelites, by whom he was imprisoned for several months in 1578. He was beatified in 1674 and canonized in 1726. His poetry was mystical, passionate and rich in images. His complete works, *Obras espirituales* (c.1618), include *Noche obscura del alma* (Dark Night of the Soul), *Llama de amor viva* (Flame of Divine Love), and *Cánticos espirituales entre el alma y Cristo su esposo* (Spiritual Canticles).][30]

Attempting to define the phrase *la gloria,* Jordan says that it is akin to the mystic ecstasy found in the painting of el Greco and in the writings of San Juan de la Cruz (380; see *saeta*).

*Judas Iscariot. [The disciple who betrayed Jesus Christ for thirty pieces of silver.]

Pilar connects Pablo's treachery to that of Judas Iscariot. She correctly recalls how Judas Iscariot killed himself (391).

Julián. A lieutenant in the Carlist cavalry, he "had led the [first] assault" and was killed early in the battle between the Carlists and Santiago's band (310, 322). He is mourned by his friend Lieutenant Berrendo (316, 318, 322; see also 326).

*Junker. [Probably the Junker Ju 86, built for Lufthansa in 1934 as an advanced airliner that could easily be converted to a bomber. The Junker was not as fast as the Heinkel 111. See also Junker in "Night Before Battle" in *The Fifth Column*.]

Although Pablo has occasionally seen Junkers (76), he has never seen such a large display of aerial power as the one presently flying overhead (see also Fiat and Heinkel; see endnote 13).

*[Kahle], Hans. [German soldier, 1899–c.1948. A professional soldier in the German Army, he was among the first foreign volunteers to come to Spain to fight for the Republic; he was involved in the early defense of Madrid. He commanded the XI Brigade in 1937 and the 45th division in 1937 and again in 1938, achieving the rank of colonel. After the war he lived in exile.][31]

The narrative correctly identifies Hans as a Communist and leader of the XI International Brigade (136); he is described in positive terms (234). At the communist headquarters in Madrid (the Hotel Gaylord), he had told

Jordan about a successful battle against the Italians, showing him maps and reporting the clever maneuvers so vividly that Jordan could "see it all" (233).[32] Like Kleber and Lucasz, he was active in the defense of Madrid.

*Kamenev, [Leon (Leo or Lev) Borisovich. Original family name: Rosenfeld. Russian politician, 1883–1936. A Leninist revolutionary, Kamenev spent several years in exile. After the Russian revolution of 1917 he formed part of the Soviet Executive but, like Zinoviev, he opposed Lenin's insistence on further revolution and had to resign. In 1918 he was elected president of the Soviet in Moscow and when Lenin died in 1924 he shared power with Zinoviev and Stalin. With his brother-in-law Trotsky, he opposed Stalin; he was twice expelled from the party (1927, 1932) and was executed in the Stalinist purges of August 1936.][33]
Karkov describes Kamenev as a political assassin and expresses his disgust for him, Zinoviev, and Rykov. Privately to Jordan he admits the necessity of politically-motivated murder (245).

Karkov. A clever and resourceful Russian journalist for *Pravda* and a high-ranking member of the International Brigade in Spain, rumored to be in direct communication with Stalin. When Andrés and Gómez are arrested by Marty, the corporal calls Karkov, who overrules Marty and thus enables Jordan's dispatch to reach Golz. Karkov is a civilized man: like Jordan he enjoys the food and drink available at the Hotel Gaylord (228) and he shares Jordan's love of Spain and Spanish literature, particularly Lope de Vega (231; see *Fuente Ovejuna*). He read and liked Jordan's book and undertakes to educate Jordan about Spain and politics (242–48, 339). He admits to literary ambitions (244). Jordan admires Karkov's intelligence and character (231, see also 232, 421, 423, 467) and is impressed that Karkov (like María) is prepared to kill himself (237–39; see 229, 356; see also journalists and Russians, three wounded).[34]
Speaks: 238–39, 242–48, 357–59, 424–26.

Karkov's mistress. She is beautiful, voluptuous, and occasionally unfaithful (232). She speaks German (357).[35]
Speaks: 357.

Karkov's wife. Thin, dark and serious, she is an interpreter. She accepts Karkov's infidelity. Karkov respects her. There are rumors that Karkov has another wife or two (232; see 356 and endnote 35).

*Kashkin. [The name and psychological identification (but not the biography) of this character come from Ivan Kashkin (Russian critic, translator and teacher, 1899–1963), whom Hemingway authorized to translate *FWBT*. Hemingway described Kashkin to Edmund Wilson as "a wonderful critic. I thought that he knew what I was trying to do better than I did" (Baker, *Letters,* 793 and 420–21). He expressed his admiration directly to Kashkin in a 1939 letter (Baker, *Letters,* 480).]

Like Jordan, Kashkin was an explosives expert who served in various parts of Spain (250) before being commissioned to work with Pablo's band. He helps them blow up the train at Arevalo (29, 31, 52, 148; the town of Arevalo is in the province of Avila, about thirty miles east and slightly north of Segovia), their last important assignment until Jordan comes to blow up the bridge. The guerrillas remember that Kashkin spoke often and fearfully of being wounded or tortured; he made Pablo's band promise to shoot him if he were wounded during the attack on the train (21). The truth about Kashkin's death emerges slowly. At first Jordan tells Pablo that when he was wounded, Kashkin killed himself (21); later he says that Kashkin died ten days after blowing up a train (23); finally Jordan reveals that he and Kashkin ran into a fascist patrol and Kashkin was wounded; when he was too weak to travel, Jordan shot him "At his request" (249; also see 149, 171, 256). Kashkin is an interesting, invisible double to Jordan: they perform the same job (24), look alike (14, 45), are similarly concerned with death, pain, and suicide, and even smoke the same cigarettes (20). Kashkin is often called "the other one." See also 91, 231–32, 237, 250–51, 253, 269, 271, 289, 309, 311.

Khotze. Spanish mispronunciation of Golz (7); see also Hotze.

*Kilpatrick, General Hugh Judson (Kill Cavalry Kilpatrick), Killy-the-Horse. [American soldier and diplomat, 1836–1881. Immediately upon graduation from the Military Academy at West Point in 1861, Kilpatrick entered service in the Union forces. He was wounded a few weeks later, but quickly recovered and served as lieutenant colonel of cavalry for much of 1862 and 1863. The Kilpatrick raid on Richmond, Virginia, designed to free Union soldiers from Libby Prison, was a failure. In 1864 Kilpatrick fought under Sherman at the Battle of Jonesboro, was wounded and, still unwell, participated in Sherman's march from Atlanta to the sea. After the war Kilpatrick was appointed minister to Chile, 1865–1868, a position he held again in 1881. He died in Chile. Because of the enormous losses the cavalry suffered under Kilpatrick's command, he was nicknamed "Kill Cavalry Kilpatrick."][36]

Jordan says he has a letter General Sheridan (q.v.) wrote to Killy-the-Horse Kilpatrick, praising Jordan's grandfather (339).

*Kleber, [Emilio. *Nom de guerre* of Lazar (or Manfred) Stern. Rumanian military man, 1895–1938. Kleber fought with the Austrians in World War I and with the Bolsheviks during the Russian Revolution. His military experience was highly valued by the Republicans; he was a commander of the XI International Brigade, which defended Madrid in 1936. Kleber was relieved of this position when the government became suspicious that he might use his popularity with his men to stage a coup. When the five International Brigades were regrouped into two Divisions, Kleber followed Lucasz as commander of the 45th Division, composed of the XII and XIV International Brigades. He returned to the USSR in 1937 and was executed by Stalin in 1938.][37]

The narrative identifies Kleber as one of the Russian-trained leaders of the International Brigades, a good soldier but "limited" and somewhat indiscreet. He was instrumental in the defense of Madrid, but General Miaja, jealous of his fame, "forced the Russians to relieve Kleber of his command" (233; see also 370). Like Karkov, Hans, and Jordan, he is one of the crowd at the communist headquarters at the Hotel Gaylord in Madrid.

*Kolchak, [Aleksandr Vasilyevich. Russian admiral and counter-revolutionary, 1874–1920. He commanded the Black Sea fleet in World War I. After the Bolshevik Revolution of 1917, he organized an anti-revolutionary government in Siberia, which was recognized by the Allies. He assumed dictatorship in 1918 and was defeated in 1919; he was shot the following year.]

Remembering Golz's triumphs, Marty mentions that Golz had fought against Kolchak (421).

*Lalanda [del Pino], Marcial. [Spanish matador, 1903–1990. Investiture as matador, 1921; confirmed in Madrid, 1922. Like many great matadors before him, Lalanda was a child prodigy and, after the death of Joselito in 1920, considered one of the major figures in bullfighting. In spite of accidents and two serious illnesses, which reduced the number of his appearances in the ring, he seemed to improve from season to season; his success was astounding. Two serious gorings in 1927 seemed only to increase his courage, and the next few years established him as one of the all-time masters of the art. His 1929 season was brilliant; in 1930 he fought an impressive 87 engagements; in 1931 the taurine critics, never given to understatement, were hard put to describe his masterful performances. Lalanda's great success allowed him to charge enormous fees, and he consequently reduced the number of his appearances to 35 in 1933, 41 in 1934, and 43 in 1935. He performed in 48 bullfights during the three years of the Civil War, in support of the Nationalist cause. After the war he returned to his more usual schedule of between 40 and 50 fights a year until his retirement in 1942.[38] Lalanda was born and lived all his life in Madrid, far from gypsy influence.]

Unlike Blanquet, de la Rosa, and Pilar, Lalanda is unable to "smell death" (251–52).

*Largo [Caballero, Francisco (the Spanish Lenin). Politician and labor organizer, 1869–1946. Largo Caballero joined the Socialist party in 1894 and was one of the organizers of Spain's general strike of 1917; he was sentenced to life imprisonment but was released in 1918 when he was elected to the Spanish Cortes (Parliament). He was the secretary general of Spain's workers' union for twenty years (1918–1938), becoming a highly respected socialist leader, like Pablo Iglesias (q.v.). When the dictatorship of Primo de Rivera fell in 1930, he was appointed Secretary of Labor in the Republican government. His socialism became more extreme; accused of fomenting the uprising in Asturias in 1934, he was jailed for a few months. For almost a year he was both Prime Minister and Secretary of War (September 1936–July 1937). After the Spanish Civil War he lived in France. Captured by the Germans in World War II, he was interned in a concentration camp; he died in Paris soon after the end of the war. After the death of Franco he was reinterred in Spain.[39] Within the Republican spectrum, Largo Caballero was to the left of the Communists. Jordan, who accepts Communist discipline and the ideology implicit in it, has moved to the right from the days when he used to approve of this Socialist leader. On the movement from left to right, see Orwell, 55–56, qtd. in Lerroux entry.]

Jordan once approved of this Spanish leader but, in his anger at Pablo's theft and treachery, he decides that all Spanish leaders, including Largo Caballero, are traitors (369–70).

*Lenin, [Vladimir Ilyich. Real name: Vladimir Ilyich Ulyanov. Russian lawyer and revolutionary, 1870–1924. A disciple of Karl Marx, Lenin encouraged workers to unite and challenge their bosses. He was exiled to Siberia for three years (1887–1900) and then went abroad to agitate for the overthrow of the Russian czars and the introduction of a socialist system to Russia. Soon after the Russian Revolution of 1917, Lenin, who controlled the Communist Party, was virtual dictator of postrevolutionary Russia, being at that time more powerful than Trotsky, Stalin and Rykov (qq.v.). He nationalized all industry, abolished private ownership of land, outlawed religion, and brutally silenced all opposition. In 1919 he established the Third International (the Communist International, or Comintern) to further the cause of world revolution.]

Jordan learned that many Spanish peasants and workers, forced to flee Spain in 1934, had gone to Russia, where they had been sent "to the military academy [the Frunze Institute, where Líster and Modesto studied] and to the Lenin Institute," supported by the Comintern (229). Ibárruri's son is said to be "studying dialectics" in Russia (311; see Ibárruri's family). Largo Caballero (q.v.) was nicknamed the Spanish Lenin.

*Lerroux [García, Alejandro. Spanish journalist, orator and politician, 1864–1949. As a young journalist he was often jailed for his revolutionary and republican campaigns, but his revolutionary fervor seemed to wane as he achieved political clout. He was accused of abandoning republicanism in favor of pragmatic political alliances. He led the government intermittently in 1934–1935 and spent the years of the Civil War in Portugal, returning to Franco's Spain in 1947.[40] George Orwell agrees with Agustín: Largo Caballero's government (1936–37) "contained ministers representing the UGT (Socialist trade unions) and the CNT (Syndicalist unions controlled by the Anarchists). . . . But every subsequent reshuffling of the Government was a move towards the right. . . . The general swing to the Right [within the Republican government] dates from about October–November 1936, when the USSR began to supply arms to the Government and power began to pass from the Anarchists to the Communists" (Orwell, 54–55).]

The narrative identifies Lerroux as a partisan leader who had moved from the left to the right of the political spectrum, a phenomenon Agustín thinks is widespread (285). Jordan compares Lerroux to Pablo (163).

*Lewis, [Colonel Isaac Newton. American soldier and inventor, 1858–1931. After graduating from West Point in 1884, Lewis served in the army, rising to the rank of Colonel. In 1891 he patented the first of many artillery designs and improvements, the most famous of which is the 1911 Lewis machine gun (the air-cooled Lewis Mark I), widely used by the Allies during World War I and later adopted by the Americans as well. "The Lewis was simple in design and easy to tear down in the field when it jammed, which was frequently" (Tunis, *Weapons*, 129–30). Col. Lewis retired from the Army in 1913, due to a service-related disability.]

The Republican Army sent a *máquina* (machine) for the train-blowing operation at Arevalo in which Kashkin was involved; that gun was "lost" (29–30) but the Republican Army later supplied two others, one for Pablo's band and one for Santiago's (271, see porters). From Rafael's description, Jordan deduces that the weapon is an "automatic rifle" or Lewis gun, which stands on a tripod and gets hot when fired (26–27, see 29). Jordan sets up but does not shoot this weapon when the Nationalist cavalry show up (266–68, 276–78, 280–81). At the bridge he fires it at the enemy tank (452, 454), and carries it up the hill (454). Santiago (el Sordo) used his *máquina* to kill Mora during his hilltop fight (307, 313, 319). The Nationalists and Carlists have this weapon too (29–30, 314). It is a valuable piece of equipment and is mentioned often.

*Líster [Forján, Enrique. Spanish communist militant, 1907—. The son of a poor family which migrated to Cuba while he was still a child, Líster went to Spain in 1932 and then to the USSR, where he worked as a sweeper while studying military science in Moscow's Frunze Institute (see Lenin, above). He returned to Spain in 1935, dedicating himself to construction work and revolution. He was one of the main organizers and later a commander of the Fifth Regiment, which later became the Popular Army of the Republic. He wrote often for the regiment's newspaper, *Milicia Popular*. He participated in all the major battles of the conflict, rising to the rank of colonel. He had a strong personality and was a successful commander. After the war he returned to the USSR, continued his military studies, and fought in the Soviet army during World War II, attaining the rank of general. After Franco's death he returned to Spain and headed the small Spanish Communist Worker's Party (PCOE); in 1986 he rejoined the Spanish Communist Party. Among his books are *Nuestra guerra, ¡Basta!* and *Memorias de un luchador*.][41]

The narrative correctly identifies Líster as a former stonemason and one of the Russian-trained leaders of the Republican Army (311). Hans reports that, like Modesto and el Campesino, Líster fought well against the Italians (234) and is "more than reliable . . . magnificent" (246). He is often at the Hotel Gaylord. Like most of the Russian-trained Communists, Líster enforced strict discipline (234, 235).

See also 193, 230, 354.

*Livingstone, Dr. [David. Scottish physician, Christian missionary and explorer, 1813–1873. Livingstone made three long exploratory journeys in Africa. When he had long been absent and was presumed dead, the Welsh explorer and journalist Henry Morton Stanley (1840–1904) was commissioned to look for him, somewhere in Africa. Stanley found him in Ujiji, greeting him with the now-famous understatement, "Dr. Livingstone, I presume?" Stanley's first book, *How I Found Livingstone* (1872), was thought to be a wild exaggeration, but Livingstone confirmed the story.]

Jordan jokes that he and María could register in a hotel as "Doctor and Mrs. Livingstone I presume" (164).

*Lope de Vega (Carpio, Félix. Prolific and popular Spanish playwright and poet, 1562–1635. Lope de Vega led an exciting life which included two marriages, several mistresses, a stint in the Spanish Armada, and various skirmishes with the law; in 1613 he became a priest whose self-flagellation covered the walls of his cell with blood. He was a prolific writer of verse and prose novels but is best remembered for his drama, which he produced at a furious rate, without much revision; he claimed to have written over 1500 plays. He was so popular and respected that Spanish nobility and Papal dignitaries sought his friendship. His death was mourned widely and publicly. Among his most famous titles are *Los ramilletes de Madrid, El perro del hortelano, El maestro de danzar* and *La viuda de Valencia*. See also DIA.]

Jordan cannot envision María as a faculty wife in Montana: her war-time experiences do not jibe with the stereotype of the ''instructor's wife'' at whose home students enjoy intellectual discussions about authors like Galdós, Lope de Vega, and Quevedo (164–65; see also *Fuente Ovejuna*).

López, Andrés (the Bull Dog of Villanconejos). He and his brother Eladio (q.v.) are members of Pablo's band (51–52). On Anselmo's recommendation, Jordan entrusts Andrés with the important dispatch in which he informs Golz that the enemy is massing forces for a counter-offensive and suggests that the Republican attack be cancelled or postponed. Andrés has to cross a number of Republican checkpoints, where he is met with suspicion because he comes from behind enemy lines. Eventually he manages to deliver the dispatch to Duval, Golz's Chief of Staff. Duval phones the message to Golz, but by this time the attack has begun and cannot be stopped (see 268, 292, 331–32, 334, 416–19; see also Gómez, Rogelio; and crowds).
   Speaks: 52–53, 57, 182, 185, 207–9, 218, 250, 259, 363–68, 372–77, 396–401, 412, 420–22, 426–27.

López, Eladio. Andrés' older brother and like him a member of Pablo's band. During the attack on the bridge he is killed by a bullet through the head (441, 455; see also 292, 361–62, 367, 385, 439).
   Speaks: 53, 182, 185, 218, 383–84, 388–89.

*López, Andrés' and Eladio's father. He was a Republican (367). Although the family is from Villanconejos [southeast of Madrid, near Aranjuez], Mr. López had moved them to Villacastín [in the province of Segovia, northwest of Madrid, about twenty miles southwest of the city of Segovia] just before the outbreak of the Civil War (375).

*Lucasz (Lucacz). [Also spelled Lukács. Real name: Mata or Maté Zalka Kemeny. Hungarian writer, 1896–1937. Lucasz was short, cheerful, fond of music and dancing. He had published a book of short stories, hoped to write a war novel, and was familiar with Hemingway's work. As a veteran of World War I and of the Russian Army, Lucasz had more military experience than most of the volunteers in the International Brigades; he was appointed Commander of the Dombrowski Battalion, attached to the XII International Brigade, which was very active in the Republican defense of Madrid and in other battles. He was the general in command of the XII International Brigade when he was killed in action at Huesca, aged 41.][42]
   The narrative identifies Lucasz as one of the Russian-trained members of the International Brigade, like Kleber and Hans. He worked with Golz

to capture a gold train in Siberia and performed bravely in the defense of Madrid (233, 421).

*Luis. The porter at the Hotel Florida in Madrid. Jordan imagines that if he hadn't met María, he would have gone by himself to Madrid after destroying the bridge, and he would have asked Luis to get him a bottle of absinthe (228; see Petra).

*manager. The former manager of Rafael tells the story of how his valuable bullfighter defected to another manager (187; see *Gómez Ortega, Rafael).
Speaks: 187.

*Mantegna, [Andrea. Italian painter and engraver, 1431–1506. Mantegna's art is characterized by skillful foreshortening, solidly modeled figures and correct anatomical details. Madrid's Prado Museum, which Jordan has visited, has several of Mantegna's masterpieces, including the famous *Death of the Virgin*.]
Jordan feels that the commitment and "feeling of consecration to a duty" represented by the International Brigades are awe-inspiring, like a "religious experience" or the wonder inspired by great art, be it architecture, music, or painting (235; see Bach, Brueghel, and el Greco in this chapter; also see Mantegna in *FTA* and in "The Revolutionist" in *In Our Time*).

*March [Ordinas], Juan. [Spanish businessman and financier, c.1880–1962. He began his career in the family business, March Hermanos (March Brothers, suppliers of farm equipment), but soon became interested in the tobacco trade, eventually supplying much of the Mediterranean and controlling the sale of tobacco in Morocco. He expanded into mines, marine and land shipping, electrical equipment, petroleum and its products. A millionaire by the age of 30, he amassed one of the largest fortunes in Spain. Although he declared himself an enemy of the Republic, which cancelled his monopoly of the tobacco trade in Morocco, he was nevertheless elected to the Cortes (Parliament) as an independent. Accused of financial irregularities, expelled from the Cortes, deprived of parliamentary immunity, and jailed in 1931, he made a spectacular escape, aided by the director of the jail. He financed several of Franco's campaigns. Like other ruthless financiers (e.g., Rockefeller, q.v. in *SAR*), he became a philanthropist towards the end of his life, establishing the March Foundation, dedicated to the advancement of the arts and sciences, in 1955. Pilar's remark expands upon a witticism attributed to the bullfighter Luis Mazzantini (1856–1926): "En este país . . . no se puede ser más que dos cosas: o tenor del Teatro Real o matador de toros'' (In this country . . . one can be only one of two things: a tenor in the Royal Theatre, or a *matador de toros;* qtd. in Cossío III 576).][43] According to Pilar, March is a criminal: she explains that only criminals, bullfighters, and tenors can get rich in Spain (184).

María (*guapa,* Rabbit, wife). The beautiful girl, nineteen years old, with whom Jordan falls in love (22–25, 43–44, 136–37, 167–69) at first sight. As the daughter of the Mayor, María was the first of the girls in her town to be shaved, branded, and gang-raped by the fascists. She was kept in a jail in Valladolid and was being taken south when the train in which the fascists traveled was blown up by Kashkin and Pablo's gang, who took her to their mountain camp where she helps and is helped by Pilar (324, 348–50). Her commitment to Jordan and to the Republican cause is absolute. Although generally docile, she refuses Jordan's order that she take a safer position (458). Like Karkov, who carries cyanide, she has a razor blade with which to commit suicide should it become necessary (170–71). Mentioned often: 28, 32, 228–29, 231–32, 267, 290–91, 305, 370–71, 385–86, 403, 457. See endnote 1.

Speaks: 22–25, 56, 58, 65–73, 82–85, 87, 92, 96–99, 116–17, 129–133, 138–140, 142, 150, 153–57, 159–61, 170–75, 179–80, 202–5, 211, 220, 223, 226, 249, 261–64, 269–70, 323–25, 341–54, 379–81, 390, 394, 405–6, 450, 456, 458, 461, 463–65. Interior monologue: 449–50.

*María's parents. Her father, a Republican, was the mayor of his village; he was shot by the fascists when they took it over (66–67, 350–51). Her mother, a Catholic, was "honorable," respecting her husband's principles and asserting her commitment to him without abandoning her own position (350); although not a Republican herself, she was also shot by the fascists (350–51; see 355).
Speak: 350–51; see 355.

*Martín, don Guillermo. A nominal fascist in Pablo's home town, he owned the store which sold the agricultural tools now being used as weapons (104) against the fascists. He is the fifth man (after Benito García, Federico González, Ricardo Montalvo, and Faustino Rivero) forced to walk between the two rows of armed people. As don Guillermo began his walk, his wife called out his name desperately. One of the drunkards in the line mocked her, and don Guillermo rushed at him, crying, to hit him. The drunk hit him hard in the face with a flail, and then other drunkards broke loose from the line and joined the attack (117–18). The general inoffensiveness of the victim and the brutality of the attack caused many villagers to abandon the two lines of armed townspeople organized by Pablo. Although she had originally approved of this method of execution because it made all the people share the guilt equally, Pilar felt "shame and distaste" after the murder of Martín (119).

*Martín, Mrs. Guillermo. She is a Catholic (117) and loves her husband, whose murder she observes from the balcony of their apartment (117–18). Late at night, after a horrible day of bloodshed, she weeps on the balcony (129).
Speaks: 118.

Marty, André. [French communist, 1886–1955. Marty was a leader of the French Communist Party and a member of the central committee of the Comintern. In 1919 he was involved in the mutiny on the Black Sea, thus gaining the trust of many Russian communists, including Stalin. He supported the Republicans during the Civil War, recruiting volunteers and obtaining supplies for the International Brigades from the French Communist Party. He was appointed head of the communist volunteers, but he was not well-versed in military tactics and was not respected as a military leader. A Stalinist, he "saw Trotskyites and spies (the two terms being equal in his mind) everywhere" (Cortada, 268). He was suspicious, malicious, and harshly authoritarian, nicknamed "the butcher of Albacete" because he ordered thousands of Republicans killed for suspected infractions of discipline. After the war he fled to France and then to the USSR; in 1953 he was expelled from the French Communist Party.][44]
Gómez immediately recognizes Marty and correctly identifies his past actions and present position (417). Marty's articles, translated into Spanish, appear in the communist party organ, *El Mundo Obrero* (417, q.v.). Marty is a destructively suspicious character: when he hears that the dispatch for Golz comes from behind enemy lines, he takes this as evidence that Golz has betrayed the Republic. Marty arrests Andrés and Gómez, takes their papers, and refuses to forward Jordan's dispatch. Karkov comes in and overrules him (416–26)
Speaks: 417–18, 419–22, 424–26.

Marty's staff. An armed motorcyclist takes a dispatch case from Marty's quarters to an unknown destination (416; see Mauser). Marty's chauffeur speaks French (417). Two officers from the International Brigades accompany Marty and two sentries guard his offices (416); a corporal arrests Gómez and Andrés at Marty's command (417–18). The corporal and two guards agree that Marty "is crazy as a bedbug" (418). See soldiers.
Speak: 416, 418–19.

*Marx brothers. [American family of comedians, including the four brothers whose stage names were Chico (Leonard, 1887–1961), Harpo (Arthur, 1888–1964), Groucho (Julius, 1890–1977), and Zeppo (Her-

bert, 1901–1979). The character Harpo was a mute harpist; the others
delivered a fast dialogue and all four were slapstick comedians. They
began their careers in vaudeville and then made several successful
movies, among them *Animal Crackers* (1928), *Monkey Business* (1931)
and *Duck Soup* (1933). Their last film was *Love Happy* (1949). Harpo's
autobiography, *Harpo Speaks,* was published in 1961. Jordan is probably thinking of their movie *A Night at the Opera* (1935).]
    Jordan thinks that María would enjoy seeing the Marx Brothers (231).

*[Mary Magdalen, Mary of Bethany. Mary Magdalen (also known as
Mary of Magdala) was a reformed prostitute, usually identified with the
unnamed woman who washed Jesus' feet with her tears, dried them with
her hair, and then anointed them (Luke 7:38). "No good evidence has
survived for calling this woman Mary Magdalene but . . . the equation
has been widely believed" since the sixth century (Calvocoressi,
155–56). The account presented in John 11:2 and 12:3 indicates that the
woman who wiped Jesus' feet with her hair, after anointing them with
valuable ointment, was Mary of Bethany.]
    Jordan jokingly asks María if she cannot dry his feet with her hair (203).

*Mauser, [Wilhelm (1834–1882) and his brother Paul (1838–1914),
German weapons manufacturers. They first earned recognition for
improving the design of the firing pin of the needle gun and opened their
own weapons factory, Mauser Brothers & Co., in 1874. They developed
a single-shot, 11 millimeter bolt-action rifle to which they later added a
tubular magazine; this design was selected in 1884 as the basic infantry
weapon of the Prussian army. Other important contributions to weaponry include a rear-loading pistol, a revolver, and a repeating rifle, all
called Mausers.]
    Anselmo tells Jordan that the *guardias civiles* were well-armed with
accurate Mausers (42). Pablo takes a Mauser pistol from a dead *guardia
civil* and forces another *guardia* to explain to him how it works; he then
shoots them with it and hands it to Pilar (100–2, 107–8). Agustín also
carries a Mauser (44), as does one of the Republican messengers (416;
see Marty's staff). Although "ugly . . . and unwieldy" (101), it is clearly
a valued weapon (see also *Guardia Civil,* Paco).

*Mayakovsky, [Vladimir Vladimirovich. Russian poet and playwright,
1893–1930. Mayakovsky is considered the poet of the Bolshevik
Revolution of 1917. Before 1917 he had to spend much time underground and abroad; after 1917 he was extremely visible, traveling,
reading his poetry to large audiences, defending the new order, which he
saw as a liberating force, and attacking the narrowness and greed of
individuals who threatened it. Both the form and the content of

Mayakovsky's poetry expressed his rejection of repressive systems: his distortion of language underlined his rejection of established, inherited systems. In his travel poetry *Amerikanskiye stikhi* (*American Verses, 1925–1926*) he admired the advanced technology he found in the US, although he was appalled by the cruelty of the capitalistic system. His poem *Pro Eto* (*In Favor of That,* 1923) is self-adulatory; *Khorosho!* (*It's Good!,* 1927) praises Soviet life; his eulogy *Lenin* (1924) was lyrical. His best known plays are *Klop* (*The Bedbug,* 1928) and *Banya* (*The Bathhouse,* 1930). As the Soviet system solidified, Mayakovsky's insistence on the primacy of the individual became obnoxious to the leadership. His early death, announced as a suicide over a failed love affair, was probably a political murder.][45]

Jordan meditates on the effects of love and sexual activity and concludes that they militate against bigotry, totalitarianism and party discipline. He figures that the Communists killed Mayakovsky because of his "Bohemianism," which encourages sexual freedom and emphasizes individuality rather than the social group (164).

*McClellan, [George Brinton. American soldier, 1826–1885. Early in his career McClellan showed himself an able organizer and fighter, distinguishing himself during the Mexican War. He resigned from the army to work for the Illinois Central Railroad, soon becoming president of the Ohio and Mississippi Railroad. Recalled into the Union Army at the start of the Civil War, he performed well at first, becoming general-in-chief of the Union forces. He hesitated to take offensive action, however, delaying so long that in 1862 President Lincoln finally issued a presidential decree ordering the Union forces to advance. McClellan relinquished his command, but even in his lesser position as head of the Army of the Potomac, he failed to act decisively, waiting for more favorable conditions and nervously overestimating the enemy's strength. When he repulsed General Robert E. Lee's attack at Malvern Hill and again when he stopped Lee's invasion of Maryland, McClellan failed to press forward and take advantage of his victories. In 1862 he was relieved of all command. In 1864 he accepted the Democratic nomination for the Presidency and was severely defeated by Abraham Lincoln. He was governor of New Jersey, 1878–1881; his autobiography, *McClellan's Own Story,* appeared posthumously in 1887.][46]

Depressed about the lack of effective military leadership in the Civil War, Jordan comments that Spain "was overrun with McClellans" on both sides of the conflict (233).

*Mejías. See Sánchez Mejías, Ignacio.

*men and boys. See *crowds, *officers, *soldiers.

*Menéndez de Avila, [Pedro. Alternative spelling: Menéndez de Avilés. Spanish naval officer and colonizer, c.1523–1574; founder of St. Augustine, Florida. Under Charles V, Menéndez was appointed captain of the Indies Fleet and commissioned to rid Spanish waters of pirates. Although he performed this task successfully, he was accused in Spain of excessive use of force and of amassing a large personal fortune. He was recalled to Spain, tried, and imprisoned for twenty months. He eventually regained royal favor and was entrusted with the governorship of Florida in 1565. To ensure Spanish hegemony, he massacred almost the entire French force stationed in Florida, displaying the bodies under an announcement which explained that they had been killed "Not as Frenchmen but as Lutherans." The French retaliated with another massacre, displaying Spanish bodies under notices which read, "Not as Spaniards but as murderers." Menéndez made several transatlantic trips in his continuing campaign against the French. He was mistrusted by many elements in the Spanish court.]

In his anger at Pablo's theft of his equipment, Jordan curses Spanish leaders of the past, including Menéndez, as destroyers of their own people. Jordan puts Pablo (and much of the present Republican leadership, see 369) in the tradition of Cortez, Pizarro, and Menéndez, all very brave men but cruel and self-seeking (354–55; see 370).

*Miaja [Menant, José. Spanish military leader, 1878–1958. He served in the Spanish Army in northern Africa before the Spanish Civil War. During the Civil War he distinguished himself as a Republican leader, organizing the defense of Madrid, in which the International Brigades were very active; he was known as "the Savior of Madrid." When the Republicans were defeated in 1939, Miaja retired to Mexico, where he died in 1958.][47]

The narrative declares that because he was jealous of the good press received by the leaders of the International Brigades (see Kleber, Lucasz, Hans and others), Miaja had engineered the ouster of Kleber (233). Angry at Pablo's treachery, Jordan rages against the historical pattern of treachery among Spanish leaders, from Cortez to the present day, and including Asensio, Largo, Prieto, and Rojo (qq.v.) as well as Miaja (369–70; see 237).

*Mike. See Strater, Henry H.

Miranda, Lieutenant-Colonel. A professional military man, he had served in Morocco and had become a Republican partly as an expression of his dissatisfaction with the Church, which forbids divorce. He understands the importance of Andrés' mission and gives Gómez and Andrés "strong" safe-conducts so they can deliver Jordan's dispatch to General Golz's headquarters (398–400; see also 412).
Speaks: 399–400.

*Miranda's mistress. She is 23 years old and pregnant (399).

Miranda's staff. A "sleepy sentry" stands guard outside Miranda's quarters. Miranda's chief of operations, Pepe, denies Andrés and Gómez access to Miranda, first claiming that "He is asleep" and later that "His fiancée is with him" (397). When Gómez threatens Pepe with his pistol, Pepe sends an orderly to fetch Miranda, who is as polite and helpful as Pepe was rude and obstructive. On Miranda's command, Pepe types out safe-conduct passes for Andrés and Gómez (397–400). See soldiers.
Speaks: 397–98.

*Miranda's wife. She left Miranda long ago, but the Roman Catholic Church forbids divorce (398–99).

*Mitchell. A gray-haired British economist who joined the Republican forces in Spain. Karkov thinks Mitchell is a fool with an unjustified reputation for being a well-informed "insider" (242–43). Although Jordan had generally admired Mitchell's writings, he did not like his reports about Spain (239) and, when he met him in Madrid, in January (four months before the action of the novel), he disliked the man immediately (241–43).[48]
Speaks: 241.

*Modesto, Juan. [Full name: Juan Modesto Guilloto León. Spanish communist soldier, 1906–1969. After military service in Morocco and a short visit to the USSR, Modesto returned to Spain. As a professional soldier, he was an important leader of the Republican Army, participated in all its major operations and was promoted to the rank of general in the last days of the war. After the war he spent a short time in the USSR and then moved either to Latin America or to Czechoslovakia. He was a strict disciplinarian, widely admired for his leadership and professionalism.][49]
The narrative presents him as Juan Modesto, formerly a cabinetmaker and now a valued Russian-trained commander of the Republican army (246, 311). Like Líster and el Campesino, he fought well against the Italians, but Jordan thinks that these men are too heavily influenced by "their Russian military advisers" (234). Karkov tells Jordan that the POUM (q.v.) has plotted but failed to kill Modesto (247). He is often at the Hotel Gaylord.

*Montalvo, don Ricardo. A landowner and a committed fascist from Pablo's home town. He suggests that all the fascists should walk out together between the two rows of armed townspeople, but Pablo sends them out one by one to be beaten and thrown over the cliff at the opposite end of the town square. Pilar reports that don Ricardo, the third

to walk down the two rows of men, cursed the Republic as he emerged from the City Hall. His dignity and bravery incited the crowd and he was killed very quickly (110–11; see 114, 116).
    Speaks: 110–11.

*Montero. A Republican who was with Jordan in Madrid on the day of the fighting at Carabanchel [January 1937]. The two of them were waiting for transport which "had been promised" (239) and with which "we can attack" (242). Jordan eventually found the driver of the stalled armored car (240; see *drivers).
    Speaks: 240, 242.

*Moors. [Nomadic peoples descended from the Arabs and Berbers of north-west Africa. In 711 the Mohammedan Moors invaded and conquered Spain, sweeping through the entire peninsula and crossing the Pyrenees into France, where they were stopped by Charles Martel in 732. They were slowly pushed back; it was not until 1492 that Granada, their final stronghold, fell to the Spanish monarchs Ferdinand and Isabella. Like the gypsies, the Moors have left a lasting mark on Spanish culture, particularly in art, architecture, medicine and cuisine. Cortada writes that "It was in Estremadura that Franco's army made use of the Moors and that the Moors developed a reputation for extreme brutality which thereafter preceded them wherever they went" (190). In *ARIT* the Moors are presented more sympathetically.]
    Pablo, María, Pilar, Jordan, and Anselmo share the general Spanish attitude that the Moors are murderous (15, 40, 117, 237; see also gypsies).

Mora, Captain (the first officer). The blond, red-faced, gun-brandishing, choleric leader of the Carlist cavalry unit which attacked Santiago's hilltop position. His sister and mother had been shot by the communists, and he curses and vilifies el Sordo's men. He falls for el Sordo's bluff: believing that the whole band is dead, he walks up the hill and is killed by el Sordo (314–19; see also Berrendo, Paco).
    Speaks: 313–18.

*Mora's family. Mora's sister and mother were killed by communists (Republicans) (316).

*Mosby, John [Singleton. American lawyer and soldier, 1833–1916. During the American Civil War, Mosby and a small group of men conducted raids on the Union forces, attacking their isolated outposts and cutting their communication and supply lines, much as Jordan is attempting to do. In their most spectacular raid, "Mosby's Rangers" went behind Union lines and captured General Edwin H. Soughton and about a hundred of his men. They were difficult to catch because they disbanded after each raid, meeting up again some time later at a secret location. When Union forces did capture and hang some of the Raiders. Mosby immediately captured and hung an equal number of Union army troops. Like Jordan's grandfather (also a leader of irregular troops, see *Jordan's family), Mosby was a Republican, an unpopular position for a Southerner. Although he had fought for the South, Mosby campaigned for the re-election of the former commander-in-chief of the Union Army, President Ulysses Grant, perhaps because Grant had restored civil rights to all Southern citizens (Amnesty Act, 1872). Mosby published *Mosby's Reminiscences and Stuart's Cavalry Campaigns* (1887) and *Stuart's Cavalry in the Gettysburg Campaign* (1908).]

Both Jordan and his grandfather admire Mosby (339, 386; see 233 and *Jordan's family), with whose ''outlaw'' soldiering they can identify.

Moscas. [(flies). Spanish nickname for the Russian Polikarpov I-16 monoplane, which had a speed of nearly 300 mph. In addition to the *moscas,* the Republicans relied on the I-15 biplane, nicknamed *chato* (snub-nosed; see Wyden, 383–84 and Ruffner and Thomas, 119, 340). The Republican air power was far inferior to that of the Nationalists; see Fiat, Heinkel, and Junker.]

Anselmo insists that the airplanes passing overhead are *moscas.* Jordan does not disillusion him, although he recognizes that they are enemy aircraft (38; see 39).

the motorcyclist. Waiting for the Republican attack to begin, Jordan sees a motorcyclist crossing the bridge he will blow up (434). See Marty's staff.

*the motorcyclist. See Gómez's staff.

El Mundo Obrero [(The Working World). Published 1936–1939, this was the official newspaper of the Spanish Communist party during the Civil War. Its editor, Jesús Hernández Tomás, made it one of the major newspapers of the Republican zone as the influence of the Communist party grew in 1937 and 1938.][50]

The narrative correctly identifies *El Mundo Obrero* as the newspaper of the Communist party in Spain. Jordan, Karkov, Gómez, and Pepe read it (245–46, 397); Marty has published in it (417).

*Napoleon [Bonaparte. Corsican-born general, 1769–1821; Emperor of the French, 1804–1814. Napoleon rose rapidly in the army and eventually conquered much of Europe. By 1820 his Grand Empire included Spain, most of central and southern Europe, and the Grand Duchy of Warsaw. He imposed his liberal economic and political reforms on the nations of his empire, appointing constitutional monarchs and enjoining them to govern according to his Civil Code, which was based on the egalitarian principles of the French Revolution. Through marriage and treaties Napoleon formed alliances with Austria, Prussia, the Scandinavian countries, and Russia. When the latter withdrew from the alliance, Napoleon and his Continental Grand Army went to war and were defeated (1812). Napoleon raised a new army but was defeated again at Leipzig, 1813. In 1814 Napoleon abdicated and was exiled to the island of Elba; he returned to France to rule for 100 days before being defeated by the British at Waterloo in 1815. He second exile was to St. Helena, the island in the south Atlantic where he died. Napoleon was a military genius, a master tactician, a politician, economist, and opportunist. See also *FTA*.]

Jordan mentions Napoleon as an example of a soldier who could do more than just fight (340).

Nationalists. A coalition of army, church, fascist, and monarchist forces which opposed the Spanish Republic. The Spanish Civil War began (July 1936) when the army rebelled against the government. Supported by German and Italian fascists, the Nationalists won the war and Spain was ruled by the dictatorial Francisco Franco (q.v.) until 1975. Fearing reprisal, most Republican leaders lived in exile after the war. See also Carlists, drivers, Falangists, Fiat, *Guardia Civil,* officers, priests, soldiers, Republicans.

*the Negro. [The *New York Times* reports only one lynching in Ohio for the years 1905–1920. It seems not to have been a racial incident: the victim, John Willey, was "lynched by irate neighbors" after being "convicted of assault, while on trial on a charge of murdering his grandmother" (29 November, 1915, 4:6). The *New York Times,* which usually identifies lynch victims as "negro," does not mention Willey's skin color: he seems to have been a white man. Jordan may be referring to an earlier incident: the lynchings, on 15 and 16 August, 1908, of two black men in Springfield, Illinois. These events were accompanied and followed by widespread race riots, during which three more people were killed, 75 were wounded, and a great deal of property was destroyed. Martial law was declared on 16 August but the violent riots continued; the soldiers did not leave Springfield until the 20th. A Grand Jury indicted several people, one of whom took poison on 27 August. The violence was widely reported and the subject of many editorials, in the *New York Times* and in other papers. Jordan may remember hearing or reading about these events; they were the most spectacular of the lynchings which occurred with depressing regularity in those years.]

Jordan remembers seeing a black hanged and then burned in Ohio
when he was about seven years old. When Pilar discourses on the
ugliness of Spanish drunkenness, Jordan tells the story of the black man
to show cruelty is universal (116–17). Rafael's song mentions "a
Negro" (60); María has never seen a black person (117). See crowds; see
also Klan in *SAR* and *Isleño* in *THHN*).

*Nin [Pérez, Andreu. Spanish (Catalan) journalist, teacher, and translator,
1892–1937. After several years in the USSR, Nin turned to politics,
serving several years as secretary general of the CNT (q.v.). Devoted to the
rights of the worker, he joined with Joaquín Maurín and others to found
POUM (q.v.). The organization was at odds with the mainline Communist
Party (under the control of Stalin) which argued that, in Spain, the fight
against the Nationalists took precedence over the struggle for the rights of
the worker. For leftist revolutionaries like Nin, the workers' rights were
inseparable from the struggle against fascism. Early in the Civil War, when
Maurín was captured by the Nationalists, Nin became the leader of the
POUM. In 1937 he disappeared; whether he was killed in Spain or in
Russia remains moot, but there is no doubt that he was killed by pro-Stalin
communists, a victim of in-fighting among the several factions within the
Republican forces. Among his books are *Las dictaturas en nuestro tiempo,
El proletariado español ante la revolución* (1931), *Las organizationes
obreras internacionales* (1932) and *Los movimientos de emancipación
nacional* (1935). He translated several Russian novels, as well as Trotsky's
works, into Spanish and Catalan.][51]
    Karkov describes Nin as "pleasant" although he dislikes his politics.
He has been gotten rid of: "We say he is in Paris" (247).

*la Niña de los Peines [(The Girl of the Combs). Professional name of
Pastora Pavón Cruz, Spanish flamenco singer, 1890–1969. Pastora
Pavón was the most popular and admired performer of this art form of
her time. She was mistress of both "cante grande" and "cante chico"
and a great improviser, much respected by contemporary artists and
writers, among them the composer Manuel de Falla and the writer
Federico García Lorca (q.v. in *DS*), whose passion for flamenco and for
gypsies led to the *Romancero gitano* (1928) and the *Poema del cante
jondo* (1931). She made several international tours and cut a number of
records. Herself trained by the famous Merced la Sarneta, she transmit-
ted her gypsy heritage to the young singers whom she trained after her
retirement in 1957. A statute was erected in her honor in Alameda de
Hércules, Sevilla, her home town.][52]
    Pilar mentions that, after one of Finito de Palencia's triumphant
performances in the bullring, la Niña de los Peines sang at the party
inaugurating Club Finito (185–86; see *Pastora).

*el Niño Ricardo, Ricardo. [Professional name of Manuel Serrapi Sánchez. Flamenco guitarist, 1905–1972. A popular performer, he accompanied all the major flamenco singers of his time, including Pastora Pavón (la Niña de los Peines), with whom he performed for more than 20 years. Much in demand as a soloist as well as an accompanist, he toured Spain and Morocco several times. His own compositions were often performed. Among his recordings are *Gitanería arabesca* and *Recuerdo de Sevilla*.][53]
        Ricardo plays the guitar at the banquet to celebrate Finito's great victory in the bullring and the founding of Club Finito (186; see Ricardo).

officers. An "overbooted," unnamed, and overwhelmed Republican officer is trying to get the stalled Republican convoy moving again (413; see the company commander). Nationalist officers travel comfortably in a car (191–92). Two dead officers (Julián and Mora) are removed from the field of battle by Barrendo (330). See soldiers.

*officers. Several nameless officers are mentioned or remembered by the characters. Jordan recalls Republican officers at Karkov's party, both foreigners and Spaniards (356–58). Rafael recalls the Nationalist officer who had to force his men to fight, shooting those who refused (30); Jordan recalls a similar situation among the Republicans (235–36). See *soldiers.
        Speak: 358–59.

*Onan. [In *Genesis,* the son of Judah who was punished by sudden death for the sin of wasting his semen.]
        When María is in pain and unable to have sexual intercourse with Jordan, she offers to do "some other thing" for him. Jordan refuses her offer, thinking that abstinence will make him stronger. He recalls that the Biblical Onan "cast his seed upon the ground" (342) but forgets what happened to him.

the orderly. An orderly sits next to a military driver (192). Also see Gómez's staff, Miranda's staff, soldiers.

Pablo. Leader of a guerrilla band of Republican sympathizers in the Guadarrama mountains. Pilar and Anselmo remember that at the beginning of the Movement Pablo was a well-organized, intelligent, brave and ruthless leader, full of "bull force" and "bull courage." He carefully organized the liberation of his home town, taking the Civil Guard by surprise, destroying their barracks, and organizing the killing of the town's fascists. Pablo is reputed to have killed countless numbers of people (26). But by May 1937, the time of the action of the novel, Pablo is more committed to liquor, his horses, and his safety than he is to the Republican cause; he resists the attack on the bridge not only because it is dangerous in itself but because it will render the Guadarrama mountains unsafe for himself and the band. In the ensuing showdown, Pilar wrests the leadership from Pablo and Pablo defects, stealing some of Jordan's equipment, but, overcome by loneliness, he returns, bringing more men and horses (391). After the attack on the bridge, he kills these newly-recruited men and the band use their horses for their getaway. Pablo is a complicated mixture of middle-aged lust (32), avarice, cunning, and cruelty, tempered by the incompletely assimilated wisdom expressed in the novel's epigraph: Pablo says that he does not feel lonely when he is "working for the good of all" and that, in the final analysis, "I do not like to be alone" (391).

Speaks: 9–16, 18, 20–22, 49–58, 60–64, 75–77, 80, 82–83, 86–88, 90, 107, 110, 127–28, 178–82, 184, 202, 204–6, 208–16, 220–24, 226–27, 250, 252, 267–68, 332–33, 361, 389–95, 402–4, 454–57, 462; see 100–102.

Pablo's band. In addition to Pablo, Pilar and María, Pablo's band includes Agustín, Anselmo, Fernando, Primitivo, the two López brothers (Andrés and Eladio), and Rafael the gypsy (qq.v.). When Pablo opposes Jordan's mission, Pilar and Anselmo challenge his leadership and Pilar is elected the band's commander (53; see 55, 56). She tells Jordan that only five of the band "are any good" (33).

*Pablo Romero. [A strain of cattle raised for the bullring. Don Felipe de Pablo Romero established his ranch in Sevilla in 1885; his bulls were first registered in Madrid and fought in the Madrid bullring in 1888. The famous old breed has been in the same family for generations (Cossío, I, 286 and 319).]

At the feria of Valladolid, Finito killed a Pablo Romero bull (185). The head of the bull is stuffed and presented to Finito, who recoils in horror (188).

*Paco. A corporal, one of the four Civil Guards who survived Pablo's attack on their barracks and surrendered to him. Pilar tells Jordan and María that Pablo shot them one by one, in the back of the head (100–2; see *Guardia Civil, Mauser).

Speaks: 101.

*Palencia. See Finito.

partizans. Spelled in this way, the word indicates a foreigner in Spain who supports the Republicans. The word is used by Jordan and the Russians (135, 162, 237, 358, 424, 425).

*la Pasionaria. See Ibárruri Gómez, Dolores.

*Pastora. [Probably a reference to Pastora Rojas Monje, flamenco *bailaora* (dancer) and sometime actress, 1889–1979, known professionally and popularly as Pastora or as Pastora Imperio because, as one writer remarked, "Esta Pastora vale un imperio" (This Pastora is worth an empire). Born in Seville and trained by her mother, also a famous *bailaora,* Pastora was a child prodigy, famous by the time she was twenty. She is credited with having added the trailing train to the flamenco dancer's costume. In 1911 she married Rafael Gómez Ortega (q.v.), the fiery matador known as el Gallo; the marriage was stormy. In 1918 she starred in Manuel de Falla's recently completed *El amor brujo* (Love, the Magician, based on an Andalucian gypsy tale) which calls for singing as well as dancing. She appeared in several movies, among them *La danza fatal* (1914), *María de la O* (1936), and *El amor brujo* (1949). She retired in 1959. Pilar mentions that Finito's party was attended by "Pastora . . . and the Niña de los Peines" (q.v.), suggesting that two gypsies named Pastora were present (185).][54]

Pastora is one of the several flamenco personalities who attended the banquet in honor of Finito's great success in the bullring at Valladolid (185). She is put in the peculiar position of defending Rafael el Gallo [her estranged husband], about whom she generally has nothing nice to say, when his former manager makes racial slurs against him (187).

patrol. See soldiers.

peasants. See crowds.

Pepe. One of the five men recruited by Pablo at the last minute to help in the attack on the bridge. After the attack Pablo kills all five men and uses their horses for the get-away (395).

Pepe. See Miranda's staff.

*Petra. A worker in the Hotel Florida whom Jordan and María might hire as a maid if they get an apartment in Madrid (347; see endnote 1; Petra also appears in *The Fifth Column,* most of which is set in the Hotel Florida, Madrid).

Pilar (Señora Commander). A handsome, large, loud, and brave middle-aged woman suffering from an undefined ailment.[55] She has some gypsy talents: she claims she can smell death and read palms. As a younger woman she, like Jordan and María, had felt the earth move when she made love. She lived with bullfighters for nine years, including five years with Finito, after whose death she joined Pablo. She is an ardent Republican and "much woman," with strong feelings and a sharp understanding both of people and of military tactics. Jordan trusts her and the guerrilla band elects her their leader (53–56; see Pablo's band), but even so her main activities seem to be cooking, encouraging Jordan, teaching María the wifely arts, and understanding and loving Pablo. She can be as obscene as Agustín, as intelligent as Jordan, as ruthless as Rafael, as brave as the young Pablo and Finito, and as loving as María. Himself a writer, Jordan admires her stories for their truth and vividness (see bullfighters, *crowds, and Quevedo). See endnote 1.

Speaks: 30–34, 53–58, 60, 65–68, 75, 77, 80–134, 138–57, 172–177, 179–82, 184–90, 202–3, 208–10, 215–20, 222–23, 249–57, 259, 266, 268, 297–301, 360–62, 383–92, 395, 402–5, 443–44, 446–48, 450, 457, 461, 464.

*Pilar. [Our Lady of Pilar appeared to the Apostle Santiago (St. James) in Zaragoza, Spain, in 40 CE. According to tradition, Santiago installed a statue of the Virgin at (or near) the site of the vision. The statue is now worshipped in the Basílica del Pilar in Zaragoza. The Virgin's feast day is October 12.][56]
Concha wrote her brother that she prayed to Saint Anthony and several Virgins, including Pilar, for his safety (303). Jordan read her letter after shooting her brother (see Carlists).

pilots. The Heinkel bombers fly so low that people on the ground can see the pilots (87). See Russians, three wounded.

*Pizarro, [Francisco. Sometimes spelled Pisarro. Spanish explorer, c. 1476–1541. Financed by Spanish sources, Pizarro made several expeditions to South America in search of the wealth of the Incas. Pizarro was hailed as a friend by Atahualpa, the last Inca chief, whom he captured, exploited, and killed, appropriating much of the Inca's treasure and land for himself and his family. He was murdered by Spanish followers of Diego de Almagro, his erstwhile partner whom Pizarro had defeated in battle (1538). His brothers Hernando, Juan, and Gonzalo also took part in the conquest of Peru; Hernando was murdered by his own men, whom he led in a revolt against Spanish representatives in Peru; Juan was killed fighting Indians; Gonzalo returned to Spain and was imprisoned for twenty years.]
Jordan ranks Pablo with the Spanish conquistadors like Cortez, Pizarro and Menéndez de Avila (qq.v.), all brave but cruel and self-seeking "sons of bitches" (354).

*Pocapena. [A Veragua bull, the fifth to be fought in Madrid on 7 May, 1922 and the second to be fought by Granero. He lacked courage and tended to veer to the right; critics noticed his preference for the area near the fence rather than the center of the ring. Sword in hand, Manuel

Granero (q.v.) cited Pocapena five or six meters from the barrier; the bull charged, veering to the right, and gored the matador in the right thigh, throwing him up into the air and then, when he landed, pushing him up against the barrier and attacking him with such force that he crushed his head. The bullfighter died moments after being brought into the infirmary. Pocapena was killed by Marcial Lalanda, whose *alternativa* had been confirmed earlier that afternoon by Juan Luis de la Rosa (q.v.), the senior of the three matadors performing that day. In the fourth fight of the afternoon, Rosa had been wounded slightly and was in the infirmary when Pocepena killed Granero.][57]

Pilar correctly identifies Pocapena as the bull which killed the matador Granero by crushing his skull (252; see also Veragua).

policeman. For increased security, a policeman sits at the *concierge*'s desk at the Hotel Gaylord, where Karkov lives (356; see the *concierge*).

*political commissar. [This position originated in the communist-organized Fifth Regiment and spread to most of the International Brigades and to some Spanish units as well. The political commissar was responsible for his unit's morale and political "education" and for disciplining spies and other undesirable or subversive elements. When regular army units were joined with volunteers and militias, political commissars were also given the task of reducing friction in these "mixed brigades." See "political commissar" in "Night Before Battle" and "battle police" in "Under the Ridge" (both stories in *Fifth Column*); in the latter story two members of the International Brigades shoot a young Spaniard, a Republican, who had injured himself in order to avoid combat.]

The narrative indicates that the system of political commissars gives political power to men like Marty, enabling them to interfere in military matters of which they are ignorant (422–23). When Karkov smoothly accuses Marty of such interference, Marty denies it, claiming he is "only a commissar" (424), although he has in fact done just that by jailing Andrés and Gómez. Jordan rejects Pilar's little pep talk, telling her that "I don't need a political commissar" (387).

*porters. Four porters, guided by Anselmo, brought Lewis guns to Pablo's and Santiago's bands (271).

*POUM. [Acronym for Partido Obrero de Unificación Marxista (Workers' Party for Marxist Unification). Among its founding members were Joaquín Maurín and Andreu Nin Pérez (q.v.). This leftist organization argued that the workers' revolution was inseparable from the struggle against fascism. It was at odds with the more right-wing communist factions, which argued that the fight against fascism took precedence over the fight for social equality and workers' rights. Maurín, who had warned the Spanish Cortes against Franco even before the Army's uprising, was arrested and killed by the Nationalists early in the Civil War; Nin was murdered by rightist elements among the communists. The organization published a newspaper, *La Batalla*, 1924–1939. The POUM and other workers' organizations and unions, like the CNT and FAI (qq.v.) were anathema to the Stalinist communists, whose accusations of Trotskyism and fascism, echoed by Karkov, are carefully analyzed by George Orwell (*Homage to Catalonia*, 179–90; also see Trotsky). In order to unify all the Republican factions, the Communist Party insisted on strict discipline, preached by political commissars (q.v.) and various political papers. Their hierarchical structure was ideologically unacceptable to the left-wing, revolutionary parties like POUM, CNT and FAI; the stronger Stalinist communists resorted to political assassination, in the name of discipline. The communist crowd at the Hotel Gaylord was of necessity opposed to POUM. After widespread arrests, POUM was ''suppressed and declared an illegal organization'' by the Republican leadership (which received aid from Stalinist Russia), June 1937, and much of its leadership ''disappeared'' (Orwell, 186).]

Karkov attacks the POUM, accusing them of plotting to kill off a variety of important Republicans, including Modesto, Prieto, Walter and himself. In his dispatches to *Pravda* Karkov attacks POUM as ''that infamous organization of Trotskyite murderers and their fascist machinations all beneath contempt,'' but he does not believe this, telling Jordan that they never managed to kill anyone and they are ''not very serious'' (247).

Pravda [(Truth). Daily newspaper founded 5 May, 1912 in St. Petersburg as an underground paper, often suppressed by the tsarist regime. In the paper's early years, a major contributor, ''actual editor and guiding spirit of the newspaper was Lenin.'' After the Russian revolution the paper became the official organ of the Central Committee of the Russian Communist Party (Bolshevik). In the 1930s ''*Pravda* played a significant part in carrying out the cultural revolution in the USSR . . . publishing . . . such famous writers as M. Gorky, V.V. Mayakovsky . . . and essays . . . by M. E. Koltsov'' and others. The paper ''educated the Soviet people in patriotism, proletarian internationalism, and political vigilance, exposed fascism, and campaigned against the imperialist war-mongers'' (*Great Soviet Encyclopedia*, XX: 505).]

As the Spanish correspondent for *Pravda* who is ''in direct communication with Stalin,'' Karkov is a very powerful man (424). He is not above using *Pravda* for purposes of intimidation (424–25) and propaganda (237, 247).

*President of Club Finito. He gives a speech during the banquet in Finito's honor (187–88).

*Price, Price Circus. [The Price Circus was founded by Thomas Price in the middle of the 19th century. It was situated on Recoletos Street, Madrid. In 1859 Price opened a branch of his circus in Barcelona but it closed after a few seasons. The original Madrid establishment, however, was very successful. Price died in 1867 and his heirs, William Parish and Matilde de Fassi, moved the circus to another site. When their building burned down in 1876, they erected a much larger structure, also in Madrid, changing the name to the Parish Circus. The Circus eventually reclaimed its original name and entertained Madrid until its closing in 1970.]⁵⁸

Pablo tries to provoke Jordan by insisting that American men wear skirts: he has seen such skirted men at the Price Circus (206). María has also been to a circus (117).

*priest. [The Roman Catholic Church supported the aristocracy and the Nationalist army during the Spanish Civil War, 1936–1939. After the war, the church stood firmly behind Franco.]

When Pablo took over his home town and rounded up all the fascists, he ordered the priest to hear their confessions. Some of the fascists are ceremonially killed by the townspeople, but most are hacked to death by the mob, the priest among them (104–5, 110–11, 121–28; see also *crowds).

*Prieto [Tuero, Indalecio. Spanish newspaperman and politician, 1883–1962. Poor and uneducated, he worked for the Bilbao newspaper *El Liberal,* eventually becoming its editor and owner. A member of the Socialist party, he achieved fame for his fiery pro-Republican oratory. He held important positions during the Second Spanish Republic (1931–1933). During the Civil War he was Minister of Defense, in charge of the Navy and Air Force (September 1936 to May 1937). The steady decline of Republican strength led to his conviction that the Republicans would lose the war. Communist factions among the Republicans, with whom Prieto had consistently been at odds, used the charge of defeatism to oust him from positions of power. He was relieved of his duties after the Republican defeat at Teruel and was sent, as Minister without Portfolio, to generate support for the Republicans in various South American countries. When the Republicans were defeated he settled in Mexico, working with the government-in-exile for the overthrow of Franco. He died in Mexico, 1962.]⁵⁹

Prieto is presented as a Republican who, like Pablo, has lost his idealism (163, 359; see also Asensio and Lerroux). Karkov tells Jordan that the POUM (q.v.) plotted but failed to kill this man (247).

Primitivo (the primitive one). A Republican, a member of Pablo's band, he is "flat-faced" (206) and somewhat deficient in understanding and imagination. He doesn't understand Finito's courage or the complexities of his situation, even after Pilar's clear exposition, and he votes against Rafael's suggestion that they sell Pablo to the enemy because "the Fascists would pay nothing for him anyway" (219). But he is solid and trustworthy, "a dependable value," as Agustín says (292). He performs his duties faithfully (266, 272, 280, 283), accepts Jordan's assurance that nothing would be gained by going to Santiago's aid (296–97), carries the wounded Fernando and offers him his own gun (440–41), and carries Jordan when he too is wounded and unable to walk (461).

Speaks: 53, 57, 184–85, 188–89, 206–9, 211, 217–20, 250, 257, 259, 270, 276, 295–300, 303, 323–25, 440–43, 451, 457.

*Putz, [Colonel Joseph. d. 1945. A French socialist, commander of a battalion of the XIV International Brigade and later commander of the entire XIV International Brigade. Although he was admired as a brave soldier and popular leader, Putz was not a communist and therefore lacked the political authority and support to maintain the position his abilities had gained him. He was posted to a local Spanish (Basque) division and thus eased out of the command structure within the International Brigades. He eventually quit the International Brigades and assumed command of a regular Spanish brigade. During World War II he fought in the French Resistance.][60]
The eternally suspicious Marty, looking for evidence that would prove Golz a traitor, notes that Golz "favors" Putz (421).

*Quantrill, [William Clarke. Confederate guerrilla leader, 1837–1865. Quantrill's Raiders attacked Union troops and positions in Missouri and Kansas. During one particularly brutal attack in Lawrence, Kansas, in 1863, more than 150 civilians were killed. Quantrill was wounded by Union troops in 1865 and died in jail in Kentucky.]
Looking at Pablo, Jordan thinks of the many guerrilla leaders who fought in the American Civil War, not just the better known ones like Quantrill, Mosby, and Jordan's grandfather, but also the many "little ones" like Pablo (233).

*Quiepo de Llano [Serra, Gonzalo. Correct spelling: Queipo. Spanish soldier and propagandist, 1875–1951. Queipo de Llano's early service in the Spanish Army was in the colonies of Cuba and Morocco. He was one of the generals, like Francisco Franco and Emilio Mola, whose uprising marked the beginning of the Spanish Civil War. During the Civil War he commanded the Nationalist forces in the South. By securing the Seville airport, he facilitated the transfer of Spanish troops from Africa back to Spain. In addition to his military contributions to the Nationalist cause, his nightly radio broadcasts raised the spirits of Nationalists throughout Spain and earned him the sobriquet "the radio General." He was handsomely decorated after the war, the title Marquis of Queipo de Llano being created for him.][61]

Anselmo reports that in the nearby town of La Granja people discussed the general's broadcast (81).

*Quevedo [Villegas, Francisco Gómez de. Spanish satirist, humorist, poet, political essayist, and novelist, 1580–1645. Quevedo lived many years in the Spanish court of Philip III, was exiled to Italy for killing a man in a duel, and returned to Spain when Philip IV came to the throne. He is known for his sharp eye, biting wit, and polished style. In *La política de Dios* (1626) he argued that monarchs should learn how to rule from the example set by Christ; in *Sueños* he castigated all classes of society. His picaresque novel, *Historia de la vida del buscón llamado don Pablos* (1626), was one of the earliest of such fictions to present a psychologically-evolving hero. He is considered one of the greatest writers of Spain's Golden Age, second only to Cervantes.]

Jordan has found it difficult to read Quevedo in the old-fashioned Spanish (11). His admiration for Pilar's story-telling abilities, particularly her rendering of the cowardly Faustino Rivero (112–15), leads him to extol her as "better than Quevedo" (134). Quevedo is, of course, studied and discussed by university students (164–65; see also Galdós and Lope de Vega).

Rabbit. Jordan's favorite nickname for María (370, 379, 380 *et passim*).[62] Pilar, who has overheard Jordan addressing María as "rabbit," echoes the word (155–56).

Rafael (the gypsy). A member of Pablo's Republican band, Rafael is fond of jokes and not overly conscientious, brave, or reliable. Early in the novel, Rafael is useful to the narrative, providing humor, gypsy flavor, and information about the gang's previous train-blowing, about Kashkin, and about the rescue of María (28–30). He is, however, less useful to Jordan, who has asked him to watch the road (e.g., 78–79, 161); the feckless Rafael wanders off to kill two hares, thus allowing a Carlist cavalryman unimpeded access to the camp (274–75; see also 266, 282, 287). Jordan, who cannot trust Rafael to stay at his post, often asks about him (178, 180–81, 272, 388). Pilar and Jordan describe Rafael as "worthless" (33, 275); Agustín agrees (293). Rafael insists that Pablo must be gotten rid of, and suggests that he be killed (60–61), sold to the fascists, handed over to Santiago (el Sordo), or blinded (219). Jordan assigns him and María the job of guarding the horses (394, 403); after the bridge is blown he teaches Rafael to shoot the machine gun (448). Unlike Anselmo, Eladio, Fernando, and Jordan, Rafael survives the bridge-blowing operation (459, 465). See gypsies.

Speaks: 18–30, 49–51, 53, 57, 59–62, 78–80, 190, 217–19, 249, 254–56, 274–75, 441, 443–44, 448.

*Rafael el Gallo. See Gómez Ortega, Rafael.

religion. See slogans.

Republicans. The two main female characters, Pilar and María, are Republicans, as are all the important male characters, such as Robert Jordan, the guerrilla bands of Pablo, Santiago (el Sordo), Alejandro and Elicio, and the people at Gaylord's in Madrid. Many of the background characters are Republicans as well: the sentries and police at the Hotel Gaylord, the driver, many of the people in Pablo's home town. Most of the foreign characters in the novel are also Republicans: the narrative presents American, British, French, German, Hungarian, and Russian volunteers of the International Brigades. Many of the Spanish factions that massed together to oppose the Nationalists are woven into the narrative as well: we see Loyalists, socialists, communists, anarchists, syndicalists and other assorted Spaniards—all Republicans. As Jordan's message travels through the Republican lines on its way to General Golz, we see that the Republican forces were a complex amalgam, weakened from within by ideological differences, incompetence, disorder and suspicion (see also crowds, soldiers, CNT, FAI, POUM). In a different sense, Jordan mentions that his grandfather was a Republican (66–67, 339).

requetés. See Carlists.

*Retana, [Manuel. Spanish impresario, administrative head of Madrid's bullfighting industry from c. 1907 until late 1926. With its tough audiences and powerful taurine critics, Madrid is the city in which reputations are made or broken. A matador who alienates or disappoints the Madrid audience will have to rebuild his reputation in the provinces before being contracted to reappear in the country's premier bullring; conversely, a matador who succeeds in Madrid will be able to pick and choose his contracts for the next season. By long tradition, *alternativas* (investitures, or the awarding of the top rank of matador) have to be granted or confirmed in Madrid; the graduated matador's seniority dates from his Madrid *alternativa.* As manager of the Madrid bullring for nineteen years, Retana was a powerful figure. In 1908, he vanquished the bullfighters who banded together to demand higher wages for fighting Miura bulls (see *Miura in *SAR*). Not a few taurine critics complained that in the 1920s Retana abused his power, willfully excluding fine bullfighters from Madrid and favoring the matador Nicanor Villalta, whose *apoderado* (agent) was Retana's own brother Matías. Towards the end of his career he seems to have expanded his hegemony, being described as the "representante de las Empresas de Madrid y Barcelona" (representative of the Madrid and Barcelona [taurine] industries, see *Sol y Sombra*'s double issue, 20 and 27 March, 1924 , p. 14). When he retired, Manuel Retana was replaced by Joaquín Gómez de Velasco as "representante de la empresa de la plaza de toros de Madrid" (representative or chief executive officer of the Madrid bull ring, *El Eco Taurino*, 1 February, 1927, unnumbered p. 7: 2).[63] The Retana whom Pilar mentions could be the powerful Manuel (nicknamed Manolo) or his brother Matías, himself an agent. It makes no difference: Rafael el Gallo was such a riveting personality that anything he did was of interest to all *aficionados*. A character named Retana appears in "The Undefeated," in *Men Without Women*.]

Pilar recalls that the former manager (agent) of Rafael Gómez Ortega told Retana the story of Rafael's defection to another manager (187).

Speaks: 187.

*Ricardo. [This character may be the gypsy guitarist Manuel Serrapi Sánchez, also known as el Niño Ricardo (q.v.).]

Pilar insists to Jordan that some people, especially gypsies, have the ability to smell death on a person who is about to die. To Ricardo's sensitive nose, the smell of death was so strong on the bullfighter Sánchez Mejías (q.v.) that he would have to leave the saloon Villa Rosa when the bullfighter would come in (254).

*Richard. A German brigade commander who talks too much. He told Karkov's indiscreet mistress that an offensive was being planned (the one involving Jordan, Pablo, Santiago, and their men), thus revealing the loose security and lack of discipline that undermines the Republican effort (357–58; see also journalists). As Fernando's report indicates, the rumors of the Republican offensive have already reached the Nationalist town of La Granja (82).

*Rincón, José. The saloonkeeper in Villaconejos, Andrés' home town. By describing him correctly, Andrés establishes his identity and is allowed to continue his journey to deliver Jordan's dispatch to Golz (375).

*Rivas, don Anastasio. A grain buyer, insurance agent, money lender, and fascist from Pablo's home town, generally disliked by the townspeople. He was the sixth man pushed out of the City Hall by Pablo and Cuatro Dedos to be killed by the armed townspeople. Their resolve and discipline shaken by the terrible murders they had committed, the villagers broke ranks, mobbed Rivas and clubbed him to death. His body was left out in the sun all day; a drunkard eventually set it on fire. That evening several bodies, including his, were carted across the plaza and thrown over the cliff and into the river (121–23, 126).

*Rivero, don Celestino. A landowner and a fascist in Pablo's home town; the father of don Faustino Rivero (112).

*Rivero, don Faustino. The oldest son of don Celestino Rivero, he had earned the townspeople's contempt by trifling with the girls and being a braggart and a coward. An amateur bullfighter, he once made himself vomit so he could plead illness and thus avoid fighting a bull which was bigger than he had anticipated. When he first emerged from the City Hall and saw the waiting lines of armed men, he ducked back into the building. Pablo forced him out again at gunpoint. The contemptuous crowd refused to hit him; he walked, untouched, halfway down the two rows of men and then fell to his knees and had to be carried to the end of the line. He was pushed screaming over the cliff, the fourth fascist to be thrown into the river that terrible day (112–15; see 116, 117, 119, 127; see also *Quevedo). Speaks: 114.

*Rojo [Lluch], Vicente. [Spanish military historian and teacher, 1894–1966. Although an army officer and military instructor, a Roman Catholic and a friend of Franco, Rojo sided with the Republicans during the Spanish Civil War, serving as chief of staff and rising to the rank of general. Under Miaja, he was instrumental in the defense of Madrid. He participated in a number of Republican campaigns and his expertise and skill were widely recognized, but because of the many Republican defeats he was nicknamed "the general of the defeats." Like Modesto, he was a professional soldier, free of political ambition. In January 1939, he recognized the inevitability of Republican defeat and advised surrender, although he soon rescinded this suggestion. After the war, he went to Bolivia, where he taught military science. He requested and was granted permission to return to Spain in the mid-1950s. Franco's government tried and convicted him of treason and then granted him a pardon. He lived in Madrid until his death. He wrote several books on military topics: *Elementos del arte de la guerra, Estampas de guerra, Culminación y crisis del imperialismo,* and *Así fué la defensa de Madrid.* He supervised the establishment of the *Colección bibliográfica militar.*][64]

The narrative identifies Rojo as "the unsuccessful professor" (6) who devised the Republican offensive which includes surprise aerial bombing, blowing up the bridge (to prevent enemy reinforcements from reaching the positions under attack), storming the pass, and repairing the bridge to allow Republican troops to advance to La Granja and perhaps even further into Nationalist-held territory. Rojo's plan depended on taking the enemy by surprise, but the Nationalists seem to have been warned and have prepared a counter-offensive. The novel presents the activities of the three days preceding the blowing of the bridge. Angry with Pablo, who has further weakened the operation, Jordan curses authority figures in general and Republican leaders (including Rojo) in particular (369).

*Romero, Pablo. See *Pablo Romero.

*Rosa [de la Garquén, Juan Luis de la. Spanish matador, 1901–1938. Investiture as matador, 1919, by Joselito; confirmed in Madrid by Belmonte, 1920. He showed early promise but his first season as fully-fledged matador (1920) was disappointing, his work with the sword being severely criticized. His next two seasons were impressive, and in 1922 he shared the bill with the popular Granero and Marcial Lalanda (qq.v.) on the day the former was killed; Rosa was wounded and in the infirmary when Granero was hurt. But 1922, when he fought 38 times, was his last good year. In 1924 he had only seven *corridas,* and he performed more and more often in Venezuela, not appearing in Spanish bullrings after 1927 except for the disastrous performance in Barcelona in 1936, which clearly indicated that his career was over. Juan Luis de la Rosa was always impressive with the cape and often spectacular with the muleta, but his sword work was, from the beginning of his career to the end, deficient, and he lacked the commitment and discipline that bullfighting requires. He was murdered in Barcelona during the Civil War.[65] Born in Cádiz, he may have been descended from gypsies.]

Pilar insists that, like Blanquet and herself, Juan Luis de la Rosa was able to smell death coming (251–53).

Speaks: 251.

*Russians, three wounded. In the early days of the Spanish Civil War, three badly wounded Russians were entrusted to Karkov. Because at that time the Russians' involvement in Spain was officially denied by both Russia and Spain, Karkov was prepared to poison the three men to prevent their falling into enemy hands and thus give other countries (i.e., Germany and Italy) justification for "open intervention" in the Spanish conflict (237–38). When he told Jordan this story, Karkov revealed that he always carried cyanide so that he could kill himself if he were captured (238). Later María shows Jordan the razor blade she carries for the same purpose (170–71). All these stories of deliberate death impress Jordan.

*Rykov, [Aleksey Ivanovich. Russian revolutionary and politician, 1881–1938. After the death of Lenin (1924), whom he originally supported, Rykov shared power with Kamenev and Zinoviev. Rykov subsequently supported Stalin against Trotsky, Kamenev and Zinoviev (qq.v.). When these were hounded out of the party, Rykov became

Soviet premier. In 1936 he was implicated in party purge trials and was executed in 1938.][66]
Karkov identifies Rykov as a political assassin (245; see Kamenev).

Saeta. [A brief, fervent prayer, sung solo, offered during religious processions, particularly during Easter. It is related to the flamenco *cante hondo,* especially in that it is improvised and springs from intense emotional involvement.]
The spiritual transport that informs *cante hondo* and the *saetas* is what María meant when she said she had been "in *la gloria*" during orgasm (379–80).

*Salvarsan. [Scientific name: arsphenamine. An arsenic-based drug, salvarsan was the first successful treatment of syphilis. It was developed in 1909 by the German bacteriologist Paul Ehrlich and was the standard treatment for syphilis until the discovery of penicillin by Sir Alexander Fleming in 1941 (four years after the action of the novel). The damage done by salvarsan, which Hemingway treats metaphorically, was the object of scientific studies during the 1930s. Aware that the incidence of salvarsan-related "accidents" had risen dramatically during World War I, scientists studied war-time statistics in order to determine correct dosages and thus safeguard the health of subsequent populations.[67] Also see *FTA.*]
In political and military terms, overdoses of remedies (i.e., Communism, which supplied the Republicans with trained leaders and much war materiel) can cause as much loss of life as the original disease (i.e., fascism). The suspicious Communist André Marty kills fellow Republicans in great numbers. He is notorious for killing more men than the bubonic plague, more than salvarsan (418–19). Pepe, Miranda's chief of operations, taunts Gómez that the Russians are more efficient purgatives than epsom salts (398). Early in the conflict, Pablo was as deadly to his enemies as the most virulent of diseases: he is reputed to have killed more people (fascists and Nationalists) than cholera, typhoid fever, bubonic plague, or typhus (26, 373).

*Sánchez. A Republican border guard. He replaces the company commander (q.v.) who interrogated Andrés when that officer leaves his post in order to take Andrés to the headquarters of Capt. Rogelio Gómez, the battalion commander (376).

*Sánchez Mejías, Ignacio. [Spanish matador and writer, 1891–1934. Sánchez Mejías was an interesting figure, attracted both by the active and the literary life. As a bullfighter he is remembered for his bravery, his disdain of pain and of danger, and his intellectual approach to the sport: he devised new, extremely risky situations (he often fought with his back against the barrier, even sitting on its railing) and solved them ingeniously. His technical skills enabled him to work his way out of the dangerous situations in which he deliberately placed himself. Sánchez Mejías also led an active literary life: he lectured, wrote plays (the best known are *Sinrazón* and *Zayas,* both premiered in 1928), essays, and an unfinished novel. After a seven-year retirement, he returned to the ring in 1934, heavier and with slower reflexes, but with the same cold disdain of danger. He was fatally gored in his fifth fight of the season (August 1934). The passionate lament *Llanto por Ignacio Sánchez Mejías* (1934), mourning the death of his friend the bullfighter, is probably Federico García Lorca's best known poem. See also *DIA.*]

Jordan explains that the bullfighter was doomed because he was too old and slow and "had been too long out of training" (253). Pilar says that in the days before he was fatally gored, the bullfighter smelled so strongly of death that people like Ricardo and Felipe González had to leave the room (253–54).

Santiago (el Sordo [the deaf one]). 52 years old, deaf in one ear, he commands a band of guerrilla fighters in the Guadarrama mountains; they helped Pablo's people blow up a train (33–34; see 46–47). Santiago is admired by Pilar (34), Anselmo (47), Jordan (162), Andrés (376), and Pablo (392). When Jordan explains his plan to him, Santiago quickly understands both the plan and its attendant problems. Even so, he undertakes the assignment and fights bravely and intelligently in the famous hill-top battle in which he and his men are all killed. Jordan and Pablo's band are understandably distressed by the sounds of el Sordo's battle (294–306). Santiago generously gives Jordan a bottle of whiskey he had obtained for him (142–43, 202–4; see 209, 329–30).

Speaks: 141–153, 308, 311–14, 317, 319, 320; short interior monologues: 312, 319, 320.

Santiago's band. Santiago commands more people than Pablo. Among Santiago's guerrillas, there are "Perhaps eight" who are "good" (33, 144). The hilltop battle involves Santiago and five of his men, three of whom are wounded by the time they reach the hilltop to begin their final battle (307) against 150 men (Santiago's estimate, 311).[68] See Ignacio and Joaquín; also see Berrendo, Julián, and Mora.

Speak: 309, 311–13.

Señor, señora, señorita (Mr., Mrs., Miss). See Comrade.

Señora Commander. Pablo sarcastically calls Pilar "Señora Commander" because she had been elected leader of their band (214).

sentries. Sentries guard strategically important positions for both the Nationalists and the Republicans. The Nationalist sentries at the bridge, as well as the sentries at the next post, are an important consideration for Jordan. Four men and a corporal guard the bridge (2); eight men and a corporal are quartered at the roadmender's hut (190; see 37, 144). Jordan observes the sentries on the bridge (1–2, 36–38, 431–34) and Anselmo hears them talking: they seem unwilling soldiers (193–96) but must nevertheless be killed (435; see 432–34) before the bridge can be blown. Santiago (el Sordo), who had undertaken to attack the hut, is killed before the bridge-blowing operation begins. These important sentries are mentioned frequently (6, 42, 78–79, 198, 438, 440). Also see *gallegos*.

Speak: 194–96.

Andrés meets several Republican sentries, guards and patrols as he travels towards Golz (372–77, 396–97, 412–14, 416–21; see the company commander, Gómez, Sánchez, Miranda's staff, Marty's staff; also see soldiers).

Speak: 412–14, 416.

*sentries. Jordan recalls the Republican sentries at the Hotel Gaylord (356), Pilar recalls Cuatro Dedos (q.v.) and the other Republicans who guarded Pablo's captives (121, 124), and Anselmo recalls the Nationalist sentry at the town of Otero: that sentry was the first man Anselmo ever killed (193). See *Guardia Civil*.

*[Shakespeare, William. English dramatist and poet, 1564–1616; author of 37 plays, including *Romeo and Juliet, King Lear, Othello, Macbeth, Hamlet, Antony and Cleopatra*. In *As You Like It,* Jacques explains that each man has "seven ages," of which the soldier is the fourth:

Then a soldier,
Full of a strange oaths and bearded like the pard,
Jealous in honour, sudden and quick in quarrel,
Seeking the bubble reputation
Even in the cannon's mouth (II.vii.148–52).]

As is proper for a professor of Spanish language and literature, Jordan occasionally refers to Spanish authors (see Quevedo). He is also familiar with Shakespeare, whose description of the soldier accurately fits Pablo, with one exception: Pablo shies away from "the cannon's mouth" and turns instead to "yonder bowl" which is full of wine (232; also see Stein).

*Sheridan, General Phil[ip Henry. American cavalry officer, 1831–1888. A graduate of West Point (1853, after a one-year suspension for fighting), he fought against the Indians in the American West. During the American Civil War, his resourceful leadership enabled him to rise

to the rank of major general in the Union Army. He was instrumental in
the fall of Petersburg, and he cut off General Robert E. Lee's line of
retreat from Appomattox. After the Civil War he served on the Mexican
border and in the Western territories. In 1883 he was appointed
Commander in Chief of the army, and in 1888 he was promoted to the
rank of general. He is author of *Personal Memoirs of P. H. Sheridan*
(2 vols., 1888).][69]

Jordan's grandfather had taught him to admire Sheridan and Stuart
(339; see 233).

*Sherman, [William Tecumseh. Union general, 1820–1891. He led the
campaign against Atlanta, Georgia, and burned most of the city after it
fell. During his "march to the sea" through Georgia in 1864, he
encouraged his troops to loot and burn. His philosophy was that the
enemy must be broken completely if victory is to be achieved.]

Jordan, who admires tough leadership, regrets the lack of leaders like
Sherman in the Spanish Civil War (233).

*SIM. [On the Republican side the initials stand for Servicio de
Inteligencia Militar (Department of Military Intelligence). On the Na-
tionalist side the same initials stand for Servicio de Información Militar
(Department of Military Information).]

Jordan's credentials are marked with the seals of the SIM and the
General Staff (10). He also carries other official Republican SIM identification (375, 332; see 396) as well as a set of false identification (285).

*Sioux. [The Sioux nation, sometimes known as the Dakotas, includes
seven North American tribes or "council fires" who shared a related
group of languages. They were famous for their strength and courage.
Originally from the eastern part of the United States, they were steadily
driven west by the Ojibwa (q.v. in *TS*) and then by the French. The Sioux
fought on the side of the English during the American War of Independence and in the War of 1812; in 1815 a treaty with the American
government granted them land, including much of what is now North
and South Dakota, Minnesota and Wisconsin. The Sioux sold some of
these lands in the 1850s. As white American settlers encroached on
Sioux lands, the Sioux retaliated and massacres were perpetrated by both
sides. Intermittent warfare continued in the late 1860s and early 1870s,
interrupted by occasional treaties but inevitably flaring up again as
settlers and gold prospectors continued their westward expansion. The
Sioux's major victories were under the leadership of Chief Sitting Bull,
who vanquished the forces of General Custer at the battle of Little Big
Horn in 1876. Sitting Bull and between two and three hundred Indians
were killed at the famous battle at Wounded Knee Creek, December

1890; after some lesser engagements the Sioux were finally defeated by the forces of Nelson A. Miles in 1891. See *Custer in this chapter; see also *Coolidge in *GE*.]
  Jordan likes the Anheuser-Busch lithograph which shows an armed General Custer surrounded by Sioux warriors (295).

slogans. A forceful speaker, Dolores Ibárruri coined several of the slogans which energized many Republicans.[70] The narrative suggests, however, that new ideologies, no matter how forcefully expressed, cannot completely dislodge the political or religious orientation of one's upbringing. La Pasionaria's rhetoric is mocked by the pragmatic communist leaders of the International Brigades: they share her aims, but they subscribe to a different system of rhetoric. Only the weak-minded among them respond to the passionate Spanish slogans (357–58). Anselmo understands that the new system, with its denial of religion, is difficult for Spaniards to adopt; his wife, for example, "would not have understood" the new ideology, and he, although he does his honest best, cannot abandon the deeply ingrained concepts of sin, atonement, and expiation (197–98) and finally turns to prayer (327). Similarly, the young Joaquín finds even la Pasionaria's political ideology an insufficient substitute for prayer: facing death, he abandons the one for the other in mid-sentence (321). Even Pablo turns to "God and the *Vírgen*" (90). And Jordan, although he accepts the necessity of communist discipline, remains committed to the American ideology on which he was raised (305; see 163–64 and *Fuente Ovejuna*). Intellectual, political, and philosophical change is possible, but native ideologies, whether religious or political, are deeply ingrained. (Before blowing the bridge, Jordan also recalls college cheers and an American political slogan which posits the state of Maine as the testing ground for national elections [438].)

*Smith, [Horace. American inventor and gun manufacturer, 1808–1893. In 1853 Smith became partners with Daniel Baird Wesson (1825–1906); they patented a new repeating action which they incorporated into a pistol. The Smith & Wesson Company (1855) continues to be one of the foremost weapons manufacturers. Hemingway's grandfather's Civil War Smith & Wesson became the suicide weapon of Ed Hemingway, Ernest's father. The coroner returned the weapon to Hemingway's mother, who gave it to him.]
  Jordan's grandfather had been issued a Smith & Wesson pistol which he had carried throughout the American Civil War and which he always kept clean and oiled afterwards. After Jordan's father shot himself with this pistol, the coroner returned it to Jordan, who dropped it into a deep lake (336–37).

the sniper. One of the Nationalists who fight Santiago on the hill. Like Berrendo, he thinks Mora is crazy and that Santiago is bluffing (314–17). Speaks: 315–17.

soldiers. The novel is crowded with unnamed soldiers. Andrés sees the large numbers of Republican troops massed for the offensive (414–15, 426–27). Nationalist cavalry worry Jordan; he kills one Carlist cavalryman and then sees several of his fellows, 24 mounted men in all (280–82). We see these men again during and after their battle with Santiago's men (325–27, 471). Santiago kills several of these soldiers; he can see four bodies and knows there are others (310; see 330, the sniper, Carlists). See sentries. Speak: 372–76, 194–96, 397, 413–14, 418–21.

*soldiers. Nameless soldiers are mentioned or recalled but do not act in the narrative. Jordan remembers seeing four men in uniform at Karkov's apartment (356). Rafael reports that the Republican Army sent two men with the machine gun for the train-blowing (29). After Kashkin and Pablo's band blew up a train, a fascist officer tried to get "the troops" (Republican prisoners) to shoot the attacking Republicans who had just blown up the train; this officer shot those who refused to attack as ordered (30); many of these troops ran away (29–30). Jordan also remembers men being shot for avoiding battle; he also thinks about the many people he has killed (235–36, 304). Dead soldiers and civilians are recalled by several characters (see *crowds and *drivers). Jordan thinks briefly of the many soldiers who will be involved in the attack Golz is planning (8); these imagined soldiers are seen by Andrés at the end of the novel (see soldiers).

el Sordo (the deaf one). See Santiago.

*Sotelo. See Calvo Sotelo, José

Star pistol. [Star was the trade name of Bonifacio Echeverría, an important Spanish pistol manufacturer in Eibar, Spain. In the period between World Wars I and II, "Many 'job shop' copies of standard . . . revolvers . . . were made in Spain. . . . These weapons were frequently made of poor materials . . . and gave Spanish-made arms a poor name. [But] Unceta . . . Gabilondo . . . and Star Bonifacio Echeverría S.A. all made quality weapons throughout this period and still do" (Ezell, 442, 444). Two important Star pistols were the Star Model A and the Super Star Model B, both of which take a 9 mm Largo shell. Each pistol weighs 2.21 lbs. (one kilo); the Super Star is somewhat longer than the Model A.][71]
    Gómez threatens Miranda's subordinate, Pepe, with a Star pistol (397) when he refuses to wake up Lieutenant-Colonel Miranda, whose written approval Andrés needs as he travels to General Golz's headquarters with Jordan's dispatch about the Nationalist counter-offensive. Santiago fires

his Star pistol six times when he pretends to shoot his men and himself (313–14). The pistols are described as "heavy" (397) and "big" (313).

*[Stein, Gertrude. American writer, 1874–1946. Stein was an important experimental writer and art collector. In 1903, she moved to Paris with her brother. Her salon at 27, rue de Fleurus attracted such important writers as Anderson, Fitzgerald, Ford, Pound and Hemingway. She collected the innovative art of the young painters of the period and was herself the subject of a portrait by Picasso. She experimented with automatic writing, colloquial dialogue, repetition, and various aspects of grammar to produce a new, unadorned style. She wrote stories (*Three Lives,* 1909), poems (*Tender Buttons,* 1914), opera (*Four Saints in Three Acts,* with music by Virgil Thomson, 1934), thinly veiled autobiography (*The Autobiography of Alice B. Toklas,* 1933, and *The Making of Americans,* published 1925), and theoretical and critical essays (*Composition and Explanation,* 1926; *How to Write,* 1931; and *Narration,* 1935). See also *MF.*]
Jordan parodies Stein and puns on her name (289).

*Stokes, [Sir Frederick Wilfrid Scott. English engineer and inventor, 1860–1927. Stokes worked for the Great Western Railway and the Hull & Barnsley Railway. From 1885 until his death he was associated with the engineering firm Ransomes and Rapier, becoming its managing director in 1897 and its chairman in 1907. Among his inventions are a rotary kiln for cement mixing and various improvements for canal sluice gates, as well as the 76 mm (3″) portable mortar that bears his name. The original Stokes mortar was a simple device, inexpensive to construct and easy to use: it consisted of a launching tube, baseplate, stand, and sights, and had a range of about one kilometer (0.6 mile). Stokes' mortar was widely used during World War I, and Stokes was knighted in 1917. His basic design was refined by Edgar Brandt in the 1930s; most modern infantry models are based on Brandt's improved designs.][72]
After the hilltop battle, Lieutenant Berrendo mourns his unit's losses, which could have been avoided if the Stokes mortar had arrived in time (315, 326). Santiago (el Sordo) hopes that his enemies do not have a trench mortar (310–12).

*[Strater, Henry Hyacinth. American painter, 1896–1987. Hemingway met Strater in Paris in 1922. Hemingway and Strater shared an interest in boxing, fishing, and other sports. Strater painted three portraits of Hemingway, two in 1922 in Rapallo, Italy, and one in Key West in 1930. His portrait of Hadley Hemingway was left behind when the Hemingways left their Paris apartment. Strater was nicknamed "Mike" by his first wife Maggie; most of his friends from the 1920s called him by that nickname.[73] In the 1920s Hemingway was also friendly with Mike Ward, q.v. in *MF.*]
Mike is a friend of Jordan's in the United States (381; see *Hickok).

*Stuart, [James Ewell Brown] (Jeb). [American soldier, 1833–1864. Early in the Civil War Jeb Stuart distinguished himself by his bravery in defense of his home state, Virginia. He was rapidly promoted, achieving the rank of Brigadier General and placed in command of the cavalry brigade of the Army of Northern Virginia. He is remembered for his daring raids and his ability to obtain information. He was mortally wounded in a battle with Sheridan's troops at Yellow Tavern.]

Taught by his grandfather to admire sound military leadership, Jordan appreciates the contributions of military men on both sides of the American Civil War. He admires both Sheridan (Union forces) and Stuart (Confederacy) as intelligent men (339; see 233; also see *Grant, *Jackson, *Sheridan, and "irregulars" like *Mosby and *Quantrill).

*Tartars [or Tatars. A conglomerate of tribes who, under Mongolian leadership, conquered parts of Asia and eastern Europe in the 13th century, reaching as far as Germany and Hungary. The word connotes fierceness and stubbornness. See *Genghis Khan, *Tamerlane and *Tartar in *THHN.*]

Jordan criticizes Líster and the other Republican leaders who, under the influence of their Russian training, execute fellow Republicans in order to maintain discipline. Líster, for example, was as "murderous" as the Tartars (234; see Marty, political commissar, and Salvarsan). Pablo, who killed many fascists in the early days of the Civil War, is also compared to the fierce Tartars (193).

*Tarzan. [Character created by Edgar Rice Burroughs (American novelist, 1875–1950). Orphaned in the African jungle, Tarzan was brought up by apes. Strong, agile, and friendly to jungle animals, Tarzan would swing from tree to tree as he rushed to aid fellow creatures in danger. His adventures are recorded in books like *Tarzan and the Apes* (1914) and in movies starring muscular actors Johnny Weissmuller, Buster Crabbe and others.]

As he crawls around under the bridge, Jordan compares himself to Tarzan (436).

*Tenorio, don Juan. [Main character of the play *Don Juan Tenorio* by José Zorrilla Moral, popular Spanish poet and dramatist, 1817–1893. The character don Juan Tenorio is based on the adventures of a lustful scion of the Tenorio family, residents of Seville since the early 14th century. Don Juan first appeared on stage in *El Burlador de Sevilla* by Gabriel Téllez (Tirso de Molina, c. 1571–1648) and has since been the subject of famous works by Molière, Mozart, Byron, Shaw and others. Zorrilla's play was so popular that the name of his main character has come to stand for any handsome young seducer.]

Because Jordan says he cares for Pilar as well as for María, Pilar calls him "a regular Don Juan Tenorio" (92).

Tercio. [A regional division of the *Guardia Civil*, q.v.]

Jordan recalls that in the terrible fighting in Madrid, the Republicans forced the *tercio* (the Madrid contingent of the Civil Guard) back in difficult, house-to-house combat (237).

*Thermopylae. [A narrow mountain pass where 300 Spartan Greeks, led by Leonidas, were defeated by the Persian army, led by Xerxes, in 480 BCE. Like the embattled Loyalists, the heavily outnumbered Greeks fought bravely at Thermopylae: "Twenty thousand Persians . . . died before that handful of [Greek] men!" (Charlotte Yonge, "The Pass of Thermopylae," in *Men at War*, ed. Ernest Hemingway, p. 275). A few Greeks surrendered; the rest were killed at that battle.]

Jordan would rather live with María than die in a battle like that at Thermopylae (164; see *Dutch boy).

*[Thompson,] Charles. [American businessman and sportsman, 1898–1978. The rich Thompson was one of Hemingway's favorite drinking and fishing companions in Key West. Meyers describes Thompson as "a well-connected local aristocrat. His family owned the marine hardware store, pineapple factory, turtle cannery, icehouse, and a fleet of fishing vessels" (*Hemingway,* 207). Thompson accompanied the Hemingways on their African safari in 1934.[74] See also *GHA*.]

Charles is a stateside friend of Jordan's (381; see also *Hickok).

TNT. [Acronym for the chemical compound named trinitrotoluene or trinitrotoluol, a powerful explosive.]

Jordan used TNT to blow up the bridge. The smell and the "acrid smoke" make him cough (445, 446, 451, 452).

*Trotsky, [Leon. Real name: Lev Davidovich Bronstein. Russian revolutionary, 1879–1940. Trotsky was an important leader in the Bolshevik revolution of 1917 and served as commissar for foreign affairs under Lenin. Trotsky advocated armed world revolution to achieve social equality among all people. In the struggle for power that followed Lenin's death in 1924, Trotsky opposed Stalin. He was expelled from the party in 1927 and from Russia in 1929. He lived in Turkey, France, Norway, and Mexico City, where he was murdered in 1940. Among his books are *Terrorism and Communism, Literature and Revolution, Lenin,* and *The Betrayed Revolution.*][75]

Karkov has filed a report with his newspaper accusing the POUM (q.v.) of supporting both Trotsky and the fascists (247). Marty's corporal reports that his superior has killed "Trotzkyites" (*sic*) among others (418; see Salvarsan).

*Tukachevsky, [Mikhail Nicolaievich. Russian military officer, 1893–1937. An officer in the Czarist army, he was taken prisoner by the Germans in World War I and escaped in 1917. Tukachevsky became a revolutionary and rose rapidly in the Red Army; he was appointed to the high rank of Marshal in 1929. Under Stalin he was accused of treason and executed with several other generals in 1937. He was a leading Russian strategist.]

In reviewing Golz's career for signs of treason, Marty mentions that he had been associated with Tukachevsky (421).

*UHP. [Unión de Hermanos Proletarios (Union of Proletarian Brothers).]

After the Falangists cut off María's braids and clipped the rest of her hair off, one of them wrote the initials UHP on her forehead with iodine, to "punish" her for her Republican connections and to brand her as captured property (352).

*Varloff. Another Russian commander whom the suspicious Marty considers a traitor to the Republican cause (421).

*Velázquez, [Diego Rodríguez de Silva. Major Spanish painter, 1599–1660. Among Velázquez's most famous works are *Las Meninas* (1656), various religious paintings and court portraits, including those of dwarfs and jesters. Four important equestrian portraits hang in the Prado Museum: they present Philip III, his wife Queen Margaret of Austria, Philip IV, and his first wife Queen Isabella of Bourbon. Other important Velázquez paintings in the Prado which include horses are the portraits of Prince Baltasar Carlos and of the Count-Duke of Olivares and, of course, the panoramic *Las Lanzas* (*Surrender of Breda*, 1625).]

Among Pablo's horses is one he took from a *guardia civil:* a big, beautiful bay stallion with white markings who "looked as though he had come out of a painting by Velásquez" (*sic*, 13). This is the horse which María gentles during the blowing of the bridge and which Pablo rides in the get-away at the end of the novel (457, 458). Jordan recalls visiting the headquarters of the International Brigades, located at Velázquez 63, Madrid (234–35).

*Veragua. [In 1835 The Dukes of Osuna and Veragua obtained from the widow of King Ferdinand VII his carefully selected and bred cattle, descended from three strains: the stock of the Marquis of Casa-Ulloa, known for their nerve; the stock of Becker, famous for their strength; and the Vistahermosa stock, known for their nobility. The bulls first performed in the Madrid bullring in 1790 (under royal patronage). In 1836 Veragua bulls were registered, shown, and fought in the Madrid Plaza de Toros under the mark of the Duke of Veragua (with the Duke of Osuna) for the first time. By 1849 the Duke of Veragua retained sole ownership of the stock; several generations of dukes registered the stock under their marks (in 1850, 1867 and 1911). The Veragua family sold stock to don Manuel Martín Alonso, who in 1930 sold it to the Domecq family, well established breeders who transferred the cattle to their ranches in Jerez de la Frontera. Since 1931 the Veragua bulls have been registered under the name Domecq. They are an old and powerful breed.][76]

The bull that killed the matador Granero in 1922 was of the Veragua breed, which was then still owned by the Duke of Veragua (252; see Pocapena).

Vicente. The Republican chauffeur who takes Jordan's dispatch from Andrés and delivers it to Duval. He offers to bring coffee for Andrés and Gómez (427–28).

Speaks: 427–28.

*Voroshilov, [Kliment Yefremovich. Russian soldier and politician, 1881–1969. The son of a poor family, Voroshilov worked in the mines as a young boy. At age 16 he joined the revolutionary movement and at age 19 organized his fellow miners into a revolutionary cell. He met and became friends with Lenin and like many revolutionaries spent most of the time between 1907 and 1914 either in jail or in exile. During World War I Voroshilov led a guerrilla band against the Germans; in 1917 he organized guerrilla warfare against the czarist armies in his native Ukraine. After the Russian Revolution he became a member of the War Council in Moscow and, because of his close friendship with Stalin, rose rapidly through the ranks. He became Defense Minister of the USSR and helped organize the great purges of the army; in 1935 Stalin appointed him the first field marshal of the USSR. During World War II Voroshilov commanded the Armies of the North. He negotiated the USSR's treaties with Finland and Hungary. After the death of Stalin, Voroshilov was president of the Supreme Soviet, 1953–1960. He is remembered as one of Stalin's closest associates.][77]

In reviewing Golz's career for signs of treason, Marty recalls that Golz had been closely associated with Voroshilov (421).

*waiters. Fernando reports that waiters in Segovia and Avila who overhear officers discussing military matters feed the rumor mills (81).

*Walter, General Walter. [*Nom de guerre* of Karl Swierczewsky. Polish military man, 1896–1947. When the Spanish Civil War erupted he recruited volunteers in Paris to accompany him to Spain to fight for the Republican cause. He commanded the XIV International Brigade and then the 35th, taking part in most of the important actions of the Republican

army. He is considered one of the best officers of the International Brigades.[78] He is thought to be the model for Golz (q.v.). See endnote 1.]
   The Communist journalist Karkov writes propaganda against the leftist POUM (q.v.), accusing them of plotting to kill Modesto, Prieto, Walter and himself (247).

*[Weaver, Leland Stanford] (Chub). [American ranchhand and hunting guide, 1899—. Hemingway met Chub Weaver in 1930 at the Nordquist Ranch in Wyoming, where they ate, drank, and hunted together during Hemingway's long stays at the dude ranch in the 1930s. Weaver visited Hemingway in Key West in 1931 (Baker, *Life*, 600). Hemingway used the nickname but not the biography of this man.]
   Jordan recalls that Chub, a childhood friend, accompanied him when he rode to the lake to dispose of the gun with which his father had committed suicide (381; see also Hickok).
   Speaks: 337.

*Wellington, [Arthur Wellesley, first Duke of Wellington. British soldier and statesman, 1769–1852. Wellington served in India from 1796 to 1805, subduing Tippoo Sahib and the Mahratta chiefs. From 1809 to 1813 he was Commander in the Peninsular War, during which Britain helped Spain repulse the French. Wellington defeated Napoleon at Waterloo, Belgium, in 1815, a defeat which led to Napoleon's exile to the island of St. Helena, where he died (see Napoleon). From 1828 to 1830 Wellington served as Prime Minister of England.]
   Jordan mentions Napoleon and Wellington as examples of soldiers who could do more than just fight (340).

*whores. Several whores attend the party in Finito's honor (185–87; see *women and girls). Pilar says that María is not a whore (291).

wife. Jordan thinks of María as his wife (164–66, 168, 261–62, 291, 344, 354). She plans and studies how to be a wife (170–72, 348–50).

*women and girls. Jordan assures Golz and Agustín that he has no time for women (7–8, 25). He mentions former girlfriends fleetingly (137, 160, 166, 291, 344). He tells María about an American woman from whom they could rent a furnished apartment in Madrid (346–47). María recalls that after the Falangists killed her parents and several other people in her home town, they tied up the survivors "in a long line of girls and women" (351); María was the first of these to be shaved, beaten, and raped. Describing the smell of death, Pilar mentions old women reputed to drink animal blood to increase their strength (254–55; see 467); she mentions women who come to a fountain for water (105) and remembers a girl who brought her a pitcher of beer in Valencia (86).

She and Agustín both mention whores (185–87, 256, 284, 293). Anselmo knows "various women of trust" in the nearby town of La Granja (284), one of whom he engages to watch the road (330).

*the Woods boys, the Woods sleeping robe. [The New York store of Abercrombie & Fitch, suppliers of sporting goods since 1892, sold a line of down-filled sleeping bags, of which several models were named "Woods": e.g., the Woods Downlite, One Star; the Woods Arctic Junior, Two Star; and the top-of-the-line Woods Arctic, Three Star. The Three Star model was available in two sizes: Medium Arctic, 33″ × 74″ (wt. 12 lbs.), which sold for $55.00; and the Large Arctic, 36″ × 82″ (wt. 14 1/4 lbs), which sold for $63.50 in New York and for $65.50 at Von Lengerke & Antoine, a Chicago store associated with Abercrombie & Fitch. The page advertising sleeping bags in the VL & A catalogue is entitled "Woods Fine Sleeping Bags and Robes," and both the price and the description of the expensive Three Star model suggest that this is the one Jordan owns.][79]
Jordan bought his comfortable down-filled sleeping bag for $65.00 (179, 180) in 1932 (74). He carries the green sleeping bag in his pack (48) and spends three nights in it with María (69–75, 258–67, 341–55, 369–71, 378–82). María intends to take good care of it (170, 381–82).

*Zeiss, [Carl. German manufacturer of optical instruments, 1816–1888. In 1846 he founded the Carl-Zeiss factory at Jena; in 1866 he was associated with Ernest Abbe (German physicist, 1840–1905; inventor of the Abbe refractometer). The Zeiss optical works achieved international fame as suppliers of all sorts of optical instruments.]
Jordan's Zeiss binoculars enable him to see the face and actions of the Nationalist sentry he will soon kill. Seeing him thus, as another man like himself, makes the task more painful (433). Jordan uses the glasses several times (1, 36–38, 325, 448); Pilar brings them to him (297).

*Zinoviev. [*Nom de guerre* of Radomilsky Apfelbaum. Russian politician, 1883–1936. As a young revolutionary, Zinoviev lived in self-imposed exile until 1917, when he returned to Russia to help the Bolsheviks assume power. After the revolution he was appointed ruler of St. Petersburg and ruled the city with an iron hand. After the death of Lenin, who had been his mentor during the years of his exile, Zinoviev, Stalin and Kamenev unofficially shared great power, although officially Zinoviev was merely Commander of Leningrad. In 1925 Zinoviev joined Trotsky; in 1926 he openly broke ranks with the leadership. The rift was officially healed but Zinoviev had lost his influence. He was executed in Moscow in August 1936.][80]
Karkov describes Zinoviev as a political assassin (245; see also Kamenev).

Scribner dust jacket for the first edition of *Across the River and Into the Trees* (courtesy Charles Scribner's Sons, an imprint of the Macmillan Publishing Company; and of the Hemingway Collection, J.F. Kennedy Library)

CHAPTER VI

ACROSS THE RIVER AND INTO THE TREES

(1950)

The action of the novel occurs in and around Venice, late November 1948 (see Brusadelli), during the last few days of Colonel Cantwell's life.[1]

*A.A.A. [Founded in 1902, the American Automobile Association (AAA, Triple A) is a federation of automobile clubs which offer domestic and foreign travel services to their members, such as local maps, guide books, and travel tips. The organization also works for the public good, attempting to make cars and roads safer and to improve travel conditions generally.[2] Hemingway owned several AAA maps, some of which, as well as his membership cards for the South Florida Division of the AAA for the years 1947 and 1948, are preserved in the Hemingway Collection (Other Materials: Maps and Objects, Wallet Contents).]

When Cantwell and Renata discuss the trips they plan to take, she mentions that they will take advantage of the AAA booklets and guides (264).

*Abd el Krim, [Mohammed ben. Moroccan nationalist leader, c. 1882–1963. The son of a Berber chieftain who was killed fighting the Spanish, Abd el-Krim organized fierce resistance against European colonialism in northern Morocco. In 1921 he gathered an army of tribesmen who were victorious against a Spanish force of more than 20,000. He wrested much of Morocco from Spain and France, but he was eventually forced to surrender to French and Spanish forces in 1926. In 1927, while being transported to France, he jumped ship and ended up in Cairo, Egypt, where he inspired the militant nationalists who liberated Morocco in 1956. Cantwell refers to the Spanish and French campaigns against the Moors in northwest Africa. The life of this passionate leader inspired the operetta *The Desert Song* and the novel and film *Beau Geste*. See Abd el Krim in *FWBT*.]

Cantwell knows that the Europeans' fight "against Abdel Krim" (sic, 230) cost many Moors (Moroccans, qq.v.) their lives.

*the Accademia. See Tintoretto.

*the actress. [D'Annunzio's companion for many years and the inspiration for several of his plays was the famous Italian actress Eleonora or Eleanora Duse (1858–1924). Duse starred in D'Annunzio's *Sogno d'un mattino di primavera* (1897; English translation, *Dream of a Spring Morning,* 1902); *La gioconda* (1899, translated into English 1901 and 1921), and several other plays which he wrote for her. His novel *Il fuoco* (1900; English translation, *The Flame of Life,* 1900) is based on their passionate relationship, but soon after he finished the novel his interest in her waned and he chose another actress for the lead in his greatest tragedy, *La figlio di Iorio* (1904; English translation, *The Daughter of Jorio,* 1907). D'Annunzio (q.v.) was the passionate lover of several women. Adeline Tintner reports that "D'Annunzio . . . had not lived in the house on the Grand Canal with Eleonora Duse . . . but with his only daughter, Renata" ("Significance," 9, 10).]

Passing the house where D'Annunzio lived with Duse in Venice, Cantwell thinks of the actress whom he admires and pities (51).

*Alberto. A character who is mentioned only once, when Cantwell decides to "ask Alberto" if he might be buried in the wooded countryside along the Brenta River (34), where many Italian families, including Renata's and Alvarito's, have their villas and country estates. Hemingway may have had the Baron Alvarito's country estate in mind.

Alvarito, the Baron (Barone). Cantwell's host for the duck-shooting expedition with which the novel begins and ends. He is a very shy young man whose main interest is hunting: he has the hunter's sharp eye (129) and is an excellent shot (292), bagging more ducks than any of the other hunters (299). He and Renata were children together (130). Alvarito looks for Cantwell before he arrives (53) and says goodbye to him, undertaking to "give my [Cantwell's] love to Renata . . . Alvarito understands" (303, 306; see children and endnote 44).

Speaks: 129–30, 300–304.

*Alvarito's widowed mother. She has a palazzo in Venice where Byron (q.v.) used to stay but now she lives mostly in the country (48; cf. Alberto; see *Renata's family and endnote 44).

*Americans. Cantwell postpones going to Harry's Bar until the chatty Americans drinking there have left (72–73, 75). See *background characters, *men and boys, and *women and girls.

the anarchist. See the barman.

Andrea. The tall, drunk Count Andrea is at Harry's Bar. He and Cantwell, both very ill, compliment each other on how well they look. Andrea introduced Cantwell and Renata (289); he is the only person Renata ever "wanted to hit" (238). See also Emily.
Speaks: 79–81.

*anthrax and botulism. [Anthrax is a very infectious, often fatal disease, characterized by malignant pustules; botulism or food poisoning can also be fatal. Both conditions are caused by bacteria, which are easy to transport and to introduce into large populations.]
The mention of atomic bombs is followed by the allusion to biological warfare, the implication being that if and when the cold war heats up, anthrax and botulism will be the weapons of choice (40, 197).

Arnaldo. The young waiter at the Gritti Palace Hotel who shows Cantwell his room. He arranges Cantwell's things for him and sees to it that he does not run out of wine (164, 172). Arnaldo is grateful for the delicious wild ducks Cantwell once gave him; Cantwell sends him four more ducks (305–6) just before he dies. Arnaldo has a glass eye (67).
Speaks: 67–76, 177.

*Arnaldo's neighbors. They explained to Arnaldo's wife how to cook the ducks and were invited to eat them (69).

*Arnaldo's wife. She cooked the ducks and saved the feathers (69–70; see also 306).

assistant manager of the Gritti Palace Hotel. He is young, goodlooking, and a potential member of the Order of Brusadelli (65). Because the manager (q.v.) is unavailable, the assistant manager attends to Cantwell and to Jackson (66; see 181).
Speaks: 66.

*Austrians. Cantwell recalls the fighting against the Austrians during World War I (16, 31, 32; see Austrians in *FTA*). See *men and boys.

*Bach, [Johann Sebastian. German organist and composer, 1685–1750. His preludes, fugues, inventions, sonatas, concerti, and church compositions are masterpieces of the Baroque period. Titles familiar to every generation of music lovers include Books I and II of *The Well-Tempered Clavier*, the Brandenburg Concertos, the Goldberg Variations, the *Magnificat*, and the *Mass in B Minor*. His influence on Western music

cannot be overestimated. Bach's Cantata 161 is *Komm' Süsser Tod* (Come, Sweet Death).]
    Renata likes Bach; Cantwell describes him as "practically a co-belligerent" (88).

background characters. Cantwell rides the gondola with a group of people (184–85); the market is full of "purchasers" (190). As he walks to Harry's Bar, Cantwell passes many people, seeing them "quickly" (78–79). At Harry's Bar he is also inattentive of the customers (q.v.) who go in and out (92). See British, customers, men and boys, porters, and women and girls.

*background characters. Many people are mentioned or recalled but not seen. Among them are the many people who, in the old days, had visited the Countess Dandolo. Cantwell recalls that at that time he had known much of the Venetian upper class (47–48; see Byron). Arnaldo mentions unseen duckhunters (69) and generalizes about gondoliers, waiters (qq.v), hair-dressers, clergy and housekeepers who gossip so much that in Venice "Everyone knows everything" (74). Cantwell and Renata plan to gossip about and snub a great many film stars (128; see the Pope). Several other people are mentioned but not seen, among them the *Americans, *Austrians, *Belgians, *French, *Germans, *journalists, *Russians, *men and boys, and *women and girls.

*Baedeker, [Karl. German publisher of guide books to foreign countries, 1801–1859. Baedeker's purpose was to enable tourists to conduct their own tours, without having to hire greedy foreign guides to point out the important sights.]
    The unidentified writer (q.v.) depends so heavily on his Baedeker that the Gran Maestro personifies the guidebook as "his lady, Miss Baedeker" (270; see also 124, 126, 130, and endnote 60).

bambini. See children.

the barman, bartender. The bartender at the entrance to Venice has known Cantwell for some time and, like most of Hemingway's bartenders and waiters, is fond of the novel's protagonist. As an anarchist he is, by definition, opposed to having one person in command of another, but he fondly suspends his principles to rejoice in Cantwell's high rank (39). He and Cantwell exchange Spanish Civil War jokes (39–41; see slogans). The bartender at Harry's Bar doesn't speak (267), and the bartender at the Gritti Palace Hotel is Giorgio (q.v.). See waiters.
    Speaks: 39–41.

the *Barone.* See Alvarito.

Beauty. One of Cantwell's many pet names for Renata is "Beauty" (94, 95, 281).

*Belgians. The Gran Maestro reports that Venice is full of Belgian tourists whom he does not admire (61; see 202 and Caesar).

*Bergman, Miss [Ingrid. Swedish-born American stage and film star, 1915–1982. Bergman was one of the most admired movie actresses from the 1940s until her death. Her first Hollywood film was *Intermezzo* (1939). Her many critical and commercial successes include *Casablanca* (1942), *For Whom the Bell Tolls* (1943), and *Notorious* (1946). She won Oscars for *Gaslight* (1944), *Anastasia* (1956), and *Murder on the Orient Express* (1974). Although her private life scandalized her fans (she left her husband, a Swedish dentist, in order to live openly with the Italian film director Roberto Rossellini, whom she later married), the beautiful Bergman was often cast in the role of the sincere, appealing, and idealized heroine. Hemingway met Bergman in 1941, when he approved her for the role of María in *FWBT*. They became and remained friends.] This movie actress had once been Renata's role model (142).

*[Blake, William. English poet, painter, and engraver, 1757–1827. His writing is mystical and sometimes obscure. Among his best known works are the *Songs of Innocence* (1789) and the *Songs of Experience* (1794). Cantwell alludes fleetingly to the first stanza of Blake's "The Garden of Love" (1794):

> I went to the Garden of Love,
> And saw what I never had seen:
> A Chapel was built in the midst,
> Where I used to play on the green.

Blake's presence becomes stronger in Cantwell's next sentence, in which he refers to Blake's "The Tyger" (*Songs of Experience*):

> Tyger! Tyger! burning bright
> In the forests of the night.
> What immortal hand or eye
> Could frame thy fearful symmetry?]

Cantwell wonders, "Why have I never seen a gondola before? What hand or eye framed that dark-ed symmetry?" (149).[3]

boatmen, *boatmen's families. Both of the boatmen Cantwell meets suffered during wartime. The boatman at the duckshoot is surly to Cantwell, though he warms to him slightly at the end. Alvarito explains

that, ever since his wife and daughter were raped by soldiers, the boatman has mistrusted all uniformed people (280–81, 302; see also gamekeeper.)
  Speaks: 2–5, 295, 297–98, 300.
  The boatman/gondolier in Venice, who lost all five of his brothers during World War I, remains friendly and "uncholeric" (42). He has six children to support. Cantwell promises him a strong engine for his boat, a promise he is unable to keep (275, 291; see also gifts and gondoliers.)
  Speaks: 42–44, 46–47, 53.

*boatmen. In addition to Cantwell and Alvarito, four other people are out duck-shooting: there are six boats out altogether; presumably each has its boatman (1, 299–300; see men and boys).

Bobby. Alvarito's hunting dog; we see him retrieving ducks (295–98). Cantwell forgets to give Bobby the sausage he had bought specially for him at the market (191, 296, 306).

*Bosch, Hieronymus [von Aeken. Flemish painter, c. 1450–c. 1516. Although records are scarce, Bosch seems to have belonged to a spiritual, ascetic organization called the Brotherhood of Our Lady, which held that the pleasures and temptations of this world lead to damnation. This moralizing mysticism is reflected in Bosch's complicated, intellectual art. Among his best known works are *The Hay Wain, The Temptation of St. Anthony, The Table of the Seven Deadly Sins* and *The Garden of Earthly Delights,* all in Madrid's Prado Museum. His paintings are satirical, symbolic, and often grotesque. See *Islands.*]
  Cantwell asserts that Bosch depicted death accurately (254).

*Boss, [Thomas. English gun manufacturer, 1790–1857. The son of a gunmaker, Thomas served an apprenticeship under his father William, who had himself been trained by Joseph Manton, a famous gunmaker and excellent craftsman. After working for some time for James Purdey (q.v.), Thomas Boss founded in 1812 the company still known as Boss & Co., Ltd., moving it to St. James's Street, London, about 1830. The company was purchased by the Robertson family in 1890; the current Chairman is John Robertson, whose son joined the company in 1990. Boss & Co., ranked among the best in the field, produces fine guns in limited editions and is known to refuse orders if there is any risk of putting its skilled workers under too much pressure and thus compromising quality. The over-and-under model which Boss & Co. introduced in 1908 or 1909 "represents probably the acme of over-and-under development purely for game shooting. Its action has a very shallow profile and the lower barrel (usually fired first) is only just above the forward, 'pointing' hand, giving a near-perfect barrel-to-hand relationship. The result is a particularly good relationship between eyes, hands and the gun."]⁴

Cantwell would like to give Boss guns to Renata (290; see gifts and Purdey).

*botulism. See anthrax.

*Bradley, General [Omar Nelson. American soldier, 1893–1981. Bradley was a graduate of several schools, including the Infantry School in Georgia, the Command and General Staff School in Kansas, and the Army War College. He commanded the First U.S. Army during the invasion of Normandy in 1944; served as Army Chief of Staff (1948–1949) and as chairman of the Joint Chiefs of Staff (1949–1953). He rose to the highest rank (five-star general). His metal-frame glasses gave him a scholarly appearance.]

Cantwell identifies Bradley as "the schoolmaster" and numbers him among the few generals he admires (125).

*Breda, [Ernesto. Italian engineer and industrialist, 1852–1918. In 1886 Breda founded the company that bears his name, in Milan. The company specializes in locomotives and other equipment for trains. During World War I it increased its production and expanded into several other Italian cities, including Venice and Rome. The Ernesto Breda Scientific Institute, established in 1917, sponsors research in metallurgy.]⁵

Taking the boat into Venice, Jackson and Cantwell pass by the "ugly" Breda works. Cantwell explains that Breda has a branch in Milan as well as the one they pass in Mestre-Venice (35).

the British. Cantwell is careful not to make fun of Montgomery in front of two British customers at Harry's Bar (85, 100).

*the British ambassador and his dull wife. They are sometimes invited for dinner at Renata's palazzo (207).

*Browning, Robert [English poet, 1812–1889] and Mrs. Robert [née Elizabeth Barrett, English poet, 1806–1861. After their marriage in 1846 the Brownings lived mostly in Italy.]

According to Cantwell, neither of these poets was much admired in Venice, though both wrote about it (48).

*Brueghel, Pieter. [Flemish painter, c. 1525–1569. Pieter the Elder is best known for his vibrant, detailed landscapes and witty presentations of peasant life. Among his many famous paintings are *The Wedding*

Dance, Hunters in the Snow, The Magpie on the Gallows, Storm at Sea, and *Landscape with the Fall of Icarus.* See *FWBT.*]

Cantwell remarks that Brueghel could not have worked properly if he, like Cantwell, had observed the countryside through the window of a speeding car (14), which blurs and distorts the landscape.

*Brusadelli, [Giulio] (the Great Patron, our Leader, the Revered One). [Italian businessman, 1878–1962. Born of a poor family, Brusadelli lost his father when he was only ten years old. In spite of these early hardships, Brusadelli eventually became the director and major shareholder of Cotonificio Dell'Acqua, a large cotton manufacturing corporation. On 20 June, 1948, the Dell'Acqua stock was listed on the stock market at L. 13,000; it was sold later that summer at L. 9,000 to Giulio Riva and several of his partners, of the rival Cotonificio Valle di Susa.[6] The sale was made "privately" and was either not declared or misrepresented to the tax authorities. It was of such proportions that it made Riva and the Valle di Susa cotton company the majority stockholders in Brusadelli's concern. The sale shook the stock market, raised the issue of monopolistic empire building, and exposed the cotton industry's sometimes shady relationships with the banks. The uproar alerted the tax authorities, and in October 1948 Brusadelli went to court in an attempt to cancel the deal and retrieve the stocks. He claimed that the sale was not legally binding because at the time he had been "in un momento di particolare disquilibrio psichico" as the result of "sforzi sessuali contro natura" (unnatural sexual exertions) demanded of him by his wife, who read pornography to him, forced him to watch "spettacolo di amori lesbici," and conned his doctor into giving him daily injections (content unspecified). He also claimed that he was the victim of a conspiracy, his wife having acted with his younger colleague Riva to weaken and defraud an old man (he was then 70 years old). In late October and early November 1948, Brusadelli dominated the headlines, the attention attracted by this unusual legal suit exacerbated by the revelation that he had failed to pay the necessary taxes on proceeds of the sale to Riva. Investigations uncovered additional tax fraud, and law suits and investigative commissions proliferated, involving not only Brusadelli's and Riva's cotton companies, but also their various subsidiaries and several domestic and foreign banks, which were suspected of laundering money. As evidence of tax evasion, stock manipulation, and other shady dealings piled up, the newspapers called for a rigorous examination of Italian business in general and of Milanese industry in particular (Milan was the center of the automobile industry). On 10 November, 1948 Brusadelli's personal property was impounded; this included furniture, antiques, Oriental rugs, tapestries, more than thirty valuable paintings, a well-equipped yacht, and several bank accounts, including one in his wife's name which held L. 110 million. Locating and evaluating all his assets and defining his tax debts was a complicated business which took several years of legal wrangling. A variety of rulings established several fines: in 1949 Brusadelli was required to pay L. 69 million in taxes and fines; the next year he was declared liable for L. 150 million; in 1952 the 60 million debt was reduced to L. 42 million with 8 million additional tax; in 1956 he was appealing a fine of L. 34 million and that summer he was sentenced to jail for failure to pay any of his taxes or fines. By this time, however, he was living in Switzerland, where he stayed until he died six years later.[7] In the context of Italy's post-war financial difficulties, the Brusadelli-Riva affair was particularly offensive. It impressed Hemingway, who had been in Italy in November 1948.]

The narrative presents Brusadelli as the thoroughly despicable character in whose name Cantwell and his friends have established an imaginary Order (q.v.). He is accurately described as a rich tax-evader, a "profiteer of Milan" (57). Renata refuses to drink a toast to "that swine" (270). The Grand Master announces that Brusadelli's property has been "confiscated" by the courts (270). To underline the ubiquitousness of such tax evaders, Hemingway briefly presents another such character, accompanied by an expensively-dressed young woman (38–39). [In November 1948 Hemingway wrote his wife that he had seen "a sort of Brusadelli type with woman to match" (Baker, *Letters,* 654).]

*Brusadelli's wife. [Anna Andreoli, Brusadelli's second wife, was half his age (about 35 years old) at the time of the 1948 scandal. Accused of entrapping her husband through sexual excesses (see Brusadelli above), she went into seclusion when the scandal broke, complaining of "un violento attaco di fegato" (severe liver problems) which prevented her appearance in court to testify in October and November 1948. She was still unavailable in December, when she was suffering "una forte crisi di nervi" (nervous break-down). The "regina del cotone" (cotton queen) did, however, issue a statement that as far as she was concerned her husband was dead (she called herself "the widow Brusadelli") and that her lawyers were preparing to clear her name. She left her husband's house (Via Brennero 1, Milan), moved in with her mother (Via Aurelio Saffi 31), and then rented a luxurious apartment where her privacy was protected by several bodyguards. To the charges of sexual abuse and entrapment, Brusadelli added the accusation (reported on 10 December, 1948) that she was involved with his nephew, whom he had formerly befriended and whom he later decided to disinherit. Early in 1949, she and Riva launched separate libel suits against Brusadelli, who dropped his charges against them in order to concentrate on his struggle with the Public Treasury (tax department). All the parties were reconciled in the summer of 1949, and the Brusadellis settled in Lugano, Switzerland, where she tended him until he died there in 1962 (see endnote 7).]

The narrative reports that Brusadelli had accused his young wife of having weakened him with her "extraordinary sexual demands" (57).

Burano. [An island in the Venetian lagoon, about six miles northeast of Venice. It is about half the size of Murano, q.v. Burano's traditional industries are fishing and lacemaking. See Visigoths.]

Cantwell points out Burano to Jackson (29).

*Burberry. [Thomas. English draper and businessman, 1835–1926. Burberry served an apprenticeship to a draper and then became involved in developing a cloth which would exclude wind and rain and yet allow enough air to circulate around the body to keep it comfortable. Burberry's material, originally called "gaberdine," is tightly woven, warm, comfortable, and practically untearable. Burberry, himself an avid sportsman, launched a line of practical, durable clothes suitable for outdoor sports such as shooting, golf, tennis, fishing, archery, and skiing. His firm, established in 1856 in Basingstoke, was very success-ful, supplying sports wear to royalty. The main office was soon moved to London and the first Paris branch was established in 1910. Burberry made tents and overalls for Captains Scott and Amundsen's trip to the South Pole in 1912. As Burberry gabardine was much more comfortable than rubberized mackintoshes, many military men opted for Burberry coats during the Boer War. Burberry developed a style known as the "trench coat," of which over half-a million were sold during World War I. The style remained popular after the war.][8]

Cantwell, who knows that the Burberry raincoat is waterproof, figures that some dishonest army contractor billed the army for top-quality protective coats and supplied cheaper goods, becoming rich in the process. The army-issued coat Cantwell has is wind-proof but not waterproof—clearly not a Burberry (184).

*Burnham. Cantwell's former driver, the predecessor of Jackson. He is now "up at the rest center . . . a fine place" (14).

*the butler. See Renata's servants; see also Maxwell, Elsa.

*Byron. George Gordon, Lord Byron. [English Romantic poet, 1788–1824. Byron spent the last eight years of his short life in Italy. He is best known for *Manfred, Don Juan,* and *Childe Harold,* a section of which is about Venice (Canto IV, 1–28). In 1816 Byron rented the Palazzo Mocenigo on Venice's Grand Canal; he had an affair with Teresa Guiccioli, a young woman married to an older man. He defines his relationship to her, that of the *cavalier servente* (attendant suitor or lover; in Byron's words, "supernumerary slave") in his satirical poem, *Beppo* (1818). Byron died in Greece, having gone there to fight for Greek independence.]

Cantwell remembers that Byron, like the Brownings and other English artists, was attracted to Venice, where he lived in the *palazzo* of Alvarito's family and conducted an affair with a gondolier's wife (48).

*Caesar. [Gaius Julius Caesar. Roman general and politician, 100–44 BCE. In his *Commentaries on the Gallic Wars,* Caesar comments that all of Gaul is divided into three parts.]

The Gran Maestro quotes Caesar correctly, saying that of the three parts, "the bravest . . . are the Belgians" (61, 202).

*Canfield, [Richard Albert (Dick). American gambler, glass manufacturer, art connoisseur and collector, 1855–1914. Canfield opened a gambling house in Rhode Island and then, after a brief period in jail, opened another one in New York at 5 East 44th Street, next door to Delmonico's. This latter gambling establishment, elegantly furnished with antiques and valuable paintings, catered to New York's upper crust. Canfield opened a similarly opulent establishment in Newport, Rhode Island, where America's rich had their summer homes. Police harassment and public disapproval eventually led to the closing of these houses and Canfield turned to glass manufacturing and to Wall Street, succeeding in both enterprises. His valuable collections included Sheraton and Hepplewhite furniture, ancient vases and pottery, and many paintings: he owned the largest private collection of the work of American artist J.A.M. Whistler (1834–1903). Canfield invented a form of solitaire which permits gambling.][9]

Cantwell plays a geographical variant of a Canfield card game: if he can find his way from the hotel to the market without getting lost, he wins (185).

*Canterbury. [Canterbury school was founded in 1915 in New Milford, Connecticut, as a private college preparatory school (grades 9–12) for Catholic boys. In the 1940s, when Ernest and Pauline Hemingway sent their sons Patrick and Gregory to this expensive school, only boys were admitted. Canterbury began admitting girls as external day students in 1970 and as boarding students in 1972.][10]

Cantwell remarks that dishonest army contractors have become so wealthy that they can afford to send their sons to expensive private schools like Groton or Canterbury (184).

*Cantwell, Gordon. The Colonel's brother, killed in the Pacific theater during World War II (257).

Cantwell, Colonel Richard (Dick, Ricardo, my Colonel, Supreme Commander). The main character of the novel is a fifty-one-year-old Colonel of Infantry in the U.S. Army who knows he is dying.[11] A graduate of the Virginia Military Institute (V.M.I., 290; also see 272), he has played polo (10), served in the Italian Army in World War I, and was an observer during the Spanish Civil War (40). He was badly wounded in the right knee during World War I, and has since been wounded twice in the hand (55, 84) and suffered "Maybe ten concussions" (10). He achieved the rank of General during World War II. Now back in his beloved Italy, he defecates ceremoniously at the place where he received his first wound (18) and, in a series of conversations with Renata, reviews his career, including the traumatic defeat at Hurtgen Forest (chapters 29–35) and his consequent demotion from General to Colonel (8, 95, 145, 169). This cathartic review and his desire to be "kind, decent and good" (65) indicate he is attempting spiritual renewal before he dies. Cantwell's economic situation is somewhat confused: he stays at the very expensive Gritti Hotel (q.v.), is well-versed in expensive guns (see Boss and Purdey), and has bought an expensive car (23–24), so that he looks like the typical "rich American" (259) whom shopkeepers love to overcharge. But he haggles over a boat ride (42) and seems unable to afford gifts for Renata (102–3, 290; see gifts, Louis XVI, Murano, *Vogue*). Similarly, he plans extravagant trips with Renata (see Muehlebach) as well as a very modest retirement, by himself, in Venice (45).

Speaks: 2–4, 6–11, 13–25, 27–30, 33–44, 46–47, 51–76, 79–111, 113–14, 116–62, 165, 172–83, 190–91, 194–229, 231–48, 251, 259–77, 282–87, 293, 295, 297–307; frequent interior monologue. Addresses portrait: 171–74, 176–80, 258; also see 195–96.

*Cantwell, Mrs. Richard. Cantwell's ex-wife, to whom he pays alimony (273), is a journalist. Cantwell describes her as an ambitious "career girl" (251) who "married me to advance herself" (212). His love affair with Renata enables him to "forget her for keeps" (214–15). See Cantwell's women, journalists, and endnote 1.

*Cantwell's family. Cantwell's grandfather owned a Purdey gun, which Cantwell's older brother inherited (92–93).

*Cantwell's women. Cantwell has been involved with other women; Renata is his fourth and last love (95; see Cantwell, Mrs. Richard).

*Carroll, [Benajah Harvey. American lawyer, churchman, editor, and diplomat, 1874–1922. Carroll held many advanced degrees, including the titles Doctor of Theology from Southern Baptist University and Doctor of Philosophy from Berlin University. He served as army chaplain during the Spanish American War (1898), was pastor of various churches in his native Texas and in Kentucky, held academic positions at Baylor University, and worked for the Houston *Chronicle* before being confirmed as U.S. Consul at Venice, a position he held from April 1914 until October 1918. Carroll was subsequently appointed to Naples and, after two years there, to Cádiz, Spain, where he died.][12]

Cantwell accurately remembers that Carroll was the American consul in Venice in 1918, when Cantwell was a young lieutenant in the Italian army (73).

*Casals, [Pau Carlos Salvador Defilló de] (Pablo). [Self-exiled Catalan cellist, composer, and conductor, 1876–1973. A Republican sympathizer during the Spanish Civil War, Casals left Spain when Franco's forces defeated the Republic in 1939. During the Civil War he had given many concerts to raise money for the Republicans; he also raised money for war victims during World War II. A world-famous performer noted particularly for his interpretations of Bach, Casals founded the Orquestra Pau Casals in Barcelona as well as long-lived musical festivals in Marlboro, Vermont and San Juan, Puerto Rico. His best known composition is the oratorio *El Pesebre* (*The Manger,* 1960). He played in the White House at the invitation of Presidents Theodore Roosevelt (1904) and John F. Kennedy (1961). His music is preserved on many records and films, and his cello is on display at the Casals Museum in San Juan, Puerto Rico.][13]

Cantwell finds Renata's voice "so lovely" that it sounds like "Casals playing the cello" (113).

*the chauffeur. He drives the Milanese profiteer's convertible (38). See also the driver.

*Chautauqua. [A movement to educate adults by sending experts to lecture throughout the USA. It was founded at Chautauqua, New York (on the shores of Lake Chautauqua) in 1873 by Bishop John Heyl Vincent and Lewis Miller, who suggested that the religious instruction offered at the Methodist Episcopalian institute they were attending at that site be expanded to include secular subjects. The first such secular camp was held at Chautauqua in 1874, and courses for home study, prepared and published by the Institute and augmented by visiting lecturers and performers, were offered to those who could not attend courses in Chautauqua. The movement was very successful until the late 1920s, Chautauqua lectures being major cultural events in many small towns. Summer camps are still held at the original site, with emphasis on music and other performance arts.][14]

At the news briefing, the assembled journalists looked like auditors at a Chautauqua lecture-meeting (238).

*children (*bambini*). Cantwell and Renata discuss her unborn children (110, 229) and he imagines having five sons (179; see Richard the Lion-Hearted). Cantwell thinks of children playing near him if he were to be buried in a garden near the Brenta River (34–35); these are probably Renata's children, and probably on Alvarito's country estate (see Alberto); Renata's villa on the Brenta was burned (34, 122). Renata offers to be Cantwell's daughter (98) and "daughter" (q.v.) is one of his favorite nicknames for her. Both Jackson and Cantwell mention that Italians have many children (15, 29). We hear about but do not see the boatman's families (q.v.), including their children.

*Cipriani, Cipriani's. [Guiseppe Cipriani was the owner of Harry's Bar (q.v.), a fine restaurant at 1323 San Marco, Calle Vallaresso, Venice. His son, Arrigo, a young teen-ager when Hemingway visited Harry Bar's with Adriana Ivancich in 1949–1950, managed the bar/restaurant after his father's retirement. The Ciprianis also own Harry's Dolci, at Giudecca 773, Venice; Cipriani a Casa (Catering) at San Marco 1323, Venice; and two fine restaurants in New York City: Bellini by Cipriani, at 777 7th Avenue, and Harry Cipriani, at 783 5th Ave. Guisseppe Cipriani wrote *L'Angolo dell' Harry's Bar* (Rizzoli, 1978); Arrigo Cipriani is the author of a novel, *Eloise and Bellinis* (New York: Little, Brown & Co).][15]
The narrative correctly identifies Cipriani as the owner of Harry's Bar. Cipriani is such a good friend that Cantwell is sure he will pay for Renata's pin and trust Cantwell to repay him sometime later (102, 266–67; but see gifts). He is mentioned often (71–72, 88–89, 91, 100).

the clergy and their housekeepers. See the Pope and the *background characters.

the clerk. Renata orders the clerk at the jewellery shop to deliver the jewelled pin to Cipriani's (260).
    Speaks: 260.

*coiffeurs, hair-dressers. See *background characters.

*[Collins, Joseph Lawton] (Lightning Joe). [American soldier, 1896–1963. During World War II Collins was active in the Pacific theater, leading the 25th Infantry Division in Guadalcanal and the XIV Corps in New Georgia. He also commanded the VII Corps during the Allied landing at Normandy and led troops at Mons, Namur, Liege and the Battle of the Bulge.][16]
    Cantwell knew "Lightning Joe" as the commander of the VII Corps and gives him good marks (125; see also 221).

the Colonel. See Cantwell.

Commendatore. [Italian rank: Knight of an order of chivalry, knight-commander.]

The cook at the Magnificent Hotel in Venice and a member of the Order of Brusadelli (q.v.). In recognition of the cook's sexual prowess, the Gran Maestro promoted him to *Commendatore* (60). Cantwell figures that the profiteer he sees outside Venice is a *Commendatore* (38).

the *concierge* at the Gritti Palace Hotel. See Domenico; see also *concierge* in *SAR* and *MF*.

Condottieri. [Plural of *condottiere,* Italian for leader. In the 14th and 15th centuries, the *condottieri* were independent military leaders who contracted themselves and their armies of mercenaries to fight for whatever cities or states paid them the highest fees. As wars among the various independent cities and states were plentiful, *condottieri* were seldom unemployed. They switched from one lord to another as economics dictated, arousing the ire of former employers and the suspicions of current ones. To succeed in their dangerous profession, the *condottieri* had to be clever strategists and effective leaders.]

The Grand Master introduces the topic of the *Condottieri.* When Cantwell begins planning the military operations they would execute as mercenary warriors, the Grand Master is out of his depth and Cantwell must abandon his military games (62–64).

contractors, contractors' sons. Dishonest contractors to the armed forces make large profits by charging the Army for well-made, expensive products but supplying inferior goods instead. They usually work in partnership with Army officers in charge of supplies (see *Meyers). The leaky raincoat Cantwell wears suggests such profiteering. Cantwell figures these contractors can now afford to send their sons to exclusive schools, like Groton or Canterbury (184, qq.v.).

*the cook. See *Commendatore.*

*correspondents. See journalists.

the Count. See Andrea

the Countess, Contessa. See Dandolo and Renata.

*Cripps, [Sir Richard Stafford. English lawyer and politician, 1889–1952. Cripps served in France as a Red Cross driver during World War

I, after which he worked in a munitions factory. He joined the Labour Party in 1929 but was at odds with it for several years and was finally expelled in 1939 for his anti-war, pro-appeasement position; he advocated a United Front with the Communists. The coalition government appointed him Ambassador to Moscow in 1940 in the belief that as founder and member of the English Socialist League he might convince Russia to support England in World War II; Cripps concluded the Anglo-Soviet pact. In 1942 he was leader of the House of Commons and a member of the war cabinet. He was sent to India in an unsuccessful bid for Indian support for the English war effort in return for post-war independence. In November 1942 he was appointed Minister of aircraft production. He was re-admitted to the Labour Party in 1945. Cripps was president of the London Board of Trade (1945–1947), Minister for Economic Affairs (1947), and Chancellor of the Exchequer (1947–1950). He administered austere post-war economic measures (high taxes, wage-freezes, continued rationing) to control inflation.][17]

Cantwell knows that, due to the weakness of the postwar economy, strict rationing is still in force in England. He jokes that "Cripps will probably ration" even the language (195).

crowds. See background characters.

*Custer, General George Armstrong. [American soldier, 1836–1876. A West Point graduate, Custer served in the Union forces and earned steady promotions by his performance in the American Civil War, achieving the rank of major general. After the Civil War Custer was appointed to the Seventh U.S. Cavalry, winning a major victory against the Cheyenne in 1868 and engaging the Sioux in battle several times over a period of years. In 1876 he and his companies, totalling less than 700 men, faced about 4,000 Sioux under the leadership of Chief Sitting Bull. Custer and over 200 of his men were killed in this famous battle at Little Big Horn; the Montana site is now a national monument. Many military historians have argued that Custer bears much of the blame for the disaster at Little Big Horn: he attacked from a position of weakness and he discarded the original timetable for the battle. Custer's apologists contend that the size of the opposing force was not known and that he was forced to attack when the Sioux became aware of his presence and the plan for a surprise attack became irrelevant. See also *FWBT*.]

Cantwell describes Custer as a handsome but stupid soldier (169). Although he knows he is dying, Cantwell pretends that he and Renata will travel together to the site of Custer's last stand, which he will explain to her (265).

*Custer, Mrs. [Elizabeth Bacon, 1842–1933. Custer's wife accompanied him on many of his frontier expeditions and wrote several books about their experiences: *"Boots and Saddles"; or, Life in Dakota with General Custer* (1885), *Tenting on the Plains; or, General Custer in Kansas and Texas* (1887), *Following the Guidon* . . . (1890, about Custer and the Washita Campaign of 1868–1869), *General Custer at the Battle of Little Big Horn* (1897), and *The Boy General; Story of the Life of Major-General George A. Custer, as told by Elizabeth B. Custer* (1901). The Custers' personal correspondence was edited by M. Merington and published in 1950.]

Cantwell mentions that Custer had "a loving wife" (169).

customers. In the morning, only a few people are seen at Harry's Bar (262); Renata watches a "morning drinker" leave (267). Later the place fills up (92; see background characters, the British).

*customers. Ettore's report that several customers are drinking at Harry's Bar, among them a Greek princess and several Americans (qq.v.), induces Cantwell to stay away until they leave (72–73, 75).

*Dandolo, Contessa Dandolo. [The Dandolo are an ancient Italian family, distinguished in the history of Venice since at least the seventh century. Four of the doges (chief magistrates) of Venice have come from this patrician family: Enrico Dandolo was doge from 1192 to 1205; he helped finance the Fourth Crusade, which brought back enormous booty to Venice, including the four bronze horses which were taken from Constantinople and installed in the façade of St. Mark's. Enrico's grandson Giovanni was doge from 1280–1289, Francesco from 1329 to 1339, and Andrea from 1343 until his death in 1354; Andrea wrote a history of Venice. The Dandolo family expanded the power, wealth, and territory of Venice. Renata, who seems to be a member of this family, says that "everybody" in her family fought.]

An elderly widow who lives in a handsome palazzo in Venice, the Contessa Dandolo colors her hair and is admired by Cantwell (47–48). Although we are not told Renata's family name, we know that Renata is also a Countess and that her ancestors have been doges of Venice (219); she seems to be a Contessa Dandolo herself (see *Renata's family).

*d'Annunzio, Gabriele. [Italian writer, soldier, and womanizer, 1863–1938. D'Annunzio's early poetry brought him fame, which his later adventures, both romantic and political, enhanced. Inspired by the great actress Eleanora Duse (1858–1924, see *the actress), he began writing plays. Duse starred in *La gioconda* (1899), *Francesca da Rimini* (1902) and several other of his plays. D'Annunzio also wrote *The Triumph of Death* (1894, a novel), *The Intruder* (1898), *The Daughter of Jorio* (1904, considered by some critics to be his masterpiece), and *Laudi Cycle* (highly praised lyrical poems, 1903–1912). During World War I he served with distinction, first in the Italian Army and then in the Air Force. In 1919 he and about 300 volunteers occupied Rijeka (Fiuma) to establish Italy's claim to land which the Allies were proposing to attach to Yugoslavia. This dramatic action, as well as his heroic war record and his chauvinism, won him many followers. D'Annunzio's extreme nationalism, expounded in rousing speeches and essays, eventually developed into fascism. He founded the Black Shirts, which later supported Mussolini.][18]

Cantwell admires D'Annunzio as a writer and man of action but objects to his self-aggrandizement and his political postures (49–52; see also 47, 49, 121, *the actress and *Notturno).

*Dante, Mister Dante [Alighieri. Italian poet, 1265–1321. Dante's love for Beatrice inspired much poetry which was later incorporated into *La vita nuova* (1292–1294). In the tripartite *Divine Comedy* (1308–1320), Dante defines the "Inferno" as a funnel-shaped series of circles in which the various sinners suffer appropriate and vividly depicted eternal punishment. "Purgatorio" is a striated mountain, populated by repentant sinners striving for salvation, and "Paradiso" is full of light, beauty, and song, the heaven where the poet meets his beloved Beatrice, who is now an angel. Critics have compared Cantwell's love for Renata to Dante's love for Beatrice; both women guide the men who love them to salvation.[19] See also *MF* and *Islands*.]

When she cannot be with Cantwell, Renata reads Dante (218). Cantwell describes the great poet as "an execrable character" but grants that he was a good writer even though his definitions of the circles of Hell were "unjust" (246), an opinion which is repeated in *Islands* (197). Dante is mentioned often in *ARIT* (90, 124–25, 129, 269); Cantwell identifies with him (246).

Daughter (*hija, hija mía, figlia*). Cantwell's favorite nickname for Renata (98–100, 107, 266 *et passim*).[20]

*Degas, [Hilaire Germain Edgar. French impressionist painter and sculptor, 1834–1917. He often painted ballet dancers and women at their toilette, as well as scenes of contemporary life, including such "unheroic" subjects as the racetrack and café life. Among his more important works are *Woman with Chrysanthemums* (1865), *Foyer of the Dance* (1872), *Absinthe, The Rehearsal,* and *Two Laundresses,* all painted in 1882. He is admired for his control of movement, color, and light.]

In the grey light, a Venetian canal reminds Cantwell of a Degas painting (71).

*della Francesca. See Franceschi, Piero de.

*de Saxe, Maurice. See Saxe, Maurice Comte de.

*Desdemona. [A Venetian lady, heroine of Shakespeare's tragedy *Othello*.]
Although Cantwell insists that he and Renata do not resemble Shakespeare's characters, he makes comparisons: Renata is more beautiful than Desdemona and he is a more experienced warrior than Othello (230).

Devil. One of Cantwell's many nicknames for Renata (114; see also *GE* and *Islands*).

*doctor. The noisy motor which drives the boatman's gondola had originally powered a doctor's car. Cantwell offers to replace it with a marine engine (43).

*Domenica del Corriere. [Illustrated supplement of the highly respected Italian daily, *Corriere della Sera* (q.v. in *FTA*), founded in Milan in 1876.]
When Renata insists that Cantwell speak of his war experiences, even if they are as dreadful to look at as the pictures which appear in newspapers, Cantwell mentions two such papers: *Domenica del Corriere* and *Tribuna Illustrata* (219, q.v.).

Domenico (Ico). The efficient *concierge* at the Gritti (274; for a description, see 194). Cantwell, who likes and trusts him (65), gives him Renata's emeralds to put in the safe (196; see also 181). The *concierge* and the second waiter handle Renata's portrait (145–46, 174).
Speaks: 106, 144, 194–98.

Donna. [Italian honorific, like the English title "Lady."]
Cantwell refers to Renata, a noblewoman, as Donna Renata (138).

the driver. See Jackson, Sergeant Ronald.

*D.S.C. [Distinguished Service Cross, a decoration offered both by the United States and Great Britain. The British D.S.C. was established in 1901, the American in 1918. For his contributions as a volunteer for the American Red Cross serving in Italy, Hemingway was awarded the

Italian *Croce al Merito di Guerra* (the War Cross) and the *Medaglia D'argento al Valore Militare* (the Silver Medal for Military Valor), both of which are now in the Hemingway Collection, s.v. Other Materials: Objects. In World War II, he was awarded the American Bronze Star Medal and the European-African-Middle Eastern Campaign Ribbon, both for his services as a war correspondent. He was not awarded any of the medals Cantwell has earned.]

During his long military career Cantwell has been awarded various honors, including the D.S.C., the Silver Star, and the V.C. (qq.v.). (18, 290; see gifts).

*du Picq, Colonel. [Full name: Charles-Jean-Jacques-Joseph Ardant du Picq. Generally known as Colonel Ardant du Picq. French soldier, military theorist and writer, 1821–1870. Colonel Ardant du Picq fought in the Crimean War (1854–1856), was captured by the Russians at Sebastopol and held prisoner from September to December of 1855. In 1860 he was named a knight of the French Legion of Honor and in 1868 he was promoted to officer of that order. He was injured by a fragment of a shell and died of his wounds at Metz in August 1870. He is considered one of the greatest and most original of the French military writers. French military thinking, which traditionally emphasized the romantic, heroic view of combat, relied on massive military formations and on the top ranks of leadership to inspire its armies to victories. Lower- and middle-echelon officers were not expected to provide much leadership, and thus the general soldiery was largely unsupervised and undisciplined. The infantry in particular suffered great losses under this plan, as foot soldiers often decamped in disorder when exposed to fire. Ardant du Picq's own combat experience and his understanding of human psychology led him to develop a less romantic, more realistic attitude: in *Etudes du combat d'après l'antique* (1868) and his *Etudes sur le combat* (published posthumously in 1880) he argued that an army's success depends on meticulous organization at all levels of the military machine, on the initiative and intelligence of commanders at all ranks and, more importantly, on the psychological state of the individual soldier. He defined the most effective formation for infantry as the widely spaced column, protected by closed ranks of riflemen. His revolutionary views were validated in action during World War I.][21]

Cantwell approves of du Picq's military philosophy and regards him as the last genuine French "military thinker" (27; see also Gamelin, Maginot, and Mangin).

*Eisenhower, General [Dwight David (Ike). American soldier and politician, 1890–1969; 34th President of the United States, 1953–1961. A graduate of the U.S. Military Academy at West Point, Eisenhower rose to the highest rank (five-star general). As Supreme Allied Commander in Europe during World War II, he directed the landing of Allied forces at Normandy in June 1944. In 1945 he became Army Chief of Staff and in 1950 he was appointed Supreme Commander of the forces of the North Atlantic Treaty Organization (NATO). He retired from the Army in 1952 and was elected President on the Republican ticket.]

Cantwell, who despises most modern military leaders, dismisses Eisenhower as being more interested in his own advancement than in the military. He presciently refers to Eisenhower as "our next President" (125, 234; see also Epworth League).

*Emily. [Since a comparison is suggested between Cantwell and Renata and Shakespeare's Othello and Desdemona, it is interesting that another name from the play appears in the novel: Emilia is the wife of Iago in Shakespeare's *Othello*.]

Wife of Count Andrea (q.v.). She and the children are wintering in Rome while Andrea drinks in Venice (80).

*Epworth League. [A Methodist organization founded in Cleveland, Ohio, in 1889, to promote Christian fellowship among young people by means of social activities. In 1939 it became part of the Methodist Youth Fellowship, which later became the United Methodist Youth Fellowship. The Epworth League was named for Epworth Rectory, the birthplace of John Wesley (1703–1791), the English clergyman and evangelist who founded Methodism.]

Cantwell dismisses General Eisenhower as "Strictly the Epworth League" but then qualifies his remark (125).

Ettore. One of the waiters at Harry's Bar. He indulges in pseudo-military talk with Cantwell, supplying gossip about the bar's patrons as if it were military intelligence. Renata says that although he is fond of joking he will not distort the truth (97).

Speaks: 75, 89–91, 101.

Fiat. [The Italian Fiat company (Fabbrica Italiana Automobili Torino) was founded in 1899 by Giovanni Agnelli and incorporated in 1906. Since 1910 Fiat has been the largest firm in Italy, specializing in cars, trucks and other vehicles, but producing aviation engines and components as well. See *FWBT*.]

Cantwell and Jackson park the car in the Fiat garage before entering Venice (36).

*Firestone, [Harvey Samuel. American industrialist, 1868–1938. Firestone founded the Firestone Tire and Rubber Co. in 1900; he produced tires of various sizes (for cars, trucks, tractors, etc.), developed non-skid tire treads, and started his own rubber plantations in Liberia. His son, Harvey Samuel, Jr. (1898–1973) headed the company from 1946 to 1963. He is author of *Man on the Move, the Story of Transportation* (New York: Putnam's Sons, 1967).][22]

Cantwell criticizes his ex-wife for not having produced children but then recognizes that blaming her Fallopian tubes for their childlessness is unfair; he mendaciously claims that the only tubes he ever complains about are those of inner-tube and tire manufacturers like Firestone, B.F. Goodrich and General Tire Corporation (273, qq.v.).

*Foch, [Marshal Ferdinand. French military leader, 1851–1929. Before the outbreak of World War I, Foch argued for a single, unified allied command but his recommendations were rejected until May 1918, when he was finally given control of allied forces. By July Foch had turned almost certain defeat into victory. Military historians are largely agreed that he achieved the Allied victory. Foch wrote *Des princips de la guerre* (1903) and *De la conduite de la guerre* (1904).]

Foch is one of the few military leaders Cantwell respects (27).

*the footman. See Renata's servants.

*[Franceschi, Piero de] (Piero della Francesca). [Italian painter, mathematician, and theorist, c. 1420–1492. Piero della Francesca (or de Franceschi) was one of the most influential Italian artists of the early Renaissance. His mathematical training helped him achieve true proportional height. His frescoes include *The Legend of the True Cross* (also known as *The History of the Cross*) in the church of St. Francesco in Arezzo; *The Resurrection* in his hometown of Borgo San Sepolcro, in Umbria; and *The Flagellation of Christ* in the Cathedral of Urbino.]

Surveying the bombed countryside, Cantwell deduces that we ought not to build beautiful villas or churches or hire artists like Giotto, Piero della Francesca, Mantegna or Michelangelo to decorate them with frescoes (13–14).

*Franco [Bahamonde, Francisco Paulino Hermenegildo Teodula (Generalissimo, el Caudillo). Spanish military and political leader, 1892–1975. At the military uprising which signaled the beginning of the Spanish Civil War, Franco took control of Spanish Morocco. In September 1936 the Nationalist forces named him head of state and Commander of Southern Forces; General Mola, who was killed in an air crash nine months later, was appointed Commander of the Army of the North. In 1939, at the end of the Spanish Civil War, Franco became the ruler of Spain, merging the Nationalist, Carlist, and Falangist factions, supported by the Roman

Catholic Church, and establishing a repressive government which tolerated no opposition or criticism. During World War II Franco supported the Axis while maintaining an official policy of neutrality. In 1946 the victorious Allies withdrew their Ambassadors from Spain, which remained isolated from the international community until 1950, when the growing threat of the USSR drew Western countries together. Franco remained head of state until his death. See also *DS*.]

Cantwell hopes that Spain will be "re-taken" from Franco, whom he despises (172).

*Frederick the Great. [Frederick II, 1712–1786; king of Prussia 1740–1786. Frederick the Great conquered and annexed upper and lower Silesia and established Prussia as a leading European power; he also expanded his country's economic, agricultural, and judicial systems. He wrote *Anti-Macchiavel* and many historical, philosophical and military essays.]

Of the many soldiers who have written about warfare, Cantwell mentions Frederick the Great, Maurice de Saxe, and T'Sun Su (qq.v.). When Renata urges Cantwell to write about modern warfare, he declines (135).

*French. To temper his disapproval of French military leaders, Cantwell cautions himself not to forget the courage and heroism of those who worked in the Resistance movement (27) and the widespread, heart-felt joy of the French when Paris was liberated from German occupation (141; see *men and boys).

the game-keeper. Alvarito's head keeper greets Cantwell and registers the day's catch after the duck shoot (299–300). The surly boatman (q.v.) also holds the position of game-keeper, at *Barone* Alvarito's estate (300).

Speaks: 299–300.

*Gamelin, [General Maurice Gustave. French soldier, 1872–1958. Gamelin served as Head of the Operations Section of the French General Headquarters during World War I, being awarded the rank of general more for his administrative than his military skills. Between the World Wars he was Commander in Chief of French forces, and in 1940 was appointed Commander of Land Forces, responsible for British and French forces in the defence of France. Convinced the Maginot line would hold, Gamelin argued for a defensive rather than offensive strategy for France. He was unable to withstand the German attack of May 1940 and is generally held responsible for the collapse of France in June that year.][23]

Cantwell does not respect Gamelin's military thinking, which he summarizes in one derisive sentence (27).

Il Gazzettino. [A daily newspaper, published in Venice, with a weekly supplement called *Il Gazzettino dell'economia.* It was founded in March 1887 by Gianpietro Talamani, one year after Talamani's arrival in Venice from his native Vodo, in the mountainous northeastern province of Belluno. During its first forty years it sported a series of subtitles: *Giornale della Democrazia Veneta* (1887–1897), *Giornale Democratico* (1898–1905), *Giornale del Popolo* (1906–1908), and *Giornale del Veneto* (1909–1926). Since 1926 it has appeared without a subtitle. Throughout its long history *Il Gazzettino* has been a serious newspaper with a national readership.][24]
     This newspaper was delivered to Cantwell's room at the Gritti (175). Renata says that Cantwell can, if he likes, announce her love for him in *Il Gazzettino* (141).

*General [Tire Corporation]. See Firestone.

*George. Cantwell remembers George, his best friend, whom he had unexpectedly met in the Ardennes (292). He wishes George could tell Renata about Cantwell as he was then, before his demotion, but George seems to have been killed (294).[25]
     Speaks: 293.

*Germans (Krauts). Cantwell admires Germans as "the best soldiers" (272); he particularly admires Rommel and Udet (qq.v.), and can't really hate any Germans (176). Renata, however, cannot "take such a tolerant attitude" towards the Germans, who killed her father and burned the family's villa (122). Cantwell remarks that the Allies killed many Germans (160–61, 230) and may have killed the "barbarous" officer Renata recalls (160–61, 122). Cantwell himself has killed at least 122 Germans (123). The German occupation of Paris is mentioned (134, 140). See *men and boys.

gifts. Gift-giving is a prominent motif in this novel. Cantwell has given Arnaldo ducks and Arnaldo gives Cantwell liquor (69). The Gran Maestro gives him a bottle of wine (150). Renata gives Cantwell three elegant gifts: an inscribed silver flask (296), a portrait of herself (97, 100–1), and several antique emeralds (103–4, 165). Like the priest in *FTA,* Cantwell chooses gifts carefully, although most of the gifts do not reach the intended recipient: sausage for the dog Bobby (191, but see 296 and 306), a Jeep engine for the boatman (275–76; the engine does not materialize), more ducks for Arnaldo (306) and, for Renata, a jewelled pin, for which Cipriani pays (267; we do not hear that Cantwell repays Cipriani). He also thinks of giving her a hand-sewn, down-filled vest (282), expensive guns, his school ring and all his possessions (290). Renata would like Cantwell to be more generous (102–3; also see Louis XVI and Murano). See Boss, D.S.C., Purdey, and V.M.I.; also see gifts in *FTA*.

*Gino. An Italian boy who lost a leg in World War I in the same attack at which Cantwell himself, then very young, was wounded (19; see Randolfo; see also Passini in *FTA*). Cantwell ceremoniously defecates at the site (18).

Giorgio (Privy Counsellor of the Order of Brusadelli). Bartender at the Gritti Palace Hotel bar, he is one of the five members of the Order (q.v.), although not part of its inner circle (54, 56). He does not like Cantwell (65; see also 63).
   Speaks: 54.

*Giotto [di Bondone. Florentine painter and architect, c. 1276–c. 1337. Giotto created frescoes for, among others, the Church of St. Francis in Assisi and the Church of Santa Croce in Florence. Most famous are the 39 Biblical frescoes in the Scrovegni Chapel, Padua. The anecdote Cantwell remembers has to do with a papal commission: "To about 1302 or 1303 would belong, if there is truth in it, the familiar story of Giotto's O. Pope Benedict XI, the successor of Boniface VIII, sent, as the tale runs, a messenger to bring him proofs of the painter's powers. Giotto would give no other sample of his talent than an O drawn with a free sweep of the brush from the elbow; but the pope was satisfied and engaged him at a great salary to go and adorn with frescoes the papal residence at Avignon. Benedict, however, dying at this time (1305), nothing came of this commission; and the remains of Italian 14th-century frescoes still to be seen at Avignon are the work, not, as was long supposed, of Giotto, but of the Sienese Simone Martini and his school" (*Encyclopedia Brittanica*, 11th ed., XII: 35).]
   Driving past ruined villas, Cantwell comments that art is a casualty of war; even a beautiful old fresco by a master like Giotto is doomed (13–14). Cantwell remembers an anecdote about Giotto (54).
   Speaks: 54.

girls. See women and girls.

*Goebbels, [Paul Joseph. German politician, 1897–1945. Goebbels was rejected for military service because of his limp, the result of polio. He earned a Ph.D. in history in 1921, worked as a journalist, and then associated himself with Hitler in 1926, becoming his minister for "enlightenment and propaganda" in 1928 and staying with him until the end. Goebbels killed himself and his family when Hitler committed suicide, 1945.]

The unidentified writer is so ugly that Cantwell compares him to Goebbels (87, 88).

gondoliers. Cantwell travels from the Gritti to the market and back by gondola (184, 194). The gondolier in whose boat Renata is brought to orgasm is described as "trustworthy" (160). But as Arnaldo points out, gondoliers are great gossips; there are no secrets in Venice (74; see also *background characters and boatmen).

*gondolier's wife. Among Byron's several mistresses was a gondolier's wife (48).

*Goodrich, [Benjamin Franklin. American industrialist, 1841–1888; founder of B. F. Goodrich Co., rubber manufacturers.]
Cantwell crudely connects his wife's Fallopian tubes to rubber tires and tubes produced by Goodrich (273; see also Firestone).

*the governess. See Renata's governess.

*Goya [y Lucientes, Francisco José. Spanish painter, 1746–1828. Although the young Goya painted lively, bright cartoons for tapestries, his outlook and art became increasingly bitter as he got older. His canvases began to depict the vices of the Court and of society as a whole. The Napoleonic Wars deepened his pessimism; his paintings and etchings (*Los Caprichos, Los Proverbios*) became increasingly bitter, distorted, tortured and even surrealistic. The horrific series *Los Desastres de la Guerra* is a powerful condemnation of war. See also *DIA*.]
Cantwell compares the ugly unidentified writer to a picture by Goya (90).

the Gran Maestro (Grand Master). A middle-aged Italian, he is the head waiter at the Gritti Palace Hotel and a parallel character to Cantwell: they fought together in the Italian Army in World War I (126), when they became good friends (55). As middle-aged men they founded the Order of Brusadelli (q.v.). They wear uniforms (55) and enjoy addressing each other by their titles and speaking military jargon: the Grand Master, for example, reports the activities of the unidentified writer in military terms. Like Cantwell, the Gran Maestro suffers from a variety of ailments, including heart disease (61). Being an ex-soldier, an expert at what he does, and a fond admirer of Cantwell, he is, as the narrator points out, an admirable man (55).
Speaks: 55–64, 107, 115–16, 119–21, 124, 130–31, 138, 140, 144, 147, 202–3, 206–7, 269–71, 273.

the Gritti. [The Gritti were a powerful, noble Venetian family. Andrea Gritti (1455–1538) was elected the 77th Doge of Venice in 1523. The venerable Gritti Palace was built during his reign. For many years an elegant hotel, it is located at Campo Santa Maria del Giglio 2467, Venice, overlooking the Grand Canal and not far from the Church of Santa Maria della Salute. The hotel's kitchen, cooking school, and restaurant are famous. The hotel has hosted royalty, military and political personalities, as well as writers, musicians, architects, and other famous folk.[26] The Hemingways stayed there when they visited Venice in 1948.]

Cantwell stays at the Gritti Palace Hotel whenever he is in Venice (see description, 52, 54, 67–68 *et passim*).

*Groton. [Groton Preparatory School is an exclusive school in Groton, Connecticut, founded in 1884 by the Rev. Endicott Peabody. Famous alumni include Franklin D. Roosevelt and Dean Acheson. The same town in Connecticut is home to another expensive and exclusive school, Groton Academy, founded in 1793, but this institution was renamed Lawrence Academy in 1846, since which time there has been only one school named Groton. Originally admitting only boys, both Groton and Lawrence Academy are now coeducational.]

Dishonest army contractors can afford to send their sons to expensive boarding schools like Groton and Canterbury (q.v., 184; see Burberry).

*haberdasher. See Truman, Harry S.

*hairdressers. See *background characters.

the hall porter. See porters.

Harry's Bar. [The bar, located at 1323 San Marco, Venice, is named for Harry Pickering, the American who helped Guiseppe Cipriani to open the bar in 1931. Guiseppe's son Arrigo still owns the bar. See Cipriani.]

Cantwell's favorite bar/restaurant in Venice is the setting for chapters 9 and 37.

*Harper's Bazaar. [The four Harper brothers were the founders of the publishing house Harper and Brothers and of several magazines, including *Harper's New Monthly Magazine* (1850), *Harper's Weekly* (1857) and *Harper's Bazar* (1867), which was a weekly women's magazine established to complement *Harper's Weekly*. *Harper's Bazar* became a monthly in 1901 and was acquired by Hearst in 1913. Hearst developed it into the modern and sophisticated magazine we know today. In 1929 the spelling *Bazar* was changed to *Bazaar*.]

Although they both know Cantwell will die soon, the two lovers plan an "ideal" future together: they will own houses and travel, and Renata will read magazines like *Harper's Bazaar* (264: see *Vogue*).

*[Hemingway,] Mary [née Welsh, 1908–1986. Mary was a journalist for the English *Daily Express* and was working in London as a researcher for several news magazines when she met Hemingway. She had been married twice (to Lawrence Cook, from 1929 to 1931, and to Noel Monks, from 1938 to 1946) before she became Hemingway's fourth wife in 1946. Her memoirs are entitled *How It Was* (1976).]
    Hemingway dedicated *Across the River and Into the Trees* to his wife Mary.

*Hill, A[mbrose] P[owell]. [American soldier, 1825–1865. A graduate of the Military Academy at West Point, Hill fought in the Mexican and Seminole Wars. When the Civil War broke out, he was made colonel of a Virginia infantry regiment, soon proving himself one of the outstanding military leaders of the Confederacy. His division formed part of Stonewall Jackson's corps; he was severely wounded in the battle of Chancellorsville, Virginia, May 1863. After Jackson's death, in 1863, Hill led the third corps of the Confederate army in many key campaigns; he was killed at Petersburg. It is said that on their death beds both Lee and Jackson called for A. P. Hill to take command; in his delirium, Lee forgot that Hill had predeceased him.]
    The dying Cantwell recalls that Jackson, just before he died, had given instructions that Hill should take command and "'prepare for action'" (307).

honey dog. One of Cantwell's many nicknames for Renata. She objects to, but then accepts, the odd name. Cantwell doesn't define the term but explains its provenance (225).

*[Ibárruri Gómez, Dolores (la Pasionaria). Spanish politician and patriot, 1895–1989. The uneducated daughter of a miner, she rose rapidly in the ranks of the Spanish Communist Party. Her fiery oratory energized the Republican cause. She coined the Republican motto, "¡No pasarán!" ("They shall not pass!") and various slogans: "To resist and to fortify is to win" and "It is better to die on your feet than to live on your knees." Her book, *They Shall Not Pass: The Autobiography of Pasionaria,* was published in 1966. Her collected speeches and articles were published in 1938. Like Hemingway, Cantwell does not have a high opinion of la Pasionaria and her rhetoric.]
    Cantwell and the bartender quote la Pasionaria's slogans when they speak of Pacciardi, who fought in the Republican International

Brigades during the Spanish Civil War (40; see Ibárruri and slogans in *FWBT*).

*Indians. Cantwell refers to Indians in Oklahoma (24) and Jackson to Indian artifacts in the museum at Rawlins, Wyoming (16). See Indians in *TS* and *FWBT*.

*Italians. Cantwell served in the Italian Army during World War I. See *men and boys; see Italians in *FTA*.

Jackson, Sergeant Ronald (T 5 Jackson). ["T" or "Tec" stands for "technical" or "technician" (*Acronyms, Initialisms, & Abbreviations Dictionary*).]
Cantwell's driver, a mechanic and a decorated veteran of World War II (22), does not share Cantwell's attitudes and postures, insisting that he is "not suffering" (24), and would rather sleep than go duck-hunting. Cantwell does not like Jackson (58–59), although he grants that he is a good driver (12). Jackson seems to have known Cantwell for some time and is familiar with his demotion, his concussions (27), and his bad temper.
Speaks: 13–17, 21–25, 27–30, 34–37, 42, 51–52, 57–58, 275, 305–8.

*Jackson, General Thomas J[onathan] (Stonewall Jackson). [American soldier, 1824–1863. After military service in Mexico and a stint of teaching at the Virginia Military Institute (see V.M.I.), Jackson became Colonel of Volunteers for the Confederate Army when the Civil War broke out. He acquired his nickname by standing against the Union forces "like a stone wall." Military historians rank Stonewall Jackson among the most effective of the Confederacy's generals, second only to Robert E. Lee. He was strict, religious, fervently committed to the Confederacy, and an outstanding tactician. He was mortally wounded after his great victory at Chancellorsville, Virginia, probably shot by his own troops who mistook him and his staff for Union cavalry. See also *FWBT*.]
As he is dying Cantwell recalls Jackson's last words, which he once memorized (307; see also Hill).

*Jackson's family. Before the war, Ronald Jackson and his brother ran a garage in Rawlins, Wyoming, which they left in the hands of a man who mismanaged it. Consequently, after his brother was killed in action (22), Jackson decided to stay on in the Army. Jackson claims that his wife would not appreciate Italian art, particularly paintings of women, and "would run me" (16) from one end of the state to the other [Rawlins is in the southern and Buffalo in the northern part of Wyoming].

*Joan of Arc. [French heroine and saint, 1412–1431. Dressed as a man, Joan of Arc routed the English and enabled Charles the Dauphin to be crowned Charles VII at Rheims in 1429. She was betrayed by the English and burned at the stake for heresy and sorcery in 1431. She was canonized in 1920. See Boutet de Monvel in *MF*.]
Cantwell decides to get a haircut so he won't resemble this heroine (169).

*Johnston, [John] (Liver Eating). [American trapper, Army scout, lawman, c.1826–1900. When the Crow Indians killed Johnston's Chinook wife, who was pregnant, Johnston vowed to kill as many Crow as he could find and eat their livers. It is said he treated between 250 and 300 Crows in this fashion. In the late 1880s Johnston and the Crows became reconciled and he was adopted into their tribe. He was a scout for the U.S. Army in the territory which in 1890 entered the Union as Wyoming.]²⁷
Jackson explains that the local museum in Rawlins, Wyoming, displays mostly Indian artifacts and pictures of 'Liver Eating' Johnston. It is no place for Italian masters (16).

*journalists. Although he recognizes that they suffered casualties, Cantwell despises journalists of both sexes (236–37). See Cantwell, Mrs. Richard; Hemingway, Mary; and Smith, Walter Wellesley, all journalists.

*King Lear [Tragedy by William Shakespeare (q.v.).]
Cantwell says that the boxer Gene Tunney (q.v.) read *King Lear* (171).

*Komm' Süsser Tod. See Bach.

*Krim, Abdel. See Abd el Krim.

*Lachaise, Père. [François d'Aix de la Chaise was a French Jesuit, 1624–1709. La Chaise was very influential in the court of King Louis XIV, whose confessor he was. The great cemetery Père-Lachaise, located in north-east Paris, is named after him. Its 115 acres contain the tombs of writers, composers, painters, dancers, philosophers, scientists, actors, and political and military leaders. The 400-acre Arlington National Cemetery, in Arlington, Virginia, is the USA's most important military cemetery.]
Cantwell does not want to be buried at Arlington or Père Lachaise or in the cemetery at Venice (228). He would prefer ''the hills'' (228, see Alberto and children).

*The Ladies' Home Journal. [Since its founding in 1883, this monthly has been an up-beat middle-class American magazine intended, as its title indicates, for women: it offers fiction, feature articles on fashion, medicine, and various aspects of housekeeping and family relationships. In recent years it has also addressed the problems of working women.] Cantwell not only reads but enjoys *The Ladies' Home Journal* (87).

*Leclerc, [General Jacques Philippe de Haute-clocque. French soldier, 1902–1947; Marshal of France, 1947. Leclerc was the Chief of Staff for the Fourth French Division in the Ardennes in September 1939 and fought with the Second Armored Group in 1940. After the fall of France Leclerc, who had been captured and had escaped from France, joined De Gaulle's Free French forces in Africa. He was the first military Governor of Chad and Cameroun. He conducted various successful expeditions, which strengthened the reputation and appeal of the Free French forces and attracted many volunteers. In December 1942 he commanded a Free French force across the Sahara Desert to join Montgomery's army in Tripoli, Libya. In 1944 he led the Second Armored Division in the Normandy invasion, and it was he who received the formal surrender of the Germans in Paris in August 1944. He also liberated Strasbourg and captured Hitler's hideaway in Berchtesgaden in 1945. He became a national hero for his part in the rebirth of the French army, but Hemingway, who met him in Rambouillet, claimed that Leclerc was an impolite "jerk." Leclerc was killed in an airplane crash.][28]
Cantwell explains to Renata that he had to hold back his troops so that Leclerc could, as arranged, liberate Paris (140). Cantwell, who claims to have known Leclerc personally, describes him as a fine soldier (218) but a "jerk" nonetheless (134; see also 217).

*Life. [*Life* was a satirical weekly, with black and white illustrations, from 1883 until 1932, when it became a monthly. In 1936 it was sold to *Time* and became a glossy illustrated weekly magazine, often featuring Hemingway, both as subject and as author: in the 1950s it serialized *The Old Man and the Sea* and *The Dangerous Summer*.]
In their imaginary future together, the two lovers will be oil millionaires who travel and read magazines like *Life* (264).

*Lightning Joe. See Collins, Joseph Lawton.

*Lombards. [Originally *Langobardi,* longbeards, an early Germanic tribe. The Lombards invaded Italy in 568, conquered much of its northern and central sections, and established the Lombard kingdom in the north of Italy; the modern Italian province of Lombardy carries their name. The Lombards eventually converted to Catholicism.]
Cantwell explains that Venice was established by people fleeing the various tribes who invaded Italy, among them the Visigoths (q.v.) and the Lombards (28).

*Longchamps. [Chain of restaurants in New York, no longer in business.]
Cantwell's physician, Wes, refuses Cantwell's invitation to the duck-shoot because he prefers to buy his ducks at Longchamps on Madison Avenue (11).

*Longhena, [Baldassare. Venetian architect, 1598–1682. Longhena is considered the major Venetian architect of the 17th century. He is known especially for the octagonal church with a huge dome, Santa Maria della Salute, at the entrance to the Grand Canal in Venice.]
Cantwell mentions that one of the beautiful Italian country houses destroyed by bombs had been designed by Longhena (13).

*Louis XVI. [1754–1793; king of France, 1774–1792. He and his wife Marie Antoinette (q.v.) were guillotined. Cantwell and Renata mention "tumbrils" (also spelled tumbrel), referring to the carts in which victims were conveyed to the guillotine during the French Revolution (139, 260, 277). Louis XVI and his court were exceedingly extravagant, "the resulting financial embarrassment" of the government being often cited as one of the causes of the French Revolution (*Encyclopaedia Britannica,* 11th ed., XVII, 44). Some historians blame Louis XVI's financial excesses on his wife.]
Cantwell and Renata "play historical personages" (261; see Rimbaud and Verlaine). When they are buying the jewelled pin for Renata, Cantwell calls Renata "Majesty," perhaps referring to her expensive tastes, and she, recognizing the reference, points out that he is very dissimilar to Louis XVI (260), perhaps referring to his failure to give her presents (see gifts).

*Lowry. A former aide to Cantwell. Cantwell recalls that when he first heard "the buzzing," his aide Lowry did not, a clear indication that the sound was internal, the result of his own physical problems. Cantwell hears the internal "buzzing" again in Venice, when he climbs steps (78). Cantwell also recalls his former driver, Burnham (q.v.).

*Lupino, Ida. [English stage actress and movie star, 1916—. The Lupinos are an English theatrical family famous since the 17th century. Ida Lupino came to Hollywood in 1934 and made many movies in the 1930s, 1940s and 1950s, among them *They Drive by Night* (1940), *High Sierra* (1941), *Ladies in Retirement* (1941), and *Roadhouse* (1948); she won an Oscar for *The Hard Way* (1942). She became a director in the 1950s.]
Renata imitates Ida Lupino's voice (207).

*Lysette. [Usually spelled Lisette. Lisette was a tough, bad-tempered mare whom only her owner, Marbot, could ride. She was bred either in the north German state of Mecklenburg or on the offshore island Rugen; horses from this area were "highly prized for speed, toughness, and spirit." She distinguished herself during the famous Battle of Eylau (8 February, 1807). Early in that fierce battle Napoleon's forces were at a disadvantage: his VII Corps, under the command of Marshal Augereau, advanced but lost its direction in the dense snowstorm that raged that day. They came too close to the Russian line and were practically annihilated: of 14,000 men, only about 3,000 survived uninjured. Marshal Augereau was wounded and most of his senior officers were killed or captured. In the confusion, one regiment of Augereau's Corps, the 14th Line Infantry, were cut off and completely surrounded by Russian troops; they refused to surrender and were killed almost to a man. The story is that Marbot, then a captain, rode Lisette bravely up to the stranded unit in order to take their Eagle and bring it back to Napoleon. Both Marbot and Lisette were injured, and Lisette turned upon the enemy, "biting off the face of one Russian and the bowels out of another." She then dashed through the enemy lines to bring the wounded Marbot and the Eagle safely back to Napoleon. The battle was costly to both sides: all told, the French lost about 15,000 men, five eagles and seven other colors; the Russians and Prussians are said to have lost about 18,000 men, or about a quarter of their original armies, as well as sixteen colors and 24 guns.[29] See Marbot.]

Cantwell remarks that in our modern, mechanized times "the gallantry" of old machinery that keeps on working has replaced the gallantry of old war horses like Marbot's fierce mare Lysette (52).

*Maginot, [André-Louis-Reve. French soldier and politician, 1877–1932. Maginot, crippled by wounds sustained in World War I, served in six successive cabinets, including two terms as Minister of War. During the second of these terms (1929–1931), he convinced the French government to construct heavy defensive fortifications on the northeastern frontier between France and Germany. These fortifications, known as the Maginot Line, were considered impregnable but were outflanked by the Germans, who entered France through Belgium in May 1940.]

Cantwell does not respect Maginot's fundamentally conservative and defensive thinking (27).

*the maid. See Renata's servants.

the Maître d' at the Gritti Palace Hotel. See Gran Maestro.

Majesty. Cantwell refers to Renata as "Majesty" (260; see Marie Antoinette and Louis XVI).

*manager. The manager of the Gritti does not appear in the novel, his work being done by the assistant manager (q.v.). The Gran Maestro promises to arrange with the manager that Cantwell be supplied with newer, better, and less expensive Valpolicella wine (131), but it is the older, "awfully dreggy" vintage which shows up on his bedside table (167, 172).

*Mangin, [Charles-Marie Emmanuel. French soldier and writer, 1866–1925. A graduate of Saint Cyr, France's top military school, Mangin began his military career in France's African colonies, where he displayed great initiative and bravery and was wounded five times. Mangin was awarded the Legion of Honor when he was only 25 years old. Promoted to the rank of general in 1913, he served with distinction during World War I, leading the offensive against the Germans; he was instrumental in the French victory at Verdun. When his attack on Chemin des Dames failed, however, he was relieved of his position. An official inquiry soon exonerated him and he was reinstated and recalled to the front, where he continued his strong offensive stance. In 1919, fearing that the unstoppable Mangin would attempt to annex more territory than the Allies were prepared to have under French domination, the French government recalled him from active military service. In 1920 he was appointed Inspector General of Colonial Forces, a post he held until his death. In his first book, *Force noire* (1910), Mangin argued that improved relations between colonizers and the native populations could best be effected by African officers; he therefore encouraged African participation in the French colonial armies. Other books include *Comment finit la guerre* (1920), *Autour du continent latin avec le 'Jules Michelet'* (1923, a travel book), *Des hommes et des faits* (1923), and *Regards sur la France d'Afrique* (1924). In 1925, Mangin was awarded the French Academy's Prize for Literature.][30]
    Cantwell seems to disapprove of Mangin's aggressive military tactics (27). He compares Mangin, Maginot, and Gamelin unfavorably with du Picq (qq.v).

*Manners, Lady Diana [Olivia Winifred Maud. English actress, 1892–1986. She was the daughter of the 8th Duke of Rutland and wife of Alfred Duff Cooper, 1st Viscount of Norwich (British author and politician, 1890–1954). In the 1920s Lady Diana Cooper was called "the most beautiful woman of the century." She was best known for her role as Madonna in Max Reinhardt's *The Miracle,* which played throughout America and Europe. Beautiful, charming, rich, well-connected, eccentric, and flamboyant, she was widely admired. See also *MF*.]
    Seeing a good-looking woman dramatically dressed in black, Cantwell thinks of Lady Diana Manners, whom he remembers as "the nun" in Reinhardt's production (86; see also Reinhardt).

mannitol hexanitrate. [Mannitol is an osmotic diuretic, which forces the body to excrete water and thus works to lower intraocular and intracranial pressure, for which it was and remains the drug of choice. But mannitol hexanitrate (also known as mannityl hexanitrate, nitromannite, and nitromannitol) is a vasodilator (like nitroglycerin, q.v.), used to alleviate or prevent attacks of stress-induced angina by increasing the flow of oxygenated blood to the heart. The undiluted compound is explosive.][31]

Cantwell, who has had three heart attacks (307) and about ten concussions (10), took extra-large doses of mannitol hexanitrate, prescribed for his heart condition, in order "to pass" his physical examination. But large doses of this medication are, as the doctor says, "definitely contraindicated" for the increased cranial and ocular pressure caused by the many concussions Cantwell has suffered (8–10). Cantwell notices that the mannitol hexanitrate sometimes makes him nauseous (9, 92). He needs to take this drug frequently (33, 92, 148, 166, 196, 198, 226, 266–67, 281, 294, 296). Sometimes he feels a "twinging" but takes deep breaths instead of medicine (78–79); sometimes he thinks of his pills but doesn't take them (231; see 175). He carries a bottle of pills in his pocket and keeps another one by his bed (164). Also see nitroglycerin and seconal.

*Mantegna, [Andrea. Italian painter and engraver, 1431–1506. Mantegna's art is characterized by skillful foreshortening, solidly modeled figures, and correct anatomical details. Important titles include the *Triumph of Caesar, Martyrdom of St. Christopher, Madonna della Vittoria* and *Dead Christ with Two Angels*. See also *FTA, FWBT*, and "The Revolutionist" in *IOT*.]

Jackson is impressed when Cantwell talks about painters like Mantegna (14).

*Marbot, [Baron Jean-Baptiste Antoine Marcelin. French soldier, 1782–1854. Marbot joined the French republican army at age 17 and rose rapidly through the military ranks. He served as aide-de-camp to Marshal Augereau of VII Corps in the war against Prussia and Russia in 1806–1807, distinguishing himself at the Battle of Eylau (1807). He was promoted to general of brigade by Napoleon just before the battle of Waterloo (1815), at which Napoleon was defeated and Marbot wounded; both were exiled. Marbot returned to France in 1819. In 1830, when Louis-Philippe became Emperor, Marbot was appointed aide-de-camp to Ferdinand, Duke of Orleans, with whom he participated in the siege of Antwerp (1832) and in various campaigns in Algeria (1835–1840). He retired from the Army when Louis-Philippe abdicated in 1848.

In the 1820s Marbot wrote two pamphlets. The first, *Remarques critiques* (1820), prompted Napoleon to leave him a legacy. In a second

pamphlet he argued for *La nécessité d'augmenter les forces militaires de la France* (On the need to enlarge the military forces of France, 1825). His *Memoir of his Life and Campaigns* (published posthumously 1891; English translation, 1902) was intended as a private document for his children, but when it was published, the vivid, romantic and often inaccurate *Memoir* revived widespread interest in the Napoleonic period. An abridged edition of the *Memoir*, entitled *Au Service de Napoléon*, was published in 1928; Hemingway read it in French (Reynolds, *Hemingway's Reading*, 154).]
Cantwell recalls Marbot's mare Lysette (q.v.). (52).

*Margaret. See Truman, Margaret.

*Marie Antoinette. [1755–1793; queen of France 1774–1792. She and her husband Louis XVI were guillotined during the French Revolution.]
Cantwell claims that Renata resembles Marie Antoinette (139) and addresses her as "Majesty" (260; see Louis XVI).

*Mark, St. (San Marco). [Author of one of the four gospels. The gorgeous Cathedral of St. Mark's in Venice stands on the site where in c. 828 a small wooden church was built to receive the remains of St. Mark, which, according to legend, were brought to Venice when the Moslems destroyed the church in Alexandria where he was originally buried. This small church was burned in 976 and a larger church was built to replace it. It has been remodeled, enlarged, and decorated over the centuries, becoming one of the most-visited sites of Italy. St. Mark's symbol is the winged lion, and his feast day is April 25.]
Cantwell tells Jackson how Mark came to be the patron saint of Venice (28–29). Renata recalls a German "shooting pigeons" in the great plaza in front of the cathedral (122).

*Mary. See Hemingway, Mary Welsh.

[Matthew 13:45–46 reads as follows: "Again, the kingdom of heaven is like unto a merchant man, seeking goodly pearls: Who, when he had found one pearl of great price, went and sold all that he had, and bought it."]
Cantwell admits that the information he has given the young night porter about Tito and his "problems" is not "any pearl of great price" (183; see also Tito).

*Maxwell, Elsa. [American writer, lecturer, radio personality, and composer, 1883–1963. Maxwell was an international society hostess whose Parisian parties were the rage of European and expatriate society in the 1920s and 1930s. In the 1940s she reported the doings of high society in a syndicated column and in her radio program, "Elsa Maxwell's Party Line." She had a brief motion picture career, appearing in *Stage Door Canteen* and other movies. She published over eighty songs and several books, including *RSVP: Elsa Maxwell's Own Story* (1954), *How To Do It, or The Lively Art of Entertaining* (1957), and *My Last Fifty Years.*][32]

To emphasize the absurdity of war, Cantwell narrates a maneuver by means of which Elsa Maxwell's butler was captured (135).

*Maxwell's butler. See Maxwell, Elsa.

*McNair, General [Lesley James. American soldier, 1883–1944. McNair saw action as a combatant in France during World War I. In World War II he served under General George Marshall, who was then Chief of Staff. In 1942 McNair was named commander of ground forces of the U.S. Army. He organized the training of American troops for combat in World War II by using simulated field conditions. He was killed on a tour of inspection at the Normandy front, 25 July 1944.][33]

Cantwell admires military men whose knowledge comes from field experience and distrusts academically trained officers because they do not risk their lives in battle. But he admits that "men from the Academy" [at West Point] have been killed on the battlefield, including McNair, though he was killed "by mistake" (251–52).

men and boys. Cantwell sees several men and boys, most of whom are involved in peaceful activities such as fishing (12–13, 21), riding a bicycle (13), drinking and "doing business" at Harry's Bar (262) or selling postcards (276) and clams (193). One old man does "odd jobs" (42–43), and a boy accompanies Cantwell to his room at the Gritti Hotel (speaks: 66). Several other "shooters" have been invited to the duck-shoot which Alvarito has organized; they enjoy an evening of drink and tall stories (278–79, see 1, also see *boatmen); we do not see them shooting. Two young men insult Cantwell as he walks to the open-air market; when he faces them threateningly, they run away (186–87; cf. the sailors).

*men and boys. Men and boys who enter the narrative only through the characters' dialogue, thoughts and memories are generally connected to guns or war. Renata recalls her ancestors, all of whom fought (219). Cantwell tells Jackson about men who shoot ducks all through the night (29) and remembers American, Austrian, French, German, and Russian troops (qq.v)—the people he fought with and against during his long military career.

Although he dislikes many individual leaders, Cantwell feels no hatred when he thinks about the enemy, be they the Austrians he fought in World War I (32–33; see also 16, 20), the Germans from World War II (122–23,

176), or the Russians who are the Cold War enemy (70). For the individual soldier Cantwell has nothing but sympathy, even for the soldiers who injured themselves in order to avoid battle (59–60). He vividly remembers the unburied bodies of soldiers who fell in World War I: thrown into a canal, they had surfaced and swelled horribly "regardless of nationality" (20) until they were buried close by (21). In a parallel memory, he recalls the unburied dead of World War II: their bodies froze in the cold weather (257). Cantwell recalls gruesome details involving soldiers on both sides: a German body being eaten by a cat and a dog and a dead American flattened by military traffic of his own Army (257). Cantwell mourns the soldiers of his regiment (242; see also chapter 33) and even feels sympathy for his prisoners of war (224). Cantwell recalls the typists and other office workers killed by Allied forces during the liberation of Paris; their bodies were thrown into the Seine River (134, 140). He also recalls civilians: the happy people when Paris was liberated (141), the brave Resistance fighters and all his "good friends" (27; see also crowds, journalists, and sailors). Cantwell knows the army does not allow privacy: wherever one goes one finds "two riflemen . . . or some boy asleep" (168). The Grand Master recalls the station guards at whom he and Cantwell threw empty containers of wine when they were young soldiers (121). Jackson mentions the "no good" man who mismanaged his business while Jackson and his brother were overseas during World War II (22) and "some bad man" who was hung and skinned by a doctor; the skin is preserved in the museum at Rawlins, Wyoming (16).

*Meyers, [Bennett Edward] (Benny). [American military administrator, 1895——. Meyers was involved with budget and procurement duties for most of his Air Force career, becoming Deputy Director of the Army Air Forces Materiel and Services in June 1944 and assuming full command of the Air Technical Service Command in May 1945; he rose to the rank of major General and was awarded the Legion of Merit in 1945. But he was also involved in a great scandal: Meyers was charged with holding Hughes aviation stock while he was employed in the Air Force Procurement Office, which awarded war contracts in excess of one billion dollars to Hughes' company. Meyers, who had supported Howard Hughes' bids for wartime aircraft contracts, admitted that he negotiated with Hughes for a loan and for a post-war job for himself, but he claimed that these negotiations occurred after he had retired from active service and were not a condition for the military contracts. In 1947 Meyers was court-martialed and found guilty; he was stripped of his war decorations and of half his retirement pay. In further action he was convicted of three counts of subornation to perjury in 1948, jailed, paroled in 1950, convicted of income-tax evasion, and rejailed in 1951.[34] Benny Meyers has come to represent corruption and dishonesty in the army.]

Cantwell knows that Meyers and other profiteers were obtaining financial gain for themselves, while he had saved lives and money for the Army until his commanding officer's orders had resulted in an "excessive butcher-bill" (188; see also 184, Brusadelli, and contractors).

*Michelangelo [Buonarroti. Italian painter, architect and sculptor, 1475–1564. Among his most famous sculptures are the *Pieta, David* and *Moses;* he painted the *Last Judgment* fresco in the Sistine Chapel, as well as the Chapel's ceiling.]
Cantwell remarks that a 20th-century patron of the arts ordering a fresco from someone like Michelangelo should take into consideration the proximity of military targets—although, considering the range of modern bombs, ensuring the safety of art of impossible (14).

*Montgomery, Field Marshal Bernard Law (Monty). [British soldier, 1887–1976. Montgomery rose to the rank of general early in World War II and attained fame as a war hero and outstanding leader during that conflict. Montgomery was one of the last officers to leave Dunkirk, June 1940, and he defeated Rommel's forces at el-Alamein in 1942, inflicting a terrible defeat on that fabled German commander and turning the tide of the North African war. He commanded British ground forces in Italy, 1943, and in Normandy, 1944, working closely with U.S. Generals Eisenhower and Bradley (qq.v.). Montgomery accepted the surrender of German forces in northern Europe, 1945, and served as military governor of the British zone of Germany. Under the command of Eisenhower, he helped organize the defense system of the North Atlantic Treaty Organization (NATO), 1951–1958. He was named Viscount Montgomery of Alamein in 1946; he published his *Memoirs* in 1958.][35]
Cantwell claims that Montgomery was a fraud (125) and complains that the liberation of Paris had to be delayed until Montgomery arrived to march at the head of the liberating troops (134). He brings the same charge against Leclerc (q.v.).

Montgomerys, Montys. Very dry martinis, made with the proportions of fifteen parts gin to one part vermouth and served "icy cold" (82). A variant is the "super Montgomery" (101). Cantwell invented this drink and named it after the general because the proportions reflect the advantage Montgomery required before he would go into battle (125–26). He and Renata drink at least three Montys before dinner. Cantwell takes care that the British patrons of Harry's Bar, to whom Montgomery is a great hero, do not hear him ordering this drink (85, 100).

*Moors. [This term includes the nomadic peoples descended from the Arabs and Berbers of north-west Africa and, by extension, any native of

Morocco. Converted to Islam, the Moors invaded and conquered Spain in 711, crossing the Pyrenees into France, where they were stopped by Charles Martel in 732. See Moors in *FWBT*. Because Moors were reputed to be brave warriors, they were often entrusted with the safety of high-born Venetian women. These ladies sometimes wore brooches which represented the head or profile of such trusted family servants; like talismans, these jewels were felt to offer security even when the protecting servant himself was absent.]

Cantwell describes Moors as "excellent soldiers"; he recalls that Othello (q.v.) was a Moor (230; see also Abd el Krim). At her request he buys Renata a jeweled ebony pin, a "little negro, or moor," which she claims will protect her in Cantwell's absence (253, 266; see 105, 259–60, 266–68, 290).

*Moroccans. [The Moroccan struggle against France ended in 1956 and two years later Spain also relinquished its claim to sections of that country (see Abd el Krim). During World War II French Morocco was allied with Vichy France.]

Because Moroccan soldiers raped his wife and daughter, the boatman hates the "Allied uniform" and is therefore rude to Cantwell, who wears it (302).

*Muehlebach. [The heirs of George Muehlebach (Swiss-born American brewer and businessman, 1835–1905) built the Muehlebach Hotel in 1914–1915, at 12th St. and Baltimore Avenue in Kansas City, Missouri. A 1918 advertisement reports that the hotel has 500 rooms, "rate from $200," and is "Ultra-modern in Equipment" and "Unique in the Courtesy of its Service." A 1931 advertisement calls it "Kansas City's Outstanding Hotel," with three dining rooms (Kansas City, Missouri, City Directory, 1918, 1931). It was a large, elegant building, and many celebrities stayed there; their photos adorned the hotel restaurant. It served as the temporary White House for President Truman (q.v.) when he returned to his home state for "lengthy visits." By 1970, the hotel had become "grimy" and "dingy"; it closed in 1986.][36]

In planning the trip he and Renata will take together, Cantwell mentions that they will stay at the Muehlebach, a "wonderful" hotel in Kansas City (263; for Cantwell's financial situation see Cantwell and gifts).

Murano. [An island in the Venetian lagoon, about a mile northeast of Venice. The island has a canal running through its center. Medieval Venetian nobility built beautiful villas and gardens on this island, and its churches are richly decorated. Murano has been famous for its glass since the 11th century. In 1621, an English glass-maker named James Howell visited Murano, "where Crystal-Glass is made; and 'tis a rare sight to see a whole Street, where on the one side there are twenty Furnaces together at work. They say here, That altho' one should transplant a Glass-Furnace from Murano to Venice herself, or to any other part of the Earth besides, and use the same Materials, the same Workmen, the same Fuel, the self-same ingredients every way, yet they cannot make Crystal-Glass in that perfection, for beauty and lustre, as in Murano: Some impute it to the quality of the circumambient Air that hangs o'er the place, which is purify'd and attenuated by the concurrence of so many Fires that are in those Furnaces Night and Day perpetually, for they are like the Vestal-fire, which never goes out" (qtd. in Marqusee, 126).]

Cantwell points out the nearby island of Murano to Jackson, explaining that their fine glass is expensive (29). He offers some resistance when Renata suggests they buy Murano glass (141–42; see gifts).

*Napoleon [Buonaparte. French military genius, 1769–1821, who rose rapidly in the military hierarchy and established himself as first consul, 1799–1804, and Emperor of the French, 1804–1814. Through marriage, conquest, and treaties Napoleon came to dominate most of Europe. He is also mentioned in *FWBT, FTA,* and *MF.*]

According to Cantwell, Napoleon believed in "luck." So does Cantwell, although he recognizes that by itself it does not guarantee success or happiness (232; also see entry for luck in *OMS*). Cantwell maligns his ex-wife, accusing her of enormous ambition, like Napoleon, but insufficient talents (212).

*Negro. Cantwell refers to racial violence in the United States when he says that Memphis is dangerous for black but not for white people (unlike the more egalitarian Chicago which is dangerous for everyone, 36). The ebony pin he buys for Renata is, of course, black (see Moors; also see the Negro in *FWBT,* blacks in *THHN,* and Klan in *SAR*).

*Newsweek. [A popular weekly American news magazine, founded in 1933 and published continuously since then.]

Imagining an "ideal" future, Renata envisions them traveling, drinking, and reading magazines together: Cantwell will read *Newsweek, Life,* and *Time,* and she will enjoy *Vogue* and *Harper's Bazaar* (qq.v.) (264; see *Islands*).

the *New York Herald Tribune,* Paris edition. [The daily American newspaper, the *New York Herald,* was founded in 1887. In 1924 it merged with the *Tribune* to become the *New York Herald Tribune* and as such launched a European edition (1924–1966) which eventually merged with the *New York Times International* to form the *International Herald Tribune* (1967–present).]

Cantwell reads the Paris edition of the *New York Herald Tribune* in his room at the Gritti Hotel (164, 166–67).

*Ney, Maréchal [Michel. French soldier, 1769–1815; one of the first sixteen marshals of France. General Ney distinguished himself during the Napoleonic Wars and, because of his great admiration for Napoleon, abandoned his republican principles and urged Napoleon, in 1803, to declare himself emperor. Napoleon admired Ney, whom he praised as "the bravest of the brave" (at the battle of Friedland, 1807), an appellation previously attached to Crillon by Henry IV of France. To reward Ney's military successes, Napoleon created him Duke of Elchingen and, during the 1812 expedition into Russia, Prince of Moskowa. During Napoleon's retreat from Russia, Ney was conspicuously brave, encouraging the defeated French army to keep up its spirits. After the fall of the Empire and Napoleon's abdication (1814), Ney suddenly became a royalist, declaring himself in favor of the restoration of Louis XVIII. When Napoleon escaped from Elba and marched into Paris, Ney promised Louis XVIII to stop him, but on meeting Napoleon he abandoned his royalist principles and joined him. Ney assisted Napoleon at the Battle of Waterloo. After this defeat he was accused of treason to the King, convicted, and shot. Ney was a great military hero and a politically controversial figure. See Crillon in *SAR*.]

For Renata, Ney and Cantwell are equally and indistinguishably "great heroes" (156). Cantwell recognizes a different resemblance, seeing himself and Ney as broken down soldiers. His remark to Renata that Ney fought so much that "Afterwards, he couldn't recognize people" (157) recalls Jackson's evaluation of Cantwell as "slug-nutty" (27). Like Ney, Cantwell fought under different regimes (in the Italian Army in World War I and in the American in World War II), rose high in the profession, and ended his career in disgrace.

night porter. See porters.

nitroglycerin. [Nitroglycerin causes the cardiac vessels to dilate and thus allows increased amounts of oxygenated blood to reach the heart muscle. Nitroglycerin tablets, placed under the tongue, are absorbed quickly into the body and offer relief from pain caused by oxygen-deprivation. See mannitol hexanitrate, also a vasodilator.]

Cantwell's doctor, Wes (q.v.), recognizes that his patient, who has taken too much mannitol hexanitrate, is "really souped up on nitroglycerin" (9).

*Notturno. [D'Annunzio's prose memoir was written in 1916, when he was temporarily blinded as the result of an airplane crash on active service;

it was published in 1921. It recalls both his wartime experiences and his romantic relationships, particularly the long affair with Eleanora Duse. Adeline Tintner finds D'Annunzio's novel *The Flame of Life,* which is based on his love affair with Duse, to be an important source for *ARIT.* She also points out the many important details in *ARIT* which derive from *Notturno,* among them the heroine's name (D'Annunzio's daughter was named Renata), her emeralds, her beautiful hair, the scene in which she sleeps, and even her nickname, "Daughter" (although this was Hemingway's favorite nickname for women he liked). Nicholas Georgiannis has also pointed out many similarities between Hemingway and D'Annunzio; he argues that *Notturno* "is close enough to *Across the River and into the Trees* to be accepted as the prototype for Hemingway's novel" (rpt. Wagner, 260). John Paul Russo offers a full discussion of Hemingway's "satiric reduction" of the man D'Annunzio and of his unwavering admiration for his book, *Notturno* ("To Die Is Not Enough" 171–75).][37]

In the middle of his attack on D'Annunzio (q.v.), Cantwell expresses his admiration for *Notturno* (52).

the Order of Brusadelli. [In the 19th century, during the struggle for the unification of Italy, various secret political organizations sprang up, the Carbonari being the most notable among them.[38] But the clubs and organizations mentioned in the novel have social and educational rather than military aims; see Chautauqua, Epworth League, and Rotary Club.]

The Order of Brusadelli is a pseudo-military secret organization founded by Cantwell and the Gritti's maître d'Hôtel in honor of their shared disillusion with war (59–60) and named after the Revered One (Brusadelli, q.v.). The Order has "only five members" (60): Cantwell is the Supreme Commander; the maître d' is the Gran Maestro; the cook at a nearby hotel was recently promoted to Commendatore; Giorgio, the Hotel Gritti's bartender, is Privy Counsellor; and the youngest member, the second waiter at the Gritti Hotel, lacks a title. After she has heard Cantwell's war stories, Renata is admitted into the Order, given the title of Super Honorary Secretary and entrusted with its Supreme Secret (270–71).[39] See endnote 1.

*Othello. [The tragic hero of Shakespeare's great play is a general, a Moor, who wins his Venetian lady Desdemona with his stories "of most disastrous chances," "hairbreadth scapes," and all the "dangers I had passed" (I.iii.132–170).]

Cantwell compares himself favorably to "the garrulous Moor" (230; see also Shakespeare).

*Pacciardi, [Randolfo] (the Honorable Pacciardi). [Italian Republican, soldier, lawyer, and journalist, 1899–1991. The son of a poor family,

Pacciardi distinguished himself in World War I, rose to the rank of battalion commander, and was decorated several times. A leading member of the Italian Republican Party, he was arrested when fascist elements became powerful in Italy. He escaped (1926) to Switzerland, from where he continued his anti-fascist activities. He was tried *in absentia* in Italy three times, and Mussolini brought such pressure to bear on Switzerland that Pacciardi was obliged to move to France. During the Spanish Civil War, Pacciardi organized and then commanded the Italian Legion of the International Brigades (the Garibaldi Battalion of the XII Brigade). He also traveled in various Western countries, urging them to support the Republican cause. During World War II Pacciardi fought against fascist Italy, commanding a unit of Italian volunteers with the British in North Africa. After the war he headed the Italian Republican Party, holding various positions in coalition governments. He was Minister of Defense from 1948 to 1953. He has been called "Italy's foremost anti-fascist military hero." He wrote a book on Mazzini (1921) and *Il Battaglione Garibaldi* (1938); he was editor for the newspapers *Italia Libera* in the U.S. and *Voce Republicana* in Italy.][40]
     Cantwell claims to have met Pacciardi, who is his contemporary, during the Spanish Civil War (39–40). Cantwell and the bartender, who consider themselves practical men, joke that they will help the idealist Pacciardi (39–41; also see 61, 70).

*the painter. An unnamed homosexual who painted Renata's portrait two years ago (96–97).

*Patton, George [Smith, Jr.] (Georgie, [Old Blood and Guts). American soldier, 1885–1945. A graduate of the American Military Academy at West Point, Class of 1909, Patton served in the tank corps in World War I, established a tank training school in France, and organized the First (later the 304th) Tank Brigade. During World War II Patton proved himself an outstanding practitioner of mobile tank warfare. He participated in the North African campaign in 1942 and commanded the United States Seventh Army in Sicily in 1943, but the high point of his career was his participation in the invasion of Normandy in 1944 and the subsequent sweep of this Third Army across France and into Germany, Austria, and Czechoslovakia "in a campaign marked by great initiative, ruthless drive, and disregard of classic military rules" (*Encyclopaedia Britannica,* 1973 edition). In a famous incident, Patton accused a shell-shocked soldier of cowardice and slapped him. His memoirs, *War as I Knew It* (1947), were published posthumously.]
     Cantwell does his best to discredit Patton: he explains that it was he and his men who cleared the way for Patton in Normandy (133). He reports that Patton was subject to crying fits (115) and that he distorted

the facts in order to advance his career and reputation (116; see also 125, 144).

*Père Lachaise. See Lachaise, Père.

pescecani. [Plural of *pescecane* (literally fish-dog); dogfish or shark, hence, a predator. When the Italian drivers discuss the war profiteers in World War I, the narrative offers the world "dogfish" instead of the more idiomatic "sharks" (*FTA* 184), thus suggesting that the men are speaking Italian (Lewis, *The War of the Words,* 147). Although derived from the Germanic Old English, "dogfish" gives the flavor of the Italian word *pescecani,* which derives from Latin.]

The narrative refers to Milanese profiteers and gamblers who come to Venice as *pescecani* (38, 43, 107, 202).

*Phoebus the Phoenician. [The reference seems to be to Phlebas the Phoenician, the object of a meditation on death in T.S. Eliot's *The Waste Land IV: Death by Water:*

> Phlebas the Phoenician, a fortnight dead,
> Forgot the cry of gulls, and the deep sea swell
> And the profit and loss.][41]

Cantwell reassures Renata that he considers his ex-wife to be "Deader than Phoebus the Phoenician" (213).

*Piero della Francesca. See *Franceschi, Piero de.

*Pitti. [Famous art gallery housed in the Pitti palace, built in the middle of the 15th century, in Florence. Together, the Pitti and Uffizi palaces house a huge art collection, including the Medici pictures, and are known as the Royal Galleries.]

When Jackson can't remember which gallery he visited in Florence, Cantwell suggests the Pitti and the Uffizi (14).

*the Pope. [At the time of the action of the novel, the Pope was Eugenio Pacelli (Italian churchman, 1876–1958) who had become Pope Pius XII in 1939. A very accommodating Pope, Pius XII did not speak out against either Hitler or Mussolini. In recent years, the Vatican has been exposed as having sheltered war criminals during Pius XII's time. Although the Catholic Church does not recognize divorce, it does, under certain conditions grant a special dispensation to permit previously married individuals to marry again in a Catholic rite.]

Although the present Pope grants his blessing to multiply-married movie stars, Renata interprets Church dogma more strictly and refuses to marry Cantwell, whose ex-wife is still living (128).

porters. Before and after their stay at Gritti Palace Hotel, Cantwell and Jackson are helped by porters at the boat landing at the entrance to Venice (42, 275). At the boat landing of the Gritti Palace Hotel, hotel employees (274) handle the luggage of arriving and departing guests. The Gritti employs at least three porters. One greets Cantwell affectionately and relays messages and information (53). The night porter is young and respectful and admits to lack of political sophistication; Cantwell considers him "member material" for the Order (q.v.) and entrusts him with the statement that Tito (q.v.) "has plenty problems" in Yugoslavia (181–83; see Matthew). The hall porter, an old employee at the Gritti, is the only one Cantwell doesn't like: he is a fascist whom Cantwell surprised once rummaging through his belongings looking for military secrets. He performs minor offices: delivers the newspaper in the morning (175) and telephones for a boatman (274).
  Speak: 53, 181–83.

*Princess. Cantwell knows but avoids a meeting with "a Greek Princess" who is at Harry's Bar (72).

Privy Counsellor. See Giorgio.

profiteer. See Brusadelli, Meyers, and *pescecani.*

*Purdey, [James (the Founder). English gunsmith, 1784–1863. James learned his trade from the great English gunmaker, Joseph Manton, and then opened his own shop in 1814. His son James (the Younger, 1828–1909) took control of the firm in 1858. Throughout its history, Purdey's has been associated with fine, hand-crafted guns. The Purdeys built guns for aristocracy, including Queen Victoria and Prince Albert; another famous customer was Charles Darwin, who in 1831 bought several weapons, spare parts, ammunition, and other equipment from Purdey's before embarking on his historic journey on the *Beagle.* In 1947, King George VI ordered two guns as a wedding present for his daughter Elizabeth's future husband, Philip Mountbatten. After World War II the firm was in serious financial difficulties, but it managed to survive, maintaining its reputation for fine workmanship. Purdey guns are numbered, Serial No. 1 having been produced in 1814 and No. 28,600 in 1983. Since 1862, the firm has been located on South Audley St., London. The present Chairman of the Board at Purdey's is Richard B. Beaumont, author of *Purdey's: The Guns and the Family* (London: David & Charles, 1984). See endnote 4.]

There is a Purdey gun in Cantwell's family, which Cantwell's older brother inherited from their grandfather (92–93). Cantwell would like to give Renata useful, valuable presents, like a fine down jacket and Purdey guns (290; also see Boss).

*Purple Heart. [This decoration, instituted in 1782 and reestablished in 1932, is awarded to Americans who, "while serving in the armed forces, are wounded in action against an enemy" (*Encyclopedia Americana,* XX, 825).]
Cantwell's driver, Jackson, has been awarded the Purple Heart as well as other decorations (22).

*Quesada, [Lieutenant General Elwood Richard] (Pete). [American soldier and administrator, 1904—. Quesada held various positions in the U.S. Air Force: he was commander of the 33rd Pursuit Group at Mitchel Field, New York; commander of the 1st Air Defense Wing; commander of the 12th Fighter Command of North Africa; commander of the 9th Fighter Command in England. "Promoted to temporary major general in April 1944, he commanded from then the 9th Tactical Air Command, flying cover and support missions in preparation for the Allied invasion on D-Day and subsequently during the battle into Germany. In June 1945 he was named assistant chief of the air staff for intelligence, and . . . chief of the Tactical Air Command" (*Webster's American Military Biographies*). After the war Quesada worked in the Office of the Joint Chiefs of Staff in Washington. In August 1949 he was chosen to head Joint Task Force III, the combined Army, Air Force, Navy, and Atomic Energy Commission group conducting the first hydrogen bomb experiments. He retired from the Air Force in 1951, after which he held several important civilian positions on the Airways Modernization Board and the Federal Aviation Administration; he was director of the Federal Aviation Agency (1958–1961). He was awarded many American and foreign ribbons, medals, and honors. Throughout his military career he was known as Pete.][42]
Cantwell recommends Pete Quesada as someone who can be trusted to provide effective "ground support" (226).

*[Quinet, Edgar. French poet, historian, and political philosopher, 1803–1875. Committed to the Republican cause and opposed to the monarchy, which was traditionally and closely allied to the Catholic Church, Quinet argued for separation of church and state, particularly in educational institutions. As a professor in Paris, he opposed the influence of the Jesuits in education by offering a series of lectures (published as *Le génie des religions*, 1842) in which he discussed all religions sympathetically but advocated none. He wrote several books about current political develop-

ments (i.e., the revolutions and political upheavals in Italy and France). Controversial and influential in his day, Quinet was awarded the French Legion of Honor in 1838 but he is seldom read today. Hemingway picked up Quinet's phrase about flowers from James Joyce, whom he visited in 1933. Joyce had memorized the long sentence, which "recapitulated Joyce's view of history . . . [and] was one of the very few passages from other authors which Joyce honored by quoting in *Finnegans Wake* in its original as well as in appropriately distorted form" (Ellman, 676). Quinet's wording is "fraiches et riantes comme aux jours des batailles" which, according to Carlos Baker and A. Walton Litz, comes from Quinet's *Introduction a la philosophie de l'historie de l'humanité, Oeuvres complètes* (Paris, 1857), II, 367 (see Baker, *Life,* 608). In *GHA* (published 1935), Hemingway mentioned not only the phrase's author but also the fact that he first heard it from James Joyce.]

Cantwell claims not to remember the author of the phrase which he misquotes (272; see Quinet in *GHA*).

*Randolfo. An Italian boy who lost both his legs in World War I in the same attack at which Cantwell, then very young, was wounded (19; see also Gino; see also Passini in *FTA*).

*Reinhardt, Max [né Goldmann. Jewish Austrian theatrical director and stage manager, 1873–1943. Reinhardt produced the pageant spectacle *The Miracle* (music by Engelbert Humperdinck, 1854–1921), which premiered in London in 1911 and toured the United States in 1923.]

Cantwell remembers that Lady Diana Manners (q.v.) played the role of the nun in *The Miracle* (86).

Renata (Beauty, Contessa, Countess, Daughter, Devil, Donna, *Hija, hija mía,* honey dog, *figlia,* my Lady, Majesty, Super Honorary Secretary). An idealized Italian girl in love with Cantwell. Although she shares his enjoyment of food, drink, and love-making, she is clearly a contrast to Cantwell, being rich, beautiful, young and aristocratic. She is described as his "last and only and true love" by Cantwell (86, 94, 110, 173, 225) and by the narrator (143, 174); she quotes the phrase herself (211).[43] Renata seems to represent spiritual values: her main activities are going to Mass and visiting the poor (142), and she insists on the Christian virtues, repeatedly exhorting Cantwell to "be gentle" (86), to "be good and kind" (158) and not to be "bad" (223) or "rough" (225). Her "office" is to love Cantwell (93) and her "wish [is] to serve" him (143, cf. the priest's definition of love, *FTA* 72). She gives him her past self (the portrait) and her inherited wealth (the emeralds), and promises to love him even after he dies (128) but refuses to marry him because his ex-wife is still living (128, 214; see Pope). Her insistence on confession, her attachment to his wounded hand which she dreams is the hand of Jesus (84–85), and his remark that she could be the Queen of Heaven (83) further emphasize the religious connection. She may be a virgin, pregnant, or menstruating.[44] She speaks Spanish, English and Italian, and reads Dante, *Vogue,* and *Harper's Bazaar* (qq.v.). See gifts.

Speaks: 80–114, 116–62, 195–96, 199–223, 225–29, 231–46, 251, 259–67, 269–77, 283–87.

*Renata's family. Renata's father (Daddy), who had commissioned her portrait (97), was killed by the Germans (122). Renata's mother (Mummy), is "lovely" (97) and "very intelligent" (93). Like Alvarito's mother, she prefers the wooded countryside to treeless Venice (205; see also 104; see Dandolo, Contessa). Renata accompanies her female forebears—her mother, aunt, and great-aunt—to church (142). She has inherited her emeralds from her grandmother (103).

*Renata's governess. She taught Renata English (151, 154, 179).

*Renata's servants. Renata's butler has a servant deliver Renata's portrait to the Gritti (101, 144). Her maid washes Renata's hair, gives her manicures and pedicures (142), and is trustworthy (104). And Renata intends to teach the footman to speak "American" (207).

*the Revered One. See Brusadelli.

*Richard the Lion-Hearted. [Richard I, 1157–1199; king of England, 1189–1199. The third son of Henry II, Richard waged war against his father, his brother, and many aristocrats on the European continent. He went on the Third Crusade, 1190–1192, with Philip II of France. On his return he was imprisoned by Leopold II of Austria, who surrendered him to the Emperor Henry VI, from whom England was able to ransom him, for an enormous sum. Richard spent most of his time defending his continental interests, leaving England to be governed by Hubert Walter. Himself a writer of lyrics, the arrogant, colorful Richard was the subject of many songs and romances.]

Renata says she will call all her sons Richard the Lion-Hearted in memory of Richard Cantwell. Cantwell refers to himself as "The crap-hearted" (229: see *children).

*Rimbaud, [Jean Arthur. French poet, soldier of fortune, adventurer, explorer, and trader, 1854–1891. The headstrong Rimbaud led an extravagant life, running way from his strict, widowed mother at age fifteen, living in Paris as a tramp, being arrested and returned to his mother, and running away again. His poem "Le Bateau ivre" brought him to Verlaine's attention. Verlaine encouraged him and they soon embarked upon a stormy homosexual relationship, traveling, drinking, writing poetry, and quarreling until Verlaine shot him (twice) and wounded him seriously. After this experience, Rimbaud completely abandoned literature; all his remarkable poetry was written between the ages of 15 and 19, during which period he published only one work, *Une Saison en Enfer* (prose). In 1874 Rimbaud began his travels through Europe, ending up in Africa where, as explorer and trader, he amassed a fortune, become a sort of tribal chieftain, and engaged in international political intrigue. Without Rimbaud's knowledge, Verlaine had published Rimbaud's poetry in a collection entitled *Les Illuminations* (1886). When Rimbaud returned to France for medical treatment a few months before he died, he discovered he was a famous poet.[45] I see no resemblance between the wild Rimbaud and Renata, but see Verlaine.]

After Cantwell has completed his confession, he and Renata pretend to be historical personalities: he calls her Rimbaud and she calls him Verlaine (259).

*Rocco, San Rocco. See Tintoretto.

*Rolex. [Fine watch company, established in 1905 by the Swiss watchmaker Hans Wilsdorf (1881–1960). The name Rolex was coined by Wilsdorf in 1912 and by 1920 was attached to all the company's products. In 1926 Wilsdorf invented the famous "Oyster" case, unique to the Rolex Watch Company, which is both water- and pressure-proof, and in 1931 he devised the "Perpetual" rotor-based watch-winding system, which is the basis for virtually all self-winding watches. During World War II a military version of the Rolex Oyster Perpetual was issued to thousands of elite troops, who brought them home when they were released from service. Its military connection increased the watch's prestige, and in the late 1940s the rugged, reliable watch enjoyed great popularity. Rolex watches are still famous for their fine craftsmanship and reliability. The company has offices around the world and offers good service to its customers.][46]

Cantwell explains that the healthy heart muscle functions as smoothly as a Rolex Oyster Perpetual, but that, unlike the watch, a malfunctioning heart cannot be sent back for repairs (138).

*Rommel, Erwin [Johannes Eugen (the Desert Fox). German soldier, 1891–1944. In World War I Rommel won Germany's highest decoration for bravery in the Battle of Caporetto. At the outbreak of World War II he commanded the Seventh Panzer Division, which attacked France. In 1941 he was appointed commander of the Afrika Korps, and much of his reputation is due to his many and extended offensives in Africa. His defeat at el-Alamein by Montgomery (q.v.) caused much celebration among the Allies, for Rommel had been considered unbeatable and unstoppable. After this defeat, Rommel was appointed to France, to prepare for the threatened Allied invasion. Suspected of participating in the 1944 plot against Hitler, he was given the choice of trial or suicide. Rommel killed himself but was given a state funeral, the official but false story being that he had died of the wounds received when his car was strafed by a British fighter. He had held the rank of Field Marshal. He wrote *Infanterie greift an* (1937) and *Krieg ohne haas* (published posthumously in 1950).][47]

Cantwell claims to have met Rommel when they were both young soldiers in World War I. Although they had fought in opposing armies, they became friends after the war (122). Cantwell would like to consult him about "certain things" (231; see also 250, 286).

*Rotary Club. [The first Rotary Club was established in 1905 by Paul Percy Harris, in Chicago. It was an organization for business and professional men, admitting only one representative from each business or profession, and thus promulgating cooperation among various businesses. The club took its name from the practice of holding meetings in rotation at its members' offices. The idea was popular and within five years the National Association of Rotary Clubs was formed, followed in 1922 by Rotary International. Membership in the Rotarian denotes excellence in one's own area of endeavor and a high degree of community involvement and awareness. The organization supports various charities.][48]

Cantwell dismisses various military leaders as being Rotarians and scorns them because they "Never fought. Ever" (125).

*Russians. Cantwell describes the Russians as "our potential enemy" (70) who might occupy Italy (91). See also *men and boys.

*S-3 ["Operations and Training Section in Army Brigades or smaller units, and in Marine Corps units smaller than a brigade; the officer in charge of this section" (*Acronyms, Initialisms, & Abbreviations Dictionary*, 597).]

Cantwell seems to expect Renata to recognize the military term "S-3" (241).

*sailors. Cantwell remembers the two young sailors who made the mistake of whistling admiringly at Renata. Cantwell, at that time a general, beat them both up (283–84).

Speak: 283.

*San Rocco, Scuola [di] San Rocco. See Tintoretto.

*Saxe, [Hermann] Maurice, [Comte de. French soldier, 1696–1750; named Marshal of France, 1743; naturalized as a French subject, 1746. The illegitimate but acknowledged son of Auguste II of Poland and Saxony, this aristocrat was noted for his great strength, independence of character, and profligate life style. He entered French service in 1720 and proved to be a brilliant commander. He led the French to victory at Fontenoy (1745), defeating the British and their allies in the War of Austrian Succession. His book *Mes Rêveries* (published posthumously in 1757) is a comprehensive, much-respected treatise on the art of war.]

Cantwell refuses to follow Count Maurice de Saxe's example in spite of Renata's urging that he "ought to write" (135).

*Schlitz. [Well-known American beer.]

Cantwell remarks that American girls "do not know their grandfather's last name" unless the grandfather happens to have made a fortune and attached his name to it, like Schlitz (247; see Schultz).

*Schultz. A common German name. Cantwell's remark that the only American girls likely to know their grandparents' names would be those of German descent (247) may be a slight on the morals of immigrants. Or, Cantwell may be suggesting that German immigrants were less likely to change their names—Schultz, for example—upon arrival at the United States than were Swedish or Russian families, whose more "foreign" patronymics were often normalized.

*seconal. [Scientific name: quinalbarbitone sodium. A sedative, used to relieve insomnia and anxiety.][49]

Having taken large doses of mannitol hexanitrate, the nauseous, nervous Cantwell feels the need for rest and a seconal tablet (9).

the second waiter. See waiters.

*servants. At the Gritti Palace, only the rooms intended for servants lack views (67). See also Renata's servants.

*Shakespeare, [William. English poet and dramatist, 1564–1616; author of *Romeo and Juliet, King Lear, Othello, Macbeth, Hamlet, Antony and Cleopatra.*]

Cantwell admires Shakespeare (171; see also 172, 230). He recommends *King Lear* to Renata (171) and compares her and himself to Desdemona and Othello (qq.v.), much to the disadvantage of Shakespeare's characters. Renata quotes Shakespeare once: "Sad stories of the death of kings" (236); her quote is accurate (*Richard II,* III.ii, 155). Cantwell quotes more or less freely from several of the plays. When he "quotes" Falstaff he increases the number of his troops to reflect the enormity of his losses. Falstaff actually says, "I have led my ragamuffins where they are peppered: there's not three of my hundred and fifty left alive; and they are for the town's end, to beg during life" (*I Henry IV*, V.iii, 37; cf. Cantwell's paraphrase, 171). Hemingway had earlier used Falstaff's words as the epigraph for his essay, "Who Murdered the Vets?" (*New Masses*, 17 September, 1935, pp. 9–10).

Less directly, Cantwell alludes to Capulet's line, "Thank me no thankings, nor proud me no prouds" (*Romeo and Juliet*, III.v,153) when he says "'Pin me no pin curls'" to Renata's portrait (179; see also *women and girls). His remark early in the novel, "A poor effort . . . But my own" (18), recalls Touchstone's phrase, "an ill-favoured thing, sir, but mine own" (*As You Like It*, V.iv, 61).

*Silver Star. [The Silver Star Medal, instituted in 1918, is awarded to a member of the United States armed forces in recognition of "gallantry in action not warranting the award of the Medal of Honor, the Navy Cross, or the Distinguished Service Cross" (*Encyclopedia Americana*, XX: 825).]
Cantwell has been awarded the Distinguished Service Cross (D.S.C., q.v.), the Silver Star, and the prestigious V.C. (q.v., 18).

slogans. Cantwell mocks the slogans of the French Revolution (26), the Spanish Civil War (40), and World War I (50). See slogans in *FWBT*.

*Smith, [Walter Wellesley] (Red). [American sports reporter, 1905–1982. Red Smith wrote about a variety of sports, among them baseball, football, boxing, horseracing and fishing. He eschewed jargon and was a literate, polished writer with a sophisticated vocabulary and a wry sense of humor. His columns appeared in the *New York Herald Tribune* (q.v.) from 1945 to 1966 (five columns a week). From 1971 to 1981 he wrote four columns a week for the *New York Times*. In 1976 Smith was awarded the Pulitzer Prize.][50]
Cantwell enjoys reading Red Smith in the Paris edition of the *New York Herald Tribune* (166–67).

*Smith, General Walter Bedell. [American soldier and diplomat, 1895–1961. During World War I Smith was commissioned as a second lieutenant of infantry. In World War II he was appointed secretary of the joint chiefs of staff, served as American secretary of the combined chiefs of staff, and became chief of staff of the European theatre of operations as well as Eisenhower's chief of staff. He negotiated the surrenders of Italy (1943) and Germany (1945). After the war Smith served as American ambassador to the Soviet Union (1946–1949), director of the Central Intelligence Agency (1950–1953), and Undersecretary of State.

He was closely allied with Eisenhower, both during World War II and during Eisenhower's presidency. Smith wrote two books: *My Three Years in Moscow* (1950; excerpted in the *New York Times* in November 1949) and *Eisenhower's Six Great Decisions* (1956).]

Cantwell blames Smith and, indirectly, Eisenhower for the disaster at Hurtgen Forest. Cantwell recalls that the "beautiful regiment" he had commanded as General was decimated as a result of "other people's orders" (242). Cantwell, who witnessed the terrible destruction occasioned by the battle, tells Renata "how it was . . . Smith doesn't know how it was yet" (245). Cantwell's interior monologue mentions some of the terrible details he remembers (chapters 33 and 35). Smith, who confidently ordered the attack (239, see 248), was "as wrong as hell" (249) but Cantwell finally exonerates his superiors (249, 250).

*Sollingen. [Usually spelled Solingen. This German city has a centuries-old reputation as the producer of fine blades. It produces excellent steel for knives, razors, scissors, and surgical instruments.]

Cantwell defecates into a hole he made with his Sollingen knife (18).

The Star Spangled Banner. [National anthem of the United States, composed by Francis Scott Key (1779–1843) during the Battle of Fort McHenry, September 13–14, 1814, towards the end of the War of 1812. Key was inspired to write the words by the sight of the flag still flying at dawn, after a night of almost continuous attack. His lyrics were set to the tune of the popular English song, "To Anacreon in Heaven." "The Star Spangled Banner" was officially adopted as the national anthem by executive order of President Wilson in 1916, and confirmed by Congress in 1931.[51] Although generally easy to sing, it requires a difficult high note on the line "And the rocket's red glare."]

Cantwell remarks that the American anthem "is foolproof" for singers until the high note at the end. Margaret [Truman's] smallish voice can be electronically amplified and modulated to sound impressive (197–98) when she sings the national anthem on the radio (but see Truman, Margaret).

The Stars and Stripes. [American military publication published in France for the American troops in Europe during World War I and then continued in the U.S. as an independent publication until 1926. It was revived as a military newspaper in 1942, first as a weekly and then as a daily. During World War II its circulation was about one million and its standard was high. The European edition continued to appear regularly after World War II, for American troops stationed overseas.][52]

Cantwell complains that during World War II Army careers were made in the widely-read *Stars and Stripes,* and not on the battlefield (236).

Super Honorary Secretary. Renata's title when she becomes a member of the Order of Brusadelli (270).

the Supreme Commander. Cantwell's title in the Order of Brusadelli (q.v.) (60, 64).

the surgeon. See Wes.

*the tailor. Renata knows of a good tailor in Rome where Cantwell can have civilian clothes made (128).

*Time. [A popular American weekly newsmagazine, founded in 1923 and published continuously until the present.]
Imagining an "ideal" future together, Renata envisions Cantwell drinking and reading newspapers and news magazines like *Time* (264; see *Life* and *Newsweek*).

*Tintoretto. [(the little dyer, the son of the dyer). Real name: Jacobo Robusti. Venetian painter, 1518–1595. Tintoretto introduced the Mannerist style to Venice. In contrast to the deep, warm colors favored by Titian (q.v.) and other masters of the High Renaissance, the Mannerists favored cold shiny surfaces, dramatic tension, and elongated figures. Titian painted the aristocracy; Tintoretto, also an excellent portraitist, painted the Venetian bourgeoisie. He decorated many Venetian palaces and churches. Venice's Accademia di Belle Arti has a fine collection. The Scuola di San Rocco, a large and sumptuous building designed by Bartolomeo Buono in 1517 as a guildhall, houses "the unrivalled series of paintings by Tintoretto, which called forth such unbounded enthusiasm on the part of Ruskin" (*Encyclopaedia Britannica*, 11th ed., XXVII, 1000).]
Cantwell daydreams about living in Venice and visiting the Accademia and the Scuola San Rocco to look at their collections of Tintorettos (45). He thinks of Tintoretto when looking at the portrait of Renata (146).

*Titian. [Tiziano Vecellio. Venetian painter, 1477–1576. This long-lived Venetian master painted grand subjects in the grand manner of the High Renaissance. His masterpieces include aristocratic portraits as well as paintings dealing with pagan and religious subjects, like the *Rape of Europa* and the *Pieta*. He found patrons both in the Church and the royal courts of Europe and was the favorite painter of Holy Roman Emperor Charles V. He is known for his sumptuous coloring, particularly his reds.]
Cantwell admires Titian, particularly his paintings of women (15–16).

*Tito, [Josip Broz. Yugoslav Communist military and political leader, 1892–1980. As premier (1945 to his death), Tito directed the unification and rebuilding of Yugoslavia. He held the various ethnic and political factions in uneasy unity, sometimes using force to maintain the constituent republics within the national confederation.]

In a silly conversation about Yugoslavian politics, Cantwell informs the young night porter that the Yugoslavian leader Tito is beset by "plenty problems" (183; see also porters and Matthew).

*Torcello. [A small island in the Venetian lagoon, just north of Burano and farther away from Venice than Burano or Murano (qq.v.). Much of Torcello's population came from mainland cities, whose inhabitants fled to Venice during the invasions of the West Goths (Visigoths, q.v.), Lombards (q.v.), and other Germanic tribes in the fifth and sixth centuries. Torcello has "two interesting churches. The former cathedral of S. Maria was founded in the 7th century. The present building, a basilica with columns, dates from 864; the nave was restored in 1008, in which year the now ruined octagonal baptistery was built. . . . The seats for the priests are arranged round the semicircular apse, rising in steps with the bishop's throne in the centre—an arrangement unique in Italy. Close by is S. Fosca, a church of the 12th century, octagonal outside, with colonnades on five sides and a rectangular interior" ("Torcello," *Encyclopaedia Britannica,* 11th ed., XXVII 50).][53]

Cantwell explains to Jackson that the people of Torcello were fine architects who "built Venice" (28, 75).

*Traveller. [Traveller was the horse of Confederate General Robert E. Lee (1807–1870). The Virginia State Memorial in Gettysburg, Pennsylvania, shows Lee astride this horse.]

Cantwell recalls the gallantry of old war horses like Traveller (52; see also Lysette).

*Tribuna Illustrata. [*La Tribuna Illustrata* was, as its name indicates, an illustrated weekly publication of the Italian newspaper *La Tribuna.* It was a politico-cultural magazine, founded in Rome, in January 1890, by Gabrielle D'Annunzio (q.v.) and published until December 1969.][54]

Renata reads newspapers and their illustrated supplements (136, 142). She tells Cantwell that she wants to hear the complete truth about war, even if it is "As bad or worse" than the illustrations [of casualties?] published in the illustrated magazines of the major newspapers like *Domenica del Corriere* or *La Tribuna* (219).

*[Truman, Harry S] (the haberdasher). [American businessman and politician, 1884–1972; President of the United States, 1945–1952, i.e., during the action and writing of the novel. With a partner, Truman ran a haberdashery store before turning to politics in the early 1920s. He ran as Franklin Delano Roosevelt's vice-president in 1944 and became

President when Roosevelt died suddenly in 1945. Truman made the difficult decision to drop the atomic bomb on Hiroshima and Nagasaki and led the country during the tense post-war years, when relations with the USSR deteriorated. Truman feared the expansion of Soviet influence into Europe; the Truman Doctrine provides support to nations threatened by communism. Truman was an amateur pianist; he usually wore bow-ties. His books include *Years of Decisions* (1955), *Years of Trials and Hope* (1956), and *Mr. Citizen* (1960). Cantwell's language when he fulminates against Truman recalls the question often asked in Congressional hearings in the early years of the Cold War: "Are you, or have you ever been, a member of the Communist party?"]

Cantwell mocks Truman when he explains to Renata, who believes he would be "an excellent president," why he is unsuited to the position: he doesn't wear bow-ties and was never "an unsuccessful haberdasher" (227).

*[Truman, Mary] Margaret. [American singer and writer, 1924—. The only child of President Truman, she married Jonathan Worth Daniels, an American newspaper editor, author, and biographer of his father-in-law (*The Man of Independence*, 1950). Like her father, Margaret Truman played the piano; her father taught her one of the first pieces she mastered, the Paderewski Minuet. She studied singing and in 1947, soon after graduating from college, embarked upon a singing career, going on several nation-wide tours. She was under contract to NBC and appeared on television and the radio, but there is no record of her having sung the national anthem on radio.[55] With Margaret Cousins she produced *Margaret Truman's Own Story: Souvenir* (New York: McGraw-Hill, 1956). Her second book was *White House Pets* (New York: D. McKay Co., 1969).]

Cantwell reports to Domenico that, in addition to the atomic bomb, the world powers have the capability for biological warfare (40, 197). He predicts that if and when the President orders the use of such secret weapons, his daughter will rally the nation behind him by singing the national anthem "on the radio" (197).

*T'Sun Su. [More commonly transliterated as Sun Tzu; also known as Sun-tzu Pingfa or Sunzi Bingfa. Sun Tzu is the pseudonym of either Sun Pin (c. 350 BCE) or, more probably, Sun Wu (c. 500 BCE), Chinese philosopher, general, and stategist. Sun Tzu wrote *The Art of War*, a short treatise in thirteen chapters (Laying Plans, Waging War, Attack by Stratagem, Tactical Dispositions, Energy, Weak Points and Strong, Maneuvering, etc.) which greatly influenced Chinese as well as Western military thinking. Hemingway's copy was entitled *Sun Tzu on the Art of War: The Oldest Military Treatise in the World*, translated from the Chinese with Introduction and Critical Notes by Lionel Giles, M.A. (London: Luzac &

Co., 1910). Giles frequently excoriates the 1905 translator, E.F. Calthrop; his scornful remarks were underlined in Hemingway's copy, which was marked both by Hemingway and by Mary Hemingway (Hemingway Collection, Other Materials: Books). *The Art of War* was reissued in English as recently as 1988 (Shambala: Boston & London; trans. Thomas Cleary).]

Cantwell mentions T'Sun Su as a military man who wrote about war. In spite of Renata's urging, Cantwell refuses to become a military writer (135).

*Tunney, [James Joseph] (Gene). [American boxer, c. 1897–1979; world heavyweight champion, 1926–1928. Tunney became world heavyweight champion when he defeated Jack Dempsey in 1926. He defeated Dempsey again in 1928 and retired as undefeated champion the next year. Like Cantwell, Tunney served in both world wars: as a marine in World War I and as director of athletics and physical fitness for the United States Navy in World War II. He wrote *A Man Must Fight* (1932) and *Arms for Living* (1941). See also Dempsey in *SAR, Islands, GHA.*]

Cantwell claims that Shakespeare is popular among tough fighting men and that the world heavyweight champion, Gene Tunney, has read *King Lear* (171).

*Udet, Ernst. [German military pilot, 1896–1941. Udet was a World War I flying ace. A stunt pilot after that war, he was often in the news for his daredevil schemes (in 1927, for example, he offered to jump off a peak in the Bavarian Alps in a motorless glider and to fly from Munich to New York nonstop) and for his narrow escapes during demonstrations of innovative flight and bail-out (parachuting) techniques. During World War II Udet was in charge of equipment for the German Air Force (Luftwaffe), a non-combatant post which he disdained and neglected, thus incurring the wrath of his superiors. His death has been variously reported as suicide (after a reprimand) and as accident (perhaps engineered by his superiors). He was given a hero's funeral.][56]

Although Germans "were in the wrong" and Cantwell himself killed at least 122 of them, he did get to know and like many of them, Ernst Udet being his favorite (122; see also 231, 250).

*Uffizi. [Famous art gallery in Florence, established by the cruel, despotic Francesco di Medici (1541–1587). See Pitti.]

When Jackson can't recall at which "big place" in Florence he saw paintings of madonnas, Cantwell supplies two names: the Uffizi and the Pitti (14).

*V.C. [Victoria Cross, Britain's most prestigious decoration, instituted by royal warrant, 29 January, 1856 and supplemented by subsequent royal warrants. It consists of a bronze Maltese cross and is inscribed "For Valour." It is awarded in recognition of "some signal act of valour or devotion" performed "in the presence of the enemy. . . . In the case of recipients who are not of commissioned rank, the Cross carries with it a pension of £10 a year" ("Medal," *Encyclopaedia Britannica,* 11th ed., XVIII: 16). Additional extraordinary acts of bravery are indicated by bars attached to the ribbon and carry an additional annuity of £5. The medal may be awarded to civilians for bravery in time of war. The shorter Indian, who lost both arms and both legs in action during World War I, was also awarded this honor (*TS* 58).]

Cantwell was awarded the Victoria Cross as well as other decorations (18; see gifts).

*Velásquez, [Diego Rodríguez de Silva. Usually spelled Velázquez. Spanish painter, 1599–1660. As court painter for Philip IV, the great Velázquez painted many portraits of the royal family and their servants. His most famous painting is probably *Las Meninas,* part of the magnificent Velázquez collection in the Prado in Madrid. See *FWBT.*]

Cantwell admires Velázquez's and Tintoretto's portraits (146).

*Verlaine, [Paul. French symbolist poet, 1844–1896. In 1871 or 1872, after having published two collections of verse and married Mlle. Mautet, Verlaine embarked upon a stormy homosexual relationship with the teen-aged Jean Arthur Rimbaud (q.v.), shooting him twice and consequently spending two years in jail, during which time he embraced Catholicism. Verlaine's propensity for drink, his mother's death, his divorce, and his poverty did not keep him from poetry, and towards the end of his life the poetry brought him academic respectability: in 1894 he was invited to lecture in London and Oxford.[57] His poetry is musical and evocative. Among his books are *La Bonne Chanson* (1870), *Romances sans Paroles* (1874), *Sagesse* (religious poems, 1881), *Jadis et naguere* (1884), *Amour* (1888), *Parallelement* (1889), *Bonheur* (1891), not all equally admired by critics. Verlaine's unhappy marriage, his passionate attachment to a teen-aged lover, his Roman Catholicism, and the lack of recognition which attended his work for most of his life may be relevant to Cantwell's situation.]

After the confession, Cantwell and Renata jokingly pretend to be Rimbaud and Verlaine (259).

*[Villon, François. French poet, 1431-date of death unknown; last date associated with him is 1463. This great poet was often in trouble with the law. Among the most exciting adventures associated with his name was the theft of a large stone known as "The Devil's Fart": while Villon was at the University of Paris the students swiped this marker and dragged it across town to the Left Bank. When the lady in front of whose house it

had stood complained of its loss, the police found it and confiscated it. The students responded by stealing it back from the police and transporting it once again to the Left Bank, swiping another stone from in front of the same lady's house (this stone they named "La Vesse," The Silent Fart), and dragging it off to join the first stone. They also seemed to have appropriated several street signs and other public properties, causing a clash between the university and the civil authorities. In another scandal, Villon and some friends managed to pick the locks of two coffers, one inside the other, and make off with the rich treasure of the College of Navarre. One of their gang bragged about the exploit and got the others convicted. Villon was accused of several other thefts, of wounding a scribe, and of killing a priest; he spent a considerable amount of time in jail and in exile. His poetry, most of it composed before 1463, is intensely personal and witty. The line "Mais ou sont les neiges d'antan?" (But where are the snows of yesteryear?) ends each of the four stanzas of his famous "Ballade of the Ladies of Bygone Times." Villon's chief works include *ballades, rondeaux,* the *Petit Testament* and the *Grand Testament.* He has been translated into English many times.]

To Villon's most famous line Cantwell adds the scatological embellishment (112).

*Visigoths. [The West Goths, an ancient Germanic tribe, like the Ostrogoths (East Goths). Under the leadership of Alaric I (c. 370–410) the Visigoths or West Goths conquered large sections of (modern) Italy and sacked Rome in 410. Their repeated incursions into northern Italy drove the inhabitants from the mainland cities to seek shelter in the secure and sparsely inhabited islands of the Venetian lagoons. As the Goths and Huns were driven back, many of the refugees would return to their former homes, but the growing strength of the Visigoths and the Lombard invasion of 568 convinced many people to abandon their mainland cities and establish themselves permanently in the area which we know as the city of Venice. Among the twelve early townships of Venice were Burano, Murano, and Torcello (qq.v.). From Rome and the northern sections of Italy, the Visigoths expanded their kingdom into southern Gaul (modern France) and northern Spain, where they converted to Catholicism and merged into the local population. See Lombards.]

Cantwell refers to the Visigoths' conquests (late 4th and early 5th centuries CE) and to the transfer of St. Mark's remains to Venice (9th century CE) when explaining the role of Torcello in the founding of Venice (28–29).

*V.M.I. [Virginia Military Institute, Lexington, Virginia. The school was founded in 1839.]

Cantwell has lost his V.M.I. school ring, otherwise he would give it to Renata (290; see gifts).

Vogue. [Founded in 1892 as a New York society weekly, *Vogue* became a semimonthly in 1910 and is now a monthly magazine which advertises expensive fashions and accessories. The magazine began publishing a British edition in 1916 and French edition in 1920. As a result of its 1936 merger with *Vanity Fair,* it began to publish fiction, including such authors as Thomas Wolfe and William Saroyan, but the fiction was phased out by 1940.][58] Cantwell sends copies of this glossy American magazine to Renata. She mentions that she saw an advertisement for a "big Buick Roadmaster" (263) in the magazine (see also *Harper's Bazaar*). Cantwell's car is a large, low-slung Buick (20) with a "big engine" (24); he's "still paying for it" (23).

*Wagon-Box Fight. [In early August 1867, Indian warriors attacked soldiers of the 27th Infantry who were the military escort for a group of civilian woodcutters. Their commander, Captain J. Powell, "lifted fourteen wagon boxes from their running gears and arranged them on the ground to form an oval corral" (Larson, *History of Wyoming,* 28–29). Thirty-two people, including four civilians, barricaded themselves within this circle of wagon boxes and, aided by a new weapon (the Springfield breech-loading rifle), suffered only a few casualties even though they were heavily outnumbered. After more than three hours, they were rescued by a relief party from nearby Fort Phil Kearny. Reports of casualties vary widely: Captain Powell is estimated to have lost between three and six men, and the Indians admitted to six warriors lost, although Powell estimated his enemy's casualties at 60 killed and 120 wounded. Following the Fetterman Massacre, in which more than 80 officers and men were killed on 21 December, 1866, the Wagon-Box Fight was hailed as a victory and "morale increased dramatically [as] the soldiers realized that their position in hostile Indian country could be protected."[59] The site of the Wagon-Box Fight, about twenty miles south of Sheridan, Wyoming, is a National Historic Landmark on the National Register of Historic Places, and is officially marked by the state's "Wagon Box Battle Monument," which lists the names of those who fought in the battle.] Cantwell suggests that he and Renata drive from Sheridan to the site of the Wagon-Box Fight (265).

waiters, waiters' families. [Like most of the waiters in Hemingway's books, the few waiters who appear in this novel embody positive values and approve of the male protagonist. Although these Italian waiters have lost family members in World War II, they view Cantwell, who fought with the Italians in World War I and against them in World War II, as a friend and not an enemy. See also waiters in *SAR*.]

Two waiters at the Gritti Hotel are members of the Order of Brusadelli: the head waiter, who serves Cantwell and Renata all their meals, is the Gran Maestro (q.v.). The second waiter is clearly "one of us" because he "believed in nothing" and because he knows that it is important to master a skill: he "was trying hard to be a good second waiter" (123–24; see *concierge*). Although he lost his wife and children in World War II, he feels kinship with rather than bitterness against Cantwell (150). Another young waiter, Arnaldo (q.v.), is fond of Cantwell and takes good care of him, buying him liquor (69) and remembering that Cantwell likes three pillows on his bed (164). Similarly, the two men who run Harry's Bar, Cipriani and Ettore, qq.v, are honest, generous, reliable men who are eager to please Cantwell and who enjoy his trust. See also bartenders and porters.

Speak: 150–51.

*Wasserman, [August von. German physician and bacteriologist, 1866–1925. In 1906 Wasserman devised the diagnostic test for syphilis which bears his name].

Cantwell refers to the accuracy of the Wasserman test (173).

Wes (City Boy). The military doctor, an old friend, gives Cantwell a good medical report although he knows that the drugs Cantwell has taken invalidate the electrocardiogram (8–11; see also 92).

*[Whitman, Walter (Walt). American journalist, printer and poet, 1819–1892. Son of a poor family, Whitman was largely selfeducated. In 1855 he published the first edition of *Leaves of Grass* and in 1856 a slightly expanded second edition; both were financial failures and, except for Emerson's high praise, critical failures as well. Whitman keep expanding and re-issuing *Leaves of Grass,* publishing ten editions in all. He extolled the individual and insisted on "common" language and the natural rhythms of English (rather than formal rhyme). "Out of the cradle endlessly rocking" became the first poem in a section entitled "Sea-Drift" in the 1881 edition of *Leaves of Grass.* Another book of poems, *Drum Taps* (1865), reflects some of his experiences as an Army nurse during the Civil War. In the second edition of *Drum Taps,* one of the four elegies mourning the assassinated Abraham Lincoln begins with the line, "When lilacs last in the door-yard bloomed." Whitman published his best prose essays as *Specimen Days and Collect* (1822). His editorials were collected and published posthumously as *The Gathering of Forces* (1920).]

Speaking of "things that say better in English," Renata quotes several examples of native American diction, including the first lines of some Whitman poems (211).

women and girls. The few unnamed women who appear in the narrative are mostly pleasant, bland figures. The woman with the unidentified writer (q.v.), perhaps his aunt, is "elderly, wholesome looking" (87, 89, 124). Four other women at Harry's are variously described in friendly, positive language (86; see Manners; Mellow finds that "A pair of lesbians turns up at Harry's Bar" [559]). Cantwell enjoys looking at two beautiful girls (78). He tries to disapprove of an expensively dressed young woman but finds it hard because "She is damned beautiful, actually" (38–39). A woman sells Cantwell some sausage (190–91).
Speaks: 191.

*women and girls. Nameless women who appear in memory are generally not admired. Unlike Renata, who sleeps with her beautiful hair loose on the pillow, an unseen Texas girl repels unseen lovers by going to bed with her hair screwed into unattractive pincurls (178–79). Some unseen women "make wonderful lace" (29), others "trap foxes" (228), several aggravate Cantwell by sitting in Harry's Bar in the afternoon (72). Cantwell disdains hearing about the wives and children of American diplomats (73). Thinking wishfully that he might spend his retirement in Venice, Cantwell imagines that he would rent a room and that his landlady might provide meals (45). See also journalists.

the writer (the pitted one, the pitted man, compatriot, pitted compatriot). An ugly American writer to whom both the narrator and Cantwell have taken a strong dislike. His outstanding characteristics are his ugliness and his attachment to his Baedeker guidebook.[60] Cantwell, Renata, and the Grand Master mention him often, always disparagingly (87–90, 97, 119, 124, 126–27, 129–30, 139, 146–47, 202, 207, 270; see also Baedeker and women and girls).

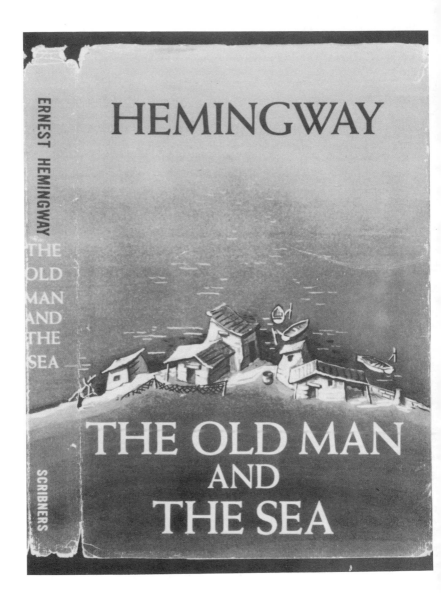

Scribner dust jacket for the first edition of *The Old Man and the Sea* (courtesy Charles Scribner's Sons, an imprint of the Macmillan Publishing Company; and of the Hemingway Collection, J.F. Kennedy Library)

CHAPTER VII

THE OLD MAN AND THE SEA

(1952)

The action takes place over four days (it begins one evening and continues over the next three days), in September, in Cojimar, Cuba, in Cuban waters and in the Gulf Stream.[1] It presents very few people and several birds, fish, and turtles, to which Santiago has well-defined and often intense responses.

albacore. Family of salt-water fish including tuna and bonito (qq.v.).

bait. Santiago uses sardines to give "scent and attractiveness" to the blue runner and yellow jack which he uses as bait (31). He can feel the marlin eating the sardines before he swallows the hook (41–42). Santiago cuts off the other three baited lines (51–52). Even so, he seems to have another line out, the "small line" with which he catches the dolphin (72); he "rebaited the line with another sardine" (73). Knowing how valuable sardines are as bait, Manolín repeatedly offers to get fresh sardines for Santiago (13, 16–18, 27). Although stored in salt (13, 15), the "sardines were rotten" after three days (98). Santiago eats raw tuna (q.v.) and offers it as bait.

*bettors. See *men in tavern.

birds. Santiago identifies with birds, who look for fish as he does. A small, tired warbler which rests on Santiago's boat occasions one of his rare shows of humor: Santiago asks it, "How old are you? . . . Is this your first trip?" and invites it to his home (54). The wild ducks flying by reassure Santiago that "no man was ever alone on the sea" (61). See also man-of-war bird.

*birds. Santiago thinks of "delicate" birds like terns and sea swallows, and of larger, more powerful ones like "the robber birds" (29).

blue runner. See bait.

bonito. [In a 1936 listing of commercially-valuable fish, the Cuban Secretary of Agriculture, Fishing Industries Division, indicates that in popular usage the names albacore and bonito are both used to refer to the same fish, whose scientific name is given as *Euthynnus sp.* (*sic*). In the same list, the *atún* or tuna's scientific name is given as *Germo alalunga,* and the bonito grande, listed separately from the bonito, has the scientific name *Sarda sarda.* All these fishes, as well as the *dorado* (q.v.), appear as members of the same sub-order and are obviously closely related (see Hemingway Collection: Other Materials, Fishing Papers).]
    Santiago uses the terms tuna (31, 40, 57, 60), bonito (58–59, 74) and albacore (30, 31) interchangeably. He catches a tuna/albacore early on his first day (38–39) and eats it raw for breakfast on the morning of the second day, calling it a tuna (57) and a bonito (58): it "was not unpleasant" to eat (58).[2]

the boy, the boy's parents. See Manolín, Manolín's parents.

*Brooklyn [Dodgers. National League baseball team. The Brooklyn Dodgers were League champions in 1916, 1920, 1941, 1947, 1949, 1952, 1953, and 1955. They broke the color line in 1947 when they signed the great Jackie Robinson, the first black man to play in the major leagues. In 1957 the team moved to the west coast, becoming the Los Angeles Dodgers. The team is also mentioned in *Islands,* 295.]
    Santiago is sure that the Yankees will win the championship in the American League, and that the Brooklyn Dodgers will be the National League champions (21; see Philadelphia).

el Campeón (the Champion). As a young man, Santiago earned this sobriquet when he triumphed in the heroic, 24-hour-long arm-wrestling match which foreshadows his victory with the marlin (70; see also *the Negro and *men in tavern). Manolín also affirms that Santiago is "the best fisherman" (23).

cat. The first time Santiago falls on his way to his shack, he stares at a cat "going about its business" (121; cf. W. H. Auden's great poem, "Musée des Beaux Arts," in which "the dogs go on with their doggy life" while "the dreadful martyrdom must run its course"). See endnote 11.

el dentuso (the toothy one). See the Mako shark.

*DiMaggio, [Giuseppe Paolo, Jr. (Joseph Paul, Joe, Joltin' Joe, Yankee Clipper). American baseball player, 1914—. DiMaggio played the outfield for the New York Yankees from 1936 until his retirement in 1951. He won the American League batting championship in 1939 and 1940, and was voted the League's most valuable player in 1939, 1941, and 1947. In 1941 he established a major league record by hitting safely in 56 consecutive games. DiMaggio's career was interrupted by military service (1943–1945) during World War II. Before enlisting, his batting average was .339; after the war, it was .304; his lifetime batting average was .325. In 1946 DiMaggio developed a painful bone spur in his left heel; it required two operations in 1947. His arm was also operated on that same year. In 1948 and 1949 he underwent surgery for a bone spur in his right heel. In spite of his medical problems, DiMaggio batted .346 in 1949 and .301 in 1950. His average went down to .263 in 1951 and he retired at the end of that season, at age 37. He had led his team to ten American League pennants and eight world championships. He was elected to Baseball's Hall of Fame in 1955. In later years he was vice-president and coach of the Oakland Athletics (1968–1989).]

Santiago admires DiMaggio for his skill, his disregard of pain, and his unshaken commitment to his team (68). He identifies with him because "his father was a fisherman" (68) and because DiMaggio, like Santiago, is coming to the end of his working life (see George Monteiro, "Santiago, DiMaggio, and Hemingway: The Ageing Professionals," 273–80). Santiago consistently attaches the epithet "the great" to DiMaggio's name (17, 21, 22, 68, 97, 103–4, 105).

*DiMaggio's father. [Original spelling of family name: DeMaggio. The Italian-born American fisherman Guiseppe Paolo (Joe) DeMaggio (1872–1949) came to the United States in 1895 and became a naturalized citizen in 1945. Born in Isola de Demme, Italy, a fishing community, he worked for other fishermen in San Francisco for many years, until he was able to buy his own boat. He and Rosalie Mercurio were the parents of four daughters and five sons. Tom, the oldest, was a promising athlete, but, being the first-born son, gave up baseball to follow his father's trade and eventually to manage the family's fish restaurant on Fisherman's Wharf, San Francisco. Three sons—Vincent (Vince), Joe, and Dominic (Dom)— became Major League baseball players. Joe DiMaggio, the eighth of the nine children, grew up in a working-class family which, while not wealthy, was not as pitifully poor as Santiago is.][3]

Santiago correctly describes DiMaggio's father as a fisherman (22, 68, 105).

dolphin (*dorado*). [Sometimes called dolphinfish to distinguish it from porpoise. See *dorado*.]

The narrative describes the dolphin as a gold-colored fish with purple spots and purple stripes down its side (71–72). Guided by the man-of-

war bird, Santiago spots a big school of dolphin early in the morning of
the first day (34) but doesn't catch a dolphin until the evening of the
second day (72–73). Both he and the dolphin eat flying fish (q.v.).
Santiago also eats a raw dolphin fillet, but without pleasure: although
dolphin is good "to eat cooked," it is "a miserable fish raw" (80)
because its flesh is "too sweet" (59). Santiago's face gets mashed
into the second dolphin fillet when the hooked marlin jumps suddenly
(82).

dorado (the golden one). [The Cuban Secretary of Agriculture, Fishing
Industries Division, includes a fish popularly known as the *dorado* in its
1936 list of commercially-valuable fish, giving its scientific name as
Coryphaena hippurus. It is classified under the sub-order "Acantopter-
igios," as are the albacore, bonito and tuna (Hemingway Collection:
Other Materials, Fishing Papers).]
    Santiago refers to the dolphin (q.v.) as *dorado* only once (74).

ducks. See birds.

*Durocher, [Leo Ernest (the Lip). American baseball player, baseball
manager, and radio and television baseball commentator, 1905–1991.
Durocher played for the New York Yankees (1928–1930), for Cincinnati
(1930–1933), and for the St. Louis Cardinals (1933–1937). He came to
the Brooklyn Dodgers in 1937 as a player and became their manager in
1939; they won the pennant in 1941. He was one of baseball's most
successful and controversial managers, often loudly at odds with his
players, the umpires, the club's owners, and even the fans. Obituaries
described him as "combative," "colorful," "irascible," "feisty" and
"fiery."[4] In 1947 Durocher was suspended for the season for "cumu-
lated unpleasant incidents" which involved betting on the horses and
associating with gamblers. From 1948 to 1955 Durocher managed the
New York Giants, who won two pennants (1951 and 1954) and the
World Series (1954) under his colorful management. From 1961 to
1964, Durocher coached the Los Angeles Dodgers; he managed the
Chicago Cubs from 1966 to 1972. He is author of *The Dodgers and Me,
the Inside Story* (1948) and, in collaboration with Ed Linn, of *Nice Guys
Finish Last* (1975). During the 1930s, 1940s and 1950s many major
league baseball teams went to Cuba over the winter to prepare for the
coming season (spring camp or spring training camp).]
    The narrative identifies Durocher as one of the major league baseball
managers who sometimes comes to Cuba for spring training camp (23).

fighting cocks. [Very aggressive gamecocks bred and trained to fight for
sport in Cuba and other Latin countries.]

Santiago admires the roosters for their ability to bear pain and to continue fighting even after their eyes have been pecked out (68; see endnote 11).

the fish. Santiago has a close acquaintance with many fish, but when he speaks of or to "the fish" he means the huge marlin (q.v.) that occupies so much of his attention for the three days of the novel. See also albacore, bait, bonito, dolphin, flying fish, shark, and sucking fish.

the fishermen. Because Santiago lives in a fishing village, most of the background characters are fishermen. Some of them "made fun of the old man" who hasn't caught anything for 84 days, while "older fishermen . . . spoke politely" and did not reveal their pity for Santiago (11). They get up early to go fishing (26). After Santiago's return, several fishermen admire and measure the huge skeleton lashed to the side of the boat (122; see tourists).
   Speak: 122.

*fishermen. The unseen community of fishermen generally serves to define Santiago's unique situation and character. Many of them have caught marlin and shark and have taken their catch to the processing plant (11); some can afford radios (39) or motorboats (29), all of which indicates that the old man's bad luck and poverty are a particular and not a general condition. Most of them are helpful and community-minded, looking after Santiago's skiff (122), worrying about him and sending out search parties (115, 124), storing their gear in a communal shack (37) and ice house (27), sharing food and newspapers (17, 20, 37), in contrast to the old man's isolation; he keeps himself and his equipment separate from the community (15). Others depend on equipment rather than skill (29–30) and some are fearful (61); they emphasize Santiago's experience, skill, and unfailing confidence and courage. Manolín's "employer" is distrustful (27) and "almost blind" (14), both literally and metaphorically, but the old man sees and understands perfectly (see endnote 11). The narrative indicates that the "old fishermen" are particularly kind (11, 115). See *men in tavern.

flying fish. [So called because their winglike pectoral fins help them fly for short distances when they jump out of the water.]
   Santiago considers the flying fish "his principal friends in the ocean" (29). He encounters them both on the journey out (29) and on the journey home (106). He knows they are attracted by light (66), that they are eaten by dolphins (33–34, 71), and that they are "excellent to eat raw" (66). He eats the two flying fish he finds in the maw of the dolphin (78–80, 85).

galano shark (shovel-nosed shark). [José I. Castro identifies the galano—the word means "elegant" or "adorned"—as the oceanic whitetip shark, which is "brown with white undersides," has yellow eyes, and is named for its "white tipped fins." Like the mako, whitetip sharks are "oceanic, pelagic fishes and likely to attack a marlin tied to a boat."[5] The Cuban Secretary of Agriculture, Fishing Industries Division, included the *tiburón galano* in its 1936 list of commercially-valuable fish, giving its scientific name as *Charcharias limbatus* (Hemingway Collection: Other Materials, Fishing Papers).]

After killing the large, brave Mako shark, Santiago fights off repeated attacks of galano sharks, which he despises (107–8). He identifies them by their brown, "white-tipped wide pectoral fins . . . [and] slitted yellow eyes," their "sweeping" tails and their "wide, flattened, shovel-pointed heads" (107–8). He knifes the first galano as it takes its huge bite of the fish and punches and stabs the second galano (108, 110). He kills the third "shovelnose" with a single blow, losing his knife in the process (111).

Just before sunset, two more galano sharks arrive. Santiago forces the first one to let go of the marlin by clubbing it twice; he delivers four powerful blows to the second one (113–14). After the battle, Santiago sees one of the sharks "swimming in circles"; he suspects that both sharks have survived his blows, although "neither one can feel very good" (114).

At midnight, many more sharks attack. "He clubbed desperately" until he loses the club; he then beats them away with the tiller but the sharks continue ripping chunks off the marlin until nothing is left "for them to eat" (118–19).

*González [y Cordero, Miguel Angel] (Mike). [Cuban baseball player, coach, and manager, 1890–1977. Between 1912 and 1932 González played catcher and first base for a variety of professional baseball teams in the major leagues.[6] González also coached in the major leagues and served as coach and manager in the minor leagues. Barbour and Sattelmeyer contend that prejudice against Latin Americans kept González out of "the managerial ranks in the major leagues" in spite of his "keen knowledge of the game" (285), but Aylesworth and Minks report that González was twice called in to manage the Cardinals: when Frankie Frisch was fired as manager in 1938, González managed the team for its last seventeen games of that season (he won nine of them); and when the Cardinals dismissed manager Ray Blades in 1940, González managed and lost the five games of the season. "He did not manage again" (Aylesworth and Minks, 32–33).]

The narrative correctly identifies Mike González as a local baseball manager (23; see Luque).

Hatuey, Hatuey Beer. [Hatuey was an Indian *cacique* (chief) of the Arawak tribe. A native of nearby Hispaniola (Haiti), he migrated to Cuba after his own people had been exterminated by the Spanish conquistadors. In Cuba he incited the native islanders to a revolt against the Spanish, who consequently burned him to death. His name has become "most widely known through a beer that the Bacardí Company makes and from ices sold from pushcarts everywhere" (Fergusson, 45; see also Roberts, 96). Harry Morgan also drinks Hatuey beer (*THHN* 30).]

Martín supplies food and two returnable bottles of Hatuey beer (20; Manolín says he will return the food containers and the (presumably) empty bottles (23).

*the Indians of Cleveland. [The Cleveland Indians, a professional baseball team, have been associated with the American League since it was recognized in 1901. The team won the World Series in 1920 and in 1948, when they defeated the Boston Braves. In 1950 the Indians "finished . . . fourth . . . six games behind the Yankees . . . [who] won the pennant in 1950 and went on to win the World Series in four games" (Barbour and Sattelmeyer, 284).]

Manolín thinks the Cleveland Indians will offer stiff competition to his favorite team, the New York Yankees (17).

Jota. [Spanish name for the letter J; also, the name of a dance.]

Manolín gives the Spanish name for the J. which is John McGraw's middle initial (22).

*lions. The lions which Santiago saw when he sailed on the coast of Africa as a boy (22) reappear in his dreams (24–25). They are "the main thing that is left" (66); when he dreams of them or of the African coast, "he was happy" (81; see 19).[7] Santiago comes from the Spanish Canary Islands, just off the shore of the western bulge of Africa (25; see endnote 2).

luck. Luck, religion, skill, courage and confidence or hope are all important to Santiago. It would be foolish to trust only to luck; one must prepare one's self to take advantage of luck when it comes (23, 32 *et passim*), and one must steadfastly believe that the luck will come (104–5). Early and late in the novel the matter of Santiago's luck comes up: Manolín's parents claim the old man is unlucky (9), a claim he confirms (32, 125) and denies (75). He considers the problem of luck carefully (116–17). While Santiago has been unable to catch anything, the boy has been catching fish steadily (9, 123, 124) in "a lucky boat" (13); he claims he will "bring the luck" (125). Superstition attends some numbers, especially 84 (9, 117), the lucky number 85 (16–18, 41), and 87 (10, 17). Santiago also believes "that if you said a good thing it

might not happen" (43).[8] William Adair discusses "Eighty-five as a
Lucky Number: A Note on *The Old Man and the Sea*" (*Notes on
Contemporary Literature,* 8.1 [1978]: 9). For the religious significance
of numbers, see Roman Catholicism.

*Luque, [Adolfo (Dolf, The Pride of Havana). Cuban baseball player and
manager, 1890–1957. Luque pitched for various major league baseball
teams, winning 194 and losing 179 with 28 saves in his twenty years in the
National League, most of them spent playing for Cincinnati (1918–1929)
and the New York Giants (1932–1935). He was one of the game's earliest
Latin American stars, "the first Latin American-born ballplayer to appear
in a World Series game" (Porter, 117). In addition to pitching, he coached
the New York Giants (1935–1937 and 1941–1945) and managed in the
Florida International League in Havana (1951) and the Mexican League
(Mexicali, 1952). Luque "served regularly as a winter league manager in
Mexico and his native Cuba for three decades from the 1930s to the
1950s" (Porter, *Supplement,* 118). Barbour and Sattelmeyer explain that
an "unwritten law prevented [Luque and González] from managing the
majors" although both men "managed in the winter leagues in Latin
America" and were clearly qualified managers (285). Hemingway's
character Thomas Hudson drinks a toast to Luque (*Islands,* 299).]
    Although Manolín can't decide whether Luque or González (q.v.) is
"the greatest manager, really," he does not hesitate in proclaiming
Santiago the undisputedly "best fisherman" (23).

the Mako shark (*el dentuso*). [A member of the family *Isuridae,* (also
known as *Lamnidae* or mackerel sharks) which includes two species: the
shortfin Mako (*Isurus oxyrinchus*), one of the largest, most commonly
seen sharks of the Atlantic Ocean; and the longfin Mako (*Isurus paucus*),
of the Indo-Pacific. The Mako are distinguished by "pointed snouts,
crescent-shaped tails, and long, slender teeth. . . . They grow to . . . about
4 metres (13 feet) and 450 kilograms (1,000 pounds)" (*Britannica
Micropedia,* 1974 ed.). The Mako "is renowned for its fighting qualities.
. . . The Maoris prize its long white teeth as ornaments" (*Collier's
Encyclopedia,* 1968 edition). Rodney Steel describes Mako sharks as
"bluish grey, shading to white on the belly . . . The pectoral fins are a
graceful sickle-like shape. . . . Makos . . . are quite slenderly proportioned"
but large and powerful, able to jump 15 feet in the air (*Sharks of the World,*
97–99). Castro describes the shortfin Mako as smaller, although "Excep-
tional females may reach 380 cm (12.5 ft.) and weigh 570 kg (1,250 lb)."
He also attests to their fierceness: "Once hooked, they put up a fierce
resistance, often leaping high into the air. They often cause injury to
anglers and damage to boats" (*The Sharks of North American Waters,*
90–91). Castro reports that the longfin Mako is found not only in the

Pacific but in all "deep, warm waters. It is common in Gulf Stream waters from the northern coast of Cuba to southeastern Florida" (92). Many sharks, not just the Mako, eat live fish, including the occasional mackerel, which the Mako resemble in that they have "accessory stabilising keels prominently developed on either side of the tail" as mackerel do; hence the name "mackerel shark" (Steel, 97). Castro writes that "mako . . . takes its name from the Maori name for that fish. It has nothing to do with the English [word] mackerel."[9] The Cuban government's 1936 listing of the common and scientific names of fish that figure prominently in the Cuban fishing industry identifies the *dientuzo* (*sic*) shark as the *Ysurus tigris* (Hemingway Collection: Other Materials, Fishing Papers).]

Santiago's epithet for the Mako shark (*el dentuso*) emphasizes its most threatening feature: its "huge jaws" with their "eight rows" of huge, sharp teeth (100–1).[10] Santiago admires the Mako, the first shark to attack his fish, for its beauty, size, bravery, and intelligence (101, 103, 106). He identifies with it and worries that he enjoyed killing it (105; see Roman Catholicism).

Manolín (the boy). From the age of five, Manolín has been Santiago's friend, fellow fisherman, and loving admirer. Now he is old enough to take care of Santiago, bringing him food and drink, worrying about keeping him warm in the winter and, to salve the old man's pride, pretending that Santiago still has the equipment which they both know has long since had to be sold (16). He has internalized Santiago's concern with skill and excellence, whether in baseball or in fishing, and remembers Santiago's triumphs; Santiago recognizes that in many ways, "The boy keeps me alive" (106). By himself on the sea, Santiago often thinks of Manolín (39, 62, 83, 96, 106, 115) and repeatedly speaks out loud his wish that Manolín were with him (45, 48, 50, 51, 56). He tells Manolín, "I missed you" (124). Manolín never loses faith in Santiago, whom he "would like to serve in some way" (12; cf. the priest's definition of love, *FTA* 72; and Renata's "wish to serve" Cantwell, *ARIT* 143). For Manolín's age, a moot point, see endnote 17.

Speaks: 10–24, 26–28, 122–26.

*Manolín's current fishing mentor. See *fishermen.

*Manolín's parents. The father (*papá*) is a man of limited vision, unable to recognize the value of intangibles such as skill, luck, and faith. He simply removes Manolín from Santiago's boat whenever the old man has a dry spell (10). His pronouncements about baseball also reveal his dependence on external, material factors: he thinks McGraw was "the greatest" manager only because he was the one he saw most often. Santiago understands that had Durocher come more frequently, Manolín's father would have considered him "the greatest manager" (23). Like the fisherman to whom he attaches his son (see *fishermen), Manolín's father does not understand or respect the boy or his values; he makes Manolín feel "as though I were inferior" (24). The boy finally denies his father's authority (125).[11] Manolín's mother figures only slightly in the narrative (9, 13).

man-of-war bird. [A raptorial sea bird with large wings, a strong hooked bill, and small webbed feet.] Santiago observes this "working" bird closely; it leads him to dolphins (34) and tuna (38) and "is a great help" (38).

marlin (the fish). A huge 18-foot-long spearfish (63, 122), weighing more than 1500 pounds (97) which takes Santiago's bait. The fish is valuable (106) and beautiful (62; it is described, 90–94). Its jumps are impressive (62, 82–83, 98; cf. the porpoise's jumps, 81). Santiago admires, loves, and pities the fish, calling it his friend (55, 75) and his brother (59, 75, 92, 95) and even wishing "I was the fish" (64).[12] Although less intelligent than man, the marlin is "more noble and more able" (63). Santiago kills the marlin on the third day; as he sails back, it is repeatedly attacked by sharks, until only the skeleton remains. Santiago gives the marlin's spear to Manolín and its head to Pedrico (124, 126).

*marlin. Santiago remembers hooking the female of a pair of marlin. He was impressed by her mate's devotion to her (49–50).[13] Santiago and the boy apologized to the marlin for killing her (50). Porpoises (q.v.) are also loving mates.

*Martín. Owner of the Terrace, the local eatery, he generously sends food, beer and coffee to the old man (20, 123).
    Speaks: 123.

*McGraw, John J[oseph (The Little Napoleon). American baseball player and manager, 1873–1934. McGraw played first and third base for the Baltimore Orioles in the 1890s and then managed the New York Giants from 1902 until his retirement in 1932. Under his management the New York Giants (q.v. in *FTA*) won ten National League championships, four of them in succession, as well as three World Series titles. He managed more games (4,879) and won more games (2,840) than any other manager except Connie Mack. McGraw was a brilliant strategist, a fine judge of young talent, and an autocratic manager. He was elected to the Baseball Hall of Fame posthumously, in 1937. Barbour and Sattelmeyer report that McGraw "was also part owner of the Oriental Park racetrack in Havana" (284).]
    McGraw used to come to Martín's restaurant, the Terrace, "in the older days." In spite of McGraw's many achievements, Santiago could

see that he was a flawed man, his commitment to baseball diluted by alcohol and horseracing (22).[14]

*men in tavern in Casablanca. [Casablanca or Casa Blanca is a small town to the north-east of Havana, across Havana Bay from the capital; pop. in 1950 was 3,433. Casablanca is also mentioned in *Islands,* 247, 251.]
    Santiago remembers the men who observed, refereed and bet on him and his competitor during the marathon hand-wrestling match in a tavern (69–70; see also *the Negro). In his current struggle, distanced from the community of men, Santiago performs all these functions himself: he observes, evaluates and encourages both the marlin and himself (including parts of himself—his head, eyes, hands, feet, legs, heart—which he sometimes addresses as if they were separate from him, e.g. 91, 92) all through their long ordeal. For other absent characters, see *fishermen.

*the Negro. "[A] fine man and a great athlete" whom Santiago defeated in a long, tough hand-wrestling contest. Santiago won the return match "quite easily" (69–70).

numbers. See luck and Roman Catholicism.

the old man. See Santiago.

papa. [Probably *papá*, Spanish for father. *Papa* means Pope and, in the Caribbean, potato (*patata* in Castilian Spanish).]
    Manolín refers to his father as "papa" (10, *sic*).

*parents. The narrative mentions DiMaggio's and Sisler's fathers and Manolín's parents (qq.v.).

*Pedrico. One of the villagers. He tends to Santiago's boat and what is left of his equipment when Santiago returns to land. Santiago gives him the head of the fish "to use in fish traps" (124, 126).

*Pedro, San. [St. Peter, chief of the Twelve Apostles. Originally named Simon, he was re-named by Jesus. He and his brother, St. Andrew, were fishermen in the Lake of Galilee. His feast day is 29 June.]
    While thinking about sin, Santiago recalls that San Pedro and DiMaggio's father were both fishermen (105).

*Perico. [Possibly a misspelling of Pedrico (q.v.).]
    Perico is a villager who gave the old man yesterday's newspaper (17).

*Perkins, Max[well Evarts. American editor, 1884–1947. Perkins was the great editor of the Scribner publishing house who tactfully and intelligently handled such different personalities as F. Scott Fitzgerald, Thomas Wolfe, and Ernest Hemingway. Fitzgerald first brought Hemingway to Perkins' attention, and Scribner began publishing Hemingway in 1926, with *The Torrents of Spring* and *The Sun Also Rises*. Hemingway mourned the death of his friend Max Perkins: "One of my best and most loyal friends and wisest counsellors in life as well as in writing is dead" (Baker, *Letters*, 621–22). Wallace Meyer, who had been with the firm for many years, succeeded Perkins as Hemingway's editor.]

Hemingway dedicated *The Old Man and the Sea* to his late editor, Maxwell Perkins, and to his publisher, Charlie Scribner.

*Philadelphia [Phillies. A professional baseball team associated with the National League since 1883. They have won the League title only twice (1915 and 1950) and have had a generally undistinguished record. If, as Barbour and Sattelmeyer argue, the story refers to the events of 1950, Santiago errs in picking the Brooklyn Dodgers to win: "in the final game of the 1950 season against Brooklyn, Sisler hit a home run in the tenth inning to win the game and the National League title for the Philadelphia Phillies" (284).]

Santiago thinks that the Brooklyn Dodgers (q.v.) will defeat Philadelphia for the National League championship, although he recognizes that the Phillies' Sisler poses a great danger (21).

porpoises. Santiago hears a pair of porpoises during the first night, when he is being towed out by the huge marlin. He claims he can distinguish between the male's "blowing noise" and the female's "sighing blow." Santiago considers them to be "good. . . . They play and make jokes and love one another. They are our brothers" (48). The next night, Santiago dreams of porpoises (81).

*Portuguese man-of-war. [A close relative of the jelly-fish, the Portuguese man-of-war is more dangerous. It has a very painful sting which can be fatal for humans.]

Santiago hates this poisonous jelly-fish (36).

*the Reds of Cincinnati. [Originally called the Red Stockings, this professional American baseball team became the Cincinnati Reds in 1890. Under its original name, the team was a founding member of the National League, which it re-entered under its new name ten years later. They won the League championship in 1939, 1940, 1961, 1970, 1972 and most recently in 1990. In 1919, when the Reds won the notorious rigged World Series against the White Sox (q.v.), the tainted victors were nicknamed the "Black Sox." All those players who had accepted bribes were banned from baseball for life.]

The old man warns the boy to be "careful" not to think that teams like the Chicago White Sox or the Cincinnati Reds could defeat DiMaggio's team, the New York Yankees (17).

*referees. See *men in tavern.

Rigel. [Scientific name: *Beta Orionis.* Rigel is a star of the first magnitude, one of three such extremely bright stars found in the constellation Orion, itself one of the most conspicuous constellations in the sky. Orion is named after a mighty hunter who figures in several legends. In one story, he was the beloved of Eos, the dawn-goddess, and was killed by Artemis, the goddess of chastity and of hunting (the counterpart of the Roman Diana). In a variant, he was loved by Artemis, who killed him by mistake. In another account, he was blinded but recovered his sight, retired to Crete, threatened to kill all the living things on the island, and was killed by a scorpion. The constellation represents Orion wearing a lion skin and carrying a club; a sword or dagger hangs from his belt.][15]
The old man sees this star but doesn't know its name (75).

*Rogelio. A Cuban villager. To encourage Manolín to go off and play, the old man assures him that Rogelio will help Santiago obtain sardines to use as bait (12). When Manolín insists, Santiago relents and allows the boy to supply him with bait and sardines (13, 27).

Roman Catholicism. [The major religion of Cuba is Roman Catholicism. Critics are well aware that Santiago's name in English is St. James (e.g., Joseph M. Flora, "Biblical Allusion," 143–47). Several critics have dealt with the religious content of the novel, including the meaning of the important numbers 84 and 87 in the Christian calendar (John Halverson, "Christian Resonance," 50–54; and G. R. Wilson, Jr., "Incarnation and Redemption," 369–73). Santiago is often seen as a Christ figure, but see Gerry Brenner's revisionist reading (*The Old Man and the Sea: Story of a Common Man*), which argues that Santiago may also be read as a conceited, overbearing, humanly flawed and therefore quite ordinary man.]
Like Anselmo in *FWBT,* Santiago had a religious wife (q.v.), worries about killing and sin (104–6), and resorts to prayer in times of stress (65, 87, 116; see Virgin of Cobre). He has witnessed Catholic processions (see 96).

Santiago (*el Campeón,* the old man). The title character is old and wrinkled but "his eyes were cheerful and undefeated" (9–10). A hand-wrestling champion and expert fisherman, he encourages Manolín to value skill and courage, to have faith, and to eschew despair and physical pain, like his hero Joe DiMaggio (q.v.). Santiago has not caught any fish for 84 days (see luck), but remains confident and eventually hooks a huge marlin (62–63) with which he struggles, using the many skills at his disposal and fighting exhaustion and pain, for most of three days and two nights. On the trip back, he gallantly fights off the many sharks which attack and finally consume his catch, leaving only the skeleton. See men in tavern, lions and endnote 1.

Speaks: 10–14, 16–24, 26–28, 33–35, 37–39, 41–46, 48, 50–68, 71, 73–75, 77, 79–80, 84–92, 95–97, 103–12, 114–17, 119–20, 124–26; much interior monologue.

*Santiago's wife. She was a religious woman who decorated her home with religious pictures which Santiago has kept on the walls, although he has put away her portrait "because it made him too lonely to see it" (16, 25; see Virgin of Cobre).

sardine. See bait.

*Scribner, [Charles] (Charlie). [American publisher, 1890–1952. Hemingway's publisher was the grandson of Charles Scribner (1821–1871), the founder of the publishing house, and the son of Charles Scribner (1854–1930), who became head of the firm in 1879 and founded *Scribner's Magazine* (q.v. in *TS*) in 1887. Charlie and Hemingway had a very friendly relationship over the many years of their association. Hemingway described him as "the best and closest friend that I had and it seems impossible that I will never have another letter from him" (Baker, *Letters,* 755). Charlie's son, born in 1921, took over the family's publishing house when his father died. Charlie had read *The Old Man and the Sea* but did not live to see it published.]

Hemingway dedicated this book to Scribner and to Perkins (q.v.).

shark. Shark and marlin are the town's principal catch. The town has a factory for processing shark (11), and for a time shark livers brought in such a good price that some of the fishermen were able to acquire motorboats (29–30). Santiago and the other fishermen drink the bad-tasting shark liver oil to strengthen their eyes and their resistance to cold (37). Sharks attack Santiago's huge marlin during the long afternoon and night as Santiago sails back to town. Fighting them off, he loses not only his marlin, but also his harpoon, his knife, his club, and part of his tiller. See also galano and Mako.

shovel-nosed shark. See galano.

*Sisler, [George Harold (Gorgeous George, the Sizzler). American baseball player, 1893–1973. Sisler was a fine first baseman and a batting champion, playing for the St. Louis Browns from 1915 to 1922. He was named the American League's most valuable player, the first player to be so honored when the award was established in 1922. In that same year a serious eye ailment forced him to retire. Sister returned to the game in 1924 but was never able to match his earlier performances. He was player-manager of the Browns until 1927, played with the Washington Senators in 1928 and with the Boston Braves until he retired in 1930. His lifetime batting average was .340. Sisler was elected to the Baseball Hall of Fame when it was established in 1939. In 1965 he was inducted into the Missouri Sports Hall of Fame and elected president of the International League (Minor Leagues). His parents were solid middle-class people; his father, Cassius, was the supervisor of a coal mine in Ohio.[16] George Sisler himself was, of course, a well-paid star.]

Manolín remarks that Dick Sisler's father had been a great baseball player and that he had never been poor (22).

*Sisler, [Richard Allan] (Dick, the great Sisler). [American baseball player, 1920—. Dick Sisler, son of the famous baseball player George Sisler (q.v.), played first base and outfield for eight years (1946–1953) for such major league teams as the St. Louis Browns, the Philadelphia Athletics, and the Cincinnati Reds. He played twice in the World Series. The young Sisler was in Cuba for winter ball from December 1945 until February 1946, becoming a national hero after an amazing hitting streak which culminated in a pyrotechnic two days: on the first day "he became the first player to hit a ball out of Tropical Stadium, 'the old ball park.' The ball cleared the outer fence and traveled at least 500 feet. On the second day, he hit three home runs in one game." For these exploits, Sisler received a medal from the Cuban government (Longmire, 96–98). Retired from professional baseball since 1953, he managed the Cincinnati Reds (1964–1965) and was also coach for the St. Louis Cardinals, the San Diego Padres, the New York Mets, and the New York Yankees.]

Manolín and Santiago, who admired Dick Sisler, regret that they had been too shy to invite him to go fishing with them (21–22).[17]

*sting ray. Thinking of DiMaggio's bone spur, Santiago mentions that he "never had anything wrong" with his heel except that it was paralyzed once when he was stung by a sting ray (104).

sucking fish. [The remora or sucking fish (*Echeneidae* family) is distinguished by a sucking disk on the top of its head, by means of which it can attach itself to large animals like whales and sharks or to the hulls of ships.]

Two yard-long gray sucking fish accompany the huge marlin (90).

terns. See *birds.

*the Tigers of Detroit (*Tigres*). [The Detroit Tigers, a professional American baseball team, have been associated with the American League since 1901. They won the League championship for three straight years, 1907–1909, and won the World Series in 1935, 1945, 1968 and 1984. In 1950 the Tigers "finished second . . . three games behind the Yankees" (Barbour and Sattelmeyer, 284).]
   Santiago chides the boy for his fears that this inferior team might defeat the New York Yankees (17).

tourists. A "party of tourists" comes to the Terrace restaurant. Due to faulty communication with the waiter (q.v.), the tourist couple who spot the remains of Santiago's marlin are left with the incorrect impression that the huge backbone is that of a shark (126–27, *tiburón* in Spanish).
   Speak: 126–27.

tuna. Manolín, who has been catching fish steadily, gave Santiago a couple of small tuna fish which the old man covers with sardines and uses as bait (31); with one of them he catches the huge marlin (41–42). On his first day out, Santiago catches a ten-pound tuna (39), part of which he eats the next morning (58–59). See bonito.

*turtles. Santiago has spent many years hunting turtles (14, 37, 71) in the waters south of Havana and off Mosquito Coast [the eastern coast of Nicaragua and easternmost section of Honduras, named after the Misskito or Mosquito Indians]. Although "turtle-ing" is hard on the eyes, Santiago suffered no damage and in fact has excellent vision (14 *et passim;* see endnote 11). He identifies with the turtles, as he does with many animals, claiming that his "heart . . . feet and hands are like theirs." He eats their eggs as he drinks the shark liver oil, to maintain his strength and stamina. He particularly likes two valuable species: the large green turtles [prized for their meat] and the small hawk-bill or hawksbill turtles [which yield valuable tortoise shell]. He feels sorry for the commercially worthless, large, inedible, yellow-spotted trunk back or leatherback turtle, and "had a friendly contempt" for the hard-shelled, large-headed loggerhead, with whose feeding and mating habits he seems familiar (36–37; he also knows turtles sleep on the surface of the water, 108).[18]

*Virgin of Cobre. [Cuba's patron saint. Hemingway donated his gold Nobel Prize medal to the shrine of the Virgen del Cobre, in Santiago de Cuba (Baker, *Life,* 528; for an unscholary account of some of the legends surrounding the Virgin, see Clark, 284–89). Cuba is rich in copper deposits, the Cobre (copper) mines near Santiago being the most productive. They first became famous during the 16th and 17th centuries, were abandoned for most of the 18th, and were re-opened early in the 19th. Cuba was the world's leading producer of copper for much of

the 19th century. Honest Lil's "blind faith" in the Virgin of Cobre is undercut by the death of young Tom (*Islands,* 279).]
Santiago's wife had decorated their shack with religious pictures, including one of this Virgin (16). Santiago swears "to make a pilgrimage" to the Virgin's shrine if he succeeds in catching the marlin (65).

waiter. A Cuban who works at the Terrace. He is unable "to explain what had happened" to the outsiders who visit the fishing village (126–27). The difficulty is not only linguistic, cultural or contextual; he himself may not understand the import of Santiago's experience.
Speaks: 127.

warbler. See birds.

*the White Sox of Chicago. [The Chicago White Sox, a professional American baseball team, have been associated with the American League since it was recognized in 1901. They were the first to hold the League championship (1901), and won the World Series in 1906 and 1917. Several White Sox players were involved in the 1919 scandal; those players convicted of deliberately helping the Cincinnati Reds win that year's World Series were banned from baseball for the rest of their lives. In 1950 this team "finished thirty-eight games out of first place" (Barbour and Sattelmeyer, 284).]
Santiago warns the boy against thinking that teams like the Chicago White Sox or the Cincinnati Reds could defeat the New York Yankees (17; see also *FTA*).

women. The narrative presents only one woman: the interested but uncomprehending tourist (q.v., 126–27).

*women. The narrative mentions two absent women: Santiago's late wife (q.v.) and Manolín's mother (13; see Manolín's parents). Santiago no longer dreams about women, not even of his wife (25).

*the Yankees. [The New York Yankees joined the American League in 1903, becoming the most powerful team in the major leagues for more than forty years (1921 to 1964). They were American League champions 29 times and won the World Series 20 times. At the time of the publication of *The Old Man and the Sea,* they were breaking their own record for straight World Series championships (four straight World Series wins, 1936–1939) by winning the World Series five years running (1949–1953).]
Santiago assures the boy that the New York Yankees "cannot lose" (17).

yellow jack. See bait.

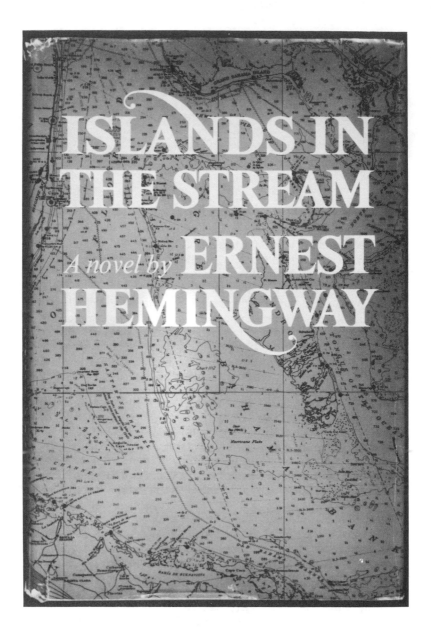

ISLANDS IN
THE STREAM

A novel by ERNEST
HEMINGWAY

Scribner dust jacket for the first edition of *Islands in the Stream* (courtesy Charles
Scribner's Sons, an imprint of the Macmillan Publishing Company; and of the
Hemingway Collection, J.F. Kennedy Library)

CHAPTER VIII

ISLANDS IN THE STREAM

(1970)

The novel was published posthumously from manuscripts edited by Hemingway's widow, Mary Hemingway, and the publisher Charles Scribner, Jr. It is organized into three titled sections. *Part I: Bimini* establishes Hudson as a disciplined, successful, twice-divorced artist whose sons arrive in late May, probably 1936 or 1937 (see Mary) for a five-week visit. The section ends with the death of the two younger sons and their mother in a car crash. *Part II: Cuba* shows a desperately unhappy Hudson, drinking and talking between submarine-hunting expeditions. We learn that a third marriage has failed and a third son has been killed. Hudson is no longer painting. The action takes place in Hudson's Cuban house and at the Floridita Bar, Havana, on 19 and 20 February, 1944 (see *Alerta* and Roosevelt). In *Part III: At Sea,* Hudson and his crew track and kill German sailors. Hudson is fatally wounded.[1]

Admiral. Peters' sobriquet for Thomas Hudson (421; see also 401).

*admiral. Hudson compares a long-whiskered shrimp to a Japanese admiral (209, cf. *ARIT* 193).

Alcalde (mayor), *Alcalde peor* (the worse mayor). See the politician; also see endnote 1.

Alerta. [Daily newspaper published in Havana, Cuba; founded September 1935. The stories about the Italian front indicate that the year is 1944, when the fighting at Anzio and Cassino dominated the headlines for February.]
Hudson reads *Alerta* and *El Crisol* (q.v.) at the Floridita Bar (258).

*Alexandra [Carolina Maria Charlotte Louise Julia. Danish princess, 1844–1925. In 1863 Alexandra married Edward, Prince of Wales.

Because the widowed Queen Victoria insisted on leading a secluded life, Alexandra and Edward became the leaders of English society both before and during Edward's reign (1901–1910). Alexandra was Queen Mother (i.e., widowed mother of the reigning monarch) from 1910 until her death in 1925.]

Bobby liked Queen Alexandra better than Queen Mary, the present Queen Mother, whose birthday is being celebrated as the novel opens (22).

Alfred. A wealthy man, he owns sugar plantations in Cuba (285), runs ''Alfred's Sin House'' and drives a sports car (284–85).

*Alice in Wonderland. [Alice's Adventures in Wonderland is a witty, philosophical exploration of games, imagination and language, starring a girl named Alice. It is the work of Charles Lutwidge Dodgson (1832–1898), English logician, mathematician, photographer, and novelist, better known by his nom de plume, Lewis Carroll. Both Alice's Adventures in Wonderland (1865) and Through the Looking-Glass (1872) were illustrated by John Tenniel (q.v.).]

Young Tom recalls a little girl he knew in Paris whose long hair reminds him of the heroine of Lewis Carroll's book as she appears in Tenniel's drawings (63). Audrey Bruce also reminds Roger of one of Tenniel's drawings (185).

*Anheuser [Eberhard, 1805–1880, and Busch [Adolphus, 1839–1913, his son-in-law, were the founders and developers of the conglomerate, Anheuser-Busch Companies, Inc., whose best known product is Budweiser beer. One of their most famous advertising promotions was the nation-wide distribution of a lithograph of Custer's last battle, which is mentioned in FWBT and THHN.]

During the shoot-out with the Germans, Willie and Hudson thirstily long for cold ''Anheuser Busch . . . in cans'' (459; also see Custer).

*Anna. The Hudsons' live-in nanny when Hudson and his second wife were still living together. The youngest boy, Andrew, spent his summers with her and her family when the older boys ''went west'' for the summer holidays, probably to Hudson's ranch in Montana (56; see also endnote 1).

Antonio. Hudson's mate and cook on the boat: he is a fine cook (366) and is, Hudson thinks, ''a much better sailor'' and even a ''better man'' than himself (396). Hudson delegates a great deal of authority to him, sending him out in the dinghy on several occasions. Antonio always behaves intelligently.

Speaks: 331–34, 349–50, 359, 369, 374, 386–87, 389, 395, 407, 409–13, 415, 419–20, 440–45, 461.

Ara. A wide-shouldered Basque whom Hudson admires and trusts. He discusses strategy intelligently (341), searches for evidence carefully (like Hudson, Ara looks for but doesn't find the hulls [i.e., spent shells] of the Germans' bullets) and reads it correctly: Hudson confirms Ara's judgment that the islanders have been dead about a week, that the surviving Germans are efficient and methodical, and that the water on the island is potable. Without the worry and doubts that hound Hudson, Ara arrives at the same philosophical position: there's not much difference between the enemy and themselves (357). Like Antonio, Ara plays a leading role in several forays in the dinghy, but in the final battle, he shoots a German who is surrendering (460) and thus invalidates the whole operation, whose aim was to take a prisoner for questioning (to obtain information, see 375 and 420). Ara "feels awful about it" and cries with remorse (462).

Speaks: 332–34, 345–46, 348, 355, 357–58, 362, 364–65, 367–72, 375, 380, 382, 384, 388–89, 392–94, 399, 402, 405–9, 416–19, 431, 433–37, 439, 465.

Archer, Fred (Freddy, Mr. Freddy). Lieutenant Commander, formerly stationed in the Far East and now attached to the American Embassy in Cuba. He speaks English, Tagalog, Cantonese, and Spanish. Archer knows that Hudson is engaged in submarine-hunting and is glad to see that he has returned safely from the latest expedition. He likes Hudson; they arrange to have dinner together (255–57), but both Hudson and the narrative forget this arrangement (see also *men and boys). Either he or Hollins (q.v.) leaves the message that Hudson is to report for duty (324).
Speaks: 255–57.

*Astor, John Jacob. [American businessman and inventor, 1864–1912. Astor was a descendant of the German-born American fur merchant of the same name (1763–1848) who was reputed to be the richest man in the United States at the time of his death. This first Astor bequeathed $400,000 for the founding of Astor Library, which consolidated with the Lenox Library and the Tilden Foundation in 1895 to become the New York Public Library. His son increased the family fortune through real estate dealings; he also contributed generously to the library. A great-grandson, William Waldorf Astor (1848–1919), moved to England and became the 1st Viscount Astor. The family established the philanthropic Astor Foundation. Colonel J. J. Astor, killed when the *Titanic* sank in May 1912, had assumed the management of the family estate in 1891. In 1897 he built the Astoria Hotel in New York, next to the Waldorf Hotel (built by his cousin William Waldorf Astor), the two luxurious hotels merging to become the Waldorf-Astoria. An inventor, J. J. Astor developed a bicycle brake and a turbine engine. During the Spanish-American War he donated a battery of artillery to the American Army and was commissioned a lieutenant colonel in the Volunteer Army, serving on General Shafter's staff during the battle of Santiago, Cuba, July 1, 1898.][2]

Complaining that he is tired of singing "Mama don't want no . . . " (q.v.) for the obnoxious yachtsman (q.v.), Louis offers another old song, about Astor and the sinking of the *Titanic* (14).

the *Atlantic Monthly.* [Founded in Boston in 1857, the *Atlantic Monthly* kept a high literary standard throughout its history. Although in its early years it reflected its New England origins, the *Atlantic* expanded its outlook and by the beginning of the twentieth century had become a national magazine, concerned with broad economic, social and political issues but always maintaining its somewhat conservative and literary orientation.]

On the fourth day after the deaths of his two younger sons and his ex-wife, Hudson fortifies himself with several drinks and reads good and bad articles in this magazine (200).

Audrey. See Bruce, Audrey.

*the Australian. Among his many wealthy friends in Hong Kong, Hudson counted an Australian (289–90; see the Chinese and Lawson; the foreman in *TS* pretends to be an Australian).

*Ayers. A married woman Roger Davis had been in love with in Paris. After a five-year relationship, he broke with her because he finally realized that "she's a phony" (98). Hudson had never liked her (99; see also *huissier*).

the baby. See children.

*Baby (Princessa). One of Hudson's many cats, an elegant Persian. She dislikes catnip (221) and, like Boise, refuses to sleep with Hudson when he is drunk (215).

*Balzac, [Honoré de. French novelist, 1799–1850. Balzac's attempt to present a comprehensive account of his society resulted in the massive *Human Comedy* (1833–1848), a collection of about 90 novels and novellas about a variety of characters from different strata of society. Individual characters and their social and psychological circumstances

are precisely described in such novels as *Eugénie Grandet* (1833), *Le Père Goriot* (1835), *La Cousine Bette* (1847), *Le Cousin Pons* (1847).]
Young Tom naively asks his father if they knew Balzac when they lived in Paris (68; see also *Droll Stories*).

*Barbara, Saint. [Third- or fourth-century saint, killed by her father for being a Christian. For this he was killed by lightning, and his daughter has become the patron saint of fireworks and firearms.]
When asked if a certain cat is a "witchcraft cat," the fisherman answers that the animal "never even heard of Saint Barbara" (211).

*the Baron. A titled, worldly older gentleman who traveled from Africa to Europe on the same luxury ship as the Prince, the Princess, and Hudson. The Baron, described as "really wicked" (226), always has "someone" in his cabin (223). He "knew" the Princess's mother (231) who was much more interesting than the Princess or her husband. He chides Hudson about his affair with the Princess and advises him not to continue the association (230–31). Hudson knows that the Baron has since died (232).
Speaks: 230–32.

bartenders. Alcoholic drinks are served in most Hemingway novels. The Floridita employs at least three bartenders; they mix generous daiquiris (282; see Constante, Pedrico, and Serafín). Both in Cojimar and in Bimini, the owner of the bar works as bartender (see also customers, proprietor, Saunders, and waiters).

*the basket-weavers. As he is driven past flower fields and "the houses of the basket-weavers," Hudson recalls that he needs to hire a basket-weaver to repair the large custom-made mat in his Cuban living room, which had been installed six months before the Japanese attacked Pearl Harbor (244, 205) and is therefore only a couple of years old.

*Batista [Zaldivar, General Fulgencio. Cuban military and political leader, 1901–1973. After the fall of the cruel and corrupt regime of Gerardo Machado (1871–1939; president and dictator, 1925–1933), Cuba had several figurehead presidents, but it was Batista who, as army chief of staff, ruled the island for most of the period between August 1933, when Machado was exiled, and January 1959, when Fidel Castro took power. Batista himself held the position of President from 1940 to 1944 and from 1952 to the end of 1958. When the growing corruption of his regime turned the people against him, Batista used the military to maintain his position and silence all opposition. See Machado in *THHN*.]

Hudson and the politician drunkenly toast all the current political leaders, including Roosevelt, Churchill, and Batista (299).

*Baudelaire, [Charles-Pierre. French poet, essayist, critic and translator, most notably of Edgar Allan Poe, 1821–1867. As a student Baudelaire became addicted to opium and infected with the venereal disease which paralysed and eventually killed him. He is best known for his first collection of poems, *Les Fleurs du Mal* (1857), several poems of which describe unsavory aspects of Parisian night life. Baudelaire was prosecuted for obscenity and blasphemy and the courts ruled that six poems had to be expurgated from the second (1861) edition. Baudelaire's prose works include his collected essays on art and literature (*L'art romantique* and *Curiosités esthétiques*), his notebooks (*Mon coeur mis a nu* and *Fusées*) and his extraordinary short story, "La Fanfarlo." He also wrote *Les Paradis Artificiels, opium et haschisch* (1860).]

Hudson accuses his wife of taking such a high moral stance that she would have prevented the creation of much art: if she had been married to Toulouse-Lautrec, Gauguin or Baudelaire, she would have kept them away from the brothels and night-life that were the subjects of their work (317–18).

*Bear, Firehole, Gibbon, and Madison Rivers. [The Bear River runs through Bear Lake county, southeastern Idaho, and into Wyoming. The Madison River runs north-south through Madison county, southwestern Montana. The Firehole River flows out of Midway Geyser Basin, Yellowstone Park, Wyoming, and runs into the Madison River, as Hudson indicates. Jack Hemingway reports that some mid-western streams are "of varying shades of brown due to the acidy bogs through which they flowed," and that "Several streams in the Madison drainage, including the Madison itself, have the same tint to a lesser degree, but for different reasons . . . the Madison drainage . . . includes the Gibbon and Firehole Rivers" (*Misadventures*, 57).]

When the color of Lil's drink reminds Hudson of the Firehole River, Hudson mentions several other American rivers of that area (277).

Beauty. One of Hudson's nicknames for his first wife (317; see Hudson, Mrs. Thomas). Henry also calls Lillian "beauty" (267, 269, 270). The nickname is also used in *GE*.

*Benítez, General. [Although Benítez is a common name and therefore difficult to track down, this is probably Manuel Benítez, "chief of the Cuban police, who had once played Latin lovers in grade-B Hollywood films" (Meyers, *Hemingway*, 368).]

General Benítez is the commander of a Cuban division which has been waiting to be sent into action in Europe. When Pedro reports that Benítez spends his time learning to ride a motorcycle, Hudson jokes that the division will be motorized (249; see also the soldier and Springfield).

Big Goats. See Goats.

*Big Harry. A fisherman who offered to become Suicides' suicide partner, but when Suicides (q.v.) finally killed himself, Big Harry was out crawfishing (157–58).
   Speaks: 157–58.

*Big-Hearted Benny. He took a drunken Eddy home after Eddy had been in a few fights on the night after David lost his big fish (146).

*Billingsley, Mr. [John Sherman (Sherm). American realtor and restaurateur, 1900–1966. Associated with the Stork Club from its opening as a plush speakeasy in 1929, Billingsley acquired a partial and eventually controlling interest in this New York nightclub after the repeal of Prohibition in 1933. He moved it to 3 East 53rd Street, furnished it elegantly, and made it the "in" spot for New York society. Billingsley courted the rich and famous for their publicity value: Walter Winchell, the syndicated gossip columnist (q.v. in *THHN*), had a permanently reserved table, and the richest and most prestigious patrons were seated in the elegant Cub Room and sometimes not charged for meals or drinks. Billingsley also generated publicity of his own by dispensing lavish and original gifts (expensive wines, pedigreed puppies, even cars) to favorite customers, and by occasionally and ostentatiously refusing admittance to some famous person for some trumped-up scandal. Billingsley managed his highly successful Stork Club from 1934 until his retirement in 1965.][3]
   Roger Davis doesn't want to offend Mr. Billingsley, from whom he would like to borrow money (101).

*Bitchy the Great. See Thanis.

Bobby. See Saunders, Bobby.

Boise (Boy). A big black and white cat with a silent purr (203), Boise is famous for his ability to suffer (233, 272). He seems to know that Hudson's work is dangerous and hardly eats when Hudson is out submarine-hunting. Hudson insists that Boise and he are in love (217, 271, 274–75), and indeed the cat seems to be Hudson's most intimate companion: he receives Hudson's confidences, shares his food, including such delicacies as mango and avocado (213), and sleeps with him.

Hudson loves the cat (208, 212) and the cat responds with a "desperate, hopeless love" (208) that has sexual overtones (238–39, 311, 316; see also endnote 1).

*Boise. [A light cruiser, commissioned in 1936 and completed in 1939. The *Boise* had a displacement of about 10,000 tons and carried over 800 men. She survived World War II and was transferred to Chile in 1947.] Hudson recalls that he and his son were given the kitten on "the first Christmas of the war" (209; 25 December, 1939 or, if Hudson is thinking of American participation in the war, 25 December, 1941; the reference to the Japanese admiral [209] ·suggests the later date). He named the kitten after the cruiser (204).

*Borgia. [Spanish-Italian noble family, known for their ambition, arrogance, and cruelty. Among the most notorious members of the family were the power-hungry and corrupt Rodrigo de Borgia (1431–1503), who became Pope Alexander VI (1492–1503); his illegitimate and cruel son Cesare Borgia (1476–1507), said to be the model for Niccolo Machiavelli's *The Prince;* and the beautiful Lucrezia (1480–1519), married three times before she was 21 and, as duchess of Ferrara, famous patroness of the arts. The Borgias practiced cruelty at home as well as abroad: accusations of fratricide, incest, and various types of treachery within the family abound.]
        Roger Davis attracts beautiful, cruel women, "Cenci or . . . Borgia types" (101).

*Bosch, Hieronymus [von Aeken, Flemish painter, c. 1450–c. 1516. Although records are scarce, Bosch seems to have belonged to a spiritual, ascetic organization called the Brotherhood of Our Lady, which argued that the pleasures and temptations of this world could only lead to damnation. Their moralizing mysticism is reflected in his complicated, intellectual art. Among his best known works are *The Hay Wain, The Temptation of St. Anthony, The Table of the Seven Deadly Sins* and *The Garden of Earthly Delights,* all of which are in Madrid's Prado Museum, which Hemingway visited often. Bosch's paintings are satirical, symbolic, and often grotesque.]
        When Bobby outlines wild, violent canvases for Hudson to paint, Hudson explains that the "old timer" Bosch had painted such canvases (21).

*Bosch, [Robert August. German engineer and industrialist, 1861–1942. In 1886 he founded the Bosch manufacturing company, which produced precision machines and electrical equipment, including the Bosch magneto and the Bosch lamp. Bosch, who held advanced social views, instituted an eight-hour working day in his firm and advocated free trade.]

When Hudson mentions the name Bosch, meaning the artist, Saunders strikes a comic note when he asks if Hudson means "The magneto man" (21).

Boy. Short for Boise (q.v.). Hudson's frequently used nickname for his cat.

*Braque, [Georges. French painter, sculptor, and illustrator, 1881 or 1882–1963. With Picasso, whom he first met in 1907, Braque is considered one of the founders of cubism. He is best known for his still-lifes. Hemingway owned at least one painting by Braque (Meyers, *Hemingway,* 166, 329); he saw several others when he visited Gertrude Stein, who was a great collector of modern art. See also *MF.*]

Hudson reminds young Tom of the many artists he knew as a little boy in Paris: the list includes Braque (71).

*Brooklyn Dodgers. [National League baseball team. The Brooklyn Dodgers were league champions in 1916, 1920, 1941, 1947, 1949, 1952, 1953, and 1955. They broke the color line in 1947 when they signed the great Jackie Robinson, the first black man to play in the major leagues. In 1957 the team moved to the west coast, becoming the Los Angeles Dodgers.]

Just as the Brooklyn Dodgers have scouts who travel widely to discover talented young baseball players, the Hong Kong millionaires have "scouts" who recruit beautiful young women for their many houses of prostitution (295).

Brown's Dock. [Jane Day writes that "Although the story takes place during World War II, the ambiance of the setting is Bimini in the mid-thirties. Some of the places mentioned in the text are real—the King's Highway, Commissioner's house, 'the old club that the hurricane blew away,' and Brown's dock" (24). Day errs about the timing of *Part I: Bimini,* the action of which does occur several years before World War II.]

Queen Mary's birthday is celebrated with fireworks on Brown's dock, Bimini. The celebrations end with a fight (29 ff.; see Captain Frank).

Bruce, Audrey (Audrey Raeburn). The beautiful young woman with whom Roger Davis intends to begin a new life. As a little girl, she used to visit Hudson's Paris studio with Dick Raeburn (q.v.); the back of her head appeared in several of Hudson's horse-racing pictures. She and young Tom share childhood memories of Paris (188–89). She claims

that as a girl she was in love with both Roger and Hudson. Now she has come to Bimini on a yacht and stays behind when her yachting companions depart. She is beautiful and reminds Hudson of his first wife (176, 183, 185; see also endnote 15). She and Roger Davis will live on Hudson's ranch (192) while Roger works on his new novel.
    Speaks: 172, 174–76, 178–91, 194.

*Bruce, Audrey's husband. Audrey is married to a rich "son of a bitch" (192). This is not the first time Roger Davis has moved in with a married woman (see Ayers).

*Bruce, Bill. The late stepfather of Audrey Bruce (185). Roger doesn't remember that Bill Bruce died (186). Audrey's mother is now Mrs. Townsend (q.v.).

*Brueghel, Pieter [the Elder. Flemish painter, c. 1525–1569. The Brueghel family's workshops were major centers of Flemish art for over a century. Pieter the Elder is best known for his vibrant, detailed landscapes and his witty presentations of peasant life. After 1560 he turned increasingly to satiric, didactic, and moralizing compositions, as in, for example, the famous "Triumph of Death" (1562). See also *FWBT*.]
    Hudson describes Brueghel as an "Old timer" who, like Bosch, painted violent, apocalyptical pictures such as the ones Bobby advises Tom to paint (21, 97).

*bullfighters. Hudson mentions that contemporary bullfighters practice with wooden rather than regulation metal swords, which are heavier, to avoid straining their wrists (249). For Hudson's other references to Spain, see *el Greco and *peasants.

Bwana M'Kubwa. [In Swahili, when one speaks of another person as *bwana,* the word means "'master, owner, possessor' of slaves, house, plantation or other property and generally 'great man, dignitary, worthy, personage'." As a term of direct address, the word means " 'master, Mr., Sir,' often *bwana mkubwa,* to show respect." The noun *mkubwa* means "superior, chief, manager, director"; it is a form of the adjective *kubwa,* "great, big, large, spacious, extensive" (*Standard Swahili,* s.v. *bwana* and *kubwa*). Harkey points out that "Africans use the compound *bwana makubwa* humorously at times, to suggest the absence of masterly qualities" (346–47).]
    Goodner refers to Tom Hudson as Bwana M'Kubwa (24).

the candidate. See the politician.

Captain Frank, Mr. Frank. Rupert's nicknames for Frank Hart (q.v.), adopted by several other people on the dock (31 ff). The song "Captain Frank in the harbor" (33–34) imitates a song about Hemingway, "Big Fat Slob," written by Nattie Saunders and a Bimini calypso band, just as Roger's fight on the dock (40–42) "is . . . reminiscent of Ernest's battle with Joe Knapp . . . publisher of *Colliers* and *McCall's* magazines" (Day 24, 23). Both the fight and the song are described in Hemingway's letter to Arnold Gingrich, 4 June, 1935 (Baker, *Letters,* 413–15) and by Fuentes (*Hemingway in Cuba,* 119). Hemingway's son Jack also recalls a song entitled "The big, fat slob's in the harbor; this the night we hab fun!" which celebrated Hemingway's "fine boxing matches" with the local strong men of Bimini (*Misadventures,* 27). A version of the song is published in the *South Florida History Magazine:*

> Big Fat Slob in the Harba
> This the night we have fun,
> Oh, the Big Fat Slob in Bimini
> This the night we got fun.
> Mr. Knapp called Mr. Ernest Hemingway
>   A Big Fat Slob
> Mr. Ernest Hemingway balled his fist
>   and gave him a knob.
> This the night we have fun.
> Mr. Knapp look at him and try to mock
>   And from the blow
>   Mr. Knapp couldn't talk.
>   At first Mr. Knapp thought
>   He had bills in stalk
> And when Mr. Ernest Hemingway walked
>   The dock rocked.
>   Mr. Knapp couldn't laugh
> Mister Ernest Hemingway grinned
>   Put him to sleep
>   With a knob on his chin (Day, 24).

Captain John. Rupert's nickname for John Goodner (29).

Captain Ralph. See Ralph.

Cartesian doubter. [The rational mathematician and logician René Descartes (1596–1650) claimed it was logically possible to doubt everything except the fact that one was involved in the act of doubting. He was thus able to prove his own existence: *Cogito, ergo sum* (I think, therefore I am).]
    Hudson describes his middle son, David, as "a Cartesian doubter and an avid arguer" (52–53).

*Cenci. [The wealthy Cenci family has a great reputation for sexual excess, cruelty, and murder. Count Francesco Cenci (1540–1598), the illegitimate son of a priest, had several illegitimate children, three stepdaughters, and twelve legitimate children, most of whom were as dissolute as he, and all of whom he seems to have abused. One son tried but failed to kill the father. According to some accounts, Shelley's among them, it was his daughter Beatrice who managed to kill Francesco; other accounts give the credit to his second wife, who was aided by several of the children. In any case, most of the family were arrested, tortured, convicted, and executed for the crime. The scandal is the subject of Percy Bysshe Shelley's tragedy, *The Cenci* (1819).]

Roger Davis' poor judgment where women are concerned got him involved with several women whose morals were like those of the Cenci (101).

*Cézanne, [Paul. French painter, 1839–1906. One of the greatest of the post-impressionists, Cézanne influenced many twentieth-century artists and artistic movements; he is considered a forerunner of cubism. Most of his landscapes depict his native Aix-en-Provence in the south of France. He often painted nude bathers, in pen and pencil, water colors, and oils. See also *GE* and *MF*.]

Observing his men bathing in the rain, Hudson is reminded of Cézanne's treatment of this subject (382).

the chauffeur. See Pedro.

*the chauffeur. Frank Hart taunts the yachtsman, claiming that his chauffeur takes care of him as if he were a child (36). When David and Andrew were killed in a car crash, Eddy speculates that a chauffeur, and not one of the victims, had been driving (195). An unnamed chauffeur drove Hudson, the Prince and the Princess to Damascus and back when their cruise boat stopped in Haifa (226).

Chief. Archer's sobriquet for Hudson (257).

children. Hudson's three sons figure prominently in Part I. One of the sea Indians carries her baby (409). See Thompson.

*children. Hudson recalls children playing in Paris (58; see nurses). The Princess (q.v.), ignorant about contraception, plans to pass off Hudson's baby as her husband's (228), but she did not get pregnant (232).

*the Chinese. [During much of its colonial history, Cuba imported Chinese as well as black African slaves to work the sugar and tobacco plantations. Importation of slaves from China had ceased by 1871, and slavery was outlawed in 1886. See also the Chinese in *THHN*.]

In *Islands in the Stream,* Cuban Chinese work at menial jobs. One unseen Chinaman works as Hudson's cook (218); Chinese grocers are mentioned (380), as are dead and wounded Chinese on a boat shelled by Germans (247). In Hong Kong, however, Hudson seems to have known only wealthy Chinese, including businessmen, generals (one of whom was an inspector of police), several pilots, and a policeman; they never revealed their names to him, only their initials (289; see also C.W.). Hudson also tells Lil, who wants to hear about his love life, about a gorgeous "emancipated" Chinese woman in Hong Kong who would not go to Tom's hotel or let him sleep at her house; they made furtive, uncomfortable love "in vehicles and conveyances" (290). Hudson also recalls sleeping with three other Chinese girls simultaneously (292–93; see also *women and girls).

*Churchill, [Sir Winston Leonard Spencer. English soldier, journalist, statesman, historian, and writer, 1874–1965. The young Churchill was a soldier and journalist in Cuba, India, Egypt, and South Africa before being elected to Parliament in 1900. As leader of the Conservative Party, Churchill served twice as Prime Minister: during World War II (1940–1945) and again in 1951–1955. Churchill wrote *Lord Randolph Churchill* (a biography of his father, 1906), *The World Crisis: 1916–1918* (4 vols., 1923–1929), *My Early Life* (1930), *Marlborough* (a history of his family, 1933–1938), *The Second World War* (6 vols., 1948–1953), and *A History of the English-Speaking Peoples* (1956–1958). He was awarded the Nobel Prize for Literature in 1953.]

Hudson and the politician drunkenly toast Batista, Churchill, and other current political leaders (299).

the clerk. Because the clerk's excessively thin moustache and plucked eyebrows offend Hudson, he simply walks past him and ignores the form the clerk proffers to all who enter the American Embassy in Havana, Cuba (253).

*Closérie des Lilas. [A café at 171, Boulevard du Montparnasse, which Hemingway frequented in the 1920s and wrote about in *MF* (the chapters entitled "A Good Café on the Place St.-Michel," "Evan Shipman at the Lilas," and "Birth of a New School"). In the garden attached to the café stands a statue of Marshal Ney (q.v. in *ARIT* and *MF).* See cafés in *SAR*.]

Hudson and young Tom reminisce about the café Closérie des Lilas (58).

*Cobb, Ty[rus Raymond (the Georgia Peach). American baseball player, 1886–1961. Cobb played for the Detroit Tigers (American League) from 1905 to 1927, during which time he established several batting records, most of which stood until the 1970s. His lifetime batting average of .367 has not been surpassed. Cobb was elected to the Baseball Hall of Fame in 1936.]

To disprove Andrew's statement that he cannot learn "things that are too old for me," David asks Andrew what Ty Cobb's lifetime batting average is. Andrew correctly states that it is .367 (65).

*Cocteau, [Jean. French poet, novelist, dramatist, critic, and filmmaker, 1889–1963. Among the best known works of this versatile genius are the plays *Orphée* (1926), *La machine infernale* (1934) and *Les parents terribles* (1938); the novel *Les enfants terribles* (1929); the long poem *L'Ange Heurtebise* (1925); and the films *Le sang d'un poète* (1932), *La belle et la bête* (1945), and *Orphée* (1950). Cocteau wrote several ballets and an opera-oratorio (*Oedipus Rex,* music by Stravinsky, 1927). In the 1950s he also painted frescoes in various French public buildings and chapels. Cocteau was interested in how classical myth, fantasy, religion, and the arts deal with the problems of human relationships and with the issue of death. He was an opium addict and a homosexual.]

Roger Davis explains to young Tom that he didn't get involved in the opium trade because he didn't want "to disturb" de Quincey and Cocteau, who had "done so well in it" (108).

colonel. See the yachtsman.

*the Colonel. An American officer who oversees Hudson's operations and to whom Hudson reports after each submarine-hunting expedition. Hudson does not look forward to seeing him (234, 240, 246, 253) because he thinks the Colonel might reprimand him for having gone out too far (206). The Colonel is not in when Hudson comes to the American Embassy but has left the message that Hudson is "to stick around" (254). When he sends Hudson out to track the Germans, he instructs him to bring back a prisoner for questioning (375, 420; see 452, 464 and Ara).

Colossus, Colossus of the North. [The Colossus of Rhodes was one of the seven wonders of the ancient world; hence, anything huge or gigantic.]

While drinking their sardonic toasts, Hudson, Lil and the *alcalde* drink against the imperialism of the United States, which they dub "the Colossus of the North." Because Hudson is a U.S. citizen, the *alcalde* calls him "Colossus," a title Hudson rejects (302).

*Columbus, Christopher. [Italian-born navigator and explorer, c. 1451–1606. With the support of the Spanish rulers Ferdinand and Isabella, Columbus made several trips to the New World, landing in the Bahamas, Cuba, Haiti, Puerto Rico, and several other Caribbean ports. He explored the Orinoco River in Venezuela.]
Hudson says that Cayo Romano is still "unspoiled," unchanged from Columbus' day (393). Hudson and Willie joke about Columbus (406–7).

Columbus boy. Hudson's sobriquet for Willie, who once read a book about Columbus and is now "an authority" on the explorer (407).

*the Commissioner. The police commissioner for Bimini "made some trouble" about Eddy's having a machine gun (86–87) and pointlessly investigated Suicides' death (158), which was obviously self-inflicted. He seems to be unpopular with the islanders, who urge Frank Hart to burn down his house (30–33).

*the Commissioner's family. Rupert distinguishes between the Commissioner, whom he would like to incinerate, and his "innocent" wife and children, to whom he intends no harm (33).

*the Constable. Bimini law enforcer. In contrast to the Commissioner, the Constable is a reliable, sensible, just, and therefore well-liked police officer. He protects blacks (12–13) as well as whites, believes Eddy's story about David's fish and protects Eddy from the disbelievers (146–47). He gives the Hudson boys permission to play their barside joke (163). Most important, he knows when to stay out of the way (32) and is interested in art: he has "an idea" for a painting he wants to commission from Hudson (151), whom he considers his friend (159).

*Constante. [Nickname of Constantino Ribailagua y Vert. Spanish-born Cuban saloon-keeper and bartender, immigrated to Cuba c. 1902, died 1952. He was the owner of the Florida or Floridita Bar (q.v.), at which Hemingway frequently drank. See endnote 1.]
Constante tends the bar at the Floridita (283), where Hudson imbibes many of his excellent drinks (215). His picture appears on the bar's promotional cards (309).

*the cook. An unseen Chinaman works as cook at Hudson's Cuban house (218). He cooks eggs which are given to Boise to eat (327). Eddy cooks for Hudson in Bimini, and Antonio cooks for Hudson's crew.

*Corydon. [The shepherd Corydon, celebrated by Theocritus and Virgil, has become a convention of pastoral poetry. Several authors have written poems or novels of this title: Hans Joachim Moser (1889–1967), Egon Fritz (1903—), Lucius Morris Beebe (1902—). André Gide's *Corydon* (1920) is an explication and defense of homosexuality. Taking the form of four Socratic dialogues, it argues that homosexuality is a biologically natural occurrence, caused by the greater sexual energies of the male and occurring in many species.]

Trying to recall the title of a book by Gide, David explains that he is not thinking of *Corydon*. Roger Davis supplies the missing title: *Si le grain ne meurt* (q.v., 179–80).

*countrymen. (Cuban peasants or farmers.) See *customers.

*the crazies. See *men and boys.

El Crisol. [Cuban daily newspaper, founded in 1934 and published in Havana.]

In February [1944], Hudson reads the war news [about the battle of Anzio] in *El Crisol* (258; see *Alerta*).

*Crittenden, Colonel [William L. American soldier, 1822–1851. Crittenden graduated from the U.S. Military Academy at West Point in 1845. His military service was spent in Texas, and he fought in the War with Mexico. He resigned from the U.S. Army in March 1849, and two years later sailed to Cuba on the ship *Pampero,* in the second of two expeditions organized by the Venezuelan-born freedom-fighter Narciso López to free Cuba from Spanish rule. The *Pampero* unloaded about 550 troops, most of them Americans, near Bahía Honda, Cuba, on the night of 11–12 August, 1851. The men were attacked by the colonial authorities and, lacking the support of the local citizenry, were soon defeated. According to some reports, Crittenden led the assault and, when it failed, he and his men were taken prisoner. Other reports indicate that Crittenden and a small contingent of about 50 men had stayed aboard the *Pampero* to wait for reinforcements and organize supplies and that, when they began to suspect that the incursion had been unsuccessful, they went ashore to investigate. In any case, Crittenden and his men were captured, tried, condemned to death, and shot. Crittenden himself was shot on 16 August, 1851, at the Castle of Atares, Havana Harbor. Narciso López's first expedition to Cuba, in July 1851, had also been unsuccessful.][4]

As he is driven from his home to Havana, Hudson identifies the sites associated with Colonel Crittenden and the unsuccessful American attempt to intervene in Cuba's affairs (246). Hudson also recalls more recent violence (see policemen).

*Crosby, [Henry Grew (Harry). American poet and publisher, 1898–
1929, by his own hand. Like Hemingway's character Frederic Henry
(*FTA*), Crosby had been an ambulance driver during World War I. In
January 1925 the wealthy young veteran (he was a nephew of the
financier J. P. Morgan, q.v. in *GE*) and his wife Caresse,[5] herself a poet,
established the Black Sun Press in Paris. They published elegant editions
of their own poetry, letters of Henry James and Marcel Proust (which
Harry Crosby had inherited), and the work of young writers like D. H.
Lawrence and James Joyce. Hemingway met the Crosbys at Sylvia
Beach's bookstore, Shakespeare & Company. Beach's description of
Crosby supports young Tom's claim that he "was always very very
nervous" (63). Beach wrote that the poet "used to dart in and out of my
bookshop . . . dive into the bookshelves like a hummingbird . . . or hover
. . . around my table" (*Shakespeare and Company,* 134–35). Crosby
drank heavily and took opium; he loved the sun, the color black, orchids,
the number thirteen, and all extravagance. Obsessed with death, he killed
his lover, the twenty-two year old Boston socialite Josephine Rotch
(Mrs. Albert Bigelow), and then committed suicide.[6] Black Sun Press
continued to publish until late 1936, being one of the longest-lived of
such expatriate-supported ventures. Crosby's last two books of poems
were *Transit of Venus* (for Josephine Rotch Bigelow) and *Sleeping
Together* (for his wife Caresse). His posthumously published diary was
entitled *Shadows of the Sun.*]
   Crosby was Tom Hudson's drinking companion in Paris. Young Tom
remembers Crosby and his long-haired little girl (62–63).

*Custer, [George Armstrong. American soldier, 1839–1876. A veteran
of the American Civil War, Custer fought against the Indians in the
territories for many years, winning a major victory against the Cheyenne
in 1868 and engaging the Sioux in battle several times. In 1876 he and
over 200 of his men were killed fighting the Sioux, who greatly
outnumbered them, at Little Big Horn. See Anheuser; see also Custer in
FWBT, THHN and *ARIT.*]
   The Germans remind Willie of Custer's embattled men (459).

customers. Various people stop off at Bimini and go to Bobby Saunders'
bar for a drink. We see two sailors drinking quietly (15, 21; see also the
yachtsman). A yacht arrives near the end of *Part I: Bimini* and its
passengers and crew drink at the Ponce, where they are treated to the
Hudsons' elaborate joke (152, 155, 164–75). Audrey Bruce describes
her fellow passengers as "good" but "dull as hell" (181; also see Hal).
Unnamed customers are also seen drinking at the Floridita, where most
of the action of *Part II: Cuba* takes place (305).
   Speak: 21–22.

*customers. Over the years, a great variety of men and women have drunk at the Ponce de León in Bimini and confided in Saunders their regrets about their mismanaged lives: he produces a humorous list (155). Saunders reports that riotous customers have overreacted to Hudson's realistic seascape, which hangs behind the bar: one tried to climb into a painted boat; another, upset by the waterspouts, threw beer at it (150–51). As Joseph remarks, "sometimes that trash comes in on yachts gets [Bobby] worn down" (11).

In *Part II: Cuba,* two flashbacks show the customers at Cuban bars in varying stages of intoxication: Hudson recalls the drunks at the bar in Cojimar on a Christmas morning several years ago (208), as well as the farmers and peasants, who dress up when they come to town, and the fishermen (q.v.), who don't (209). He also recalls the many and varied customers, Cubans and Americans, who drank with him (215).

Speak: 208, 210–11.

*C.W. One of the many Chinese millionaires, known only by their initials, who were Tom Hudson's friends in Hong Kong; they seem to be brothel-owners. Tom tells Honest Lil that once, when Hudson was very frustrated by the Chinese girl (see *the Chinese), C.W. surprised him with a gift of three beautiful girls, with whom Tom had a "wonderful" night (292–95). C.W. was eventually shot (295).

*Cynara. [The poem "Non sum qualis eram," by Ernest Christopher Dowson (English poet, 1867–1900), takes its title from Horace (*Odes,* 4.1) "in which the poet pleads with Venus to stop tormenting him with love since he is growing old and is no longer what he was when under the sway of Cynara . . . the girl he used to love" (Abrams, II: 1723, n.1). Dowson's speaker, however, seems to be a young man, driven to passionate excesses by his love for Cynara. The poem repeats the refrain, "I have been faithful to thee, Cynara! in my fashion" at the end of each of its four stanzas, as the poem's speaker tries to explain to Cynara, who seems to have caught him in the act, that he indulges in drink, food, dance, and prostitutes only in order to forget her. He insists that his debauchery is unsuccessful because he cannot stop loving her. "I was desolate and sick of an old passion," he says four times; his love for Cynara is always with him. The poem is said to have been inspired by Dowson's unrequited devotion for Adelaide Foltinowicz, the young daughter of a Polish restaurant keeper. Dowson led an "irregular life," his tuberculosis much aggravated by "Late nights and excessive drinking" (Abrams, II: 1722). The famous refrain of Dowson's poem is parodied by David Bourne (*GE* 204).]

Hudson insists that he doesn't love his current wife but is still in love with his first wife, with whom he has just made love. He cites his recent passionate behavior as evidence of his love for her, but she discounts the lovemaking, as the speaker of Dowson's poem discounts his, and paraphrases its refrain (316). Hudson does manage to convince young Tom's mother that he does love her, and not his current wife (316–17).

*Damon and Pythias. [When the tyrant Dionysius of Syracuse condemned Pythias (Pintias) to death, Damon pledged himself as hostage so that Pythias could be freed temporarily to arrange his affairs. Pythias returned, and Dionysius, impressed by their honesty and their faith in each other, released them both and begged to be their friend. They have since become a symbol of fidelity and disinterested friendship.]

The man who tried to seduce young Tom approached the subject of homosexuality through classical and Biblical references. He mentioned David and Jonathan as well as Damon and Pythias (179; see also Edwards).

*Danforth, Danforth anchor. [The American Robert A. Danforth and his nephew Robert D. Ogg developed the highly respected lightweight type anchor for which Danforth has become the generic name. Danforth anchors catch quickly, are very stable, and have great holding power. Two or three of these lightweight anchors are often used simultaneously, with long ropes or anchor lines to help stabilize the boat. Introduced in 1939, the Danforth anchor became popular during World War II.][7]

Hudson's well-equipped boat carries the recently-developed Danforth anchors. Hudson jokes that the anchor lines make the boat look like "a goddam spider" (359).

*Dante [Alighieri. Italian poet, philosopher, political thinker, and literary theorist, 1265–1321. Dante is considered the greatest poet of Renaissance Italy. Among his most famous works are *La Vita Nuova* (1292–1294) and *The Divine Comedy* (1308–1320), in which he describes Heaven, Purgatory, and, in great detail, the various discomforts and tortures inflicted upon the sinners who have been condemned to Hell.]

Sitting quietly in his luxurious stateroom on his way to France to claim the bodies of his two sons, Hudson recognizes that he is in hell, though his surroundings bear no resemblance to the place Dante described (197; see *ARIT*).

*David and Jonathan. [David the son of Jesse and Jonathan the son of Saul were devoted friends. Jonathan took David's part when Saul turned against him, pleading for David's life even though David's existence threatened Jonathan's own position as heir to the throne of Israel. David's beautiful lament for Saul and Jonathan is recorded in I Samuel 14, 18–31.]

Mr. Edwards, a Parisian homosexual who taught young Tom to play backgammon and who was hoping to seduce him, tried to explain homosexuality indirectly, mentioning David and Jonathan (179; see Damon and Pythias).

*[da Vinci,] Leonardo. [Italian painter, sculptor, architect, scientist, and universal genius, 1452–1519. Among his best known works are the Milan fresco *The Last Supper* and the oil painting *Mona Lisa.*]
    Tom recognizes that it is "silly" to wish that one could "draw like Leonardo" (97).

*Davis, David (Dave). Roger Davis's younger brother, who died at age eleven in a canoe accident which Roger survived (75). Hudson advises Roger to write about the accident and about his guilt feelings for having survived his brother (77).

Davis, Roger (Roge). Tom's oldest and best friend; their friendship dates back to their youth in Paris. Roger has one novel and several film scripts to his credit (see *The Storm;* see also 156). He is a dangerous fighter who almost killed one man in Hollywood (46–47; see *men and boys) and badly mauls another in Bimini (40–42; see the yachtsman). Like Tom, he has "behaved stupidly and badly with women" (98, 46; see also Ayers, Kathleen, Thanis and *women and girls). Unlike the disciplined Hudson, he "had thrown away and abused and spent his talent" (103), first as a painter (39, 76) and then as a writer, writing well-paid "junk" (76; see 71, 103). Unlike Tom, Roger does not avoid human contact: he loves Tom's children and guides David tenderly and expertly in his struggle with the big fish (110–11). Roger gets a new start at the end of *Part I: Bimini,* going to Montana with Audrey Bruce (q.v.) to write a serious novel (76). Hudson, who believes in Roger and whom Roger respects, encourages him to write about a traumatic accident in which his younger brother was killed (see David Davis).
    Speaks: 26–28, 30, 37–51, 54, 63–66, 68–71, 74–78, 87–88, 94–95, 98–103, 110–19, 121–26, 128–30, 133, 135–39, 141–43, 153–56, 158–60, 166–69, 172, 174–81, 183–87, 192, 194.

*Davis' father. Roger is under the impression that his father never forgave him for surviving the accident in which his brother was killed (75).

*the dealer. Most of Hudson's work is sold through a dealer in New York, who holds an annual show of his work. Hudson and his dealer keep in close touch through visits and letters (10); Hudson refers a potential customer to the New York gallery (173). Hudson's work is selling well and is well-received by critics and the art establishment (8, 17; see also paintings).

*de Mille, Cecil B[lount. Hollywood magnate, 1881–1959. De Mille produced and directed huge, popular movies, including *The King of Kings* (1927), *The Greatest Show on Earth* (1952) and *The Ten Commandments* (1923; remade with Charlton Heston in 1956)].

A former Hollywood scriptwriter, Roger jokes about himself, claiming that he is so "corrupted" that he can only write clichés. Outlining a hackneyed Hollywood plot, he introduces Cecil B. de Mille as a character (77).

*de Montfried. See *Montfried.

*Dempsey, Jack [William Harrison (the Manassa Mauler). American boxer from Manassa, Colorado, 1895–1983. In a surprise victory over Jess Willard, then reigning champion, Dempsey became world heavyweight champion in 1919; he lost the crown to Gene Tunney in 1926 and retired from boxing in 1928, although he fought many exhibition fights in the early 1930s. He served in the Coast Guard during World War II. Dempsey was 6' 1-1/2" tall. In 1912, when he began his fighting career, he weighed about 148 pounds; his weight during his heavyweight prime ranged from 187 to 194. Willard was taller (6'7") and heavier: his weight ranged from 235 to 265.][8]

Arguing that weight is not the determining factor in fighting, Hudson mentions that Dempsey won the heavyweight crown from a heavier opponent (236; see Willard).

*de Quincey, Mr. [Thomas. English writer, critic, and essayist, 1785–1859. De Quincey was addicted to opium from 1813 to the end of his life. Among his best-known works are the autobiographical *Confessions of an English Opium Eater* (1822; enlarged ed., 1856), in which he describes his addiction and its effects, and the *Autobiographic Sketches* (1834–1853).]

Roger Davis, reputed to write "vicious stories" (71), explains to young Tom that he didn't get involved with opium [in the physical and literary sense] because it was the province of de Quincey and Cocteau (108).

Devil. Hudson's nickname for his first wife (306, 326; see 344 and Hudson, Mrs. Thomas; the nickname is also used frequently in *GE* and *ARIT*). Andrew Hudson is described as "a devil" (53).

*the doctor. Hudson knows that doctors are not always ethical. He mentions to his ex-wife that he can obtain medical certificates from a couple of "good doctors" which will excuse her from her performance duties and thus enable her to spend more time with him (314). He recognizes, however, that doctors are necessary: he remarks that the mauled yachtsman needs a physician (42) and when he himself is wounded, he hopes to make it to a good doctor (463). Hudson's father was a doctor (see Hudson's family).

the doorman. He opens the car door for Hudson's ex-wife when she arrives at the Floridita Bar (305).

the driver. See Pedro.

*the driver. Young Tom repeats Davis' report that the writer Montfried (q.v.) would rely on the stars rather than on maps when instructing Parisian taxi drivers how to reach the address he wanted (107).

*Droll Stories. [Balzac's Contes drôlatiques (1832–1837) are lively, lusty, Rabelaisian stories containing much 16th-century language. See also Balzac and Gautier.]
    Young Tom admires Droll Stories and wishes he had been personally acquainted with Balzac, as he was with James Joyce, so that he could read the spicy stories to his schoolmates without getting into trouble with the headmaster (q.v., 68).

*Dumas, [Alexandre Davy de la Pailleterie (Dumas père). Prolific French dramatist and novelist, 1802–1870, famous for his multi-volumed historical novels, such as The Three Musketeers and The Count of Monte Cristo.]
    When young Tom points out to Roger Davis that his new novel contains a character who had died in an earlier book, Davis comments that Dumas had also resuscitated a deceased character (167).

*Eakins, [Thomas. American painter and sculptor, 1844–1916. Eakins is best known for The Gross Clinic (1875), a large painting which depicts medical students observing an operation. He often painted portraits of his friends engaged in outdoor sports such as swimming and boating. One such painting, Max Schmitt in a Single Scull (1871), shows the painter himself rowing a scull away from the viewer. Working in the realist tradition, Eakins emphasized accurate perspectives and anatomical details.]
    Observing the men bathing in the rain, Hudson thinks they should be painted by Eakins but then decides he could paint the scene himself (382–83).

Eddy. A native of Bimini, he works as Tom's cook/companion; he also keeps the fishing equipment in good shape (104–5). He is fond of Tom, the boys, and his job, which he does well. Like Roger Davis, he has a troubled past which he doesn't talk about and a tendency to drink and get into fights, as a result of which the Commissioner has forbidden him to have a gun on shore (86–87). Unlike the aloof Hudson, Eddy responds actively, immediately, and uninhibitedly to experience. He shoots the shark that threatens David, tenderly helps the boy fight the huge fish he has hooked and, when the line breaks, dives into the water after it (139). During that night's celebratory drinking, he brags about David's fish and indefatigably fights the many people who don't believe the story (146–47; see 153 and *men and boys). Eddy worries as actively as he does everything else: sometimes his worries about the boys and the "Bad things in the ocean" (80) keep him awake all night. Even so, "Eddy isn't tragic. . . . Eddy's happy because he does something well and does it every day" (161). Tom worries about him, admires and respects him (89). He is also momentarily jealous of David's admiration for Eddy (90–91). Hemingway's cooks are often superior characters: see Antonio; see also Juma in *GE*).
  Speaks: 80–89, 91–94, 104–6, 109, 111–13, 115–17, 119, 121–24, 127–28, 130–34, 136–41, 146–49, 158–59, 195–96.

Edward, Uncle. A handsome old black man (12) who is the subject of some of Hudson's paintings (17).
  Speaks: 12–13.

*Edwards, Mr. A Parisian homosexual who taught Tommy backgammon and then attempted to seduce him (179–80).
  Speaks: 180 (quoted, perhaps incorrectly, by David).

*Einstein, [Albert. German-born American mathematician and physicist, 1879–1955. Einstein formulated the general theory of relativity, for which he was awarded the 1921 Nobel Prize, and was perhaps the most famous scientist of his day.]
  To support their alibi that they are scientists gathering specimens, Hudson's men outfit themselves with machetes and "wide straw hats such as Bahaman spongers wear." The fellow with the biggest and therefore "most scientific" hat jokingly compares himself to Einstein (332).

elevator operator at the American Embassy in Cuba. He exchanges pleasantries with Hudson as he takes him up (253); Hudson later walks down the four flights of stairs (257).
  Speaks: 253.

Eugenio (George). One of the Basques on Hudson's crew, he is a minor character, briefly described (387). He goes with Antonio to interview the light-keeper (394–95).
    Speaks: 372, 387.

father. When the boys call Hudson "papa" one after the other, Roger Davis jokingly picks up the refrain and addresses him as "father" (54).

*fathers. See mothers.

*Fats (el Gordo). One of the many cats at Hudson's Cuban home (see endnote 1), so called because of his girth. He frequently fights with another one of the cats (Goats, q.v.), including one fierce fight while Hudson is gone (232–33). Mario is afraid that Fats will someday kill Goats (236).

*Firehole River. See Bear.

*fishermen. Hudson recalls Cuban fishermen he met in happier days, when his sons were still alive: he approvingly describes them as "unfishermanlike" but very expert and skilled professionals, and "cheerful, self-confident men" (208–9). One of them offered to give Hudson a cat and Tom invited him for a drink; they spoke Spanish together (210–11; see *customers). While stalking the Germans, Hudson correctly figures that they have commandeered a local fisherman (also referred to as "the guide" and "the pilot") to guide them through the dangerous keys (379–82, 385, 396). The husbands of the Indian women (q.v.) are fishermen (409). Thinking of them and of other fishermen like them, Hudson promises himself that he will send someone back to remove or disconnect the explosives rigged up on the Germans' turtle boat (454). Willie and Ara dismantle the explosives (464–65).
    Speaks: 210–11.

*fisherwomen. Hudson remembers fisherwomen in Marseilles (230).

*Flechtheim, [Alfred. German-Jewish art dealer and publisher, 1878–1937. The Flechtheim Galleries in Berlin and Dusseldorf showed and sold important contemporary art. Flechtheim founded *Der Querschnitt,* an irregularly published magazine devoted to modernist paintings, drawings and photographs. The magazine also published literary pieces, including Hemingway's story "The Undefeated" as well as some of his unimpressive poetry. Hemingway was proud of owning *Monument in Arbeit,* which he bought at Flechtheim's in Berlin in the late 1920s (Meyers, *Hemingway,* 215).]

When he was a young man living in Europe, Hudson bought Paul Klee's *Monument in Arbeit* at the Flechtheim Gallery in Berlin (238).

Flit. [Kenneth Johnston describes 1937 advertisements in the *Saturday Evening Post* featuring flit guns, soldiers, and dead insects. He identifies the "flit gun" as "a small, hand-pumped, insecticide spray gun" (" 'The Butterfly and the Tank': Casualties of War," 184, n.7). The flit was held in a horizontal cylinder at the front of the gun, perpendicular to the long neck of the gun. The flit was pumped out in a spray.]
Hudson has a Flit gun (383). He uses the trade name "Flit" as a noun (404) and a verb (370).

La Florida, la Floridita. [Roberts locates the restaurant La Florida at the corner of Obispo and Monserrate Streets, Havana. In the 1950s the restaurant was "One of the really fine places . . . Game, poultry and shellfish are specialties." Its bar, which has "a clientele apart from the restaurant . . . is famous for its Daiquiri cocktails, which many drinkers aver to be the best of the city" (Roberts, 246, 249). For an anecdotal history of the Floridita, see Fuentes, *Hemingway in Cuba,* 228–33. A brass nameplate and a wall-hung bust mark Hemingway's favorite place at the long wooden bar.]
Most of *Part II: Cuba* takes place in this bar.

*the flower-growers. Driving from his house into Havana, Hudson passes their fields (244; see also the basket-weavers).

*Flynn, Errol [Leslie Thomson. Tasmanian-born actor, 1909–1959. Errol Flynn was a popular American film star, projecting an image of rich, carefree gaiety. In private life he is said to have been an ineffectual, irritable drunk. He often played the sophisticated, romantic lead, or the swashbuckling hero in films such as *Captain Blood* (1935), *The Charge of the Light Brigade* (1936), *The Adventures of Robin Hood* (1938), *The Sea Hawk* (1940), *Gentleman Jim* (1942), and many other movies in the 1940s and 1950s. "Under the influence of Ronald Coleman, Clark Gable, and William Powell, small thin moustaches were popular" in the mid-1930s (Jenkins, *The Thirties,* 37). Flynn sported such a moustache in many of his movies.][9]
The effeminate clerk at the American Embassy in Havana gloats that not even Errol Flynn has a moustache as elegantly narrow as his (253).

*Ford, Mr. [Ford Madox Hueffer. English novelist, critic, historian, 1873–1939. Among Ford's many novels are the short but sophisticated *The Good Soldier* (1915) and the enormous *Parade's End* (1924–1928). Ford collaborated with Joseph Conrad in *The Inheritors* (1901) and

Romance (1903). He founded and edited *The English Review* (1908–1911) and edited the *Transatlantic Review* (1924–1925). Although Ford published the early Hemingway and invited him to work on the *Transatlantic Review,* their relations were not always friendly. Hemingway mocked the older Ford as being old-fashioned and unattractive. Ford, who had been gassed in World War I, had difficulty breathing; he wheezed. See also *MF* and *TS.*]

Young Tom remembers that when he heard James Joyce's claim that Ford was "mad," he mistakenly assumed that Ford was suffering from rabies or hydrophobia (63–64).

*F. Puss. [Feather Puss was Hemingway's nickname both for Hadley and for a cat they had in Paris. See also *MF.*]

F. Puss is a large cat who kept strangers away from young Tom when he was a baby in Paris (57, 61, 449).

Frank, Captain Frank. See Hart, Frank.

Fred, Freddy. An islander hired to serve drinks on John Goodner's boat, the *Narwhal,* which is moored at Bimini (24, 40). He may be the same character as Fred Wilson (q.v.), although Wilson seems older, more verbal, and more sophisticated than the servile Freddy.

Speaks: 24, 26.

*the Frenchmen. A group of Frenchmen had attempted to colonize the beautiful Cayo Romano but had been driven away by the swarms of mosquitoes which appear when the wind drops (393: see also *men and boys).

Friendless.[10] Former name of Hudson's cat, Goats (q.v.).

*Friendless' Brother. In spite of the name, Friendless' Brother is a female. An offspring of Boise, she and Goats, her brother, were the only two of Hudson's cats that would sleep with him when he was drunk (215).

*Furhouse. One of Hudson's many cats, Furhouse loves catnip (221; see endnote 1).

*the gardener. He had advised Mario to feed Goats lightly until the cat had recovered from injuries incurred in one of its frequent brawls with Fats (236; see servants).

*Garrick, [David. English actor, producer, poet, and dramatist, 1717–1779. Considered the greatest actor of his age, Garrick was famous for his portrayals of Richard III, Lear, Macbeth, and other Shakespearean characters. From 1747, Garrick was one of the managers of Drury Lane, redesigning the theatre (e.g., eliminating the apron and introducing footlights and sidelights) and making it one of London's most famous and profitable playhouses.]

Hudson compares himself to Garrick when his first wife teases him about his "great roles," and particularly his unconvincing performance as "the Faithful Husband" to one of his subsequent wives while visibly lusting after her (313).

*Gauguin, [Eugène-Henri Paul. French impressionist and post-impressionist painter, 1848–1903. As he developed his art, Gauguin turned away from his bourgeois background (he had been a banker) and from his society's materialism, abandoned conventional design, and turned increasingly to bright, often shocking color. Gauguin, who moved to Tahiti in 1891, was one of the first painters to be influenced by primitivism. Famous paintings include *Nava, Nave, Mahane* (1896), *The Yellow Christ* (1889), and *Where Do We Come From? What Are We? Where Are We Going?* (1897–1898).]

While he lives his tightly circumscribed and emotionally detached life in Bimini, Tom Hudson recalls and seems to share Renoir's puzzlement at Gauguin's need to move to Tahiti (7). Later he accuses his ex-wife of holding to a too-rigid moral code, claiming she would have prevented Toulouse-Lautrec and Gauguin from consorting with the women whom they painted (317–18).

*Gautier, [Théophile. French poet, novelist, journalist, and critic, 1811–1872. As a young man, Gautier devoted himself to the study of 16th- and early 17th-century literature, adopting some of the old-fashioned, extravagant language and impressing his elders with his erudition. Gautier became famous not only for his rich diction and fantastic, romantic poetry but also for his outrageous clothes and personal style. His fiction includes *Mademoiselle de Maupin* (1835), *Les Jeunes-France* (1833, a humorous exposé of the follies of young Romantics), *La morte amoureuse* (a ghost story), *Roman de la momie* (about Egypt, 1856), and *Le capitaine Fracasse* (1863, a picaresque novel, based on a 17th-century romance). His poem "Art" (in the collection *Emaux et Camées,* 1852) proclaims technical difficulty as the basic principle of art and defines his commitment to form rather than moral or intellectual content: art for art's sake. Gautier also worked as a journalist for thirty years. His *Histoire du romantisme* was published posthumously (1874).]

Young Tom, who has enjoyed *Droll Stories* and *Mademoiselle de Maupin* (qq.v.), wishes he had been friends with Balzac and Gautier, as

he was with Joyce, so that he could bring their racy books to school
without getting expelled (68–69; see also the headmaster).

*the general. The first Mrs. Hudson discreetly does not identify the
military man with whom she is involved (307–8, 316). Hudson gives
him the rank of general (447). Hudson's second wife is compared to a
general (6).

*the generals. See the Chinese.

George. The crew's nickname for Eugenio (q.v.) (372).

*George. [George III (1738–1820); King of England (1760–1820)
during the American Revolution. When John Hancock signed the
Declaration of Independence (1776), he wrote his name in large letters
and said that the King should be able to read *that* without his spectacles.]
    When the Hudsons are playing their elaborate joke in Bobby's bar,
Hudson offers to paint the novel Davis pretends to be unwilling to finish.
Roger joins the foolery, advising Hudson to "Paint it big enough so
King George can read it without his spectacles" (168).

the Germans (the Krauts). A group of sailors, the surviving crew of a
German submarine destroyed about ten days before the action of *At Sea*
(Hudson had been "faintly instrumental" in that operation, 356; see
353). The Germans killed nine villagers (civilians), burned their bodies,
and took their turtle boat and dinghies, hoping, so Hudson figures, to
reach German-sympathizers in Havana (427; see also 452) and thence
home. They also executed one of their own men (338). Another German,
taken prisoner by Hudson, dies of gangrene; he earns Hudson's admiration for his courage and integrity (see the prisoner). Of the eight or nine
Germans left, one is killed by Hudson's men when they board the turtle
boat (425–26). In the final shoot-out, at least four Germans and their
guide were killed, and another German, wishing to surrender, was shot
by Ara. The action of *Part III: At Sea* deals with Hudson's attempt to
catch up to and capture this group of German sailors.

*Gibbon River. See Bear.

*Gide, [André Paul Guillaume. French novelist and critic, 1869–1951.
Among his many novels are *The Immoralist* (1903), *Strait Is the Gate*
(1909), *Lafcadio's Adventures* (1914), and *The Counterfeiters* (1926). His
plays include *Bathsheba* (1912) and *Oedipus* (1931). He also wrote
Journals (1939, 1944, 1950), essays, and short stories, and was one of the
founders and editors of the influential journal *Nouvelle Revue Française*

(1909—). Gide championed the individual, arguing for independence from convention and tradition and for the validity of the individual's impulses, no matter how unusual. He rejected constraints but realized that unrestrained impulse can lead to madness and endanger both the individual and his society. At first condemned for his unconventional actions and fictions, Gide was finally recognized as a philosopher and moralist. He was awarded the 1947 Nobel Prize for Literature. See also *Corydon* and *Si le grain ne meurt*. Although deeply committed to his wife, Madeleine Rondeaux, whom he married in 1895, he was openly homosexual.]

When a homosexual approached Tommy, the boy mentioned that he had read Gide's autobiography *Si le grain ne meurt* and was therefore well acquainted with homosexuality, although he took "only an academic interest" in it (179–80).

Gil. A Basque on Hudson's boat, he has sharp eyes and serves as lookout while Hudson and his crew search for Germans. During the final battle, Gil accurately hurls grenades (456) and home-made bombs (brass fire extinguishers filled with explosives) into the Germans' hide-out (460). The heat of battle brings out the best in him, giving him "control" over his pitching arm (463). He dresses Hudson's wounds (459, 463).

Speaks: 348–49, 395–96, 405, 408, 410–14, 453, 455, 457, 461, 463–64.

G'Ning, G'Ning. Young Tom's nickname for himself when he was a baby (57).

G'Ning, G'Ning the Terrible. His parents' nickname for him (57).

Goats (Big Goats, Friendless). One of Hudson's favorite cats, he is a son of Boise. He is a feline hero, physically impressive and psychologically intact (217). Goats responds to the word "medicine" (214; see Seconal), fights with Fats (236), and likes to go for walks with Hudson (214).

Goodner, John (Johnny, Captain John). Like Tom Hudson and Roger Davis, he is a mainlander with a troubled past who now lives in Bimini: Goodner spent time in jail for having sexual relations with a minor (25). He invites Davis and Hudson to dinner and drinks on his boat, the *Narwhal,* and engages them in a humorous "theological discussion" (28). Although he is carefully described (23) and introduced as Hudson's and Davis' social and intellectual equal, he soon disappears from the narrative. [*Islands* was based on manuscripts which Hemingway did not see fit to publish during his lifetime. He may have intended to discard or to develop Goodner; we cannot know.]

Speaks: 23–29, 38, 43, 45.

el Gordo. Spanish name of Fats (q.v.)

governor. The Cuban candidate for mayor calls Hudson "Colossus" and "governor" (302). See the yachtsman.

*el Greco. [Pseudonym of Kyriakos Theotokopoulos, painter and sculptor, c. 1541–c. 1614. He was born in Crete but was active in Italy, where he was known simply as "the Greek." He came to Spain in 1576 or 1577 and, unable to get a court appointment, settled in Toledo. His highly individual style is noted for its emphasis on vertical lines, particularly in the elongated human figures, and, in the religious pictures, the almost mystical religious fervor. Although el Greco is noted for his portraits and religious paintings, the *View of Toledo* is among his most famous paintings. Late in 1949, before leaving for Europe, Hemingway went to the Metropolitan Museum where he particularly admired el Greco's *View of Toledo,* telling Lilian Ross that "This is the best picture in the Museum for me, and Christ knows there are some lovely ones" ("How Do You Like It Now, Gentlemen?" *The New Yorker,* 13 May, 1950; rpt. Weeks, *Collection,* 35). Another view of Toledo hangs in el Greco's home in Spain.]

Himself a painter, Hudson is obviously acquainted with el Greco's famous painting, *View of Toledo.* The Cuban countryside reminds Hudson of a section of Toledo he has seen himself, different from the view painted by el Greco (245–46).

*Gris, Juan. [Real name: José Victoriano González. Spanish cubist painter, 1887–1927. Soon after he came to Paris in 1906, Gris had become part of the group of intellectuals and artists who gathered in Picasso's studio. He is known mainly for his still-lifes. Hemingway owned his *The Guitar Player* and *The Torero,* which was the frontispiece for *Death in the Afternoon.* Gris' *Woman with a Basket* was chosen for the front cover illustration of Hemingway's posthumously published novel, *The Garden of Eden.*]

Gris' *Guitar Player* hangs in Hudson's bedroom in Cuba. He loves the painting because in it Gris had succeeded in representing nostalgia, which Hudson had "always tried to do," although unsuccessfully (237–38).

*guards. Hudson tells Lil about a Sikh guard in charge at the Women's Prison in Kowloon who would return to Hudson the pigeons which fell into the prison yard when Hudson shot them (287). He also recalls the guards in the gardens in Paris, whom he also associates with the killing of pigeons (60).

*the guide. See *fishermen.

*Gutiérrez, [Luis F.] (Pincho). [Cuban boxing promoter and manager. Gutiérrez managed the Cuban boxer Kid Chocolate, world welterweight (junior lightweight) champion (1931–1933) and featherweight champion (1932–1934). Gutiérrez worked as a sports commentator in Cuba in the 1940s and 1950s.][11]
The effeminate clerk at the American Embassy in Havana, whom Hudson disdains, smooths his plucked eyebrows and ruffled feelings and comforts himself with the thought that not even Gutiérrez's moustache is as narrow as his (253; also see Flynn).

Hal. One of Audrey Bruce's yachting companions, he was at the Ponce de León bar in Bimini when the Hudsons played the trick in which the boys pretend in various way to be the victims of drink and drunkards. As part of the joke, Bobby pretends to dislike the large canvas which hangs in the bar. When Hal offers to buy the canvas, Bobby insists that "There's no picture there" (170). After the trick is over, Hudson apologizes for their foolery and offers to buy Hal a drink. The persistent Hal tries unsuccessfully to buy a picture from Hudson (172–75, 181).
Speaks: 168–70, 172–75.

*Handley Page, [Sir Frederick. English aviation pioneer and airplane designer, 1885–1962. In 1909, Handley Page founded the first English aircraft company, Handley Page Ltd., which he managed for over forty years. In 1917 he produced a two-engine bomber which was successful although not produced in sufficient quantities to affect the course of World War I. Handley Page is credited with the invention of the "slotted wing," which allows a steeper, safer climb. He was knighted in 1942.][12]
Having flown into Kenya, the Prince and Princess are glad to sail back because the luxury liner would certainly be more comfortable than flying in "the Handley Pages" (225).

*"Happy Days Are Here Again." [Music by Milton Ager, lyrics by Jack Yellen; copyright 1929. The optimistic song, used in Roosevelt's election campaign, begins as follows:

> So long, sad times! Go 'long, bad times
> We are rid of you at last.
> Howdy, gay times! Cloudy gray times,
> You are now a thing of the past.
> 'Cause happy days are here again
> The skies above are clear again.

Let us sing a song of cheer again
Happy days are here again.][13]

Hudson noticed that this song was featured prominently in "funeral processions" in Hong Kong (289).

Harper's. [*Harper's New Monthly Magazine* was founded by James Harper in 1850 and managed by his brother Fletcher Harper. Under the editorship of Henry J. Raymond (1850–1856), *Harper's New Monthly Magazine* published mostly British authors, including Dickens, Thackeray, Trollope, and Hardy. When Henry M. Alden became editor (1869–1919), the focus turned to American fiction. In 1925 the name of the magazine was shortened to *Harper's Magazine* and it was and is commonly called just *Harper's*. See *TS*.]
By the fourth day after the deaths of his two younger sons and his ex-wife, a drink-fortified Hudson can concentrate enough to read *Harper's, The New Yorker, The Ring,* and *The Atlantic Monthly* (200).

Hart, Frank (Captain Frank, Mr. Frank). A banjo player (28), heavy drinker, and troublemaker. Although he has been cleared of some unidentified charge (33), he bears the Commissioner of Bimini (q.v.) a grudge and, with Rupert Pinder egging him on, shoots off a number of flares, some of them aimed at the Commissioner's house. Hart also incites Roger Davis to fight the drunken yachtsman. See Captain Frank.
   Speaks: 30–37, 40, 42–43.

*the headmaster. Young Tom's exegesis of the Molly Bloom soliloquy in Joyce's *Ulysses* was greatly appreciated by his fellow schoolboys but not by the headmaster, who threatened to expel Tom and to confiscate the book. Tom dissuaded his headmaster from both courses of action (67–68, 74).

*Henderson. Probably one of Hudson's associates or superiors in the submarine-hunting task-force (in *Part II*). When Hudson goes to the American Embassy to make his report to the Colonel, Hollins inquiries after Henderson (254).

Henry. A member of Hudson's crew, he is eager to serve in whatever capacity he can and to do his duty well. He performs both domestic and military duties competently but without distinction. Although he and Willie don't get along, he comes to admire Willie for his bravery (431).
   Speaks: 338–42, 344, 346–48, 360–61, 364, 369, 371–72, 374, 387–92, 399–400, 405–7, 419–21, 429, 431–35, 437–39, 451–52, 454, 457–58, 461–62.

*Henry's Sin House. Cuban house of prostitution which Willie and Henry Wood intend to visit (266); Henry Wood goes to Alfred's Sin House instead (see Alfred).

*Hershey, [Milton Snavely. American confectioner and philanthropist, 1857–1945. After building up and selling a successful caramel manufacturing business, Hershey began experimenting with chocolate. His factories produced many confections, including the famous Hershey chocolate bar and the distinctively-shaped and individually-wrapped Hershey's kisses. In 1903 Hershey bought land near Harrison, Pennsylvania, where he developed an entire community for the workers of the Hershey Chocolate Corporation, endowing and supporting its schools, local utilities, hospital, hotel, and museum. Hershey, Pennsylvania, boasts a beautiful park; the museum has a fine collection of Stiegel glass. In order to make himself independent of the sugar trust and to ensure a large and steady supply of sugar for his confections, Hershey established his own sugar refinery in Santa Cruz, Cuba, in 1916. He bought land, built a railroad and several mills and, as he had done in Pennsylvania, provided homes and medical facilities for the workers and a school for orphans. In appreciation of Hershey's large investments in its economy, Cuba honored him with a gold medal in 1924 and with the Grand Cross of the National Order of don Carlos Manuel de Céspedes in 1933, the latter being the highest award Cuba can bestow on a foreigner.[14] Hemingway was similarly honored by Cuba on his 55th birthday.]

While toasting national and local leaders, Hudson and the politician (q.v.) drink to Hershey's sugar-producing industry, the Central Hershey (299).

*Hitler, Adolf. [Austrian-born German politician, 1889–1945; chancellor and dictator, 1933–1945. Hitler was responsible for the murder of more than six million Jews during the course of World War II. He also arranged for the wholesale slaughter of gypsies, homosexuals, Catholics, Slavs and other groups of non-Aryans.]

Hudson and the politician drunkenly toast Hitler, Stalin, and other political leaders (299).

*H.J., H.M. See *C.W. and *the Chinese.

*Hogarth, [William. English painter and engraver, 1697–1764. Hogarth is best known for his social and political satires: *The Harlot's Progress* (1732), *The Rake's Progress* (1735), *Marriage à la Mode* and *The Election*. The famous *Gin Lane* woodcut (c. 1751) depicts the degradation and social decay that result from drink.]

On the drive from his house to the American Embassy, Hudson

reproves himself for not doing something to alleviate Cuba's poverty. Instead, he insulates himself from it by drinking "the way they drank in Hogarth's *Gin Lane*" (246).

Hollins, Mr. A Marine lieutenant stationed at the American Embassy in Havana. He is the warrant officer who tells Hudson that the Colonel is not in but that he has left instructions for Hudson to "stick around" (254). Later that day, Lieutenant Hollins tells Hudson's houseboy that Hudson should report for duty immediately (324). There seems to be some hostility between Hudson and Hollins: Hudson seems defensive about his civilian status, and the office-bound Marine probably resents Hudson's active involvement in war work. Hollins finds the Colonel difficult to work for (254–55).
    Speaks: 253–55.

Honest Lil. See Lillian.

Horseman. [A literal translation from the Spanish "caballero" (gentleman, noble, knight), which is derived from "caballo" (horse). Gregory Hemingway's book *Papa* alerted me to the family's translation of "caballeros" as "horsemen" rather than the more usual "gentlemen" (*Papa* 83).]
    Andrew Hudson, an excellent rider (53) whose triumphs with horses had been reported in newspapers (55), is called "horseman" by his brothers (57, 64, 133, 142, 160, 187).

houseboys. In Bimini, Joseph (q.v.) works as Hudson's houseboy. In Cuba, Hudson employs two houseboys. He is fond of Mario (q.v.). but the other houseboy is surly and Hudson, who does not like him, has fired him twice (233). This surly houseboy is the first person Hudson sees on his return home after twelve days at sea (232–33). See servants.
    Speaks: 232–33, 324.

*houseboy's family. The houseboy's father intercedes for his son and convinces Hudson to rehire the boy each time he fires him (233). See Mario's family.

Hudson, Andrew (Andy, Horseman). The youngest of Hudson's three sons, he is an "excellent athlete . . . marvelous with horses" (53); his ambition is to be a baseball pitcher (71). Tom Hudson thinks of him as "quite wicked" (53, see Devil). Andrew is afraid of the dark and of goggle-fishing. With his brother and mother, he is killed in a car crash (195; see endnote 1).
    Speaks: 54–57, 59–68, 70–72, 74, 78, 87–93, 95, 109–13, 119–21,

133, 137, 140, 142, 159–60, 166, 168–70, 172, 174, 176, 181–82, 185, 187–90, 193.

Hudson, David (Davy, Dave, Sport). Hudson's middle son is intelligent and fair, as admirable as Andrew is bad (52; see *Descartes). His older brother extols him as "the best of us" (125). David loves swimming and fishing (80). When a huge shark approaches him, he shows no fear. Later he hooks a huge fish and fights him bravely for about six hours (109–39), during which time he identifies with the fish (142), much as Santiago identifies with the marlin (q.v. in *OMS*). He understands himself (162) and his father's painting (163). With Andrew and their mother, he dies in a car crash (195). He seems to have a crush on his half-brother Tommy's mother (see endnote 15).
   Speaks: 54–57, 60, 62–68, 70–71, 73–74, 78–80, 87–93, 109–16, 119, 121, 123–24, 126, 131–34, 137, 139–43, 159–65, 168, 174, 177–83, 185–89, 193.

Hudson, Mrs. Thomas (Beauty, Devil, the girl). Hudson's first wife, the mother of young Tom, is a very beautiful actress (183, 311).[15] In *Part I* she is reported to be filming in France (6); in *Part II* she is engaged in war work, entertaining troops for the United Service Organizations (USO). She appears unexpectedly and, although she is currently involved "with someone" (307), she goes home with Hudson for a passionate reunion which is followed by the sexual jealousy and the bickering that originally wrecked their marriage (306–18). Hudson treats her tenderly and generously when he breaks the news of their son's death and takes his leave of her (319–27). He thinks of her early in *Part II* (220); later in that section he drinks heavily to blot out the death of young Tom and his other losses (282 *et passim*). In *Part III: At Sea*, he has changed tactics, abstaining from drink in order to keep her and his dead sons out of his mind (but see 383, 385, 447–50, and the dream sequence on 343–45). He not only thinks of her often (e.g., 238), but talks about her to the boys (57, 60–62, 65) and to Honest Lil (279–80). He knows he is still in love with her (7, 96, 98). See *huissier,* the general.
   Speaks: 306–27, 344–45 (dream sequence).

*Hudson, Mrs. Thomas. Although he admits her "good qualities" (6), Hudson generally dislikes his second ex-wife, the mother of Andrew and David, whom he divorced in 1933 (198). He feels that she makes plans for the boys without consulting him and forces everyone to adjust to her "unmalleable decision" (6). Hudson recalls her drinking and notes that while the boys visit Hudson, she buys clothes in Paris (6). David mentions his mother occasionally (64, 66, 163). She and her two sons are dead at the end of *Part I* (195).

*Hudson, Mrs. Thomas. Hudson reads letters from his third wife (203–5, 248), whom he married in the seven- or eight-year interval between *Part I* and *Part II*. Lil describes her as "very beautiful" but not the right woman for him (297). Hudson claims that he married her only because his first wife was in love with someone else (315); he tells his first wife that he doesn't love the current Mrs. Hudson (316, 317), who is now covering the war in the Pacific (307). He recalls her without affection (248).

Hudson, Thomas (Admiral, Bwana M'Kubwa, chief, Colossus, father, governor, Mr. Tom, Papa, Tom, Tommy, Tomás). [English portrait-painter, 1701–1779. Hudson was successful and prosperous, "the most fashionable portrait-painter of the day . . . true and faithful in his likenesses, but . . . without the necessary touch of genius to secure permanent fame." His subjects included the Duke of Marlborough, Handel, and George II. Hudson married twice: as a young man, he married the daughter of his teacher, and "in later life . . . a widow with a good fortune." A minor English poet by the same name lived in the 17th century (*Dictionary of National Biography*, X: 153–54).]

The central character of the novel is a successful middle-aged painter (see *the dealer), with a house in Bimini (3–4), a house in Cuba (192, 196, 203 ff), a ranch in Montana (8, 56, 102–3, 192; see Old Paint), and a boat (the setting for most of *Part III*). He is familiar with Spain (see *bullfighters, *el Greco, and *peasants), Africa (16; see *the Prince), and Hong Kong (286–95). His comfortable financial situation is largely due to his grandfather (see *Hudson's family), although his own work (mostly paintings of local characters and scenes) sells well. He is twice divorced and the father of three sons, all of whom are eventually killed. As a young man, Hudson seems to have fought in a war[16] and to have lived happily with his first wife and son (young Tom) in Paris. In *Part I,* divorced from her and from his second wife, he lives alone in Bimini, painting local scenes in the mornings and drinking and fishing in the afternoons. By exercising strict discipline (he saves the newspaper for breakfast, does not drink before noon, and works every day, even when the boys are visiting) he has been able to come to terms with loneliness. In spite of his emotional detachment, he is affected by the boys' visit and he expects to suffer greatly when they leave; when he hears the younger ones have been killed, he is devastated.

In *Part II* (February 1944) Hudson is separated from his third wife, living with servants and cats in a large house in Cuba and, instead of painting, patrolling Cuban waters in search of German submarines; the boat on which he had taken his boys fishing is now fully equipped for the anti-war effort (239, 256). Hudson is drinking heavily at the Floridita Bar, trying to come to terms with the recent loss of his son Tom (323, 418), shot down in Europe. In *Part III* he tracks the survivors of a recently-sunk German submarine, finds them, engages them in battle, and is fatally wounded, but not before he comes to understand that he, his crew members, and the Germans all make mistakes, all have moments of bravery and of weakness, and that finally there's no real difference between himself and the enemy who has shot down his son (356). See also *men and boys in *ARIT*.

Speaks: 9–11, 13–19, 21, 23–28, 30–31, 33, 35, 37, 42, 44–52, 54–63, 65–69, 71–84, 86–94, 98–99, 101–21, 123, 125–27, 129–32, 134–35, 138–56, 159–66, 168–69, 172–73, 175, 183, 190–92, 194–96, 203–5, 207, 210–14, 216–18, 220–45, 247–50, 252–57, 259–326, 331–34, 336–42, 344–55, 357–76, 380–82, 384, 386–403, 405–26, 429–45, 447, 449–63, 465–66; occasional short interior monologues.

Hudson, Thomas (Tom, Young Tom, Tommy, Mr. Tom, Schatz). Hudson's oldest son spent his early years in Europe (57), mostly in Paris where, with his father and Roger Davis, he was often in the presence of great writers and artists (71–72). He sounds improbably adult when he reminisces about his early childhood: he not only "remembers" a recipe for preparing leeks (65), but is prepared to write "my memoirs right now" (72). After such a stimulating childhood, school is boring (108). He is described by his father as "a happy boy" (52) and by himself as a worrier (114); his father recalls his son's earlier worries, about the return of the ice age and the extinction of the passenger pigeon (447). A flight lieutenant during World War II, young Tom flew Spitfires (q.v.); he was killed shortly before the beginning of *Part II*.

Speaks: 52, 54, 57–74, 87–90, 92–94, 106–9, 111, 114–15, 117–23, 125–27, 129–35, 137, 139–40, 159–60, 163–64, 167–68, 171–72, 174–76, 180–82, 184–89, 193, 210–12, 447.

Hudson's crew (the boys, the gentlemen, my mob). They usually gather at his house in Cuba before and after a submarine-hunting expedition (207, 233; see also 255, 257, 326). See Antonio, Ara, Eugenio (George), Gil, Henry, Juan, Peters, and Willie. Also see scientists.

*Hudson's family. Hudson's late father was a doctor. Hudson recalls pictures in his father's medical books (238) and hunting expeditions with him (417). The income derived from his grandfather's oil leases frees him from financial pressures and lets him enjoy a high standard of living (8). Hudson's mother is not mentioned.

*Hudson's women. See *women and girls.

Huff Duff. [American Air Force slang, during World War II, for a
high-frequency direction finder (from the initials H.F.-D.F.), or radio
radar.][17]

Hudson says that cats' whiskers and "that incrustation" on pigeons'
beaks work like the "Huff Duff" on radar equipment he depends on
during his night-time expeditions (239).

*the *huissier.* [French for the bailiff. *Black's Law Dictionary* defines *huissiers* as follows: "In French law. Marshals; ushers; process-
servers; sheriff's officers. Ministerial officers attached to the courts,
to effect legal service of process required by law in actions, to issue
executions, etc., and to maintain order during the sitting of the courts"
(874). In November 1926 Hemingway explained to Hadley, his first
wife, how the divorce process works in France: "a *huissier* would
serve me with demand to return to you—which if I refused would be
followed by a second service some months later—then we would both
have to appear for a formal refusal to reconcile . . . before a *juge
d'instruction* . . . and then you would be given a decree of divorce"
(Baker, *Letters,* 227). The wording on the original document indicates that, after Hadley had defined the marriage as happy and had
demanded that her husband resume conjugal life, the husband had
formally refused her summons. His refusal, probably spoken in the
first person, was written down in the third: Hemingway had said "qu'il
refuse de recevoir sa femme au domicile conjugal et la prie de le laisser
tranquille—qu'il le trouve très bien tout seul" (that he refuses to
receive his wife in the conjugal home and asks her to leave him
alone—that he does very well all alone). Hemingway was "Requés de
signer a déclaré vouloir le faire et il a signé" (requested to sign, which
he agreed to do and did; Hemingway Collection: Other Materials,
Divorce Papers).]

When Roger breaks up with Ayers, he and Hudson recall the
"formula" of the divorce process, including the sentences which one
must speak "to a *huissier*" (99).

Ile de France. [Large, luxurious French liner which made her maiden
voyage in 1927. In 1934, Pauline and Ernest Hemingway sailed back to
the United States on the *Ile de France* (after their trip to Africa). Late in
1949 Mary and Ernest Hemingway sailed to Europe on this boat,
returning to the U.S. on the same boat in 1950. In 1956, several years
after the action of *Islands in the Stream,* the *Ile de France* helped rescue
passengers from the *Andrea Doria,* which had collided with the *Stockholm.*]

At the end of *Part I,* the grieving Hudson sails to France on the *Ile de
France* (197–200).

Indians. Two dark-haired "sea Indian" women who live in a thatched hut on Cayo Guillermo tell Antonio that they saw a turtle boat recently and indicate its direction; they thus help Hudson and his crew track the Germans (409–10; see also 277, 432 and children).

*Indians. [The Ojibway or Ojibwa are a large North American Indian tribe now residing along Lake Superior and Lake Winnipeg; they speak an Algonquin language (see *TS*). The *yucatecos* are descendants of the Yucatecs, the Indian peoples inhabiting the Yucatán Peninsula. They spoke a Mayan language. The populations of the Caribbean are a mixture of European (from the Spanish conquistadors), African (from the slave trade), and Indian (from the local populations)—a mixture Lil identifies as *mulatos*. See also Indians in *FWBT*.]

Hudson and Lil mention Caribbean and North American Indians, like the *yucateros,* the Ojibway, and the sea Indians (q.v.) (277). After his years in Hollywood. Roger Davis worries that he can only think in terms of clichés, e.g., "the beautiful Indian girl" who needs to be rescued by the hero, prosaically named Jones (q.v.) (77; see *women and girls).

*the inspector of police. See the Chinese.

Joe. See Joseph.

John. See Goodner, John.

*Jonathan. The oldest son of King Saul. See David and Jonathan.

*Jones. [A common name. In 1536 the Act of Union of England and Wales decreed that the Welsh adopt English-style surnames. People called themselves after their place of residence (Hill), their professions (Baker, Smith, Tailor or Taylor) or, even more frequently, after their fathers. Thus, the son of John adopted the patronymic Jones, the son of David called himself Davis or Davies, the son of William took the family name Williams.]

Roger Davis, who has being writing Hollywood scripts, worries that now he can only think in stereotypes: the heroine is predictably "beautiful," the hero is named Jones (77; see also 'Old Betsy').

Joseph (Joe). Hudson's black houseboy in Bimini. He grew up with the Hudson boys and admires them without discriminating among them (10). He has varied duties: makes drinks for Tom, brings in the mail, picks up after the boys (51–52), takes them out fishing (74, 79, 84), reports when they wake up (148), sees to their bait (105), makes sure Hudson has enough tonic water (152), and carries the boys' bags out to

the amphibian plane that takes them away (193). He is among the first to hear that David and Andrew have died (195).
Speaks: 9–11, 49, 51, 89, 144–46.

*Josey. A friend of Louis, with a reputation for fine singing (14).

*Joyce, Mr. [James. Irish novelist and poet, 1882–1941. Joyce developed the technique of "stream of consciousness." Hemingway, who met and drank with Joyce in Paris in the 1920s, read and admired his work. Joyce is the author of *Dubliners* (1914), *Portrait of the Artist as a Young Man* (1916), *Ulysses* (1922), and *Finnegans Wake* (known as *Work in Progress* for many years before its publication as *Finnegans Wake* in 1939). Joyce's weak eyes required several operations; he wore a patch over his left eye.]
Like Hemingway, Tom Hudson and Roger Davis knew Joyce in Paris. Young Tom claims friendship with the famous author (64), describes him accurately (63), and mentions him often (63–70, 71–74). The Hudsons discuss *Ulysses* (66–68; see also the headmaster).
Speaks: 63–64.

Juan. A minor character, one of Hudson's crew on the boat (346–48).
Speaks: 348.

Jungle man. Covered with scratches and swollen from mosquito bites suffered while reconnoitering an uninhabited key, Willie jokingly refers to himself as "jungle man" (437); Hudson picks up the term (441, 460).

*Kathleen. One of Roger Davis' several girlfriends, she is beautiful but deeply flawed (100–2). She eventually commits suicide (156; see also Ayers and Thanis).

*Kerr, [Richard Henry (Dickie,] Dick). [American baseball player, 1894–1963. As a pitcher for the Chicago White Sox (1919–1921), Kerr pitched the third and sixth games of the 1919 World Series and, unaware that eight of his teammates had been bribed to lose the Series, he played to win. Even so, the White Sox lost to Cincinnati. When the scandal of the fixed World Series broke, Kerr's teammates were banned from professional baseball for life. During his three years with the White Sox Kerr won 53 and lost 34. He broke with the team over a salary dispute after the 1921 season; he was reinstated in 1925 but by then his pitching arm had lost much of its power. Kerr coached and managed for a few years; he also worked in the cotton business in Texas and Arkansas.][18]
Young Andrew Hudson, whose ambition is to be a pitcher, mentions

Dick Rudolph (q.v.) and Dick Kerr (71), great pitchers of the preceding decade whose names are unfamiliar to his brothers.

*Klee, Paul. [Swiss abstract painter, 1879–1940. Through color, form and space, Klee attempted to suggest the essential spiritual significance of material objects. He developed a new "language" in painting. Klee taught at the Bauhaus (1921–1931); his lectures were published in *The Thinking Eye* (1956). Hemingway bought Klee's *Monument in Arbeit* with the royalties from *FTA* (Meyers, *Hemingway*, 215); he took the painting with him to Cuba.]

Like Hemingway, Hudson bought *Monument in Arbeit* in Berlin and has it in his bedroom in Cuba. At first, the painting had seemed "corrupt" to Hudson and had frightened his wife, but now "he loved to look at it" (238).

*Knickerbocker, Cholly. [This was the pen name of two journalists. It was first used by Maury Henry Biddle Paul (1880–1942), who was the society editor of the *New York Evening Mail* (1918–1923), the *New York American* (1919–1937), and the *New York Journal-American* (1937–1942). But the Knickerbocker in *Islands* is probably Igor Loienaski Cassini (1915—), whose gossip column about the rich and famous was syndicated in more than fifty Hearst newspapers. This Cholly Knickerbocker was also known as the "Boswell of the Jet Set."][19]

Audrey Bruce had read Cholly Knickerbocker's report that Hollywood scriptwriter Roger Davis is preparing "to write a . . . great novel" (191; see endnote 1).

Kraut. [German for herb, plant, cabbage. English slang for German (pejorative).]

Hudson refers to the Germans (q.v.) as Krauts. Willie calls their language "Kraut" (442).

*Lawrence, T[homas] E[dward. British archaeologist, adventurer, and writer, 1888–1935; changed his name to T. E. Shaw in 1927. During World War I, Lawrence and other British officers were sent to help the Arabs in their revolt against the Turks. With Prince Feisal of Mecca, Lawrence led the successful Arab forces (1916–1918) and wrote of these experiences in *The Seven Pillars of Wisdom* (1926, 1935; the shortened version, *Revolt in the Desert,* appeared in 1927). His popularity with the Arabs led to his being called "Lawrence of Arabia." He is also mentioned in "Homage to Switzerland" (*WTN*).]

During his brief stay in the Middle East, Hudson was so involved with the Princess (q.v.) that he saw only "a small part of the Holy Land and a small part of the T.E. Lawrence country" (226).

*Lawson, Henry [Archibald Herzberg. Australian poet and short story writer, 1867–1922. Deaf from age 9 or from age 14 (reports differ), the child of an unhappy marriage, and an alcoholic by his mid-30s, Lawson extolled the endurance and heroism of people forgotten by society. His Australian slum- and bush-dwellers inevitably lose their heroic struggle against social and natural forces. Lawson's short stories are carefully constructed and display his command of Australian idiom and his "restrained, anti-climactic prose style" (*Penguin Companion to Literature: Britain and the Commonwealth,* 308). Collections of his stories include *The Country I Come From* (1901), *Joe Wilson and His Mates* (1901), *Children of the Bush* (1902), and *While the Billy Boils* (1896), which Hemingway owned (Reynolds, *Hemingway's Reading,* 148).]

Roger likes Lawson's "Australian stories," which he reads at Hudson's house (49).

the lepers. See *men and boys.

Lieutenant. See Hollins.

the Lieutenant. A suntanned, intelligent and "cheerful" Cuban (351) who runs the radio station at Cayo Confites and relays supplies to Hudson. He has seen through the official story that Hudson is conducting scientific research, and has also figured out that the turtle boats he had seen two days earlier were carrying Germans from the submarine that had been sunk ten days previously. On his own initiative, he has put his station in a state of defense. When Hudson offers to share supplies with him, the Lieutenant volunteers more information (352–54). He seems to have helped himself to some of Hudson's supplies, which were not offered to him (444).
Speaks: 351–54.

*the lieutenant. Hudson doesn't expect the lieutenant at Cayo Frances to make "any trouble" or offer any interference when Hudson stops off there to "get my orders" and unload the dead Peters (427).

Lieutenant Commander. See Archer, Fred.

*the lightkeeper. The lighthouse keeper works and lives on or near the inhospitable Cayo Romano. Antonio, who knows him, is commissioned by Hudson to ask him if he has seen the Germans or their turtle boat. Antonio reports that neither the keeper nor the old man has seen Hudson's quarry (386, 394–95; see the Indians; see also men and boys).

Lillian (Beauty, Honest Lil, Lil, Lilly). An aging, fat Cuban prostitute with a beautiful face and the proverbial heart of gold who is a general

favorite at the Floridita Bar (273). She proclaims that she has always been straight and honest, has never liked "piglike things" and has never had sexual dealings with women (276). Although Hudson hides Tom's death from her, she recognizes that he is unhappy and tries to cheer him up by insisting that he tell her happy stories and by offering to take him home with her. After many drinks and several stories, she seems to intuit the cause of Hudson's suffering (298). She cries easily (198).
    Speaks: 267–83, 285–98, 299–303.

*Lillian's husband. He was "difficult" and "crazy" (275).

Lilly. Nickname for Lillian, used once, by Willie, when he apologizes to her for having insulted her and made her cry (272).

*the lion-tamer. Young Tom recalls that the lion-tamer, his wife, Mr. Crosby (q.v.), and Thomas Hudson had a drink together in Paris (62; see Wahl).

*Littless. One of Hudson's many cats. All we know of Littless is that it likes catnip (221).

Louis. A black native of Bimini, hired by the yachtsman to go bonefishing. When the yachtsman gets drunk, he insults Louis and requires him to sing the same song over and over (14; see "Mama Don't Want . . ."). Louis feels sorry for the yachtsman's wife and tries to cheer her up by showing her conch pearls (13–15).
    Speaks: 13–15.

Lucius. A black islander standing in line in Bimini to give Captain Ralph his order for supplies from the mainland. When Hudson arrives with his shopping list, Ralph makes Lucius wait while he attends to Hudson. Both Ralph and Hudson call Lucius "boy" (149–50; see men and boys).

*Luger, [George. Austrian firearms developer, 1849–1923. Working for Mannlicher, Luger became known as an inventor. In 1896, he joined the newly established Deutschen Waffen- und Munitions-werke (DWM). In 1898, Luger invented a semiautomatic hand weapon that had a toggle-joint breech mechanism; on recoil after firing, this mechanism would open to receive a new cartridge from the magazine in its grip. The pistol was known as the Parabellum 1900 in Europe and as the Luger in the United States.]
    The bullets Hudson and Ara dig out of the dead villagers and the executed German are "9 mm Luger," equivalent to "our .38's" (338).

*Luque, Adolfo [(Dolf, The Pride of Havana). Cuban baseball player, coach and manager, 1890–1957. Luque pitched for various North American major league baseball teams, winning 194 and losing 179 with 28 saves in his twenty years in the National League. He was one of the game's earliest Latin American stars and "the first Latin American-born ballplayer to appear in a World Series game" (Porter, *Supplement,* 117). In addition to pitching, he coached for the New York Giants for several years and "served regularly as a winter league manager in Mexico and his native Cuba for three decades from the 1930s to the 1950s, developing such future major league stars as New York Giants and Brooklyn Dodgers pitching ace Sal Maglie and Cleveland Indians . . . infielder Bobby Avila [who in] 1954 . . . became the first Latin American to win a major league batting title. Luque remained an active pitcher in Cuba, recording his final CUWL game at the remarkable age of 56 in 1946" (Porter, *Supplement,* 118). Barbour and Sattelmeyer argue that prejudice kept Latin Americans out of managerial positions in the major leagues (285). Luque is discussed by Santiago and Manolín (*OMS* 23).]

When drinking toasts to various world and local leaders, Hudson and the politician at the Floridita include Luque (299).

*Lutecia. See Natera, Lutecia.

*Macbeth, Lady. [In Shakespeare's tragedy *Macbeth,* the ruthless Lady Macbeth incites her husband to regicide. Overcome by guilt, she sleepwalks in her nightgown and attempts to wash the imagined blood from her hands.]

When the pajama-clad yachtsman threatens Roger Davis with a gun, Davis coolly taunts him by comparing him to Lady Macbeth (45).

*Mademoiselle de Maupin. [Théophile Gautier's first and best-known novel (1835), written when Gautier was only 24 years old. In a long preface, the author attacks conventional respectability and, more particularly, the critics' prudery. The novel itself rejects the romantic ideal of pure love and espouses pagan eroticism. It presents the adventures of a heroine who rejects her traditional upbringing, dresses as a man, and goes out in search of adventure. She meets a poet, for whom she embodies the "ideal woman" he had longed for all his life.]

Interested in racy literature, young Tom reads Joyce in English and Balzac and Gautier (qq.v.) in French. He finds *Mademoiselle de Maupin* a challenge but is enjoying his rereading of the risqué text. He would like to show it to his teen-aged school fellows, but he realizes his headmaster (q.v.) would disapprove (68).

*Madison River. See Bear.

["Mama Don't Want No Peas An' Rice An' Coconut Oil." Popular song copyrighted in 1931 by Edward B. Marks Music. Lyrics by L. Wolfe Gilbert; music by Charlie Lofthouse (L. Charles). The song, "based on a traditional folk melody from the Bahamas," emphasizes Mama's great appetite for liquor and sex:

> When you're cruising down in Nassau by the sea,
> And you're all pepp'd up on gin and bacardi,
> Then you'll dance and sing all night
> Till the Island heaves in sight
> And you'll hear the natives sing merrily:
> Mama don't want no peas an' rice an' coconut oil (x 3)
> Just a bottle of brandy handy all the day.
>
> Mama don't want no gin because it will make her sin (x 3).
> She says it keeps her hot and bothered all the time.
>
> Mama complain she got a pain right across her chest (x 2).
> Mama complain she got a pain and there is a reason very plain.
> Because the food that Poppa gave her won't digest.
>
> Mama she likes the rum, it fills her soul with fun (x 3)
> And it makes her feel like whoopee all the time.
>
> Mama lay down last night to sleep she was feeling cold (x 3)
> So she said that Poppa must be getting old.
> Mama lay down to sleep last night she closed the door (x 2)
> Mama lay down to sleep last night and she closed her eyes so tight
> Then she said to Poppa "there is nothing more."][20]

Louis complains to Hudson that the yachtsman asks him to sing this song "Over and over." Louis offers to sing other old songs but the arrogant, drunken yachtsman is adamant (14).

*Manet, [Edouard. French painter, 1832–1883. Manet is sometimes called the father of impressionism. Two of his masterpieces, *Le Dejeuner sur l'herbe* (1863) and *Olympia* (1865), created a scandal when first shown. Manet's revolutionary style, a shocking departure from the realism which dominated French painting in his day, repelled most contemporary art critics but attracted painters like Pierre-Auguste Renoir and Claude Monet. He painted actresses, laundresses, absinthe drinkers, prostitutes, bullfighters, and other unconventional, contemporary subjects. See also *MF*.]

As a poor young artist in Paris, Hudson had earned the money for a used pair of shoes by painting the portrait of the proprietor of the Café Select "a little in the style of Manet" (448; see also *Select).

*Mannlicher, [Count Ferdinand of. Austrian weapons designer, 1848–1904. Mannlicher began his long association with the Austrian Arms Company in 1866, introducing more than 150 innovations and improvements to its various models. Among his important inventions are the straight-pull bolt-action design and the turning-bolt clip-loading system, both of which made possible a more rapid loading and firing of pistols and rifles. His breech-loading repeater rifle became an official weapon of the Austro-Hungarian Army in 1885. The .256 Mannlicher-Schoenauer is a small, full-stocked carbine used for shooting deer in wooded or alpine conditions. Although the arm was mass-produced, "it was beautifully made and supremely elegant," highly appreciated by sportsmen in Europe and in America. Mannlicher designed the rifle's action, and Otto Schoenauer "designed the complicated and expensive but extremely efficient rotary magazine used in the rifle." Schoenauer was the director of the Austrian Arms factory at Steyr, one of the largest in the world, where the rifle was made.]²¹

Hudson is proud of his well-worn, well cared-for .256 Mannlicher-Schoenauer, which is lovingly described (82). He fires it at the huge hammerhead shark which is headed for David but misses (82–83, 85). It is Eddy who kills the shark and saves David's life.

the Marine. See Hollins. Willie (q.v.) is a former Marine (394, 431).

Mario. The first houseboy, whom Hudson likes (233). Mario keeps track of all the animals at Hudson's Cuban house (232, 242), worries about them (236) and about Hudson (237). He also fetches the newspapers and the mail (233), takes messages (234), and mixes drinks (234, 240). See endnote 1.
    Speaks: 233–37, 240–43.

Mario's brother. Pedro and Hudson see Mario's younger brother as they leave the house on their way to the American Embassy in Havana (243).

*Mario's father. He seems to have found a job (233).

*Mary. [Princess Victoria Mary Augusta Louise Olga (1867–1953) had been engaged to Albert Victor, the eldest son of Edward VII and therefore Prince of Wales. When Albert Victor died of pneumonia in 1892, his younger brother George (1865–1936) became Prince of Wales and fiancé of Mary; they were married in 1893. As the Consort of George V, Mary was Queen of England (1910–1936). As the widow of George V and mother of George VI, "the present King Emperor" (22),²² she was Queen Mother from 20 January 1936 until her death. The fact that she is Queen Mother indicates that the events of the novel could not

have taken place before 1936. Her birthday was the 26th of May.[23] Janet
Flanner's Profile, entitled "Her Majesty the Queen," appeared in two
parts, in the May 4 and May 11 issues of *The New Yorker* magazine, in
1935, the year in which Mary and the already ailing King George V
celebrated the Silver Jubilee of their reign. The essay describes Mary's
history, personality, career, clothes and some of her jewelry, including
"three historical crowns" and her fabulous pearls, "some of the finest
known, including a rope that Mary, Queen of Scots, brought from
France, and which on her death Queen Elizabeth paid three thousand
pounds for. . . . There are also pearls given by Drake to Queen Elizabeth
. . . [and] two pearl earstuds of such size that one of her ancestors cut one
open with his sword to see if it was real." Another set of pearls includes
a necklace "which falls to her waist [and] contains about a hundred and
fifty enormous pearls" (Flanner "Her Majesty," Part I: 24). Flanner
does not mention conch pearls, but Mary was a gracious and diplomatic
queen and it is not unlikely that at some point she made the remark
Hudson attributes to her, perhaps in response to a gift of conch pearls.]

Mary's birthday is cause for much celebratory drinking (11, 22, 24,
30–32) and for the firing of flares and firecrackers in Bimini (32) [which,
like the rest of the Bahamas, was a British crown colony from 1729 to
1973, when it was granted independence]. Queen Mary is the only
woman Hudson ever heard of who likes conch pearls (14–15).

"Mary, Pity Women." [Poem by Rudyard Kipling (1865–1936) in
which a poor, uneducated, pregnant and probably unmarried woman
begs her lover not to leave her. The speaker of the poem addresses the
woman:

> What's the good o' pleadin', when the mother that bore you
> (Mary, pity women!) knew it all before you?
> Sleep on 'is promises an' wake to your sorrow
> (Mary, pity women!), for we sail to-morrow!
> (Kipling II: 284–85)]

Seeing his ex-wife's grief, Hudson is reminded of this poem's
suffering woman and wonders who wrote it. His wife identifies the
author as "Some bastard of a man" and rejects his offer to recite the
poem. Hudson leaves her a few minutes later to sail off in search of
the Germans who survived the sinking of their submarine (324).

*Masson, [André-Aimé René. French surrealist painter and graphic
artist, 1896–1987. Wounded in World War I, Masson was profoundly
affected by his wartime experiences. He settled in Paris after the war and
was influenced by the current interest in representing the unmediated

impulses of the subconscious. Like Gertrude Stein and others who practiced automatic writing, Masson was drawn to automatism and spontaneous painting; he was also active in the surrealist and abstract impressionistic movements. His work during the post-war years is turbulent, violent, and erotic. To avoid further contact with war, Masson left Spain, where he had lived since 1934, when the Spanish Civil War broke out; he went to the United States during World War II, not returning to France until 1945. His later work is less somber than the work of the 1920s. Masson was an officer of the Legion of Honor. Hemingway owned five Massons (Reynolds, *The Paris Years,* 173).]

Hudson owns and loves Masson's painting of the forest at Ville d'Avray, which hangs in his bedroom in Cuba (238).

*Mays, Carl [William ("Sub"). American baseball player, 1891 or 1893–1971. Mays pitched for Boston (1915–1919), New York (1919–1923, 1929), and Cincinnati (1924–1928). In his fifteen years in the major leagues, he won 208, lost 126, with 27 saves. He "excelled as a right-handed 'submarine pitcher'" (Porter, *Biographical Dictionary,* 392). He made history in August 1920 when one of his "fast-rising submarine" pitches accidentally hit Roy Chapman, who became the only major leaguer to die from an accident on the field.]

Peters tosses a grenade at the German boat the way Carl Mays pitches a baseball (424).

*Medici. [The powerful Medici family of Tuscany has produced a great many political leaders and patrons of the arts. Marie de' Medici (1573–1642) became Queen of France when she married Henri IV. After he was assassinated in 1610, she was regent for her son Louis XIII. During her regency she commissioned the architect Solomon de Brosse to build a palace reminiscent of the Pitti palace at Florence, where she had grown up. Built on land owned by the Duke François of Luxembourg, the palace and surrounding gardens today carry his name. Situated in these beautiful gardens, the Medici Fountain (1624) faces a long pool. Statues of the cyclops Polyphemus and of Leda and the Swan were added in the 19th century. Near the lake is a series of statues of the Queens and other illustrious women of France. Many other statues decorate the gardens.]

Hudson and young Tom recall their walks in the Luxembourg Gardens. On their way out of the gardens they would walk by the Medici Fountain, where Hudson sometimes killed pigeons (58, 60).

men and boys. The islanders who populate the background of *Part I: Bimini* are generally black and usually referred to as "boy," so that the word does not always signify youth. One boy teases Uncle Edward

(12–13), another is sent out for bait (104–5), other boys work in the radio shack (195), fish (28), and play pool (15). Many men and boys gather to play the guitar, sing, and drink during the Queen Mother's birthday celebrations (29 ff); they observe the fight between Davis and the yachtsman (qq.v.), after which some of them help the crew of the injured yachtsman carry him back into his ship (40, 42). Somewhat sobered by the violence, they then wander off, many of them going to Saunders' bar for a nightcap (43). Several weeks later, we see men and boys standing in line to pick up supplies that Captain Ralph has brought over on his weekly run from the mainland (149; also see Lucius); others lounge about and amuse themselves (150).

In *Part II: Cuba* we see several unnamed men drinking at the Floridita Bar (305; see also customers): Henry Wood drinks with two friends (270), one of whom likes "piglike things . . . in bed" (275). The black bathroom attendant at the Floridita studies Rosicrucianism (304; see Rosicrucian). Hudson passes a poor black couple as he is driven into Havana (247–48). Sections of Havana are populated almost exclusively by blacks: only the occasional white is seen (251). In the blowy February weather, unidentified people "looked cold" (252). In *Part III: At Sea* Hudson and his men see an old man out fishing (388). The lighthouse keeper describes this old man as talkative; he would have mentioned the Germans or their turtle boat if he had seen them (395; also see lightkeeper).

Speak and sing: 12–13, 33–34, 248, 304.

*men and boys. Several off-stage male characters are mentioned. In Bimini, an unseen boy reports to Joseph that Roger Davis has gone sculling (49); when Davis returns, he reports that he had also "sat around with some of the boys" (50). Andy mentions a black "boy" who will help him practice his pitching (70) and Eddy twice mentions the "boy" he has sent to fetch bait for the Hudsons' fishing expedition (104, 105). Hudson's sons recall the boys at school (67–68, 71, 74, 88, 108, 180). Hudson recalls getting "in trouble" with a man who witnessed the Hudsons' practical joke during which David plays the role of a drunk; the man apparently thought Hudson an unfit father (162). Hudson recalls another man, who advised him he could book a place on the luxury liner from Mombasa to Haifa to Marseilles (225). Mario reports that a man in the nearby Cuban village died after consuming bananas and rum (235) and nervously warns Hudson against the combination (237). At the American Embassy in Havana, Fred Archer twice mentions that he'd like Hudson to meet two new Embassy workers (256). Reminiscing about Paris, Hudson and Tom recall several unnamed, unseen Frenchmen: a roast chestnut vendor (62), a lion tamer in Paris (62), and men playing "bowling games" in the Jardin du Luxembourg (60). Outlining several large, apocalyptic paintings he

wants Hudson to paint, Bobby Saunders mentions black people, "rummies," devils, churchman, etc. in a scene of violent confusion (18–20; see
also *Titanic*). Other unseen violence: one local Bimini man had lost an arm
in "the last war" (22) and a man in California was severely injured by
Roger Davis (q.v.), in front of many witnesses (46–47, 184; Roger also
beats up the yachtsman, q.v.). Several local "fighting men" have fought
with Eddy (q.v.); other, even tougher men are expected to show up and do
the same (145; see also the veterans in *THHN*). In *Part II: Cuba* Hudson
recalls the crowd's interest in a gory murder case (see policemen and
*women and girls). He and Lil discuss inmates of the insane asylum and
leprosarium; Lil would like to see them (275). See also *customers,
fishermen and *Indians.
    Speaks: 245.

*Michelangelo [Buonarroti. Italian painter, sculptor, architect and poet,
1475–1564. This great Renaissance artist insisted on the nobility of the
individual human being. His most famous sculptures are probably the
David (1500–1504) and *Moses* (1513–1516). Legend (supported by
the book and movie, *The Agony and the Ecstasy*) reports that he painted
the frescoes on the ceiling of the Sistine Chapel in the Vatican
(1508–1512) while lying on his back on the scaffolding; the recent
restoration suggests that he painted standing up.[24] Michelangelo painted
the famous *The Last Judgment* (1534–1541), behind the high altar of the
Sistine Chapel, several years after completing the ceiling.]
    When the Hudsons are playing their trick in Bobby Saunders' bar,
Hudson offers to paint the novel that Davis claims he is unable to finish.
Roger jokingly advises Tom to "Paint it upside down like Michelangelo." The joke soon acquires sexual overtones (168).

*Milton, [John. English poet, 1608–1674. After ten years of problems
with his eyes, Milton became completely blind in 1652. His son died that
same year and his first wife early the next year, leaving him with three
young daughters, Anne, Mary, and Deborah, whom he seems to have
neglected and who, in turn, felt little affection for their despotic father,
objecting when he required them to take dictation or read to him,
services Milton also obtained from friends, servants, and secretaries.
Several paintings portray Milton dictating to his daughters, one of whom
is often pictured with a musical instrument at hand, to indicate Milton's
love of music. George Romney, the great English portraitist, painted
Milton and his Daughters in 1792. The next year Henry Fuseli painted
Milton, a painting which idealizes the daughter who stands, bathed in
light, writing (Fuseli painted a total of 47 paintings on subjects taken
from Milton, as well as several paintings based on Shakespeare's plays).
Eugene Delacroix's *Milton Dictating Paradise Lost to his Daughters*

(1826–1828), is a sympathetic, realistic presentation of a domestic scene, with flowers on the table and a painting, appropriately derived from Raphael's fresco, *The Expulsion of Adam and Eve from Paradise,* on the wall. Decaisne's *Milton,* which was exhibited together with Delacroix's painting, is known today from Leon Noel's 1830 lithograph: it presents the poet and his daughters in an outdoor setting. The Hungarian Mihaly Munkacsy painted Milton and his daughters in 1874; this "immense canvas . . . which hangs over the staircase in the New York Public Library, fairly crackles with hatred and resentment" (Wagenknecht, 121).[25] Milton is author of the poems *L'Allegro* and *Il Penseroso* (both written in 1632); the famous defense of free speech, *Areopagitica* (1644); *Paradise Lost* (1665), *Paradise Regained* (1671), *Samson Agonistes* (1671) and the sonnet "On His Blindness."]

As part of the Hudsons' elaborate joke, Roger Davis pretends to be drunk and young Tommy plays the part of the "patient and brave and long-suffering" youngster who tries to get him away from the bar so he can finish his novel. When Tommy warns Roger that continued drinking will deprive him of his eyesight, Roger retorts that if that happens he'll "dictate. Like Milton" (167).

*Miró, [Joan. Spanish (Catalan) surrealist painter, 1893–1983. Miró came to Paris in 1919 and affiliated himself with the Dadaists. In 1925 he exhibited with the surrealists and was acclaimed by the critic Bernard Dorival as "the best and perhaps the only great painter" of the group. When Paris fell to the Germans in 1940, Miró returned to Spain, then ruled by Franco; in 1947 he went to the United States. His paintings are abstract, full of bright color and humor. Famous canvases include *The Farm* (1922, bought by Hemingway in 1925), *The Tilled Field* (1924), *Dog Barking at the Moon* (1926), and *Women and Kite Among the Constellations* (1939). Miró is also noted for book illustrations, prints, tapestries, ballet designs, and two pairs of huge mosaic murals: *Night* and *Day,* and *Sun* and *Moon* (the latter pair at the UNESCO building in Paris).]

Hudson reminds young Tom of the many artists he knew as a little boy in Paris, including Miró (71; see also *DIA* and *MF*).

*Mister X, our friend. Hudson's and Lil's nicknames for Hudson's penis (273–74, 290–91).

*Montfried, Mr. [Henri] de. [Correct spelling: Monfreid. French writer, 1879–1974. His work is based on his adventures in Ethiopia and the Persian Gulf: *Les secrets de la mer Rouge* (1932), *La croisière du haschisch* (1933), *Le cimetière des éléphants* (1952), *Le trésor des filibustiers* (1961), and *Testament de pirate* (1963). Young Tom Hudson seems to have read the first two of these books; he could not have read the others, which were published after he was killed in World War II.][26]

Young Tom, who had read two of de Montfried's (*sic*) books, has heard that this author was involved in "the slave trade" and "the opium trade" (like de Quincey and Cocteau, qq.v.). Both Roger Davis and Tom Hudson had known him in Paris, where many stories circulated about this unconventional writer (107–8).

*Morris, William. [English poet, artist, craftsman, and socialist, 1834–1896. Morris designed stained glass, wallpaper, furniture, fabrics, and other household items. He and his friends established an association of craftsmen dedicated to fine workmanship and good taste in all aspects of daily life.]

To shock the visiting mainlanders, the Hudsons play a joke in which David plays the part of the reformed alcoholic (see Sport) and Andy pretends to drink lots of gin. As part of the elaborate joke, Tom Hudson, Roger Davis, and Bobby Saunders discuss a plan for manufacturing, bottling, and selling their own gin; by controlling all aspects of the design and production of their product, they would follow the principles set forth by William Morris (169).

*mothers and fathers. Goodner explains that young girls in California mature rapidly and "get hungry" for sex, and that a man might easily seduce or be seduced by an underage girl and end up in jail (hence the slang terminology, "jailbait" or "San Quentin quail" (q.v.), in reference to minors). Young girls all have "mothers and fathers or one or the other" to protect them (25–26) and prosecute the man—Goodner (q.v.) speaks from personal experience. For other mothers in the novel, see Mary, Mrs. Townsend, Willie's family, and the first two Mrs. Hudsons; see also Peters' grandmother. For fathers and grandfathers, see Bruce, Raeburn, Townsend, Natero Revello's family, Hudson, and Hudson's family.

*the mourners. See "Happy Days Are Here Again."

the *Narwhal.* [Goodner's cruiser is probably named after the narwhal, a small whale (order *Cetacea*) of the sub-order *Odontoceti* (the modern toothed whale). Its scientific name is *Monodon monoceros.* The male is distinguished by a single, straight tusk or tooth, which in medieval times was thought to be related to the tusk of the unicorn. This tusk, which seems to serve no useful function for the whale, grows to a length of almost three meters and is made of excellent ivory. The blubber of the narwhal yields oil, and its gray skin is sometimes used for leather.]

Johnny Goodner's big cabin cruiser, to which Tom Hudson and Roger Davis come to dinner, is called the *Narwhal* (22–29).

*Natera, Lutecia. Her husband Ignacio invites Hudson for lunch in her name (264).

Natera Revello, Ignacio. A thin, unattractive, inappropriately dressed Cuban (258) whom Hudson dismisses as "a snob and a bore" and "a rummy" (259–60). Natera, who has had a run-in with the American Ambassador (259, 262), is "edgy" (262). Drinking with Hudson and having to pay for all the drinks (he has bad luck rolling dice) doesn't improve his temper (259–62). Hudson tells Ignacio about his son's death but rejects Natera's trite and insensitive expressions of condolence (262–64), which include a garbled patriotic remark (263; Natera does misquote: he meant to say *Dulce et decorum est pro patria mori* [Horace, *Odes* 3.2]). Hudson also rejects Natera's invitation to lunch (264–65). See endnote 1. Speaks: 259–65.

*Natera Revello's family. When Hudson asks Natera if his name is Ignacio Natera Revello the third ("the turd"), Natera says that Hudson knows the names of all the Natera brothers, their father, and grandfather: "Don't be silly," Natera says, oblivious of the insult (260).

Negrita. An old but prolific black bitch of which Hudson is fond. He asks about her when he returns home and is told that she is pregnant again (232, 242; see endnote 1).

*Negrete, Jorge. [Mexican screen star, folk and pop singer, 1911–1953. Through his films, records, stage and television appearances, Negrete was well-known throughout Latin America.]
    The clerk at the American Embassy in Havana thinks that not even Negrete has a moustache as narrow as his (253; see also Flynn and Gutiérrez).

the Negro, Negroes. See men and boys; also see women and girls.

Newsweek. [A popular American news magazine, founded in 1933 and published weekly. Its column "Transition" reports deaths, births, marriages, and other milestones in the lives of famous people.]
    When Hudson reads the short obituaries of his two sons and his ex-wife in *Newsweek,* he feels that the newswriter regretted the boys' deaths (198; see also *Time*).

The New Yorker. [Sophisticated weekly, founded in 1925 by Harold Ross and published continuously since then. It publishes fiction, cartoons, and several regular features: "Goings on About Town" (a schedule of the week's events in New York), "The Talk of the Town," and "Profiles for the Nation." Lillian Ross's profile of Hemingway ("How Do You Like It Now, Gentlemen?" in the issue of 13 May, 1950) angered its subject. The profile of Queen Mary appeared in two parts, on 4 and 11 May, 1935 (see Mary).]

Hudson, who subscribes to this witty magazine, recalls a profile of Queen Mary in *The New Yorker* (15). Grieving for his sons, he cannot concentrate on the most recent issue, though after a few days and several drinks he finds that he can read and appreciate it (198, 200).

*Nokomis. [The U.S.S. *Nokomis,* originally named the *Kwaswind,* was a steam yacht built in 1917 for Horace E. Dodge and purchased from him that same year by the Navy for service in World War I: *Nokomis* served with the U.S. Patrol Squadron, protecting American troop transports en route to France by sea. After the war the 243-foot boat was converted into a survey vessel and used to survey Mexican and Caribbean waters; the *Nokomis* surveyed the north coast of Cuba, including several cays, the results being published in Hydrographic Office Charts 1311, 1417, 2625, and 5162. She was retired from the Navy Hydrographic Office in 1934 and decommissioned in 1938.[27] Nokomis was the name of Hiawatha's grandmother and nurse.]

Navigating the channel between the keys and the northern shore of Cuba, Hudson notes differences between actual conditions and what is described on the navigation charts (454).

*Normandie. [Built by Chantiers & Ateliers de St. Nazaire, Penhoet, France, the *Normandie* was completed in 1935. She was a large (83,000 tons), luxurious ship, with ten decks and a dining room which seated 1000. She was also fast: in 1935 she set the transatlantic speed record of just over four days. In 1936 she was enlarged and declared the largest ship in the world. In 1941 she was appropriated by the United States for conversion into a military transport, to be named *Lafayette.* On February 10, 1942, she caught fire in New York port from a carelessly handled acetylene torch; the water used to extinguish the fire made her so heavy that she turned on her side and sank partially. After efforts to raise and restore her proved impracticable, she was scrapped in 1946. Hemingway traveled on this elegant French liner when he returned to the United States from Spain in May, 1937.]

The windows of the bedroom in Hudson's house in Cuba remind his first wife of the *Normandie* (313–15, 327). Hudson, his first wife, and his second wife seem to have run into each other on this boat. Hudson recalls being upset about the fire on board the boat (313; see also *DS*).

*nurses. Hudson remembers the French nurses (nursemaids) watching their charges playing in the park (58). Young Tom recalls that the nurse who watched over him in Austria "was beautiful" (59). Andrew used to spend the summers with his nurse Anna (q.v.).

*Obispo. [Spanish for Bishop. The street was named for a Spanish bishop whose residence was on this street, "at the corner of the Plaza de Armas." Although the street has since been renamed "'Pi y Margall after a Spanish historian who had spoken up for Cuba," it is invariably called by its old name (Roberts 156).]
   Hudson orders his driver to drive down this street (252).

*officers. Hudson was friendly with several British officers in Hong Kong (290), among them a high-ranking officer in charge of supplying wolfram (tungsten) to the United States, where it was "of vital importance in our preparations for war" [i.e., World War II]. The wolfram was mined in Nam Yung in Free China and had to be transported over enemy or enemy-controlled territory on its way to the U.S. When Hudson pointed out to him that wolfram was plentiful in Hong Kong, from which it could be flown out safely, the officer "was not at all interested" (288).
   Speaks: 288.

*Ojibway. See *Indians.

*'Old Betsy.' [In American slang, the phrase refers to "a gun or pistol, specifically one's favorite gun" (*OED*, 2nd ed., 1989).]
   Roger Davis claims that as a writer he is "so corrupted" that he can only write clichés about a maiden in distress and a hero whose "trusty flintlock" is predictably named Old Betsy (77).

*Old Paint. A horse that used to throw David at the Hudsons' ranch in Montana, as a result of which David is now scared of horses (55–56).

Old Willie, Mr. Willie. Hudson's nicknames for Willie (q.v.) (431).

*the optometrist. After a few drinks, Natera Revello and Hudson discuss optometrists. Natera claims to know who are the "best" optometrists in New York and London (261). He is "a snob" (259).

*O'Reilly, [Alejandro. 18th-century Irish-born Spanish general. O'Reilly was sent by the Spanish Ministry of War to inspect and report on Spain's holdings in the New World. In 1763 he "commanded the Spanish forces that took over Havana when it was evacuated by the English" (Roberts, 156). In 1765 he inspected the fortifications and garrison of Cuba and Puerto Rico, ordering the remodeling and enlargement of El Morro fortress and the walls surrounding the city of San Juan. His major claim to fame lies in his having put down an anti-Spain rebellion in Louisiana. Louisiana had been ceded by France to Spain in 1762, but the French-speaking population of Louisiana resisted Spanish rule. O'Reilly arrived in New Orleans in 1769 with 3,600 troops, arrested the leaders of the revolt, executed five of them, and imprisoned the rest in Havana. Early in the 20th century O'Reilly Street in Havana was "one of the finest retail business streets."][28]

Hudson instructs his chauffeur to drive along O'Reilly Street (257).

*OSS, USO. [Each of these initialisms stands for several organizations, most of which are not relevant to the military or to World War II. In the context of the passage, OSS can stand for "Office of Strategic Services (World War II)" or "Office of Support Services (Army)"; USO for "Unit Security Officer" or, more probably, "United Service Organizations" (*Acronyms, Initialisms & Abbreviations Dictionary,* 509, 717). Jack Hemingway writes that when he transferred "to the 2677th OSS Regiment, provisional . . . nobody . . . knew what the letters OSS stood for. . . . I only learned then, myself, that it stood for Office of Strategic Services. Most people thought it had something to do with entertaining GIs, Special Services, or sports . . . the appellation so often applied to OSS staff personnel [was] 'Oh, so social!'" (127, 132).]

Hudson's wife identifies her unit as USO: Hudson mentions OSS (308).

*Paco. He owns or works at the Basque Bar. He and Hudson are the only ones who can convince Henry to eat when he's been drinking (265–66).

paintings. Hudson is a successful painter, whose work sells regularly and fetches a good price. He paints local characters and seascapes (17). Both before and after it is painted, Hudson and Bobby discuss Hudson's large canvas depicting three waterspouts, which is to hang in the bar at the Ponce de León (17–19, 150–51, 172; see also Hal). Hudson also plans and sketches two paintings of David's long but finally unsuccessful struggle to land his big fish (148, 153–54, 160–61, 163). He celebrates Andy's catch by painting a wahoo (193). Powerful, intelligent paintings can be frightening (17; see Edward and Mrs. Saunders). Hudson owns paintings by other artists (see Gris, Klee and Masson); they hang in his bedroom (237–38).

*paintings. The narrative mentions many unfinished paintings and recalls some finished ones. Hudson thinks he might paint his sons and Roger swimming in clear water (69–70). He recalls that he painted the first plover young Tom shot, and that the boy took the picture to school with him (446). He also remembers sketching young Tom asleep but the boy looked like the effigy of a dead knight and Hudson superstitiously did not finish the painting (446). After young Tom's death, Hudson offers Tom's mother his letters and any painting she chooses, including a portrait he had done of her (325; see also 219 and dealer). Hudson recalls that, to pay for a pair of shoes, he painted a portrait of the proprietor of the Café Select (q.v.) in Paris (448). Some of Willie's understanding and admiration of Hudson is revealed in his desire to buy one of his paintings (451). Constable has a "valuable idea" for a painting he wants Hudson to paint for him (151). Roger Davis also used to paint (76, 100; see 98).

Papa. Andrew, David, and Tom's name for their father, Thomas Hudson.

*Pascin, Jules. [Real name: Julius Pincos. Bulgarian-born painter, 1885–1930. In 1905, Pascin left Bulgaria for Paris, where he lived most of his life, spending the war years (1914–1918) in the United States and becoming an American citizen before returning to Paris in 1918. Pascin's subject was the underworld; he is best known for his bitter and ironic studies of prostitutes. His paintings show a troubled and cynical atmosphere. Pascin hanged himself in Paris, 1930, just before the opening of his important one-man exhibition. See also *MF.*]
   Pascin is another of the many painters Tom Hudson, Roger Davis, and young Tom knew in Paris. Hudson remembers Pascin as a fine painter with a penchant for wine, women, and drugs. He also remembers Pascin's joking description of young Tom as a "beer-swilling monster" and correctly reports that Pascin died a suicide (72–74).

*peasants. Hudson mentions that the peasants of the Spanish province of Extremadura (*sic;* see Estremadura in *FWBT*) can barely make a living off the land which, ironically, is rich in wolfram or tungsten, "needed for hardening steel" and therefore valuable (287–88).

Pedrico. A Cuban bartender with a peculiar smile (258), who serves Hudson, Honest Lil, Henry Wood, and the other patrons of the Floridita Bar (258–61, 267, 270). See endnote 1.

Pedro. Hudson's Cuban driver. Although Hudson dislikes and disapproves of Pedro, he recognizes that he is a skillful driver. But his real reason for not firing him is that Pedro has acquired so much information about Hudson's undercover war-time activities that he cannot afford to alienate him (244–45). When Pedro complains of the cold, Hudson gives him one of his son Tommy's sweaters (242). See endnote 1.
   Speaks: 241–45, 248–50, 252, 310, 326.

*Peirce, Waldo. [American impressionist painter, 1884–1970. An ambulance driver in France during World War I (he was awarded the Croix de Guerre), Peirce stayed in Europe after the war. He and Hemingway met in Paris and traveled together to Spain. Peirce painted the bulls and bullfights in Pamplona as well as landscapes, seascapes, and still-lifes. He also painted murals for several American government buildings. Some of his best-known works are *Circus at Night, Haircut by the Sea* (1933; it depicts Peirce's third wife, Alzira, and his twin sons and was purchased by the Metropolitan Museum of Art), and *Autumnal Weekend* (1945). His portrait of Hemingway is part of the Hemingway Collection, J.F. Kennedy Library.]

To Hudson's list of the great European painters he met in Paris, young Tom adds the American Waldo Peirce (71).

Peters, Mr. Peters. An incompetent radio operator who has been assigned to Hudson's boat because he can speak German (397), Peters is unable to make contact with the radio station at Guantánamo (340, 343; Guantánamo Bay in southeastern Cuba was a U.S. Naval Reserve) and ruins the boat's new radio (345, 369). He drinks heavily and Hudson and his crew mistrust him (419, 452). Towards the end of the sea chase he begins to joke (see next entry) and is killed when he, Hudson, and Willie board the Germans' turtle boat (425, 426).

Speaks: 362–63, 367, 400–1, 404, 421–24.

*Peters' grandmother. Because Peters' jokes involve his grandmother (421, 422), Hudson refers to him as "grandma's boy" (424). Willie also jokes about his grandmother (407) and his mother (421).

*Phelps, Miss. Imaginary secretary of Roger Davis, invented as part of the joke the Hudsons enact in Bobby Saunders' bar (167).

*Picasso, [Pablo Ruíz. Spanish painter, sculptor, and ceramicist, 1881–1973. Picasso was one of the founding forces of cubism and surrealism. His most famous works include *Les Demoiselles d'Avignon* (1907) and *Guérnica* (1937). Hemingway met him through Gertrude Stein. See Picasso in *MF*.]

Like Braque, Miró, and Pascin, Picasso is one of the many artists the Hudsons and Roger Davis knew in Paris (71).

pictures. See paintings.

*the pilots. The Germans' guide is also referred to as their pilot (419, 421). See the Chinese and the fishermen.

Pinder, Rupert. A very strong, tall, black islander, whose exhibitions of strength are still remembered years later (29). When Hudson and Davis have dinner with Goodner, Rupert sits with several other blacks on the dock, singing and drinking. He takes charge of the evening's activities, asking Goodner to supply drinks and urging Frank Hart to shoot flares at the Commissioner's house and burn it down (32–34). Although he "fancied himself as a fighting man" (29), he mainly incites others to violence.
  Speaks: 29–34, 38, 42–43.

*policemen. A Cuban policeman murdered and dismembered his ex-girl-friend. As Hudson is driven past the place where parts of her body had been found, he recalls the excitement engendered by the case (245; see endnote 1). Hudson recalls a wealthy policeman he knew in Hong Kong (289; see also the Chinese).

the politician (*alcalde peor,* the candidate). He is a cynical man who explains to Hudson the shady workings of the political mind, explaining why, for example, Cuban politicians always promise but will never provide the aqueduct which Cuba needs (299). The two men and Lil toast various politicians and well-known personalities, Cuban and foreign, as well as local rackets that enrich individuals and impoverish the general population. They then design a political platform for the politician, a platform which promises, among other things, improved levels of leprosy, cancer, tuberculosis, and syphilis for all Cubans. Honest Lil praises the politician, who is currently out of office (300).
  Speaks: 298–305.

*Ponce de León, [Juan. Spanish explorer, 1460–1521. Ponce de León established the oldest settlement in the Western Hemisphere, in Puerto Rico, which he governed from 1509 to 1512. He arrived in Florida in 1513, ostensibly searching for the Fountain of Youth, which according to some legends is in Bimini. Many buildings, streets, and neighborhoods in Latin America bear his name.]
  The Ponce de León (also known as Mr. Bobby's, Bobby's place, the Ponce) is Bobby Saunders' bar and hotel in Bimini. Both the drunken yachtsman and Audrey Bruce rent rooms at the Ponce de León (15, 192). The bar serves as a social center where messages may be left and information exchanged. Tom Hudson and Roger Davis visit the bar almost every day; the boys play their 'pretend-rummy' trick there (163–72). A large painting by Hudson hangs behind the bar.

*the porters. They brought Hudson's bags and magazines to his stateroom on the *Ile de France* (197).

*Pound, Mr. Ezra [Weston Loomis. American expatriate poet and critic, 1885–1972. Pound lived in London (1908–1920), Paris (1920–1924) and, for many years, in Italy, from whence he broadcast his anti-semitic and pro-fascist views. He was arrested for treason by the American forces during World War II, declared to be mentally incompetent, and hospitalized in a mental institution named St. Elizabeth's. Pound exerted a profound influence on twentieth-century literature, both with his own work and through the assistance he rendered to other writers, most notably Yeats, Eliot, Joyce, and Hemingway. Pound was an innovator, experimenting with meter, helping found the Imagist and Vorticist movements, and insisting that twentieth-century artists must "Make it new." He is best known for poetry: *Hugh Selwyn Mauberley* (1920) and the *Cantos* (1915–1940). See also *MF.*]

Pound is another of the many writers and painters whom Hudson knew in Paris in the 1920s. Young Tom had interpreted Joyce's remark that "Ezra's mad" to mean that the poet suffered from rabies, and had imagined Pound foaming at the mouth like a mad dog (63–64).

*the Prince. A pleasant, innocuous young aristocrat whom Hudson met in Nairobi. He and his wife and Hudson sail together from Mombasa to Haifa to Marseilles (225). The Prince plays cards late every night to avoid the Princess (q.v.), who tries to satisfy her desire for Hudson by increased sexual activity with her husband, to whom she wants to remain faithful (228).

Speaks: 225.

*the Princess. Hudson remembers his affair with a princess during a luxury cruise. Although she claimed to be in love with Hudson, she was unwilling to be unfaithful to her husband (see the Prince). Instead, she attempts to relieve her unconsummated passion for Hudson by nightly intercourse with her husband. Eventually she does sleep with Hudson, by whom she hopes to become pregnant (222–29; see *children). Hudson has also had affairs with some Italian princesses (222).

Speaks: 222–29.

*Princessa. [Correct Spanish spelling: Princesa.]

The servants' name for Baby (q.v.), one of Hudson's many cats in Cuba (221).

the prisoner. Willie and Ara find an injured German sailor, unable to travel and therefore abandoned by his fellows. They bring him aboard Hudson's boat, but he soon dies of his gangrenous wounds. Hudson is

impressed by the young man (362–63, 368–69). He gives orders for burial and marks the place on his chart (369).
Speaks: 363.

*prisoners. Hudson has been instructed by the Colonel (q.v.) to bring back a prisoner for questioning (375, 420, 452, 464). Although he tracks, finds, and defeats the Germans in battle, he fails to obtain a prisoner: Ara (q.v.) shoots a German who is trying to surrender (460).

*the proprietor. The proprietor of the bar in Cojimar, Cuba, speaks roughly to his drunken customers and gives the kitten Boise to Hudson (208–10; see also *customers and *Select).
Speaks: 208–10.

prostitutes. See whores.

*Pythias. See Damon and Pythias.

*quail, St. Quentin quail. ["Quail" is American slang for "a sexually attractive girl, especially one under the legal age of consent." Having sexual intercourse with such a girl could result in a jail term at San Quentin prison in San Quentin, Marin County, California.][29]
Goodner doesn't know all the details of Roger Davis' brush with the law, but he does know that Roger was not involved with "St. Quentin quail" (*sic*) or "jailbait" (25–26).

*Queen, Queen Mother. See Mary and *Queen Mary*.

Queen Mary. [British luxury liner, built in Scotland in the 1930s. The 81,000-ton, 975' long *Queen Mary* was launched from Clydebank in 1936 and was a new boat at the time of the action of *Part I: Bimini*. She is now docked and displayed at Long Beach, California.]
Saunders and Hudson, drinking toasts to celebrate Queen Mary's birthday, are appalled when a sailor from one of the yachts in the harbor defines her merely as "the one the *Queen Mary*'s named after" (22).

*Quentin, St. Quentin. See quail.

Raeburn, Audrey. See Bruce, Audrey.

*Raeburn, Dick. Audrey Bruce's father or stepfather (see also Bruce and Townsend). Audrey was fond of Raeburn, who used to bring her with him when he visited Hudson's studio in Paris. Young Tom remembers how Raeburn died (186–87).

Ralph, Captain. Captain of the boat that brings the mail, food, gasoline, and other supplies from the mainland United States to the island of Bimini and then transports the island's exports back to the States. Although many islanders are queued up to put in their orders, Captain Ralph attends to Tom Hudson first (149–50).
     Speaks: 149–50.

*Renoir, [Pierre Auguste. French impressionist painter, 1841–1919. Renoir broke with the impressionist movement in the 1880s; his later work is associated with the postimpressionists. He is especially famous for his studies of nudes and his pictures of women and children, including such masterpieces as *Madame Charpentier and her Children* (1878), *Bathers* (1884 or 1887), and *After the Bath* (1895). Except for trips to Algeria and Italy in the early 1880s, Renoir did not leave France. When he first became afflicted with rheumatism (c. 1890), he sought relief in the sunny, southern provinces, his visits to Aix and Marseilles becoming longer and more frequent as the disease advanced. In 1899 he moved south permanently; in 1907 he bought a house and property there.]
     Now that he is permanently settled in Bimini, Hudson has come to share Renoir's dislike of travel. Renoir, who always preferred to paint at home, could not understand Gauguin's going to Tahiti (7).

Revello. See Natera Revello, Ignacio.

The Ring [*:World's Foremost Boxing Magazine*. Established in New York in 1922 by American boxing expert Nathaniel (Nat) S. Fleischer (1888–1972) and published continuously since then, this monthly has a circulation of 200,000. It is now subtitled *World's Official Boxing Magazine*.]
     Traveling from New York to France to claim the bodies of his dead sons, Hudson reads several magazines, including *The Ring* (200).

Rodríguez, Mr. [Two Cubans by this name achieved fame as professional ballplayers in the major leagues in the United States: Antonio Héctor Rodríguez (Hec; born 1920) played one year with the Chicago White Sox in the American League (1952); he obtained 108 hits, including one homer, and 17 stolen bases in his one major league season. José Rodríguez (1894–1953) played three years with the New York Giants in the National League (1916–1918).][30]
     The handsome Cuban radio announcer, formerly "a gambler and . . .

ballplayer'' (309), admires Hudson's first wife, whose films he has seen.
He invites her, Hudson, and Ginny Watson for lunch; only Ginny
accepts the invitation (309–10).
  Speaks: 309–10.

Roge. Thomas Hudson's affectionate nickname for Roger Davis (76,
125). Wilson also addresses Davis in this familiar way (43).

*Roosevelt, [Franklin Delano. American politician, 1882–1945; 32nd
President of the United States, 1933–1945. Early in his Presidency
Roosevelt launched the New Deal and other plans for economic
recovery, including the Social Security Act and the Works Progress
Administration (WPA, 1935); he ended Prohibition. Roosevelt guided
the United States through World War II but died suddenly on 12 April,
1945; the action of the novel therefore takes place before that date (see
Alerta). He was the first president to run for a third term.]
  Hudson and the Cuban politician drunkenly offer a toast to President
Roosevelt and to other political leaders (299) in February (302).

Rosicrucian. [A secret religious, mystic society tracing itself to ancient
Egypt. Their secret symbols are said to include the rose, the pyramid,
and the cross (hence the name, although an alternative explanation is that
the society was founded or re-established by Johan Valentin Andrea
(1586–1654; he called himself Christian Rosenkreutz). Rosenkreutz
published *Fama Fraternitatis* (1614) and *Confessio Rosae Crucis*
(1615). It seems unlikely that the secret society would have had black
members in the 1940s.]
  The bathroom attendant at the Floridita Bar is studying a Rosicrucian
publication (304).

*Roy. Owner of a shop in Bimini that sells souvenirs and supplies (15,
29–30).

*Rudolph, [Richard] (Dick). [American baseball player, 1887–1949. In
the spectacular season of 1914, Rudolph was the most important of the
three pitchers who brought the Braves from last place in the National
League (July 11) to a pennant victory, after which the Braves defeated
the overwhelmingly favored Philadelphia Athletics in four straight
games in the World Series. Rudolph pitched the first and fourth games
of that Series, defeating Chief Bender (q.v. in *TS*) in the first game. His
record of 27 wins (12 consecutive games) stood as a Boston pitching
record for over thirty years. His team was nicknamed ''the Miracle
Braves'' that season. Rudolph was with the Boston Braves from 1914 to
1927, serving as coach for his last few seasons on the team and

becoming a manager and coach in the Eastern League after his retirement from the majors. He was only 5' 9-1/2'' tall.][31]

Taunted about his lack of stature, young Andrew Hudson, an aspiring pitcher, retorts that he will grow as tall as Rudolph and Kerr (71).

Rupert. See Pinder, Rupert.

sailors. Most of Bobby Saunders' customers (q.v.) are sailors. The Germans (q.v.) whom Hudson and the others track are sailors, the surviving crew of a submarine.

*Sande, Earl. [American jockey, 1898–1968. By 1918, Sande was ranked among the best jockeys of his time. He brought in 967 winners and was elected to the Racing Hall of Fame. In 1921, 1923, and 1927, he earned more money than any other jockey; during the course of his career he earned almost three million dollars. Sande began to work the racetracks in 1913 and rode his first formal race in 1917. He retired in 1928 to become a trainer but returned to racing in 1930, riding Gallant Fox to win the three-year-olds' competition; he won the Triple Crown victory that same year. Sande retired in 1931, returned to racing soon after, and retired again in 1932. The 1932 retirement lasted until 1953, when he came out of retirement for a brief period. At 5'6'', he was rather tall for a jockey.][32]

David teases his younger brother Andrew, who wants to be tall, that he will be short, like Earl Sande (71). The name of the retired jockey is supplied by Roger Davis (71).

Saunders, Mr. Bobby. The owner and bartender of the Ponce de León, he is an old friend of the Hudsons. His suggestions for a painting about waterspouts (17–20) result in a large realistic canvas which he hangs behind the bar (see *customers and paintings). He defends Eddy (147), whom he has known since childhood (151). He likes jokes and participates convincingly in the drinking trick put on by Hudson, Roger, and the boys (164–75).

Speaks: 16–22, 150–58, 165–66, 168–74, 194.

*Saunders, Mrs. Bobby. Bobby explains that he will hang Hudson's waterspout painting in the bar instead of at home because the painting would frighten his wife (17; he mentions her again, 173).

Schatz. [German for "treasure."]

Thomas Hudson's nickname for Tom, his oldest son (52, 59, 62; the same nickname is applied to the son in "A Day's Wait" in *Winner Take Nothing*).

*Schmeisser, [Hugo. German submachine designer. Hugo Schmeisser designed the 9mm MP 18/1 and the 9mm MP 28/2, both of which were out of production by the late 1930s. Because he was the only German submachine designer to obtain an international reputation, many machine pistols (submachine guns) were colloquially but incorrectly called Schmeissers by the Allies, even when the weapons were not of his design. The weapon which Hudson identifies as a Schmeisser is probably the widely used 9mm MP 40, which was the most common single type in German service. It was designed by Erma-Werke (Erfurter Maschinenfabrik). The only individual designer known to have been associated with it was Henrich Vollmer, who developed a telescoping main operating spring. During World War II Hugo Schmeisser was general manager of the Haenel factory, which subcontracted the manufacture of the MP 40, a mass-production development of the more expensive MP 38. By 1942, when brass and lead were in short supply, much German 9mm ammunition for machine pistols was loaded with sintered iron and packed in steel cases. Several varieties of such ammunition were developed, among them the Tombak plate iron-cored bullets, which were lacquered black to prevent confusion with earlier models, or with ammunition intended for use in pistols rather than in machine pistols.][33]

Hudson identifies the weapons used by the Germans whom he is stalking as Schmeissers (337, 426, 437–38). The bullets have black tips (336, 338), which makes them easily identifiable (337). The Germans' ammunition is packed "in a metal case" (426).

*Schnautz. The dog young Tom remembers the Hudsons had when they lived in Austria (59).

scientists. As they patrol the waters off Cuba, Hudson and his crew pose as marine scientists gathering data and specimens. Hudson himself is transparently disguised as a "painter of marine life for the Museum of Natural History" (316; see also 332–33, 352, 353, 359; see Einstein and Hudson's crew).

*Sebastian, Saint. [Roman martyr of the late third century. When the Emperor Diocletian learned that Sebastian was a Christian, he ordered him killed, The Emperor's archers, having shot Sebastian full of arrows, left him for dead. Sebastian recovered and was then beaten to death on Diocletian's orders. He is usually depicted in his martyrdom, his body pierced by many arrows and his eyes cast upwards. The Louvre displays two such pictures, one by the 15th-century painter Le Perugin and one by Andrea Mantegna (q.v. in *FTA*). His feast day is January 20.]

The expression on the face of Hudson's second houseboy (in Cuba) recalls St. Sebastian; the comparison is unflattering to both parties (232).

Seconal (the medicine). ["Seconal" is a sedative made by the Lilly
Pharmaceutical company; see "Quinalbarbitone Sodium," *Martindale
The Extra Pharmacopoeia*, 776–77. Hemingway's character Cantwell
also requires the soothing effect of this drug (*ARIT* 9).]
    A drunk Hudson takes a "big double Seconal" to prevent a hangover
(216).

*Select. [The Café Select opened in 1925 at 99 Boulevard du Montpar-
nasse. Its owner, Monsieur Select, "wore 'long melancholy moustaches
like Flaubert'" (qtd. in Hansen, 121).]
    When he was young and in need of money, Hudson had painted a
portrait of the proprietor of the Café Select, Paris, à la Manet (448; also
see paintings and proprietor).

Serafín. One of the bartenders at the Floridita, he is described briefly
(282). He encourages Hudson to break his drinking record (283) and
offers him food (281). See endnote 1.
    Speaks: 281–83.

servants. In Bimini, Hudson employs Eddy and Joseph (qq.v.). At his
Cuban house, he employs two houseboys (one is named Mario), a cook,
a gardener, and a chauffeur (Pedro). Except for Mario, the Cuban
servants are mostly unsatisfactory. See 212, 216, 218, 220, 221, 230,
323.

*servants. The Chinese woman in Hong Kong didn't want her servants
to know she was having an affair with Hudson (290–91).

*Shoenauer. Correct spelling: Schoenauer. See Mannlicher.

*Si le grain ne meurt. [*If It Die . . . An Autobiography*. Published in
1924, Gide's autobiography focusses on the events which preceded and
led up to his marriage to his cousin Madeleine Rondeaux in October
1895, when Gide was in his mid-30s. It includes accounts of his two
visits to North Africa (1893 and 1894), on the second of which he ran
into Oscar Wilde, whom he had met earlier, and Wilde's companion and
erstwhile lover, Lord Alfred Douglas, nicknamed Bosy; both Wilde and
Douglas picked up Arab boys. Wilde, who encouraged Gide to defy
convention and explore his suppressed homosexual tendencies, arranged
for him to spend a night with Mohammed, whose "perfect little body, so
wild, so ardent, so sombrely lascivious" left Gide "in a state of
passionate jubilation" (Gide, *If It Die . . .*, 289).]
    David describes *Si le grain ne meurt* as generally boring but re-
deemed by some "dreadful" (i.e., sexy) passages (180). As a young

boy, Tommy discouraged a homosexual by telling him that having read *Si le grain ne meurt,* he was well informed about homosexuality although he himself did not practice it (180; see Gide and Wilde).

*the Sikh guard. See guard.

*Sikorsky, [Igor Ivanovich. Russian-born American aeronautical engineer, 1889–1972. Sikorsky studied aeronautical engineering in Russia, Germany, and France; he moved to the United States in 1919 and became an American citizen in 1928. He worked for the United States Air Force and for Pan American Airlines, for whom he created the large, elegant Flying Clipper. In 1933 he established the Sikorsky Aero-Engineering Corporation, later a division of United Aircraft Corporation. His designs set several world records for altitude and speed. Sikorsky was a pioneer of the helicopter, on which he worked intermittently all his life. He presented one of his first models, which could hardly rise, to the Czar of Russia. In 1939 he produced the US-300, the first helicopter to have only one rotorblade, which was widely used during World War II. Sikorsky wrote *The Story of the Winged-S* (1941) and *The Invisible Encounter* (1947).]

The plane which transports passengers from Bimini to the nearby mainland is an "old Sikorsky amphibian" (193; see also Wilkinson and Wilson).

the soldier. A thin Cuban soldier stands in front of headquarters (248). Although there are signs that the Cubans are preparing to contribute to the war effort (see Benítez, Springfield), Hudson does not seem very impressed with their efforts.

*the soldier's wife. She has washed his uniform repeatedly (248).

sonny. See the yachtsman.

*Spitfire (Spitty). [A fast, highly maneuverable British fighter plane, developed during the 1930s and used in great numbers during World War II. The Spitfire was a single-seater with eight machine guns: the pilot flew and shot at the same time.]

Hudson says that young Tom, a flight lieutenant, was shot down in his Spitfire (264; see also 446 and endnote 1).

Sport. Bobby Saunders's nickname for David when they are playing the trick in which Andy pretends to drink gin and David plays the part of the reformed alcoholic (165, 171).

the Springfield. [Various models of rifle were developed by Col. James Gilchrist Benton (American soldier and inventor, 1820–1881), who commanded the Washington Arsenal during the American Civil War and the Springfield, Massachusetts arsenal after the war. As Benton refused to patent his improvements and inventions under his own name, the rifles were known after the town. The famous Springfield Model 1903, a .30 caliber breech-loading repeating rifle, was much used during World War II.][34]

Hudson notices a Cuban soldier carrying a Springfield (248; see also Benítez).

*Stalin. [(Made of Steel). Real name: Joseph Vissarionovich Dzhugashvili. Russian politician, 1879–1953; Premier of the Soviet Union, 1941–1953. A Bolshevik revolutionary, the young Stalin was arrested six times and, in 1913, exiled for life to Siberia. After the 1917 Revolution he formed part of Lenin's cabinet and, when Lenin died in 1924, he assumed political leadership, together with Kamenev and Zinoviev. He managed the expulsion of Trotsky, Zinoviev, Kamenev (qq.v. in *FWBT*) and other political rivals from the party, thus consolidating his own position as head of the Politburo of the Communist party. In the 1930s he resorted to wholesale "purges," which effectively eliminated political opposition. It is still not known how many people were killed at Stalin's orders. Stalin assumed the Premiership from Molotov in 1941, holding the position during and after World War II.]

Drinking at the Floridita Bar in Cuba, Hudson and the politician toast all the current political leaders, including Stalin (299).

*the steward. Hudson recalls the various stewards he encountered on his sea journeys. He remembers the bath steward on the smelly ship on which he sailed with his first wife (279). On the luxurious cruise ship which Hudson boarded in Mombasa, the wine steward tells Hudson the time (229; see also the waiter) and another steward calls the passengers for lunch (226). The room steward on the *Ile de France* brought drinks and food to Hudson's stateroom (198–99).

Speaks: 229.

*Stillwell, General [Joseph Warren (Vinegar Joe). Correct spelling: Stilwell. American soldier, 1883–1946. A graduate of West Point, Stilwell served in France during World War I. After the war he studied Chinese and served as military attaché to China. In 1942 he was appointed commander of the Chinese 5th and 6th armies in Burma; later that year he became commander of the American forces on the China-Burma-India front (1942–1944). Routed by the Japanese in Burma, he and his troops retreated to India, arriving on foot after a desperate

140-mile march through jungle. Friction with Chiang-Kai-shek resulted in his being recalled to the United States (1944), where he was appointed commander of the United States Army Ground Forces. Stilwell served in the Pacific once again, as commander of the 10th Army on Okinawa, June-September 1945. *The Stilwell Papers,* a collection of his diaries and letters, was published posthumously in 1948.]

Hudson sees a Cuban soldier and compares his headgear to that of General Stillwell (*sic,* 248–49).

*The Storm. Young Tom identifies this as the title of a work by Roger Davis (perhaps the screenplay Davis wrote for Hollywood, or perhaps just another detail Tom invents for the elaborate charade the Hudsons are putting on in Bobby's bar [167]).

*Suicides. Nickname for a drunken customer at Bobby's bar who frequently threatens to commit suicide and does finally kill himself. Suicides' condition—he is a manic depressive—is humorously mispronounced as "Mechanic's Depressive" (157–58; see Big Harry).

Speaks: 157–58.

*Taskforce. Like most of Hudson's many cats, Taskforce loves catnip (221).

*Tenniel, [John. English illustrator, satirical artist and cartoonist, 1820–1914. Tenniel is best known for his work in *Punch* and his illustrations of Lewis Carroll's *Alice in Wonderland* (1865).]

Audrey remembers that, years ago, Roger had said that she looked like a Tenniel illustration. He had intended the remark as a compliment, but at the time it made Audrey cry (185).

*Thanis (Bitchy the Great). The first of the three beautiful but unsavory girls with whom Roger Davis got involved after he broke up with Ayers (q.v.). Thanis was a successful fortune hunter (100; see also Kathleen).

*thieves. Willie refers to Luke 10:30 when he says, "I have fallen among thieves" (422).

*Thompson, [John Taliaferro. American soldier and inventor, 1860–1940. Thompson held many patents for improvements and innovations in automatic small arms. In 1920 he patented the Thompson submachine gun (Tommy gun), the weapon of choice of the gangsters who flourished during the Prohibition years (1920–1933) because it is accurate, fast, and reliable.]

As part of Bimini's celebrations of Queen Mary's birthday, the islanders shoot off weapons and flares, including tracer bullets from a Tommy gun (30). When Hudson and his men stalk the Germans, they carry Thompsons (374–75, 379, 419, 423–24, 439, 457), which they call *niños* ("children," see 374–75).

Time. [A popular American weekly news magazine, founded in 1923 and published continuously until the present. The *Time* column "Milestones" records births, marriages, divorces, deaths, and other important events involving the rich and famous.]

The deaths of Hudson's ex-wife and his two sons are reported in *Time* (198).

*the *Titanic.* [Considered unsinkable, this luxurious 800'-long White Star liner sank the night of April 14–15, 1912, after hitting an iceberg on her maiden voyage from Southampton to New York. The confident *Titanic* had sailed with insufficient lifeboats, and most of the third-class passengers were killed, as were many extremely wealthy first-class travelers. It is estimated that about 1,500 of her almost 2,200 passengers perished. The shocking event resulted in more stringent safety laws about lifeboat drills and equipment, the introduction of 24-hour radio watches, and more careful planning of travel routes to avoid dangerous areas. There are hundreds of *Titanic* songs, but no copyrighted version mentions J. J. Astor. Louis may be offering his own version of one of the *Titanic* ballads. One of the more popular ones had the following refrain, which tacked on another hundred to the already high death toll:

> You know that it was bad with those people on the sea.
> They were singing 'Nearer My God to Thee.'
> They all were homeward bound; sixteen hundred had to drown.
> It was sad when that great ship went down.

A more facetious version runs as follows:

> Now, the moral of the story, as you can plainly see:
> Is to wear a life preserver and never go out to sea.
> Keep your feet on the ground; ever pure and faithful be.
> It was sad when that great ship went down.][35]

Complaining that he is tired of singing "Mama don't want . . ."(q.v.) for the obnoxious yachtsman, Louis offers another old song, which recalls the death of J. J. Astor (q.v.), a *Titanic* passenger (14). Bobby Saunders outlines a painting of the sinking of the *Titanic* which he thinks Hudson should paint (18–19; see also *yachtsman).

Tomás. A fisherman calls the elder Thomas Hudson by the Spanish version of his name (210–11). Serafín calls him Señor Tomás (281).

Tommy. See Hudson, Thomas (father and son).

Tommy gun. See Thompson.

*Toulouse-Lautrec[-Monfa, Henri Marie Raymond de. French painter and lithographer, 1864–1901. Toulouse-Lautrec's psychologically astute portraits depict the famous and infamous people who frequented the brothels, theatres, and cafés of Montmartre. Toulouse-Lautrec is famous for his posters of the Parisian night-life and for *Elles,* a series of lithographs depicting the lonely and isolated life of prostitutes and of their clients.]

Hudson accuses his first ex-wife of taking such a high moral stance that, had she been married to Toulouse-Lautrec or to Gauguin (q.v.), she would have kept them at home, and thus deprived them of access to the subject matter of their paintings (317–18).

*Townsend, Geoffrey. Current husband of Audrey Bruce's mother, with whom she lives in London (186).

*Townsend, Mrs. Audrey Bruce's twice-widowed mother. Audrey reports that her mother had hardly changed from the way she was when Roger knew her in Paris: she has retained her looks and her addiction to drugs (185–86; see also Dick Raeburn and Bill Bruce).

*Tunney, [James Joseph] (Gene). [American boxer, c. 1897–1979. Tunney became world heavyweight champion when he defeated Jack Dempsey in 1926; he defeated Dempsey again in 1928 and retired as undefeated champion the next year. Tunney served in both world wars: as a marine in World War I and as director of athletics and physical fitness for the United States Navy in World War II. He wrote *A Man Must Fight* (1932), a book which Hemingway owned (Reynolds, *Hemingway's Reading,* 193), and *Arms for Living* (1941).]

In proposing their many humorous toasts, Hudson and the politician drink to Gene Tunney (299).

*T.V. See *the Chinese.

*Ulysses. [James Joyce's masterpiece, first published by Sylvia Beach in 1922. It presents the events of a single day, June 16, 1904, in the lives of Leopold Bloom and Stephen Daedalus. Noel Riley Fitch notes that in

Hemingway's copy of *Ulysses,* "Only the pages of the first half and the last portion (Molly's soliloquy) are cut" (*Sylvia Beach and the Lost Generation,* 121).]

Young Tom got into trouble at school for explicating the notorious Molly Bloom soliloquy to his interested schoolmates. Although the headmaster wanted to confiscate the book, he returned it when Tommy pointed out that the book belonged to his father and that it was an autographed first edition and therefore valuable (67; see also *Droll Stories* and *Mademoiselle de Daupin*).

Uncle Edward. See Edward.

*Uncle Woolfie. See Woolfie.

*USO. See OSS.

*Verey, [Edward Wilson. Correct spelling: Very. American naval officer and weapons expert, 1847–1910. Very served in the American armed forces during and after the American Civil War, achieving the rank of lieutenant in 1871 (peacetime promotion was very slow). Interested in artillery, Very is remembered for the Very signal pistol, which allows flares to be fired into the air. Very was issued an American patent in 1877 and a German patent in 1878, his name becoming the generic term for the signal pistol. The original flare cartridge, invented by Benjamin Franklin Coston and patented by his widow in 1859, burned in its holder or pistol, which the signaller had to hold aloft until all the lights had emerged. Very's much more successful cartridges could actually be fired from the pistol and would expel their balls or stars of red, green, and white fire high in the air. After resigning from the Navy in 1885, Very became vice-president of the American Ordnance Company. He later developed an interest in lighthouses, for which he devised a lighting system.][36]

To celebrate Queen Mary's birthday, Frank Hart shoots off several flare cartridges from the Verey (*sic*) gun; the emerging fire balls fall dangerously close to the Commissioner's house (30–35).

*Virgen del Cobre. [Cuba's patron saint, q.v. in *OMS* .]

Honest Lil surrounds young Tom's picture with religious images: the Sacred Heart of Jesus and the Virgin of Cobre (279; cf. Santiago's wife in *OMS*).

*Wahl, Le Capitaine [(*homme aux crocodiles*). Pantomimes involving crocodiles, caymans, serpents, and other dangerous, exotic reptilians were popular in Paris in the 1920s. In one pantomime, entitled "the

Pearl of Bengal,'' beautiful slaves were thrown to the crocodiles. Wahl's act presented a hundred "trained" crocodiles, among whom he would disport himself. In 1926 Wahl acquired the controlling interest of the Swiss circus where he performed.]

Young Tom remembers many details about a circus he saw in Paris, including the crocodiles presented by Wahl and "a beautiful girl," the colors and smells of the circus, and the fact that his father and Crosby (q.v.) had a drink with the lion-tamer (62).

*the waiter. A waiter at the Café Select sold Hudson a pair of racing shoes (448). A waiter at another Parisian café showed his affection for the Hudsons by serving them "doubled-sized drinks" (448; see André, Emile and Jean in *MF*). A waiter on the luxury ship that is taking Hudson and the Princess from Mombasa to Marseilles serves them champagne (228).

Speaks: 228.

Watson, Ginny. A "nice, ugly . . . woman" (305–6) who serves as secretary to Hudson's first wife. She accepts Rodríguez's invitation for lunch (309–10).

Speaks: 308–10.

*West, Mae. [American actress, film star, playwright, and scriptwriter, 1892–1980. Mae West started her career in vaudeville; she introduced the shimmy to New York (1918–1919). During her long career she made many films; among the most famous are *She Done Him Wrong* (1933), *Go West Young Man* (1937), *My Little Chickadee* (1939), and *Myra Breckinridge* (1969). She wrote many of the plays and films in which she starred, as well as her autobiography, *Goodness Had Nothing to Do With It* (1959). She was famous for her voluptuous figure and suggestive double-entendres. The inflatable life jacket used by airmen was named after her.]

Natera tactlessly offers a description of young Tom in his pilot's regalia, including parachute and a Mae West vest, to the boy's recently-bereaved father (264).

["Western Wind." Anonymous medieval lyric: "Western wind, when will thou blow?/ The small rain down can rain./ Christ, that my love were in my arms,/ And I in my bed again."]

After cursing the east wind, Hudson quotes this poem (413–14; Frederic Henry quotes parts of this same poem, *FTA* 197).

*Whitty, Dame [Mary Louise] May. [British actress, 1865–1948. By the time she was 20, the successful Whitty was performing with the leading actors and managers of her day. Among her many successes was her

1899 performance as the lead in W. B. Yeats' *Countess Cathleen*. A suffragette and a pacifist, Whitty turned to charity work during World War I, in recognition of which she was created Dame of the British Empire in 1918. In 1935, at age 70, she was widely praised for her performance in *Night Must Fall* (1935). She was also successful in films: *The Thirteenth Chair* (1937), *The Lady Vanishes* (1938), and *Mrs. Miniver* (1942).]

Explaining how he ended up in jail for having sexual intercourse with a minor, Johnny Goodner remarks that girls mature early in California: at fifteen girls look like women in their mid-20s, and in their mid-20s they look to be the age of Dame May Whitty, who at the time of Goodner's remark was over 70 (25).

whores. Mostly we hear about but don't see prostitutes, because the Cuban government has deported them (251), and prostitution seems to be outlawed. But Honest Lil (q.v.), who has been a prostitute for 25 years (273), and enough of "the old respectable whores" (215) show up at the Floridita Bar that the management has made rules about where they are to sit (270; i.e., the far end of the long bar, 215, 273).

*whores. The rough word "whores" appears more frequently than "prostitutes" in this novel. Hudson recalls poor prostitutes in Marseilles (230) and the high-class prostitutes of Hong Kong (292–93; see the Chinese). He also remembers the day the Cuban prostitutes were deported (251; Roberts writes that during the Prio administration, "a sudden spasm of reform . . . led to the closing of all the known houses and the jailing of free lances" but does not mention deportation of prostitutes [224]). Willie and Henry Wood talk about prostitutes (267; see 266–69). See also *women and girls.

*Wilde, Oscar [Fingal O'Flahertie Wills. Irish poet, novelist and dramatist, 1854–1900. Wilde belonged to the Aesthetic movement, which advocated art for art's sake. He is remembered for his novel, *The Picture of Dorian Gray* (1891), and his drawing room comedies, like *Lady Windermere's Fan* (1892) and *The Importance of Being Earnest* (1895). After a notorious trial and two years' imprisonment for homosexual activity (1895–1897), Wilde published "The Ballad of Reading Gaol" (1898) and *De Profundis* (posthumously, in 1905).]

As a little boy, young Tom had indicated that he was familiar with homosexuality by referring to a book by Gide which mentions Oscar Wilde. Roger supplies the title: *Si le grain ne meurt* (q.v., 179–80).

*Wilkinson. Pilot whom Hudson hires to fly him to the mainland. When Hudson hears that the boys have been killed, he wants Wilkinson to pick

him up in Bimini and to make him a plane reservation from Miami to
New York (196).

*Willard, [Jess. American boxer, 1881–1968; world heavyweight cham-
pion, 1915–1919. Several "White Hopes" challenged the exuberant
black champion Jack Johnson (c. 1876–1946), who was the object of
much racial hatred. Willard obtained the title by knocking out Johnson
in Cuba; he lost his title in 1919 to Jack Dempsey (q.v.), who was much
smaller and lighter. Willard was 6'7'' tall and his weight ranged between
235 and 265.][37]

Hudson mentions Willard and Dempsey to support his contention
that weight is not important in determining the outcome of a fight
between men or cats, although it is a crucial factor in cockfights
(236).

Willie (Columbus boy, jungle man, Mr. Willie, Old Willie). An American explosives expert on Hudson's boat, he is a "medically discharged
marine" (431) with a glass eye (365), extensive plastic surgery on his
face (465) and a "bad head" (391–94). He recovered from his wounds
in San Diego (407) and served in the Philippines, where he picked up
some Spanish (447). He drinks heavily and speaks offensively, both at
the Floridita Bar in Havana, where he insults Lil (270) and her
colleagues (268); and on Hudson's boat, where he quarrels with Henry.
But he is capable of understanding and even of sympathy: his prejudice
against the Germans is shaken when he sees how carefully they provided
shelter and supplies for their dying comrade (see the prisoner). Willie
worries about Hudson's refusal to talk about the death of Tom (271) and
expresses his affection for him (466). Like Hudson and Davis, he has
difficulty sleeping, a clear sign of unresolved suffering. His expertise
and commitment to duty win him Hudson's and Henry's admiration,
expressed through nicknames (431).
    Speaks: 265–72, 364–68, 373, 375–76, 380–82, 387–88, 390–92,
297–98, 402–3, 405–8, 419–26, 429–31, 436–37, 441–43, 449–51, 454,
458–60, 462, 465–66.

*Willie's family. Willie refers to his mother (421) and grandmother
(407).

*Willy. One of Hudson's many cats, addicted to catnip (221). Like Boise
and Baby, he refuses to sleep with Hudson when he is drunk (215).

Wilson. Pilot of the Sikorsky amphibian which takes the boys away and
then returns the next day to take Audrey Bruce and Roger Davis back to
the mainland (193–94, but see Wilkinson).

Wilson, Fred (Freddy). He sings and plays the guitar (28) and later joins Frank Hart and Rupert Pinder (qq.v.) in baiting the drunken yachtsman whom Roger Davis beats up. Wilson confides his philosophy to Davis: "Only suckers worry" (43; see also the grain broker in *THHN*). Although by himself Wilson offers no problems, he tends to be influenced by the troublemakers with whom he associates (43–44; see also 45).

Speaks: 29, 30, 31, 33, 35, 36, 41, 43.

*Wilson, Mrs. Fred. Mocking the yachtsman, Wilson advises him to satisfy his wife sexually and thus cure her insomnia. Wilson mentions that this advice has been relayed to him by his own wife, who in turn obtained it from her analyst (35).

women and girls. In addition to Audrey Bruce, an unnamed, attractive girl watches the Hudsons' practical joke in Saunders' bar (165, 171). Taken in by the charade, she gets upset, cries, and leaves the bar. Other women and girls are seen in the background (150). An old, poor Cuban woman and her husband accept money from the third Mrs. Hudson.

Speak: 171–72, 248.

*women and girls. Several unnamed, undefined, and unseen women have shared Hudson's bed (8–9; see also Lil and the Chinese). Hudson also remembers two of Roger Davis' unnamed former lovers, whom he abandoned in expensive New York night clubs (one at Club 21 and the other at El Morocco). Another woman's love affair ended more violently: she had been dismembered by her lover (245, see policemen). Although the houses of prostitution have been closed (251), Henry Wood and Willie have found two prostitutes (266, 268). The huge, heavy Wood lusts after a "little tiny girl" who refuses him as a customer (267; also see *whores).

Bobby would like Hudson to paint storm-tossed women as well as women being loaded into the lifeboats during the sinking of the *Titanic* (18). Hudson remembers women on a windy day in Marseilles (230). He also remembers women and children in Hong Kong gathering wolfram-rich soil for illegal sale to Americans, and he remembers hearing the voices of other women who had been incarcerated for that same crime (287–88; also see officers). Cuban girls disappointed in love or abandoned by their lovers sometimes commit suicide by drinking dye (281; see also *mothers and fathers). On a happier note, Hudson and Tom remember the lion tamer's wife in Paris and the beautiful girl in Wahl's circus (62; see also nurses). Young Tom mentions the women whom Montfried (q.v.) squired about Paris in taxis (107). Part of the Hudsons' joke is Tommy's claim that the same heroine appears in all of Davis' potboiler fiction, even though she is occasionally killed off (167; see 175 and *Indians).

Wood, Henry. A huge, cheerful, hard-drinking man who is involved in Hudson's submarine patrols. He blushes easily and sweats profusely. After twelve days at sea, he is intent on women (266–68, see *women and girls); he goes to Alfred's Sin House (284). Hudson and Willie worry about him because he doesn't eat when he drinks (267–70, 284; also see Paco and endnote 1).
  Speaks: 267–70, 284.

*Woolfie, Uncle. A gray Persian cat, he is beautiful, stupid and unadventurous (221).

the yachtsman (colonel, governor, sonny). An obnoxious drunken tourist (13) makes a rumpus at the Ponce, throwing dishes and refusing to pay his bill and, later, back in his yacht, insulting Fred Wilson and Frank Hart and finally provoking Roger Davis into a fight (35–37). When Roger beats him up he threatens to shoot him but doesn't (39–45; see also customers, men and boys, *the yachtsman's wife). He calls the revellers on the dock "swine"; Fred Wilson and Frank Hart respond by calling him colonel, governor, and sonny (35–36).
  Speaks: 14, 35–37, 39, 42.

*the yachtsman. [It is thought that, because of the shortage of crewmen for the life-boats, the officers of the *Titanic* allowed first-class passenger Major Arthur Godfrey Peuchen, vice-commodore of the Royal Canadian Yacht Club, to enter one of the life-boats before the evacuation of women and children was complete.]
  Bobby Saunders suggests that Hudson paint the sinking of the *Titanic* and include "every detail," including this yachtsman, of whom he obviously disapproves (18).

*the yachtsman's wife. She has a terrible life with the drunken yachtsman (q.v.); Louis tries to cheer her up by showing her conch pearls (15). When the celebrations on the dock get loud, the yachtsman complains that his wife can't sleep, which results in predictably lewd and rude suggestions (35–37).
  Speaks: 14.

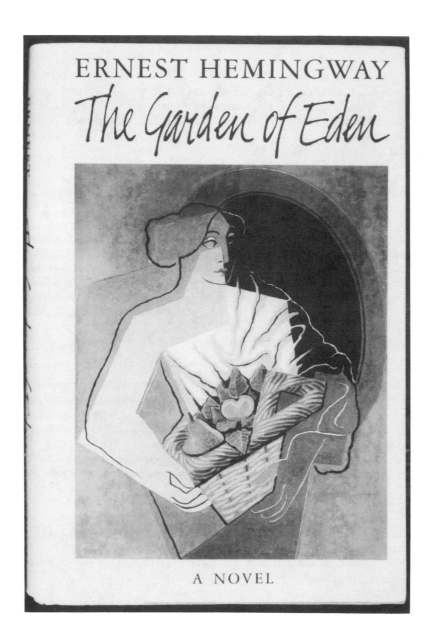

ERNEST HEMINGWAY

The Garden of Eden

A NOVEL

Scribner dust jacket for the first edition of *The Garden of Eden* (courtesy Charles Scribner's Sons, an imprint of the Macmillan Publishing Company; and of the Hemingway Collection, J.F. Kennedy Library)

CHAPTER IX

THE GARDEN OF EDEN

(1986)

The action of this book takes place between late May/early June and September (the year is not identified but is probably 1927; see Coolidge) in France and Spain. The focus is on the work and private life of a young American writer. Other plots and a number of characters were deleted from Hemingway's manuscript when it was prepared for posthumous publication.[1]

absinthe. See Pernod.

the African stories. Three untitled stories during the writing of which their author, David Bourne, comes to understand his eight-year-old self, his relationship to his father, and the demands of his art. All three stories are set in east Africa, where David lived as a boy, and all three deal with what seems to be the same secret evil. His wife Catherine jealously burns the three manuscripts; after his initial anger and despair wear off, David finds that thanks to what he has learned about his subject and his craft, he can not only recover but improve the stories.

1) In the first story, "sand-scoured bones" are somehow related to the unidentified "evil in the shamba" (94). David is able to write this story quickly, in two days, because he has thought it through to the end (93). The plot and characters of this story are not reported in the novel.

First story: 93–94, 107–8.

2) The second story is about some guilty secret shared by David's father and his servant (129). The secret may be related to "the massacre in the crater" mentioned by Catherine (223). The action of the story takes place over three days, during which David's father, followed by his porters, walks across arid territory (128, 138) to reach an Edenic landscape which features "the river and . . . fig trees" (139); here David finally manages to know "what his father had thought" (146–47). The

story, probably a third-person narrative told from the father's point of view, takes David four or five days to write.

Second story: 108, 123, 128–29, 138–39, 146–48, 153; see the Kamba servant and Maji-Maji.

3) The third story, like the first, connects bones to a secret evil shared by David's father and Juma (q.v.). In this fully reported story the secret evil is not only identified but also attached to David: the bones are those of a "skull as high as David's chest" (180; also see *bibis*), the skull of a huge elephant which David's father and Juma had killed, probably illegally, in order to harvest its valuable tusks. That slaughter is repeated in the third story, in which another huge elephant is tracked and killed, this time with David's participation. During the three days of the elephant hunt (the first sighting occurs in the evening; the elephant is killed late in the afternoon of the third day), David's attitude to his father changes from childish hero-worship to rejection. Writing this "very young boy's story" (201) David comes to understand his father's and his own guilt and their responses to it. He grows artistically as he grapples with the difficulties of communicating the events of the hunt and the feelings connected to the events. *The Garden of Eden* documents both the story of the elephant hunt and the five-day process of writing that story.

Third story: 159–60, 164–66, 171–74, 179–82, 197–202.

André. The waiter at the cafe near the Bournes' hotel at Grau du Roi enjoys fishing (7). When David hooks an impressively big fish, André jumps into the water to help bring it in, after which he excitedly embraces and kisses both David and Catherine (7–10; also see waiters).

Speaks: 7–10, 24.

*the armorer. David recalls that, as a pilot during World War I, he would work with "the mechanic and the armorer" to keep himself from worrying. The ground crew "did the work perfectly" but it was "comforting" to him to be involved in the pre-flight activity (224).

askari. [In Swahili, *askari* is a military term, meaning soldier, guard, armed attendant. David refers to the long-dead elephant as the friend (not guard) of the elephant currently being hunted, but the Swahili word for friend or companion is *rafiki* or *mwenzi (Standard Swahili).* Another Swahili dictionary defines *askari* as "comrade at arms," a definition more compatible with David's word, "friend."][2]

David's father tells him that Juma killed the elephant's *askari* (173, 180).

Atlantic Monthly. [Founded in Boston in 1857, the *Atlantic Monthly* kept a high literary standard throughout its history. Although in its early years it reflected its New England origins, the *Atlantic* expanded its outlook and by the beginning of the twentieth century had become a national magazine, concerned with broad economic, social and political issues but always maintaining its somewhat conservative literary orientation.][3]

Having burned his manuscripts, Catherine wants to reimburse David. She intends to consult the editors of several literary magazines, including the *Atlantic,* to have them fix a price for the stories. She will then order her bankers to deposit twice that sum in David's account (226; see the lawyers and endnote 17).

Aurol, Madame. Owner, manager and cook of the small hotel near la Napoule, where Catherine and David stay both before and after their trip to Madrid (they "go back to la Napoule" where they had once stayed briefly [71]). She is friendly and concerned, teasing David about his women and urging him to eat (166–67, 233–35). David insists she have caviar and champagne with him (130, 234). She realizes that Catherine is not well and cries when she has to tell David that Catherine has gone. She receives a black eye from her husband (240, 243).

Speaks: 75–76, 129–31, 166–67, 233–35.

Aurol, Monsieur. Owner and manager of the hotel. He speaks seldom, and then only in clichés (94, 129).

Speaks: 83; see 94.

Aurol's nephew (the boy, the waiter). An "apprentice waiter" (76), he serves meals and drinks, sets and clears the table, and runs a few errands (85, 95, 97, 109, 127, 129, 131, 133, 147, 156, 183, 186, 233–34). David teaches him how to make a drink (133) but otherwise takes almost no notice of him.

Speaks: 109.

background. The novel presents very few minor characters, and these are generally undefined in terms of profession or sex. The narrative reports that there was very little tourism at the time of the action, that the townspeople are friendly (6) although somewhat taken aback at Catherine's haircut (16). Nice is less friendly, and "Someone said something" to Catherine (110). The Bournes seem to have no living relatives and no friends, and Marita seems similarly disconnected from family and society. When she and David discuss their future, friends don't seem important: David seems not to need them, and she wants men friends for him—no women—but doesn't seem to need friends herself (244–45). Altogether, the background of this novel is strikingly unpopulated. Even bartenders, customers, maids, and waiters (qq.v.) appear seldom and, except for the Aurols, are not used to highlight the main characters or themes. Similarly, the African stories (q.v.) present very few secondary characters. But we must not forget that the posthumously edited and published novel was carved out of a much larger manuscript.

the bartender. He serves wine to David and Colonel Boyle and enjoys Boyle's chaffing (59–60). Waiters (q.v.) also serve drinks.
   Speaks: 60.

Beauty. David's nickname for Catherine (125) and for Marita (139). The same nickname is used in *Islands*.

bibis. [In Swahili, "a term of respectful reference and address to women, now fallen into evil days in some places because of its use to refer to concubines of Europeans" (*Standard Swahili*, 34).]
   David thinks scornfully of his father and Juma, "drunk with their *bibis*" (181; see Juma's family).

*The Bookman. [A monthly magazine devoted to literature and criticism, published from 1895 to 1933. *The Bookman* published English and American authors but favored Americans. It was a conservative magazine, modeled on the English *Bookman*. Under the editorship of John Farrar (1921–1927), the magazine paid more attention to current literary movements, although its attitude was not always encouraging. From 1921–1924 the magazine had a department, "The Literary Spotlight," which presented "short, sometimes caustic sketches of contemporary writers" (Mott, *History of American Magazines*, IV:439).]
   David scornfully denies that the conservative *Bookman* can evaluate his fiction (60).

Bourne, Catherine Hill (boy, beauty, brother, Devil, girl, Peter, stranger). David Bourne's 21-year-old wife is a beautiful, strong-willed heiress who enjoys sex, food, drink, sleep, and nude swimming and sunbathing. Early in the novel she promises him that "We'll do everything you want" (27). But she is jealous and possessive of his work and likes to have her own way, particularly on sexual issues: "I'm how you want but I'm how I want too" (29). Her first Lesbian affair disturbs her, as does David and Marita's growing involvement, which she instigates. Throughout, she attempts new beginnings, but her many resolutions—to be a girl, to study Spanish (71), to stop drinking (143), to keep David (169), to exercise regularly (175)—don't last. Early in the novel Catherine describes herself as "destructive" and wonders if her exaggerated appetites are "normal" (5). Her deterioration is marked by quick mood changes, an increased need for sleep (125, 135), visual distortion (162), loss of appetite (118, 162, 170), lapses of memory (118, 119,

134–35, 189, 193), verbal abuse (215–16) and destructive behavior: she burns David's work.[4] Although she suspects that she is "crazy" (100, 137), she rejects professional help (158, 161) and instead drives off, leaving a farewell note. She may have inherited her unstable constitution; absinthe may have aggravated her condition (see Hill and Pernod); but see Willingham's coherent reading of Catherine in terms of *l'écriture féminine:* "Catherine's suffering and presumed descent into madness relate directly to her debilitating insecurities in the face of the patriarchal dominance of the arts" (47).

Speaks: 5–7, 9–18, 20–22, 24–31, 35–41, 43–50, 52–56, 62–71, 76–92, 95–106, 109–15, 117–25, 133–37, 142–45, 149–52, 154–58, 162–63, 168–70, 175–78, 187–93, 195–96, 209–10, 212–28.

*Bourne, Catherine's family. For Catherine's parents, see Hill. Catherine's uncle is a gambler who lives in Paris and frequents the races at Longchamps and Auteuil. Boyle thinks that he is "silly" and "really worthless" and that the rest of the family led similarly empty and, finally, dangerous lives (61).

Bourne, David (Catherine, Dave, Davey, Davie, girl, stupid). A successful young American writer, honeymooning in Spain and in the south of France (see endnote 1). His wife's unusual demands disturb him, but he acquiesces, first letting her control their sexual life, then having his hair cut and dyed to her specifications, and finally sleeping with and falling in love with a girl she has supplied. Although he does not control the events of his daily life, David is disciplined about his writing, which is autobiographical: his first novel, *The Rift,* was about his boyhood in Africa; the second was about flying in World War I. The narrative he is writing is about his relationship to Catherine and Marita. His African stories explore the issues of love, death, and the relations between fathers and sons. David "had many problems" which "for years he had put off facing" (13, 123); he deals with these in the stories (128, see 93–94). Born in Oklahoma in 1897 and raised in East Africa (111, 157), he has a smattering of French, Spanish, and Swahili (see 215–16).

David speaks: 5, 7–13, 15–18, 20–22, 24–31, 35–41, 43–56, 58, 60–62, 64–71, 76–79, 81–92, 95–106, 109–22, 124–27, 129–31, 133–37, 139–45, 149–58, 161–63, 167–70, 174–77, 183–85, 187–96, 203–5, 209–10, 212–14, 216, 218–36, 239–45; see 238.

The eight-year-old Davey speaks: 165–66, 173, 180–81, 198–99, 201–2.

*Bourne, [David's family]. David's father was a "professional hunter" (171) and ivory poacher (180, 197–98) in East Africa. David loved and admired him (111), but while still a boy he came to reject him for failing to understand the values represented by the elephant, who replaces the father as David's "hero" (201). The African stories suggest that David's father may have committed suicide (129, 146–48). He is the subject of much of David's fiction (111; see African stories). Catherine mentions the "wife" and "friends" of David's father (210); David does not mention his mother and seems to have no siblings.

Speaks: 147, 164–66, 171–73, 180–82, 198–202; see 238.

boy. When Catherine insists that she and David "change" sex, he addresses her as "boy" and she calls him "Catherine" and "my girl" (56).

the boy, the waiter. See Aurol's nephew.

Boyle, Colonel John. Handsome, distinguished, well-dressed and self-confident, he is an old friend whom David is happy to meet unexpectedly in Madrid. Boyle knew Catherine's father and uncle (see Hill) but meets her now for the first time, even though he had noticed her at the Prado Museum and had somehow recognized that at that point she was a boy. He puts Catherine at ease, is nonjudgmental of her trans-sexual experiments, and encourages her to tan her skin even darker. His remarks to David foreshadow the coming pain: "everything is right until it's wrong" and David should therefore try to enjoy himself as long as possible (65).[5] His clipped language recalls that of Brett Ashley, Mike Campbell, and Wilson-Harris in *SAR*. See endnote 1.

Speaks: 60–65.

*the British. After World War I, British tourism to France has fallen off (167). See the English, the Germans, and the Russians.

brother. David calls the shorn Catherine "brother" (15, 22). She says he is her brother (21–22, 29).

the Bug. Catherine and David's nickname for their car (175, 225, 227; see next entry).

*Bugatti, [Ettore Arco Isidore. Italian manufacturer of race cars, 1881–1947. Bugatti produced small, fast, expensive racing cars. His most expensive model was the Type 41 (Golden Bugatti, also known as La Royale), produced in the 1920s, of which only six or eight were made.]

The Bournes' "small blue car" (99), nicknamed the Bug, was bought by Catherine (209, 228).

Catherine. David's wife, Catherine Bourne, calls him by her own name when, in some undefined fashion, he ''becomes'' a girl during lovemaking (17, 56; see also girl and Peter).

*Cézanne, [Paul. French painter, 1839–1906. Cézanne spent most of his life in his native Aix-en-Provence, in the south of France. His landscapes depict the scenery around Bouffan, Auvers, the gulf of Marseilles at l'Estaque, as well as the fine gardens of his father's country house, near Aix, and the surrounding countryside. His many paintings of bathers show the banks of the small river Arc, which flows past Aix. Cézanne is known as the ''Master of Aix.'' See also *MF*.]
    Catherine wants to drive through ''all the Cézanne country'' (71).

Chasseur Français. [*Le Journal de la chaussure française*. Quarto published in Paris since 1913 (*Catalogue Collectif des Périodiques*).]
    David and Catherine buy this magazine in Cannes (88).

*Cheyenne. See *Coolidge.

Chicago Tribune. [From 1917 to 1923 and again from 1929–1934, the *Chicago Tribune* published a European edition with the same title. Published in New York, this edition must have reached European readers after some delay. The narrative mentions that David reads ''the Paris papers of the day before'' (43).][6]
    David buys the Paris edition of this American newspaper (59).

*children. Catherine speaks vaguely of having a baby (27); she is upset when she is menstruating (71). She charges David's father with having begotten ''little horrors'' in Africa (189). David's first novel is set in 1905, when he was an eight-year-old child (157; also see African stories). Catherine compares the burning of David's manuscripts to murdering a child (237; see also boy, girl).

the clerk. David leaves a message for Catherine with the clerk at the Palace Hotel in Madrid (59).

clippings, cuttings. See Romeike.

*clowns. During a quarrel about language, Catherine enjoins David not ''to be a clown.'' He replies that language is not necessary to ''The best clowns'' (155).

the coiffeurs. See hairdressers.

the *concierge.* The assistant *concierge* at the Spanish hotel hands David a
note Catherine has left for him (38; see also *concierge* in *TS, SAR* and *MF*).
Speaks: 38.

*Coolidge, [John Calvin (Silent Cal). American lawyer and politician,
1872–1933; thirtieth President of the United States, 1923–1929.
Coolidge became President when his predecessor, Warren G. Harding,
died in office in 1923. The Republican Coolidge was elected President
in 1924 but refused his party's nomination in 1928. He spent the summer
of 1927 vacationing at Custer State Park in South Dakota. He and Mrs.
Wilson arrived at the State Game Lodge in the Black Hills on 16 June,
1927, fished in South Dakota through July and much of August, left
for Yellowstone Park on 22 August, caught trout in Yellowstone Park on
24 August, returned to the Black Hills on 29 August and left for
Washington, D.C. on 10 September, after a long, much-reported and
-photographed vacation described as his "busiest vacation in three
years" (*NY Times,* 21 August, 1927, 9: 2). David's references to the
Sioux and the Black Hills strongly suggest that this is the vacation he
had just read about. In other years Coolidge vacationed in Swampscott,
Massachusetts (1925), in the Adirondacks, New York and in Vermont
(1926), and in Wisconsin (1928).

The Sioux or Dakota Indians who had occupied the Black Hills were
forced to relinquish most of their territory to white settlers during the
first half of the 19th century. In the 1870s, the discovery of gold in the
Black Hills (southwestern South Dakota and northeastern Wyoming)
brought a flood of prospectors to the already-diminished lands reserved
for the Sioux. These white gold-seekers were unsuccessfully resisted by
a series of Sioux chiefs, the last major battle being fought at Wounded
Knee, 29 December, 1890 (see *Sioux in *FWBT*). Similarly, the
discovery of gold in Colorado in 1858 brought prospectors into that
area's Cheyenne lands. By 1861 the Cheyenne had agreed to live in a
reservation in southeastern Colorado, where they were reduced to
poverty and endured near-starvation.]

After reading a letter from his publisher, who is looking forward to his
next book, David has a sudden revulsion against American concerns and
issues. He rails against President Coolidge, who goes "fishing . . . in a
fish hatchery." He also berates Americans who dispossessed "the Sioux
and the Cheyenne" (59) and "bathtub-ginned-up writers wondering if
their baby does the Charleston" (60).[7]

*Crillon, [Louis des Balbes de Berton de. French soldier, c. 1541–1615.
Crillon was a distinguished soldier who fought for Kings Henry III and
Henry IV. In 1788 his descendant, François-Félix-Dorothée Berton des
Balbes, Count of Crillon, acquired a mansion facing on the Place de la

Concorde. In 1907 the family sold it to a hotel organization, which turned it into the elegant Hotel Crillon.][8]

David and Catherine met at the bar of the Hotel Crillon, sometime in March; they seem to have married soon after (237, 216; see 57).

crowd. A small crowd gathers around David when he catches a fifteen-pound sea bass; Catherine calls it "your mob" (9–10; see also background).

*crowd. Comparing her burning of David's manuscripts to the killing of a child, Catherine imagines "the crowd gathering to scream" after the murder (237; see also *women and girls).

customers. We see "some customers," "three Spaniards," and "more people" at hotel bars (38, 66). When they eat in cafés, the Bournes see "three Spaniards" and are "conscious" of other customers but make no attempt to communicate with them (38, 36). See background.

Dave, Davie. Catherine Bourne's nicknames for her husband, David (17, 27).

Davey. His father consistently addresses the eight-year-old David Bourne by this nickname (164–66, 171–72, 200–2, 238).

*Dent, [Joseph Malaby. English publisher, 1849–1926. In 1872 Dent established his own bookbinding business, and in 1888 he began his first publishing business, called the Temple Library. He published the Temple series of Shakespeare's work (the Temple Shakespeare, 1894) and the Temple Classics (1896). In 1904 he inaugurated the famous Everyman's Library series, under the general editorship of Ernest Rhys. His son, Hugh Railton Dent (1874–1938), managed J.M. Dent after his father's death and edited *The Memoirs of J.M. Dent* (1921).][9]

David reads Hudson's *Far Away and Long Ago* (q.v.) in the Dent edition (94–95; see also Galignani).

*dentist. David explains to Catherine that one should consult a doctor for psychiatric or psychological problems just as one would go to a dentist for dental problems (158).

*Derain, [André. French postimpressionist painter, 1880–1954. Derain seems to have been susceptible to the ideas and philosophies of many of his contemporaries: various critics find that his early work was influenced by Van Gogh and the Pointillists Seurat and Signat; he responded to Gauguin's colors, Cézanne's distortions of perspective, and Picasso's experiments with cubism, which he later rejected. Derain is most often associated with the Fauve movement. He painted suburban townscapes and landscapes, designed costumes and scenery for the ballet *La Boutique fantastique* (1919), and illustrated *Pantagruel* (1945).][10]

Catherine intends to commission various painters (Derain, Dufy, Laurencin, Pascen [*sic*], Picasso) to illustrate "the narrative" (189). Puzzled and amused by her possessive attitude towards the book, David at first humors her, although he objects to Derain (189). As her condition degenerates, Catherine talks more seriously of the illustrations (225) for what she has come to consider as "my book" (237).

Devil. David begins to use this nickname for his wife Catherine when she has her second "dangerous" haircut; later he calls her exclusively by this nickname (45, 69, 77, 88, 104, 106, 109, 112, 115, 117, 119, 135, 137, 142, 143, 155, 175, 176, 177, 190, 196, 219, 220, 224, 225, 227). The nickname is also used in *ARIT* and *Islands*.

Dial. [Monthly magazine, published from 1880 until 1929. Established in Chicago, the *Dial* was a staid journal of criticism. Under the editorship and co-ownership of Scofield Thayer (1919–1926), who moved it to New York, it became one of the leading "small" literary magazines, publishing innovative art, fiction and poetry and encouraging young talent.[11] The *Dial* rejected Hemingway's submissions. See also *TS* and *MF*.]

David is scornful of this (or any) literary magazine's authority to evaluate him or his fiction (60).

*doctor. David recommends that Catherine see a psychiatrist (158).

*Dufy, [Raoul. French painter and designer, 1877–1953. One of the popularizers of Fauvism, Dufy achieved fame with his graceful, gay, brilliantly colored paintings of rich, luxurious scenes. He also designed textiles and theatrical sets.]

Dufy is one of the artists Catherine intends to commission (189; see Derain).

Eclaireur de Nice. [The weekly paper *L'Eclaireur du dimanche et la Vie pratique,* published in Nice from 1920 to 1937, carried a supplement titled *L'éclaireur de Nice (Catalogue Collectif des Périodiques)*.]

Monsieur Aurol and David read *L'Eclaireur de Nice* (83, 133).

*the editor. Catherine figures that editors of literary magazines can appraise David's stories (which she burned) so that she can reimburse him for the loss (226; see *Atlantic Monthly* and lawyers).

*the elephant. A huge, old elephant with enormous tusks is at the center of David's third African story. He comes to symbolize dignity, faithfulness and friendship and is contrasted to Juma and to David's father who, motivated by greed, kill him. The identification between David and the elephant is suggested by physical proximity (159), by the fact that the elephant's shadow covers him and his dog, and, more specifically, by the connection between the elephant's tusk and the boy's leg (160; cf. the connection between David and the first elephant's skull, 180). The elephant's strength and his love for his dead friend impress David, who regrets having put his father on its trail (181). The massive elephant is difficult to kill: badly wounded, it attacks Juma, lurches away, is shot twice more, crashes down, but is still not dead (199). David's sympathy for and identification with the elephant cause him to reject his father (182, 201).

*the engineer. David writes about the day when Catherine, driving fast, passed a moving train "car by car," enabling her to see "the engineer and fireman" (78; Scripps also sees an engineer and a fireman in a moving train, *TS* 9).

*the English. [Wealthy English people frequent Biarritz, a fashionable resort in south-west France made popular by Napoleon and his second wife, the Empress Eugénie. Restaurants, fashion houses, and other shops and services cater to this clientele, among them the coiffeurs who dress the ladies' hair and, at the end of the season, give their sons the regulation haircut as defined by their schools (see Eton; see also the English in *SAR*).]
    Catherine has her hair cut in Biarritz, where "good coiffeurs" serve the wealthy English tourists who send their sons to Eton (46; see also Peter). David notes that after World War I, fewer Britons can afford luxurious travel (167).

*Eton. [A prestigious English public (i.e., private) school for boys, established in 1440. Boys live at the school and are required to abide by a strict dress code, which defines how they may wear their hair. Other prestigious schools (Rugby, in Warwickshire, est. 1567; and Winchester, in Hampshire, est. 1387) are equally strict. See Eton in *TS;* see also Harrow in *THHN*.]
    Catherine wants her hair cut to resemble the regulation hair style worn by schoolboys at schools like Eton, Winchester, and Rugby (46).

*Far Away and Long Ago [Subtitled *A History of My Early Life.* Published in 1918, this autobiographical account of W. H. Hudson's youth in Argentina reveals its author's sympathy with nature and his rejection of rules and technology. According to John Galsworthy, "All Hudson's books breathe this spirit of revolt against our enslavement by towns and machinery.'' Galsworthy praises Hudson's "love of simple folk and simple things, championship of the weak, revolt against the caging and cruelties of life, whether to men or birds or beasts'' ("Foreword," *Far Away and Long Ago*). Hemingway, who admired Hudson, remarked that he ''writes the best of anyone'' (qtd. in Reynolds, *Hemingway's Reading,* 138–39); see also entries for Hudson and *Nature in Downland*].

David considers *Far Away and Long Ago* a "lovely book'' (94).

*the fireman. See the engineer.

fishermen, fishing fleet, fishing people. At Aigues Mortes, fishermen catch bass close to shore (3) and fish for mackerel out at sea (4, 7, 20). They return with a good catch (10). In view of this, it is interesting that David eats canned mackerel (109, 236–37).

*the French. David and Mme. Aurol discuss the "drinking habits'' of the French (167).

*the Frenchwoman. See *women and girls.

*Galignani, [Giovanni Antonio. Italian-English publisher in Paris, 1752–1821. Galignani lived some time in London and then settled in Paris, where he opened an English library in 1800. In 1814 he began to publish the English-language daily, *Galignani's Messenger*. His two sons, Jean Antoine (1796–1873) and Guillaume (1798–1882), continued publishing the newspaper after their father's death. The paper was sold in 1890 and ceased publication a few years later. The Galignani library and bookstore moved to their present address, 224, rue de Rivoli, in 1856. In the 19th century, the bookstore was a smaller concern than the library and the newspaper; in the 20th century the bookstore became the dominant aspect of Galignani, which advertises itself as "The First English Bookshop Established on the Continent."][12]

Catherine orders books (including several by W. H. Hudson, q.v.) for David from Galignani's in Paris (94–95; see also 194).

*the Germans. After World War I tourism from Germany has fallen off because the defeated Germans have no money (167).

girl. David and Catherine call each other ''girl'' (17, 56, 85–86). The narrative usually identifies Marita as "the girl.''

the girl. See the maid.

*Goldberg, Rube. [American cartoonist, 1883–1970. Goldberg is best know for his "crazy inventions," complicated mechanical contraptions designed to perform simple tasks, like opening a door or striking a match.]
David tells Marita of Catherine's plan to have his stories, which she burned, "appraised in some fantastic Rube Goldberg manner" so she can reimburse him for the loss (213). Both David and Marita see this plan as clear evidence that Catherine has ceased to function normally.

*el Greco. [Pseudonym for Kyriakos Theotokopoulos, painter and sculptor, 1548?–1614?, born in Crete but active in Spain and Italy. The Prado Museum has an impressive collection of el Greco paintings, including the *Aged Nobleman* (1585–1595), *The Licentiate Jeronimo de Cevallos* (1584–1594). *The Baptism of Christ* (1597–1600), *The Crucifixion* (1600–1610) and *Pentecost* (1604–1614). His paintings are characterized by elongated figures and emphasis on vertical lines. "What is known of El Greco's biography does not permit us to regard him as a man of deep devotional feeling; he appears rather as a refined humanist, who took pride in his culture and enjoyed life. However, he is generally regarded as a mystic painter" (Luca de Tena, 58). The painter's mystic qualities impressed Robert Jordan (*FWBT*); his *View of Toledo* is mentioned in *Islands*. The Prado has an extensive collection of el Greco paintings on religious subjects, as well as several of his portraits of aristocrats.]
Catherine talks about el Greco's paintings (52, 62) which she has seen at the Prado Museum in Madrid.

Guardia Nacional (the G.N.'s, Whatyoumacallits nationals). [Catherine mistakenly refers to the Spanish civil guard (*guardia civil*) as the national guard. The nation-wide *guardia civil* was established by three royal decrees (28 March, 12 April, and 13 May, 1844) to replace various independent provincial law-enforcement agencies. Its supreme commander holds the military rank of field marshal.[13] Because they are closely associated with the army and represent a strong central government which deals harshly with the citizenry, the *guardia civil* in Spain inspired great respect. Their peculiar black patent leather hats and very visible weapons make them easily recognizable. They work in pairs. Absinthe, known to be a dangerous substance, is banned in France but not in Spain (see Pernod). Coming from France, Catherine nervously hides the evidence from the armed Spanish police. For their role in the Spanish Civil War, see Guardia Civil in *FWBT*.]
Although not illegal in Spain, absinthe is consumed discreetly in Madrid, without the paraphernalia which would advertise its presence. The waiter who serves the absinthe is nervous about it, and Catherine drinks hers down quickly "because two G. N.'s were in" (38–39).

hairdressers. Haircuts, hair color, and hairdressers play an important part in this novel. Increasingly extreme haircuts and hair color accompany the Bournes' sexual adventures, and it is Catherine's haircut which attracts Marita to them. The attitudes of the three hairdressers in the novel range from nonjudgmental tolerance to personal involvement. The local coiffeur at Aigues Mortes is the first to cut Catherine's hair; at her request, he gives her "a true boy's haircut," the same haircut he had given David the previous week (15); he was neither "surprised" nor "worried" by her unusual request (16). For her second haircut Catherine seeks out "the best place" (46) in Biarritz (see Eton), where her hair is "smooth close clipped" (45). The third coiffeur, who cuts and bleaches David's as well as Catherine's hair, is personally involved, staying after hours and thoughtfully deliberating the issue (see Jean).

*Harper's. [Harper's New Monthly Magazine was founded by James Harper in 1850. Under the editorship of Henry J. Raymond (1850–1856). Harper's published mostly British authors. When Henry M. Alden became editor (1869–1919), the focus turned to American fiction and a separate English edition was published abroad. The next editor, Thomas B. Wells, modernized the magazine: he shortened its name to Harper's Magazine, dropped illustrations, and addressed current cultural, social and political issues. Although the emphasis on longer, serialized fiction has varied over the years, Harper's has published outstanding short stories throughout its history.][14]
Catherine intends to consult the editor of Harper's and the Atlantic Monthly (q.v.) about the value of the burned stories, which she now sees only in financial terms (226; see also *the lawyers and endnote 17).

Haya. [Swahili for "shame, modesty, bashfulness; . . . humility, respect" (Standard Swahili and Madan).]
David chooses this nickname for Marita because she blushes so frequently. This nickname, bestowed on Marita when she objects to being called "Heiress," is used in only one scene (141–42).

Heiress. The Bournes' name for Marita, who, like Catherine, is quite rich (120, 121, 124, 137, 141, 144, 187, 210, 212, 214, 215, 237; she is also called Beauty and Haya).

*Hill, Mr. and Mrs. Catherine's parents. Colonel Boyle describes the late Mr. Hill as a "very odd . . . difficult and charming man" who "used everything," and not just absinthe, to get through life (61, 63). He may have been a suicide: Boyle blames him for the car crash which killed him and his wife. Catherine's mother is described as "very lonely" and "very fair" (61, 63).[15] After Catherine burns his stories, David regrets that her parents "ever met . . . and . . . made you" (224). Boyle suggests that her heredity bodes ill for Catherine. See also Catherine's uncle.

*Hoche, [Lazare. French soldier, 1768–1797. Hoche spent most of his life in the army, with a short and unsuccessful stint as minister of war (1797). He rose to the rank of general. The Avenue Hoche radiates out of the Place de l'Etoile (now called Place Charles de Gaulle); the English (not American) Catholic Church of St. Joseph (Eglise Saint-Joseph Catholique Anglaise) is at 50, Avenue Hoche; this is probably the church where the Bournes married. Paris has several American churches, but none is on the Avenue Hoche: Hemingway's small, now-crumbling red guidebook lists the Protestant Eglise Americaine de Paris, located at 21, rue de Berri (Hemingway Collection, Other Materials: Maps). The American Church of the Holy Trinity (built 1885–1888) is on Avenue George V. Catherine and David probably married in May (see Crillon).]

The American church at which Catherine and David got married a couple of months after their first meeting is on Avenue Hoche (237).

*Hudson, W[illiam] H[enry]. English naturalist and writer, 1841–1922. Born in Argentina of American parents, Hudson became British in 1900. He wrote autobiography, fiction, and many nature studies of both English and Argentinean flora and fauna. Hemingway read many if not all of his books: *The Purple Land that England Lost* (1885), *The Naturalist in La Plata* (1892), *Hampshire Days* (1903), *Green Mansions* (1905), *The Land's End: A Naturalist's Impression in West Cornwall* (1908), *Afoot in England* (1909), *South American Sketches* (1909), *Adventures Among Birds* (1913), *The Book of a Naturalist* (1919), *Birds in Town and Village* (1920), *A Hind in Richmond Park* (1922).]

David seems to own several of Hudson's books (94–95, 194; see also Dent and Galignani). He admires Hudson's *Far Away and Long Ago* and his *Nature in Downland* (qq.v.).

*Humpty Dumpty. [Character in a Mother Goose rhyme.[16] Humpty Dumpty is an egg who fell off a wall and broke into pieces: "All the king's horses and all the king's men / Couldn't put Humpty together again."]

In one of the African narratives, David's father affectionately refers to the injured Juma as "you bloody Humpty Dumpty" (200).

*Indian. Catherine mentions the dark skin and the wealth of Indians (30–31, 111).

*Isidro, San. [San Isidro, Labrador (St. Isadore, the Laborer, 1082–1170) is the patron saint of Madrid, his birth- and burial-place. His feast day, 15 May, marks the beginning of a week of fiesta, highlighted by daily bullfights. The Seville fiesta (*Feria de Abril*) runs from the 18th to the 25th of April.]

Discussing where they could go next, David mentions that the fiestas of Seville and Madrid are already over, thus helping us fix the time of the action (30).

Isotta Fraschini (the Isotta). Marita's car, an old, big convertible with "Swiss plates" (89), needs major repairs (107). David intends to get it fixed because it is dangerous (135–36, 147; see also 98, 99, 100, 209).

Jean, Monsieur Jean. The "very good . . . very enthusiastic" (76–77) young coiffeur at Cannes who shares Catherine's passion for extreme hair-dos. He seems aware of the significance of hair cuts and hair color (77, 80). He does Catherine's hair regularly (79, 95, 176), experiments with special rinses to lighten it (142), has a drink with her (133–34), and keeps his shop open specially for her and David who, in spite of strong misgivings, allows Monsieur Jean to cut and bleach his hair (82, 177). Marita first approaches the Bournes to ask who their hairdresser is (90).

Speaks: 79–81.

*the Jelkses. The Bournes tell Marita that the Jelkses are one of America's "oldest families" (96; see the Jukeses).

*the Jukeses. ["Jukes" is the fictitious name of a New York family which was the object of important sociological studies. In 1875, Richard Louis Dugdale, finding that several members of the same family were in prison, traced them back seven generations, to a backwoodsman named Max, whose two sons married two of the Jukes sisters (one was dubbed "Margaret the Mother of Criminals"). Most of the 700 Jukeses about whom Dugdale collected information had suffered from poor health, 140 had been jailed for various crimes, and 280 had been welfare recipients. In his book *The Jukes, A Study in Crime, Pauperism, Disease and Heredity* (New York, 1875, 1877, 1910), Dugdale concluded that criminal tendencies were hereditary, the genetic tendency being activated by environmental or social factors. A follow-up study, *The Jukes in 1915* by Arthur Estabrook, found that the Jukes' condition had improved in the years following Dugdale's study. The "Kallikak" family were also studied by the sociologists.]

Catherine and David play on Marita's ignorance when they explain to her the peculiar drinking habits of America's "oldest families," among whom they include themselves and the Jukeses and the Jelkses (96; see also the Morgans and the Woolworths).

*Juma. [In Swahili, a week, or Friday, the Moslem sabbath (also *Ijumaa*, the day of assembly). Most of the days of the week begin with "Juma": thus, Sunday is *Jumapili*, Monday is *Jumatatu*. "*Juma* is a very common personal male name" (*Standard Swahili* and Madan).]
    Juma is an African hunter with "filed teeth," several wives (but see *bibis*), and a fondness for drink (180–81). He is probably the unnamed Kamba servant (q.v.) in David's second African story, and figures prominently in the third story. He works as a cook for David's father, helped bring up David, and is a skilled tracker to whom David's father defers (171). Juma correctly identifies the elephant and its destination from its spoor. He is attacked by the wounded elephant and suffers a torn ear, a huge gash in his head (199), and several broken ribs (201); he continues the hunt in spite of his injuries. When David refuses to finish off the fallen elephant, Juma kills it just as, a few years ago, he had killed the elephant's friend: by shooting him in the ear at close range (199). After the hunt, Juma displays the elephant's tail as a trophy (200). The young David rejects both Juma and his father after the hunt (202). Other cooks with impressive non-culinary skills are Antonio and Eddy (*Islands*).

*Juma's family. The boy David figures that the polygamous Juma will probably buy another wife with his share of the ivory-money (181; see *bibis*).

*the Kamba servant and brother. [The Kamba, like the Kikuyu (q.v. in *GHA*), are a people of East Africa, east of the Rift Valley (Tanzania and Kenya), whose language probably derives from Bantu.]
    A character in David's second African story who "shared the guilt and knowledge of the delay" (129) with the main character of the story. In the third African story, this character (or a parallel character) is named Juma (q.v.).

keys. Keys are mentioned often (38, 40, 70, 78, 153, 163, 203, 234). David carefully locks up his work room and the suitcase where he keeps his manuscripts (78, 153–54, 166, 174, 182–83, 209, 219; see 43 and 186 and Vuitton).

*Kibo Mawenzi (Kibo). [Local name for Kilimanjaro, the highest mountain in Africa. The mountain comprises two peaks: Kibo is over 19,000 feet tall, Mawenzi is almost 17,000 feet. Kilimanjaro is in northeastern Tanzania, near the border with Kenya. The name "Mawenzi" or *Mwenzi* derives from the verb "*enda,* go—including a wide range of meanings under the general idea of motion." *Mwenzi* is one who goes with another, "a friend, companion, associate, acquaintance . . . match, double"

(*Standard Swahili*); Ashton defines *mwenzi* simply as "companion" (364). The related noun *Mwenenzi* means "one who goes, traveler" as well as "one who causes to go, hence, powerful, mighty." A different verb, *enea* ("become abundant . . . permeate") yields the noun *Mwenezi*, "one who allots (distributes, gives out), esp. as a title of God, the Giver of good to all" (*Standard Swahili*, 83–85; s.v. *enda* and *enea*).]

Kibo, David's dog, accompanies David on the night when he first follows the elephant (159–60, 165), an episode which takes up the first half of the story. David identifies his childhood self with Kibo (173, 197), "a wonderful dog" (163). Catherine loves Kibo and identifies him with David (163); she had thought of preserving the parts of the story in which he appears, but then decided to burn them with the rest of the African stories (220, 222).

*Laurencin, Marie [(*La Fauvette*). French painter and designer, 1885–1956. Laurencin's delicate watercolors often depicted women, usually elegant, sophisticated but sad or troubled young women, painted in pastels.]

Intending to commission various artists (189) to illustrate David's narrative (based on their life together), Catherine envisions a Laurencin painting of herself and Marita in the early stages of their sexual involvement which took place "in the car" (189; see 113; see also Derain).

*the lawyers. Catherine's business affairs are handled by her lawyers and bankers in Paris. She intends to have them arrange compensation for David's loss of the stories (226, 231; see also 22, 25).[17]

*Leda. [In Greek mythology, the queen of Sparta, mother of Clytemnestra and the twins Castor and Pollux. Impregnated by Zeus, who assumed the form of a swan, she gave birth to Helen of Troy. The Prado's sculpture collection includes one Leda, in white marble, a copy of a famous statue by Timotheos (4th cent. BCE). The statue, including the plinth, is 1.43 meters (4' 8"). The swan's head and legs are intact; its body, as well as Leda's head and both arms, have undergone restoration.[18] A statue of Leda and the Swan also adorns the Luxembourg Gardens in Paris, which Boyle may have visited.]

Colonel Boyle compares Catherine, whom he saw looking at paintings at the Prado, to a "young chief . . . looking at that marble of Leda and the Swan" (62).

*lion. Catherine remarks that she is "lion color" (30) and the narrative often attaches the adjective "tawny" (the color of most lions) to her. David playfully brags that a good meal will enhance his sexual powers, making him "like a lion" (167). The Bournes' hotel looks out over the Gulf of the Lions (3).

London Daily Mail. [This London paper launched an overseas edition in 1904. This edition received its own name, the *Overseas Daily Mail*, in 1919. It is published in London but the name of the city is not part of its name (*British Union Catalogue of Periodicals*, 1955—).]
 David buys the Paris edition of the *London Daily Mail* (*sic*, 59).

the maid. During the off-season Aurol hires only one maid servant. She looks after the Bournes' rooms (76, 78).

*the Maji-Maji. [An East African tribe whose protest against German agricultural policy escalated into a full-scale revolt against German rule in East Africa. The revolt (1905–1907), in which the Kolelo peoples also participated, was brutally suppressed by the Germans. There were several such revolts against colonial rule at that time.]
 David's second African story is set against the background of this violence in Tanganyika (now Tanzania; 157, 246).

Marita (Beauty, Haya, Heiress, stupid). The dark young woman whom the Bournes meet at Cannes. Although she is shy and blushes easily and often, she is sexually sophisticated, first seducing Catherine and then, at Catherine's instigation, becoming David's mistress as well. Comfortable with her bisexuality, she seems to be in love with both of them at the same time (98–102). Eventually she rejects Catherine and identifies with David; she appreciates his books and stories, is able to read his face (239) and his mind (232), and feels the loss of his manuscripts as intensely as he does (238). In addition to being beautiful, rich and intuitive, she is undemanding and compliant (112, 145). She buys caviar, champagne and a mirror for the Aurols' bar (121–22, 126, 130).
 Speaks: 89–91, 95–99, 101–5, 109–12, 116, 119–22, 124–27, 133–37, 139–42, 144–45, 149–57, 161–62, 170, 174–75, 183–85, 187–94, 203–5, 209, 212–17, 220, 228–32, 234–36, 239–45.

*the mechanic. See the armorer.

men and boys. Some men congratulate David heartily on his big fish (9). Workmen install the mirror which Marita has bought for Aurol's bar (129; see also background and waiters).

*men and boys. In David's third African story, a young girl and "her younger brother" bring beer to David and his father, who sit in honor "on old men's stools," near the tusks which "the men" had carried in

(202; also see porters). Boyle compares Catherine to a young warrior chieftain who has temporarily evaded "his councillors" (62).

*Michelin, [André (1853–1931) and his brother Edouard (1859–1940), French manufacturers of rubber products, founded the Compagnie Générale des Etablissements Michelin in 1888. The company's major product was tires. In 1891 they introduced a bicycle tire that could be demounted in a few minutes; four years later they produced a demountable automobile tire. To advertise this product, they entered the 1895 Paris-Bordeaux road race, driving a car equipped with their demountable pneumatic tires. Although they did not win the race, their public relations stunt was successful and the tires sold well. The Michelin Company expanded rapidly, first to Italy (1906) and then to other countries. The first Michelin Red Guide appeared in 1900: it listed places of interest in France, mentioning hotels and garages and describing the amenities offered by means of symbols. It succeeded in its purpose, which was to promote tourism by car. The popular Michelin Guide and maps were limited to France until 1957; now the company publishes a series of guides and maps to other European countries as well.]

David writes about a car trip: Catherine drove and he consulted a Michelin map (78; see the engineer).

Miroir de Sports. [First published under the name *Miroir Clé, Miroir de Sports* was an illustrated sports magazine, published in Paris from 1912 to 1939 (*Catalogue Collectif des Périodiques*).]

David and Catherine buy *Miroir de Sports* in Cannes (88, 94).

*Molo. African servant in David's second African story (147).

*the Morgans. [Probably a reference to the family of John Pierpont Morgan, 1837–1913, and his son of the same name, 1867–1943, wealthy American financiers. A member of this family, Henry Grew Crosby, is mentioned in *Islands*.]

Catherine and David play on Marita's ignorance when they explain to her the peculiar drinking habits of America's "oldest families," among whom they include themselves and the Morgans (96; see also the Jukeses).

the narrative. Like all of David's writing, the narrative is autobiographical, about his and Catherine's life together—in a sense, the narrative is the book we are reading. At the beginning the writing goes "simply and easily" (37), and in four days of writing David brings the narrative "nearly up to now" (75–77). But as he attempts to write of their sexual complications the work slows down and he abandons the narrative in order to write the African stories (q.v.). For David, knowing the ending is a necessary condition for writing a good story (93); he cannot continue the narrative because he doesn't know how it will end (108). David refuses to let Catherine read the narrative until he can "get it right" (77), but she reads it anyway and gives it to Marita to read (184). She claims she made it "economically possible" and intends to hire various artists to illustrate it (189; see Derain).

Nature in Downland. [Published in 1906, this book by naturalist and writer W. H. Hudson (q.v.) describes birds, insects and other fauna and flora of the English downs, notably that of Sussex, at various times of the year.]
Although he had put off reading this book because of its "most unpromising title," David is completely absorbed once he starts reading it (194–95; see also Dent and Galignani).

Ndiyo. [In Swahili, "one of the commonest forms of simple affirmation, 'yes, it is so'" (*Standard Swahili,* 332).]
Asked a question, Molo answers in the affirmative: "Ndiyo" (147).

the nephew. see Aurol's nephew.

*The New Republic. [American journal of opinion, founded in 1914 by Willard D. Straight. This magazine dealt with current events and politics until the 1920s, when it began to emphasize literature, music, and other arts. Its political position has always been liberal and left-wing, its literary position somewhat conservative.]¹⁹
David is scornful of this prestigious literary magazine (60).

The New York Herald, Paris edition. [In 1924 the daily *New York Herald* (founded in 1887) merged with the *Tribune* to become the *New York Herald Tribune* and as such launched a European edition (1924–1966), which eventually merged with the *New York Times International* to form the *International Herald Tribune* (1967–present).]
The Bournes read the Paris edition of the *Herald* (59, 209, 210).

Ngoma. [In Swahili, a drum or dance (Ashton 367, 373). *Standard Swahili* defines *ngoma* as a drum, explaining that, as it is "the usual accompaniment of all merrymaking and ceremonial, *ngoma* is extended to include (1) any kind of dance; (2) music in general" (336). Kandinsky recommends that the narrator of *GHA* see "The big ngomas. The big dance festivals. The real ones" (*GHA* 16).]
In celebration of their triumph, the elephant hunters sit in the place of honor while "the big drum" beats and the *Ngoma,* which promises to be an extended affair, gets underway (202).

Nina. Marita's "handsome" (96) companion in Nice and Cannes. She and Marita admire the Bournes' hair styles, but Nina jealously objects to Marita's approaching the Bournes (89–91). Later Marita reports that they fought and Nina "went away" (96). The Bournes refer to Nina as "a wolf" and "That bitch" (91).
 Speaks: 90–91.

La Nouvelle Revue Française. [French journal of literature and literary criticism. Founded in 1909, the monthly stopped publication between September 1914 and May 1919 but has been published continuously since then. Originally the leading literary review of the influential publisher Gallinard, the *Nouvelle Revue Française* published French modern and experimental writers, with the notable exception of the surrealists. Paulhan, who became editor in 1925, was interested in foreign literatures (Dostoievsky, Rilke, Pirandello) and in philosophical issues. Over the years the journal has become more conservative: the modern *Nouvelle Revue Française* is not open to avant-garde literature. The journal is mentioned disparagingly in *SAR* 36.]
 Thinking that she can make financial restitution, Catherine intends to consult this and other journals about the value of David's stories (226; see also *Atlantic Monthly*).

*the Original Romeike's. See Romeike.

*Pascen. [Correct spelling: Pascin. Jules Pascin was the professional name of Julius Pincos. Bulgarian-born painter, 1885–1930. In 1905, the twenty-year-old Pascin left Bulgaria for Paris, where he lived most of his life, spending the war years (1914–1918) in the United States and becoming an American citizen before returning to Paris in 1918. Pascin's subject was the underworld; he is best known for his bitter and ironic studies of prostitutes. His paintings show a troubled and cynical atmosphere. Pascin hanged himself in Paris, 1930, just before the opening of his important one-man exhibition. He is described as a drunk, a drug addict, and a fine painter in both *Islands* and *MF*.]
 Among the artists she intends to commission to illustrate David's narrative, Catherine lists Pascen (*sic,* 189; see also Derain).

*passengers. The train Catherine took had "very few passengers" (234).

the patron. See Aurol, Monsieur.

Pernod, [Henry-Louis. "In 1797 . . . Henry-Louis Pernod in France first produced the drink called absinthe, using the recipe originated by [Dr.] Ordinaire" (Lanier, 282). Pernod's company (founded 1805) also produced "Anis Pernod." The main ingredient of absinthe is wormwood, which is so toxic that absinthe has been banned in Switzerland and France; its importation into the U.S. has been illegal since 1912. Absinthe has the reputation of being an aphrodisiac and of being addictive; excessive use is said to result in disorientation, insomnia, and even insanity. Pernod has become a trade name. When they are in Spain, Brett Ashley and Robert Jordan also drink absinthe (*SAR,* 167; *FWBT,* 50–51, 56–57).]

In Spain, where it hasn't been outlawed (but see *Guardia Nacional), Catherine and David drink absinthe: "ordinary Pernod" and "the real Pernod" (38–39, 62–66, 69). Catherine talks about its effects (49, 53; but see absinthe in *FWBT*). Colonel Boyle describes it as "truth serum" and indicates that Catherine's father "used everything," including Pernod (63).

Peter. Catherine's name for herself when she is a boy (17) is a slang word for penis. By its association with "Peter Pan" it also suggests arrested development or eternal childhood. Both these aspects are echoed in her desire for a schoolboy haircut (see the English, Eton, and hairdressers).

*Picasso, [Pablo Ruíz. Spanish painter, sculptor, and ceramicist who worked mostly in France, 1881–1973. Picasso was one of the founding forces of cubism and surrealism. His many famous works include *Les Demoiselles d'Avignon* (1907) and *Guérnica* (1937).]

Catherine intends to commission Picasso, among others, to illustrate the narrative David is writing about his and her life together (189; see also Derain).

*policeman. When David insists that Catherine tell him where she burned the stories, Catherine complains that he sounds "like a policeman" (220).

*the porters. Native workers appear in David's African stories (128–29, 139), including "people" and "men" who transport the elephant's tusks (200, 202); see also *men and boys.

the postman. He delivers the Bournes' mail, forwarded from their Paris banks, and has a couple of drinks before continuing with his deliveries (22). Later the mail is forwarded to the bank in Madrid, where David picks it up (58).

the priest. He ministers to the residents of the walled city of Aigues Mortes. Catherine and David attend Mass at his church and contribute generously to the collection. He disapproves silently of their shorts, but bows to them when they wear trousers in the evenings (6–7).

the proprietor. The owner of a restaurant in Madrid suggests the Bournes have sirloin for lunch (53).
   Speaks: 53.

*the publisher. David's New York publisher seems to think of David as a promising writer. He had given David a sizable advance for his second novel, expresses an interest in publishing the third, and keeps in touch with him. He reads, evaluates, and forwards the reviews, reports that present sales are good, cautiously avoids predictions, and hints that he is waiting for the next novel (23, 59; see also endnote 7). He offers external evidence that David is a serious, talented writer.

*the reader. David thinks about his implied reader as he considers the problems of how to present action vividly (201) and how to handle the narrative point-of-view (129). David's intention is to draw the reader into the story; cf. *the reader in *TS,* who is external to the action and is humorously apostrophized.

*The Rift.[20] David's first novel, an autobiographical account about his childhood in Africa (111). Marita was moved by it (111). David's second novel derives from his experiences as a pilot in World War I; its title is not given in *GE* (112).

*Romeike, [Henry. Swiss or Russian originator of a newspaper clipping service, 1855–1903. Dissatisfied with his job as a shopkeeper, Romeike hit on the idea of providing individuals with newspaper clippings about themselves. He began his service in Paris, transferred it to London in 1881 and, with the help of a partner, established a branch in New York in 1884. The American branch of Romeike's was very successful, and Henry Romeike himself moved to the United States in 1887. Eventually branches of the business were established in various other countries. In the mid-1920s Hemingway himself enjoyed receiving clippings supplied by Romeike, but by 1935 critical reviews were considered to be dangerous: writers who take their reviews seriously can "lose confidence" and become unable to write (*GHA* 23–24).][21]
   David's publisher forwards Romeike's clippings (the advertisements for and the reviews of his recently published second novel) to David (216, 221; see 23, 59). Resentful and jealous of David's success, Catherine picks a fight with David as they read the first batch of clippings (23–25; see also 215 and endnote 1). The clippings, testimony to David's successful career, are a sore point with Catherine, who mentions them often (39, 49, 78, 112, 215) before she burns them and the African stories (216, 219, 221).

*Rube Goldberg. See Goldberg, Rube.

*Rugby. See Eton.

*the Russians. David recognizes that the American Bournes are a new kind of tourist, replacing the aristocratic European clientele who used to frequent the south of France before World War I and the Russian revolution. Now, he notes, there are no more Russian aristocrats and the post-war British and Germans (qq.v.) are less inclined to luxury (167).

shamba. [In Swahili, "a plantation, an estate, farm, garden, plot of cultivated ground" (Standard Swahili, 416). Elsewhere in Hemingway, the word is defined as "plantation" (GHA, 17).]
   David thinks of his father and Juma drinking and carousing "at the beer shamba" (181).

*Sioux. See *Coolidge; also see *Sioux in FWBT.

stranger. David calls Catherine "stranger," and she picks up the Hollywood-western tone and replies in kind (38).

stupid. Both Catherine and David call Marita "stupid" (110, 185): Catherine and Marita address David by the same epithet (27, 243).

*Van Gogh, [Vincent. Dutch post-impressionist painter, 1853–1890. Van Gogh's early paintings portrayed Dutch working people, mainly farmers, in somber colors; when he moved to Paris and later to Provence. his colors became brighter and more expressive. His vivid colors and thick brush strokes give the paintings of his later period great intensity. The sunny painting of Van Gogh's Bedroom (1888; 28-1/2" by 36") presents his bed, several pictures on the walls, a mirror and towel hanging on the wall near a table on which stand a bowl, a pitcher, and several toiletries; and two plain, armless yellow wooden chairs with rough cane seats, one next to the bed and one by a door. Hemingway might have seen this famous painting at the Art Institute of Chicago. A similar rough, homey chair is the subject of Van Gogh's Chair, also painted in Arles, 1888–1889. The pipe and opened packet of tobacco that lie on the chair suggest that someone is about to return, sit down, and smoke; they give the painting a comfortably inhabited air.]
   As the novel opens, David and Catherine are staying in a hotel room that recalls Van Gogh's rendition of his bedroom (4), including "Van Gogh chairs" (11).

Vogue. [Founded in 1892 as a society weekly, *Vogue* became a semimonthly in 1910 and is now a monthly magazine which advertises expensive fashions and accessories. The magazine began publishing a British edition in 1916 and a French edition in 1920. As a result of its 1936 merger with *Vanity Fair,* it began to publish fiction, including such authors as Thomas Wolfe and William Saroyan, but the fiction was phased out by 1940.][22]

Catherine and David buy the French edition of *Vogue* in Cannes (88). Marita leafs through an issue of this magazine (190).

*Vuitton, [Louis. French manufacturer of fine trunks and suitcases, 1821–1892. Vuitton perfected his box- and trunk-making skills by packing the dresses and accessories made by Parisian haute-couture houses. In 1854 he established his own firm, the house of Louis Vuitton, at 4, rue des Capucines. In 1860 he moved his successful business to Asnières. He is credited with inventing the flat-topped trunk, which could be stacked and moved easily; previously, trunks had curved tops (so the rain would not collect on them). With the coming of passenger boats, which stacked luggage inside (in the hold as well as in the passengers' cabins), Vuitton's elegant, flat-topped, compartmentalized trunks and cases came to be much in demand among aristocrats and other rich travelers, who took great quantities of daytime and evening clothes, hats, shoes, linens, children's equipment, writing accessories, and other necessaries on their long voyages. Vuitton's son Georges (1857–1936) furthered the fortunes of the company, as did his grandson Gaston-Louis (1883–1970). In 1894 Georges published an illustrated history of travel goods entitled *Travelling;* the founder's great-grandson, Henry-Louis Vuitton (1911—) is the author of *A Trunk Full of Memories* (Paris: Image, 1989). In 1871 the Vuittons moved their shop to 1, rue Scribe, Paris, and in 1912 they opened their store at 70, Champs Elysées. They also had branches in various other countries. The Vuitton Musée du Voyage in Asnières exhibits items made for royalty, opera stars, and other famous people. All Vuitton cases, whether custom-made or not, are numbered and registered in ledgers stored at their main store, Ave. Marceau, Paris. In 1987, the company of Louis Vuitton merged with Moet-Hennessy, makers of champagne.][23]

The Bournes have an expensive car and designer luggage: David keeps his notebooks in "the big Vuitton suitcase" (218; see keys).

waiters. One waiter serves breakfast (43), others bring soup (51–52) and drinks (24, 38, 58, 69, 230, 232), and one refuses to serve David a beer (58; see also André, Aurol's nephew, and background).

Speak: 24, 38, 43, 51–52, 58.

*Winchester. See Eton.

women and girls. An unnamed woman from the fish market kisses David when he lands a big fish (9). See background and the maid.

*women and girls. In David's third African story, a girl and her brother serve beer (202). Catherine presents the image of a screaming Frenchwoman, overwhelmed by the pain of seeing her child killed, to indicate that she understands "how terrible it was" that she destroyed David's stories (237; also see *children, *crowd). When Catherine decides to sleep with Marita, she tells David that she has been approached before by "people wanting to do it with me" (114; see 105). According to Marita, Catherine's first Lesbian affair may not be her last (190–91). David playfully brags of his sexual prowess, and warns "the women of the south" of France to "take care" (167). He locks his work-room, knowing that the cleaning woman has a pass key (78).

*the Woolworths. [The family of Frank Winfield Woolworth, 1852–1919, American merchant who founded the successful national chain of American five- and ten-cent stores that bear his name. See also *FTA*.]
   Catherine and David jokingly include themselves and the Woolworths among America's decadent "oldest families" (96; see also the Jukeses and the Morgans).

Yankee Doodle Dandy. [Popular tune, thought to date back to the American Revolution. The refrain is: Yankee Doodle, keep it up / Yankee Doodle Dandy / Mind the music and the step / And with the girls be handy.]
   Rebuffed by Marita and jealous of the relationship developing between David and Marita, Catherine is nervous and touchy. She criticizes David's colorless language and enjoins him to explain the word "dandy," which is an "Americanism," to Marita. Marita connects the word to the song (134).

Photo of Ernest Hemingway (courtesy Lloyd Arnold and the Hemingway Collection, John F. Kennedy Library)

ENDNOTES

Because I have treated Hemingway's characters as imaginative constructs, the endnotes offer only minimal information about the historical and literary prototypes of such characters. Readers interested in this aspect of the characters, or in the life of the author, or in the complicated relationship between Hemingway's biography, psychology, and fiction, will find much to please them in the biographically-oriented work of Carlos Baker, Michael Reynolds, Jeffrey Meyers, Bernice Kert, Scott Donaldson, Kenneth Lynn and, more recently, James Mellow. Hemingway's contemporaries (Beach, Crosby, Loeb, McAlmon, Stein, Strater, Toklas, and many others) have also written volumes about him and their relationships with him. This wealth of material is only briefly summarized in the first endnote to each chapter.

Frequently cited works by Ernest Hemingway are identified by the following abbreviations:

ARIT	*Across the River and Into the Trees*
DIA	*Death in the Afternoon*
DS	*The Dangerous Summer*
Fifth Column	*The Fifth Column and Four Stories of the Spanish Civil War*
FTA	*A Farewell to Arms*
FWBT	*For Whom the Bell Tolls*
GE	*The Garden of Eden*
GHA	*Green Hills of Africa*
IOT	*In Our Time*
Islands	*Islands in the Stream*
MF	*A Moveable Feast*
MWW	*Men Without Women*
OMS	*The Old Man and the Sea*
SAR	*The Sun Also Rises*
THHN	*To Have and Have Not*
TS	*The Torrents of Spring*
WTN	*Winner Take Nothing*

Although I have consulted several editions of the *Encyclopaedia Britannica,* the *Encyclopedia Americana,* and Webster's dictionaries, I do not cite these basic sources in the endnotes. Material taken from annual supplements to these two encyclopedias, however, is identified as such. Other encyclopedias and dictionaries are cited, and all direct quotes are fully documented. The Hemingway Collection is housed at the John F. Kennedy Library, Columbia Point, Boston, Massachusetts.

INTRODUCTION

1. Archibald MacLeish, *Collected Poems,* 145; Nobel Prize citation, 1954, Stockholm, Sweden.

2. Susan Beegel used the phrase in her 1988 study, *Hemingway's Craft of Omission: Four Manuscript Examples.*

3. Ernest Hemingway, *Death in the Afternoon,* 192.

4. George Plimpton, "The Art of Fiction XXI," 84.

5. Early criticism addressed itself to identifying the historical prototypes for the characters in Hemingway's fictions. Not a few of Hemingway's friends and relatives wrote defensive autobiographies. These were followed by scholarly biographies, the more important full-length studies being Carlos Baker's *Ernest Hemingway: A Life Story* (1969) and the multi-volumed effort of Michael Reynolds, still in progress. Also of note are Scott Donaldson's *By Force of Will: The Life and Art of Ernest Hemingway* (1977), Jeffrey Meyers' *Hemingway: A Biography* (1985), Kenneth S. Lynn's *Hemingway* (1987), and James R. Mellow's *Hemingway: A Life Without Consequences* (1992).

6. Sandra Whipple Spanier, "Hemingway's Unknown Soldier," 82. Looking at *A Farewell to Arms,* for example, Michael Reynolds concluded that Hemingway had researched his topic carefully (*Hemingway's First War: The Making of A Farewell to Arms*), and Robert W. Lewis agreed, noting that Hemingway got many of his facts from Trevelyan ("Hemingway in Italy: Making it Up," 233).

7. Brian Way, "Hemingway the Intellectual," 153, 151.

8. Qtd. in Brasch, "Invention from Knowledge," 22–23.

CHAPTER I: *THE TORRENTS OF SPRING*

1. *Historical and Literary Prototypes.* The writer Scripps O'Neil and the World War I veteran Yogi Johnson suggest aspects of Hemingway's own life. A veteran of World War I, Hemingway spent the fall and winter of 1919 in Petoskey, Michigan, trying to adjust to civilian life. Late in 1925, when he wrote this novel, Hemingway, like O'Neil, was detaching himself from his wife (his elder by eight years) and was involved with a younger woman whom he soon married. The culture-vulture Diana suggests the intellectuals who, in Hemingway's opinion, talked about but did not always make art. Mandy's anecdotes poke fun at the talkative Ford Madox Ford, whom Hemingway attacked frequently (see endnote 1 in *SAR* and the entry for Ford in *MF*).

   Many of the characters in this novel are thinly-veiled parodies of characters in Sherwood Anderson's best-seller, *Dark Laughter*: Scripps O'Neil, his first wife, and their daughter are based on Anderson's Sponge Martin and his family; Scripps' undefined yearnings and his bigamous marriage derive from Anderson's character Bruce Dudley and his adulterous relationship with Aline Grey. The Indians who work in the pump factory recall the nameless employees in Fred Grey's wheel factory. Hemingway also parodies Anderson's style, particularly his penchant for lists. Sherwood Anderson had recently joined the publishing house of Boni and Liveright, where his *Dark Laughter* was a best-seller. Hemingway's deliberate and obvious parody of Anderson, written in just ten days, was designed to force Boni and Liveright, to whom he was contracted, to reject his book and so free him to sign on with Scribner's. The ploy worked and both *TS* and *SAR* (written before *TS* but never submitted to Boni and Liveright) were published by Scribner's. Taylor Alderman suggests that Hemingway's subtitle may derive from Madison Grant's *The Passing of the Great Race* (1916; 4th rev. ed. published by Scribner, 1921), and Daniel Barnes discusses the presence of folktales in the novel.

2. A. P. Herbert, "Preface" to *The Beggar's Opera by John Gay: To Which Is Added the Music to Each Song,* p. vii.

3. "*The Bookman,*" Mott, *A History of American Magazines,* IV: 432–41.

4. Rebecca J. Bates, Curatorial Assistant of the Harvard University Archives, supplied information about Charles Brickley's post-Harvard activities, including clippings from the *Boston Herald,* 30 December,

1949, and the *Boston Globe,* 30 October, 1967 (letter to author, 27 February, 1991). Arthur Daley's testimonial, "The Best of the Drop-Kickers," appeared in the *New York Times,* 5 January, 1950.

5. See Jarvis, *Historical Glimpses—Petoskey,* 106.

6. "Indians, Education of the," *Encyclopedia Americana.*

7. Emily Clark, Assistant Librarian of the Chicago Historical Society, informs me that the Anarchist Memorial Monument was dedicated on 25 June, 1893, and that the sculptor was Albert Weiner or Weinert. The inscription at the base represents one version of August Spies' last words. Ms. Clark supplied two other versions: "There will come a time when our silence will be more powerful than the voices you strangle today," and "Our silence in the grave will be more powerful than our speeches would be." Ms. Clark enclosed a sketch (from the *Chicago Tribune,* 27 June, 1893, 7: 1–2) and a photograph (from the Society's Prints and Photographs Department) of the large, impressive monument (letter to author and enclosures, 1 June, 1991).

8. *"The Dial,"* Mott, *A History of American Magazines,* III: 539–43; Hoffman, Allen and Ulrich, *The Little Magazine,* 196–206.

9. "Dodge, Mabel," *Reader's Encyclopedia.* Lawrence did not like Mabel Dodge Luhan, as his acid description of her indicates: "Mabel Dodge: American, rich, only child . . . has had three husbands—one Evans (dead), one Dodge (divorced), and one Maurice Sterne (a Jew, Russian, painter, also divorced). Now she has an Indian, Tony, stout chap. She has lived much in Europe—Paris, Nice, Florence—is a little famous in New York and little loved, very intelligent as a woman, a 'culture-carrier,' likes to play the patroness, hates the white world and loves the Indian out of hate, is very 'generous,' wants to be 'good' and is very wicked, has a terrible will-to-power, you know—she wants to be a witch and at the same time a Mary of Bethany at Jesus's feet—a big white crow, a cooing raven of ill omen, a white buffalo" (qtd. in Moore, *The Intelligent Heart,* 369–70).

10. For information about Emerson's jobs at Harvard, see "Emerson," *American Authors.*

11. "Enright, Ethel," Obituary, *Encyclopaedia Britannica,* 1969 Book of the Year.

12. The complete title is *An Apology for the Life of Mrs. Shamela Andrews. In Which, the many notorious Falshoods (sic) and Misrepresentations of a Book Called Pamela, are exposed and refuted; and all the matchless Arts of that young Politician, set in a true and just Light.* As late as 1946, the authoritative *Oxford Companion to English Literature* (3rd ed.) wrote that the authorship of *Shamela* "is uncertain (it was perhaps by Fielding)"; the issue seems not to have been settled until Charles B. Woods' "Fielding and the Authorship of *Shamela*," *Philological Quarterly* 25 (1946): 256–72.

13. "Harper," *Encyclopedia Americana;* "Harper's Bazar," "Harper's Monthly Magazine," and "Harper's Weekly," *Oxford Companion to American Literature;* "Harper's," *Reader's Encyclopedia of American Literature.*

14. Letter to author, from Emily Clark, of the Chicago Historical Society, who found these landmarks in the 1923 Chicago city directories (27 December, 1990).

15. Rebecca J. Bates, Curatorial Assistant of the Harvard University Archives, offered this observation (letter to author, 28 December, 1990).

16. "Caricature, Cartoon, and Comic Strip," *Encyclopaedia Britannica, Macropaedia,* 1974, III: 920; "Musial, Joe," Obituary, *Encyclopedia Americana,* 1978 Annual.

17. "Lauder," *Cambridge Guide to World Theatre* and *Who Was Who on Screen.*

18. "Le Gallienne," *Oxford Companion to the Theatre,* 478.

19. "*The Literary Digest,*" Mott, *A History of American Magazines,* IV: 569–79.

20. Mahan Obituary, *New York Times,* 24 July, 1975; 30.

21. In *The Tabula,* the literary magazine of the Oak Park/River Forest High School, Hemingway published a story called "The Judgment of Manitou" (1916). William White notes that the story "has been reprinted at least three times: in Constance Cappel Montgomery, *Hemingway in Michigan* (New York: Fleet Publishing Corporation, 1966), 44–45; Matthew J. Bruccoli, editor, *Ernest Hemingway's*

Apprenticeship: Oak Park, 1916–1917 (Washington, D.C.: NCR Microcard Editions, 1971), 96–97; and David D. Anderson, editor, *Michigan: A State Anthology* (Detroit: Gale Research Company, 1983), 219'' (*The Hemingway Newsletter,* No. 9, January 1985: p. 4).

22. The fact that his wife, Gretchen von Briesen, came from a wealthy German family, probably further injured his reputation at this stage.

23. Reynolds, *The Paris Years,* 337–38; Webster's *Guide to American History,* 328 (on the Preparedness Movement); Obituaries in *New York Times* and *Tribune,* both 9 January, 1954. Gould P. Colman, University Archivist, Cornell University, supplied further information about Menken (letter and enclosures, 21 May 1991).

24. Peterson, *Magazines in the Twentieth Century,* 135.

25. I am grateful to Karl J. Crosby, Serial Reference Specialist of the Library of Congress, Washington, D.C., for information about the unfortunate politics of *American Mercury* after 1950 (letter to author, 15 January, 1991). See also ''Magazines,'' *Reader's Encyclopedia,* 691; and ''*The American Mercury,*'' Mott, *A History of American Magazines,* V:3–26.

26. Meyers obituary, *New York Times,* 27 July, 1971, 34:4.

27. ''Home, Sweet Home'' was composed in 1821 by Sir Henry Bishop (1786–1855). The tune first appeared in an album of national airs, entitled ''Sicilian.'' With the addition of Payne's lyrics it was incorporated in Bishop's opera *Clari, the Maid of Milan.* The lyrics are by John Howard Payne (1791–1852):

'Mid pleasures and palaces though we may roam,
Be it ever so humble, there's no place like home.
A charm from the skies seems to hallow us there,
Which seek thro' the world, is ne'er met with elsewhere.

The refrain is: ''Home! home! sweet, sweet home. / There's no place like home'' (from *Songs the Children Love to Sing,* arranged by Albert E. Wier [New York and London: D. Appleton and Co., 1916], 24–25). See also ''Bishop'' and ''Clari'' in *The Oxford Companion to Music.*

28. "Phelps," *Oxford Companion to American Literature* and *Reader's Encyclopedia.*

29. "Printemps," *Oxford Companion to Film.*

30. Interview with Brad Leech, October 1991. Zelda Gilman and Candy Eaton, of the Little Traverse Historical Society, also supplied information about the Petoskey of Hemingway's time.

31. *"The Saturday Evening Post,"* Mott, *A History of American Magazines,* IV: 671–716; "Magazines," *The Reader's Encyclopedia,* 687.

32. *"Saturday Review,"* Oxford Companion to American Literature.

33. *"Scribner's Magazine,"* Mott, *A History of American Magazines,* III: 457 ff. and IV: 717–32; "Magazines," *Reader's Encyclopedia,* 687.

34. "Stuart," *Dictionary of American Biography.*

35. "Met Museum Given Major Private Collection," *New York Times,* 25 August, 1982.

36. Maude Adams had played the title role in *Peter Pan* in various productions (1905, 1912, 1915); Marilyn Miller replaced her when the play was presented again in 1924. Hemingway had mentioned Maude Adams in the text, but agreed cheerfully with Max Perkins' suggestion to delete her name: "We will change Maude Adams to Lenore Ulrich or Ann Pennington which should be funnier and will make the same joke without mentioning Miss Adams' name" (Baker, *Letters,* 198). Maude Adams would certainly have been an "aging" Peter Pan if she had performed the role again in 1924. My thanks to Peter Hays for providing much of this information. See also Ulric obituary, *Encyclopedia Americana,* 1971 Annual.

37. Mott, *A History of American Magazines,* III: 354 and 479. See "Van Doren, Carl," *Oxford Companion to American Literature;* "Van Doren, Irita," *Dictionary of American Biography, Supplement 8,* 666–68; "Van Doren, Irita," *Who Was Who in America,* IV.

38. *"Vanity Fair,"* Oxford Companion to American Literature.

CHAPTER II: *THE SUN ALSO RISES*

1. *Historical and Literary Prototypes.* Hemingway's biographers, friends, enemies and acquaintances have established that many of the characters in the novel are based on historical figures: Robert Cohn is based on Harold Loeb, whose mother was a Guggenheim; Pedro Romero on Cayetano Ordóñez (Niño de la Palma); Brett Ashley on Lady Duff Twysden; Mike Campbell on Pat Guthrie (according to several biographers, Twysden and Guthrie were cousins as well as lovers: see Fitch, *Walks in Hemingway's Paris,* 139; Diliberto, 197; Mellow, 292); Juan Montoya on Juan Quintana; Bill Gorton on Bill Smith and Don Stewart; Frances Clyne on Kitty Cannell; Mr. and Mrs. Braddocks on Ford Madox Ford and Stella Bowen; Harvey Stone on Harold Stearns; Jake Barnes on Hemingway and so on (see biographies and autobiographies by Baker, Reynolds, Meyers, Hotchner, McAlmon, and Loeb, among others, in Works Cited, as well as Hemingway himself in *DS*). Nicholas Joost disagrees with most biographers by identifying the prototype of Frances Clyne as Lily Lubow (Joost, 73). In her biography of her parents, Honoria Murphy Donnelly writes that her father's sister-in-law, Noel Haskins Murphy, "inspired a minor character named Edna in *The Sun Also Rises*" (*Sara & Gerald,* 134). Another minor character is Vicente Girones, fatally gored during the running of the bulls. He is based on Esteban Domeño Laborra, an unmarried 22-year-old from nearby Sangüesa, who was similarly gored on Sunday morning, 13 July, 1924, by one of the Santa Coloma bulls that were fought that afternoon by Chicuelo, Nacional, and Algabeño. Domeño died Monday morning and was buried the next afternoon. He was the first casualty of an *encierro* (see the local newspapers, *La voz de Navarra,* 15 July, 1924, 1: 1–3, and 16 July, 1924, 6:1; and *El pensamiento Navarro,* 16 July, 1924, front page). Although the novel is based on the events of 1925, Girones' death recalls an event from the previous year. No one was killed during the *encierros* of the 1925 fiesta.

   James Hinkle offers "Some Unexpected Sources for *The Sun Also Rises,*" *Hemingway Newsletter* 2.1 (1982): 26–42. More than one critic has noticed the similarity between Jake Barnes' name and the names and Paris addresses of Natalie Barney (q.v. in *MF*) and the writer Djuna Barnes; Barney lived at 20 rue Jacob and Barnes at the Hotel Jacob et d'Angleterre. The Biblical echoes suggested by Jake's name are explored by, among others, Bates Hoffer in "Jacob: As the Sun Rises," *Linguistics in Literature* 3.2 (1978): 93–108. Mellow reports that F. Scott Fitzgerald disparaged both "the original Duff [and] the imagined Lady Brett Ashley . . . [as] replays of Iris March, the feckless heroine of Michael Arlen's *The Green Hat*" (293).

2. Peter Hays, English Department, University of California at Davis, offered information about the Alexander Hamilton Institute. The Institute has a long list of publications.

3. Bullfighters are often known by nicknames which, if the bullfighter becomes famous, may be adopted by several members of the family. Nicknames may indicate ethnic origin (e.g., *el gitanillo,* the gypsy) or a salient physical feature (*el gordito,* the fat one). Most often, they indicate the bullfighter's birthplace: "el Algabeño" refers to García's hometown, La Algaba (Seville). Hemingway's reference to a hand wound suggests the elder Algabeño, but the dates and the character of the bullfighter suggest the son. Hemingway seems to be conflating the two, although he distinguishes clearly between them in *DIA.* For the father, see "García Rodríguez, José," Cossío, III: 331–33, and "Algabeño," Silva Aramburu, 257. For the son, see "García Carranza, José," Cossío, III: 329–31, and "Algabeño II," Silva Aramburu, 280. The younger Algabeño's Pamplona performances are reviewed in the local daily *El pensamiento Navarro,* 13 and 14 July, 1923, and 12 and 15 July, 1924. The Saturday issue (11 July, 1925) announced the arrival of Belmonte and the expected arrival of Algabeño for that afternoon's *gran corrida extraordinaria.* The Madrid Red Cross *corrida* is also reviewed in this issue, including the fact that Algabeño had been injured by both the bulls he had fought on 10 July. The injuries were not seen as serious then, but the Madrid daily *ABC* explained that Algabeño had had to cancel Pamplona because his arm was inflamed (12 July, 1925, 31:1).

4. Alexander Pollock Moore of Pennsylvania (1867–1930) was appointed Ambassador to Spain in March 1923, presenting his credentials in Madrid on May 16 of that year and holding that position until 20 December, 1925 (letter from J. Dane Hartgrove, of the Civil Reference Branch, National Archives and Records Administration, Washington, D.C.). Hartgrove adds that "Our records do not contain . . . information with regard to contacts between high-level U.S. embassy personnel and Spanish bullfighters" (letter to author, 4 February, 1991). The Ambassador and his party drove to Pamplona for the *corrida de prueba* of 9 July and the *gran corrida extraordinaria* of 11 July, driving back to San Sebastián each evening. The fact that Márquez and Lalanda have driven over to San Sebastián might connect them to the Ambassador's entourage; Montoya expects them to spend the night there.

Ambassador Moore wrote Leandro Nagore, the Mayor of Pamplona, to ask for seats to the Belmonte fight of 11 July. The Mayor seems to have complied, probably inviting him to sit in the President's box. In a letter written from Villa Arbaicenea, San Sebastián, and dated 13 July, the Ambassador thanked the Mayor for the hospitality extended to Mrs. Morris *(sic)*, Miss Leary and himself and invites the Mayor to visit him in San Sebastián or in Madrid (see *El pensamiento Navarro,* 8 July, 1925, 1:6; 10 July 1925, 2:2; and 12 July, 1925, 2:2. The paper misspelled the name in the thank-you note, 15 July, 1925, 1:5). Baker notes that in the manuscript the Ambassador is named Ferdinand J. Watson of Ohio; he is accompanied by his niece and another woman, also an American, called Mrs. Carelton *(Life,* 152).

5. Ashley is not listed in Debrett's or in Burke's *Peerage and Baronetage.*

6. The provenance of the phrase "Irony and Pity" which Gorton sings, probably loudly and mockingly, has occupied a number of critics. Matthew J. Bruccoli traces it to Gilbert Seldes' favorable review of Fitzgerald's *The Great Gatsby,* in the 1925 *Dial.* Hemingway disliked both Seldes and the *Dial* and was jealous of other authors' successes, even when he admired their work, as he did Fitzgerald's novel (see "'Oh, Give Them Irony and Give Them Pity'," *FHA* [1970]: 236; see also Seldes in *MF*). Robert Murray Davis proposes that the phrase is a quote from Paul Elridge's *Irony and Pity: A Book of Tales* (see "Irony and Pity Once More," *FHA* [1973]: 307–08). And Scott Donaldson argues that the phrase comes from Anatole France's *Le Jardin d'Epicure* (1895; English translation 1908; see "'Irony and Pity': Anatole France Got It Up," *FHA* [1978]: 331–34). James Hinkle discusses the humor implicit in Gorton's singing of the phrase in "What's Funny in *The Sun Also Rises"* (*HR* 4.2 [1985]; rpt. in Wagner, *Six Decades,* see pp. 86, 88).

7. "Belmonte García, Juan," Cossío, III: 108–18 and IV: 375; "Sobre el toreo de Belmonte," Cossío, IV: 963–69; "Belmonte," Silva Aramburu, 268–69; and "Juan Belmonte y García," Martínez, 195. Belmonte's 1925 performance in Pamplona was reviewed in the local daily *El pensamiento Navarro,* 12 July, 1925, 1:1–6, and by the Madrid daily *ABC,* 12 July, 1925, 31:1 and 3.

8. Botín's menu details the restaurant's history. Also see Allen Josephs, "At the Heart of Madrid," *Atlantic* 244 (July 1979): 74–77.

9. "Bottechia, Ottavio," *Dizionario Biografico degli Italiani* XIII and *Dizionario Enciclopedico Italiano.*

10. Bryan was author of *First Battle* (1896) and the collected *Speeches* (1909). For his education and death date, see "Bryan, William Jennings," *Dictionary of American Biography,* ed. Allen Johnson (New York, Scribners, 1929), III: 191, 197. As Reynolds has noted, in the days preceding the Pamplona fiesta, which begins early in July, Bryan was still alive; Jake's announcement is premature (*The Paris Years,* 132). Frederic Joseph Svoboda writes that "the comic discussion between Jake and Bill" which begins "with a verbal parody of William Jennings Bryan," includes Bishop Manning and Wayne B. Wheeler because, among other things, "both of them were notable misusers of the language" (*Hemingway,* 17). I believe the parody is based on ideological and generational conflicts as well: the actions of most of the novel's characters indicate their rejection of the strict, reactionary positions on religion, divorce, politics, and drink held by these influential men—and by Hemingway's parents as well.

11. This is doubly an impossibility, since the Veuve Cliquot is (1) a woman and (2) long since dead. For a more thorough explanation of this joke, see Hinkle, 90. Hinkle found sixty jokes in this novel. For more information on Cliquot and Mumm, see Forbes, 454.

12. Harold Loeb, on whom the character of Robert Cohn is based, was the son of Rose Guggenheim, a great heiress, and Albert Loeb, a successful stockbroker. Harold and his first wife Marjorie had two children, Susan and James.

13. Veronique Brown-Claudot, Public Relations, Hotel de Crillon, 10 Place de la Concorde, Paris 75008, supplied brochures about the hotel and its history and offered additional information in a personal interview, Paris, 18 December, 1991.

14. "Jack Dempsey," Menke, 246 and *Collier's Encyclopedia* IV: 443–44 and VIII: 98.

15. "Gigantes y cabezudos," *Gran Enciclopedia Navarra* V: 349–52. For handsome illustrations of all these figures, see *Sanfermines,* 160–73.

16. "Fermín, San," *Gran Enciclopedia Navarra* V: 91; "Sanfermines," *Gran Enciclopedia Navarra* X:172–180, esp. 172 and 177; "Fermín, San," *Gran Enciclopedia Rialp* X: 21–22; "San Fermín's Cult," *Sanfermines,* 31–39; and "The Procession,"

Sanfermines, 58–67. The *Diccionario Enciclopédico Abreviado* (1954) also mentions a French saint by the same name, a fourth-century prelate who was the Bishop of Amiens. His feast day is the first of September.

17. Not much is written about Tiger Flowers, but see Morrison, *Boxing: The Records,* 60–64. Scoop Gallello, boxing historian and President of the International Veteran Boxers Association, New Rochelle, N.Y., generously provided information about the boxers Kid Francis, Kid Ledoux, and Tiger Flowers (telephone interview, 6 December, 1991; letters to author with enclosures, 24 March and 12 December, 1991 and 14 February, 1992).

18. Donaldson mentions that the Fratellini clowns had been admitted to the French Academy in 1924 and that they had been written up in the *New York Times Magazine* that same year (15 June, 1924), two years before the publication of *The Sun Also Rises* (" 'Irony and Pity': Anatole France Got It Up," 333–34).

19. Obituaries, *Americana* Annual 1974, 445; *New York Times,* 19 February, 1973, 17:1.

20. "Gayarre, Julián," *Enciclopedia Universal Ilustrada;* "Gayarre, Sebastián Julián," *Gran Enciclopedia Rialp;* "Gayarre Garjón, Sebastián Julián," *Gran Enciclopedia Navarra* V: 323–27.

21. "Gómez Ortega, José," Cossío, III: 364–79; "Joselito," Cossío, IV: 959–63; "Gómez Ortega, Joselito," Silva Aramburu, 267–68; "José Gómez Ortega," Martínez, 193–94.

22. "Gómez Ortega, Rafael," Cossío, III: 384–90; "Rafael Gómez, 'el Gallo'," Silva Aramburu, 262–63.

23. "Hernández, Rafael (Rafael)," Cossío, II: 633; "Hernández Ramírez, Rafael," Cossío, VI: 947 (section entitled "Escritores taurinos").

24. For a succinct review of details linking Brett and Georgette, see E. Roger Stephenson "Hemingway's Women," 36.

25. The manuscript identifies Hoffenheimer as Joseph Hergesheimer (American writer, 1880–1954); he and Mencken were good friends. Hemingway changed the name at Scribner's insistence (Baker, *Letters,* 213).

26. Although Hemingway mocks Hubert's parents, he had shared their sentiments only a few years before the writing of this novel. In August 1920, he hoped to "buy a car in the Spring and then [drive] over all the country next summer. I hate buzzing all over Europe when there is so much of my own country I haven't seen" (Baker, *Letters,* 37).

27. Ben Primer, University Archivist, Princeton University, supplied information about Spider Kelly, including *The Nassau Sovereign,* February 1940; the quoted material is from page 15 (letter to author, 9 October, 1990).

28. "Lalanda del Pino, Marcial," Cossío, III: 475–80 and IV: 523–24; "Marcial Lalanda," Silva Aramburu, 277; "El matador de toros Marcial Lalanda muere en Madrid a la edad de 87 años" and "El más grande," both articles published in the daily newspaper *El país* (26 October, 1990): 41. Lalanda's performances in Pamplona were reviewed on the front pages of *El pensamiento Navarro,* 10, 12 and 14 July, 1925, and in the Madrid daily *ABC,* 10 July, 1925, 18:3 and 14 July, 1925, 14:1.

29. Of the many books which deal with the Paris Hemingway knew, the most informative are Arlen J. Hansen's *Expatriate Paris: A Cultural and Literary Guide to Paris of the 1920s* (New York: Arcade Publishing/Little, Brown & Co., 1990) and John Leland's *A Guide to Hemingway's Paris* (Chapel Hill, N.C.: Algonquin Books, 1989). Robert E. Gajdusek's *Hemingway's Paris* (New York: Scribner's, 1978) is lavishly illustrated. For information on Paris in the 1930s and later, see Herbert R. Lottman, *The Left Bank: Writers, Artists, and Politics from the Popular Front to the Cold War* (Boston: Houghton Mifflin, 1982).

30. Leblanc's sexual orientation and marital status, like her birthdate, are difficult to ascertain. Michael Reynolds identifies her as a Lesbian, "a singer and the loving friend for whom Margaret Anderson had left Jane Heap" (*The Paris Years,* 310). James Hinkle describes her as "the ex-mistress of Maeterlinck, an actress, singer, and past-middle-aged eccentric who regularly bicycled around Paris in a flowing medieval robe of gold-flowered velvet" (Wagner, 89). The *New York Times* agrees, discreetly noting that "She was known during the years of their companionship as Mme. Maeterlinck" (29 October, 1941, 23:3). Noel Riley Fitch identifies her as "the former wife of Maurice Maeterlinck" (*Sylvia Beach and the Lost Generation,* 156). Hinkle finds that Georgette Hobin's

484 Endnotes pages 91–94

dislike of the Flemish suggests a Hemingway insult to Maeterlinck, who was "insistently" Flemish ("Some Unexpected Sources," 38).

31. The quoted material is from "Boniface VII," *Encyclopaedia Britannica,* 11th ed., IV: 207. Also see "Lemoine, Jean," *Grand Dictionnaire Encyclopédique Larousse,* 1984 ed., and Leland 9 and 35–36.

32. "Lenglen, Suzanne," *New Columbia Encyclopedia* and *Oxford Companion to Sports and Games.*

33. Reynolds identifies Lett as "Arthur Lett-Haines, lover of Cedric Morris the painter" (*Paris Years,* 310–11 and 387, n. 24). In Hilda Doolittle's post-World War II novel, *Bid Me to Live* (New York: Grove, 1960), a character named Lett Barnes is a poet and the friend of the main character, Julia Ashton. Hilda Doolittle (1886–1961, known as H.D.) was one of the expatriate crowd in Paris. It is interesting although probably coincidental that both the first and last names of her character echo the names of characters in *The Sun Also Rises.*

34. My thanks to Professor Joseph J. Feeney, S.J., Department of English, Saint Joseph's University, Philadelphia, Pennsylvania, who helped me understand that the joke about Bishop Manning is based on incongruity. He pointed out that the Protestant Episcopalian Manning had no connection to Loyola and that H. L. Mencken did not go to college at all (letter to author, 8 August, 1991). Bishop Manning graduated from the University of the South, Sewanee, Tennessee, in 1893 (*Encyclopedia Americana*). See also "Bishop Manning, 83, Dies in Retirement," *New York Times,* 19 November, 1949, pp. 1 and 9; and "Pomp of Centuries at Manning Rites," *New York Times,* 23 November, 1949, 30.

35. "Márquez y Serrano, Antonio," Cossío, III: 542–45 and IV: 552; "Antonio Márquez," Silva Aramburu, 277. For detailed reviews of the 1925 performances, see the local daily newspaper *El pensamiento Navarro,* 8 July, 1925, 1:3; 10 July, 1925, 1:3; and 14 July, 1925, 1:2–3. Also see the taurine reviews in the Madrid daily *ABC:* "Cuatro toros de Cándido Díaz," *ABC,* 10 July, 1925, 18:3; and "Seis toros de Pablo Romero," *ABC,* 14 July, 1925, 14:1.

36. See Harold Hinsdill Smedley, *Fly Patterns and Their Origins,* 63–64. For information about fishing and fishing tackle, I am

grateful to Ernest Schwiebert and to Alanna Fisher, Curator, The American Museum of Fly Fishing, Manchester, VT. The fly is described in A. J. McClane's *Standard Fishing Encyclopedia* (see Wet Flies) but I prefer Schwiebert's more sensuous description: "the McGinty was brightly colored and a bit gaudy. It was tied with a tail of scarlet hackle fibers, alternating wraps of black and yellow chenille intended to suggest the fat body of a honey bee, a throat of chocolate brown cock's hackle, and a white-tipped wing of blue mallard wing feathers" (letter to author, 21 December, 1991). By World War II its popularity had faded.

37. "Indice alfabético y fecha en que, por vez primera a su nombre, se han corrido toros, como nuevos, en las plazas de Madrid, desde el año 1765," Cossío, I: 318; see also I: 283–84 and IV: 213. For the great Miura controversy, see Cossío, III: 952–53 and "El pleito de los Miuras," Silva Aramburu, 260–62. Silva Aramburu's date, 1808 (top 262), is clearly a typographical error, the correct date being 1908. The *corrida* of 8 July, 1925 was reviewed in the local daily, *El pensamiento Navarro* on the front page of 9 July. Although the bulls were a disappointment in the ring, they had provided plenty of excitement during the *encierro* at 6:00 AM, almost goring two young men on Calle Estafeta.

38. "Anlló y Orrío, Ricardo (Nacional)," Cossío, III: 41–42 and V: 623; and "Anlló y Orrío, Juan (Nacional II)," Cossío, III: 39–40. Nacional II died 6 October, 1925 as a result of a headwound suffered during a ringside brawl.

39. In response to his editor's remarks that using recognizable names in the book might result in libel suits, Hemingway wrote, "Roger Prescott is now Roger Prentiss. I believe I went to school with a Roger Prentiss but at least he was not Glenway [Wescott]" (Baker, *Letters,* 213). Jake's strongly negative response to homosexuals (20–21) is shared by Count Mippipopolous (63). William Kerrigan and Leon Seltzer find that the Count resembles Jake in that he too is "physically impotent" (Seltzer, 4). Having transcended his impotence at the time Jake meets him, the Count can be seen as a role model for Jake, "a sort of successful Jake Barnes" who embodies the attitudes and pleasures Jake will have to cultivate in order to compensate for his loss (Seltzer, 8).

40. "Sanfermines," *Gran enciclopedia Navarra* X: 176–177; "The 'riau-riau'," *Sanfermines,* 49–54. Federico García romantically describes the "¡Riau! ¡Riau!" as "a defiant, centuries-old and

eternal cry, an expression of the brave Navarrese spirit'' (''El encierro de Pamplona,'' in *La fiesta nacional: Libro de oro de la tauromaquia,* ed. Antonio Fernández Martín [Barcelona, 1951], p. 194, my translation).

41. ''Romero, Pedro,'' Cossío, III: 825–34; ''Pedro Romero y lo rondeño,'' Cossío, IV: 866–70; ''El coloso del siglo: Pedro Romero,'' Silva Aramburu, 233–35.

42. Ordóñez's performances were reviewed on the front pages of *El pensamiento Navarro* of 8, 10, 12 and 14 July, 1925, and in the Madrid daily *ABC,* 10 July, 1925, 18:3 and 14 July, 1925, 14:1. He was awarded only one ear in Pamplona, for his first bull of 12 July: according to Baker, he had dedicated that bull to Hadley Hemingway and gave her the ear (*Life,* 151–52).

43. ''Sarasate Navascués, Pablo,'' *Gran Enciclopedia Navarra* X: 273–74.

44. When Bill Gorton compares himself to a cat, the image recalls Harvey Stone to Jake's mind (73).

45. ''Villalta y Serris, Nicanor,'' Cossío, III: 995–96; ''Villalta,'' Silva Aramburu, 282.

46. The Villar *corrida* was reviewed in *El pensamiento Navarro,* 8 July, 1925, 1:1–5: it was a good *corrida.*

47. ''Wheeler, Wayne Bidwell, *Dictionary of American Biography* (New York: Scribner's, 1936), XX: 55.

CHAPTER III: *A FAREWELL TO ARMS*

1. *Historical and Literary Prototypes.* Various biographers have found traces of Hadley Richardson Hemingway, Pauline Pfeiffer Hemingway, and Agnes Hannah von Kurowsky, who nursed Hemingway when he was wounded in Italy, in the character of Catherine. Von Kurowsky herself has suggested Elsie Jessup (another American Red Cross nurse) as ''the pattern for some of Hemingway's characterization of Catherine Barkley'' (qtd. in Reynolds, *Hemingway's First War,* 174) and Bernice Kert suggests that Catherine's ''Scottish origins and mannerisms were derived from Duff Twysden'' (*The Hemingway Women,* 218). Count Giuseppe Greppi,

who died at the age of 102, is probably the prototype for Count Greffi, and the various nurses and doctors who tended Hemingway in the Red Cross Hospital in Milan served as models for Miss Gage, Miss Ferguson, Mrs. Walker and the Head Nurse. Henry Serrano Villard, who knew Hemingway, Von Kurowsky, and many others associated with the American Hospital in Milan, shared his papers and memories with James Nagel, the result being *Hemingway in Love and War* (Boston: Northeastern U.P., 1989), which presents Villard's and von Kurowsky's letters, photographs, and diaries, as well as other valuable primary materials. The Guttingens' inn recalls the Gangwisch Pension in Switzerland. Among the many biographical critics who have examined the relationship between biography and fictional characters are Carlos Baker (*Life*, 152 ff.) and Michael Reynolds (*Hemingway's First War*, 160–80).

Edward Engelberg finds that Frederic Henry's name and development derive from Flaubert's Frédéric Moreau, noting that in the "first" version of *L'Education Sentimentale*, "completed in 1845 [and] published 1909–1912 . . . The hero's name is Henry" (191). Robert O. Stephens argues that Hemingway is rooted in Stendhal's *The Charterhouse of Parma*, most notably "in the comparable passages of battle and retreat" but also in Hemingway's "subtle uses of Fabrizio's pattern of development and discovery" when he created Frederic Henry (279). Reynolds also discusses the journalistic, historical and fictional sources of *A Farewell to Arms*, noting the connection to Stendhal and also identifying Stephen Crane's *The Red Badge of Courage* as an influence (*Hemingway's First War*, 148–160). He also points out that the name Rinaldo Rinaldi appears in Hugh Dalton's 1919 book, *With British Guns in Italy* (*Hemingway's First War*, 150). In "Hemingway and Peele," Robert Fleming discusses the relevance of George Peele's poem "A Farewell to Arms" to Hemingway's first chapter.

2. Letter to author, 13 January, 1992. The Spanish tenor Plácido Domingo, who recorded the aria "O paradis sorti de l'onde" in 1981, "was the prime mover for recent revivals of this opera in San Francisco and London" (Martin Bernheimer, "Plácido Domingo, Carlo Maria Giulini," Introduction for *Opern-Gala*, Deutsche Grammophon Compact Disc 400 030-2, Hamburg: Polydor International GmbH, 1981).

3. *"Alpino, truppe alpine," Dizionario Enciclopedico Italiano* I: 312.

4. The United States declared war on April 1, 1917.

5. For the genealogy, see "Savoia (Savoia-Aosta), Emanuele Filiberto di" and "Savoia, Tav. VII" in *Dizionario Enciclopedico Italiano* X: 862, 889; "Amadeo Ferdinando Maria di Savoia" in *Dizionario Enciclopedico Italiano* I: 351; and "the Royal House of Italy," in *Burke's Royal Families* I: 365–67.

6. The 1920 Astra Model 200, which is based on the 1911 Victoria Model, has a very short barrel (56mm long; total length is 110mm), as Henry's weapon does. Like its predecessor the Victoria, it is 6.35 caliber weapon, mainly useful for self-defense. Hernández Menéndez offers pictures and a diagram of the Astra 200 (p. 189) but not of the Victoria. For the Astra 7.65, Model 300, produced in 1921, see Hernández Menéndez, 190 and Sopena Garreta, 164. For the quality of Astra weapons, see the entry for Star in *FWBT*.

7. The hitchhikers they pick up underscore the contrast between the gentler Aymo and the rougher Bonello: Aymo picks up two harmless, frightened girls (see virgins), but the self-centered Bonello's riders are two sullen engineers who refuse to help those who help them (see Sergeants from the Engineering Corps). Bonello kills one of them and later defects; presumably, he survives the war. But Aymo is shot, probably by the Italian rear guard. The narrator reflects that sometimes "they killed you gratuitously like Aymo" (327).

8. Henry grows the beard at Catherine's instigation. Her remarks that growing it "might be fun" and "exciting" (298, 300) and his rejoinder that "It will give me something to do" recall Lady Bracknell's approval of Jack's smoking: "A man should always have an occupation of some kind" (Oscar Wilde's *The Importance of Being Earnest* [first performed 1895, published 1899], Act I).

9. "*Bersagliere*," *Dizionario Enciclopedico Italiano* II: 239.

10. Mariani G. Luigi, Manager of the Grand Hotel des Iles Borromees, Stresa, supplied details about the hotel. Mr. Luigi writes that the barman Emilio does not appear in the hotel's records, but adds that he "could have existed" (letter to author, 31 August, 1991).

11. Reynolds writes that "The facts could be no more accurate if they were in a military history, which is where Hemingway very likely found many of them" (*Hemingway's First War,* 103). My point is that they are reported by a British individual, not an American or an Italian.

12. "Cadorna, Luigi," Herwig and Heyman, 103–5; and in *Dizionario Enciclopedico Italiano* II: 590.

13. Robert W. Lewis notes that G. M. Trevelyan, author of *Scenes from Italy's Wars* (London: T.C. and E.C. Jack, 1919) mentions this fact: "They call the Carabinieri 'aeroplanes,' on account of their wide-winged hats." Lewis argues that Hemingway got many of his facts from Trevelyan ("Hemingway in Italy: Making it Up," 233). See "carabiniere," *Dizionario Enciclopedico Italiano* II: 759.

14. The manager of Hotel Cavour supplied information about the new hotel (letter to author, 8 August, 1991).

15. The first of the several messages printed on the Field Service Post Cards read "I am quite well." Paul Fussell remarks that "The egregious *quite* seems to have struck users of the card as so embarrassing that they conveniently forgot it as the years passed." Fussell adds several examples of veterans who, like Henry, misre-member the message as "I am well" (*The Great War and Modern Memory*, 185).

    Both in wartime and peacetime censors concern themselves with morality. When Henry jokingly warns Ferguson not to "write anything that will bother the censor" (25), he probably means "anything spicy or sexy." Ferguson either misses or rejects his sexual banter and prefers to interpret his "anything" as "anything unpatriotic": "Don't worry. I only write about what a beautiful place we live in and how brave the Italians are" (25). Catherine, who probably intends to write sexy letters to Henry, asks, "Do they read your letters?" (155).

16. Henry twice takes Ferguson's place next to Catherine, when Catherine and Helen are sitting in pleasant, even romantic settings: the garden at the British hospital in Gorizia (25) and the dining room at the hotel in Stresa (246). Both times Catherine and Ferguson are alone together when Henry arrives, and both times Catherine shifts her attention from Ferguson to Henry, a shift of which Ferguson is aware and which pains her. Henry's remark that, unlike Othello, he is "not jealous" immediately makes Catherine think of Ferguson (257), whose stormy tears (246–47) were due to exactly that cause. Fern Kory remarks that in thinking back over the events of his life with Catherine, Frederic realizes that Ferguson is "a person with her own story." She is, but her "story" focuses on Catherine and not, as Kory argues, on "some experience beyond, or, more likely, previous to the present situation" ("A Second Look," 22–23). I

disagree with Kory's conclusion that "Ferguson took an active role in making Catherine's romance possible," that "She encourages the relationship" (25). She simply recognizes that Catherine is in love with a man, and either cries or walks away when he shows up.

17. Although Henry probably does speak Italian with an accent (see the barber), he was singled out by the battle police for being an officer, not for having an accent. Other officers who are shot have Italian accents. The "floorwalker" comparison is confused and improbable, but Frederick was tired and under great stress when he made it. It is a striking enough comparison for him to remember it later, when he writes the scene.

18. Lewis discusses "reversals and disguises" (*Hemingway on Love*, 41–42). Even the title of the novel suggests games: George Peele's poem was commissioned by Sir Henry Lee (1530–1610) to explain and excuse his retirement from chivalric games and tournaments.

19. The Gran Italia, like Biffi's, is at the Galleria Vittorio Emanuele, Milan.

20. Atkins makes the valid point that "the culture of the past is an enigma to most people in the present." To Henry, the busts all looked the same; they "all looked like a cemetery" (*FTA*, 28). Similarly, he notes the decay of the frescoes (*FTA*, 29). Atkins describes Henry's remarks as "A straightforward admission that the past was dead and could not speak to us over the gap of time. . . . the art and skill of the past have been debased to a decoration of a war that is destroying all it stands for" (*The Art of Ernest Hemingway*, 180, 183). Interestingly enough, when the same villa is connected to the British, it is described in positive terms, with the emphasis on the pastoral: "It was really very large and beautiful and there were fine trees in the grounds" (*FTA*, 25). Catherine, who walks with Henry in the garden, is compared to a statue at the end of the novel (*FTA*, 332).

21. *"Granatiere," Dizionario Enciclopedico Italiano* V: 541.

22. Even while Frederic Henry is in uniform, Helen Ferguson and Catherine Barkley address him as "Mr. Henry" (25, 29), as if he were a civilian. Scott Donaldson's statement "that nowhere in the novel does Catherine Barkley refer to her lover by name" is correct only in that she never calls him by his first name. Donaldson's discussion of Henry's name is thorough and interesting, particularly

his noticing that Henry is often called "a boy" and addressed as "baby" and "darling" (*By Force of Will*, 153). After the defection, the still-uniformed narrator is called Tenente and Signor Tenente by the porter and his wife, although they are playing "dumb" (240). Thereafter he is called Henry and Mr. Henry by several other characters (240, 241, 297, 307, 316, 319, 331). Simmons and the hospital staff repeat his last name rather insistently.

23. Several critics have addressed the question of when the first-person narrator wrote the narrative. Gerry Brenner argues that *FTA* was written soon after Catherine's death and shortly before Frederic Henry's suicide and that Henry "is a disoriented and, ultimately, untrustworthy narrator" (*Concealments in Hemingway's Works*, 31–35). More recently, James Phelan argued that Henry is "speaking from the time of the action" ("Distance, Voice, and Temporal Perspective in Frederic Henry's Narration: Successes, Problems and Paradox," in Donaldson, *New Essays*, 56). Most critics, myself among them, believe that the narrative was written quite some time after the events. In the late 1960s, Delbert Wylder wrote that "the narrator is reflecting upon an experience which took place long . . . ago" (68). In 1973 Arnold E. Davidson argued that the passage of time allowed "the development of consciousness and the growth of awareness" which define the difference between the "protagonist-narrator" and the "protagonist actor" (127). James Nagel argues convincingly that the novel is "a retrospective narrative told by Frederic Henry a decade after the action has taken place" ("Catherine Barkley and Retrospective Narration in *A Farewell to Arms*," in Wagner, *Ernest Hemingway: Six Decades*, 171). Dale Edmonds finds that ten years have elapsed between events and narration ("When Does Frederic Henry Narrate *A Farewell to Arms?*"). See also my entries for the priest and Ruth, both of whom are also discussed by Nagel.

24. Robert Jordan (*FWBT*) also recalls both his grandparents. I believe that Henry is the only male character in the Hemingway opus to have a stepfather. A female character, Audrey Bruce, has at least two stepfathers (see Bill Bruce, Dick Raeburn and Geoffrey Townsend in *Islands*).

25. In contrast, British equipment receives high praise: Henry carries "an English gas mask," which he approvingly describes as "a real mask" (29). The gas mask hangs in his room (11) but he takes it with him when he goes "up to the posts" (29). We never see him or anyone else wear one, although when he is drunk Henry remarks

that "Anything can go in a gas mask. I've vomited into a gas mask," the implication being that he was wearing it at the time, not holding it (77). Rinaldi accuses him of bragging (77).

26. Henry reads in the old newspapers that "They had stopped racing in France" and realizes "That was where our horse Japalac came from" (136). Japalac probably stopped at San Siro on his way to safety in the south of Italy. Even the "terrible lot" (127) of horseflesh which runs at San Siro is later evacuated to Rome "and there was no more racing" (133).

27. The Japalac episode encapsulates Barkley's and Henry's responses to the war and indicates that Catherine is far ahead of Henry in the process of disengaging from convention and society and making a separate peace. The four young people feel "we *ought* to back" the French horse Japalac (my emphasis), as if this action carried moral significance. Catherine "was sure his color had been changed" when she "agreed we ought to back him," but at this stage none of them realizes that there is more crookedness involved in the racing than just dyeing the horse. She quickly understands that the betting process is dishonest as well and that she and her friends have been taken in by it: she acknowledges that "if it hadn't been crooked [i.e., if the odds hadn't been so long] we'd never have backed him at all." She honestly admits that "I would have liked the three thousand lire" and then distances herself from the whole system, preferring to "back a horse we've never heard of and that Mr. Meyers won't be backing." The whole process—being tricked into participation (by appearances, rhetoric, or romantic ideas), expecting victory, realizing that the whole undertaking is immoral, abandoning it, and then embarking upon independent action (at which point they can see "the mountains off in the distance") even though it is sure not to be profitable or triumphant—all this summarizes her experience of the war and her commitment to life and love outside society. Henry and Mr. Meyers are a little slower to catch on: Catherine mocks their "touching faith" when she hears they have bet on another hot tip. Of course, the same thing happens: the winning horse "did not pay anything." Catherine learns more quickly than the others and doesn't hesitate to discard false systems. She doesn't attempt to understand or beat the system or to give it another chance; she simply undertakes separate, independent action. In this episode, as in others, Henry follows her lead. Thus, the episode foreshadows their defections (from nursing, from war, from Italy, in that order) and hints at the happiness that independent action can bring (in the mountains). It does not touch upon

Catherine's difficult labor and death, events which are unrelated to society or personality and against which no amount of courage or brains can prevail.

28. McAdams is a fictional name. J. Dane Hartgrove of the National Archives in Washington, D.C. informs me that three American diplomats served as vice-consuls in Milan during World War I: they were N. Lyle Robb, Ilo C. Funk, and Roy L. McLaughlin. McLaughlin, whose nickname could have been Mac, served in Milan from October 1918 until November 1919 (letter to author, 4 February, 1991).

29. The episode is interesting both for the vanity and self-pity Henry displays: he had just had himself shaved and had self-consciously "walked along the side street practising not limping." More self-pity emerges in the phrase "went home to the hospital." And Henry insists on wearing his cap to look "more military," posing in full military regalia as he occupies the position recently held by two "giggling girls." Jackson J. Benson, however, find that "a genuine wave of affection passes between Henry and the artist" (*Hemingway: The Writer's Art of Self-Defense,* 108).

30. Robert Lorenz, researcher for the Museum of Montreux, writes that in the 1920s the Montreux shop was managed by an employee, not a member of the family (letter to author, with enclosures, 26 August, 1991). M. Guenot, of the Registre du Commerce des districts de Vevey et de Lavaux, provided information on the Montreux branch (letter and enclosure, 21 April, 1992) and B. Stadler, of the Staatsarchiv des Kantons Zurich, supplied information about the Zurich branch of the company (letter and enclosures, 17 March, 1992). Additional information was sent me by Robert Buscaglia, Office de l'état civil, Geneva (letters, 23 and 24 June, 1992), and by Jean-Etienne Genequand, Archiviste d'Etat adjoint, Archives d'Etat, Geneva (letter and enclosures, 7 July, 1992). François Och kindly supplied information about his family's business and its history, including xeroxes of several brochures from the years 1905 to 1920 (fax of 19 May, 1992; letter and enclosures, 26 June, 1992).

31. It is interesting that Rinaldi holds such a low rank, particularly in view of Henry's remark that a surgeon who "was any good . . . would be made a major" (98). Rinaldi seems to be a good doctor; he has "fine surgeon's hands" and claims that he is "becoming a lovely surgeon" (166–67) who will publish in *The Lancet* (q.v.). But Rinaldi mistreats his syphilis with mercury. When his com-

manding officer, the Major (q.v.), points out that the arsenic-based salvarsan (q.v.) is the proper treatment, Rinaldi incorrectly calls it "A mercurial product" (175). Henry makes no remarks about Rinaldi's being only a lieutenant, but he does connect rank and competence in another context, pointing out that the incompetent doctors who examined him in Milan are merely captains and that the skillful Dr. Valentini is a major (98–99). Most of the doctors (q.v.) at the field hospital are "medical captains" (i.e., awarded the rank because of their medical, not their military, qualifications).

32. Letter to author from the Press Office, Teatro alla Scala, Milan, 13 January, 1992.

33. Henry himself gets a "violent bump" on the forehead when he deserts (229). Two months later he still has "a big bump" (298).

34. Letter to author from the Press Office, Teatro alla Scala, Milan, 13 January, 1992.

35. "Victor Emmanuel III," Herwig and Heyman, 347–48; "Victor Emmanuel III," *Who Was Who in World War II*, 213–14.

36. Reynolds reports that Frederic Henry's description of the King is accurate (*Hemingway's First War*, 92). See also games and play—acting.

37. Like Catherine, Cantwell has outgrown the picturesque (*ARIT*, 34); Catherine and David Bourne also dislike the picturesque (*GE*, 87). The word is used three times by Renata (*ARIT*, 147, 218–19).

38. Henry is essentially monogamous. Although he frequented prostitutes, Rinaldo recalls him "trying to brush away the Villa Rossa from your teeth in the morning . . . cursing harlots . . . trying to clean your conscience with a toothbrush" (168). Even before he falls in love with Catherine, he prefers a relationship with one woman to the more promiscuous behavior of his fellow officers (30).

CHAPTER IV: *TO HAVE AND HAVE NOT*

1. *Historical and Literary Prototypes.* The characters of Helene and Tommy Bradley are said to be based on Jane and Grant Mason; McLendon, who seems ignorant of Hemingway's affair with Jane Mason, identifies Martha Gellhorn (q.v. in *FWBT*) as the prototype

for Helene Bradley and Hemingway as Richard Gordon (*Papa*, 174–75). Several critics argue that Richard Gordon is based on John Dos Passos (e.g., Robert Fleming, "The Libel of Dos Passos in *To Have and Have Not*," 597–601). Helen Gordon shares many characteristics, most notably her Roman Catholicism and crumbling marriage, with Pauline Pfeiffer Hemingway, and Helen's husband Richard is, like Hemingway, writing an inept novel of social significance. Most of the "other characters in the novel are based on his friends and enemies" (Meyers, *Hemingway*, 294). Carlos Baker identifies the prototypes for these and other characters: Freddy Wallace is based on Joe (Josie) Russell, the owner of the boat *Anita* and of Sloppy Joe's bar in Key West; Robert Simmons (Bee-Lips) on Key West lawyer George Brooks; John MacWalsey on Arnold Gingrich and Professor Harry Burns; and so on. Baker remarks that in *THHN* Hemingway "continued to indulge his taste for personal satire" (*Life*, 295). McLendon describes George Brooks as small, thin, drunken, and given to stupid practical jokes; he identifies Albert 'Old Bread' Pinder and Hamilton 'Sack of Ham' Adams as prototypes for Hemingway's down-and-out character Albert Tracy, although in the early 1930s Pinder was well-off, the owner of a "large new charterboat" (*Papa*, 152–55, 157, 63–64). Also see endnote 5.

Some of the Morgan material was first published in the magazines *Cosmopolitan* (1934) and *Esquire* (1936).

2. "Allen, Gracie Ethel Cecile Rosalie," Obituary, *Encyclopaedia Britannica*, 1965 Book of the Year.

3. Morgan suspects that "the coast guard will pinch" some of the stolen money (174). The coast guard men virtuously and repeatedly insist to the sheriff that they "didn't want to touch" the money and that "Everything's just like it was. The money and the guns. Everything" (248, 249–50).

4. Mary Louise Brown, Curator of Collections and Assistant Archivist of the Anheuser-Busch Companies, kindly supplied information about the lithograph and its history (letter to author and enclosures, 19 November, 1990).

5. The wealthy, good father is probably based on Pauline Pfeiffer Hemingway's rich uncle, Gustavus Adolphus (Gus) Pfeiffer, whose wealth came from Sloan's Liniment, the Richard Hudnut line of perfumes, and William Warner Pharmaceuticals. Gus Pfeiffer financed most of the Key West house as well as Pauline and Hemingway's safari to Africa. Hemingway dedicated *A Farewell to*

Arms to this generous uncle-in-law. Michael Reynolds points out that Hemingway's first wife, Hadley Richardson, had also inherited drug-store money. The Richardson Drug Company, founded by Hadley's grandfather, "was the largest drug company west of the Mississippi" in the 1880s (*The Young Hemingway,* 151). Hadley's father mismanaged his inheritance and committed suicide in 1905; Hadley's trust fund helped to support her and Hemingway in Paris.

6. The writer in this novel is married to Helen Gordon, "a very pretty dark girl . . . the prettiest stranger in Key West that winter" (138) and probably the most beautiful woman in the novel, but he cannot hold her. The novel's attack against writers is pretty thorough. The narrative mocks Richard Gordon's published and unpublished fiction and presents him as an imperceptive, despicable human being who uses his profession as an excuse for self-indulgence. He is insulted by his wife and his mistress, slapped and beaten up, until he finally looks like "Some poor goddamned rummy" to Marie Morgan (255).

7. Information about Key West personalities and place names was supplied by Tom Hambright, Local and State History Department, Monroe County May Hill Russell Library, Key West, Florida. Hambright concludes that Walton is a fictitious name: "The 1927 Key West City Directory lists two Walton's, both are African American women. Whalton is the more common Key West name. There are seven listings under that name" in the directory (letter to author, 31 December, 1992).

8. The grain broker "used to say that only suckers worried" (236, 238), a sentiment repeated by Freddy Wilson (*Islands,* 43). Hemingway himself told Lillian Ross that "Only suckers worry about saving their souls" (*Portrait,* 68). Worry can be deadly: Hudson says that "worry kills big businessmen right in their prime" (*Islands,* 312).

9. The Exhibition of 1883, sponsored by the Prince of Wales and held in South Kensington, London, was "devoted to a display of the various industries connected with fishing. . . . The Crystal Palace held a successful International Exhibition in 1884" (*Encyclopaedia Britannica,* 11th ed, X: 69a). Ernest Schwiebert offers information on the Hardys and their company in *Trout Tackle: Part Two* (New York: E. P. Dutton, Inc., 1984) and in a letter to the author, 21 December, 1991. Surviving invoices indicate that Hemingway bought Hardy rods and other equipment in 1932–1935 (Hemingway Collection: Other Materials, Service/Store Receipts). Some of this equipment is displayed at the American Museum of Fly Fishing in Vermont.

10. In the 1940s, "the newly developed lighter diesel engines displaced the gasoline engines in the marine market, due to their inherently greater fuel economy, longer life and reduced fire hazard." Kermath's forte was the production of gasoline marine engines. The company attempted to enter the diesel market, "buying truck/industrial [diesel] engines . . . and converting these to marine use. This was not a successful strategy," and the company collapsed in the spring of 1956, selling "the real estate, the machinery and equipment, the vehicles, the special tools, the drawings, the inventory of engines and parts (finished and unfinished)" at public auction. For this detailed information about Kermath, I am grateful to Gabor M. Korody, founder of the Korody-Colyer Corporation (manufacturers of diesel engine parts, now a division of the Swedish SKF AB), who attended the 1956 Kermath auction and acquired much of the Kermath equipment on behalf of the California-based company of which he was then vice-president. Mr. Korody writes that a Canadian subsidiary of the Kermath Manufacturing Company, known as Kermath Marine Limited and owned by the Smith family, eventually came to California and bought the equipment used for the production of gasoline engines: "Kermath in Detroit went out of business so fast [in 1956], that their licensee in Toronto did not even know about the auction" (letter to author, 9 February, 1992). My thanks also to Walter Ferguson, founder of the Southern Diesel Co., 244 S.W. 6th St., Miami, FL (telephone interviews, November 1991), and to Paul J. O'Pecko, Reference Librarian, Mystic Seaport Museum, Mystic, CT for information about the Kermath and Palmer companies and engines (letters to author and enclosures, 12 November, 1991 and 21 February, 1992).

11. "Lindbergh, Charles A.," Obituary in *Encyclopedia Americana 1975 Annual.*

12. She seems to have undergone a hysterectomy shortly before the action of the novel, and now feels that "I'm old . . . I've had that thing." Morgan reassures her that "You'll never be old. . . . That don't make no difference when a woman's any good" (113–14). When Freda enquires, Morgan reports that Marie is "fine now . . . feeling good now" (103).

13. Richard Hart, Reference Librarian at the Greenwich Library, Greenwich, CT, supplied relevant materials from Horace W. Palmer's *Palmer Families in America* (Neshanic, NJ: Neshanic Printing Co., 1966, see pp. 56–57) and Spencer Mead's *Ye Historie of Ye Town of Greenwich* (1911; rpt. New York: Knickerbocker

Press, 1979, pp. 346, 618), as well as a few pages (unnumbered) of the 1985 reprint of the 1907 Palmer Brothers catalogue (letter to author and enclosures, 31 March, 1992). Also see endnote 10.

14. "Ral" or "rail" is Army slang for syphilis. The etymology is sketchy: "Orig. Southern use. Some Armed Forces use. Orig. ral; rail is a variant" (Wentworth and Flexner, *Dictionary of American Slang*).

15. The *Queen Conch* seems to be a fictional boat built by a fictional boatbuilder. No boat by that name is listed in the records of the U.S. Coast Guard (U.S. Dept. of Transportation), or in any of the 1930s issues of *Merchant Vessels of the United States*. In 1945, eight years after the publication of *THHN*, a boat named *Queen Conch* was built in Miami; this boat, whose last home port was Key West, burned in 1957 (letters and enclosures from R.M. Browning, Jr. and Eleanor P. Fischer, of the Office of the Historian of the U.S. Coast Guard, 28 February, 1992). I have not been able to find a boatbuilder with the family name of Robby, but Robby may easily be the boatbuilder's first name.

16. Morgan has been charging $35 a day for taking people out fishing (25, 96); Adams is probably charging Harrison a similar amount. Morgan pays Eddie $4 a day and the boy who prepares the bait earns $1 a day (11). Tracy had struck against the low government pay scale, but widespread unemployment has forced him to return to work (96).

17. "Sidney, Sylvia," in James Vinson, *The International Dictionary of Films and Filmakers*, Volume III: *Actors and Actresses* (Chicago: St. James, 1986).

18. Freddy Wallace and Wallace, his bouncer, have the same name but are two different people, as evidenced by the fact that Freddy speaks to Wallace: "Hey, Wallace . . . Put that fellow over against the wall" (208). Wallace is also the first name of the rich composer Johnston. Not only names but also descriptions are repeated: five characters in this novel are "tall" and "thin" or "cadaverous": Nelson Jacks (203), Roger Johnson (199), James Laughton (129), Robert Simmons (91), and Herbert Spellman (195). The phrase carries over into Hemingway's next novel: Robert Jordan and González are also "tall and thin" (*FWBT*, 3, 109), and so is Natera (in the posthumous *Islands*, 258).

19. Karl J. Crosby, Serial Reference Specialist at the Library of Congress, Washington D.C., found this magazine in the *Union List of Serials,* 3rd. ed. (1965), p. 4088, but was unable to determine when it ceased publication; the Library's holdings take it through 1949 (letter to author and enclosures, 15 January, 1991).

20. "Winchell, Walter," in *The New Century Cyclopedia of Names,* Vol. III, and in *Encyclopedia Americana.*

CHAPTER V: *FOR WHOM THE BELL TOLLS*

1. *Historical and Literary Prototypes.* Most biographical critics agree that the character of Robert Jordan is based on Robert Hale Merriman (university teacher, volunteer to the International Brigades, commander of the Lincoln Battalion, killed in 1938 at age 28) and on Hemingway himself. Jordan's family closely resembles Hemingway's: Hemingway's grandfathers were Civil War veterans, his father committed suicide, and his mother was a strong-minded woman whose son blamed her for his father's death. After examining Hemingway's grandfather's Civil War diaries, James Nagel argues that the character of Jordan derives from this ancestor with whom Hemingway strongly identified ("The Grandfather in *For Whom the Bell Tolls:* Biographical and Thematic Resonance," paper read at the Fifth International Hemingway Conference, Pamplona, Spain, 16 July, 1992). Most scholars agree that María is loosely based on Martha Gellhorn (q.v.). Peter Wyden reports that in Spain Hemingway had heard about a nurse's aide named María, who was "shy, serene, about 24. . . . She was a Communist, like her father, who had been executed in Andalusia when the war broke out. Maria had been imprisoned and, over the months, raped 24 times" (Wyden, 468). Less authoritative is McLendon's statement that "Maria was patterned directly after Jenny Jennings, the wife of Key West writer John Jennings" (*Papa,* 192). The fictional maid Petra is based on "Ernest's chambermaid at the Hotel Florida" in Madrid (Baker, *Life,* 347). Most of the politicians and military figures appear under their own names or their military code names. The two who are fictionalized are only thinly disguised: Mijail Koltsov, the *Pravda* correspondent, appears as Karkov (see endnote 34), and Karl Swierczewsky (General Walter) appears as Golz, q.v. Linda Miller argues that Pablo and Pilar are based on Gerald and Sara Murphy ("Invention Is the Finest Thing: Role Models in *For Whom the Bell Tolls,*" paper read at Up in Michigan II, a conference of the

Hemingway Society, October 19, 1991, Petoskey, MI). Mellow argues that Pablo "was based on the gypsy bullfighter Rafael el Gallo" (518), who appears undisguised in the narrative (see entry for *Gómez Ortega, Rafael). And in "*For Whom the Bell Tolls* as Contemporary History," the Seventy-Fifth Lecture in the Council on Research and Creative Distinguished Research Lecture Series, the Graduate School, University of Colorado at Boulder, Jeffrey Meyers writes that Golz's chief of staff, Duval, is "based on the French colonel, Jules Dumont" (*Research and Creative Work*, 1 [1988]: 12).

2. "ABC, diario de Madrid," and "ABC, diario de Sevilla," Rubio Cabeza, 12. William J. Irwin's essay on this newspaper claims that the Seville edition was inaugurated in 1929 (Cortada 5). *ABC* is still a widely read and highly respected paper.

3. Mary Louise Brown, Curator of Collections and Assistant Archivist of the Anheuser-Busch Companies, supplied information about the lithograph and its history (letter to author and enclosures, 19 November, 1990).

4. See "Asensio Torrado, José," Rubio Cabeza, 68 and Cortada, 58–59. A contemporary of José Asensio Torrado (1892–1961) was Carlos Asensio Cabanillas (1896–1969), who was also a professional soldier, but on the Nationalist side. Carlos Asensio was a graduate of the Academia de Infantería (1914) and the Escuela Superior de Guerra (1935). He served in the Spanish colonies in northern Africa until the outbreak of the Spanish Civil War, when he and his troops fought against the Republicans, whom Jordan supports. He rose to the rank of Brigadier General during the Spanish Civil War and was heavily decorated by the Franco regime after the war (see "Asensio Cabanillas, Carlos" in Rubio Cabeza, 68, in Cortada, 57–58, and in *Enciclopedia Universal Ilustrada, Suplemento 1936–39*). Because all the leaders Jordan accuses of betraying their people ("Largo, Prieto . . . Miaja, Rojo, all of them") are fellow Republicans, I assume that the Asensio whom Jordan is criticizing is the Republican José and not the Nationalist Carlos.

5. "Belenguer Soler, (Enrique) Blanquet," Cossío, III: 104–5; "Foxá Torroba, Agustín de," Cossío, VI: 929. See also Belenguer in *DIA*.

6. "Burns, Emile," *Who Was Who Among English and European Authors*. Mary Hemingway's inventory of the Hemingway library indicates that in 1936 Hemingway acquired or read *A Handbook of Marxism* (Reynolds, "Supplement to *Hemingway's Reading*," 102).

The *Handbook* was published in New York by Random House in 1935 and by International Publishers in 1936. In London it was published by V. Gollancz, Ltd. in 1937. Both the American and English editions were 1087 pages long. Karkov recalls 1500 pages.

7. "Calvo y Sotelo, José," *Enciclopedia Universal Ilustrada, Apéndice 2*: 893, and *Suplemento 1936–39,* 368–75; "Calvo Sotelo, José," Cortada, 100–1.

8. "Jiménez Moreno, (Manuel) Chicuelo," Cossío, III: 462–65 and IV: 515. See also Jiménez Moreno in *DIA.*

9. According to *The Book of the XV Brigade,* the XV International Brigade included a British Battalion, an American Battalion (composed of the Lincoln and Washington Brigades), the Canadian MacKenzie-Papineau Battalion and a Spanish Battalion (23). *The Book of the XV Brigade* praises Copic; Richardson (72–73) and most encyclopedias provide a more negative view.

10. "El Debate," Kern, *Historical Dictionary of Modern Spain.* According to Cortada, the paper resumed publication, probably after Franco's death in 1975. Cortada writes that the paper was established in 1908; Rubio Cabeza gives the date as 1910.

11. "Durán Martínez, Gustavo," Rubio Cabeza, 264; "Durán, Gustavo," Cortada, 173; Meyers, *Hemingway,* 369–74, 382–84; Baker, *Life,* 309 ff.

12. "Durruti, Buenaventura," *Enciclopedia Universal Ilustrada, Suplemento 1977–78,* 121; and Cortada, 173–75; "Durruti Domínguez, Buenaventura," Rubio Cabeza, 264 65.

13. Bryan Kennedy, Researcher for Smithsonian Books, provided information about the Fiat and Junker aircraft and helped me identify planes mentioned by Hemingway (letter to author, 27 November, 1989); also see the several Fiat entries in Rubio Cabeza, 316.

14. "Galicz ('Gal'), Janos" and "Jarama, Battle of," Cortada, 230 and 277. Verle B. Johnson, author of the Cortada entry, "Jarama, Battle of," summarizes the enormous battle: "Nationalist sources variously place Nationalist casualties from 6,360 to about 10,500, and cited Republican documents placing Loyalist casualties at 7,963. . . . However, losses of at least 10,000 (25 percent) on each side seem more likely. On balance, the battle represented a defensive

victory for the Republicans'' (in Cortada, 277). Richardson writes that ''losses sustained by . . . the International Brigades . . . in the Jarama fighting were extremely heavy. . . . on the order of 75 percent casualties'' (85). He discusses Gall's and Merriman's participation in the Battle of Jarama (84–87), concluding that ''the role of the Internationals was probably decisive'' in the defense of Madrid (87).

15. In 1938 Hemingway wrote to Eugene Jolas, ''Have had lovely experiences with Miss Dietrich, Miss Garbo and others in dreams too, they always being awfully nice (in dreams)'' (Baker, *Letters,* 465).

16. ''Zaisser, Wilhelm'' and ''Brigadas Internacionales,'' Rubio Cabeza, 793 and 137; ''Gómez (Wilhelm Zaisser),'' Cortada, 244.

17. ''Gómez Ortega, José,'' Cossío, III: 364–79; ''Joselito,'' Cossío, IV: 959–63; ''Gómez Ortega, Joselito,'' Silva Aramburu, 267–68; ''José Gómez Ortega,'' Martínez, 193–94. Joselito is also mentioned in *SAR* and *DIA.*

18. ''Gómez Ortega, Rafael,'' Cossío, III: 384–90; ''Rafael Gómez, 'el Gallo','' Silva Aramburu, 262–63. See also *DIA* and *SAR.*

19. ''González, Valentín,'' Rubio Cabeza, 388–90; and ''Campesino, el (Valentín González),'' Cortada, 101–2.

20. Belmonte had been scheduled to officiate at Granero's *alternativa* in 1920, but was unable to attend, his place being taken by Rafael el Gallo. For further details, see ''Granero, Manuel,'' Cossío, III: 409–11; and ''Manolo Granero,'' Silva Aramburu, 278. Granero's fame has not faded in the 70 years since his death. The fatal goring is recreated in Madrid's Wax Museum (Museo de cera, Plaza de Colón) and he is still written about: a recent essay discussed bad omens, prescient nightmares, and other foreshadowings of Granero's death, the same topic which Pilar discourses upon (see ''Manuel Granero, gran figura valenciana,'' *ABC,* 22 July, 1992: 90–91). Like Finito, Granero was honored by the formation of a fan club.

21. *''Tercio,'' Diccionario de la lengua española; ''Guardia,'' Enciclopedia universal ilustrada* XXVI: 1587–91; ''Civil Guard,'' Cortada, 131–32.

22. Pilar is probably speaking specifically of Rafael (this individual, who happens to be a gypsy, is corrupt), but it is possible that she is explaining Rafael's desire for Pablo's death in terms of a generalization about all gypsies: Rafael wants to kill Pablo because, like all gypsies, he has no compunctions about killing (i.e., all gypsies are corrupt). Anselmo is unambiguously generalizing about gypsies when he says that they do not think it a crime to kill an outsider, a person who is not a member of their tribe (40). Jordan also generalizes: Rafael "is truly worthless" as all gypsies "are worthless" (275–76).

23. "Harlow, Jean," *Who Was Who in America, IV.*

24. "Heinkel, Ernst Heinrich," *Meyers Enzykopadisches Lexikon;* "Heinkel, Ernesto," *Enciclopedia Universal Ilustrada, Suplemento 1936–39.*

25. In *"For Whom the Bell Tolls* as Contemporary History," Jeffrey Meyers identifies the Hungarian commander as Lucasz (11–12).

26. "Ibárruri Gómez, Dolores," Rubio Cabeza, 425–27; see next endnote.

27. Dolores Ibárruri (la Pasionaria) writes about her son in the chapter, "Mi Rubén," in her book *Me faltaba España.* Her family is also discussed by Andrés Carabantes and Eusebio Cimorra, *Un mito llamado Pasionaria* (249–55); and in Jaime Camino's interviews with Dolores Ibárruri, published in *Intimas conversaciones con la Pasionaria* (176–78).

28. Spain had another, less famous leader with the same name. Pablo Iglesias Martínez was an Army officer (lieutenant colonel) who, when the Army rose up against the Republic, dissuaded his subordinates from joining the rebellion; thus the uprising of Jaén failed, July 1936. He ordered the army personnel and their dependents transported to the sanctuary of la Vírgen Santa María de la Cabeza, where they were besieged for over 200 days, often attacked by the Republican air force (to which the Nationalist Army was anathema) but refusing to surrender his soldiers to the Republicans. His family were among the besieged, who suffered from starvation and terrible sanitary conditions. See "Jaén, alzamiento en" and "Santa María de la Cabeza, Santuario de," in Rubio Cabeza, 439 and 706. For the socialist Pablo Iglesias, see *Encyclopaedia Britannica,* 1973 ed.

29. Jordan and Anselmo detail the physical correspondences between bears and men and list the similarities which both gypsies and Indians have noted: the bear "drinks beer . . . enjoys music and . . . likes to dance" and even steal (*FWBT*, 40). The connection between bear and man is reiterated in *Islands in the Stream:* "bears, of course, are very close to men" because they joke and drink alcohol (*Islands*, 52, 213).

30. "Juan," *Diccionario Enciclopédico Abreviado* (1972); "Juan," *Enciclopedia Universal Ilustrada.* In his essay, "For Thine Is the Power and the Glory: Love in *For Whom the Bell Tolls*," Robert Crozier discusses the mystical poetry of St. John of the Cross as it relates to the phrase *la gloria.*

31. The date and place of Kahle's death are disputed. Rubio Cabeza indicates that he moved to Canada and then to England, where he was assassinated by Soviet agents in 1948 (449). Hugh Thomas claims that he died in Mecklenburg in 1952 (*The Spanish Civil War*, 954). Cortada supports the latter version (283).

32. Hans' description of this battle is quoted in Andreu Castells Peig, *Las brigadas internacionales de la guerra de España* (Barcelona: Editorial Ariel, 1974), 186.

33. "Kamenev, León Borisovich," *Enciclopedia Universal Ilustrada, Apéndice 6,* 677, and *Suplemento 1936–39,* 458.

34. The character of Karkov is based on Mikhail or Mijail Koltsov, Russian politician and journalist (1898–1942), who went to Spain at the beginning of the Civil War as a correspondent for *Pravda* but was suspected of being a personal agent of Stalin. Koltsov is thought to be responsible for the political murders in Paracuellos del Jarama and in Torrejón de Ardoz (near Madrid, November 1936); under his frequently used pseudonym Miguel Martínez he had ordered political prisoners transported from the Madrid jails to these "safer" places, to prevent their being set free by the Nationalists who were about to take Madrid. It is estimated that well over 2,000 political prisoners were massacred during the course of the month. The facts are still disputed, but the event tarnished the reputation of the Republic. Koltsov was author of *Combatientes del ejército rojo* (1937), *Diario de la guerra de España* (published posthumously in 1963), and *Hombres del ejército rojo* (n.d.). Baker identifies Koltsov as a correspondent for both *Izvestia* and *Pravda* (*Life*, 306). Morrow claims that Koltsov was killed "Late in 1938 . . . one of the

victims of Stalin's continuing, megalomaniac purge of suspected military and political leaders'' (503). See ''Koltsov, Mijail,'' Rubio Cabeza, 453–54.

35. Peter Wyden identifies the mistress of Mikkhail Koltzov, on whom the character Karkov is based, as the German novelist Maria Osten (real name: Maria Greshoner). Wyden describes Koltzov's wife Lisa as ''tall, bony''; Maria was ''shapely'' (*The Passionate War,* 328).

36. ''Kill Cavalry Kilpatrick'' and ''Kilpatrick, Hugh Judson,'' Sifakis, 271; see also ''Kilpatrick'' in *Encyclopedia Americana.*

37. ''Kleber, Emilio,'' Rubio Cabeza, 453; and Cortada, 284.

38. ''Lalanda del Pino, Marcial,'' Cossío, III: 475–80 and IV: 523–24; ''Marcial Lalanda,'' Silva Aramburu, 277; ''Lalanda, Marcial,'' Rubio Cabeza, 456–57; ''El matador de toros Marcial Lalanda muere en Madrid a la edad de 87 años'' and ''El más grande,'' both articles published in the daily newspaper *El país* (26 October, 1990): 41. Lalanda is also mentioned in *SAR* and *DIA.*

39. ''Largo Caballero, Francisco,'' *Enciclopedia Universal Ilustrada, Apéndice 6,* 1022, and *Suplemento 1945–48;* Rubio Cabeza, 457–58; Cortada, 287–91.

40. ''Lerroux García, Alejandro,'' *Enciclopedia Universal Ilustrada,* 161–62; *Apéndice 6,* 1155–56; and *Suplemento 1949–52,* 300.

41. ''Líster Forján, Enrique,'' Rubio Cabeza, 467–68. Cortada describes him as ''a one-time quarryman,'' reports he was already a general in 1937, and concludes that he ''was one of the most important combat commanders of the Spanish Republican Army'' (299–300).

42. For Lukacs' character and death, see Wyden, 336–37 and Landis, 55 and 181. Also see ''Zalka, Mata o Matei,'' Rubio Cabeza, 793; and '' 'Lukács,' General (Mata Zalka Kemeny),'' Cortada, 307.

43. ''March Ordinas, Juan,'' *Enciclopedia Universal Ilustrada, Suplemento 1961–62,* 257; Rubio Cabeza, 509–10; Cortada, 318–19; and ''March Ordinas, Juan Albert,'' Obituary, *Encyclopaedia Britannica,* 1962 Book of the Year.

44. "Marty, André," Rubino Cabeza, 522–23 and Cortada, 268, 322. Richardson writes that "Marty blamed the failings and shortcomings in the Brigades on traitors, spies, and agents provocateur. . . . a key part of the task of the new [political] commissars was to root out these elements" (102–3).

45. "Mayakovsky, Vladimir," *Columbia Dictionary of Modern European Literature.*

46. "McClellan, George Brinton," *Webster's American Biographies.*

47. "Miaja Menant, José," *Enciclopedia Universal Ilustrada, Suplemento 1957–58,* 241; Rubio Cabeza, 534–35; Cortada, 335–36.

48. In answer to his editor Maxwell Perkins' objections to the character we now have as Mitchell, Hemingway "cut the part about the man Mitchell drastically and removed all libel without, I think removing the flavour of Karkov's mind" (Baker, *Letters,* 513). Keith Potter, of the Research Department of the British publication *The Economist,* writes me that "we have never heard of Mitchell. We can only presume that he is a fictional character" (letter to author, 1 May, 1991).

49. "Guilloto León, Juan Modesto," Rubio Cabeza, 407–8; and "Modesto Guilloto, Juan," Cortada, 339.

50. According to Rubio Cabeza, the newspaper was founded in Madrid, August 1930, was suspended in October 1934, and began publishing again in 1936 (558). Luis Haranburu and Peru Erroteta claim that the paper first appeared in Madrid on 14 November, 1931, soon after the Republican government was established (28). Kern adds that Dolores Ibárruri (la Pasionaria) often published in this paper. Also see *"El Mundo Obrero"* in Cortada and Kern. A newspaper by this name began publication in Paris, 1946.

51. Orwell writes that Nin and many other POUM members were arrested 15 June, 1937, the night the POUM was suppressed. The Republican government accused POUM members "of being in Fascist pay. And already the rumours were flying round that [POUM] people were being secretly shot in jail. . . . the rumor reached Barcelona that he [Nin] had been shot . . . in prison by the secret police. . . . From that day to this, Nin has never been heard of alive again" (221). Cortada reports that Nin was killed on 20 June,

1937, five days after his arrest, at "a Soviet camp . . . near Madrid" (365). Maurín, co-founder of the POUM, "was a prisoner in the hands of the Fascists and . . . believed to have been shot by them" (Orwell, 231). See "Nin i Pérez, Andreu," *Enciclopedia Universal Ilustrada, Suplemento 1977–78,* 160; "Nin Pérez, Andrés," Rubio Cabeza, 573–74; "Nin, Andrés," Cortada, 365.

52. "Pavón, Pastora," *Enciclopedia Universal Ilustrada, Suplemento 1959–60,* 306; "Niña de los Peines," *Gran Enciclopedia de Andalucía* VI: 2548. The second of these articles lists her death date as 1968.

53. "Serrapi Sánchez, Manuel," *Enciclopedia Universal Ilustrada, Suplemento 1971–72,* 271. The *Gran Enciclopedia de Andalucía* lists his dates as 1904–1974 (VII: 3010). Like Pastora Pavón and Pastora Rojas Monje, Serrapi was from Seville.

54. Pilar describes Pastora as "uglier than I am" (185), but photographs show her to be reasonably attractive. See "Espectáculos," *Enciclopedia de la Cultura Española* III: 7; and "Rojas Monje, Pastora," *Enciclopedia Universal Ilustrada, Suplemento 1979–80,* 157.

55. Pilar is 48 years old (141; see 30). She may be suffering from a liver ailment (88; we never see her drinking wine and she refuses Santiago's whiskey, 142) or from heart disease (climbing hills is difficult for her, 153–54, 297, 457; she remarks upon the steepness of a hill, 131). She says she needs exercise (65), she needs to rest (96), and she looks ill (157, 172–73).

56. "Pilar," *Diccionario Enciclopédico Abreviado* (1954).

57. "Granero, Manuel" and "Lalanda, Marcial," Cossío, III: 410–11 and 476. See endnote 20.

58. "Circo," *Enciclopedia Universal Ilustrada, Suplemento 1969–70.*

59. "Prieto y Tuero, Indalecio," *Enciclopedia Universal Ilustrada, Suplemento 1961–62,* 297–98; and in Cortada, 406–8 (entry by Edward Malefakis). Also see "Prieto, Indalecio," Obituary, *Encyclopaedia Britannica,* 1962 Book of the Year.

60. See Richardson 71, 99.

61. "Queipo de Llano y Serra, Gonzalo," *Enciclopedia Universal Ilustrada, Suplemento 1936–39* and *Suplemento 1949–52;* Cortada, 411–13 (entry by Raymond L. Proctor).

62. "Conejo" (rabbit) is vulgar slang for the female pudenda. Critics have variously argued that Hemingway was ignorant of Spanish slang, that Jordan was ignorant, that Hemingway was making a joke, that he was being offensive, that Jordan was innocently translating from English ("rabbit" is inoffensive, as in "scared as a rabbit") although Stephenson claims that "'Rabbit-pie' was—and is—a fairly common Americanism for prostitute" and finds it significant that "Maria serves Robert . . . rabbit stew" ("Cats Don't Live in the Mountains," 43). Even Andrés' hometown of Villa-conejos has been dragged into the debate.

63. When Gómez de Velasco left his position at the Asociación de Matadores de Toros y Novillos to take over the management of the Madrid bullring, his colleague Esteban Salazar moved with him; both men are identified as Retana's replacements in the French taurine weekly, *Le Toril,* 8 January, 1927, 3: 2. For an angry editorial against Manuel Retana, which accused him of favoritism, profiteering, manipulation of the press—in short, of destroying the art of bullfighting—see *Toreros y Toros,* 30 March, 1924, unnumbered pp. 2 and 3. This weekly was dead set against Retana in 1923 and 1924, as evidenced by the issues Hemingway saved (see Hemingway Collection: Other Materials). Many Spanish taurine publications list the names and addresses of the *apoderados* of the leading *matadores de toros* and *matadores de novillos,* through whom communications with most bullfighters were channeled. Matías Retana represented only one or two other bullfighters in addition to his main client, Nicanor Villalta; they could be reached at Retana's address: 3, Calle de Caramuel, Madrid. A powerful contemporary *apoderado* was Manuel Rodríguez Vázquez, whose clients in the 1920s included, among others, such famous men as Diego Mazquiarán (Fortuna), Ricardo Anlló (Nacional), Juan Anlló (Nacional II), and Rodolfo Gaona; this *apoderado* was, according to *Toreros y Toros,* one of several people angling for Manuel Retana's job (issue of 10 June, 1923, 10:3). A common complaint was that certain matadors (many of them clients of Rodríguez Vázquez) were not contracted to perform in Madrid as often as their fame and skill warranted: the front cover of Barcelona's journal *La Corrida* marveled that Nacional's following was undiminished in spite of "vetos y boicots" imposed against him (21 June, 1923), and Madrid's *El Tauro* remarked that the Madrid establishment was

prejudiced against important matadors like Valencia II and Nacional II (5 July, 1923, 3:1 and 4:1). A front page editorial in *Sangre y Arena* complained of Retana's treatment of Manuel García (Maera) (9 July, 1924, 1:1–2).

64. "Rojo Lluch, Vicente," *Enciclopedia Universal Ilustrada, Suplemento 1965–66,* 425; Rubio Cabeza, 685–86; Cortada, 420.

65. "Rosa de la Garquén, Juan Luis de la," Cossío, III: 834–36. Also see *DIA.*

66. "Rykov, Aleksey Ivanovich," *Everyman's Encyclopedia.*

67. "Salvarsán," *Enciclopedia Universal Ilustrada, Suplemento 1942–44,* 444–45.

68. In addition to Joaquín and Ignacio, there are "the man with his chin in the dirt," "another," and "another"; this last man shares his wine with his fellows. When Santiago pretends to shoot all his men and himself, he fires six shots (314). Later Anselmo sees six headless bodies on the hill (329).

69. "Sheridan, Philip Henry," *Webster's American Biographies.*

70. On 19 July, 1936, the day after the generals' insurrection, Ibárruri gave the Republicans their most famous slogan when she said, "Todo el país vibra de indignación ante esos desalmados que quieren hundir la España democrática y popular en un infierno de terror y muerte. Pero, ¡no pasarán!" (The whole nation trembles with indignation against those soulless [generals] who intend to sink democratic and popularly-ruled Spain in a hell of terror and death. But, they shall not pass!). In September 1936, she explained that "Consciente de lo que nuestra lucha significa, el pueblo español prefiere morir de pie a vivir de rodillas" (Conscious of what our struggle signifies, the Spanish folk prefers to die on its feet than to live on its knees). And in November 1936, she told the women of Spain, "Pensad que es mejor ser viudas de héroes que mujeres de cobardes" (Think that it is better to be the widows of heroes than the wives of cowards). She cheered her fellow Republicans to battle, telling them that "Resistir y fortificar es vencer" (to resist and to fortify is to win) [my translations].

71. The Super Star Model B is shown in cross-section diagrams in Hernández Menéndez 200-3, who also includes ballistics details.

Hernández Menéndez writes that this gun, based on the Colt 1911-A1, is produced in several calibers, including Parabellum 9mm Largo. The Star 9mm was adopted as an official weapon for the *Guardia Civil* in October 1922 (Sopena Garreta, 172–74).

72. D. J. Penn, Keeper of the Department of Exhibits and Firearms of the Imperial War Museum, London, supplied biographical information about Sir Wilfrid Stokes (letter to author, 14 February, 1991).

73. Michael Culver, Curator of the Museum of Art of Ogunquit, ME (established by Strater), and David F. Setford, Senior Curator of the Norton Gallery and School of Art, West Palm Beach, FL (where Strater often exhibited) supplied information about Henry Hyacinth (Mike) Strater. Strater wrote that his middle name caused him to take up boxing early in his life (reported in an informal chronology compiled by Strater and Richard Madigan, former director of the Norton Gallery, and sent me by the current curator, 2 April 1991). Strater occasionally boxed with Hemingway.

74. "Charles Thompson Dies; Was Friend of Hemingway," *Miami Herald,* 19 February, 1978.

75. Orwell discusses Trotskyism and rejects the accusation that POUM was "Trotskyist" (189–91). Orwell was a member of POUM and participated in the Barcelona fighting.

76. See Cossío, I: 269–70 and IV: 230–31.

77. "Voroshilov, Kliment Yefremovich," *Enciclopedia Universal Ilustrada, Suplemento 1969–70,* 319; and Rubio Cabeza, 785–86.

78. "Swierczewski, Karl," Rubio Cabeza, 738.

79. Abercrombie & Fitch's New York catalogue calls the bag the Woods Arctic, Three Star. The VL & A calls the same bag the Arctic Senior, Three Star. The catalogues of the two stores advertise it in very similar language, explaining that it is suitable "For extremely cold temperatures, from freezing down to 20° below zero. Filled with Woods Ever-live down in overlapping tubes, with Harwood patent down equalizers to prevent down from shifting. . . . Cover is of soft, high count, windbreaker, water-repellent Egyptian cotton, olive drab color. Lining of light gray kersey wool, remarkable for its warmth, resistance to moisture and durability"

(Abercrombie & Fitch Co., 1939 catalogue). Carol Smith, of the Corporate Headquarters of Abercrombie & Fitch, Columbus, OH, also sent me a few pages of the 1940 Fall and Winter catalogue of Von Lengerke & Antoine store in Chicago; these are the earliest catalogues she could find. Jordan obviously bought his sleeping bag a few years earlier, but the price seems to have remained stable. Ms. Smith believes that Jordan's phrase "the Woods boys" refers to the store or people who supplied the bag and other sports goods to be used in the woods by outdoorsmen, and not to a family named Woods (telephone interview and letter to author with enclosures, 27 and 28 January 1993). Hemingway himself seems to have owned a sleeping robe like Jordan's; getting ready for a trip, he wrote a reminder to himself: "Get Woods eiderdown robe from boat with blanket. Pack it and rubber mattress" (Hemingway Collection: Other Materials: EH's Papers, To Do's).

80. "Apfelbaum, Radomilsky," *Enciclopedia Universal Ilustrada, Apéndice I,* and *Suplemento 1936–39.*

CHAPTER VI: *ACROSS THE RIVER AND INTO THE TREES*

1. *Historical and Literary Prototypes.* Baker reports that Hemingway defined Cantwell as a composite of Charles T. (Buck) Lanham (q.v. in *DS*), Charlie Sweeny (q.v. in *MF*, where his name is misspelled Sweeney), and of himself "as he might have been if he had turned to soldiering instead of writing" (*Life*, 475). Biographical critics have also identified Colonel Cantwell with E. E. (Chink) Dorman-Smith (q.v. in *MF*; see Meyers, *Hemingway*, 470–71). Renata has generally been identified with Adriana Ivancich; her name may derive from Renata Borgatti (Baker, *Life*, 477) or Renata D'Annunzio (Tintner, 10; see **Notturno*). The Barone Alvarito derives from Gianfranco Ivancich (Adriana's brother, q.v. in *DS*) and from the Baron Nanyuki Franchetti (Hemingway's host for a duck-shooting expedition in December 1948). The unidentified writer has been identified as Sinclair Lewis (see endnote 60); and the Colonel's ex-wife is probably based on Hemingway's third wife, Martha Gellhorn (q.v. in *FWBT*). Cipriani appears under his own name. During his 1948–1949 trip to Venice, Hemingway "was presented with a scroll which made him Cavaliere di Gran Croce al Merito in the Knights of Malta" (Baker, *Life*, 468); this honor may have inspired him to invent the Order of Brusadelli (q.v.).

   The more important literary influences are mentioned in the narrative itself; see the entries and attendant endnotes for Dante,

D'Annunzio, *Notturno,* and Shakespeare; also see endnote 3 below.

2. "American Automobile Association," *Encyclopedia of Associations,* Vol. I, Part I, Item 397.

3. Phrases in this passage echo the early work of Hemingway as well as the poetry of William Blake. Hemingway's last heroine recalls his first: Renata "looks as lovely as a good horse or as a racing shell . . . she looked like the figure-head on a ship. The rest of it, too" (149). Almost twenty-five years earlier, Hemingway had written that Brett Ashley "was built with curves like the hull of a racing yacht" (*SAR,* 22). Elsewhere, we read that Renata has "dark hair, of an alive texture" (80); "it was very heavy hair and as alive as the hair of peasants" (112). The description echoes Hemingway's impression of Gertrude Stein's "lovely, thick, alive immigrant hair" (*MF,* 14). Hemingway had met Stein in Paris in the early 1920s.

4. Letter to author from D. J. Penn, Keeper of the Department of Exhibits and Firearms at the Imperial War Museum, London, 29 July, 1991. Mr. Penn not only supplied information on the Boss and Purdey firearms companies but also explained that "Two shotguns are required for formal, driven game shooting when birds are put up by a line of beaters and driven over the standing 'guns,' who each have a loader (usually a game keeper, servant or chauffeur) who unloads and reloads the second gun while the first is in use. Competently performed, this partnership allows virtually continuous shooting for the brief duration of each drive." Mr. A. J. W. Lokatis, Director of Boss & Co., 13 Dover St., London, provided detailed information about the Boss and Robertson families, the guns, and their prices, in a letter of 3 October, 1991. Mr. Lokatis wrote me that in the year *ARIT* was published, a pair of Boss over-and-unders would have cost about £1,000; in January 1990 "the first .410 O/U sold for in excess of $100,000." The records of Boss & Co. do not list Hemingway "as an account or order" but he may have been given a Boss or perhaps purchased one second-hand. According to Baker, Hemingway shot himself with "a double-barreled Boss shotgun with a tight choke. He had used it for years of pigeon shooting." That gun was cut into pieces which were buried "in a secret place" (*Life,* 563, 668).

5. "Breda, Ernesto," *Dizionario Enciclopedico Italiano.*

6. Cotonificio Valle di Susa was a powerful conglomerate headed by Riva in association with Banca Vonwiller and Banca Credito Commerciale of Milan; with Warner Abegg, a Swiss-American financier associated with Credit Suisse; and with Marinotti, who controlled the manufacture of synthetic fibers in Italy. Riva's take-over of Brusadelli's cotton industries enlarged an already impressive empire, affecting Italian and Swiss banks and markets. Riva was Brusadelli's friend and protégé as well as his business rival; there are hints that they may have been related. The negotiations preceding the sale stipulated that Brusadelli would remain as president of Dell'Acqua (see endnote 7, particularly *L'Unita* of 23 and 24 October, 1948).

7. The various side-shows which accompanied the major events also drew the attention of the press. Notable among these was a "strange and unexpected" motion in favor of Brusadelli, signed by over 8,000 of his companies' employees; only those workers who had not come to work on the day the motion was circulated did not sign. The newspapers editorialized that the "pressioni illecite" (illicit pressure) exerted upon the signatories invalidated the document. Brusadelli's defense against the charge of creating a monopoly was as unconvincing as his workers' adulatory document: he claimed that he was ignorant of the connection between the individuals who bought his stock (Riva and Werner Abegg) and the company Valle di Susa. The Brusadelli scandal was not reported in the English-language press, and I am grateful to the following for supplying information: Gianfranca Balestra, of the Department of Foreign Languages and Literatures, Universita Cattolica del Sacro Cuore, Milan, Italy (letter to author, 16 December, 1991); D. Fullin, Centro Documentazione, *Corriere della Sera* (letters and enclosure, 27 August, 1991 and 28 February, 1992); and Pierluigi Tagliaferro, Vicedirector of *Il Gazzettino,* who generously sent me a thick packet of news items relating to the Brusadelli scandal, including reports published by his own newspaper and by *Gazzetta Veneta Sera, L'Unita, Corriere della Sera,* and *Il Popolo;* the coverage extends from October 1948 to November 1962 (letter to author and enclosures, 12 May, 1992).

8. David Hull, Manager of Store Operations, Burberrys Limited, New York, NY, gave me several of the company's publications about Thomas Burberry, the Burberry gaberdine, and the history of the firm (personal interview, 5 December, 1991).

9. "Canfield, Richard A.," *Dictionary of American Biography,* III: 472–73.

10. Patrick M. Finn, Director of Admissions, sent information about the school (letter and enclosures, 12 December, 1991).

11. He says he is 51 years old (75), but he occasionally rounds it off to "half a hundred" (63, 180, 217). If he is as old as Pacciardi (40), he was born in 1899.

12. "Carroll, jr., Benajah Harvey," *Register of the Department of State, December 15, 1916* (Washington, D.C.: Government Printing Office, 1917), 79. Joseph Dane Hartgrove, Civil Reference Branch, National Archives, Washington, D.C. wrote me about Consul Carroll (letter to author and enclosure, 22 March, 1991).

13. "Casals, Pablo," *Encyclopedia Americana,* 1974 Annual.

14. "Chautauqua movement" and "Vincent, John Heyl," *The New Columbia Encyclopedia.* From 1880 to 1914 the Chautauqua Literary and Scientific Circle published *The Chautauquan,* a magazine which "in its early years gave much of its space to readings for that great organization for adult education; eventually it introduced greater variety, with strong emphasis on public affairs" (*"Magazines," The Reader's Encyclopedia of American Literature,* 688).

15. Arrigo Cipriani, srl, supplied this information (unsigned letter of 3 October, 1991).

16. "Collins, Lieutenant General 'Lightnin' Joe' Lawton," *Who Was Who in World War II,* 61.

17. "Cripps, Sir (Richard) Stafford," *Who Was Who in World War II;* and in Laqueur, 123.

18. "D'Annunzio, Gabriele," *Cassell's Encyclopedia of World Literature* (1973), II: 361–62; and in *The Penguin Companion to Literature: Europe,* 214.

19. For a careful examination of the relationship between Dante and *ARIT,* see Kathleen Verdun, who argues that Hemingway accepted the current literary traditions about Dante without studying the man or his work: "In point of fact, Hemingway seems hardly to have known Dante at all" ("Hemingway's Dante," 635); see also Gerry Brenner, who finds that Dante was an important influence (*Concealments in Hemingway's Works,* 153–63).

20. Cantwell likes to show off his Italian, French, and Spanish (e.g., 120, 266). Similarly, Robert Jordan indicates his knowledge of Spanish, French, and German (*FWBT,* 166–67).

21. "Ardant du Picq, Charles-Jean-Jacques-Joseph," Balteau, III: 441– 42; "Ardant du Picq, Charles," *Grand Dictionnaire Encyclopedique Larousse,* 1982; "Ardant du Picq," Carrias, 257–59. Hemingway owned Ardant du Picq's *Battle Studies: Ancient and Modern Battle,* translated from the French by Colonel John N. Greely and Major Robert C. Cotton (Harrisburg, PA: Military Service Publishing Co., 1947); see Brasch and Sigman, 12.

22. "Firestone, Harvey S., Jr.," Obituary in *Encyclopedia Americana,* 1974 Annual; and in *New York Times Biographical Edition* (1973), 962–63.

23. "Gamelin, General Maurice Gustave," *Who Was Who in World War II.*

24. Pierluigi Tagliaferro, Vice-director of *Il Gazzettino,* supplied information about the newspaper, as well as a book produced in 1987 to celebrate the paper's centennial (letter and enclosures, 12 May, 1992).

25. George's remark that "Everybody's right until he's wrong" (293) is echoed in the two posthumous novels. Colonel Boyle warns David Bourne: "Remember everything is right until it's wrong" (*GE,* 65). In terms of geography, Hudson claims that "Any place is good," but Roger Davis disagrees: "They're good and then they go bad." Hudson agrees with his assessment (*Islands,* 77).

26. "Gritti," *Dizionario Enciclopedico Italiano,* V: 611. Vincenzo Finizzola, Manager of the Hotel Gritti Palace, Venice, sent interesting information about the hotel as well as recipes from its kitchen and bar (letter to author and enclosures, 13 June, 1991).

27. "Johnston, John 'Liver Eating'," Sifakis, 260.

28. "Leclerc, General Philippe," *Who Was Who in World War II;* and "Leclerc, Jacques Philippe de Hauteclocque," *The Historical Encyclopedia of World War II.*

29. For much of this interesting information about Lisette I am indebted to Howard Bass, of Thoroughbred Racing Communications, Inc.,

who consulted John R. Elting's *Swords Around a Throne* (letter to author, 21 September, 1990). Marbot's own descriptions of Lisette's actions against the enemy are vivid. He reports that when she was wounded, she turned on the Russian grenadier whose bayonet had injured her "and at one mouthful tore off his nose, lips, eyebrows, and all the skin of his face, making of him a living death's-head, dripping with blood." She then kicked and bit several other Russians, and when one hapless officer grabbed her bridle, "she seized him by his belly, and carrying him off with ease, she bore him out of the crush [of battle] to the foot of the hillock, where, having torn out his entrails and mashed his body under her feet, she left him dying on the snow." After all this, Marbot writes, "she made her way at full gallop" back to Napoleon's forces, where more misadventures awaited her and her rider. Both Marbot and Lisette recovered from their wounds ("Lisette at Eylau," from *The Adventures of General Marbot*, rpt. in *Men at War: The Best War Stories of All Time*, ed. with an Introduction by Ernest Hemingway [1942; rpt. New York: Bramhall House, 1979], 535 ff.).

30. "Mangin, Charles," *La Grande Encyclopédie;* and *Dizionario Enciclopedico Italiano* (1970).

31. "Mannitol" and "Mannityl Hexanitrate," *Martindale: The Extra Pharmacopoeia,* 562–63 and 1650–51. John Paul Russo also concludes that Wes' remarks about mannitol hexanitrate are correct and that he is fully aware of the seriousness of Cantwell's condition (" 'To Die Is Not Enough'," 177, n.7). In 1949 Hemingway himself was taking mannitol hexanitrate six times a day, for blood pressure. He was also taking the sedative seconal twice a day, as well as vitamins (Hemingway Collection: Other Materials, Medical Records 1944–1955).

32. "Maxwell, Elsa," *American Women: 1935–40: A Composite Biographical Dictionary;* obituary in *Encyclopedia Americana,* 1964 Annual.

33. "McNair, Lesley James," *The Historical Encyclopedia of World War II,* 309.

34. Karl E. Cocke and William J. Webb, Acting Chief of the Staff Support Branch, the Center of Military History, Washington D.C., sent me information about the military career of Bennett Edward Meyers (letters to author and enclosures, 15 February, 1991). The

post-war scandal and trials are documented in the *New York Times,* 1947, 1948, 1950, 1951.

35. "Montgomery, Field Marshal Bernard," *Who Was Who in World War II,* 173–74; "Montgomery of Alamein, Bernard Law Montgomery, 1st Viscount," Obituary in *Encyclopedia Americana,* 1977 Annual.

36. For information about the Muehlebach family and their holdings, see *Kansas City und sein Deutschthum im 19 Jahrhundert* (Cleveland: German-American Biographical Publishing Co., 1900; copyright held by Jacob E. Mueller), 125–27, 142, and 324. The hotel's history and demise were recorded in the *Kansas City Star,* 20 May, 1987 and 14 June, 1987. Cantwell says that the hotel "has the biggest beds in the world" (263). Ms. Lisa Schwarzenholz, Archivist of the Wyandotte County Historical Society and Museum, writes that she has "often heard stories from older people who remember the Muehlebach who have referred to the large beds. Apparently the rooms were equipped with 'king-sized' beds instead of the standard 'queen-size' beds of most American hotels" (letter to author, 14 November, 1991). Ms. Schwarzenholz identifies the Country Club where Cantwell used to play polo (263) as the Kansas City Country Club, which had moved to 6200 Indian Lane, Mission Hills, KA, in 1926. The Polo Field, at the southern end of the Country Club, was near Malcolm Lowrey's house at 6435 Indian Lane, where Pauline and Ernest Hemingway stayed in the summer of 1928 and the fall of 1931.

37. John Paul Russo thinks that "Cantwell's Italian must have been fluent because *Notturno* has never been translated" ("To Die Is Not Enough," 171). Tintner points out that it has been translated into French but not into English ("Significance," 11). Dante has also been identified as a source for *ARIT;* see endnote 19.

38. "Carbonari," *The New Columbia Encyclopedia;* "Italy-History," *Encyclopedia Americana,* XV: 488–89.

39. A sentence recalling the Supreme Secret occurs in Hemingway's letter to Charles Scribner, 19 August, 1949, at which time Hemingway was finishing the novel: "But riding is riding and fun is fun and as old Blicky used to say, 'It's always so quiet when the goldfish die'." Carlos Baker thinks Blixen (q.v. in *MF*) may be referring to Auden's line, "But it's madly ungay when the goldfish die" (*Letters,* 665, n.2) but the repetition and rhythm of the first part of

the sentence—"riding is riding and fun is fun"—seem to me markedly different from Auden's "Good little sunbeams must learn to fly" which precedes "But it's madly ungay when the goldfish die." I have not, however, been able to find a source for the first half of the Supreme Secret.

40. "Pacciardi, Randolfo," Cortada, 384; *Current Biography 1944,* 531–33; *Dizionario Enciclopedico Italiano* (1970); "Randolfo Pacciardi; Fascists' Foe was 91," Obituary in *New York Times,* 16 April, 1991, D23. Pacciardi was reappointed Italian Minister of Defense in January 1950 and visited the United States in October 1950 (see *New York Times,* 27 January, 1950, 10:4; 28 January, 1950, 5:6; and 27 October, 1950, 6:4). For his record during the Spanish Civil War, see Richardson, 103–10.

41. Nicholas Joost and Alan Brown argue that Hemingway had Phlebas the Phoenician in mind as early as *SAR* and that Frederic Henry's leap into the river (*FTA*) is also a version of "death by water" (Joost and Brown, 439).

42. For information on Lieutenant General Quesada, I am indebted to Perry D. Jamieson, of the Historical Services Division, Office of the Air Force Historian, Bolling Air Force Base, Washington D.C. (letter to author and enclosures, 15 May, 1991); and to Karl E. Cocke and William J. Webb, Acting Chief of the Staff Support Branch, Center of Military History, Washington D.C. (letter to author and enclosures, 15 February, 1991). Also see "Quesada, Elwood Richard," *Webster's American Military Biographies,* 338.

43. Another phrase which is repeated in this novel is "shining white and beautiful," used to describe New York (34) and airplanes (223). The text identifies both this and "my last true and only love" as quotes (34, 211). Phrases from *ARIT* surface in Hemingway's correspondence as well: he wrote "high in the sky and shining and beautiful" in a love letter to Mary Welsh, 13 September, 1944 (Baker, *Letters,* 570); and mentioned Brusadelli and the goldfish of the Supreme Secret in letters as well (Baker, *Letters,* 654 and 665; see endnote 39 above). For Renata's resemblance to characters in other Hemingway books, see endnote 3 in this chapter; for her language, see endnote 37 in the chapter on *FTA*.

44. Charles M. Oliver summarizes the several arguments for and against Renata's being pregnant by Cantwell and intending to marry Alvarito ("Hemingway's Study of Impending Death," 151, n.3).

Mellow, noticing that both Renata's and Alvarito's mothers are widowed and that both like to live in wooded areas, concludes that the similarity between them is "an unconscious slip that tends to suggest that the young *barone* and Renata have the same mother and therefore are brother and sister, clearly not the intention of the novel" (559). Russo thinks it "highly unlikely that Renata has ever had intercourse with Cantwell" (178, n.13).

45. "Rimbaud, Jean Arthur," *Cassell's Encyclopedia of World Literature* (1973), III: 410.

46. See "The Oyster Perpetual," in Alfred Chapuis and Eugene Jaquet, *The History of the Self-Winding Watch, 1770–1931* (Geneva: The Rolex Watch Co., Ltd., 1952; English ed., rev. 1956), 232–34. Diana Harkin, Advertising, and Marc A. Shafir, Management Consulting and Public Relations, Rolex Watch U.S.A., New York, NY; and John Hunt, Publicity Manager, Rolex, London, supplied information on the Rolex company and its founder. Mr. Shafir thinks that Hemingway himself owned a Rolex Oyster Perpetual. He writes: "Although we have no present documentation on it, one of our older associates has in the past said that he saw one on the great man's wrist in Florida in the very late forties-early fifties" (Fax, 7 April, 1992).

47. "Rommel, Field Marshal Erwin," *Who Was Who in World War II*, 173–74.

48. "Rotary International," *The New Columbia Encyclopedia.*

49. "Seconal" is made by the Lilly Pharmaceutical company; see "Quinalbarbitone Sodium," *Martindale: The Extra Pharmacopoeia*, 776–77. The drug is also taken by Thomas Hudson (*Islands*, 216) and by Hemingway himself (see endnote 31).

50. "Smith, Red (Walter Wellesley Smith)," Obituary, *Encyclopaedia Britannica*, 1983 Book of the Year.

51. "Star-spangled Banner, The," *The New Columbia Encyclopedia.*

52. *"Stars and Stripes, The" Oxford Companion to American Literature*, 719.

53. Russo gives a Freudian reading of Torcello's skyline: "Torcello with its square tower signifies completeness, phallocentrism, the

masculine virtue of being closed up in oneself, autonomy," unlike Venice, which "signifies the feminine, the unattainable, the sense of lack, the lure of death" ("To Die Is Not Enough," 161).

54. D. Fullin, Centro Documentazione, *Corriere della Sera,* Milan, Italy, supplied information about Italian newspapers (letter to author, 27 August, 1991).

55. Benedict K. Zobrist, Director of the Harry S Truman Library, writes that "we were unable to find any evidence that Miss Truman sang the "Star-Spangled Banner" on the radio during World War II" (letter to author, 24 April, 1992). As he points out, she was still a student during World War II.

56. "Udet, Lieutenant General Ernst," *Who Was Who in World War II,* 211; and in *Der Grosse Bruckhaus.*

57. "Verlaine, Paul," *Cassell's Encyclopedia of World Literature* (1973), III: 684.

58. *"Vogue,"* Mott, *A History of American Magazines,* IV: 756–62; and *Catalogue Collectif des Périodiques.*

59. Information about the Wagon-Box Fight was supplied by Thomas P. Wollenzien, President, Sheridan County Historical Society (letter to author, 26 July, 1993); by Paul Fees, Senior Curator, Buffalo Bill Historical Center, Cody, WY (letter to author, 13 September, 1993); and by Professor Robert Roripaugh, Department of English, University of Wyoming (letter to author, 11 July, 1993).

60. The unidentified writer is Sinclair Lewis, who met Mary Hemingway at the bar of the Hotel Gritti early in 1949, disparaged Ernest to her, and left without paying the bar bill. Hemingway wrote Charles Scribner that Lewis was at the Gritti with "the mother of his ex-mistress Marcella Powers" and that when he wasn't drinking or writing "he would go out with Mrs. Powers and peer at whatever was 3 starred in Baedeker." As Baker points out, Hemingway's description of Lewis as a "poor Baedeker peering bastard with his Mistress's (who left him) mother defiling Venice with his pock-marked curiosity and lack of understanding" matches his attack on the unidentified writer of *ARIT* (Baker, *Letters,* 660–61).

CHAPTER VII: *THE OLD MAN AND THE SEA*

1. *Historical and Literary Prototypes.* Baker identifies Manolito, "the young son of the café-owner at Cojimar," as "a rough model for Manolo, the boy in the story" and Carlos Gutiérrez "as one distant prototype of Santiago" (*Life,* 501–2). Meyers affirms the Manolito-Manolín connection and writes that Santiago is a composite of Hemingway, Gregorio Fuentes, and Carlos Gutiérrez (*Hemingway,* 486).

    Carlos Baker discusses Conrad's story "Youth" as a literary source for Hemingway's "parable of youth and age" (*The Writer as Artist,* 4th ed., 309–11). Bruce Morton finds that Hemingway mined his essay "Marlin Off Cuba" (1935) when writing *OMS.* A one-paragraph outline of *OMS* appeared in Hemingway's "On the Blue Water: A Gulf Stream Letter," April 1936, though in that report the old man did not make it back to shore: "He was crying in the boat when the fishermen picked him up, half crazy from his loss, and the sharks were still circling the boat" (rpt. White, 253–54).

2. When Malcolm Cowley mentioned the shifting terminology, Hemingway reassured him that "It is all right about the bonito. . . . This fish was a small tuna, but the old man being from the Canaries would call him 'albacore' and think of him generally as 'Bonito' " (qtd. by James D. Brasch, "Invention from Knowledge: The Hemingway-Cowley Correspondence," in Nagel, 221–22).

3. "DiMaggio's Father Dies on Coast at 77," *New York Times,* 4 May 1949, 29:6. Additional information about the careers and families of Joe DiMaggio and of George and Richard Sisler was provided by Dr. Robert W. Brown, President of the American League of Professional Baseball Clubs, 350 Park Avenue, New York (letters to author, 20 March and 17 May, 1991); Jeff Elijah, International Baseball Association, 201 S. Capitol Ave., Indianapolis, IN (letter to author and enclosures, 26 March, 1991); and Gary Van Allen, Research Associate of the National Baseball Hall of Fame and Museum, Inc., Cooperstown, NY (letter to author and enclosures, 1 May, 1991). For a discussion on how DiMaggio and other baseball players function in *OMS,* see Barbour and Sattelmeyer, "Baseball and Baseball Talk," 281–87.

4. Thomas Rogers, "Leo Durocher, Fiery Ex-Manager, Dies at 86," *New York Times,* 8 October, 1991, D25: 1–3; "Leo (the Lip) Durocher, at 86; fiery baseball manager, player," *The Boston Globe,* 8 October, 1991, 15: 1–2; see also Bob Ryan's essay, "Durocher:

Gas Houser was fiery to the finish,'' pp. 27 and 31 of this edition of the *Globe*.

5. Letter to author, 19 January, 1992. The appellation ''shovel-nosed shark'' is usually used in reference to a different shark, the bonnethead (scientific name: *Sphyrna tiburo*), a member of the hammerhead family of sharks (the *Sphynidae*) whose distinctive shovel- or bonnet-shaped head distinguishes it from other members of the hammerhead family. It is smaller than the Mako, obtaining a maximum size of a little over a meter. It prefers warm waters and ''travels in schools of five to fifteen individuals. Migrating schools of hundreds and even thousands of these sharks have been reported'' (Castro, *The Sharks of North American Waters*, 156). It generally feeds on small fishes. But Castro finds that Hemingway's phrase ''shovel-pointed'' ''must be in comparison to the pointed head of the mako. It has nothing to do with the shovel-nosed bonnethead which is not found in the pelagic environment'' (letter to author, 16 January, 1992). Dr. José I. Castro is Senior Research Scientist, U.S. Department of Commerce, National Marine Fisheries Service, Southeast Fisheries Center, Miami, FL. Although in the novel the galano is described as having a ''brown, triangular fin'' and ''brown head and back'' (107–8), elsewhere Hemingway mentioned ''a large black shark of the type we call *galanos* on the Cuban coast'' (''On Being Shot Again: A Gulf Stream Letter,'' June 1935, rpt. White, 214).

6. For a detailed list of González's appointments, see Reichler, *The Baseball Encyclopedia*, 970. Reichler lists González's birth date as 24 September, 1890 and his death date as 19 February, 1977. The obituary published in *The Sporting News* (2 April, 1977) agrees that he died in Havana, Cuba, at age 86; another obituary reports he died in Mexico City at age 84. A 1938 newspaper clipping, celebrating González's appointment as ''the first Cuban ever to pilot a major league club,'' insists that he was born in 1894; that would make him 82 when he died. There is general agreement, however, that when he was scouting for new players González coined the phrase ''Good field, no hit'' and that '' 'Smart dummy' was ol' Mike's finest accolade'' (''Broeg on Baseball,'' 29 January, 1972, clipping from the National Baseball Files sent to author by Gary Van Allen, Research Associate, National Baseball Hall of Fame and Museum, Inc., Cooperstown, NY, 23 November, 1992).

7. Peter Hays has pointed out that lions are the only social cat, living in packs. Although Santiago lives alone and generally remains aloof from the village fishermen, he is aware that he lives in a good

community. His need for the boy and his admiration for the lions and for Joe DiMaggio, "the ultimate team player," underline the importance he attaches to community (Hays, "Exchange between Rivals," 157). A lion skin is worn by Orion; see entry for Rigel.

8. Superstition about the power of speech appears in other novels as well. David Hudson insists his brother not speak about the huge fish he has hooked (*Islands,* 111, 113, 119); such talk "seems bad luck" (*Islands,* 120). If one doesn't talk about dreams, they may be realized (*Islands,* 384). Talking about or in other ways acknowledging (externalizing) death is bad luck: Morgan is shocked and "scared" when Simmons speaks of death (*THHN,* 109, 111), and Hudson does not paint a canvas because in the preliminary sketch, the subject, his son Tom, reminded him of a dead knight and painting him thus "could be bad luck" (*Islands,* 446). Like Santiago, Cantwell thinks himself unlucky and recognizes that luck, while not sufficient, is necessary—a belief he claims to share with Napoleon (*ARIT,* 232; see *Islands,* 444).

9. Letter to author, 19 January, 1992. In "'Out in the Stream: A Cuban Letter,'" August 1934, Hemingway also admired the mako's "intelligence and courage" but wrote that "a mako shark [will] not eat a hooked or dead marlin or swordfish . . . [it] will swim around and round a hooked marlin and never hit him" (rpt. White, 189). In the novel it is a mako which takes the first bite out of Santiago's marlin.

10. This dental arrangement obtains in all sharks, although, as Weeks points out, "Only two rows . . . are functional; the others are replacements which become functional as the forward teeth are lost or destroyed." Weeks adds that not all of the Mako's functional teeth are equally large and dangerous; he concludes that Hemingway presented the Mako "more menacing than he actually is," although he recognizes that the Mako is "the biggest and most dangerous of the sharks" ("Fakery," 190–91). Hemingway mentions the mako's "curved-in teeth" in "Out in the Stream: A Cuban Letter" (rpt. White, 189).

11. See Bennett, "Manolín's Father," 417–18. Manolín's father attaches his son to a fisherman who is practically blind, physically and spiritually; Santiago has very keen vision, like a cat (67; the cat is associated with eyes, 108). He claims he could not bear to lose his eyes (68) and drinks shark liver oil because "it was good for the eyes" (37).

12. Santiago describes both himself and the fish as "strange" (14, 67), and feels the damage done to the fish, by himself and by the sharks, as if had been done to him (103, 115). David Hudson also identifies with the fish he has hooked (*Islands,* 142–43).

13. Weeks objects to Santiago's ability to differentiate between male and female marlin. He quotes Gilbert Voss, an ichthyologist: "The sexes are not recognizable in these animals except by internal dissection" ("Fakery," 189).

14. In *MF* we read that following the horses requires one to become knowledgeable about "jockeys and trainers and owners and too many horses and too many things," many of them dishonest or illegal. Hemingway claims he gave up horses because keeping up with it all in order to make a profit "was hard work" and "took too much time" (62). Because McGraw's continued interest in horses suggests corruption, greed, and an incomplete commitment to baseball, Santiago refrains from describing McGraw as "the greatest," in spite of his many achievements.

15. Several critics have objected to the reference to Rigel, which "does not appear in Cuban skies at sunset in September but some five hours after Santiago sees it" (Weeks, "Fakery," 192). According to Baker, Hemingway admitted the mistake and said of the various people who pointed out the error to him, that "They were so good to write" (qtd. in Baker, *Life,* 514). The inaccuracy has been justified by Bickford Sylvester on the grounds of poetic license: having achieved a larger vision of the universe and of man's place in it, Hemingway no longer needed to rely on "the way it was," the principle which had informed the earlier fiction ("Hemingway's Extended Vision," 138). Kenneth G. Johnston presents a thorough justification of the star Rigel and its function in the novel: he points out that it "is the brilliant white star embedded in the upraised left foot" of Orion and thus suggestive of DiMaggio's bone spur. Similarly, he relates Orion's club to DiMaggio's baseball bat and to Santiago's clubbing of the sharks, and connects Orion's lion skin, worn as a shield and symbolizing "courage and invulnerability," to Santiago's dreams of lions, which serve him as a shield against old age. Johnston finds that the reference to Rigel "significantly enriches" the novel ("The Star in Hemingway's *The Old Man and the Sea,*" 92). The name Rigel derives from the Arabic word for foot (*OED*).

16. "Sisler, George," Obituary, *Encyclopedia Americana,* 1974 Annual, 450. See endnote 3.

17. Poverty made the old man shy, an attitude Manolín shares. Unlike the Cuban characters of this novel, the Sislers were middle-class people: "the great Sisler's father [i.e., George] was never poor" and "he, the father, was playing in the Big Leagues [and earning a good salary] when he [i.e., Dick] was my age" (22). This passage establishes Manolín's age: C. Harold Hurley's argument that the second "he" refers to Dick and not George Sisler, makes good sense: it defines Manolín as ten years old, the age of Dick Sisler at the time of his father's retirement from the Boston Braves ("Manolín's Age," 71–72). (George Sisler was born on 24 March, 1893, and was 22 years old and a college graduate [University of Michigan] when he made his debut on 28 June, 1915, playing for the St. Louis Browns; Manolín seems much younger than this.) By Hurley's reckoning, Manolín would have been born sometime in 1942, and would have been three or four years old when Dick Sisler visited Cuba (December 1945–February 1946), old enough to know that Sisler was an impressive baseball player and to know that "He hits the longest ball I have ever seen" (*OMS*, 21), especially as Sisler was the talk of the town for several years afterwards. Manolín insists he has a good memory: he remembers clearly his first fishing trip with Santiago, when he was five years old (12). Manolín recalls seeing Sisler and agrees that he was too shy to speak to him and relay Santiago's invitation to go fishing. And Santiago, embarrassed by poverty, had himself also been "too timid" to invite Sisler; he would be less shy with DiMaggio, the son of a fisherman, who had "Maybe" once been "as poor as we are" (22). The referent of "he" is ambiguous, but seems to be "the great DiMaggio." For that family's finances, see entry for DiMaggio's father.

18. Like Santiago, Bobby Saunders speaks slightingly of the "common loggerhead," which is "Not even a green turtle" (*Islands*, 19).

CHAPTER VIII: *ISLANDS IN THE STREAM*

1. *Historical and Literary Prototypes.* Most biographical critics agree that the character of Hudson, although slightly older than his creator (see endnote 16) is based on Hemingway himself. His first ex-wife seems to be a combination of the first Mrs. Hemingway (Hadley Richardson, q.v. in *SAR*) and long-time friend Marlene Dietrich, whom Hemingway met late in 1934 (Baker, *Life*, 258) and whose lover he may have been (Donnelly, 134). The second ex-wife, mother of the two younger boys, is based on Pauline Pfeiffer Hemingway; and the current Mrs. Hudson, who is pursuing her

career in the Pacific, on Martha Gellhorn (q.v. in *FWBT*). Hudson's three sons are based on Hemingway's, all of whom survived their father. The two older boys were in a car crash which most biographers date to May 1933 although Jack Hemingway recalls it as occurring in 1934 (*Misadventures,* 257); Patrick and Gregory were in another car crash in 1947 (Meyers, *Hemingway,* 245). The oldest son, John Hadley Nicanor (Jack), was wounded and captured by the Germans in October 1944; he was liberated, recaptured, and released in May 1945 (Meyers, *Hemingway,* 412). The children's nurse, Anna (56) is based on Ada Stern, "a silent, blue-eyed Germanic spinster from Syracuse" (Meyers, *Hemingway,* 225) who entered the Key West household in 1932, when Patrick was about four years old and Gregory was a baby. She supervised the children, all of whom hated her, for over ten years (Kert, 239, 269, 368, *et passim*). The character of Roger Davis derives from Hemingway and from Scott and Zelda Fitzgerald, who between them provide several of the elements that define Roger: painting, formulaic fiction written for money, scriptwriting in Hollywood, and mental illness. The Fitzgeralds' good looks and exuberant doings made them newsworthy items; similarly, Roger is mentioned by Cholly Knickerbocker and knows Sherm Billingsley. As for the secondary characters, Meyers writes that "Gregorio [Fuentes], Paxtchi [Ibarlucia] and [Don] Saxon are portrayed as Antonio, Ara and Willie in *Islands in the Stream*" (*Hemingway,* 609, n.33; see also 386) and that Winston Guest was the prototype for Henry Wood (387). Guest was nicknamed "Wolfie" because one of Hemingway's children thought he looked like Lon Chaney, Jr. in *The Wolfman* (Baker, *Life,* 376); the nickname surfaces in the cat Uncle Woolfie. Honest Lil at the Floridita bar and Hudson's servants in Cuba also seem to be based on people Hemingway knew in Cuba (Meyers, *Hemingway,* 328–29). The indefatigable Baker has even found the historical prototype of Ignacio Natera Revello: "the portrait of Ignacio is based on a real-life resident of Havana, Alvaro González Gordon. The portrait is exact, even to the green-tinted spectacles" (*The Writer as Artist,* 4th ed., 398; see also 399, n.37). Norberto Fuentes confirms this identification and identifies the historical prototypes of some of the other characters whom Hudson meets at the Floridita: the fictional Constante, Pedrico and Serafín are based on the historical Constantino (Constante) Ribailagua y Vert, Manuel (Pedrito) López Laza, and Serafín García Lago; the politician is based on Raul García Menocal, and so on (*Hemingway in Cuba,* 224, 233–34). Fuentes repeats Mary Hemingway's identifications of the Hemingway servants: e.g., Juan the chauffeur, René the "loving butler," Ramón the Chinese cook. Fuentes, who blurs fact and fiction and whose book is riddled with contradictions, identifies Hemingway's chauffeur, Juan Pastor (whose last name Mary Hemingway does not supply), as the prototype of Hudson's chauffeur, Pedro (*Hemingway Rediscovered,* 128, 138; but see *Hemingway in Cuba,* p. 76, where Fuentes mistakenly claims that Hudson's chauffeur is called Juan) and René Villarreal as the prototype of Hudson's houseboy Mario (*Hemingway in Cuba,* 37–38). Less verifiable is Fuentes' identification of the policeman-*cum*-murderer with a Cuban medical student named René Hidalgo or Hidaldo (*Hemingway in Cuba,* 88–89). There is general agreement that Hudson's hunting of German submarines is based on Hemingway's own patrols aboard the *Pilar* during 1942 and 1943 (Baker, *Life,* 374–85). Hemingway had many cats at Finca Vigía, his Cuban house, among them Furhouse, Boise, Fats, Friendless, Friendless' Brother, and Uncle Wolfie. He also had a black bitch named Negrita (Baker, *Letters,* 552, 555). The trip to the Far East recalled in *Part II* reflects Hemingway and Gellhorn's trip in 1941 (Baker, *Life,* 360–64).

Baker finds that several details in the sea chase section of *Islands* derive from Conrad's story "The Heart of Darkness" (*The Writer as Artist,* 4th ed., 405–7). Wirt Williams has found more literary influences than most other critics: e.g., Dante's *Inferno,* Conrad's "The Secret Sharer" and *Lord Jim,* Dostoevsky's *The Brothers Karamazov,* Sartre's *No Exit,* and Vergil's *Aeneid* (Williams, 201–21).

2. Information about John Jacob Astor's military rank and career was supplied by Karl E. Cocke and William J. Webb, of the Staff Support Branch, The Center of Military History, Department of the Army, Washington D.C. (letter to author, 15 February, 1991).

3. "Billingsley, John Sherman," Obituary, *Encyclopaedia Britannica,* 1967 Book of the Year; *Who Was Who,* IV; *Dictionary of American Biography,* Supplement 8.

4. See George W. Cullum, *Biographical Register of the Officers and Graduates of the U.S. Military Academy at West Point,* 3rd rev. and extended ed. (Boston: Houghton, Mifflin, 1891), 249. Suzanne Christoff, Assistant Archivist, U.S. Military Academy at West Point, supplied information on William Crittenden (letter to author, 16 January, 1991). The loss of life at Bahía Honda was considerable, only 170 of the 548 men surviving; see "Cuba," *Enciclopedia Universal Ilustrada,* XVI (1913): 836. Crittenden's brief career is summarized in Cullum, II: 249, Item 1271; see also "Crittendem

(*sic*), Guillermo'' in *Enciclopedia Universal Ilustrada,* XVI (1913): 411–12.

5. Mrs. Crosby was born Mary Phelps Jacob; her first husband was Richard Rogers Peabody. She married Harry Crosby in 1922 and Bert Young in the mid-1930s. Her autobiographical book, *The Passionate Years* (1953), is a tribute to Harry Crosby, at whose instigation she changed her name to Caresse (Beach, 135).

6. The dramatic story of drugs, assignation, murder, and suicide among the rich was in the *Daily News* and other New York newspapers of 11 and 12 December, 1929. For a full account, see Geoffrey Wolff, ''The Man Who Fell in Love with Death: Harry Crosby's Transit to the Sun,'' *Atlantic Monthly,* July 1976: 37–46. Rebecca J. Bates, Curatorial Assistant, Harvard University Archives, Cambridge, MA, provided a wealth of material on Harry Grew Crosby, Class of 1922 (letter to author and enclosures, 8 May, 1991).

7. See ''Anchor,'' McEwen and Lewis, *Encyclopedia of Nautical Knowledge,* 15; and R. D. Ogg, *Anchors and Anchoring,* 5th ed, a brochure produced by the Danforth/White Co., Portland, ME (1967). For information about the Danforth anchor, I am indebted to R. P. Dinsmore, of the Woods Hole Oceanographic Institution, Woods Hole, MA (letter to author and enclosures, 11 February, 1991); and to Lysle B. Gray, Executive Director of the American Boat and Yacht Council, Inc., Millersville, MD (letter to author and enclosures, 22 January, 1991).

8. ''Jack Dempsey,'' Menke, 246; and *Collier's Encyclopedia* IV: 443–444 and VIII: 98. See ''Dempsey'' in *SAR* and *GHA.*

9. ''Flynn, Errol,'' *International Dictionary of Films,* III; and Thomson, *Biographical Dictionary of Film.*

10. In the summer of 1942, when the three Hemingway boys were visiting their father in Cuba, ''He signed them on as apprentice crew to sail on an 'Operation Friendless (code name)' '' (Kert, 369; see Baker, *Life,* 375).

11. In 1954 he was sentenced to four years' imprisonment for political activities; Batista gave him a Presidential pardon after Gutiérrez had served two months of his sentence (*New York Times* 25 June, 1954, 5: 1; and 13 August, 1954, 5: 6).

12. "Page, Sir Frederick Handley," Obituary, *Encyclopaedia Britannica,* 1963 Book of the Year.

13. Professor Bruce A. Rosenberg, English Department, Brown University, Providence, RI; and Jean Rainwater, Librarian, and Rosemary Cullen, Curator, of that university's John Hay Library, Harris Collection, kindly tracked down this and other songs for me.

14. "Hershey, Milton Snavely" and "Hershey," *Collier's Encyclopedia,* XII: 89. Lisa C. Schlegel, Public Relations Representative for Hershey Foods, supplied information about Hershey's activities in Cuba (letter to author and enclosures, 22 February, 1991).

15. The first Mrs. Hudson, an actress, is so beautiful that "Everyone had tried to look like her for many years and some came quite close" (305). Thomas Hudson, Roger Davis, and David all remark on Audrey Bruce's resemblance to Tommy's mother. Unlike his brothers, young David is not smitten with Audrey because, as he has confided to Roger Davis, he is "in love with someone else," with a person whom Audrey resembles (178). David remarks that "Maybe she [Audrey] saw her in the cinema and tried to look like her" (178; see also 176–77, 185). See endnote 1.

16. Hudson was born in 1891, forty years after Crittenden and his men were executed in July 1851 (*Islands,* 246). He recalls "feeling the firing of heavy guns when he had lain on the earth close by some battery a long time ago when he had been a boy" (5).

17. "Huff-duff," Wentworth and Flexner, *Dictionary of American Slang.*

18. "Kerr, Richard Henry," Obituary, *New York Times,* 5, May, 1963, 87: 1.

19. The chronicler was also chronicled: in the *Saturday Evening Post,* 19 January, 1963, 236: 287; in *Esquire,* February 1963, 59: 61–62, and April 1964, 61: 94ff; and in *Newsweek,* 18 February, 1963, 61: 23, this latter article suggesting that Cassini was "an unlicensed representative" of the Dominican Republic.

20. "Mama Don't Want . . ." (1931), rpt. 1989 in Lax and Smith; also rpt. in *First Time Ever: 650 Outstanding Songs.*

21. Mr. D. J. Penn, Keeper of the Department of Exhibits and Firearms at the Imperial War Museum, London, supplied information on the .256 Mannlicher-Schoenauer, for which he shares Hemingway's enthusiasm (letter to author, 29 July, 1991).

22. Like his predecessors, from Queen Victoria to his father George V, George VI was King of Great Britain and Northern Ireland and Emperor of India. After India became independent, the monarchs of Great Britain no longer carried the title of Emperor.

23. See Alison Weir, *Britain's Royal Families: The Complete Genealogy.* Flanner gives Mary's name as "Victoria Mary Augusta Louise Olga Pauline Claudine Agnes, but her mother [the Duchess of Teck] called her 'May' or sometimes 'my Mayflower' " ["Her Majesty," II: 28).

24. Peter Plagens, "The Agony and the Ecstasy: Is Michelangelo's masterpiece better than ever?" (*Newsweek,* 116.23 [3 December, 1990]: 55).

25. Noam Flinker, English Department, Haifa University, supplied material on various portraits of Milton and his daughters.

26. "Monfreid, Henri de," *Grand Dictionnaire Encyclopédique Larousse,* 1984 ed.

27. See Nelson, 86–88, 98; and *Dictionary of American Naval Fighting Ships,* V: 102. Information on the *Nokomis* was supplied by R. M. Browning, Jr., Historian, U.S. Coast Guard, Washington D.C., and Lysle B. Gray, Executive Director of the American Boat and Yacht Council, Inc., Millersville MD (letters to author and enclosures, 22 January, 1991); R. P. Dinsmore, of the Woods Hole Oceanographic Institution (letter and enclosures, 11 February, 1991); and A. J. Booth, Deputy Director of Naval History, Department of the Navy, Washington D.C. (letter and enclosures, 4 February, 1991).

28. The incident involving O'Reilly is mentioned in "Louisiana—8. History" and "New Orleans," *Encyclopedia Americana,* XVII: 791 and XX: 191; and in "Cuba," *Enciclopedia Universal Ilustrada,* XVI: 832. The quoted material at the end of the entry is from *Encyclopaedia Britannica,* 11th ed., XIII: 76. Roberts (quoted at the beginning of the entry) writes that the street was re-named for the fourth president of Cuba, Alfredo Zayas, but that "Except for a few provincials and foreigners, O'Reilly is what people use" in spite of

the fact that in the 1950s, when Roberts is writing, "The new signs are [already] in place from end to end of the street" (Roberts, 156).

29. "San Quentin quail," Wentworth and Flexner, *Dictionary of American Slang.*

30. "Rodríguez, Antonio Héctor" and "Rodríguez, José," Myron Smith, *Baseball*, 728.

31. "Rudolph, Richard," Obituary, *New York Times,* 22 October, 1949, 17:4.

32. "Sande, Earl," Obituary, *Encyclopaedia Britannica,* 1969 Book of the Year; and *Encyclopedia Americana,* 1969 Annual.

33. Louis Schmeisser, also a designer and manufacturer of weapons, was associated with the Rheinmetall Weapons Manufacturing Co., many of whose guns are also known as Schmeissers (see Chinn, I: 216, 453). But Mr. D. J. Penn, of the Imperial War Museum, London, thinks it highly likely that the Germans are using the MP 40, with which Hugo (not Louis) Schmeisser was associated. My thanks once again to Mr. Penn for detailed technical information about German weapons and ammunition.

34. "Springfield," Tunis, *Weapons.* The Springfield 1903 is described in *Colliers Encyclopedia,* 1968 ed., XII: 781–82. The biography of Col. Springfield is readily available (e.g., *Encyclopedia Americana,* 1961 ed., III: 528).

35. Alfredo Seville, *Abecedary.* Wayne D. Shirley, Music Specialist, The Library of Congress, Washington D.C., tracked down several songs for me (letter to author, 1 July, 1991).

36. D. J. Penn, Imperial War Museum, London, supplied information about Edward Wilson Very (letter to author, 14 February, 1991).

37. "Jess Williard," Menke, 245–46; and *Collier's Encyclopedia* IV: 444.

CHAPTER IX: *THE GARDEN OF EDEN*

1. *Historical and Literary Prototypes.* The character of David Bourne recalls various details of Hemingway's own life: his women have

more money than he, he has hunted in Africa, he is an American living in Europe, he is in love with two women, he suffers the loss of manuscripts, he learns to despise his father, and he follows the same writing schedule and rituals as Hemingway. Catherine and Marita contain elements of Hadley Richardson, Pauline Pfeiffer, and Pauline's sister Virginia (Jinny), who was a lesbian. Catherine's madness and her jealousy of her husband's work recall Zelda Fitzgerald, attacked by Hemingway in *MF* for undermining her husband's work. Grau du Roi is where Hemingway and Pauline Pfeiffer honeymooned in the late spring of 1927; they went to Spain that summer (Meyers, *Hemingway*, 194). Having examined the entire manuscript, Mark Spilka finds that Catherine is based on Pauline Pfeiffer and that Barbara Sheldon, a character excised when the manuscript was prepared for publication, is closely modeled on Hadley Richardson. He suggests that the name Marita results from a combination of the first names of Hemingway's third and fourth wives, Martha Gellhorn and Mary Welsh. Spilka finds that all four wives were involved in androgynous experimentation ("Hemingway's Barbershop Quintet," 44–45). Colonel John Boyle may be based on the dashing adventurer Charles Sweeny (q.v. in *MF,* where the name is misspelled Sweeney). Rose Marie Burwell finds that the character is based on Colonel John Boyes, whose book about elephant-hunting, *The Company of Adventurers,* Hemingway owned ("A Source for the Androgynous Elephant in *The Garden of Eden,*" paper read at the Fifth International Hemingway Conference, 19 July, 1992, Pamplona, Spain). Burwell reports that Boyes organized a private, well-disciplined native army in East Kenya; he wrote about his experiences in *John Boyes: King of the Wa-Kikuyu* (London: Methuen & Co., 1911). The book was popular in Britain, a sixth edition appearing in 1926. There was also an American edition, entitled *A White King in East Africa* and subtitled "The Remarkable Adventures of John Boyes, trader and soldier of fortune, who became king of the savage Wa-Kikuyu" (New York: McBride, Nast & Co., 1912).

Mark Spilka finds a source for Hemingway's African stories (q.v.) in Kipling's *Jungle Books* ("Hemingway's Barbershop Quintet"; see also "The Kipling Impress," in Spilka's *Hemingway's Quarrel with Androgyny,* 91–124). Hemingway quotes Kipling in *SAR* (s.v. *"The Colonel's Lady and Judy O'Grady") and in *Islands* (s.v. "Mary, Pity Women"). For a discussion of Kipling's influence on Hemingway, see Jeffrey Meyers, "Kipling and Hemingway"; and Reynolds, *The Paris Years,* 6, 66. David's African narratives recall Joseph Conrad's "Heart of Darkness."

2. E.O. Ashton's *Swahili Grammar* explains the prefix system and has a short vocabulary list. Arthur Cornwallis Madan's *Swahili-English Dictionary* (1903, hereafter cited as Madan) was the basis for the authoritative *A Standard Swahili-English Dictionary,* prepared by the Inter-Territorial Language Committee for the East African Dependencies, under the general editorship of Frederick Johnson (Oxford U.P., 1939, reprinted frequently and cited in the text as *Standard Swahili).* The definition "comrade at arms" was supplied by Rose Marie Burwell, who found it in *A Dictionary of the Swahili Language,* compiled by Ludwig Krapf and first published in 1882. Burwell also informs me that "when bulls get very old, and are displaced by younger males, they sometimes go off alone or in pairs, and live away from the herd" (letter to author, 3 December, 1992).

3. *"Atlantic Monthly," Oxford Companion to American Literature,* 43; and in Mott, *History of American Magazines,* II (1850–1865); "Magazines," *The Reader's Encyclopedia of American Literature,* 688.

4. Catherine's pejorative language echoes the rejection letters Hemingway received at the beginning of his career: she calls his stories "sketches or vignettes or pointless anecdotes" (210), complains about "mistakes in spelling and grammar" both in English and in French (215), and rejects his inelegant diction: "He can't write like a gentleman nor speak like one in any language" (216; see also 134, 154–55).

5. Colonel Cantwell's best friend, George, makes a similar remark: "Everybody's right until he's wrong" *(ARIT,* 293).

6. Newspapers in Microform, Foreign Countries 1948–1983, Library of Congress Catalogues (Washington, D.C., 1984).

7. David's reported thoughts seem to reflect what he has just read in the letter from the publisher ("It was an unusual summer in New York, cold and wet") and, probably, the news items he had just read in the papers. The drunken writer may be Fitzgerald. David's sudden anger—against the 19th-century Americans who displaced the Indians, against the current American president and current American culture—may well be due to the fact that he has no "next book" ready for his publisher: he makes no other anti-American statements in the novel.

8. Veronique Brown-Claudot, Public Relations, Hotel de Crillon, 10 Place de la Concorde, Paris 75008, supplied brochures about the hotel and its history and offered additional information in a personal interview, Paris, 18 December, 1991. Also see *Crillon in *SAR.*

9. "Dent, Joseph Malaby," *Everyman's Encyclopedia,* V: 352.

10. "Derain, André," Obituary, *Encyclopaedia Britannica,* 1955 Book of the Year.

11. *"The Dial,"* Mott, *A History of American Magazines,* III: 539–43.

12. "Galignani, Giovanni Antonio," Obituary, *Encyclopaedia Britannica,* 1938–46 Book of the Year; "Galignani, Wm.," *Dictionary of National Biography;* "Galignani's," Hyamson. The informative in-house booklet, "A Famous Bookstore," details the history of the Galignani family and firm. It is available free of charge at the store.

13. *"Guardia,"* *Enciclopedia Universal Ilustrada,* XXVI: 1587–91.

14. "Harper's Bazar," "Harper's Monthly Magazine," and "Harper's Weekly," *Oxford Companion to American Literature;* "Harper's," *Reader's Encyclopedia of American Literature.*

15. When time becomes distorted for Catherine, she insists that she is old, "older than my mother's old clothes" (163).

16. The Mother Goose rhymes and tales were published in France in the late 17th century as *Contes de ma Mère L'Oye.* Nursery rhymes were first published in England by John Newbery in the 18th century. Newbery's grandson published a *Mother Goose* in England in 1791; it appeared in the United States in 1833.

17. Catherine's legalistic (145) and financial (226) approach to David's stories may derive from her "poor little rich girl" background: orphaned early in life, she seems to have internalized the values of the bankers and lawyers who handle her inherited wealth.

18. "Leda," in Antonio Blanco and Manuel Lorente, eds., *Catálogo de la Escultura (Museo del Prado)* (Madrid: Patronato Nacional de Museos, 1981), 11–12. The statue is also listed in E. Barrón's 1908 *Catálogo de la Escultura (Museo del Prado),* on which Blanco and Lorente's 1981 catalogue is based.

19. *"The New Republic,"* Mott, *A History of American Magazines,* V: 191–224; "Magazines," *Reader's Encyclopedia of American Literature,* 688.

20. The title seems to be fictional. The Union Catalogue lists *A Rift in the Cloud* (1904), by Frank Edward Cleaveland, and *The Rift in the Clouds* (1872), by Catherine Marsh, but no book entitled simply *The Rift.*

21. "Romeike, Henry," *Dictionary of American Biography.* Surviving invoices indicate that Hemingway subscribed to the service in 1924 and 1926 (Hemingway Collection: Other Materials, Service/Store Receipts; also see Baker, *Letters,* 214).

22. *"Vogue,"* Mott, *A History of American Magazines,* IV: 756–62; and *Catalogue Collectif des Périodiques.* Renata also reads this magazine (*ARIT,* 263.)

23. "Vuitton, Claude-Louis" and "Vuitton, Henry-Louis," *Qui est Qui.* Patricia Champier, Manager of the Louis Vuitton shop at 51 Copley Place, Boston, MA, made available to me the French and English versions of Henry-Louis Vuitton's book and shared with me her knowledge of the Vuitton family (Interviews, October 1991). In 1927 Hemingway ordered a "malle bibliothèque" (a suitcase for books; see Hemingway Collection: Other Materials, Service/Store Receipts).

LIST OF WORKS CONSULTED

Abrams, M.H. et al., eds. *The Norton Anthology of English Literature.* 5th ed. 2 vols. New York: W.W. Norton, 1986.

Acronyms, Initialisms, & Abbreviations Dictionary. 1960. 5th ed. 3 vols. Ed. Ellen T. Crowley. Detroit, MI: Gale Research Co., 1976.

Alderman, Taylor. "Fitzgerald, Hemingway, and *The Passing of the Great Race.*" *Fitzgerald-Hemingway Annual* (1977): 215–17.

Alinei, Tamara. "The Corrida and *For Whom the Bell Tolls.*" *Neophilologus* 56 (1972): 487–92.

American Authors 1600–1900: A Biographical Dictionary of American Literature. Ed. Stanley J. Kunitz and Howard Haycraft. New York: H. W. Wilson Co., 1938.

American Women: 1935–40: A Composite Biographical Dictionary. Detroit: Gale, 1981.

Anderson, Sherwood. *Dark Laughter.* New York: Boni & Liveright, 1925.

Ashton, E.O. *Swahili Grammar.* 2nd ed. London: Longmans, 1947.

Atkins, John. *The Art of Ernest Hemingway: His Work and Personality.* London: Spring Books, 1952.

Auge, Claude and Paul, eds. *Nuevo Pequeño Larousse Ilustrado, Diccionario Enciclopédico.* Trans. from the French by Miguel de Toro y Gisbert. Paris: Librairie Larousse, 1951.

August, Jo, comp. *Catalog of the Ernest Hemingway Collection at the John F. Kennedy Library.* 2 vols. Boston: G.K. Hall & Co., 1982. Addendum (1983–1992) prepared by Megan Floyd Desnoyers,

Lisa Middents, and Stephen Plotkin; available at the Hemingway Room, J.F.K. Library.

Aylesworth, Thomas, and Benton Minks. *The Encyclopedia of Baseball Managers, 1901 to the Present Day.* New York: Crescent Books, 1990.

Bailey, William G. *Americans in Paris: 1900–1930, A Selected, Annotated Bibliography.* New York: Greenwood, 1989.

Baker, Carlos. *Ernest Hemingway: A Life Story.* 1969. New York: Collier/Macmillan, 1988.

———. *Hemingway: The Writer as Artist.* Princeton: Princeton U.P., 1963.

———. *Hemingway: The Writer as Artist.* 4th ed. Princeton: Princeton U.P., 1972.

———, ed. *Ernest Hemingway: Critiques of Four Major Novels.* New York: Scribner, 1962.

———, ed. *Ernest Hemingway: Selected Letters 1917–1961.* 1981. London: Panther Books, Granada Publishing, Ltd., 1985.

Bald, Wambly. *On the Left Bank 1929–1933.* Ed. Benjamin V. Franklin Athens, Ohio: Ohio U.P., 1987.

Barbour, James, and Robert Sattelmeyer. "Baseball and Baseball Talk in *The Old Man and the Sea.*" *Fitzgerald/Hemingway Annual* (1975): 281–87.

Barea, Arturo. "Not Spain But Hemingway." In *The Literary Reputation of Hemingway in Europe.* Ed. Roger Asselineau. New York: New York U.P., 1965, 197–210.

Barnes, Daniel R. "Traditional Narrative Sources for Hemingway's *Torrents of Spring.*" *Studies in Short Fiction* 19 (1982): 141–50.

The Barnhart Dictionary of Etymology. New York: H.W. Wilson, 1988.

Bartlett, John. *A Complete Concordance or Verbal Index to Words, Phrases and Passages in the Dramatic Works of Shakespeare.* London: Macmillan, 1962.

————. *Familiar Quotations.* 15th ed. Ed. Emily Morison Beck. Boston: Little Brown & Co., 1980.

Baudot, Marcel, et al., eds. *The Historical Encyclopedia of World War II.* Trans. from the French by Jesse Dilson. New York: Facts on File, 1980.

Beach, Sylvia. *Shakespeare and Company.* 1959; rpt. London: Plantin Paperbacks, 1987.

Beaumont, Richard. *Purdey's: The Guns and the Family.* London: David & Charles, 1984.

Beegel, Susan F. *Hemingway's Craft of Omission: Four Manuscript Examples.* Ann Arbor: UMI Research Press, 1988.

————, ed. *Hemingway's Neglected Short Fiction: New Perspectives.* Ann Arbor: UMI Research Press, 1989.

Bennett, Fordyce Richard. "Manolin's Father." *Fitzgerald/Hemingway Review* (1979): 417–18.

Benson, Jackson J. *Hemingway: The Writer's Art of Self-Defense.* Minneapolis: U. of Minnesota P., 1969.

Benstock, Shari. *Women of the Left Bank: Paris, 1900–1940.* Austin: U. of Texas P., 1986.

Beversluis, John. "Dispelling the Romantic Myth: A Study of *A Farewell to Arms.*" *Hemingway Review* 9.1 (1989): 18–25.

Black's Law Dictionary: Definitions of the Terms and Phrases of American and English Jurisprudence, Ancient and Modern with Guide to Pronunciation. By Henry Campbell Black. 4th ed. St. Paul, MN: West Publishing Co., 1951.

Bluefarb, Samuel. "The Sea—Mirror and Maker of Character in Fiction and Drama." *English Journal* 48 (1959): 501–10.

Blum, Daniel C. *Great Stars of the American Stage: A Pictorial Record.* New York: Grenberg, 1952.

The Book of the XV Brigade: Records of British, American, Canadian and Irish Volunteers in the XV International Brigade in Spain

1936–1938. Pub. and with a preface by Frank Graham, 6 Queen's Terrace, Newcastle-Upon-Tyne, England, 1975.

Brasch, James Daniel. "Invention from Knowledge: The Hemingway-Cowley Correspondence." In Nagel, 201–36.

———, and Joseph Sigman. *Hemingway's Library: A Composite Record.* New York: Garland, 1981.

Brenner, Gerry. *Concealments in Hemingway's Works.* Columbus: Ohio State U.P., 1983.

———. "Epic Machinery in Hemingway's *For Whom the Bell Tolls.*" *Modern Fiction Studies* 16 (1970): 491–504.

———. *The Old Man and the Sea: Story of a Common Man.* Twayne's Masterwork Studies No. 80. New York: Twayne, 1991.

Broeg, Bob. *Super Stars of Baseball: Their Lives, Their Loves, Their Laughs, Their Laments.* St. Louis, MO: The Sporting News, 1971.

Bruccoli, Matthew J. *Some Sort of Epic Grandeur: The Life of F. Scott Fitzgerald.* New York: Harcourt Brace Jovanovich, 1981.

———. " 'Oh, Give Them Irony and Give Them Pity'." *Fitzgerald/Hemingway Annual* (1970): 236.

Burhans, Clinton S. "*The Old Man and the Sea:* Hemingway's Tragic Vision of Man." *American Literature* 31 (1960): 446–455.

Burke, W. J., and Will D. Howe. *American Authors and Books: 1640 to the Present Day.* 3rd rev. ed. New York: Crown, 1972.

Burke's Peerage and Baronetage. London: Burke's Peerage, Ltd., 1975.

Burke's Royal Families of the World. London: Burke's Peerage, Ltd., 1977.

Byrd, Lemuel Brian. "Characterization in Ernest Hemingway's Fiction: 1925–1952, with a Dictionary of the Characters." Unpublished Dissertation, University of Colorado, 1969, c. 1970. Facsimile printed by University Microfilms International (UMI) Dissertation Information Service, 1989.

Cairis, Nicholas T. *Cruise Ships of the World*. London: Pegasus, 1989.

Callaghan, Morley. *That Summer in Paris*. New York: Dell, 1963.

Calvocoressi, Peter. *Who's Who in the Bible*. 1987. London: Penguin, 1988.

The Cambridge Guide to Literature in English. Ed. Ian Ousby. Cambridge: Cambridge U.P., 1988.

The Cambridge Guide to World Theatre. Ed. Martin Banham. Cambridge: Cambridge U.P., 1988.

Camino, Jaime. *Intimas conversaciones con la Pasionaria*. Barcelona: Dopesa, 1977. Interviews in Moscow, conducted during the filming of *La vieja memoria* (produced by Profilmes de Barcelona).

Carabantes, Andrés, and Eusebio Cimorra. *Un mito llamado Pasionaria*. Barcelona: Editorial Planeta, 1982. Colección Documentos, Documento 76.

Carrias, Eugene. *La Pensée Militaire Française*. Paris: Presses Universitaires de France, 1960.

Carroll, Lewis. *Alice's Adventures in Wonderland, Through the Looking-Glass,* and *The Hunting of the Snark*. Illustrations by John Tenniel. New York: Random House/Modern Library, n.d.

Carson, David L. ''Symbolism in *A Farewell to Arms*.'' *English Studies* 53 (1972): 518–22.

Cassell's Encyclopedia of World Literature. Ed. S. H. Steinberg. 2 vols. New York: Funk & Wagnalls, 1953.

Cassell's Encyclopedia of World Literature, rev. and enlarged. General ed. J. Buchanan-Brown. 3 vols. New York: William Morrow & Co., 1973.

Castells Peig, Andreu. *Las Brigadas Internacionales de la Guerra de España*. Barcelona: Editorial Ariel, 1974.

Castro, José I. *The Sharks of North American Waters*. College Station, Texas: Texas A & M U.P., 1983.

Catálogo de Periodistas Españoles del Siglo XX. Antonio López de Zuago Algar. Madrid, 1980–81.

Catalogue Collectif des Périodiques du Début de XVIIe Siècle à 1939. 5 vols. Paris: Bibliotheque Nationale, 1977–1981.

Cawkwell, Tim, and John M. Smith. *The World Encyclopedia of Film.* London: Studio Vista Publishers, 1972.

Chamber's Encyclopedia. New rev. ed. London: International Learning Systems, 1973.

Charters, James (Jimmie the Barman) as told to Morrill Cody. *This Must Be the Place: Memoirs of Montparnasse.* Ed. with a preface by Hugh Ford. Introduction by Ernest Hemingway. London: Herbert Josephs, Ltd., 1934; rpt. New York: Collier Books, 1989.

Chinn, George M. *The Machine Gun.* 3 vols. Washington, D.C.: U.S. Government Printing Office, 1951.

Clark, Sidney A. *Cuban Tapestry.* New York: Robert M. McBride & Co., 1936.

Cochran, Robert W. "Circularity in *The Sun Also Rises.*" *Modern Fiction Studies* 14 (1968): 297–305.

Cohen, Milton A. "Circe and Her Swine: Domination and Debasement in *The Sun Also Rises.*" *Arizona Quarterly* 41.4 (1985): 293–305.

Collier's Encyclopedia. Ed. in chief, Louis Shores. 24 vols. Crowell-Collier Educational Corp., 1968.

Columbia Dictionary of Modern European Literature. General ed. Horatio Smith. New York: Columbia U.P., 1947.

Concise Dictionary of American Biography. 3rd ed. New York: Scribner's, 1980.

The Concise Oxford Dictionary of Music. 3rd ed. Ed. Michael Kennedy. Oxford: Oxford U.P., 1980.

Cortada, James W. *Historical Dictionary of the Spanish Civil War, 1936–39.* Westport, CT: Greenwood Press, 1982.

Cossío y Martínez de Fortún, José María de. *Los Toros: Tratado técnico e histórico.* 11 vols. Madrid: Espasa-Calpe, 1943—.

Cowley, Malcolm. *Exile's Return: A Literary Odyssey of the 1920s.* 1934; rpt. Compass Books, 1956.

Crozier, Robert D., S.J. "For Thine Is the Power and the Glory: Love in *For Whom the Bell Tolls.*" *Papers on Language and Literature* 10 (1974): 76–97.

————. " 'The Paris Church of Passy': A Note on Hemingway's Second Marriage." *Papers on Language and Literature* 15.1 (1979): 84–86.

Cullum, George W., comp. *Biographical Register of the Officers and Graduates of the U.S. Military Academy at West Point, New York, from its Establishment in 1802, to 1890.* 3 vols. 3rd ed., rev. and extended. Boston: Houghton, Mifflin & Co., 1891.

Davidson, Arnold E. "The Dantean Perspective in Hemingway's *A Farewell to Arms.*" *Journal of Narrative Technique* 3.2 (1973): 121–30.

Davis, Robert Murray. "Irony and Pity Once More." *Fitzgerald/Hemingway Annual* (1973): 307–8.

Day, Jane. "Bimini, Bahamas: Hemingway's Island in the Stream." *South Florida History Magazine* 4 (Fall 1989): 5–9, 24.

Debrett's Peerage and Baronetage. London: Debrett's Peerage, Ltd., 1939, 1990.

Diccionario de la Lengua Española. 19th ed. Madrid: Real Academia Española, 1970.

Diccionario Enciclopédico Abreviado. Madrid: Espasa-Calpe, 1954.

Diccionario Enciclopédico Abreviado. 7th ed. 7 vols. Madrid: Espasa-Calpe, 1972.

Dictionary of American Biography. 1964 ed. 10 vols. New York: Scribner's, 1964.

Dictionary of American Naval Fighting Ships. Vol. 5. Washington, D.C.: Office of the Chief of Naval Operations, 1970.

Dictionary of Literary Biography. Vol IV: *American Writers in Paris, 1920–39.* Ed. Karen Lane Rood. Detroit: Gale Research, 1980.

Dictionary of National Biography. Founded in 1822 by George Smith. Eds. Sir Leslie Stephen and Sir Sidney Lee. 21 vols. plus Index and Supplements. Oxford: Oxford U.P., 1917—.

Dictionnaire de Biographie Française. Ed. Jo. Balteau et al. Paris: Librairie Letorzey et Ane, 1939.

Diliberto, Gioia. *Hadley.* New York: Ticknor & Fields, 1992.

Dizionario Biografico degli Italiani. Rome: Instituto della Enciclopedia Italiana, 1960—.

Dizionario Enciclopedico Italiano. 12 vols. Rome: Instituto della Enciclopedia Italiana, 1970.

Donaldson, Scott. *By Force of Will: The Life and Art of Ernest Hemingway.* New York: Viking, 1977.

————, ed. *New Essays on A Farewell to Arms.* Cambridge: Cambridge U.P., 1990.

Donnelly, Honoria Murphy, with Richard N. Billings. *Sara & Gerald: Villa America and After.* New York: Holt, Rinehart and Winston, 1984.

Doody, Terrence. "Hemingway's Style and Jake's Narration." *Journal of Narrative Technique* 4 (1974): 212–25.

Dunning, John. *Tune in Yesterday.* New York: Prentice-Hall, 1976.

Edmonds, Dale. "When Does Frederic Henry Narrate *A Farewell to Arms?*" *NMAL: Notes on Modern American Literature* 4 (1980): Item 14.

Eliot, T.S. *The Complete Poems and Plays: 1909–1950.* New York: Harcourt Brace, 1952.

Ellis, James. "Hemingway's *The Sun Also Rises.*" *Explicator* 36.3 (1978): 24.

Ellman, Richard. *James Joyce.* New York: Oxford U.P., 1959.

Emmons, Frederick E. *American Passenger Ships.* Newark: U. of Delaware P., 1985.

Enciclopedia de la Cultura Española. Vol. III. Madrid: Editora Nacional, 1963.

Enciclopedia Universal Ilustrada Europeo-Americana. 70 vols. plus *Apéndices* (10 vols), Index, and annual *Suplementos* beginning 1936. Madrid: Espasa-Calpe, 1908—.

Encyclopaedia Britannica. 11th ed. 24 vols. New York: The Encyclopaedia Britannica Company, 1910–1911.

Encyclopaedia Britannica. 14th ed. 24 vols. Chicago: Encyclopaedia Britannica, Inc., 1973.

Encyclopaedia Britannica. 15th ed. 30 vols, including the Marcropaedia (19 vols.), Micropaedia (10 vols.), Propaedia (1 vol.). Chicago: Encyclopaedia Britannica, Inc., 1974, 1990.

Encyclopedia Americana. 30 vols. plus Annuals, 1962–1978. New York: Americana Corporation, 1961.

Encyclopedia of Associations. 4 vols. Ed. Katherine Gruber. Detroit, MI: Gale Research Co., 1985. Volume I: *National Organizations of the U.S.* Part I: Trade, Business, and Commercial Organizations.

Engelberg, Edward. "Hemingway's 'True Penelope': Flaubert's *L'Education Sentimentale* and *A Farewell to Arms.*" *Comparative Literature Studies* 16 (1979): 189–206.

Everyman's Encyclopedia. 5th ed. 12 vols. Ed. E. F. Bozman. London: Dent, 1967.

Ezell, Edward Clinton. *Small Arms of the World: A Basic Manual of Small Arms.* Harrisburg, PA: Stackpole, 1977.

Fergusson, Erna. *Cuba.* New York: Alfred A. Knopf, 1946.

First Time Ever: 650 Outstanding Songs. Melville, NY: MCA/Mills, n.d.

Fitch, Noel Riley. *Sylvia Beach and the Lost Generation: A History of Literary Paris in the Twenties and Thirties.* New York: Norton, 1983.

———. *Walks in Hemingway's Paris: A Guide to Paris for the Literary Traveler.* New York: St. Martin's Press, 1989.

Flanner, Janet. "Profile: Her Majesty the Queen—Part I." *The New Yorker* XI.12 (4 May 1935): 20–24.

———. "Profile: Her Majesty the Queen—Part II." *The New Yorker* XI.13 (11 May 1935): 28–32.

Fleischer, Nathanial S., ed. *Nat Fleischer's All-Time Ring Record Book.* Norwalk, CT: C. J. O'Brien Suburban Press, 1941—.

Fleming, Robert E. "Hemingway and Peele: Chapter 1 of *A Farewell to Arms.*" *Studies in American Fiction* 11.1 (1983): 95–100.

———. "The Libel of Dos Passos in *To Have and Have Not.*" *Journal of Modern Literature* 15.4 (1989): 597–601.

———. "Portrait of the Artist as a Bad Man: Hemingway's Career at the Crossroads." *North Dakota Quarterly* 55.1 (1987): 66–71.

———. "Re Sources for *The Sun Also Rises.*" *Hemingway Newsletter* 8 (June 1984): 3.

Flora, Joseph M. "Biblical Allusion in *The Old Man and the Sea.*" *Studies in Short Fiction* 10 (1973): 143–47.

———. *Ernest Hemingway: A Study of the Short Fiction.* Boston: Twayne, 1989.

Forbes, Patrick. *Champagne.* London: Gollancz, 1982.

Ford, Ford Madox. *It Was the Nightingale.* 1933; rpt. New York: the Ecco Press, 1984.

Fuentes, Norberto. *Hemingway in Cuba.* Secaucus, NJ: Lyle Stuart Inc., 1984.

————. *Hemingway Rediscovered.* Photographs by Roberto Herrera Sotolongo. New York: Scribner's, 1988.

Fussell, Paul. *The Great War and Modern Memory.* London: Oxford U.P., 1975.

Gajdusek, Robert E. *Hemingway's Paris.* New York: Scribner's, 1978.

Ganzel, Dewey. "Cabestro and Vaquilla: The Symbolic Structure of *The Sun Also Rises.*" *Sewanee Review* 76 (1968): 26–48.

Gellens, Jay, ed. *20th Century Interpretations of A Farewell to Arms.* Englewood Cliffs, NJ: Prentice-Hall, 1970.

Gerogiannis, Nicholas. "Hemingway's Poetry: Angry Notes of an Ambivalent Overman." 1981; rpt. Wagner, *Six Decades,* 257–72.

Gide, André. *Corydon.* New York: Farrar, Straus and Giroux, 1950.

————. *If It Die . . . An Autobiography.* New York: Vintage Books, 1965.

Grand Dictionnaire Encyclopedique Larousse. 10 vols. Paris: Librairie Larousse, 1982–1985.

Le Grande Encyclopédie. Paris: Larousse, 1974.

Gran Enciclopedia de Andalucía. Gen. ed. José María Javierre. 10 vols. Sevilla: Promociones Culturales Andaluzas, Ediciones Ariel, 1979.

Gran Enciclopedia Navarra. 11 vols. Gen ed., Juan Luis Uranga Santebestan. Pamplona: Caja de Ahorros de Navarra, 1990.

Gran Enciclopedia Rialp. 24 vols. Madrid: Ediciones Rialp, 1971–1976.

Graves, Robert. *Fairies and Fusiliers.* New York: Alfred A. Knopf, 1918.

Great Soviet Encyclopedia. 3rd ed. Moscow: Sovetskaia Entsiklopediia Publishing House, 1970—. English translation, 31 volumes and Index. New York: Macmillan, 1973–1983.

Grebstein, Sheldon Norman, ed. *Studies in For Whom the Bell Tolls.* Columbus, OH: Charles E. Merrill, 1971.

Green, Gregory. "The Old Superman and the Sea: Nietzche, the Lions, and the 'Will to Power'." *Hemingway Notes* 5.1 (1979): 14–19.

Greenclose, Barbara S. "Hemingway's 'The Revolutionist': An Aid to Interpretation." *Modern Fiction Studies* 17 (1971–1972): 565–70.

Griffin, Peter. *Along with Youth: Hemingway, The Early Years.* New York: Oxford U.P., 1985.

Gross, Barry. "Dealing with Robert Cohn." In Lewis, *Hemingway in Italy and Other Essays,* 123–30.

Gurko, Leo. *"The Old Man and the Sea."* *College English* 17 (1955): 11–15.

Hagemann, Meyly Chin. "Hemingway's Secret: Visual to Verbal Art." *Journal of Modern Art* 7.1 (1979): 87–112.

Halliwell, Leslie. *The Filmgoer's Companion.* 4th ed. New York: Hill and Wang, 1974.

Halverson, John. "Christian Resonance in *The Old Man and the Sea."* *English Language Notes* 2 (1964): 50–54.

Hanneman, Audre. *Ernest Hemingway: A Comprehensive Bibliography.* Princeton: Princeton U.P., 1967.

———. *Supplement to Ernest Hemingway: A Comprehensive Bibliography.* Princeton: Princeton U.P., 1975.

Hansen, Arlen J. *Expatriate Paris: A Cultural and Literary Guide to Paris of the 1920s.* New York: Arcade Publishing (Little, Brown & Co.), 1990.

Haranburu Altuna, Luis, and Peru Erroteta. *Dolores Ibárruri.* San Sebastián: Kriselu, 1977.

Harkey, Joseph H. "The Africans and Francis Macomber." *Studies in Short Fiction* 17 (1980): 345–48.

Harrison, Charles Yale. *Generals Die in Bed.* 1928; rpt. Hamilton, Ontario: Potlatch Publications, 1975.

Hays, Peter L. *Ernest Hemingway.* New York: Continuum, 1990.

————. "Exchange between Rivals: Faulkner's Influence on *The Old Man and the Sea.*" In Nagel, 147–64.

Hemingway, Ernest. "Introduction." *Men at War: The Best War Stories of All Time.* Ed. Ernest Hemingway. 1941; rpt. New York: Bramhall House, 1979.

————. "Marlin Off Cuba." In *American Big Game Fishing.* Ed. Eugene V. Connett. New York: Derrydale Press, 1935, 55–81.

Hemingway, Gregory H., M.D. *Papa: A Personal Memoir.* Boston: Houghton Mifflin, 1976.

Hemingway, Jack. *Misadventures of a Fly Fisherman: My Life With and Without Papa.* Dallas, TX: Taylor Publishing Co., 1986.

Hemingway, Leicester. *My Brother, Ernest Hemingway.* Cleveland: World, 1962.

Hemingway, Mary Welsh. *How It Was.* New York: Knopf, distributed by Random House, 1976.

Herbert, A.P. "Preface." *The Beggar's Opera by John Gay: To Which is Added the Music to Each Song.* Introduction by A. P. Herbert and illustrations by Mariette Lydis. New York: The Heritage Press, 1937, vii–xviii.

Hernández Menéndez, Carlos. *Historia de las armas cortas.* Madrid: Editorial Nebrija, 1980.

Herwig, Holger H., and Neil H. Heyman, eds. *Biographical Dictionary of World War I.* Westport, CT: Greenwood Press, 1982.

Hinkle, James. "Seeing Through It in *A Farewell to Arms.*" *Hemingway Review* 2.1 (1982): 94–95.

————. "Some Unexpected Sources for *The Sun Also Rises.*" *Hemingway Newsletter* 2.1 (1982): 26–42.

————. "What's Funny in *The Sun Also Rises.*" *Hemingway Review* 4.2 (1985): 31–41; rpt. Wagner, *Six Decades,* 77–92.

The Historical Encyclopedia of World War II. Trans. from the French by Jesse Dilson. London: Macmillan, 1980.

Hoffman, Frederick J., Charles Allen, and Carolyn F. Ulrich. *The Little Magazine: A History and a Bibliography.* Princeton: Princeton U.P., 1946.

The Holy Bible and International Bible Encyclopedia and Concordance, authorized or King James version. New York: Garden City Publishing Co., 1940.

Hotchner, A. E. *Papa Hemingway: A Personal Memoir.* New York: Bantam, 1966.

Hoyt, J. K. *The Cyclopedia of Practical Quotations.* Rev. ed. New York: Funk & Wagnalls, 1896.

Hurley, C. Harold. "Just 'a Boy' or 'Already a Man?': Manolin's Age in *The Old Man and the Sea.*" *Hemingway Review* 10.2 (1991): 71–72.

Hyamson, Albert M. *A Dictionary of Universal Biography of All Ages and of All Peoples.* 2nd ed. London: Routledge & Kegan Paul, Ltd., 1951.

Ibárruri, Dolores. *Memorias de Dolores Ibárruri (Pasionaria): El Unico Camino y Me Faltaba España.* Barcelona: Editorial Planeta, 1985. Colección Documento, Documento 178.

The International Dictionary of Films and Filmmakers. Vol. III: *Actors and Actresses.* Chicago: St. James, 1986.

Jarvis, Nancy H., ed. *Historical Glimpses—Petoskey.* Petoskey, MI: Little Traverse Historical Society, 1986.

Jenkins, Alan. *The Thirties.* New York: Stein and Day, 1976.

Jobes, Katherine T., ed. *20th Century Interpretations of The Old Man and the Sea.* Englewood Cliffs, NJ: Prentice-Hall, 1968.

Johnson, Lee. *The Paintings of Eugene Delacroix: A Critical Catalogue.* Oxford, Eng.: Clarendon Press, 1981.

Johnston, Kenneth G. " 'The Butterfly and the Tank': Casualties of War." *Studies in Short Fiction* 26.2 (1989): 183–86.

———, "Hemingway and Mantegna: The Bitter Nail Holes." *Journal of Narrative Technique* 1 (1971): 86–94.

————. "The Star in Hemingway's *The Old Man and the Sea.*" *American Literature* 42 (1970): 388–91.

Joost, Nicholas. *Ernest Hemingway and the Little Magazines: The Paris Years.* Barre, MA: Barre Publishers, 1968.

————, and Alan Brown. "T. S. Eliot and Ernest Hemingway: A Literary Relationship." *Papers on Language and Literature* 14.4 (1978): 425–49.

Josephs, F. Allen. "Hemingway's Poor Spanish: Chauvinism and Loss of Credulity in *For Whom the Bell Tolls.*" *Hemingway: A Revaluation.* Ed. Donald R. Noble. Troy, NY: The Whitston Publishing Co., 1983, 205–223.

Kampis, Antal. *The History of Art in Hungary.* Trans. Lili Halapy. London: Corvina in cooperation with Collet's Publishers, 1966.

Kearns, Cleo McNelly. *T. S. Eliot and Indic Traditions: A Study in Poetry and Belief.* Cambridge: Cambridge U.P., 1987.

Kenner, Hugh. *The Pound Era.* Berkeley: U. of California P., 1971.

Kern, Robert W., ed. *Historical Dictionary of Modern Spain, 1700–1988.* Westport, CT: Greenwood Press, 1990.

Kerrigan, William. "Something Funny about Hemingway's Count." *American Literature* 46.1 (1974): 87–93.

Kert, Bernice. *The Hemingway Women.* New York: W. W. Norton, 1983.

Kipling, Rudyard. *Rudyard Kipling's Verse.* Volume II: *Inclusive Edition, 1885–1918.* London: Hodder & Stoughton, 1919.

Knoff, Josephine Z. "Meyer Wolfsheim and Robert Cohn: A Study of Jewish Type and Stereotype." *Tradition: A Journal of Orthodox Jewish Thought* 10.3 (1969). Rpt. *Ernest Hemingway's The Sun Also Rises.* Ed. Harold Bloom. New York: Chelsea, 1987, 61–70.

Kobler, Jasper F. "Confused Chronology in *The Sun Also Rises.*" *Modern Fiction Studies* 13 (1967): 517–20.

Kory, Fern. "A Second Look at Helen Ferguson in *A Farewell to*

Arms.'' In Lewis, _Hemingway in Italy and Other Essays,_ 21–33.

Krapf, Ludwig, comp. _A Dictionary of the Swahili Language._ 1882; rpt. Westport, CT: Negro U.P., 1969.

Landis, Arthur H. _The Abraham Lincoln Brigade._ New York: Citadel, 1967.

Lanier, Doris. ''The Bittersweet Taste of Absinthe in Hemingway's 'Hills Like White Elephants'.'' _Studies in Short Fiction_ 26.3 (1989): 279–88.

Laqueur, Walter, ed. _A Dictionary of Politics._ Rev. ed. New York: The Free Press, 1973.

Larson, Kelli A. _Ernest Hemingway: A Reference Guide 1974–1989._ Boston: G.K. Hall, 1991.

Larson, T. A. _History of Wyoming._ 2nd ed., rev. Lincoln: U. of Nebraska P., 1965, 1978.

Lax, Roger, and Frederick Smith. _The Great Song Thesaurus,_ 2nd ed. New York: Oxford U.P., 1989.

Leland, John. _A Guide to Hemingway's Paris._ Chapel Hill, NC: Algonquin Books, 1989.

Lewis, Robert W. _A Farewell to Arms: The War of the Words._ Twayne's Masterwork Studies No. 84. New York: Twayne Publishers, 1992.

———. ''Hemingway in Italy: Making It Up.'' _Journal of Modern Literature_ 9.2 (1981–82): 209–36.

———. _Hemingway on Love._ Austin: University of Texas Press, 1965.

———, ed. _Hemingway in Italy and Other Essays._ New York: Praeger, 1990.

Light, James F. ''The Religion of Death in _A Farewell to Arms._'' _Modern Fiction Studies_ 7 (1961): 169–73.

Loeb, Harold. _The Way It Was._ New York: Criterion Books, 1959.

Longmire, Samuel E. "Hemingway's Praise of Dick Sisler in *The Old Man and the Sea*." *American Literature* 42.1 (1970): 96–98.

Lottman, Herbert R. *The Left Bank: Writers, Artists, and Politics from the Popular Front to the Cold War*. Boston: Houghton Mifflin, 1982.

Luca de Tena, Consuelo, and Manuel Mena. *Guide to the Prado*. Madrid: Silex, 1986.

Lynn, Kenneth S. *Hemingway*. New York: Simon & Schuster, 1987.

McAlmon, Robert. *Being Geniuses Together 1920–1930*. Revised with supplementary chapters by Kay Boyle. Garden City, NY: Doubleday, 1968.

McEwen, W. A., and A. H. Lewis. *Encyclopedia of Nautical Knowledge*. Cambridge, MD: Cornell Maritime Press, 1953.

McLane, A. J., ed. *McClane's Standard Fishing Encyclopedia and International Angling Guide*. New York: Holt, Rinehart and Winston, 1965.

MacLeish, Archibald. *The Collected Poems of Archibald MacLeish*. Boston: Houghton Mifflin Company, 1962.

McLendon, James. *Papa: Hemingway in Key West*. Miami: E. A. Seemann, 1972.

Madan, Arthur Cornwallis. *Swahili-English Dictionary*. Oxford, Eng.: Clarendon Press, 1903.

Maddox, Brenda. *Nora: The Real Life of Molly Bloom*. Boston: Houghton Mifflin, 1988.

Manvell, Roger, ed. *International Encyclopedia of Film*. London: Michael Joseph, Ltd., 1972.

Marqusee, Michael, comp. *Venice: An Illustrated Anthology*. London: Conran Octopus, Ltd., 1988.

Martindale: The Extra Pharmacopoeia. 27th ed. Ed. Ainley Wade. London: The Pharmaceutical Press, 1977.

Martínez Salvatierra, José. *Los Toros, La Fiesta Nacional Española.* Barcelona: Ediciones Sayma, 1961.

Mason, A. E. W. *The Four Corners of the World.* New York: Scribner's, 1917.

Maurois, André. *A History of France.* Trans. Henry L. Binsse. New York: Grove Press, 1960.

Mellow, James R. *Hemingway: A Life Without Consequences.* Boston: Houghton Mifflin, 1992.

Menke, Frank G., ed. *Encyclopedia of Sports.* 4th rev. ed. London: 1969.

Meyerbeer, G. *L'Africaine, Opera en Cinq Actes, Partition Piano & Chant.* Paris: Brandus & Cie., n.d.

Meyers Enzyklopadisches Lexikon. 25 vols. Mannheim: Bibliographisches Institut, Lexiconverlag, 1974 ed.

Meyers, Jeffrey. *Hemingway: A Biography.* London: Grafton, 1985.

———. "*For Whom the Bell Tolls* as Contemporary History." *Research and Creative Work* 1 (Fall 1988): 1–19.

———. "Kipling and Hemingway: The Lesson of the Master." *American Literature* 56.1 (1984): 87–99.

Milford, Nancy. *Zelda Fitzgerald: A Biography.* London: Bodley Head, 1970.

Miller, Madelaine Hemingway. *Ernie: Hemingway's Sister "Sunny" Remembers.* New York: Crown, 1975.

Moliner, María. *Diccionario de Uso del Español.* Madrid: Editorial Gredos, 1983.

Monteiro, George. "The Reds, the White Sox, and *The Old Man and the Sea.*" *Notes on Contemporary Literature* 4.3 (1974): 7–9.

———. "Santiago, DiMaggio, and Hemingway: The Ageing Professionals of *The Old Man and the Sea.*" *Fitzgerald/Hemingway Annual* (1975): 273–80.

Moore, Harry T. *The Intelligent Heart: The Life of D. H. Lawrence.* New York: Grove Press, 1962.

Morris, Richard B., ed. *Encyclopedia of American History, Bicentennial ed.* New York: Harper and Row, 1976.

Morrison, Ian. *Boxing: The Records.* Enfield, Middlesex: Guinness Superlatives, Ltd., 1986.

Morton, Bruce. "Santiago's Apprenticeship: A Source for *The Old Man and the Sea.*" *Hemingway Review* 2.2 (1983): 52–55.

Mother Goose: The Classic Purnell Edition. Rearranged and edited by Eulalie Osgood Grover. Illustrated by Frederick Richardson. Maidenhead, Eng.: Purnell & Sons, Ltd., 1975.

Mott, Frank Luther. *American Journalism: A History: 1690–1960.* 3rd ed. New York: Macmillan, 1962.

———. *A History of American Magazines.* Vol. III: 1865–1885. Cambridge: Harvard U.P., 1938.

———. *A History of American Magazines.* Vol. IV: 1885–1905. Cambridge: Harvard U.P., 1957.

Nagel, James. "Catherine Barkley and Retrospective Narration in *A Farewell to Arms.*" In Wagner, *Ernest Hemingway: Six Decades of Criticism,* 171–85.

———, ed. *Ernest Hemingway: The Writer in Context.* Madison: The U. of Wisconsin P., 1984.

National Cyclopaedia of American Biography. New York: James T. White, 1891—.

Nelson, Stewart B. *Oceanographic Ships, Fore and Aft.* Office of the Oceanographer of the Navy, 1971.

The New Century Cyclopedia of Names. Ed. Clarence L. Barnhart. 3 vols. New York: Appleton-Century-Crofts, 1954.

The New Columbia Encyclopedia. Ed. William H. Harris and Judith S. Levey. New York: Columbia U.P., 1975.

The New Lexicon Webster's Dictionary of the English Language. Encyclopedic Edition. New York: Lexicon Publications, 1988.

Nolan, Charles J., Jr. "Shooting the Sergeant: Frederic Henry's Puzzling Action." *College Literature* 11.3 (1984): 269–75.

Ogg, R. D. *Anchors and Anchoring.* 5th ed. A brochure of the Danforth/ White Co., Portland, ME, 1967.

Oldsey, Bernard. "The Sense of an Ending in *A Farewell to Arms.*" *Modern Fiction Studies* 23 (1977–78): 491–510.

————. *Hemingway's Hidden Craft: The Writing of A Farewell to Arms.* University Park: Pennsylvania State U.P., 1979.

Oliver, Charles M. "Hemingway's Study of Impending Death: *Across the River and Into the Trees.* In Lewis, *Hemingway in Italy and Other Essays,* 143–152.

Oren, Dan A. *Joining the Club: A History of Jews in Yale.* New Haven: Yale U.P., 1985.

Orwell, George. *Homage to Catalonia.* 1938. London: Martin Secker & Warburg, Ltd., 1951, 1954.

The Oxford Companion to American Literature. 4th ed. Ed. James D. Hart. New York: Oxford U.P., 1965.

The Oxford Companion to English Literature. 3rd ed. Ed. Sir Paul Harvey. Oxford: Oxford U.P. at the Clarendon Press, 1946.

The Oxford Companion to English Literature. 5th ed. Ed. Margaret Drabble. Oxford: Oxford U.P., 1985.

The Oxford Companion to Music. 9th ed. Ed. Percy A. Scholes. London: Oxford U.P., 1955.

The Oxford Companion to Sports and Games. Ed. John Arlott. London: Oxford U.P., 1975.

The Oxford Companion to the Theatre. 4th ed. Ed. Phyllis Hartnoll. Oxford: Oxford U.P., 1983.

The Oxford Dictionary of Quotations. London: Oxford U.P., 1941.

Palmedo, Roland, ed. *Skiing: The International Sport.* New York: The Derrydale Press, 1937.

Palmer, Horace W. *Palmer Families in America.* Neshanic, NJ: Neshanic Printing Co., 1966.

Partridge, Eric. *Eric Partridge's Dictionary of Slang and Unconventional English.* 8th ed. Ed. Paul Beale. London: Routledge & Kegan Paul, 1984.

————. *Name into Word: Proper Names that Have Become Common Property: A Discursive Dictionary.* London: Secker and Warburg, 1949.

The Penguin Book of American Folk Songs. Ed. Alan Lomax. Harmondsworth, Eng.: Penguin, 1964.

The Penguin Companion to Literature: Britain and the Commonwealth. Ed. David Daiches. London: Penguin, 1971.

The Penguin Companion to Literature: Europe. Ed. Anthony Thorlby. London: Penguin, 1969.

Peterson, Theodore. *Magazines in the Twentieth Century.* Urbana: U. of Illinois P., 1964.

Phelan, James. "Distance, Voice, and Temporal Perspective in Frederic Henry's Narration: Successes, Problems and Paradox." In Donaldson, *New Essays,* 53–73.

Plimpton, George. "The Art of Fiction XXI: Ernest Hemingway (Interview)." *The Paris Review* 18 (Spring 1958): 60–89.

Porter, David L., ed. *Biographical Dictionary of American Sports: Baseball.* Westport, CT: Greenwood Press, 1987.

————, ed. *Biographical Dictionary of American Sports: 1989–1992. Supplement for Baseball, Football, Basketball and Other Sports.* Westport, CT: Greenwood Press, 1992.

Qui est Qui en France: Dictionnaire biographique, 1988–89. 20th ed. Paris: Jacques Lafitte, 1989.

The Quotation Dictionary. Ed. Robyn Hyman. New York: Macmillan, 1962.

The Reader's Encyclopedia of American Literature. Ed. Max J. Herzberg. New York: Crowell, 1962; London: Methuen, 1963.

Reichler, Joseph L., ed. *The Baseball Encyclopedia.* 4th ed., rev. and expanded. New York: Macmillan, 1979.

Reynolds, Michael S. *Hemingway: The Paris Years.* Cambridge, Eng.: Basil Blackwell, 1989.

———. *Hemingway's First War: The Making of A Farewell to Arms.* Cambridge, Eng.: Basil Blackwell, 1987.

———. *Hemingway's Reading, 1910–1940: An Inventory.* Princeton: Princeton U.P., 1981.

———. *The Sun Also Rises: A Novel of the Twenties.* Boston: Twayne, 1988.

———. "A Supplement to *Hemingway's Reading: 1910–1940.*" *Studies in American Fiction* 14.1 (1986): 99–108.

———. *The Young Hemingway.* Cambridge, Eng.: Basil Blackwell, 1986.

Richardson, R. Dan. *Comintern Army: The International Brigades and the Spanish Civil War.* Lexington: U.P. of Kentucky, 1982.

Rigdon, Walter. *The Biographical Encyclopaedia & Who's Who of the American Theatre.* New York: James H. Heineman, 1966.

Roberts, W. Adolphe. *Havana: The Portrait of a City.* New York: Coward-McCann, Inc., 1953.

Rolfe, Edwin. *The Lincoln Battalion: The Story of the Americans Who Fought in Spain in the International Brigades.* New York: Random House, 1939.

Ross, Lillian. "How Do You Like It Now, Gentlemen?" *The New Yorker,* 13 May, 1950; rpt. in *Hemingway: A Collection of Critical*

Essays. Ed. Robert P. Weeks. Englewood Cliffs, NJ: Prentice-Hall, Inc., 1962, 17–39.

———, Portrait of Hemingway. New York: Avon, 1961.

Ross, Morton L. "Bill Gorton, the Preacher in *The Sun Also Rises.*" *Modern Fiction Studies* 18 (1972–73): 517–27.

Rouch, John S. "Jake Barnes as Narrator." *Modern Fiction Studies* 11 (1965–66): 361–70.

Rovit, Earl. *Ernest Hemingway.* Boston: Twayne, 1963.

Rubio Cabeza, Manuel. *Diccionario de la Guerra Civil Española.* 2 vols. Barcelona: Planeta, 1987.

Ruffner, Frederick G., Jr., and Robert C. Thomas, eds. *Code Names Dictionary: A Guide to Code Names, Slang, Nicknames, Journalese and Similar Terms.* Detroit: Gale Research Co., 1963.

Russell, H.K. "The Catharsis in *A Farewell to Arms.*" *Modern Fiction Studies* 1 (1955): 25–30.

Russo, John Paul. "To Die Is Not Enough: Hemingway's Venetian Novel." In Lewis, *Hemingway in Italy and Other Essays,* 153–180.

Saintsbury, George. *A Last Scrap Book.* London: Macmillan, 1924.

Salvat Universal: Diccionario Biográfico. 16th ed. 20 vols. Barcelona: Salvat Editores, 1986–88.

Sanfermines: 204 Hours of Fiesta. Pamplona: Larrión & Pimouler, 1992.

Sanford, Marcelline Hemingway. *At the Hemingways: A Family Portrait.* Boston: Little, Brown and Co., 1962.

Scafella, Frank, ed. *Hemingway: Essays of Reassessment.* New York: Oxford UP, 1991.

Scharff, Robert, ed. *Ski Magazine's Encyclopedia of Skiing.* New York: Harper & Row, 1979.

Schneider, Daniel J. "Hemingway's *A Farewell to Arms:* The Novel as Pure Poetry." *Modern Fiction Studies* 14 (1968): 283–96.

Schneider, Hannes. "The Development of the Ski School in Austria." Trans. from the German by Roland Palmedo. In *Skiing: The International Sport.* Ed. Roland Palmedo. New York: The Derrydale Press, 1937, 89–112.

Schwartz, Nina. "Lovers' Discourse in *The Sun Also Rises:* A Cock and Bull Story." *Criticism* 26.1 (1984): 49–69.

Schwiebert, Ernest. *Trout Tackle: Part Two.* New York: E. P. Dutton, Inc., 1984.

Scott, Arthur L. "In Defense of Robert Cohn." *College English* 18 (1957): 309–14.

Seltzer, Leon F. "The Opportunity of Impotence: Count Mippipopolous in *The Sun Also Rises.*" *Renascence* 31 (1978): 3–14.

Seville, Alfredo. *Abecedary.* New York: Hawthorn Books, Inc., 1966.

Shipman, David. *The Great Movie Stars: The Golden Years.* London: Hamlyn, 1970.

Sifakis, Carl, ed. *The Dictionary of Historic Nicknames.* New York: Facts on File Publications, 1984.

Silva Aramburu, José (Pepe Alegrías). *Enciclopedia taurina.* Barcelona: Editorial de Gassó Hnos., 1961.

Smedley, Harold Hinsdill. *Fly Patterns and Their Origins.* Muskegon, MI: Westshore Publications, 1943.

Smith, Myron J., Jr., comp. *Baseball: A Comprehensive Bibliography.* Jefferson, NC: McFarland., 1986.

Smith, Paul. *A Reader's Guide to the Short Stories of Ernest Hemingway.* Boston: G. K. Hall, 1989.

Smoller, Sanford J. *Adrift Among Geniuses: Robert McAlmon, Writer and Publisher of the Twenties.* University Park: Pennsylvania State U.P., 1975.

Sokoloff, Alice Hunt. *Hadley: The First Mrs. Hemingway.* New York: Dodd, Mead, 1973.

Sopena Garreta, Juan. *Historia del armamento español.* Volume III: *Las armas de fuego, 1700–1977.* Barcelona, 1979; rpt. 1984.

Spanier, Sandra Whipple. "Hemingway's Unknown Soldier: Catherine Barkley, the Critics, and the Great War." In Donaldson, *New Essays,* 75–108.

Spilka, Mark. *Hemingway's Quarrel with Androgyny.* Lincoln: U. of Nebraska P., 1990.

————. "Hemingway's Barbershop Quintet: *The Garden of Eden* Manuscript." *Novel* 21.1 (1987): 29–55.

Stallman, R. W. "*The Sun Also Rises*—But No Bells Ring." In his *The Houses that James Built and Other Literary Studies.* East Lansing: Michigan State U.P., 1961, 173–91.

A Standard Swahili-English Dictionary. Prepared by the Inter-Territorial Language Committee for the East African Dependencies. Gen. ed. Frederick Johnson. East Africa: Oxford U.P., 1939; rpt. 1969.

Steel, Rodney. *Sharks of the World.* New York: Facts on File, 1985.

Stephens, Robert O. "Hemingway's Old Man and the Iceberg." *Modern Fiction Studies* 7 (1961): 295–304.

————. "Hemingway and Stendhal: The Matrix of *A Farewell to Arms.*" *PMLA* 88.2 (1973): 271–80.

Stephenson, E. Roger. "Hemingway's Women: Cats Don't Live in the Mountains." In Lewis, *Hemingway in Italy and Other Essays,* 35–46.

Stevenson, Burton, ed. *The Home Book of Quotations, Classical and Modern.* 6th ed. New York: Dodd, Mead & Co., 1952.

Stoneback. H. R. " 'Lovers' Sonnets Turn'd to Holy Psalms': The Soul's Song of Providence, the Scandal of Suffering, and Love in *A Farewell to Arms.*" *Hemingway Review* 9.1 (1989): 33–76.

Strater, Henry. "Portrait: Hemingway." *Art in America* 49.4 (1961): 84–85.

Strauch, Edward. "*The Old Man and the Sea:* A Numerological View." *Aligarh Journal of English Studies* 6.1 (1981): 89–100.

Svoboda, Frederic Joseph. *Hemingway and The Sun Also Rises: The Crafting of a Style.* Lawrence: U.P. of Kansas, 1983.

Sylvester, Bickford. "Hemingway's Extended Vision: *The Old Man and the Sea.*" *PMLA* 81.1 (1966): 130–38.

———. " 'They Went Through This Fiction Every Day': Informed Illusion in *The Old Man and the Sea.*" *Modern Fiction Studies* 12 (1967): 473–77.

Thomas, Hugh. *The Spanish Civil War.* Rev. and enlarged ed. New York: Harper & Row, 1977.

Thomson, David, ed. *Biographical Dictionary of Film.* 2nd ed. rev. New York: Morrow, 1976.

Tintner, Adeline R. "The Significance of D'Annunzio in *Across the River and Into the Trees.*" *Hemingway Review* 5.1 (1985): 9–13.

Toklas, Alice B. *What Is Remembered.* London: Michael Joseph, Ltd., 1963.

"Tracking Sharks in the Western North Atlantic." *Seaword* 12.2 (1984). Mystic, CN: Mystic Marinelife Aquarium, Division of Sea Research Foundation.

Truman, Margaret, with Margaret Cousins. *Margaret Truman's Own Story: Souvenir.* New York: McGraw-Hill, 1956.

Tunis, Edwin. *Weapons: A Pictorial History.* New York: World, 1954.

University of Delaware's Sea Grant Marine Advisory Service. "Shark." College of Marine Studies, University of Delaware, Newark, DE, 1980.

Variety (January 18, 1961: obit. Harry Pilcer).

Verdun, Kathleen. "Hemingway's Dante: A Note on *Across the River and Into the Trees.*" *American Literature* 57.4 (1985): 633–40.

Villard, Henry Serrano, and James Nagel. *Hemingway in Love and War.* Boston: Northeastern U.P., 1989.

Vuitton, Henry-Louis. *A Trunk Full of Memories.* Paris: Image, 1989.

Wagenknecht, Edward. *The Personality of Milton.* Norman: U. of Oklahoma P., 1970.

Wagner, Linda W. "The Poem of Santiago and Manolin." *Modern Fiction Studies* 19 (1973–74): 517–29.

———, ed. *Ernest Hemingway: Six Decades of Criticism.* East Lansing: Michigan State U.P., 1987.

———, ed. *New Essays on The Sun Also Rises.* Cambridge: Cambridge U.P., 1987.

Waldhorn, Arthur. *A Reader's Guide to Ernest Hemingway.* New York: Farrar, Straus, and Giroux, 1972.

Watson, Milton H. *Flagships of the Line.* England: P. Stephens, 1988.

Way, Brian. "Hemingway the Intellectual: A Version of Modernism." *Ernest Hemingway: New Critical Essays.* Ed. A. Robert Lee. London: Vision Press, Ltd., 1983, 151–171.

Weapons: A Pictorial History. Edwin Tunis. New York: World, 1954.

Webster's American Biographies. Ed. Charles Van Doren. Springfield, MA: G & C Merriam Co., 1974.

Webster's American Military Biographies. Ed. Robert McHenry. New York: Dover Publications, 1978.

Webster's Biographical Dictionary. Springfield, MA: G & C Merriam Co., 1972.

Webster's Guide to American History. Springfield, MA: G & C Merriam Co., 1971.

Webster's New Twentieth Century Dictionary of the English Language.
Unabridged. 2nd ed. Ed. in chief, Jean L. McKechnie. New York:
World Publishing, 1956.

Webster's Third New International Dictionary of the English Language.
Unabridged. Ed. in chief, Philip Babcock Gove. Springfield, MA:
G & C Merriam Co., 1966.

Weeks, Robert P. "Fakery in *The Old Man and the Sea.*" *College
English* 24.3 (1962): 446–55.

————, ed. *Hemingway: A Collection of Critical Essays.* Englewood
Cliffs, NJ: Prentice-Hall, 1962.

Weir, Alison. *Britain's Royal Families: The Complete Genealogy.*
London: Bodley Head, 1989.

Welk, Lawrence. *Lawrence Welk's Sing-A-Long Book.* New York:
Crown, 1975.

Wells, H. G. *Mr. Britling Sees It Through.* New York: Macmillan, 1916.

Wentworth, Harold, and Stuart Berg Flexner, eds. *Dictionary of American Slang.* New York: Thomas Y. Crowell, 1960. 2nd supplemented ed., 1975.

White, William, ed. *Ernest Hemingway: By-Line.* 1967. London:
Grafton, 1989.

Who Was Who in America. 4 vols. Chicago: Marquis-Who's Who, Inc.,
1968.

Who Was Who in World War II. Ed. John Keegan. New York:
Crescent/Bison, 1984.

Who Was Who on Screen. 2nd ed. Ed. Evelyn Mack Truitt. New York:
R. R. Bowker, 1977.

Who's News and Why. Ed. Anna Rothe. New York: H.H. Wilson Co.,
1945.

Who's Who in the Bible. Ed. Peter Calvocoressi. Harmondsworth, Eng.:
Penguin, 1987.

Who's Who in Paris Anglo-American Colony. 1905.

Wickes, George. *Americans in Paris.* Garden City, NY: Doubleday, 1969; rpt. New York: Da Capo Press, 1980.

Wier, Albert E., arr. *Songs the Children Love to Sing.* New York and London: D. Appleton and Co., 1916.

Williams, Wirt. *The Tragic Art of Ernest Hemingway.* Baton Rouge: Louisiana State U.P., 1981.

Willingham, Kathy. "Hemingway's *The Garden of Eden*: Writing with the Body." *The Hemingway Review* 12.2 (1993): 46–61.

Wilson, G. R., Jr. "Incarnation and Redemption in *The Old Man and the Sea.*" *Studies in Short Fiction* 14 (1977): 369–73.

Wiser, William. *The Crazy Years: Paris in the Twenties.* New York: Atheneum, 1983.

Wolff, Geoffrey. "The Man Who Fell in Love with Death: Harry Crosby's Transit to the Sun." *Atlantic Monthly* (July 1976): 37–46.

Woods, Charles B. "Fielding and the Authorship of *Shamela.*" *Philological Quarterly* 25 (1946): 256–72.

Wyden, Peter. *The Passionate War: The Narrative History of the Spanish Civil War, 1936–1939.* New York: Simon and Schuster, 1983.

Wylder, Delbert. *Hemingway's Heroes.* Albuquerque: U. of New Mexico P., 1969.

Young, Philip. *Ernest Hemingway: A Reconsideration.* University Park: Pennsylvania State U.P., 1966.

Zaragoza, Cristóbal. *Ejército popular y militares de la República, 1936–1939.* Barcelona: Planeta, 1983.

INDEX

Note: In the Index, as in the text, spelling follows the Scribner editions of Hemingway's texts. Endnotes are glossed only when they contain information not mentioned in the text. Historical prototypes and literary sources for Hemingway's characters are excluded from the Index because they have been systematically presented in the first endnote for each chapter. Similarly, bibliographical sources appear in the Endnotes but not in the Index. When several page numbers follow a heading or sub-heading, those which refer to major mentions in the text have been set in bold type, to distinguish them from subsidiary mentions.

—A—
AAA (American Automobile Association), 283
ABC (Madrid), 199
Abd el Krim, 199–200, 283
Absinthe, **57, 200,** 245, 447; in art, 409; and Pernod, 100, **464–65**
Accademia (Venice), 337
Adams, Cassilly, 201–2
Adams, Willie, **165,** 176, 189; and boat, 186, 191, 196
Adjutant, 115
Admiral, 365
Afghan War, 15
"Africana" (Meyerbeer), 115–16
Agincourt, 200
Agüero, Martín, 88, 110
Agustín, **200–1,** 210, 248, 264; and political opinions, 217, 242
Alaric I, 342
Albert (Prince Consort), 328
Alberto, 284
Alejandro, 201, 217
Alerta (Havana), 365
Alexander VI (Pope), 372
Alexander Hamilton Institute, 57–58
Alexandra (Queen of England), 365–66
Alfonso XI (street name), 222
Alfonso XIII (King of Spain), 216
Alfred, 366, 441
Algabeño, 58–59
Alger, Horatio, 59

Algonquin, 20, 26, 35, 37, 41, 52, 403
Alice in Wonderland (Carroll), 366, 433
Allen, Gracie, 165–66
Almagro, Diego de, 259
Alpini, 116, 160
Alternativa (investiture), 265
Alvarito, **284,** 287–88
Alzira III (boat), **166,** 179, 186
Amadeo Ferdinando (Duke of Aosta), 117
American Ambassador: in Cuba, 417; in Italy, 129, 133; in Spain, **59,** 89, 93, 97
American Embassy (Cuba): clerk, 377, 389, 395, 417; other personnel, 387, 413. *See also* Archer, Colonel Fred; Hollins
American Mercury. See Mercury
American Museum of Fly Fishing, 176, 496n.9
American Red Cross, 301–2
Americans, **59, 116,** 153, **201, 284,** 380; historical figures in WWII (generals), 289, 302–3, 319, 320–21, 326, 329, 335–36, 432–33; sports figures in war, 87, 340, 349, 385, 435; as tourists, 90, 299; and war, 26, 145, 320. *See also* President
El Amor Brujo (de Falla), 258
Anarchists: in Chicago, 11, **17–18,** 24; in Italy, 150, 286; in Spain: and barbers, 204; and communists, 204, 210, 242; and drunkenness, 215. *See also* FAI: CNT
Anderson, Sherwood, **11,** 22, 35; Hemingway's parody of, 14, 15, 20, 27–28,

Index

Index

ABOUT THE AUTHOR

MIRIAM B. MANDEL taught at Douglass College of Rutgers—the State University of New Jersey and Clemson University before moving with her family to Israel in 1979. In addition to her work on Hemingway, she has translated critical essays on the fiction of Ramón del Valle-Inclán and published articles on Jane Austen, Joseph Conrad, F. Scott Fitzgerald, A. E. Houseman, Katherine Mansfield, and the teaching of composition. She has also read papers before learned societies in Australia, Canada, France, and Spain. She is a Senior Lecturer in the English Department of Tel Aviv University.